# CORE

## TEACHING READING

### SOURCEBOOK

# CORE

# teaching reading

# SOURCEBOOK

*for kindergarten through eighth grade*

BILL HONIG · LINDA DIAMOND · LINDA GUTLOHN

*Contributing Author* Jacalyn Mahler

ARENA PRESS *Novato · California*

ARENA PRESS
20 Commercial Boulevard
Novato, California 94949-6191
800-422-7249
www.AcademicTherapy.com

CORE
5855 Christie Avenue, Suite A
Emeryville, California 94608
888-249-6155
www.corelearn.com

International Standard Book Number: 1-57128-119-3

0 9 8 7 6 5 4 3

4 3 2 1 0

## CREDITS

Editorial Director: Linda Gutlohn
Book Design and Production: Lucy Nielsen
Senior Editor: Jacalyn Mahler

Consultants: Mary Lantz, Orna Lenchner, Ruth Nathan, Tina Pelletier, Jean Peterson, B. J. Thorsnes, Isabel Valle, Kendra Wagner

Writers: Bruce Barthol, Susan Blackaby, Fran Lehr, Ink, Inc.

Editorial Staff: Mary Barbosa, Shelle Epton, Sally Gallinger, Tom Hassett, Jeri Hayes, Anna Holly, David Sweet

Special acknowledgment is given to the contributions of Marion Joseph, Ruth Nathan, Anne Cunningham, Sheila Mandel, B. J. Thorsnes, CORE instructors, Rick Brownell, and Murrell Peddicord to the development of this book.

## ACKNOWLEDGMENTS

For each of the following selections, grateful acknowledgment is made for permission to adapt and/or reprint original or copyrighted material.

American Federation of Teachers: "Align Decoding Instruction with the Stages of Reading Development" excerpted from "Teaching Decoding," by Louisa C. Moats in the Spring/Summer 1998 issue of the *American Educator,* the quarterly journal of the American Federation of Teachers. Copyright © 1998 by the American Federation of Teachers. Reprinted by permission of Louisa C. Moats and the American Federation of Teachers.

Fran Avni: "There's a Starfish Hidden Under My Bed," by Fran Avni. Copyright © 1997 by Fran Avni. Reprinted by permission of Fran Avni. For information about the audiocassette "I'm All Ears," school concerts, and workshops, contact Fran Avni at 510-595-9132 or FAVNI@aol.com.

Susan Blackaby: *Common Sense: An Anansi Tale*, by Susan Blackaby. Copyright © 1999 by Susan Blackaby. *Pioneers on the Oregon Trail,* by Susan Blackaby. Copyright © 1999 by Susan Blackaby. Used by permission of the author.

Brookline Books: "How Many Words Do People Know?" excerpted from *Vocabulary Development* by Steven A. Stahl. Copyright © 1999 by Steven A. Stahl. Reprinted with permission of the copyright holder.

California Department of Education: "Standards for Print Concepts and Alphabet Recognition," "Standards for Phonemic Awareness," "Standards for Decoding and Word Recognition," "Standards for Spelling," "Standards for Vocabulary and Concept Development," "Standards for Reading Comprehension," and "Standards for Literary Response and Analysis" from *English-Language Arts Content Standards for California Public Schools: Kindergarten Through Grade Twelve.* Copyright © 1999 by the California Department of Education. Adapted by permission of the California Department of Education. "Criteria for Reliable Research" adapted from "Characteristics of Reliable Research," in *Read All About It!: One-Day Workshop* by the Comprehensive Reading Leadership Program. Copyright © 1997 by the California State Board of Education. Adapted by permission of the California Department of Education. "Students Who Are English Language Learners" and "Instructional Grouping" adapted from *Reading/Language Arts Framework for California Public Schools: Kindergarten Through Grade Twelve,* developed by the Curriculum Development and Supplemental Materials Commission. Copyright © 1999 by the California Department of Education. Adapted by permission of the California Department of Education.

*Acknowledgments continued on page A.41*

# CONTENTS

# PREFACE

Since 1995 CORE has been committed to helping *all* students learn to read. To realize this goal, CORE works collaboratively with schools and districts to implement effective, research-based reading practices. CORE offers educators a three-part professional program: (1) on-site workshops, professional seminars, ongoing coaching, and classroom demonstrations; (2) criteria for the selection of reading materials; and (3) support for the systemic changes needed for program implementation.

In conjunction with CORE's professional development services, the CORE Literacy Series provides information about and models of proven practices in the teaching of reading. The three books in this series are *CORE Teaching Reading Sourcebook, CORE Assessing Reading,* and *CORE Reading Research Anthology.*

The *CORE Teaching Reading Sourcebook: For Kindergarten Through Eighth Grade* is a comprehensive resource for teaching reading. It combines the best features of an academic text and a practical, hands-on teacher's guide. The Sourcebook provides educators with the proven research and instructional strategies necessary for a balanced and comprehensive reading program. Its text organization and design format reflect the elements of explicit instruction by presenting the What?, Why?, When?, and How? of teaching reading. Generic teaching strategies (How?) serve as a bridge between research and practice.

The Sourcebook covers all aspects of an effective, research-based reading program, including key components of balanced reading instruction. It features an overview of literacy concepts, reference information about the structure of English and Spanish, information for teachers of students who are English language learners, guidelines for assessment and instructional organization, and reproducible masters for classroom use.

# SECTION I

# The Big Picture

I

# CONTENTS

## Section I: The Big Picture

CHAPTER

1

# Reading: The Context for Change

what?
why?
when?
how?

# Reading: The Context for Change

**1.2**

*"Reading is the most important skill for success in school and society. Children who fail to learn to read will surely fail to reach their full potential."*

—HALL & MOATS, 1999

For some children, learning to read seems to happen as if by magic. In fact, the Reading Reality, as shown in the pie chart below, is that about 5 percent of children already know how to read when they start school. For another 20 to 35 percent, learning to read in school is relatively easy, regardless of the instructional method used. However, about 60 percent of children find learning to read a challenge, and for 20 to 30 percent of this group, reading will be one of the most difficult tasks they will have to master throughout their years of schooling. The National Institute of Child Health and Human Development (NICHD) has found these percentages in every classroom in the country.

## A National Reading Crisis

Reading is the cornerstone of all school-based learning, yet reading failure is pervasive. The results of the 1998 National Assessment of Educational Progress (NAEP) showed 38 percent of fourth-grade students and 26 percent of eighth-grade students reading at a "below basic" level of achievement (National Center for Education Statistics 1999). This means that a significant number of students exhibit little or no mastery of the knowledge or skills necessary to perform work at each grade level.

There are several factors that put students at risk for reading failure, including poverty, phonological processing difficulties, language barriers, parents' low-reading abilities, and/or bio-

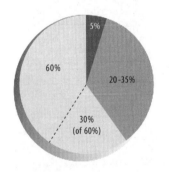

**Reading Reality**

■ Students who can read at the start of school (5%).

■ Students who find learning to read relatively easy (20% to 35%).

□ Students who find learning to read challenging (60%). And 30% of this 60% experience *extreme difficulty* learning to read.

## Children Most at Risk for Reading Failure*

**Children raised in poverty**

**Children with phonological processing and memory difficulties**

**Children with speech and hearing impairments**

**Children who are English language learners**

*\*Without proper instruction*

**CORE Reading Research Anthology**

for background information

logical or psychological learning deficits (Lyon 1998). Data indicate that parents' low-reading abilities may have put many students at risk for reading failure. According to a 1993 study of adult illiteracy in the United States, 47 percent of adults are either illiterate or can only perform simple literacy tasks (National Center for Education Statistics 1993). Yet many children from more advantaged, literacy-rich environments also have trouble learning to read. According to the 1998 NAEP, 16 percent of the eighth-grade students reading "below basic" are children of college-educated parents who presumably encourage literacy in the home.

In order to participate fully in society, literacy is essential. Illiteracy cannot help but have a direct, negative effect on quality of life, usually in the form of lost opportunities and lower wages. Access to fundamental information regarding nutrition, health, safety, and general well-being and to information that expands and enriches understanding, such as culture, history, literature, science, and mathematics, is limited. Literacy is the key to staying in step with the daily discoveries and insights of the information age, both for the common good and for personal growth.

1.3

According to Thomas Jefferson, "Democracy has no orthodoxy, but it can survive and flourish only with a literate citizenry." Literacy can be defined as "the ability to read and write." What are the ways that illiteracy or weak reading skills could impact a person's life? A society?

**1.4**

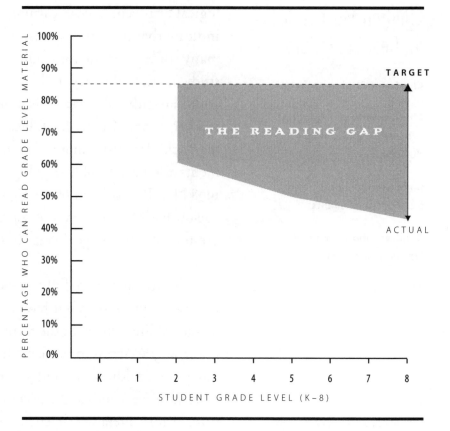

## The Reading Gap

The "reading gap" is a term used to describe the difference between the target level of reading proficiency, which should be possible for students to achieve, and the actual level of reading proficiency. With proper instruction, about 85 to 90 percent of students in any given classroom or district should be able to read grade-level texts independently. This means they should be able to read literature selected for a particular grade as well as content-area texts. Unfortunately, however, few classrooms attain this goal.

The dotted line on the graph above represents the target of 85 to 90 percent of students reading at grade level. The sloping line represents the actual percentage—the reality—in a sample district. In this district, only 60 percent of second graders could read grade-level texts independently. This district's second-grade reading gap was 25 to 30 percent. The reading

> *"Reading failure [reflects] not only an educational problem, but a significant public health problem as well."* —NICHD

gap tends to get wider as students encounter more difficult texts. In the same district, only 50 percent of fifth graders were able to read grade-level texts independently—a 35 to 40 percent gap; and only 43 percent of eighth graders were able to meet this benchmark—a 42 to 47 percent gap.

## Reading Gap Factors

Various factors influence the reading gap. Only some of them can be addressed within the classroom, however.

Teachers can
- base teaching methods on replicated research
- help students who are having difficulty learning to read
- create a supportive classroom environment

Teachers cannot
- improve the family situation at home
- improve the economic situation at home
- make English the primary language spoken at home

Connect to Theory

At the end of the most recent school year, what would you estimate was the reading gap in your classroom? About what percentage of your students were able to read grade-level texts independently? Estimate and then indicate your actual percentage by marking the point on the graph on the facing page. Figure out your reading gap by calculating the difference between the target (85 to 90 percent) and your class's actual percentages.

How wide was your reading gap?

Now think about the group of students in your current classroom who are reading substantially below target level. What are some of the indicators that a student is having difficulty with reading?

## Observable Indicators of Reading Difficulty

1.6

**Reads textbooks with difficulty**

**Struggles with many individual words**

**Reads slowly and laboriously**

**Can't figure out unfamiliar words, especially multi-syllabic words**

**Can't remember what was read**

**Tries to sound out irregular words**

**Does not know meanings of decoded words**

**Doesn't think deeply or strategically about what is read**

**Fails to make appropriate interpretations about what is read**

**Avoids reading**

**Spells poorly**

**Is afraid or embarrassed to read**

**Has difficulty with complex concepts**

# Reading Failure Is Preventable

Illiteracy may become a problem of the past. This is a pivotal juncture in the history of reading instruction: Never before has there been so much converging research and such an abundant professional knowledge base that shows so clearly how to foster and nourish reading proficiency. Enough is now known about how students learn to read to prevent most reading difficulties from starting, as well as to help those who are already experiencing reading problems. According to experts, only about 2 to 5 percent of students will not learn to read.

Recent advances in brain-imaging technology, studies by cognitive scientists, neurobiologists, and reading researchers, and the work of effective teachers have enabled us to better understand brain processes and reading and language development. These studies all indicate the need for a thorough, more balanced approach to teaching reading from the start.

Researchers Pressley, Rankin, and Yokoi (1996) studied a sample of the very best Kindergarten, first-, and second-grade teachers who had exceptional success promoting literacy achievement in students. They found that regardless of whether the teachers characterized themselves as whole language or skills-based, they all successfully taught reading by using a balanced and comprehensive approach—an approach that included direct teaching of phonemic awareness and phonics as well as an abundance of rich and varied literature and writing practice. In another study that began in 1994, Wharton-McDonald and Pressley (1998) observed outstanding and more typical first-grade literacy teachers. As in the 1996 study, the outstanding teachers in this study taught reading by employing a balanced and comprehensive approach.

**CORE Reading Research Anthology**

for background information

## NICHD Research*

**Studied the reading development of 34,501 children and adults**

**Studied 21,860 good readers for up to 12 years to understand normal reading development**

**Studied 12,641 individuals with reading difficulties for up to 12 years to understand why many students do not learn to read**

**Studied 7,669 students during Kindergarten and first grade (including 1,423 good readers) at 11 sites in the U.S. and Canada to pinpoint who is at risk for reading failure**

*\*Studies that have been or currently are being conducted*

## Factors That Influence Reading Development

Research has identified and replicated findings pinpointing seven key factors that influence reading development in students, regardless of risk factors such as socioeconomic level or physical impairments:

1. Development of phonemic awareness and of the alphabetic principle (how print maps to speech)

2. Ability to decode words

3. Automaticity with enough words

4. Acquisition of vocabulary along with the application of reading comprehension strategies

5. Extensive reading of both narrative and expository texts

6. Maintaining the motivation to learn

7. Adequate teacher preparation and materials

1.7

## Reading Research

### NICHD and Reading Research

The National Institute of Child Health and Human Development (NICHD) was established in 1965. Since that time, studies have involved 1,012 classroom teachers working in 985 classrooms in 266 schools. There are 41 study sites located in North America, Europe, and Asia. NICHD researchers work to identify (1) the critical environmental, experiential, cognitive, genetic, neurobiological, and instructional conditions that foster strong reading development; (2) the risk factors that predispose youngsters to reading failure; and (3) the instructional procedures that can be applied to ameliorate reading deficits at the earliest possible time.

1.8

## The National Reading Panel identified the following criteria for their reading studies:*

**Address achievement of one or more skills in reading**

**Generalize achievement to the larger population**

**Examine effectiveness of approach by comparing treatments using an experimental method**

**Use only high quality research reviewed by peers**

*\*Report of the National Reading Panel, 2000*

## Criteria for Reliable Research

Ideally, all educational strategies and methodologies should be research-based—based upon the best, most current, proven, and reliable research that is both quantitative and qualitative. Quantitative research usually includes statistical data and analysis, while qualitative research often involves case studies. In order for research to be deemed reliable, it must meet certain criteria.

- **Results are replicated.**
  Three or more studies are conducted with the same result.

- **Findings can be generalized.**
  The studies are controlled enough to document cause-effect relationships among specific groups of people.

- **The scientific method is used.**
  Hypotheses are generated on the basis of what is already known, and the experiment is designed to disprove the hypothesis; Y is varied to measure the effect on X.

- **Rigorous standards are met.**
  The study design, execution, and interpretation have undergone a rigorous peer review.

- **Convergent findings are compatible.**
  Whether or not a study is qualitative or quantitative, results make sense in light of findings from studies conducted in related disciplines.

- **Findings are longitudinal.**
  Groups of students have been studied over long periods of time.

SOURCE
Adapted from *Read All About It!: One-Day Workshop* (1997) by the Comprehensive Reading Leadership Program. Sacramento: California Department of Education.

*By the end of the school year, first graders should be reading independently.*

## The Earlier the Better

First graders should be reading independently by the end of the school year. Studies conducted by the NICHD substantiate that by the end of first grade, many students lose self-esteem, confidence, and motivation to learn if they have not learned to read. Only recently have researchers begun to understand that the optimal time to develop reading proficiency is relatively short.

Students who are not reading at grade level by the end of first grade have a 1 in 8 chance of ever catching up to grade level without extraordinary and costly interventions (Juel 1988, 1994). Study findings suggest that students who fail to learn to read early in their school careers risk falling further and further behind in their development of literacy skills, and subsequently become more at risk for school failure. There is strong evidence that these students become frustrated and drop out at higher rates than their classmates.

## The "Matthew Effect"

**Good readers get increasingly "richer" in reading ability, while nonproficient readers get increasingly "poorer."**

In his reviews of research on early literacy development, Stanovich (1986, 1993b) also addressed the consequences of early reading failure. He reasoned that since poor readers are often given texts that are too difficult for them to read, they are precluded from gaining the benefits—development of language, vocabulary, and background knowledge—that competent readers normally derive from reading. According to Stanovich (1986), students who struggle with reading are less likely to engage in reading-related activities, thus greatly reducing their exposure to text and further opportunities for practice. He observed that the less students read in the first grade, the less likely they are to read in subsequent school years.

**CORE Reading Research Anthology**

for background information

1.10

This lack of exposure to text and the resulting lack of productive practice on the part of less-skilled readers contributes to the gap between good and poor readers that tends to increase as these students progress through the grades. This phenomenon—in which students who learn to read early continue to improve in reading, or get "richer," and students who do not learn to read early get "poorer," or become increasingly distanced from the "rich" in reading ability—Stanovich calls the "Matthew effect."

## VARIATION IN AMOUNT OF INDEPENDENT READING

| Percentile Rank[a] | Minutes of Reading per Day | | Words Read per Year | |
|---|---|---|---|---|
| | BOOKS | TEXT[b] | BOOKS | TEXT[b] |
| 98 | 65.0 | 67.3 | 4,358,000 | 4,733,000 |
| 90 | 21.2 | 33.4 | 1,823,000 | 2,357,000 |
| 80 | 14.2 | 24.6 | 1,146,000 | 1,697,000 |
| 70 | 9.6 | 16.9 | 622,000 | 1,168,000 |
| 60 | 6.5 | 13.1 | 432,000 | 722,000 |
| 50 | 4.6 | 9.2 | 282,000 | 601,000 |
| 40 | 3.2 | 6.2 | 200,000 | 421,000 |
| 30 | 1.8 | 4.3 | 106,000 | 251,000 |
| 20 | .7 | 2.4 | 21,000 | 134,000 |
| 10 | .1 | 1.0 | 8,000 | 51,000 |
| 2 | 0 | 0 | 0 | 8,000 |

[a] Percentile rank on each measure separately. [b] Books, magazines, and newspapers.

Adapted from "Growth in Reading and How Children Spend Their Time Outside of School" (1988) by R. C. Anderson, P. T. Wilson, and L. G. Fielding. *Reading Research Quarterly* 23 (3), p. 292.

**CORE Reading Research Anthology**

for background information

## Better Readers Read More

Anderson, Wilson, and Fielding (1988) found a significant, positive relation between the measures of amount of reading, particularly the amount of book reading, and the measures of reading comprehension, vocabulary, and reading speed. The table on the facing page provides a dramatic representation of the amount of reading done independently out of school by 155 fifth-grade students. Notice that the fifth-grade students who read the most, those in the 98 percentile rank, read books as much as 65 minutes per day, while the fifth-grade students who read the least, those in the 10 percentile rank, read books as little as .1 minute per day.

Better readers get to read a lot more words. They read more on their own and continually build their vocabularies. Consequently, good readers keep getting better at reading and can read increasingly complex materials. They are exposed more often to new vocabulary, literature, concepts, and information. Weak readers read little, do not increase their vocabularies, and consequently struggle as texts get more complex. The table on the facing page shows the variation in the number of words read by the most skilled and the least proficient readers. Notice that the best fifth-grade readers, those in the 98 percentile rank, read about 4,358,000 words per year, while the poorest readers, such as the ones in the 10 percentile rank, read only about 8,000 words per year. The proficient reader reads approximately 544 times as many words as the less-skilled reader.

1.11

**See also...**

**CORE Reading Research Anthology**

for background information

1.12

## Diverse Learners

In almost any classroom, one can expect to find students with a wide range of learning needs. These students have a variety of skills, abilities, and interests, as well as varying proficiency levels in English.

### Students with Learning Difficulties or Disabilities

Students with learning difficulties or disabilities may have language, memory, auditory, and/or visual processing problems. Some students with these serious reading problems often are labeled "dyslexic."

### Students Who Are Advanced Learners

Students who are advanced learners are those who demonstrate, or are capable of, performance in language arts at a level significantly ahead of same-age peers. They are often labeled "gifted."

### Students Who Are English Language Learners

Students who are English language learners are those whose first language is not English. These students can be at various stages of English literacy development.

## Closing the Gap: Comprehensive Literacy Strategies

*The solution to our present predicament is for all schools to implement balanced and comprehensive literacy programs for all students.*

Getting students off to a successful start for a lifetime of reading is the job at hand. With good instruction and motivation, most will continue to read and become strong readers. Bringing all students to higher levels of literacy is the challenge teachers must meet; bringing disadvantaged, vulnerable, reluctant, and learning-impaired students to higher levels of literacy is the challenge teachers must overcome. Understanding the nature of reading, how proficient readers read, and how to teach students to read will help teachers face those challenges head-on.

The solution to our present predicament is for *all* schools to implement balanced and comprehensive literacy programs for *all* students. This approach requires understanding which skills need to be developed at which points and shifting the curricular emphasis over time. A comprehensive approach requires employing all of the literacy strategies shown in the chart below. This is what it will take to bring all students up to full literacy. It will not be easy, but it is a fundamental need.

## COMPREHENSIVE LITERACY STRATEGIES

| Pre-K | K | 1 | 2 | 3 | 4 | 5 | 8 |
|---|---|---|---|---|---|---|---|

PRINT CONCEPTS

ALPHABET RECOGNITION

PHONEMIC AWARENESS

DECODING: SYSTEMATIC, EXPLICIT PHONICS

INDEPENDENT, WIDE READING

SPELLING

VOCABULARY DEVELOPMENT

COMPREHENSION STRATEGIES

ORAL LANGUAGE DEVELOPMENT

WRITING

INTERVENTION

HOME/SCHOOL CONNECTION

| Pre-K | K | 1 | 2 | 3 | 4 | 5 | 8 |
|---|---|---|---|---|---|---|---|

CHAPTER

2

# Reading: Constructing Meaning from Text

what?
why?
when?
how?

# *what?* *Sources of Meaning: Words and Passages*

**2.2**

*"In forging a strategy to ensure reading success for all, it is essential to focus on practices grounded in research."*

—LEARNING FIRST ALLIANCE, 1998

Reading is about constructing meaning from text—comprehension. Reading is more than deciphering words. The ultimate goal of reading instruction is to enable students to understand what they read. Research has given us a clear picture of how best to help students become proficient readers and get meaning from text. This research also helps to clarify the roles of decoding, automatic word recognition, and contextual clues in reading instruction.

Reading has been viewed as a process of either building from the bottom up or from the top down. In the former view, the reader derives meaning from the detailed code knowledge provided by the text; in the latter view, the reader derives meaning from the prior, or background, knowledge he or she brings to the text. In reality, reading is both a bottom-up and a top-down process. Good readers begin with attention to the word, which, according to Marilyn Adams (1990), serves along with the text "as the blueprint for constructing meaning." Then they add their stored knowledge of words and letters, their prior knowledge of the topic, syntactic knowledge, text-structure understanding, experiences, and ability to string words together into a meaningful whole.

# Constructing Meaning

**Recognizing Words**

................................................

• Print Concepts
• Alphabet Recognition
• Phonemic Awareness
• Decoding
• Spelling
• Vocabulary Development

**Understanding Passages**

................................................

• Comprehension Strategies
• Text Structure
• Independent, Wide Reading
• Book Discussions

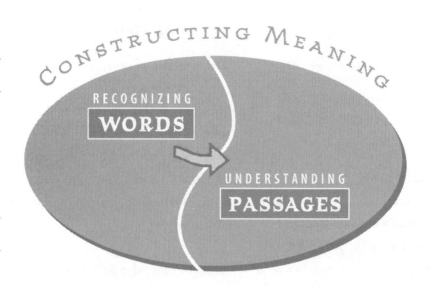

**AUTOMATICITY**

rapid, effortless, and unconscious word recognition

Readers construct meaning from two major sources: words and passages (strings of words). Proficient readers recognize and obtain meaning from words rapidly, effortlessly, and unconsciously—*automaticity*. Automaticity leaves readers' minds free for the more complex task of actively and consciously extracting meaning from the passage as a whole. Readers need to recognize each word as fast and effortlessly as possible, so that they can pay attention to the more mentally demanding task of figuring out the overall meaning. Word recognition difficulties are at the root of most reading problems.

Passage understanding is primarily an active, engaged cognitive process of weaving individual words into phrases, clauses, sentences, and paragraph, thinking about what the author is saying, and connecting it to prior knowledge. A reader's prior, or background, knowledge consists not only of prior personal experiences, conceptual learning, topic and text-type knowledge, and reading experiences, but also prior stored knowledge about how print works, and about letters and letter patterns and their spelling pairings.

## Automatic Word Recognition

The process of converting the printed word into its spoken form is called *decoding.* Decoding involves looking at a word and connecting the letters and sounds, and blending those sounds together to form a spoken word. Decoding leads to *word recognition* when the reader connects the spoken form of a word to its meaning. When the reader automatically recognizes strings of words in text, this results in comprehension of the whole text.

In first grade, the ability to decode words correlates highly with comprehension. This is because the words in beginning reading texts are usually familiar and part of the student's oral vocabulary; so, the words only need to be decoded to be understood. In later grades, knowledge of vocabulary and text structure also aid in comprehension.

The Connecticut Longitudinal Study (Foorman et al. 1997) demonstrates that first-grade decoding ability continues to be a major factor in comprehension as students progress through the grades. In first grade, the ability to decode words accurately correlates .89, or about 80 percent, with comprehension. By the fourth grade, how well a student learned to decode in first grade correlates .64, or about 40 percent, with comprehension. In ninth grade, the correlation between first-grade decoding ability and comprehension is .52, or about 27 percent. Therefore, first-grade reading ability continues to have an impact in the upper grades. This is because learning to decode words in first grade enables reading, which in turn enables readers to increase the number of words they recognize automatically.

**2.4**

**DECODING**
the process of converting the printed word into its spoken form; sounding out a word

**WORD RECOGNITION**
the process of decoding a word and then connecting the spoken form of the word to its meaning

| CORRELATION BETWEEN DECODING & COMPREHENSION IN THE CONNECTICUT LONGITUDINAL STUDY | | | | | | | | |
|---|---|---|---|---|---|---|---|---|
| GRADE 1 | .89 | | | | | | | |
| GRADE 2 | .75 | .83 | | | | | | |
| GRADE 3 | .70 | .74 | .77 | | | | | |
| GRADE 4 | .64 | .71 | .74 | .73 | | | | |
| GRADE 5 | .58 | .63 | .68 | .67 | .70 | | | |
| GRADE 6 | .59 | .65 | .67 | .68 | .66 | .69 | | |
| GRADE 7 | .53 | .61 | .65 | .65 | .67 | .68 | .69 | |
| GRADE 8 | .49 | .58 | .62 | .62 | .64 | .65 | .65 | .63 |
| GRADE 9 | .52 | .58 | .60 | .62 | .60 | .63 | .63 | .61 | .63 |
| COMPREHENSION / DECODING | GRADE 1 | GRADE 2 | GRADE 3 | GRADE 4 | GRADE 5 | GRADE 6 | GRADE 7 | GRADE 8 | GRADE 9 |

2.5

(Foorman et al. 1997)

## Correlation Between Grade 1 Decoding and Comprehension

· **Grade 1: about 80%**

· **Grade 4: about 40%**

· **Grade 9: about 27%**

Because of the close relationship between decoding and comprehension, it is difficult to get meaning without recognizing just about every word. (Imagine what it would be like to try to understand someone who garbles about every fourth word.) Research now indicates that good readers process almost all the words in a given text. According to the eye movement research, the eye lights on each word for about one quarter of a second and then jumps to the next word (Kolers 1976). The same research found that proficient readers actually process almost every letter. Thus, contrary to the popular notion that good readers skip, skim, and sample text, the opposite is true. Proficient readers actually read almost every word and letter when reading.

Connect to Theory

2.6

## PART 1

Proficient readers must read just about every word in order to understand the text. Prove this for yourself. In the sentence below, try omitting each word one at a time and see which words you can leave out and still maintain the author's intent without losing meaning.

Virtually each word is important or it wouldn't be there.

*Explanation:* In the above sentence, the only words that can be omitted without affecting meaning are *is* and *it*—function words that can be inferred from the text. Omitting the word *virtually* alters the meaning of the sentence from "almost each word is important" to "all the words are important."

## PART 2

Do proficient readers notice all the letters in the words in text? Read the sentences below.

One, tow, buckle my show.
The color of the flag is rid, white, and blue.

*Explanation:* Did you notice all the letters? In English many words are distinguished by just one letter, such as the words *sit* and *sat.* Failure to fully process each letter of each of these words would result in the incorrect, or slow, recognition of the word. In fluent reading, sequentially scanning the letters in a word activates a search for that word stored in the memory.

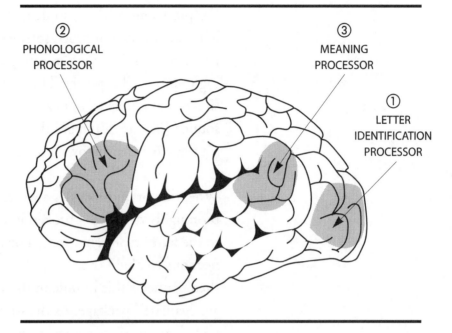

**②**
PHONOLOGICAL
PROCESSOR

**③**
MEANING
PROCESSOR

**①**
LETTER
IDENTIFICATION
PROCESSOR

## Becoming Automatic with Words

According to scientists at Yale University's Center for Learning and Attention, the brain reads by breaking words into sounds. After the eye notices the printed letters in a word, the letter identification processor connects the letters to the phonological processor, where the sounds associated with the letters are identified. The blended bundle of letters and sounds then connects to the brain's meaning processor, where the concept of the word is identified.

① The *letter identification processor* is located in the extra-striate cortex of the occipital lobe. It pinpoints letters, such as *c - a - t.*

② The *phonological processor* is located in the inferior frontal gyrus. It identifies sounds associated with letters, such as /k/ /a/ /t/.

③ The *meaning processor* is located in the superior temporal gyrus. It identifies the meaning of the word *cat*—"a furry pet that meows."

See also . . .

**CORE Reading Research Anthology**

for background information

For proficient reading, students have to have well-developed letter identification processors, well-developed phonological processors, and enough meaning and conceptual understanding to put it all together. The illustration on the previous page shows that letters (*c, a, t*) are stored in one area of the brain, sounds (/k/ /a/ /t/) in another, and the meaning of the word ("a furry pet that meows") in yet another.

**2.8**

When the brain processes a word for the first time, it must be thoroughly decoded—broken into the sounds that correspond to the letter representations. The brain then uses neural connections to blend those sounds and letters into a word, and then connects this bundle to the word's meaning to create an amalgamated package. As the word is read over and over, the neural connections get stronger and stronger until recognition is automatic. After reading a word successfully several times, most students will automatically recognize it. Some students may require as many as 50 to 100 exposures. Partial storage of only the first and last letters of a word, or only the letters without the sounds, doesn't give the brain enough information to store and retrieve efficiently.

When weaker readers come across a word for the first time, they do not sound it out thoroughly or analyze it alphabetically. This is also true for hearing-impaired students who read two to three years below grade level, because they have only the letter identification system operating. Similarly, if a reader does not initially read a word successfully enough times, the neural connections will not become strong enough for automaticity.

One of the best strategies for developing automaticity is to read—and reread—text in which approximately 19 out of 20 words can be easily recognized. As a result, more and more words become part of a student's stored word knowledge—"sight" words in the truest sense. Once students have stored many letter patterns and sounds, they begin to "read" using letter-pattern chunks, such as *st . . . ate* for the word *state*. This reading in chunks represents a "consolidation" of students' phonic knowledge.

Once words have become automatic, they are available for recognition either in whole texts or in word lists. David Share and Keith Stanovich (1995) call this process "the self-teaching process of reading." The success of this process depends on each student developing the *decoding tool*—the ability to initially sound out a word and then read it successfully enough times until it becomes automatic. Students who never develop full alphabetic decoding lack the tool to become automatic with a growing number of words. They are forced to resort to memorization or slower, less accurate contextual strategies to recognize words (Stanovich 1986).

In short, the brain needs patterns to store and access complicated information. Memorizing words one by one is too overwhelming. There are too many words in our language, and recognition must be immediate. Memorizing spelling patterns without connecting them to their sounds is insufficient for automatic word recognition. The combination of information about a word—its sounds and its letters—is needed to isolate

**DECODING TOOL**
the ability to initially sound out a word and then read it successfully enough times until it becomes automatic

**READING FLUENCY**
the accuracy and rate with
which students read

and find that exact word and its meaning. When students are able to recognize large numbers of words automatically and accurately, reading fluency—the accuracy and rate with which students read—improves. Full decoding is crucial to the development of word automaticity and fluency.

2.10

## Dyslexia

Dyslexia is a difficulty with language. Individuals with dyslexia may have difficulty with a variety of language-related tasks; they may have trouble recognizing, manipulating, and learning the speech sounds that correspond to letters in our writing (Hall and Moats 1999). According to Sylvia Richardson, M.D. (1994), "the major defining characteristic of dyslexia is specific deficit in the processing of phonological information. The dyslexic has particular difficulty breaking the symbol-sound code of the language—in understanding the alphabetic principle." Sally Shaywitz (1996) defines dyslexia as "an unexpected difficulty learning to read despite intelligence, motivation, and education."

*"For people with dyslexia, intelligence is not the problem. The problem is language."*

—INTERNATIONAL
DYSLEXIA ASSOCIATION

While the precise causes of dyslexia are unknown, genetic research shows that in many cases the condition is hereditary (Berninger 1997). Current findings from the brain research laboratory at Harvard Medical School indicate that the anatomy and functioning of the brain appear to be different for individuals who are affected by this disability. Normally, the brain's left hemisphere supports language comprehension and expression more than the right, and the left side is usually larger than the right. In people with dyslexia, both hemispheres are equal in size. Researchers have also observed unexpectedly low levels of activity in those areas of the brain responsible for reading. It is still not known whether appropriate instruction can change those brain activation patterns.

**Connect to Theory**

Why do you think the ability to sound out a simple, previously unread word or nonsense word, such as *pel* or *min* in mid–first grade would be a good predictor of reading comprehension in second and third grades, and still account for one quarter of reading comprehension in ninth grade?

*Explanation:* Sounding out nonsense words like *pel* and *min* requires an understanding of letter/sound correspondences—a basic tool for deciphering new words. As students apply this phonics knowledge to read a growing number of words, they become more automatic and more fluent readers. In addition, these nonsense words make up the syllables in the longer, more complex words students will encounter in upper-grade texts.

## Two Common Myths

① **English is too irregular to make phonics worthwhile.**

② **Context clues can substitute for decoding as a way to recognize words.**

## Decoding vs. Context Clues

There have been two major objections to making decoding a central part of reading instruction. The first objection is that English is so irregular that studying phonics is not worthwhile. The second objection is that context clues can replace decoding as a method to automatically recognize individual words.

As for the first objection, actually about 87 percent of English words are regular enough to be decoded. Out of this 87 percent, 50 percent are completely regular and 37 percent have only one irregular sound, for example, the word *put* (Hanna, Hanna, Hodges, and Rudorf 1966).

**2.12**

The passage below reflects a sixth grader's actual reading of a text selection from *The Call of the Wild* by Jack London. Read the excerpt and try to use the context provided to determine the missing words.

He had never seen dogs fight as these w____ish c____ f____t, and his first ex____ t____t him an unf____able l____n. It is true, it was a vi____ ex____, else he would not have lived to pr____it by it. Curly was the v____. They were camped near the log store, where she, in her friend____ way, made ad____ to a husky dog the size of a full-____ wolf, th____ not half so large as ____he. ____ere was no w____ing, only a leap in like a flash, a met____clip of teeth, a leap out equal____ swift, and Curly's face was ripped open from eye to jaw.

*Explanation:* Since many of the missing words tend to be less common, it is impossible to use context to predict all of them. As the reader struggles to use context, meaning is sacrificed. Since so few words can be recognized, insufficient data exist to effectively make use of context clues. Using context does not lead to the alphabetic storage necessary for automatic word recognition.

As for the second objection, context can be used to predict only about 25 percent of the words that students encounter in text (Gough, Alford, and Holley-Wilcox 1981). In expository text, where specific word meaning is crucial to understanding, the percentage is much lower. In addition, contextual strategies are too slow for fluent reading.

Poor readers, who often have weak decoding skills, over-rely on context clues to try to make meaning from text (Nicholson 1991; Stanovich 1986). If a reader figures out a word by using context clues alone, the process for becoming automatic with that word is not initiated. Therefore, the word will not be recognized more easily the next time it is encountered.

Although context is inadequate as a decoding or automatic word recognition tool, it is an important vehicle for learning the meaning of words not yet in the reader's oral vocabulary. Furthermore, context helps to resolve ambiguity. (Is the word *read* pronounced "reed" or "red"?) It also serves as an ongoing monitoring tool (Does it sound right? Does it make sense?) and as a backup for decoding. It is only when good readers can't use their knowledge of sound/spelling relationships to figure out an unfamiliar word that they should rely on context clues.

# what?

## Teaching Reading: Recognizing Words

**2.14**

### Recognizing Words

To read efficiently, word recognition must be automatic. How do we foster automatic word recognition? Automatic word recognition depends on rapid and efficient decoding, which in turn depends on phonics and word attack skills, which in turn depend on foundation skills that make the sound/print connection: print concepts, alphabet recognition, and phonemic awareness. Spelling supports the development of all of the above. In other words, students need to have well-developed phonemic awareness, alphabet and phonics knowledge, and adequate practice in applying that knowledge by sounding out words in text.

Connect to Theory

What do you think are the top two predictors of a Kindergarten student's success in learning to read in first grade?

a. Amount of television watched
b. Amount read to at home
c. Phonemic segmentation ability
d. Ability to recognize alphabet names and shapes
e. Prediction of former Kindergarten teacher
f. Score on oral vocabulary test (Peabody Picture Vocabulary)
g. Whether or not student attended preschool
h. Ability to decode made-up words

*Answer: According to Share et al. (1984), the top two predictors are (c) and (d).*

## Print Concepts

Some students begin Kindergarten with many hours of book-handling experience. They can identify the cover of a book and the pages within it; understand that words are read from left to right on a page; understand that the lines of text are read from top to bottom; and recognize that the white spaces between words are word junctures. There are, however, students who begin school without these rich literacy experiences and require careful attention to develop these print concepts.

**See also . . .**

2.15

## Alphabet Recognition

English—like many other languages—is an alphabetic language. One of the best predictors of first-grade reading success is a Kindergarten student's ability to visually recognize the letters of the alphabet and to name them (Adams 1990). This includes recognizing the letters in both their uppercase and lowercase forms. If students cannot recognize and discriminate one letter shape from another, teaching phonics will make little sense.

## Phonemic Awareness

**See also . . .**

A *phoneme* is a speech sound. *Phonemic awareness* is the understanding that spoken language is composed of phonemes, or speech sounds. Phonemic awareness involves the ability to blend, segment, and manipulate phonemes in spoken words. It is an auditory skill that does not involve the use of print.

**PHONEME**

a speech sound

**PHONEMIC AWARENESS**

understanding that spoken language is composed of phonemes

2.16

The lack of phonemic awareness is the most powerful predictor of difficulty in learning to read. If students cannot hear and manipulate sounds in spoken words, they have an extremely difficult time learning how to map those sounds to letters and letter patterns—the essence of decoding (Adams 1990). In Kindergarten, as little as 15 to 20 minutes per day of explicit phonemic awareness instruction can prevent reading difficulties in most students (Adams et al. 1998).

Try some simple phonemic awareness tasks for yourself.

1. How many sounds are there in *cup*?
2. What is the first sound in *rose*?
3. What is the last sound in *pencil*?
4. Say the word *top* backward.
5. Say the word *enough* backward.

*(See Appendix for answers.)*

**Section IV: Decoding**

Chapter 8: Phonics

Chapter 9: High-Frequency Words

Chapter 10: Multisyllabic Words

Chapter 11: Reading Fluency

WORDS

## Decoding

Decoding involves converting the printed word into its spoken form. It is the tool that enables students to become proficient readers who recognize words effortlessly and rapidly. Beginning readers use phonics skills "to attack" the pronunciation of words that are not readily recognized. As students progress in their reading development, they draw on other word attack skills: the recognition of irregular words, the recognition of word parts (syllables, affixes, base words, and phonograms), and the use of context to confirm pronunciation and resolve ambiguity.

**DECODING**

the process of converting the printed word into its spoken form

There are four major areas where students stumble in learning to decode. First, they may not be phonemically aware enough to segment or blend sounds in words—skills necessary to learn phonics. Second, they may not have learned enough basic ways in which consonant and vowel sounds are represented by letters in English words. Third, they may have learned how sounds are represented by letters, but have difficulty applying that knowledge in decoding or sounding out a previously unread word. Fourth, they may not have practiced reading enough words represented by these basic patterns to become automatic with a large number of words.

**2.17**

## Phonics

**PHONICS**

study and use of sound/spelling correspondences to identify written words

**ALPHABETIC PRINCIPLE**

how print maps to sound

The difference between phonemic awareness and phonics is that phonemic awareness involves sounds in *spoken* words and phonics involves the relationship between sounds and *written* symbols. *Phonics* is the study and use of sound/spelling correspondences and syllable patterns to help students identify written words. Phonics is useful to students in determining the pronunciation of words and in learning to recognize the spellings that correspond to the pronunciation of word parts. A primary difference between good and poor readers is the ability to use sound/spelling correspondences to identify words (Juel 1991).

In the English alphabetic system, individual letters are abstract and without meaning. In order to read words, readers must figure out the relationship between printed letters (graphemes) and their sounds (phonemes); they must know how print maps to sound—the *alphabetic principle.* This requires connecting about 43 sounds with the 26 letters of the alphabet.

**Section II: Word Structure**

Because of English language inconsistencies and linguistic complexities, many students have a difficult time learning to read unless the basic and most common sound/spelling correspondences, along with some high-frequency words, are

## Text Types

**decodable text**

connected reading material in which most of the words are wholly decodable and the majority of the remaining words are previously taught high-frequency and story words

**2.18**

**predictable text**

contains repeated text patterns; fosters print concepts and language; useful in Kindergarten and with emergent readers; usually not decodable

**authentic text**

literature trade books in a wide range of genres and formats; good for reading aloud; provides vocabulary and conceptual development; fosters enjoyment of reading; develops critical reasoning skills and strategies

explicitly taught in a systematic manner. Obviously, with approximately 43 sounds and only 26 letters, some sounds must be represented by more than one letter. For example, the /f/ sound can be represented by several letters or letter combinations (*f, ff, ph,* and occasionally *gh*). Conversely, one letter, for example, the letter *a,* can stand for more than one sound. Some sounds, such as /ch/ and /sh/, are represented by a pair of letters. Therefore, the sound/spelling sequence of instruction should progress from simple to more complex sound/spellings. For this reason, short and long vowels are taught before vowel teams and *r*-controlled vowels; and infrequent and more difficult linguistic patterns are introduced later.

*Implicit Phonics*    In an implicit phonics approach, students are expected to infer sound/spelling correspondences from reading whole words and analyzing their phonic elements. For example, students would be asked to induce the /m/ sound for the letter *m* from hearing the teacher read and point to the words *man, muffin,* and *mother.* The individual sound/spellings are introduced incidentally, as students encounter them in stories or other texts. This approach does not follow a phonics curriculum of increasingly more difficult phonic elements and generalizations.

*Systematic, Explicit Phonics*    There is compelling evidence that systematic, explicit phonics is the most effective type of instruction, especially for students who are "at risk" (Adams 1990; Chall 1996). Systematic, explicit phonics is a carefully organized, instructional program in which the most frequent sound/spellings are introduced systematically and sequentially, directly taught in isolation, and blended into whole words. Some basic strategies, or methods, for teaching students to blend sound/spellings to form words include sound-by-sound blending and whole-word blending. Systematic, explicit phonics instruction includes practice in spelling, word building, word sorting, and most important, practice in reading words in decodable texts.

*Decodable Text*   Decodable text is a critical part of explicit phonics instruction. This type of connected text contains (1) wholly decodable words that conform to previously introduced letter/sound correspondences and (2) previously introduced, high-frequency and "story" sight words. These texts give beginning readers the support necessary to apply their newly acquired phonics skills to the materials they are reading. The decodability of a particular text can only be determined by examining the relationship between a reading program's instructional sequence of phonic elements and the words in text selections.

2.19

## High-Frequency Words

Only 100 words account for approximately 50 percent of the words in English print (Fry, Fountoukidis, and Polk 1985). These high-frequency words are often quite abstract but crucial for comprehension. Since fluent, connected reading depends on the automatic recognition of these words, they are sometimes referred to as "sight" words. The Dolch List (Dolch 1955) and Instant Words (Fry 1993) are two examples of high-frequency word lists—lists of words that appear most frequently in primary reading texts.

Beginning in Kindergarten, students should receive explicit, systematic instruction in high-frequency words. Some high-frequency words are completely regular in their sound/spelling patterns—*and, on, be, this, can.* Many high-frequency words, however, are irregular with spelling patterns that do not follow the most common letter/sound correspondences—*of, to,*

**HIGH-FREQUENCY WORDS**
A small group of words that account for a large percentage of the words in print. Many high-frequency words are irregular, that is, not readily decodable by sounding out.

*you, was, said.* Because students cannot sound out these irregular words they need to use different strategies to learn them, including spelling them out letter-by-letter before encountering them in print and using contextual clues. Using contextual clues helps to clarify and monitor, to resolve ambiguity, and to check the accuracy of word recognition.

## Multisyllabic Words

For students in second grade and above, knowing how to decode unfamiliar multisyllabic words is essential because most of the new words they will encounter in print are "big" words. Explicit instruction in syllabication and morphemic analysis will help students "to attack" longer, unfamiliar words. *Syllabication* is the process of analyzing the patterns of vowels and consonants in a word to determine where the word breaks into syllables. *Morphemic analysis,* also called "structural analysis," involves identifying and isolating word parts such as affixes, base words, and word roots.

## Reading Fluency

Reading fluency is the accuracy and rate with which students read. It significantly affects the reader's ability to comprehend, and it is the mark of a proficient reader. Fluency involves recognizing words automatically, understanding the phrasing of text, and applying rapid phonic, structural, and contextual analysis to identify unknown words. LaBerge and Samuels (1974) described the fluent reader as "one whose decoding processes are automatic, requiring no conscious attention." An additional dimension to fluency is known as *prosody,* or the natural rhythms and tones of spoken language.

---

**2.20**

**SIGHT WORDS**
Words that are immediately recognized as a whole. The term sometimes refers to high-frequency irregular words that are explicitly taught as a whole because they cannot be sounded out.

**SYLLABICATION**
the process of analyzing the patterns of vowels and consonants in a multisyllabic word to determine where the word breaks into syllables

**MORPHEMIC ANALYSIS**
identifying and isolating word parts (prefixes, suffixes, base words) in multisyllabic words

**See also...**

## Spelling

Poor spellers are often poor readers. This is because spelling requires an understanding of how letters and letter patterns map to sounds. Learning to *spell* a word correctly reinforces automatic recognition when reading because all of the graphemes become embedded in students' minds and get attached to sound and meaning. Researchers have found a correlation between children's knowledge of spelling and their reading accuracy and fluency, comprehension, articulation, and vocabulary and concept development (Bear 1991; Gentry 1998; Henderson 1981).

**ORTHOGRAPHY**

spelling patterns in words

Research has also shown that children learn to spell in a predictable series of developmental stages (Henderson et al. 1972, 1986; Beers, Cramer, and Hammond 1995; Bear et al. 1996; Moats 1995). During each stage, they use spellings that reflect their orthographic knowledge. To promote concept development, spelling lists and word study must be linked to individual students' stage of development. Just as reading materials should match students' reading levels, spelling instruction should focus on words that have patterns that are neither too hard nor too easy. When students are presented with words that they are not ready to learn, spelling becomes a matter of memorization—"known" on Friday and "forgotten" on Monday.

## Patterns for Word Study

**Sound Pattern**

words grouped together that have a common sound

**Visual Pattern**

words grouped together that have a common spelling pattern

**Meaning Pattern**

words grouped together that have common base words or structural patterns

Although the English spelling system is complex, it is orderly and patterned. The most effective way to teach English spelling is through active word study that leads students to discover these rules and underlying patterns. Word lists should be made up of high-utility words, grouped by sound, visual, or meaning pattern. When students look at words and sort them into categories based on common patterns, they make the connection between spelling, pronunciation, and meaning. Word-sorting activities not only increase students' spelling ability, but their reading ability as well (Hall, Cunningham, and Cunningham 1995).

2.21

WORDS

**2.22**

## Vocabulary Development

Vocabulary knowledge is fundamental to reading comprehension; one cannot understand text without knowing what most of the words mean. There are two types of word knowledge: *definitional knowledge* and *contextual knowledge.* Definitional knowledge is similar to that information included in a dictionary definition. Contextual knowledge comes from exposure to a word in multiple contexts from different perspectives. Stahl and Fairbanks (1986) found that vocabulary instruction providing both definitional and contextual information can significantly improve students' reading comprehension.

Connect to Theory

Traditionally, much vocabulary instruction has involved some form of definitional approach. But definitions alone can lead to only a relatively superficial level of word knowledge. Even when definitions are accurate, they do not always contain enough information to allow a person to use the word correctly. This is especially true of definitions for words or concepts with which the learner is unfamiliar. Take some definitions of words that represent truly unfamiliar concepts—such as those listed below—and try to do what students are often asked to do: "For each word, write a sentence in which it is used correctly."

flam: a drumbeat of two strokes of which the first is a very quick grace note

lepton: any of a family of particles (as electron, muons, and neutrinos) that have spin quantum number ½ and that experience no strong forces

stirp: a line descending from a common ancestor

Adapted from *Teaching Vocabulary to Improve Reading Comprehension* by William E. Nagy. Newark, DE: International Reading Association, 1988. Definitions appear in *Merriam Webster's Collegiate Dictionary,* 10th Edition.

**Chapter 1: Reading: The Context for Change, "Variation in Amount of Independent Reading," p. 1.10**

**CORE Reading Research Anthology**
for background information

Students face two challenges in vocabulary development: acquiring new word knowledge and increasing the depth of that knowledge over time. Instruction in specific words and concepts helps students develop depth of word knowledge and instruction in independent word-learning strategies helps students determine the meanings of unfamiliar words they encounter while reading. Independent word-learning strategies focus on morphemic analysis and external context clues.

**2.23**

Differences in students' word knowledge are largely due to the amount of text they read. According to Nagy (1988), "Increasing the volume of students' reading is the single most important thing teachers can do to promote large-scale vocabulary growth." It follows that students need to develop strong beginning reading skills to be able to engage successfully in the volume of reading necessary for them to learn large numbers of word meanings through reading (Anderson and Nagy 1991). This development of strong reading skills is the most effective word-learning strategy available (Baker, Simmons, and Kameenui 1998).

The graph of Nagy and Anderson's 1984 study shows the difference in the estimated number of words read in school by middle-grade students. It is estimated that for in-school reading, the least-motivated readers might read 100,000 words a year, while the average readers might read 1,000,000. The figure for highly motivated middle-grade readers might be as high as 50,000,000. If these estimates are anywhere near the mark, they show staggering individual differences in students' volume of language experience and therefore, their opportunity to learn new words.

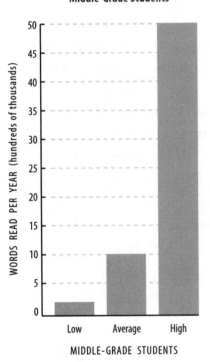

**Words Read per Year by Middle-Grade Students**

(Nagy and Anderson 1984)

# what?

## Teaching Reading: Understanding Passages

Understanding a passage requires stringing the concepts of individual words together into a meaningful whole. Automatic and accurate word recognition is necessary for passage understanding. To the extent that readers struggle with words, they necessarily lose track of meaning. A reader who is simply struggling from one word to the next has no energy left to process information and consequently does not understand what has been read.

In order to achieve passage understanding, word recognition skills must be supported by rich and abundant literary experiences in school as well as at home. Understanding passages involves a host of processes, all aimed at making meaning of the individual words, paying attention to how words are combined, and drawing conclusions about content. Passage understanding depends on reading fluency, vocabulary knowledge, reading strategies, syntactic understanding, engagement with texts through literary discussions, and amount of independent reading.

**See also . . .**

**Section VII: Comprehension**

Chapter 16: Strategic Reading

Chapter 17: Narrative Text

Chapter 18: Expository Text

PASSAGES

## Comprehension Strategies

Comprehension is the process of constructing meaning from written texts. For this to occur, the words in the text, along with their meanings, must first be accessible to the learner. Instruction should focus on developing comprehension strategies while using explicit instruction that develops students'

## Main Reasons for Poor Comprehension

**Lack of automaticity with word recognition**

**Limited vocabulary**

**Poor syntactic knowledge**

**Lack of understanding of text organization**

**Lack of internalized reading strategies**

**Insufficient reading experiences**

**METACOGNITION**
reflecting on one's own thinking or controlling one's own learning

metacognitive awareness. In explicit comprehension strategies instruction, students learn *what* the strategy is, *why* it is important, and *how, when,* and *where* to apply it.

Comprehension strategies promote students' comprehension and retention of what they read (Pressley and Woloshyn 1995). Strategic readers may be described as readers who select appropriate strategies that fit the particular text, purpose, and occasion (Paris et al. 1991). There are certain key comprehension strategies that students need to master to become proficient, strategic readers. These include using prior knowledge, predicting, identifying the main idea and summarization, questioning, making inferences, and visualizing (Pressley et al. 1989). "Good strategy users" possess metacognitive knowledge about strategies. Metacognitive reading strategies aid in readers' awareness of whether or not they comprehend what they are reading, and help readers decide what strategies to employ to increase comprehension (Pressley et al. 1989; Weisberg 1988).

PASSAGES

## Text Structure

Text structure and student awareness of text structure are highly related to reading comprehension (Dickson, Simmons, and Kameenui 1998). In general, text structure refers to the organizational features of text that serve as a frame or pattern with which to guide readers and help them identify important information and logical connections between ideas (Englert and Thomas 1987; Meyer et al. 1980; Seidenberg 1989). There are generally two types of text structures: narrative text and expository text. Narrative text is usually a story written to entertain. Expository text is usually written to communicate information. Most narrative text is organized around a set of elements known as story grammar. These elements include setting, characters, plot, and theme. Common expository text structures include cause-effect, compare-contrast, description, problem/solution, and time order.

PASSAGES

## Independent, Wide Reading

Wide, or extensive, reading is one of the most effective methods of increasing fluency, vocabulary, and comprehension, and becoming educated about the world (Shany and Biemiller 1995; Stanovich 1993a). Each school or district should invest time and effort in establishing an independent reading requirement (the number of books to be read per year) and an independent reading plan for each student. This plan should:

- ensure that students read enough books for vocabulary and knowledge growth

- include a way of matching books to students' reading levels

- emphasize breadth so that both narrative and expository genres are represented

- include a method for checking and tracking

PASSAGES

## Book Discussions

Regular classroom book discussions are essential to an effective reading program. During a book discussion, small groups of students are encouraged to reflect deeply about text, debate and argue over the author's intent, and support their interpretations with textual evidence. This opportunity to talk about and share books can help students refine and enrich their understanding of an assigned reading and stimulate interest in independent reading. There are three common types of book discussions: literature circles, reading workshops, and Questioning the Author (QtA).

# Section References

Adams, M. J. 1990. *Beginning to read: Thinking and learning about print.* Cambridge, MA: MIT Press.

Adams, M. J., B. R. Foorman, I. Lundberg, and T. Beeler. 1998. *Phonemic awareness in young children.* Baltimore, MD: Paul H. Brookes.

Ambruster, B., F. Lehr, and J. Osborn. 2001. *Put Reading First: The Research Building Blocks for Teaching Children to Read.* Partnership for Reading. Washington, DC: U.S. Dept. of Education.

Anderson, R. C., and W. E. Nagy. 1991. Word meaning. In R. Barr, M. L. Kamil, P. B. Mosenthal, and P. D. Pearson (eds.), *Handbook of reading research*, Vol. 2 (pp. 690–724). New York: Longman.

Anderson, R. C., and W. E. Nagy. 1992. The vocabulary conundrum. *American Educator* (Winter), pp. 14–18, 44–46.

Anderson, R. C., P. T. Wilson, and L. G. Fielding. 1988. Growth in reading and how children spend their time outside of school. *Reading Research Quarterly* 23(3), pp. 285–303.

Baker, S., D. C. Simmons, and E. J. Kameenui. 1998. Vocabulary acquisition: Instructional and curricular basics and implications. In D. C. Simmons and E. J. Kameenui (eds.), *What reading research tells us about children with diverse learning needs: Bases and basics.* Mahwah, NJ: Erlbaum.

Bear, D. 1991. *Determining criteria for the development of a qualitative scale of higher levels of orthographic knowledge.* Unpublished study. Reno, NV: University of Nevada-Reno.

Bear, D., M. Invernizzi, S. Templeton, and F. Johnston. 1996. *Words their way: Word study for phonics, vocabulary, and spelling instruction.* Upper Saddle River, NJ: Prentice-Hall.

Beers, J., R. Cramer, and D. Hammond. 1995. *Spelling: An overview of research and current research information and practices.* Glenview, IL: Scott, Foresman.

Berninger, V. 1997. Educational and biological links to learning disabilities. *Perspectives* 23.

Chall, J. S. 1996. *Learning to read: The great debate* (3rd ed.) New York: McGraw-Hill.

Dickson, S. V., D. C. Simmons, and E. J. Kameenui. 1998. Text organization: Research bases. In D. C. Simmons and E. J. Kameenui (eds.), *What reading research tells us about children with diverse learning needs: Bases and basics.* Mahwah, NJ: Erlbaum.

Dolch, E. W. 1955. *Methods in reading.* Champaign, IL: Garrad.

Englert, S. S., and C. C. Thomas. 1987. Sensitivity to text structure in reading and writing. A comparison between learning disabled and non-learning disabled students. *Learning Disability Quarterly* 10, pp. 93–105.

Foorman, B. R., D. J. Francis, S. E. Shaywitz, B. A. Shaywitz, and J. M. Fletcher. 1997. The case for early reading intervention. In B. A. Blachman (ed.), *Foundations of reading acquisition and dyslexia: Implications for early intervention* (pp. 243–264). Mahwah, NJ: Erlbaum.

Fry, E. 1993. *Reading teachers book of lists.* (3rd ed.) Upper Saddle River, NJ: Prentice-Hall.

Fry, E., D. Fountoukidis, and J. Polk. 1985. *The new reading teacher's book of lists.* Upper Saddle River, NJ: Prentice-Hall.

Gentry, J. R. 1998. *Five questions teachers ask about spelling.* Zaner-Bloser Spelling Research Series. Columbus, OH: Zaner-Bloser.

Gough, P. B., J. A. Alford, Jr., and P. Holley-Wilcox. 1981. Words and context. In O. J. L. Tzeng and H. Singer (eds.), *Perception of print*. Mahwah, NJ: Erlbaum.

Hall, D. P., P. M. Cunningham, and J. W. Cunningham. 1995. Multilevel spelling instruction in third grade classrooms. In K. A. Hinchman, D. L. Leu, and C. Kinzer (eds.), *Perspectives on literacy research and practice*. Chicago: National Reading Conference.

Hall, S. L., and L. C. Moats. 1999. *Straight talk about reading: How parents can make a difference during the early years*. Lincolnwood, IL: NTC/Contemporary Publishing Group.

Hanna, P. R., J. S. Hanna, R. E. Hodges, and E. H. Rudorf, Jr. 1966. *Phoneme-grapheme correspondences as cues to spelling improvement*. Washington, DC: U.S. Office of Education.

Henderson, E. H. 1981. *Learning to read and spell: The child's knowledge of words*. DeKalb, IL: Northern Illinois University Press.

Henderson, E. H., T. Estes, and S. Stonecash. 1972. An exploratory study of word acquisition among first graders at midyear in a language experience approach. *Journal of Reading Behavior* 4, pp. 21–30.

Juel, C. 1988. Learning to read and write: A longitudinal study of 54 children from first through fourth grades. *Journal of Educational Psychology* 80(4), pp. 437–447.

Juel, C. 1991. Beginning reading. In R. Barr, M. L. Kamil, P. B. Mosenthal, and P. D. Pearson (eds.), *Handbook of reading research*. Vol. 2. Mahwah, NJ: Erlbaum.

Juel, C. 1994. *Learning to read and write in one elementary school*. New York: Springer-Verlag.

Kolers, P. 1976. Buswell's discoveries. In R. A. Monty and J. W. Senders (eds.), *Eye movements and psychological processes*. Mahwah, NJ: Erlbaum.

LaBerge, D., and S. J. Samuels. 1974. Toward a theory of automatic information processing in reading. *Cognitive Psychology* 6, pp. 292–323.

Learning First Alliance Board of Directors. 1998. Action paper. Learning First Alliance Summit on Reading and Mathematics. Washington, DC: January 26–28, 1998.

Lyon, G. R. 1998, April 28. Statement of Dr. G. Reid Lyon Before the Committee on Labor and Human Resources. Washington, DC.

*Merriam Webster's Collegiate Dictionary* (10th ed.). 1996. Springfield, MA: Merriam-Webster.

Meyer, B. J. F., D. M. Brandt, and G. J. Bluth. 1980. Use of top-level structure in text: Key for reading comprehension of ninth-grade students. *Reading Research Quarterly* 16, pp. 72–103.

Moats, L. C. 1995. *Spelling: Development, disability, and instruction*. Timonium, MD: York Press.

Nagy, W. E. 1988. *Teaching vocabulary to improve reading comprehension*. Newark, DE: International Reading Association.

Nagy, W. E., and R. C. Anderson. 1984. How many words are there in printed school English? *Reading Research Quarterly* 19, pp. 304–330.

National Center for Education Statistics. 1993. *Adult literacy in America: A first look at the results of the National Adult Literacy Survey* (Stock No. 065-000-00588-3). Washington, DC: U.S. Government Printing Office.

National Center for Education Statistics. 1999. *NAEP 1998 reading report card for the nation and the states*. Washington, DC: U.S. Department of Education.

National Institute of Child Health and Human Development. 2000. *Report of the National Reading Panel, Teaching Children to Read: Reports of the Subgroups*. Bethesda, MD: National Institutes of Health.

Nicholson, T. 1991. Do children read words better in context or in lists? A classic study revisited. *Journal of Educational Psychology* 83, pp. 444–450.

Paris, S. C., B. A. Wasik, and J. C. Turner. 1991. The development of strategic readers. In R. Barr, M. L. Kamil, P. B. Mosenthal, and P. D. Pearson (eds.), *Handbook of reading research*. Vol. 2 (pp. 609–640). New York: Longman

Pressley, M., F. Goodchild, J. Fleet, R. Zajchowski, and E. D. Evans. 1989. The challenges of classroom strategy instruction. *Elementary School Journal* 89, pp. 301–342.

Pressley, M., J. Rankin, and L. Yokoi. 1996. A survey of instructional practices of primary teachers nominated as effective in promoting literacy. *Elementary School Journal* 96, pp. 363–384.

Pressley, M., and Woloshyn, V. E. (eds.). 1995. *Cognitive strategy instruction that really improves children's academic performance*. Cambridge, MA: Brookline Books.

Richardson, S. O. 1994. *Doctors ask questions about dyslexia: A review of medical research*. The International Dyslexia Association.

Seidenberg, P. L. 1989. Relating text-processing research to reading and writing instruction for learning disabled students. *Learning Disabilities Focus* 5(1), pp. 4–12.

Shany, M. T., and A. Biemiller. 1995. Assisted reading practice: Effects on performance for poor readers in Grades 3 and 4. *Reading Research Quarterly* 50(3), pp. 382–395.

2.28

Share, D. L., A. F. Jorm, R. Maclean, et al. 1984. Sources of individual differences in reading achievement. *Journal of Educational Psychology* 76, pp. 1309–1324.

Share, D. L., and K. E. Stanovich. 1995. Accommodating individual differences in critiques: Replies to our commentators. *Issues in Education: Contributions from Educational Psychology* 1, pp. 105–121.

Shaywitz, S. E. 1996. Dyslexia. *Scientific American* 275.

Shaywitz, S. E., B. A. Shaywitz, J. M. Fletcher, and J. D. Escobar. 1990. Prevalence of reading disability in boys and girls: Results of the Connecticut Longitudinal Study. *Journal of the American Medical Association* 264, pp. 998–1002.

Stahl, S. A., and M. M. Fairbanks. 1986. The effects of vocabulary instruction: A model-based beta-analysis. *Review of Educational Research* 56(1), pp. 72–110.

Stanovich, K. E. 1986. Matthew effects in reading: Some consequences of individual differences in the acquisition of literacy. *Reading Research Quarterly* 21(4), pp. 360–406.

Stanovich, K. E. 1993a. Does reading make you smarter? Literacy and the development of verbal intelligence. In H. Reese (ed.), *Advances in child development and behavior.* Vol. 24. San Diego, CA: Academic Press.

Stanovich, K. E. 1993b. Romance and reality. *The Reading Teacher* 47(4), pp. 280–291.

Weisberg, R. 1988. 1980's: A change in focus of reading comprehension research: A review of reading/learning disabilities research based on an interactive model of reading. *Learning Disability Quarterly* 11(2), pp. 149–159.

Wharton-McDonald, R., and M. Pressley. 1998. Literacy instruction in nine first-grade classrooms: Teacher characteristics and student achievement. *Elementary School Journal* 99(2), pp. 101–139.

# Word Structure

# CONTENTS
# Section II: Word Structure

CHAPTER

3

# Structure of the English Language

what?
why?
when?
how?

# What Is a Phoneme?

The English language alphabet has 26 letters that are used singly and in combination to represent about 42 to 44 different sounds, or phonemes. A phoneme is a speech sound. It is the smallest unit of sound that makes a difference in meaning. For example, the phonemes /p/ and /s/ are different; the word *pit* has a different meaning from *sit*.

Linguists disagree on the actual number of phonemes, or sounds, in the English language. The number varies according to dialect, individual speech patterns, changes in stress, and other variables.

## Phoneme Categories

**Consonant Phonemes** There are about 25 consonant phonemes, or sounds. Eighteen consonant phonemes, such as /d/ and /t/, are represented by a single letter. Seven phonemes, such as /ch/ and /sh/, are represented by two letters. The letters *c, q,* and *x* do not have a unique phoneme assigned to them. The sounds that they represent are more commonly represented by other letters and spellings: the sound /k/ or /s/ for *c,* the sounds /kw/ for *qu,* and the sounds /ks/ for *x.* To produce a consonant sound, the air flow is cut off either partially or completely.

See also . . .

**CORE Reading Research Anthology**

for background information

**Vowel Phonemes** Generally, there are about 18 vowel phonemes, or sounds. The letters *a, e, i, o,* and *u* are classified as vowels. These five letters are used to represent many different sounds. Every syllable has a vowel sound. To produce a vowel sound the air flow is unobstructed by any portion of the mouth.

## Consonant Phonemes (American English)

| Phoneme | Key Word | Phoneme | Key Word |
|---------|----------|---------|----------|
| /b/ | bus | /t/ | tent |
| /d/ | dot | /v/ | van |
| /f/ | fan | /w/ | web |
| /g/ | gold | /y/ | you |
| /h/ | hat | /z/ | zebra |
| /j/ | giraffe, jog | /ch/ | chair |
| /k/ | cat, key | /sh/ | shoe |
| /l/ | log | /zh/ | television |
| /m/ | milk | /th/ | think |
| /n/ | no | /TH/ | this |
| /p/ | pen | /hw/ | what |
| /r/ | red | /ng/ | wing |
| /s/ | city, six | | |

## Vowel Phonemes (American English)

| Phoneme | Key Word | Phoneme | Key Word |
|---------|----------|---------|----------|
| /ā/ | take | /ə/ | ago |
| /ē/ | teeth | /aw/ | saw |
| /ī/ | tie | /o͞o/ | tube |
| /ō/ | rope | /o͝o/ | good |
| /a/ | bat | /oi/, /oy/ | oil |
| /e/ | egg | /ou/, /ow/ | house |
| /i/ | rib | /ûr/ | girl |
| /o/ | pot | /är/ | art |
| /u/ | nut | /ôr/ | or |

# What Are the Classifications of Consonant Phonemes?

**3.4**

Consonant phonemes may be classified according to place of articulation, manner of articulation, and whether they are voiced or unvoiced. They can be further classified as either continuous or stop sounds. To produce a consonant phoneme the air flow is cut off either partially or completely.

## CONSONANT PHONEME CLASSIFICATIONS

| | |
|---|---|
| **Place of Articulation**<br>Where in the mouth is the sound produced? | ▶ Lips (bilabial)<br>▶ Lips and teeth (labiodental)<br>▶ Tongue between teeth (dental)<br>▶ Tongue behind teeth (alveolar)<br>▶ Roof of mouth (palatal)<br>▶ Back of mouth (velar)<br>▶ Throat |
| **Manner of Articulation**<br>How is the sound produced? | ▶ PLOSIVES: formed by closing or blocking off the air flow and then exploding a puff of air; for example, /b/ as in *box*.<br>▶ NASALS: formed when the mouth is closed forcing air through the nose; for example, /m/ as in *man*.<br>▶ FRICATIVES: formed by narrowing the air channel and then forcing air through it, creating friction in the mouth; for example, /v/ as in *voice*.<br>▶ AFFRICATIVES: formed by a stop followed by a fricative; for example, /ch/ as in *chip*.<br>▶ GLIDES: formed in similar ways as vowels; for example, /y/ as in *yes*.<br>▶ LIQUIDS: formed by interrupting the air flow slightly, but no friction results; for example, /l/ as in *line*. |
| **Voiced or Unvoiced** | ▶ VOICED: the vocal cords vibrate; for example, /z/ as in *zoo*.<br>▶ UNVOICED: the vocal cords do not vibrate; for example, /s/ as in *sit*. |
| **Continuous or Stop** | ▶ CONTINUOUS: a sound that can be pronounced for several seconds without distorting the sound; for example, /s/ as in *sun*.<br>▶ STOP: a sound that can be pronounced for only an instant; for example, /p/ as in *pop*. |

# CONSONANT PHONEME ARTICULATION

| ▽PLACE   MANNER▷ | Plosives | Nasals | Fricatives | Affricatives | Glides | Liquids |
|---|---|---|---|---|---|---|
| Lips | **/b/** /p/ | **/m/** | | | **/w/** /hw/ | |
| Lips and teeth | | | **/v/** /f/ | | | |
| Tongue between teeth | | | **/TH/** /th/ | | | |
| Tongue behind teeth | **/d/** /t/ | **/n/** | **/z/** /s/ | | | **/l/** |
| Roof of mouth | | | **/zh/** /sh/ | **/j/** /ch/ | **/y/** | **/r/** |
| Back of mouth | **/g/** /k/ | **/ng/** | | | | |
| Throat | | | | | /h/ | |

*Boldface phoneme indicates voiced sound.*

# CONSONANT PHONEMES

| **Continuous Sounds** | /f/, /l/, /m/, /n/, /r/, /s/, /v/, /w/, /y/, /z/ |
|---|---|
| **Stop Sounds** | /b/, /d/, /g/, /h/, /j/, /k/, /p/, /kw/*qu*, /t/, /ks/*x* |

Help make the vague concept of sound, or phoneme, more concrete by teaching students how to hear, feel, and experiment with sounds. Use the following excerpt from the *Phonological Awareness Training for Reading* (1994).

3.6

**/ m /**

Place of Articulation: Lips
Manner of Articulation: Nasal
Voiced

When I ask you to say /m/, what part of your mouth moves? *(the lips)* How? *(They come together.)* Does any air come out? *(yes)* Try holding your nose. Can you still say /m/? *(no)* That is because the air comes out through your nose.

**/ p /**

Place of Articulation: Lips
Manner of Articulation: Stop
Unvoiced

Your lips help make /p/ also. Do they stay together? *(no)* They start out closed and then they open. Does any air come out? *(a lot!)* This sound stops the air for a moment, and then the air rushes out. Put your hand in front of your mouth and feel the air when you say /p/.

**/ t /**

Place of Articulation: Tongue behind teeth
Manner of Articulation: Stop
Unvoiced

Now say the sound /t/. Do you feel a lot of air coming out? *(yes)* Try to close your lips and say /t/. Can you do it? *(no)* Another part of your mouth makes /t/. Can you feel what part? *(the tongue)* Where does it stop the air? *(on the hard ridge behind your upper teeth)*

**/ b /**

Place of Articulation: Lips
Manner of Articulation: Stop
Voiced

Do you remember when we practiced making /p/? What stopped the air? *(the lips)* Could you feel a lot of air come out? *(yes)* Now I want you to use your mouth in the same way, but use your voice also. This sound is /b/. Do you think you really use your voice? Cover your ears and say /p/ and /b/. Which one sounds louder? *(/b/)* That is because you are using your voice. Say *big, pig.* When you change the sound, you change the meaning.

**/k/**

Place of Articulation: Back of mouth
Manner of Articulation: Stop
Unvoiced

Try making /k/. Does a lot of air come out? *(yes)* Let's find out what stops the air. Do your lips move? *(no)* Do you put your tongue up behind your top teeth? *(no)* Where is your tongue? *(The front is low because the back of the tongue stops the air.)* Where? *(in the back of the mouth)*

**/n/**

Place of Articulation: Tongue behind teeth
Manner of Articulation: Nasal
Voiced

Say the sound /n/. Keep making the sound and put your hand in front of your mouth. Do you feel any air come out? *(no)* Hold your nose. Can you still make the sound? *(no)* In what other sound did air come out through the nose? *(/m/)* Make that sound now. What did you have to move? *(your lips)* We don't use our lips for the /n/ sound. Make /m/, then /n/. Where did your tongue go? Say *map, nap.* The tongue is in a different place even though the air comes out the nose.

**/d/**

Place of Articulation: Tongue behind teeth
Manner of Articulation: Stop
Voiced

Try making /d/. Does a lot of air come out? *(yes)* How do you know that? *(by putting your hand in front of your mouth)* Cover your ears when you make /d/. Do you use your voice in making this sound? *(yes)* Say /d/, /t/, /d/, /t/. How are these sounds different? *(We use our voice for /d/ but not for /t/.)*

**/g/**

Place of Articulation: Back of mouth
Manner of Articulation: Stop
Voiced

Look at me as I say the sound /g/. Can you see any part of my face move? *(no)* (If someone notices your throat, you should recognize the good observation and come back to it in a moment.) Now you make the sound and see if a lot of air comes out. *(yes)* If you didn't put your hand up to check, you were only guessing. Do you use your voice? How can you be sure? *(cover your ears)* Notice where your tongue stops the air when you start to make the sound. (Start to make the sound and then stop.) Is it the front of your mouth or the back? *(the back)* Now say /g/, /k/, /g/, /k/. We make these sounds in the same place, but we use our voice for one. Which one? *(/g/)*

CONTINUED ▷

**/ l /**

Place of Articulation: Tongue behind teeth
Manner of Articulation: Liquid
Voiced

3.8

Make the sound /l/. Does a lot of air come out? *(no)* If you said yes, try putting your hand in front of your mouth and saying /l/, /t/, /l/, /t/, or *melt.* The air is not stopped for /l/, so you don't feel a puff of air when you make this sound. Make /l/ and hold it. Can you make /t/ and hold it? *(no)* The air has to stop on /t/ and then rush out. For /l/, it comes out at the sides of the tongue. Can you tell where the tip of the tongue is? *(on the upper ridge behind the front teeth)*

**/ f /**

Place of Articulation: Lips and teeth
Manner of Articulation: Fricative
Unvoiced

Try making /f/. Can you make this sound and hold it? *(yes)* Watch me make the sound /f/. What part of my mouth moved? *(Children will probably say lips.)* Look again closely. Do both lips move? *(no, just one)* Which? *(the lower one)* Make the sound /f/ yourself. The lower lip comes up close to your upper teeth and makes the air sound noisy. Hold the /f/ and hear how noisy the air is.

**/ h /**

Place of Articulation: Throat
Manner of Articulation: Glide
Unvoiced

Try saying /h/, /h/, /h/. Can you feel a puff of air? *(yes)* Keep your hand in front of your mouth and say *e–e–e.* Now say *he, he, he.* Did you feel a difference from when you said *e–e–e? (yes)* Now try *o–o–o, ho, ho, ho.* When we put a quiet puff of air before another sound, it is the /h/ sound. Say *I, hi,* or *eat, heat.* Does the /h/ sound make a difference in the meaning? *(yes)*

**/ r /**

Place of Articulation: Roof of mouth
Manner of Articulation: Liquid
Voiced

Make the sound /r/. Can you hold this sound for a long time? *(yes)* /r/ does not stop the air. Stop making /r/, but keep your tongue ready to say the sound. Now take a deep breath. The part of your tongue that feels cool is the part that helps to make this sound. It is the under part of the tip of your tongue. This part comes close to a part of your mouth. What part of your mouth does the tongue come close to? *(the roof of the mouth)* Say *at.* Now put the /r/ first and say *rat.* Do *at* and *rat* mean different things? *(Yes, the /r/ makes a difference in meaning.)*

## /w/

Place of Articulation: Lips
Manner of Articulation: Glide
Voiced

I am going to get my mouth ready to say this next sound, but I won't say it. See if you can guess what it is. (Round your lips to pronounce /w/, but do not say it.) Can you tell me what sound I was going to make? *(/w/)* Now everyone make the /w/ sound. What part of your mouth moves? *(your lips)* What do they do? *(get round and tight)* Do you use your voice to say the /w/ sound? *(yes)* Say *itch,* then *witch.* Does the /w/ sound make a difference in meaning? *(yes)*

## /sh/

Place of Articulation: Roof of mouth
Manner of Articulation: Fricative
Unvoiced

Now we are going to make another sound where the lips are round but not as tight. Try /sh/. Can you hold this sound? *(yes)* (Have a child stand in the corner of the room and make the /sh/.) Could everyone hear (child's name) make the /sh/? *(yes)* The air is very noisy. Remember, the air gets noisy when it rushes past a close or narrow place. The lips help make this place. So does the top of the front part of the tongue. It comes close to part of your upper mouth.

## /s/

Place of Articulation: Tongue behind teeth
Manner of Articulation: Fricative
Unvoiced

Watch me change from /sh/ to this sound, /s/. How do my lips change? *(They are no longer rounded.)* Does the air make a lot of noise in /s/? *(yes)* Are your teeth close together or far apart? *(close)* The top of your tongue makes this sound also, but it has moved from the ridge to come close to another part of your mouth. Can you tell where? *(It comes close behind your teeth.)* Say *she, see,* or *shock, sock.* Does /s/ make a difference in meaning? *(yes)*

SOURCE
Adapted from *Phonological Awareness Training for Reading* (1994) by Joseph K. Torgesen and Bryan R. Bryant. Austin, TX: PRO-ED.

# What Are the Classifications of Vowel Phonemes?

**3.10**

To produce a consonant phoneme, the air flow is cut off either partially or completely; in order to produce a vowel phoneme, the air flow is unobstructed, or continuous. Vowel phonemes are classified as continuous sounds. They are further classified according to tongue position and mouth position.

**Tongue Position**
1. Is the tongue high, mid, or low in the mouth?
2. Is the tongue near the front, central, or back of the mouth?

**Mouth Position**
1. How rounded are the lips?
2. How tense are the mouth and jaw muscles?

In the chart on the facing page, the most common English spellings are listed under each vowel sound. Notice that to pronounce the /ē/ sound in the word *three,* the mouth position is wide and smiling; the jaw muscles are tense. To pronounce the /o/ sound in the word *hot,* the mouth position is round and wide open; the jaw muscles are relaxed. To pronounce the /o͞o/ sound in the word *moon,* the mouth position is round and partially open; the jaw muscles are tense.

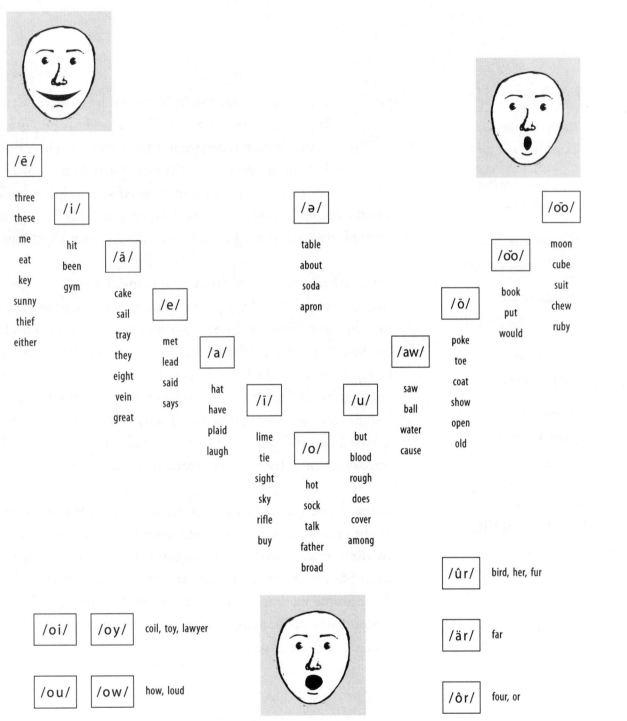

/ē/

three
these
me
eat
key
sunny
thief
either

/i/

hit
been
gym

/ā/

cake
sail
tray
they
eight
vein
great

/e/

met
lead
said
says

/a/

hat
have
plaid
laugh

/ə/

table
about
soda
apron

/ī/

lime
tie
sight
sky
rifle
buy

/o/

hot
sock
talk
father
broad

/u/

but
blood
rough
does
cover
among

/aw/

saw
ball
water
cause

/ō/

poke
toe
coat
show
open
old

/o͝o/

book
put
would

/o͞o/

moon
cube
suit
chew
ruby

/ûr/    bird, her, fur

/är/    far

/ôr/    four, or

/oi/    /oy/    coil, toy, lawyer

/ou/    /ow/    how, loud

# *What Is a Sound/Spelling?*

**3.12**

## Phonic Elements

Since phonemes, or sounds, cannot be written, we use letters to represent or stand for sounds. A *grapheme* is the written representation (a letter or a cluster of letters) of one sound. Phonics instruction involves teaching the relationship between sounds (phonemes) and the spellings (graphemes) used to represent them. These are referred to as phoneme/grapheme pairings, or sound/spellings.

There are hundreds of different graphemes for the 42 to 44 English phonemes. Many phonemes are represented by more than one grapheme, or letter. For example, the long-*e* sound can be represented by the spellings *e, ea, ee*; the /b/ sound can be represented by the letter *b*; and the /sh/ sound can be represented by the letters *sh*. The word *sat* has three phonemes (/s/ /a/ /t/) and three graphemes (*s, a, t*) represented by three letters. The word *chop* has three phonemes (/ch/ /o/ /p/) and three graphemes (*ch, o, p*) represented by four letters.

In the English language, phonic elements and generalizations can be used to categorize the common sound/spellings, which are used to form words. For the most part, after the single letter phonic elements (consonants and short vowels), it is the multiple spelling representations for the same sounds that students find challenging. The phonic elements are summarized on the facing page.

# PHONIC ELEMENTS (SOUND/SPELLING CATEGORIES)

| | |
|---|---|
| **Single consonants** | (b, c, d, f, g, h, j, k, l, m, n, p, q, r, s, t, v, w, x, y, z) |
| **Consonant blends** | Two consonants that appear together in a word, with each retaining its sound when blended. (Examples: fl, gr, sp, mp) |
| **Consonant digraphs** | Two consonant letters that together stand for a single sound. (Examples: sh, th, wh) |
| **Silent consonants** | Two consonant letters may represent the sound of only one of them. The other consonant is "silent." (Examples: gn, kn, wr) |
| **Short vowels** | (a, e, i, o, u) |
| **Long vowels** | (ā, ē, ī, ō, ū) Long vowels occur at the end of an open syllable. |
| **Long vowels with silent *e*** | (a_e, e_e, i_e, o_e, u_e) |
| ***r*-controlled vowels** | The letter *r* affects the sound of the vowel(s) that precedes it. The preceding vowel and *r* are treated as a single sound. (er, ir, ur, ar, or, air) |
| **Vowel digraphs*** | Also known as vowel pairs. These pairs make one sound. (Examples: ai in *bait,* ee in *feet,* ie in *pie,* oa in *coat*) |
| **Variant vowel digraphs*** | Sounds that are not commonly classified as long or short vowels. (Examples: aw, au, o͝o, o͞o) |
| **Diphthongs*** | A blend of vowel sounds in one syllable. (Examples: oi in *boil,* oy in *toy,* ow in *now,* ou in *cloud*) |
| **Schwa (ə)** | The vowel sound sometimes heard in an unstressed syllable. |

3.13

*These vowel pairings are sometimes referred to as* vowel teams.

## COMMON CONSONANT SOUND/SPELLINGS

**3.14**

| Phoneme | Spelling (Initial Position) | Key Word | Spelling (Final Position) | Key Word |
|---------|-----------------------------|----------|---------------------------|----------|
| /b/ | b | bat | b | hub |
| /d/ | d | day | d | bad |
| /f/ | f<br>ph | fat<br>phone | f<br>ff<br>ph<br>gh | beef<br>off<br>graph<br>laugh |
| /g/ | g<br>gu<br>gh | get<br>guitar<br>ghost | g<br>gue<br>gg | big<br>plague<br>egg |
| /h/ | h<br>wh | how<br>who | | |
| /j/ | j<br>g | jump<br>giant | ge<br>dge | cage<br>dodge |
| /k/ | c<br>k<br>ch | cat<br>kite<br>choir | k<br>ck | look<br>clock |
| /l/ | l | let | ll | wall |
| /m/ | m | mat | m<br>mb<br>mn | ham<br>lamb<br>hymn |
| /n/ | n<br>kn<br>gn | net<br>knock<br>gnat | n<br>gn | man<br>sign |
| /p/ | p | pet | p | top |
| /r/ | r<br>wr | rat<br>write | r | jar |

| Phoneme | Spelling (Initial Position) | Key Word | Spelling (Final Position) | Key Word |
|---|---|---|---|---|
| /s/ | s | sat | ce | face |
| | c | cent | se | case |
| | ps | psychology | ss | kiss |
| | | | s | bus |
| /t/ | t | tip | t | fit |
| | | | bt | doubt |
| | | | ed | skipped |
| /v/ | v | vine | ve | love |
| /w/ | w | wave | | |
| /y/ | y | yellow | | |
| /z/ | z | zoo | se | these |
| | | | ze | sneeze |
| | | | zz | buzz |
| | | | s | has |
| | | | z | whiz |
| /ch/ | ch | chop | ch | beach |
| | | | tch | match |
| /sh/ | sh | shoe | sh | rash |
| | s | sugar | | |
| /zh/ | si (medial position) | vision | | |
| | s (medial position) | measure | | |
| | z (medial position) | azure | | |
| /th/ | th | thank | th | path |
| /TH/ | th | this | the | bathe |
| /hw/ | wh | what | | |
| /ng/ | | | ng | sing |

## INITIAL CONSONANT BLEND SOUND/SPELLINGS

| Sounds | Spelling | Key Word | Sounds | Spelling | Key Word |
|---|---|---|---|---|---|
| **l - blends** | | | **s - blends** | | |
| /bl/ | bl | block | /sk/ | sc | scan |
| /cl/ | cl | clip | /sk/ | sk | skate |
| /fl/ | fl | flow | /sm/ | sm | small |
| /gl/ | gl | glad | /sn/ | sn | snow |
| /pl/ | pl | plan | /sp/ | sp | spell |
| /sl/ | sl | slap | /st/ | st | star |
| **r - blends** | | | /sw/ | sw | sway |
| /br/ | br | brat | **3 - letter** | | |
| /cr/ | cr | crow | /skr/ | scr | scream |
| /dr/ | dr | drain | /spl/ | spl | splash |
| /fr/ | fr | free | /spr/ | spr | spring |
| /gr/ | gr | green | /skw/ | squ | squash |
| /pr/ | pr | pray | /str/ | str | strap |
| /tr/ | tr | train | **Other** | | |
| | | | /dw/ | dw | dwarf |
| | | | /kw/ | qu | quack |
| | | | /tw/ | tw | twine |

## FINAL CONSONANT BLEND SOUND/SPELLINGS

| /kt/ | ct | fact | /mp/ | mp | damp |
|---|---|---|---|---|---|
| /ft/ | ft | raft | /nd/ | nd | bend |
| /ld/ | ld | wild | /nk/ | nk | sink |
| /lf/ | lf | self | /nt/ | nt | rent |
| /lk/ | lk | milk | /pt/ | pt | kept |
| /lt/ | lt | salt | /sk/ | sk | desk |
| /lp/ | lp | help | /sp/ | sp | crisp |
| /lt/ | lt | quilt | /st/ | st | best |

3.16

## CONSONANT DIGRAPH SOUND/SPELLINGS

| Phoneme | Spelling | Initial Position Key Word | Final Position Key Word |
|---------|----------|---------------------------|-------------------------|
| /sh/ | sh | shoe | rush |
| /ch/ | ch | chin | lunch |
| /th/ | th | think | path |
| /TH/ | th | that | clothe |
| /hw/ | wh | whale | |
| /f/ | ph | phone | graph |
| /f/ | gh | | laugh |
| /ng/ | ng | | ring |

## COMMON SILENT CONSONANT SOUND/SPELLINGS

| Phoneme | Spelling | Key Word | Phoneme | Spelling | Key Word |
|---------|----------|----------|---------|----------|----------|
| /j/ | dg | dodge | /m/ | lm | calm |
| /g/ | gh | ghost | /m/ | mb | dumb |
| /n/ | gn | gnat | /s/ | ps | psychology |
| /n/ | kn | know | /r/ | rh | rhino |
| /k/ | lk | talk | /r/ | wr | wrong |

## COMMON VOWEL SOUND/SPELLINGS

| | | | | | | | | | |
|---|---|---|---|---|---|---|---|---|---|
| /ā/ | a_e (late) | ai (bait) | ay (say) | ea (steak) | ei (veil) | ey (they) | eigh (sleigh) | | |
| /ē/ | e (me) | ee (feet) | ea (bead) | y (many) | ie (field) | e_e (these) | ey (key) | i_e (machine) | ei (receive) |
| /ī/ | i_e (time) | y (try) | i (mild) | ie (pie) | igh (high) | ye (lye) | | | |
| /ō/ | o (so) | o_e (hope) | oa (coat) | ow (low) | oe (toe) | ou (soul) | ew (sew) | | |
| /a/ | a (sat) | a_e (have) | | | | | | | |
| /e/ | e (pet) | ea (head) | ai (said) | a (many) | | | | | |
| /i/ | i (six) | y (gym) | e (pretty) | i_e (give) | ee (been) | ui (build) | | | |
| /o/ | o (log) | a (watch) | | | | | | | |
| /u/ | u (but) | o (ton) | o_e (love) | ou (young) | | | | | |
| /ə/ | a (alone) | e (system) | i (easily) | o (gallop) | u (circus) | | | | |
| /ûr/ | ur (turn) | ir (girl) | er (her) | or (work) | | | | | |
| /är/ | ar (car) | | | | | | | | |
| /ôr/ | or (or) | our (four) | ar (war) | | | | | | |
| /aw/ | aw (saw) | au (cause) | a[l] (walk) | a[ll] (ball) | ou (cough) | | | | |
| /oi/ /oy/ | oi (boil) | oy (toy) | | | | | | | |
| /ou/ /ow/ | ou (cloud) | ow (now) | | | | | | | |
| /o͞o/ (yo͞o)* | oo (hoot) | u (ruby) | ue (blue) | ew (new) | u_e (tube) | o (do) | ou (soup) | | |
| /o͝o/ | oo (book) | u (put) | o (wolf) | ou (would) | | | | | |

*As in cute *and* fuel.

3.18

## The Most Frequent Spellings of the 43 Sounds of English

It is useful to know which sound/spellings are important enough to teach, and which, because of their lower frequency in words, can be learned on an as-needed basis. The following chart shows the most frequent spellings of the 43 phoneme sounds covered in this book. The percentages provided in parentheses are based on the number of occurrences in which each sound/spelling appeared in the 17,000 most frequently used single and multisyllabic words (Hanna et al. 1966).

REFERENCE

Hanna, P. R., J. S. Hanna, R. E. Hodges, and E. H. Rudorf, Jr. 1966. *Phoneme-grapheme correspondences as cues to spelling improvement.* Washington, DC: U.S. Office of Education.

# SOUND/SPELLING PERCENTAGES

CONSONANTS

| | |
|---|---|
| /b/ | b (97%), bb |
| /d/ | d (98%), dd, ed |
| /f/ | f (78%), ff, ph, lf |
| /g/ | g (88%), gg, gh |
| /h/ | h (98%), wh |
| /j/ | g (66%), j (22%), dg |
| /k/ | c (73%), cc, k (13%), ck, lk, q |
| /l/ | l (91%), ll |
| /m/ | m (94%), mm |
| /n/ | n (97%), nn, kn, gn |
| /p/ | p (96%), pp |
| /r/ | r (97%), rr, wr |
| /s/ | s (73%), c (17%), ss |
| /t/ | t (97%), tt, ed |
| /v/ | v (99.5%), f (of) |
| /w/ | w (92%) |
| /y/ | y (44%), i (55%) |
| /z/ | z (23%), zz, s (64%) |
| /ch/ | ch (55%), t (31%) |
| /sh/ | sh (26%), ti (53%), ssi, s, si, sci |
| /zh/ | si (49%), s (33%), ss, z |
| /th/ | th (100%) |
| /TH/ | th (100%) |
| /hw/ | wh (100%) |
| /ng/ | n (41%), ng (59%) |

VOWELS

| | |
|---|---|
| /ā/ | a (45%), a_e (35%), ai, ay, ea |
| /ē/ | e (70%), ea (10%), ee (10%), ie, e_e, ey, i, ei, y |
| /ī/ | i_e (37%), i (37%), y (14%), ie, y_e, igh |
| /ō/ | o (73%), o_e (14%), ow, oa, oe |
| /a/ | a (97%) |
| /e/ | e (91%), ea, e_e (15%) |
| /i/ | i (68%), y (23%) |
| /o/ | o (79%) |
| /u/ | u (86%), o, ou |
| /ə/ | a (24%), e (13%), i (22%), o (27%), u |
| /ûr/ | er (40%), ir (13%), ur (26%) |
| /är/ | ar (89%) |
| /ôr/ | or (41%) |
| /aw/ | o, a, au, aw, ough, augh |
| /oi/ | oi (62%), oy (32%) |
| /ou/ | ou (56%), ow (29%) |
| /o͞o/ | oo (38%), u (21%), o, ou, u_e, ew, ue |
| /yo͞o/ | u (69%), u_e (22%), ew, ue |
| /o͝o/ | oo (31%), u (54%), ou, o (8%), ould |

# *What Is a Syllable?*

A syllable is a unit of pronunciation. Each syllable contains only one vowel sound. There are six basic syllable types that characterize most of English spelling: closed, open, *r*-controlled, vowel team, vowel–silent *e,* and consonant-*le.* These syllable types are useful to teach so that students can automatically recognize larger, recurring chunks in printed words. This skill is useful in both reading and spelling.

A syllable has two primary parts: the onset and the rime. The rime is the vowel and everything after it. The onset is the consonant, consonant blend, or digraph that may come before the rime. For example, in the one-syllable words *sing, bring,* and *thing,* the rime is *ing* and the onsets are *s, br,* and *th.* The two-syllable word *pancake* has two onsets and two rimes. Some one-syllable words, such as *I, it,* and *out,* have no onset.

## Onset and Rime

| Word | Onset | Rime |
|:---:|:---:|:---:|
| I | – | I |
| it | – | it |
| out | – | out |
| sing | s | ing |
| bring | br | ing |
| thing | th | ing |

## TYPES OF SYLLABLES

| | |
|---|---|
| **closed** | A syllable in which a single vowel is followed by a consonant. The vowel sound is usually short. (cat, rabbit, picnic) |
| **open** | A syllable ending with a single vowel. The vowel sound is usually long. (me, veto) |
| **r-controlled** | A syllable in which the vowel(s) is followed by the single letter *r*. The vowel sound is neither long nor short. (chart, fern, pour, target, whisper) |
| **vowel team** | A syllable containing two or more letters that together make one vowel sound. The vowel sound can be long, short, or a diphthong. (plain, show, heavy, boy, cow, cloudy, boiling) |
| **vowel–silent e** | A syllable with a long vowel–consonant–silent *e* pattern. (shape, cube, slide, behave) |
| **consonant-*le*** | An unaccented final syllable containing a consonant plus –*le*. (apple, table) |

## SYLLABLE PATTERNS

| Pattern | Division | Key Word | Definition |
|---|---|---|---|
| VCCV | VC/CV | rab • bit | If a word has two consonants in the middle, divide between them. When a consonant digraph stands between two vowels, divide the syllables before or after the digraph. |
| VCV | V/CV<br>VC/V | mu • sic<br>clos • et | If a word has one consonant between two vowels, divide the word before or after the consonant. The V/CV division is the most common. |
| VCCCV | VC/CCV | hun • dred | Words with three or more consonants in the medial position almost always contain a blend, and almost always have a closed first syllable. |
| VCCCCV | VC/CCCV | in • struct | Words with four or more consonants in the medial position almost always contain a blend, and almost always have a closed first syllable. |
| VV | V/V | ne • on | If a word has two vowels together that make two different sounds, divide between the two vowels. |

# What Is a Phonogram?

3.22

A phonogram is a letter (or series of letters) that stands for a sound, syllable, syllable part (rime), or series of sounds. Phonograms are often referred to as word families. The words *sunk, chunk,* and *trunk* belong to the same word family because they all contain the ending *–unk.* In these three words the ending *–unk* is a phonogram; it is also the rime.

A relatively small number of phonograms can be used to generate a large number of words. Wylie and Durrell (1970) point out that nearly 500 primary-grade words can be derived from only 37 "rhyming" phonograms.

| "Rhyming" Phonograms | | | | |
|------|------|------|------|------|
| ack | ail | ain | ake | ale |
| ame | an | ank | ap | ash |
| at | ate | aw | ay | eat |
| ell | est | ice | ick | ide |
| ight | ill | in | ine | ing |
| ink | ip | ir | ock | oke |
| op | ore | or | uck | ug |
| ump | unk | | | |

REFERENCE
Wylie, R., and D. Durrell. 1970. Teaching vowels through phonograms. *Elementary English* 47.

# "Rhyming" Phonogram Word List

| | |
|---|---|
| **ack** | back, black, crack, flack, hack, jack, knack, lack, pack, quack, rack, sack, slack, stack, tack, track |
| **ail** | bail, fail, frail, grail, hail, jail, mail, nail, pail, quail, rail, sail, snail, tail, trail, wail |
| **ain** | brain, chain, drain, gain, grain, lain, main, pain, plain, rain, slain, sprain, stain, strain, swain, train, twain, vain |
| **ake** | bake, brake, cake, drake, fake, flake, lake, make, quake, rake, sake, shake, snake, stake, take, wake |
| **ale** | bale, gale, hale, kale, male, pale, sale, scale, shale, stale, tale, vale, wale, whale |
| **ame** | blame, came, fame, flame, frame, game, lame, name, same, shame, tame |
| **an** | ban, bran, can, clan, fan, man, pan, plan, ran, scan, span, tan, than, van |
| **ank** | bank, blank, clank, crank, dank, drank, flank, frank, lank, plank, prank, rank, sank, shank, spank, stank, swank, tank, thank, yank |
| **ap** | cap, chap, clap, flap, gap, lap, map, nap, pap, rap, sap, scrap, slap, snap, strap, tap, trap, wrap, yap, zap |
| **ash** | bash, brash, cash, clash, crash, dash, flash, gash, gnash, hash, lash, mash, rash, sash, slash, smash, splash, stash, thrash, trash |
| **at** | bat, brat, cat, chat, drat, fat, flat, gnat, hat, mat, pat, rat, sat, scat, slat, spat, sprat, that, vat |
| **ate** | crate, date, fate, gate, grate, hate, late, mate, pate, plate, rate, skate, slate, spate, state |
| **aw** | caw, claw, craw, draw, flaw, gnaw, haw, jaw, law, maw, paw, raw, saw, slaw, squaw, straw, taw, thaw, yaw |
| **ay** | bay, bray, cray, day, flay, fray, gay, gray, hay, jay, lay, may, nay, pay, play, pray, quay, ray, say, slay, spay, splay, spray, stay, stray, sway, tray, way |

CONTINUED ▷

## "RHYMING" PHONOGRAM WORD LIST (CONTINUED)

| | |
|---|---|
| **eat** | beat, bleat, cheat, cleat, eat, feat, heat, meat, neat, peat, pleat, seat, teat, treat, wheat |
| **ell** | bell, cell, dell, fell, hell, jell, knell, quell, sell, shell, smell, spell, swell, tell, well, yell |
| **est** | best, blest, chest, crest, fest, guest, jest, nest, pest, quest, rest, test, vest, west, zest |
| **ice** | dice, lice, mice, nice, price, rice, slice, spice, splice, thrice, trice, twice, vice |
| **ick** | brick, chick, click, crick, flick, hick, kick, lick, nick, pick, prick, quick, sick, slick, stick, thick, tick, trick, wick |
| **ide** | bide, bride, chide, glide, hide, pride, ride, side, slide, snide, stride, tide, wide |
| **ight** | blight, bright, fight, flight, fright, knight, light, might, night, plight, right, sight, slight, tight |
| **ill** | bill, chill, dill, drill, fill, gill, grill, hill, kill, mill, pill, quill, shrill, sill, skill, spill, still, thrill, till, will |
| **in** | bin, chin, din, fin, gin, grin, kin, pin, shin, sin, skin, spin, tin, thin, win |
| **ine** | brine, dine, fine, line, mine, nine, pine, shine, spine, swine, tine, thine, vine, wine |
| **ing** | bring, cling, ding, fling, king, ping, ring, sing, sling, spring, sting, string, swing, thing, wing, zing |
| **ink** | blink, brink, clink, drink, fink, ink, kink, link, mink, pink, rink, sink, slink, stink, think, wink |
| **ip** | blip, chip, clip, dip, drip, flip, grip, hip, kip, lip, nip, pip, quip, rip, ship, sip, skip, slip, strip, tip, trip, whip, zip |
| **ir** | fir, sir, stir, whir |

| | |
|---|---|
| **ock** | block, chock, clock, cock, crock, dock, flock, frock, hock, jock, knock, lock, mock, pock, rock, shock, smock, sock, stock |
| **oke** | bloke, broke, choke, coke, joke, poke, smoke, spoke, stoke, stroke, woke, yoke |
| **op** | cop, chop, crop, drop, flop, fop, glop, hop, lop, mop, plop, pop, prop, shop, slop, sop, stop, top |
| **ore** | bore, chore, core, fore, gore, lore, more, pore, score, shore, snore, sore, spore, store, swore, tore, wore, yore |
| **or** | for, nor |
| **uck** | buck, chuck, cluck, duck, luck, muck, pluck, puck, shuck, snuck, struck, stuck, suck, truck, tuck |
| **ug** | bug, chug, drug, dug, hug, jug, lug, mug, plug, pug, rug, slug, smug, snug, thug, tug |
| **ump** | bump, chump, clump, dump, frump, grump, hump, jump, lump, plump, pump, rump, slump, stump, sump, thump, trump |
| **unk** | bunk, chunk, clunk, dunk, drunk, flunk, funk, hunk, junk, lunk, punk, skunk, slunk, spunk, stunk, sunk, trunk |

**3.25**

# What Are Some Spelling Generalizations?

**3.26**

**Section V: Spelling**

**Chapter 13: Spelling Instruction**

There are some spelling generalizations that are useful to know because they apply to many words and can help students notice spelling patterns in words. The following chart lists generalizations for forming plurals and adding suffixes.

## USEFUL SPELLING GENERALIZATIONS

| **Forming Plurals** | For most singular nouns, add –s to form the plural. |
| --- | --- |
| | cup ▷ cups, book ▷ books |
| | When a singular noun ends with s, ss, ch, sh, x, or z, add –es. |
| | kiss ▷ kisses, tax ▷ taxes, dish ▷ dishes, lunch ▷ lunches |
| | When a singular noun ends with a consonant + y, usually change the y to i and add –es. |
| | cherry ▷ cherries, penny ▷ pennies |
| | When a singular noun ends with a consonant + o, usually add –es. |
| | hero ▷ heroes, potato ▷ potatoes, tornado ▷ tornadoes |
| | When a singular noun ends with a vowel + o, usually add –s. |
| | studio ▷ studios, radio ▷ radios |
| | When a singular noun ends in f and fe, usually change the f to v and add –es. |
| | knife ▷ knives, calf ▷ calves |

| | |
|---|---|
| **Adding Suffixes** | **Words ending in *e*** |

**Words ending in *e***

- When a word ends in silent *e,* usually drop the *e* when adding a suffix that begins with a vowel.

write ▷ writing, move ▷ movable

Exception: When a word ends with vowel + *e,* usually keep the *e* when adding a suffix that begins with a vowel.

see ▷ seeing, hoe ▷ hoeing

- Keep the *e* when adding suffixes *–ful, –ness, –less, –ly.*

hope ▷ hopeless, care ▷ careful

**Words ending in *y***

- When a word ends with consonant + *y,* usually change the *y* to *i* when adding a suffix.

easy ▷ easily, carry ▷ carried

Exception: Keep the *y* if the suffix begins with *i.*

carry ▷ carrying

- When a word ends with vowel + *y,* usually keep the *y* when adding a suffix.

play ▷ player, joy ▷ joyful

**Words ending in *ic***

- When a word ends with *ic,* add a *k* when adding a suffix that begins with *e, i,* or *y.*

mimic ▷ mimicked, picnic ▷ picnicking, garlic ▷ garlicky

**Words that require doubling the final consonant**

- When the last syllable of a word ends with a short vowel + consonant and the last syllable is stressed, usually double the final consonant when adding a suffix that begins with a vowel.

hot ▷ hottest, stop ▷ stopped, begin ▷ beginning

# What Is a Morpheme?

Morphology is defined as the study of meaningful parts of words and how they are put together. Morphemes are the smallest meaningful spoken units of language. *Morphos* means "form or structure" in Greek; *eme* means "an element or little piece of something." The majority of morphemes in English came from one of three ancient languages: Latin, Greek, or Anglo-Saxon.

A morpheme may be one syllable (*pig*) or more than one syllable (*elephant*). It may be a whole word or a part of a word. There are two basic types of morphemes: free and bound.

▷ *Free morphemes* can stand alone as words; they do not have to be combined with other morphemes to make words. Base words and root words are examples of free morphemes.

▷ *Bound morphemes* must be attached to, or "bound" to, other morphemes to make words. Affixes (prefixes, suffixes) and word roots are examples of bound morphemes.

## Free Morphemes

**Anglo-Saxon Base Words**   These base words, or root words, can stand alone, but they also may take prefixes and suffixes; for example, *friend/friendly* and *happy/unhappy.*

**Compound Words**   A compound word is a word made up of two free morphemes. The majority of compound words are of Anglo-Saxon origin. Some compound words have a meaning that differs from the meanings of their two parts. (See the examples marked with an asterisk.) Other compound words have the same meaning as the two word parts would have if they appeared as separate, adjacent words.

| | | | |
|---|---|---|---|
| baseball* | earthquake | outside* | sunshine |
| blackboard* | egghead* | somebody* | toenail |
| bluegrass* | firearm* | splashdown* | washcloth |
| daytime | highlight* | | |

3.29

## Bound Morphemes

AFFIXES

**Inflectional Suffixes**   An inflectional suffix, or ending, is a letter or group of letters that is added to the end of a word. Although it does not change its part of speech, it adjusts the word to fit the meaning of the sentence. If the word is a noun, an inflectional suffix may show possession *(hers)*, or plurality *(boxes)*. If the word is a verb, an inflectional suffix may show tense *(walked)*, active or passive voice *(it was driven)*, or state *(she had been singing)*. If the word is an adjective, the inflectional suffix may show comparison *(louder, loudest)*.

**Derivational Prefixes**   A prefix is a group of letters that is "fixed" to the beginning of a word. A derivational prefix modifies the meaning of the word to which it is attached.

**Derivational Suffixes**   A suffix is a letter or group of letters that is "fixed" to the end of a word. A derivational suffix modifies the meaning of the word to which it is attached. It may also change the part of speech, pronunciation, and spelling.

WORD ROOTS

**Latin Word Roots**   Most Latin word roots can't stand alone. They appear in combination with one or more affixes.

**Greek Word Roots**   Most Greek word roots can't stand alone. They appear in combination with each other.

**3.30**

## MOST FREQUENT PREFIXES

| Prefix | Meaning | Key Word | Origin |
|---|---|---|---|
| anti– | against | antifreeze | Latin |
| de– | opposite | defrost | Latin |
| dis–* | not, opposite of | disagree | Latin |
| en–, em– | cause to | encode, embrace | Latin |
| fore– | before | forecast | Latin |
| in–, im– | in | infield | Latin |
| in–, im–, il–, ir–* | not | injustice, impossible | Latin |
| inter– | between | interact | Latin |
| mid– | middle | midway | Latin |
| mis– | wrongly | misfire | Latin |
| non– | not | nonsense | Latin |
| over– | over | overlook | Anglo-Saxon |
| pre– | before | prefix | Latin |
| re–* | again | return | Latin |
| semi– | half | semicircle | Latin |
| sub– | under | submarine | Latin |
| super– | above | superstar | Latin |
| trans– | across | transport | Latin |
| un–* | not | unfriendly | Anglo-Saxon |
| under– | under | undersea | Anglo-Saxon |

*Most frequent. The four most frequent prefixes account for 58 percent of prefixed words in printed school English.*

REFERENCE
White, T. G., J. Sowell, and A. Yanagihara. 1989. Teaching elementary students to use word-part clues. *The Reading Teacher* 42.

# MOST FREQUENT SUFFIXES

| Suffix | Meaning | Key Word | Origin |
|---|---|---|---|
| –able, –ible | can be done | comfortable | Latin |
| –al, –ial | having characteristics of | personal | Latin |
| –ed* | past-tense verbs | hopped | Anglo-Saxon |
| –en | made of | wooden | Latin |
| –er | comparative | higher | Anglo-Saxon |
| –er, –or | one who | worker, actor | Anglo-Saxon |
| –est | comparative | biggest | Anglo-Saxon |
| –ful | full of | careful | Anglo-Saxon |
| –ic | having characteristics of | linguistic | Latin |
| –ing* | verb form/present participle | running | Anglo-Saxon |
| –ion, –tion, –ation, –ition | act, process | occasion, attraction | Latin |
| –ity, –ty | state of | infinity | Latin |
| –ive, –ative, –itive | adjective form of a noun | plaintive | Latin |
| –less | without | fearless | Anglo-Saxon |
| –ly* | characteristic of | quickly | Anglo-Saxon |
| –ment | action or process | enjoyment | Latin |
| –ness | state of, condition of | kindness | Anglo-Saxon |
| –ous, –eous, –ious | possessing the qualities of | joyous | Latin |
| –s, –es* | more than one | books, boxes | Anglo-Saxon |
| –y | characterized by | happy | Latin |

*Most frequent. The four most frequent suffixes account for 72 percent of suffixed words in printed school English.*

REFERENCE

White, T. G., J. Sowell, and A. Yanagihara. 1989. Teaching elementary students to use word-part clues. *The Reading Teacher* 42.

3.32

## COMMON LATIN WORD ROOTS

| Root | Meaning | Key Word | Root | Meaning | Key Word |
|------|---------|----------|------|---------|----------|
| aud | hear | audible | man | hand | manual |
| bene | well, good | benefit | mem | mind | memory |
| centi | hundred | centipede | migr | move | migrate |
| contra | against | contrary | miss | send | missile |
| cred | believe, trust | credible | ped | foot | pedal |
| dict | say, speak | dictate | pop | people | popular |
| duct | lead | conduct | port | carry | porter |
| equi | equal | equitable | rupt | break | erupt |
| extra | outside | extravagant | sign | mark | signal |
| fac | make | factory | spect | look | inspect |
| fig | form | figure | sta/stat | stand | statue |
| flec | flex, bend | flexible | struct | build | construct |
| form | shape | formulate | trac/tract | pull | tractor |
| fract | break | fracture | urb | city | suburb |
| init | beginning | initial | vid/vis | see | video/visible |
| ject | throw | reject | voc | voice | vocal |
| junct | join | junction | volv | roll | revolve |

# COMMON GREEK WORD ROOTS

| Root | Meaning | Key Word | Root | Meaning | Key Word |
|------|---------|----------|------|---------|----------|
| amphi | both | amphibian | micro | small | microscope |
| aster | star | asterisk | mono | single | monorail |
| auto | self | automatic | ology | study of | biology |
| biblio | book | bibliography | opt | eye | optical |
| bio | life | biology | para | beside | parallel |
| chron | time | chronic | phil | love | philosophy |
| geo | earth | geology | phon | sound | phonograph |
| graph | write, record | photograph | photo/phos | light | photograph |
| hemi | half | hemisphere | pod | foot | podiatrist |
| hydr | water | hydrolic | psych | mind, soul | psychic |
| hyper | over | hyperactive | scope | see | microscope |
| ist | one who | dentist | sphere | ball | hemisphere |
| logo | word, reason | logic | syn | together | synonym |
| macro | large | macrobiotic | tele | from afar | telephone |
| mech | machine | mechanic | therm | heat | thermometer |
| meter | measure | altimeter | | | |

CHAPTER

4

# Structure of Spanish and Other Languages

what?
why?
when?
how?

# What Is the Spanish Letter/Sound System?

*Note: Most Spanish speakers in North, Central, and South America pronounce both ll and y as /y/.*

From a phonetic standpoint, Spanish is a much simpler language than English. There is a nearly one-to-one correspondence between the 22 phonemes in the Spanish that is spoken in the Americas* and the 29 letters that represent these sounds. One significant difference between Spanish and English is the ease with which students are able to learn the letter/sound correspondences of the five Spanish vowels. Each vowel letter has a distinct and relatively consistent sound that forms the nucleus of every syllable. The five vowels are categorized as open (/a/), semi-open (/e/, /o/), and closed (/i/, /u/), depending on how wide the mouth is opened and the position of the tongue and lips. Because of the grapheme/phoneme consistency and structural importance of vowels, beginning Spanish readers are taught vowel letters and their corresponding sounds before they are introduced to consonant letters and their sounds.

The phonetic variations of Spanish consonants are a challenge for many beginning readers. As the chart of Spanish consonants later in this chapter shows, the *c* and *g* (like their English counterparts) have both a "hard" and a "soft" sound (e.g., *cocina* and *gigante*). In addition, the Spanish consonant phonemes /s/, /b/, and /y/ have more than one spelling. Students typically take several years to master these contrasts, drawing on visual memory specific to words or word families (Moran and Calfee 1993). Although the spelling of the consonant phonemes /k/, /g/, and /x/ varies, it follows predictable rules that are governed by the vowel sound that follows the consonant phoneme. Therefore, students can be taught how to use syllabic context to decode and spell words with these sounds.

REFERENCES

Moran, C., and R. Calfee. 1993. Comprehending orthography: Social construction of letter-sound systems in monolingual and bilingual programs. *Reading and Writing: An Interdisciplinary Journal* 5, pp. 205–225.

Real Academia Española, Comisión de Gramática. 1996. *Esbozo de una nueva gramática de la lengua española.* Madrid: Espasa Calpe.

See also...

**"Spanish Phonic Elements with Positive Transfer to English," p. 4.18**

## SPANISH VOWELS

| Vowel Type | Letter | Phoneme* | Key Words | Notes |
| --- | --- | --- | --- | --- |
| Open | a | /a/ | ama, casa | This is the short-*o* sound in *father* and *spa*. |
| Semi-Open | e | /e/ | edad, mesa | This is the short-*e* sound in *messy*.** |
| | o | /o/ | oso, mono | This is the long-*o* sound in *no* and *old*. |
| Closed | i | /i/ | iba, niña | This is the long-*e* sound in *machine*. |
| | u | /u/ | uno, duda | This is the long-*oo* sound in *ruby* and *July*. |
| | y | /i/ | y | This is the long-*e* sound in *city*. |

*Phonemes are represented by phonetic symbols used in Spanish.*
**Commonly taught in U.S. schools as the long-a sound in* weigh.

**4.4**

## SPANISH VOWEL COMBINATIONS

### Hiatos

*Hiatos* are two consecutive vowels that appear in different syllables. There is a pause between two distinct sounds.

▸ One Open and One Semi-Open, or Two Semi-Open

ae   ao   ea   eo   ee   oa   oe

Key Words:  trae, real, leo, cree, toalla

▸ One Open or Semi-Open, and One Accented Closed

ía   íe   ío   úa   úe   úo   aí   eí   oí   aú   eú

Key Words:  día, río, actúo, país, leí, Raúl

### Diptongos

*Diptongos* are two consecutive vowels that appear in the same syllable. The sounds are blended together.

▸ One Open or Semi-Open, and One Closed

ai/ay   ei/ey   oi/oy   au   eu   ou

ia   ie   io   ua   ue   uo

Key Words:  baile, voy, aunque, lluvia, cielo, cuando, puede

▸ Two Closed

iu   ui/uy

Key Words:  ciudad, ruido, muy

### Triptongos

*Triptongos* are three consecutive vowels that are blended within one syllable.

▸ Open or Semi-Open, and Two Closed

iai   iei   iau   ioi   uai/uay   uei/uey   uau

Key Words:  apreciáis, miau, averiguáis, buey, guau

# SPANISH CONSONANTS

| Letter | Phoneme* | Key Words | Notes |
|--------|----------|-----------|-------|
| b | /b/ | boca, baño | |
| c | /k/ | cama, cosa, cuna | Phoneme /k/ is spelled *c* before *a, o,* and *u* and *qu* before *e* and *i*. |
| | /s/ | cena, cita | |
| ch | /ch/ | chato, ocho | |
| d | /d/ | deja, dos | Similar to /th/ between vowels (*nada*) and at the end of words (*pared*). |
| f | /f/ | fiesta, fecha | |
| g | /g/ | gato, guerra, guía | Hard *g* before *a, o, ue, ui*. |
| | /x/ | giro, gente | Spanish phoneme /x/ is a guttural sound, similar to English /h/. |
| h | silent | hijo, hermano | |
| j | /x/ | jabón, rojo, jugo dije, jinete | Spanish phoneme /x/ is spelled *j* before *a, o,* and *u*. It can be spelled *j* or *g* before *e* and *i*. (See note for phoneme /x/ spelled *x*.) |
| l | /l/ | loma, malo | |
| ll | /y/ | llama, pollo | Although *ll* and *y* represent two distinct phonemes, most Spanish speakers say both /y/. |
| m | /m/ | más, ama | |
| n | /n/ | nido, una | |

*A simplified system of phonetic symbols has been used to represent the sounds of* ch, ll, ñ, rr, *and* y.

CONTINUED ▷

**4.5**

## SPANISH CONSONANTS (CONTINUED)

**4.6**

| Letter | Phoneme* | Key Words | Notes |
|--------|----------|-----------|-------|
| ñ | /ñ/ | año, niño | Phoneme /ñ/ has a sound similar to that of the letters *ni* in the English word *onion*. |
| p | /p/ | papá, pera | |
| q | /k/ | queso, quita | For /kw/ sound in Spanish, *cu* + vowel. |
| r | /r/ | oro, cara | More forcibly rolled than English /r/. |
| | /rr/ | rosa, alrededor, barro | Initial *r* has /rr/ sound, as does *r* after *l*, *n*, or *s*. When phoneme /rr/ occurs between two vowels, it is spelled *rr*. |
| s | /s/ | sapo, silla, mesa | Similar to the *s* of *cause* when followed by *b, d, g, l, m, n*. |
| t | /t/ | tú, todo, pata | Softer than English /t/. |
| v | /b/ | vaca, oveja | There is no Spanish phoneme /v/. |
| x | /ks/ | máximo | This is the only letter in Spanish that represents two phonemes. |
| | /x/ | México, Oaxaca | This spelling of phoneme /x/ can be found in certain place names. |
| y | /y/ | yema, yo | |
| z | /s/ | zapato, paz | |
| k | /k/ | kilogramo, kiosco | Only appears in words of foreign origin. |
| w | /ōo/ or /b/ | wat, wáter | Only appears in words of foreign origin. |

*A simplified system of phonetic symbols has been used to represent the sounds of ch, ll, ñ, rr, *and* y.

# SPANISH CONSONANT BLENDS

| Sounds | Spelling | Key Words | Sounds | Spelling | Key Words |
|---|---|---|---|---|---|
| **r - blends** | | | **l - blends** | | |
| /br/ | br | brazo, abrigo | /bl/ | bl | blusa, habla |
| /cr/ | cr | crema, crudo | /cl/ | cl | clase, aclara |
| /dr/ | dr | drama, dragón | /fl/ | fl | flaco, flores |
| /fr/ | fr | frío, ofrece | /gl/ | gl | globo, glaciar |
| /gr/ | gr | gris, agregar | /pl/ | pl | plancha, pluma |
| /pr/ | pr | primo, aprende | /tl/ | tl | nahautl, tlacuache |
| /tr/ | tr | traigo, atrás | | | |

# SPANISH CONSONANT DIGRAPHS

| Phoneme | Spelling | Key Words | Notes |
|---|---|---|---|
| /ch/ | ch | choque, ancho | Usually taught as part of the Spanish alphabet. |
| /y/ | ll | llama, calle | Usually taught as part of the Spanish alphabet. |
| /rr/ | rr | perro, barril | |

# What Are the Guidelines for Spanish Phonics Instruction?

**4.8**

**CORE Reading Research Anthology**

for background information

**CORE Assessing Reading**
**"CORE Spanish Phonics Survey"**

Explicit Spanish phonics instruction has been shown to improve Spanish-speaking students' reading achievement in both Spanish and English (Carrillo 1994; Durgunoğlu et al. 1993). Although there is no "set in stone" sequence for teaching Spanish sound/spelling relationships, the following are some general guidelines:

- Unlike phonics instruction in English, Spanish phonics instruction should begin with the five vowels.

- Instruction should progress from simple to more complex sounds. Consonant sounds should be taught before digraphs (*ch, ll, rr*), blends (*cr, tr, bl, pl,* etc.), and vowel combinations (*hiatos* and *diptongos*).

- Consonants should be taught in combination with vowels so that students can apply what they learn to decodable text. Instruction should begin with the consonants that are most useful in generating and decoding Spanish words.

- The sequence of instruction should stagger consonant sounds so that the type varies: bilabial (/p/, /b/, /m/), labiodental (/f/), dental (/t/, /d/), alveolar (/s/, /n/, /l/, /r/, /rr/), palatal (/ch/, /ñ/, /y/), and velar (/k/, /x/, /g/).

REFERENCES

Carrillo, M. 1994. Development of phonological awareness and reading acquisition: A study in Spanish. *Reading and Writing: An Interdisciplinary Journal* 6, pp. 279–298.

Durgunoğlu, A. Y., W. E. Nagy, and B. J. Hancin-Bhatt. 1993. Cross-language transfer of phonological awareness. *Journal of Educational Psychology* 85(3).

In addition, students should receive systematic instruction that includes constant review and repetition of sound/spelling relationships. With these guidelines in mind, the following chart presents a possible sequence of Spanish phonics instruction.

## SUGGESTED SEQUENCE FOR GRADE 1 SPANISH PHONICS INSTRUCTION

| | | |
|---|---|---|
| **Vowels** | Initial Vowel | o, a, i, u, e |
| **Consonants and Consonant Digraphs** | Open Syllables with | m, s, p, t, c (/k/), n, b, l, f, r (initial) & rr, g (/g/), d, v, ch, ñ, j, ll, r (medial), c (/s/), g (/x/), y, q, gu + *e* or *i* (/g/), z, h, güe & güi, k, x, w |
| | Closed Syllables ending in | l, m, n, r, s, d, z, x |
| **Consonant Blends** | Open Syllables with | cr, pr, tr, br, gr, dr, fr, bl, cl, fl, pl, gl |
| | Closed Syllables with | cr, pr, tr, br, gr, fr, bl, cl, fl, pl |
| **Vowel Combinations** | Hiatos | ae, ea, ee, eo |
| | Diphthongs in Open Syllables | ia, ie, ua, ue, ui & uy, io, ai & ay, oy |
| | Diphthongs in Closed Syllables | ie, ua, ue |

# What Are the Syllable Types and Patterns in Spanish?

Spanish is in many respects a syllabic language: the spoken language is built upon a relatively small collection of distinctive syllables, and the printed language is easily decoded syllable by syllable (Moran and Calfee 1993). The vast majority of Spanish syllables fall into two categories: open CV (55.94 percent) and closed CVC (20.16 percent) (Guirao and Manrique 1972).

The guiding principle in syllable division is to make syllables end in a vowel as far as possible, so a single consonant between vowels is joined to the vowel or vowels that follow: *ca•la•ba•za*. The digraphs *ch, ll, rr* are considered single consonants and never separated: *ca•rre•te•ra*. Prepositional prefixes form separate syllables, except when the prefix is followed by *s* + a consonant: *con•sul•tar* vs. *cons•tan•te*. Vowels forming a diphthong or triphthong must not be separated: *llu•via*. Hiatos as well as diphthongs and triphthongs that are dissolved by an accent mark form separate syllables: *le•er* and *dí•a*. The liquids *l* and *r* when preceded by any consonant other than *s* are not separated from that consonant unless the consonant is part of a prefix: *a•bra•zo* vs. *sub•ra•yar*. Two separate consonants standing between vowels are divided: *pron•to*.

REFERENCES

Guirao, M., and A. M. B. Manrique. 1972. Fonemas, sílabas y palabras del español de Buenos Aires. *Filología* 16, pp. 135–165.

Moran, C., and R. Calfee. 1993. Comprehending orthography: Social construction of letter-sound systems in monolingual and bilingual programs. *Reading and Writing: An Interdisciplinary Journal* 5, pp. 205–225.

Quilis, A., and J. Fernández. 1997. *Curso de fonética y fonolgía españolas.* Madrid: Consejo Superior de Investigaciones Científicas.

Ramsey, M. M., and R. Spaulding. 1956. *A textbook of modern Spanish.* New York: Holt, Rinehart and Winston.

## Spanish Syllable Types

| Syllable Type | Definition | Key Words |
|---|---|---|
| Open | An open syllable ends in a vowel. In Spanish, most syllables are open and begin with a consonant. | la, de, ojo, hilo, sopa, corre, abeja, bonito, muchacho, graciosa |
| Closed | A closed syllable ends in a consonant. | el, ir, vez, pon, árbol, tambor, saltan, barcos, puentes, comparten |

## Spanish Syllable Patterns (FROM MOST TO LEAST FREQUENT)

| Pattern | Division | Key Words |
|---|---|---|
| CV | CV/C | so • pa,  mu • cha • cho |
| CVC | CVC/C | ven • der,  tor • men • tas |
| V | V/CV, CV/V | u • va,  e • cha,  tí • o,  le • a |
| CCV | CCV/C<br>CCV/CC | cla • se,  glo • bos<br>pro • ble • ma |
| VC | VC/C | us • ted,  ár • bol,  im • por • tan • tes |
| CCVC | CCVC/C | gran • de,  cris • tal |
| VCC | VCC/CC<br>VCC/C | abs • trac • to<br>ins • pi • rar |
| CVCC | CVCC/C | cons • tan • te,  pers • pec • ti • va |
| CCVCC | CCVCC/C | trans • for • mar |

# What Are the Important Issues in Spanish Spelling?

**4.12**

**CORE Assessing Reading**

**"CORE Spanish Spelling Inventory"**

The Spanish language is often described as having a "shallow" or "transparent" orthography because of its high degree of sound-to-grapheme correspondence. Fourteen phonemes map directly onto their corresponding graphemes: *a, e, o, u, ch, d, f, l, m, n, ñ, p, r, t*. Therefore, students are able to quickly learn how to spell an abundance of words that they say and hear every day: *luna, dedo, uña, noche, muchacho* (moon, finger, nail, night, boy). The spelling of four other phonemes—/k/, /rr/, /g/, and /x/ in /xa/, /xo/, /xu/—follows context-dependent rules that students can learn through explicit instruction and writing practice. Although the sounds /i/, /b/, /s/, /y/, and /x/ in the syllables /xe/ and /xi/ can be represented by more than one Spanish grapheme, the possibilities of choice are fairly limited when compared with the orthographic variations found in English. Research has shown that when making decisions about how to spell unknown words, writers rely on their memory store of known words (the lexical route) and the most common spelling of particular sounds (the phonological route) (Cuetos 1993).

Syllable type also affects spelling difficulty, with closed syllables being more difficult for students to spell than open syllables. One important study found the following spelling errors to be those most frequently made by first graders: (1) the omission of the consonant phonemes /s/, /n/, /l/, and /r/ before other consonants; (2) the omission of the liquids /l/ and /r/ in the stop + liquid clusters *pr, pl, cr, cl,* and *tr;* (3) the omission of the final consonant in closed syllables; and (4) the omission of vowels in diphthongs and in syllables made up of a cluster + a vowel (Manrique and Signorini 1994).

**CORE Reading Research Anthology**

for background information

The following chart shows the most frequent spellings of several common Spanish sounds for which there is more than one written representation. The chart on the next page shows a recommended sequence of beginning Spanish spelling instruction.

REFERENCES

Cuetos, F. 1993. Writing processes in a shallow orthography. *Reading and Writing: An Interdisciplinary Journal* 5, pp. 17–28.

Manrique, A. M. B., and A. Signorini. 1994. Phonological awareness, spelling and reading abilities in Spanish-speaking children. *British Journal of Educational Psychology* 64, pp. 429–439.

4.13

## SPANISH SPELLING FREQUENCIES

| Phoneme* | Most Common | Least Common | Phoneme* | Most Common | Least Common |
|----------|-------------|--------------|----------|-------------|--------------|
| /a/ | a | ha | /ya/ | lla | ya |
| /e/ | e | he | /ye/ | lle | ye |
| /i/ | i | hi | /yo/ | llo | yo |
| /o/ | o | ho | /yu/ | llu | yu |
| /u/ | u | hu | /xe/ | je | ge |
| /ba/ | va | ba | /xi/ | gi | ji |
| /be/ | ve | be |
| /bi/ | vi | bi |
| /bo/ | vo | bo |
| /bu/ | bu | vu |

*Phonemes are represented by phonetic symbols used in Spanish, including a simplified system for the sound of ll and y.*

4.14

| SUGGESTED SEQUENCE FOR BEGINNING SPANISH SPELLING INSTRUCTION | |
| --- | --- |
| **Words with One-to-One Phoneme/Grapheme Correspondence** | Open Syllables<br>Examples: la, uno, pato, dedo, teme, noche, fecha, arena, tomate, muchacho |
| | Closed Syllables<br>Examples: el, un, del, pon, mar, ancha, alto, tarde, falda, mundo, perder |
| **Words That Provide Syllabic Context (Open Syllables)** | Phoneme /i/ spelled *i*<br>Examples: iba*, idea, iguana*, miro, niña, nido, tira, chile, pide, dinero |
| | Phoneme /k/ spelled *c* and *qu*<br>Examples: cada, cae, que, pequeño, quema, quita, come, cosa*, cuna |
| | Phoneme /rr/ spelled *r* (initial) and *rr* (intersyllabic)<br>Examples: rata, regalo*, rima, ropa, ruta, corre, perro, carro |
| | Phoneme /g/ spelled *g* and *gu*<br>Examples: gato, agarra, guerra, guitarra, gota, gorra, digo, agudo |
| | Phoneme /x/ spelled *j* in *ja, jo, ju*<br>Examples: jarra, caja, ceja*, aguja, mojado, ojo, dejo, jugo, juguete |
| **Phonemes with Variant Spellings (Open Syllables)** | Phoneme /s/ spelled *s*<br>Examples: sale, saca, seco, semana, sigue, silla*, solo, queso, su, suma |
| | Phoneme /b/ spelled *b*<br>Examples: baño, arriba, jugaba, beso, bebe, recibe, bigote, boca, bonito, burro |
| | Phoneme /x/ spelled *g* in *ge, gi*<br>Examples: gemelo, recoge, ligera, generoso, corrige, gira, agita |
| | Phoneme /y/ spelled *ll*<br>Examples: ella, llamo, lleno, calle, gallina, llora, pollo, anillo, lluvia* |
| | Phoneme /s/ spelled *c, z*<br>Examples: cena, cerrado, cereza, cine, cocina, zapato, taza, calabaza, zorro |
| | Phoneme /b/ spelled *v*<br>Examples: va, vaca, vaso, ve, vela, vecino, oveja, vine, vida, aviso, vivo |
| | Phoneme /x/ spelled *j* in *je, ji*<br>Examples: jefe, deje, dije, maneje, traje*, viaje*, jinete, mejilla, jirafa |
| | Phoneme /y/ spelled *y*<br>Examples: ya, yate, payaso, yema, oye, yo, rayo, yuca, ayuda |

*Some high-utility words are included in the sequence before all of the associated spelling skills are taught.*

## Suggested Sequence for Beginning Spanish Spelling Instruction

| | |
|---|---|
| **Closed Syllables** | Ending in *l*<br>Examples: sol, real, azul, barril, golpe, salto, bolsillo, volver, colgar, calmado |
| | Ending in *n*<br>Examples: junto, vende, banco, gente, cinco, lindo, gigante, cansada, diferente, joven |
| | Ending in *r*<br>Examples: sur, barco, cerca, verde, parque, partir, correr, cortan, persona, sorpresa* |
| | Ending in *s*<br>Examples: mes, lista, desde, isla, mosca, pasto, lejos, buscan, sospecha, escalera |
| | Ending in *d*<br>Examples: red, salud, pared, bondad, multitud, maldad, soledad |
| | Ending in *z*<br>Examples: pez, paz, luz, voz, vez, nariz, arroz, feliz, diez*, niñez, conozco |
| **Blends** | Examples: creo, primo, triste, abre, libro, grupo, frase, blanco, clase, flor, plato, globo |
| **Plurals ending in** *–s, –es, –ces* | Examples: sillas, calles, vacas, primos, flores, relojes, voces, peces, luces |
| **Silent *h*** | Examples: hace, hablaba, helado, cohete, hermano, hijo, hombres, horrible, ahora, humano |
| **Words with *m* before *p* and *b*** | Examples: campo, rompen, tampoco, compran, tambor, timbre, hambre, siempre*, limpio*, cumpleaños, imposible |
| **Diphthongs** | Examples: hay, baile, rey, reina, voy, estoy, cielo, miedo, viene, estudio, sucio, ciudad, cuando, juego, pueblo, hueso, fuerte, muy |
| **Words with *n* before *v*** | Examples: enviar, envase, envolver, invita, inventar, convence, invierno, investigar, invisible |

*Some high-utility words are included in the sequence before all of the associated spelling skills are taught.*

4.15

# What Are the Differences Between English and Spanish Sound/Spellings?

**4.16**

 See also...

**CORE Reading Research Anthology**

for background information

The following chart identifies important differences between English and Spanish phonology and orthography. Teachers of Spanish-speaking students can use this information to better understand students' performance in both reading and spelling. When teachers recognize that a particular error is a result of a student correctly applying the rules of Spanish, they can work with the student to identify differences between the two language systems and thereby build on the student's existing repertoire of literacy skills.

## ENGLISH/SPANISH LANGUAGE DIFFERENCES

| | |
|---|---|
| **b & v** | In Spanish *b* and *v* are pronounced with the same sound, like the letter *b* in *balloon*. Therefore, students may have problems spelling words with the letter *v*. |
| **c, s, z** | In Spanish the following letters have the same sound, like the sound of the letter *s* in *sent*:<br>•*c* preceding *e* or *i*  •*s*  •*z*<br>Students may be confused when spelling words with any of these three letters. |
| **ch & sh** | The *sh* digraph does not exist in Spanish. Therefore, students may pronounce *sh* as /s/ and have difficulty spelling words with *sh*, possibly substituting *ch*. The *ch* consonant digraph is usually taught as part of the Spanish alphabet. It has the /ch/ sound in *cheese*. |
| **double consonants** | The only double consonants in Spanish where both letters are pronounced are *cc*—pronounced like /ks/ in *accent*—and *nn*. In Spanish *ll* and *rr* are not considered double consonants because they represent a single sound. English words containing double consonants may be difficult to read and spell. |
| **–ed** | The variations in the sound of *–ed* in past-tense verbs may be confusing, especially when *–ed* has the soft-*t* sound as in *wrapped*. |

| | |
|---|---|
| **final consonant blends** | Because Spanish words do not usually end with final consonant blends, English words that do may cause confusion in spelling. Students will generally pronounce the first consonant and not the second. The most common combinations that can create difficulties are *ng, nd, st, nk, mp, nt, ft,* and *rl.* |
| **g & j** | In Spanish, *g* before *e* or *i,* and *j* represent a strong guttural sound with no equivalent in English. The English *h* has a sound that most closely approximates the Spanish consonant sound /x/. Students may pronounce words such as *general* as *heneral, giraffe* as *hiraffe,* and *juvenile* as *huvenile.* These pronunciation differences can lead to spelling confusion. |
| **h** (initial position) | The only silent letter in Spanish is *h.* Students may not write the letter *h* in the initial position of words, and may not pronounce it when reading. |
| **k** | In Spanish, the letter *k* is found only in words of foreign origin and may, therefore, be unfamiliar to students. They may use the letter *c* or *qu* followed by *e* or *i* to write the sound for the letter *k.* |
| **plurals** | English plural words are likely to cause problems in both pronunciation and spelling for Spanish-speaking students. First, the pronunciation of the final *–s* in English varies. It can have the /s/ sound of *books* or the /z/ sound of *stores.* Second, students may have problems writing the plurals of English words ending in consonants, as most take *–s* and not *–es* as is the case in Spanish. |
| **q** | The /kw/ sound in the English word *question* is always written *cu* plus a vowel in Spanish. The letter *q* always appears with *ue* or *ui* in Spanish and has the /k/ sound as in *kite.* |
| **s-blends** | There are no Spanish words that begin with *s*-blends. A vowel always precedes consonant clusters with *s,* so Spanish-speaking students may add the sound of the letter *e* (/ā/) when they pronounce words that begin with *sc, sk, sl, sm, sn, sp, sq, st,* or *sw.* |
| **th** | The *th* digraph does not exist in Spanish spoken in the Americas. Students may pronounce *th* as *d* since its sound is similar to the soft *d* in Spanish. For example, *that* might become *dat.* |
| **vowels** | In Spanish, vowels have a single and relatively invariable sound:<br>•*a* as in *spa*   •*e* as in *weigh*   •*i* as in *marine*   •*o* as in *open*   •*u* as in *tune*<br>Spanish-speaking students may have trouble with the various English vowel sounds and vowel combinations, substituting them with Spanish vowel sounds and combinations. |
| **w & wh** | The letter *w* and the digraph *wh* do not exist in Spanish, except in words of foreign origin. The pronunciation of the letter *w* depends on the language the word comes from and is either the /ōo/ or /b/ sound. This may cause confusion in spelling. In addition, students may pronounce and write *wh* as *w.* |

# What Spanish Phonics Skills Are Transferable to English Phonics?

**4.18**

See also . . .

Chapter 3: Structure of the
English Language

Students who can read in Spanish have mastered a number of important skills. Even beginning Spanish readers have learned that letters represent the different sounds of spoken language and that individual sounds can be blended into meaningful units. Rather than being a deficit, literacy in Spanish provides a strong foundation for learning English phonics.

As teachers introduce Spanish readers to English phonics, they can draw on a large number of phonic elements that are common to both languages. The following chart lists these common sound/spelling patterns.

## SPANISH PHONIC ELEMENTS WITH POSITIVE TRANSFER TO ENGLISH*

| | |
|---|---|
| /b/ spelled *b* | /s/ spelled *s* and *c* in *ce, ci* |
| /d/ spelled *d* | /t/ spelled *t* |
| /f/ spelled *f* | /y/ spelled *y* |
| /g/ spelled *g* in *ga, go, gu* | /ch/ spelled *ch* |
| /g/ spelled *gu* in *gue, gui* | *l*-blends (bl, cl, fl, gl, pl) |
| /k/ spelled *c* in *ca, co, cu* | *r*-blends (br, cr, dr, fr, gr, pr, tr) |
| /l/ spelled *l* | /ō/ spelled *o* |
| /m/ spelled *m* | /o͞o/ spelled *u* |
| /n/ spelled *n* | diphthong /oi/ spelled *oi, oy* |
| /p/ spelled *p* | |

*Sound/spelling patterns are the same in both languages.*

Certain features of the Spanish letter/sound system are likely to cause difficulties for students who are transitioning from reading in Spanish to reading in English. Teachers can use the following chart to identify these elements with "negative transfer" and help students understand the differences between Spanish and English. In addition, there are many features of the English sound/spelling system that don't exist in Spanish. The second chart lists the phonic elements that have no counterparts in Spanish and thus have "zero transfer." Students will need systematic, explicit instruction in these English phonics skills.

## SPANISH PHONIC ELEMENTS WITH NEGATIVE TRANSFER TO ENGLISH*

| | |
|---|---|
| *g* before *e* and *i*, and *j* represent the guttural sound /x/, similar to English /h/ | *v* is pronounced /b/ |
| *h* is a silent letter | *z* is pronounced /s/ by Spanish speakers in the Americas |
| *ll* is a consonant digraph, usually taught as part of the Spanish alphabet. Most Spanish speakers pronounce *ll* as /y/. | The five Spanish vowels are relatively invariable in sound:<br>*a* represents the short-*o* sound in *watch* and *father*<br>*e* represents the long-*a* sound in *eight*<br>*i* represents the long-*e* sound in *machine* |
| *que* and *qui* are pronounced /k/, never /kw/ | *o* represents the long-*o* sound in *no, old, rose*<br>*u* represents the long-*u* sound in *July, tube* |
| *rr* is a consonant digraph that represents the forcibly rolled phoneme /rr/ | |

## ENGLISH PHONIC ELEMENTS WITH ZERO TRANSFER FROM SPANISH**

| | |
|---|---|
| all short vowels and schwa | /v/ spelled *v* |
| long vowels with silent *e* | digraphs *sh, th, wh, ph, gh, -ng* |
| long-vowel digraphs and double vowels (except the diphthongs *oy* and *oi*) | *s*-blends |
| /j/ spelled *j* and *g* in words like *jump, giant,* and *cage* | consonants in final position (a limited number of consonants can appear at the end of Spanish words: *n, s, l, m, r, x, t, d, z, j*) |
| /k/ spelled *k* (In Spanish, the letter *k* only appears in a small number of borrowed words.) | final consonant blends |
| /w/ (Letter *w* only appears in Spanish in a limited number of borrowed words and is pronounced /b/ or /o͞o/.) | three-letter consonant blends |

*Letter/sound correspondences are different. **Sound/spelling patterns do not exist in Spanish.*

## What Role Do English/Spanish Cognates Play?

Thanks to their shared Latin and Greek roots, there are many words in English and Spanish that look and sound similar and have the same meaning. These cognates provide an important link between English and Spanish. Teachers can use cognates to develop students' oral vocabulary and phonemic awareness. By focusing students' attention on the morphological patterns of language, the study of cognates also helps English language learners with word attack and spelling skills.

The lists on the following pages provide some basic age-appropriate cognates. Both words in each pair begin with the same initial phoneme. The lists are intended as a starting point and should be expanded depending on students' individual interests and needs. For example, teachers can work with students to create lists of cognates related to particular subject areas: communities, foods, technology, geography, or mathematics. Cognates also lend themselves to word sorts that focus on the orthographic differences between English and Spanish word endings: *–tion* and *–ción, –ent* and *–ente, –cy* and *–cia.*

A note of caution: not all words that are spelled alike in English and Spanish have the same meaning. The Spanish word *pan* means "bread," and *red* means "net." In addition, words that sound the same in English and Spanish sometimes mean very different things. There are many false cognates, also known as "false friends." Some examples are the Spanish words *actual* (which means "current," not "actual"), *embarazada* (which means "pregnant," not "embarrassed"), and *campo* (which means "field," not "camp").

Borrowed words provide another useful bridge between English and Spanish. American English has borrowed more words from Spanish than from any other language. There are countless examples used in everyday speech, including *barbecue, canyon, tornado, plaza, chocolate, ranch, tomato, corral, banana, burro, jaguar,* and *potato.*

REFERENCE
McCrum, R., W. Cran, and R. MacNeil. 1987. *The story of English.* New York: Viking Penguin.

## ENGLISH/SPANISH COGNATES, KINDERGARTEN

| English | Spanish | English | Spanish |
| --- | --- | --- | --- |
| baby | bebé | lion | león |
| boat | bote | medicine | medicina |
| button | botón | monster | monstruo |
| center | centro | music | música |
| circus | circo | number | número |
| class | clase | pajamas | pijama |
| color | color | park | parque |
| computer | computadora | pear | pera |
| different | diferente | plant | planta |
| doctor | doctor | restaurant | restaurante |
| family | familia | rose (flower) | rosa |
| favorite | favorito/favorita | sandals | sandalias |
| flower | flor | secret | secreto |
| fruit | fruta | telephone | teléfono |
| grade | grado | television | televisión |
| lemon | limón | tiger | tigre |
| letter | letra | title | título |
| line | línea | turtle | tortuga |

## ENGLISH/SPANISH COGNATES, GRADE 1

| English | Spanish | English | Spanish |
|---------|---------|---------|---------|
| bicycle | bicicleta | mathematics | matemáticas |
| bottle | botella | minute | minuto |
| breeze | brisa | mountain | montaña |
| calendar | calendario | north | norte |
| centimeter | centímetro | ocean | océano |
| circle | círculo | part | parte |
| club | club | person | persona |
| dentist | dentista | piano | piano |
| difficult | difícil | poem | poema |
| dinosaur | dinosaurio | popular | popular |
| double | doble | practice | practicar (verb) |
| equal | igual | princess | princesa |
| famous | famoso/famosa | problem | problema |
| favor | favor | rectangle | rectángulo |
| group | grupo | sack | saco |
| guitar | guitarra | sum | suma |
| kilogram | kilogramo | taxi | taxi |
| list | lista | tower | torre |
| map | mapa | triangle | triángulo |

# ENGLISH/SPANISH COGNATES, GRADE 2

| English | Spanish | English | Spanish |
|---------|---------|---------|---------|
| artist | artista | palace | palacio |
| castle | castillo | perfect | perfecto/perfecta |
| celebration | celebración | pilot | piloto |
| coast | costa | planet | planeta |
| collection | colección | possible | posible |
| culture | cultura | prepare | preparar |
| desert | desierto | president | presidente |
| dictionary | diccionario | professor | profesor |
| fossil | fósil | program | programa |
| future | futuro | second | segundo |
| mask | máscara | service | servicio |
| memory | memoria | similar | similar |
| menu | menú | submarine | submarino |
| modern | moderno/moderna | surprise | sorpresa |
| museum | museo | telescope | telescopio |
| nation | nación | temperature | temperatura |
| natural | natural | terrible | terrible |
| necessary | necesario/necesaria | traffic | tráfico |
| orbit | órbita | tunnel | túnel |

# *What English Sounds Pose Problems for Speakers of Other Languages?*

**4.24**

**Chapter 3: Structure of the
English Language**

Research has shown that phonemic awareness instruction is most effective when students are taught how to discriminate, articulate, and manipulate the various sounds of the English language. The chart on the facing page lists the English sounds that have proven to be the most difficult for students who are learning English as a second language. The difficulty may arise because a given phoneme does not exist in the primary language. For example, there is no *th* digraph in Japanese, so Japanese-speaking students have to learn to identify and articulate an entirely new sound when they encounter such basic words as *the* and *that*. Sometimes difficulties arise because of the contrast between a sound/spelling pattern in the primary language and the pattern in English. An example of this kind of negative transfer occurs when Spanish-speaking students encounter the English sound/spelling pattern of the consonant *v*, which in Spanish is pronounced /b/.

## PROBLEM ENGLISH SOUNDS FOR SPEAKERS OF OTHER LANGUAGES

| Native Language | Problem English Sounds |
|---|---|
| Chinese | b ch d dg f g j l m n ng ō sh s th TH v z<br>l-clusters  r-clusters |
| French | ā ch ē h j ng oo oy s th TH s schwa |
| Greek | aw b d ē g i j m n ng oo r s w y z schwa end clusters |
| Italian | a ar dg h i ng th TH v schwa l-clusters end clusters |
| Japanese | dg f h i l th TH oo r sh s v w schwa l-clusters r-clusters |
| Korean | b l ō ow p r sh t TH l-clusters r-clusters |
| Spanish | b d dg h j m n ng r sh t th v w y z<br>s-clusters end clusters |
| Urdu | ā a d ē e f n ng s sh t th TH |
| Vietnamese | ā ē k l ng p r sh s y l-clusters r-clusters |

**4.25**

SOURCE

From *The ESL Teacher's Book of Lists* (1993) by Jacqueline Kress. Upper Saddle River, NJ: Prentice-Hall. Reprinted with permission of Center for Applied Research in Education/Prentice-Hall, Inc.

**4.26**

## PROBLEM ENGLISH CONTRASTS FOR SPEAKERS OF OTHER LANGUAGES*

| Contrast | Chinese | French | Greek | Italian | Japanese | Korean | Spanish | Urdu | Vietnamese |
|---|---|---|---|---|---|---|---|---|---|
| ā/a |  |  | x | x | x | x |  | x |  |
| ā/e |  |  | x | x | x | x | x | x | x |
| a/e | x |  | x | x | x | x | x | x | x |
| a/o | x | x | x | x | x | x | x | x | x |
| a/u | x |  | x | x | x |  | x | x |  |
| ē/i | x | x | x | x | x | x | x | x | x |
| e/u | x |  | x | x |  |  | x | x |  |
| ō/o | x |  | x | x | x |  | x | x | x |
| o/aw | x |  | x |  | x | x | x | x | x |
| o/u | x |  | x | x | x |  | x |  | x |
| u/o͞o | x | x | x | x |  |  | x | x | x |
| u/oo | x |  | x |  | x |  | x |  | x |
| u/aw | x |  | x | x | x | x | x | x |  |
| o͞o/oo | x | x |  | x |  | x | x | x |  |
| b/p | x |  |  |  |  | x | x |  | x |
| b/v |  |  | x |  | x | x | x |  |  |
| ch/j |  |  |  | x |  | x | x |  | x |
| ch/sh | x | x | x |  | x | x | x |  | x |
| d/TH | x |  |  | x | x | x | x | x | x |
| f/th |  |  |  | x |  | x | x | x | x |
| l/r | x |  |  |  | x | x | x |  | x |
| n/ng | x | x | x | x | x |  | x | x |  |

*Chart identifies pairs of English sounds that are difficult for English language learners to distinguish.

# PROBLEM ENGLISH CONTRASTS FOR SPEAKERS OF OTHER LANGUAGES

| Contrast | Chinese | French | Greek | Italian | Japanese | Korean | Spanish | Urdu | Vietnamese |
|---|---|---|---|---|---|---|---|---|---|
| s/sh | | | x | x | x | x | x | | x |
| s/th | x | x | | x | x | x | x | x | x |
| s/z | x | | x | x | | x | x | | x |
| sh/th | | | | x | x | x | x | x | x |
| t/th | x | | | x | x | x | x | x | x |
| th/TH | x | x | | x | x | x | x | x | x |
| TH/z | x | x | x | x | x | x | x | x | x |

SOURCE

From *The ESL Teacher's Book of Lists* (1993) by Jacqueline Kress. Upper Saddle River, NJ: Prentice-Hall. Reprinted with permission of Center for Applied Research in Education/Prentice-Hall, Inc.

# SECTION III

# Sound/Print Connection

# Section III: Sound/Print Connection

Some children arrive at school with a good understanding of how print works, thorough alphabet knowledge, awareness of letter sounds, and even the ability to read easy words. Others, however, still need to master these skills and concepts. This section lays the early foundation for reading instruction by addressing the skills and concepts that help students make the connection between sound and print: print concepts, alphabet recognition, and phonemic awareness. Of the three, print concepts are relatively easy for most students to learn. Alphabet recognition requires more instruction, but most students will learn alphabet letters without too much difficulty. Phonemic awareness is much more difficult, often requiring more intensive, explicit instruction.

## Standards for Print Concepts and Alphabet Recognition

**KINDERGARTEN**

- Identify the front cover, back cover, and title page of a book.
- Follow words from left to right and from top to bottom on the printed page.
- Understand that printed materials provide information.
- Recognize that sentences in print are made up of separate words.
- Distinguish letters from words.
- Recognize and name all uppercase and lowercase letters of the alphabet.

**GRADE 1**

- Match oral words to printed words.
- Identify the title and author of a reading selection.
- Identify letters, words, and sentences.

## Standards for Phonemic Awareness

**KINDERGARTEN**

- Track (move sequentially from sound to sound) and represent the number, sameness/difference, and order of two and three isolated phonemes (e.g., /f/, /s/, /th/; /j/, /d/, /j/).
- Track (move sequentially from sound to sound) and represent changes in simple syllables and words with two and three sounds as one sound is added, substituted, omitted, shifted, or repeated (e.g., vowel-consonant, consonant-vowel, or consonant-vowel-consonant).
- Blend vowel-consonant sounds orally to make words or syllables.
- Identify and produce rhyming words in response to an oral prompt.
- Distinguish orally stated one-syllable words and separate into beginning or ending sounds.
- Track auditorily each word in a sentence and each syllable in a word.
- Count the number of sounds in syllables and syllables in words.

**GRADE 1**

- Distinguish initial, medial, and final sounds in single-syllable words.
- Distinguish long- and short-vowel sounds in orally stated single-syllable words (e.g., *bit/bite*).
- Create and state a series of rhyming words, including consonant blends.
- Add, delete, or change target sounds to change words (e.g., change *cow* to *how; pan* to *an*).
- Blend two to four phonemes into recognizable words (e.g., /k/ /a/ /t/ = cat; /f/ /l/ /a/ /t/ = flat).
- Segment single-syllable words into their components (e.g., cat = /k/ /a/ /t/; splat = /s/ /p/ /l/ /a/ /t/; rich = /r/ /i/ /ch/).

SOURCE
Adapted from *English-Language Arts Content Standards for California Public Schools: Kindergarten Through Grade Twelve* (1999). Sacramento: California Department of Education.

# CONTENTS
# Section III: Sound/Print Connection

v

|||

# Print Concepts

what?
why?
when?
how?

# Print Concepts

*"Experiences with print (through reading and writing) help preschool children develop an understanding of the conventions, purpose, and functions of print. These understandings have been shown to play an integral part of the process of learning to read."*

—GUNN, SIMMONS & KAMEENUI, 1998

*Print concepts* is an umbrella term encompassing several concepts about printed text that students need to grasp in order to learn to read. Some of these concepts relate to the features of written language, while others relate to directionality, or the way that printed text is organized. Knowledge of print concepts is fundamental to beginning reading. Although some students enter Kindergarten with a good understanding of these concepts, others may not. These students will need instruction and practice in the key print concepts.

Following is a list of the concepts about print that emergent readers need to develop. Together with these concepts, reading-ready students need a firm grasp of the basic terms that are used in the language of instruction—*word, letter, beginning, middle, end, first, last, next, sentence*—and the names of common punctuation marks.

- The purpose of reading (Print carries a message.)
- The different forms of print (Print is print regardless of case, size, font, or color.)
- The relationship between print and spoken words (Print corresponds to speech, word for word.)
- How stories work (Stories have a beginning, middle, and ending.)
- The concept of a word and word boundaries
- The difference between a letter and a word
- The parts of a book (front cover, back cover, title page, and table of contents)
- Directionality (left to right; top to bottom)

Many students have developed basic print concepts before they enter first grade. The following chart shows important benchmarks in the acquisition of print concepts and the expected time of mastery for these benchmarks.

## PRINT CONCEPTS DEVELOPMENT SEQUENCE

| | |
|---|---|
| **Birth to 3 Years** | ▸ Can distinguish individual books by looking at their covers <br> ▸ Looks at pictures in books and understands they represent things in the real world <br> ▸ May attend to some print elements, such as letters in names |
| **3 to 4 Years** | ▸ Recognizes print in the environment <br> ▸ Holds books correctly and pretends to read them <br> ▸ Knows that books tell stories <br> ▸ Understands that different kinds of print serve different purposes; for example, stories versus street signs |
| **Kindergarten** | ▸ Knows the parts of a book and their functions <br> ▸ Begins to track print when listening to a familiar text being read or when rereading own writing <br> ▸ Knows the difference between a letter and a word <br> ▸ Learns basic conventions of directionality: word boundaries and left-to-right sweeps <br> ▸ Uses word boundaries to distinguish words within sentences <br> ▸ Recognizes single letters and can locate the first letter in a word |
| **Early Grade 1** | ▸ Matches oral words to printed words with one-to-one correspondence <br> ▸ Knows additional conventions of print, including titles and authors <br> ▸ Full print awareness |

# why? *Print Concepts*

Experiences with print (through reading and writing) help children develop an understanding of the conventions, purpose, and functions of print (Gunn et al. 1998). They come to realize that print—not pictures—carries the story. They also learn about the physical structure of written language. For example, students learn that text begins at the top of the page, moves from left to right, and carries over to the next page when it is turned. They further learn that words are units separated by white spaces.

Because all children are not exposed to the same range of print-related experiences, they come to school with varying levels of print awareness and knowledge. This variation in knowledge of the functions of print is related to daily routines in the child's home. Those who come from homes where they have handled books and been read to regularly are likely to have a good grasp of basic print concepts.

**ELL** English print concepts may be difficult for students who have learned to read in languages that are nonalphabetic (e.g., Chinese, Japanese, Urdu) or that use different writing systems (e.g., Arabic, Korean, Vietnamese, Russian), different signals (e.g., inverted punctuation in Spanish), and different directional conventions (e.g., Hebrew, Arabic, Chinese, Urdu).

## Research Findings . . .

*In addition to alphabet recognition and phonemic awareness, reading-ready children need to have a sense of story and a basic understanding of the concepts of print. . . .*

—BLEVINS, 1998

*The performance of children on tests designed to measure concepts about print has been found to predict future reading achievement and to be strongly related to other, more traditional measures of reading readiness and achievement.*

—TUNMER ET AL., 1988

*Some directional confusions may be found in all beginning readers who are learning the arbitrary rules we use to write down languages. Such confusion persists for some children who are having difficulty in learning to read.*

—CLAY, 1993

## Suggested Reading . . .

*Becoming Literate: The Construction of Inner Control* (1991) by Marie Clay. Portsmouth, NH: Heinemann.

*Reading Recovery: A Guidebook for Teachers in Training* (1993) by Marie Clay. Portsmouth, NH: Heinemann.

*What Reading Research Tells Us About Children with Diverse Learning Needs: Bases and Basics* (1998) edited by Deborah C. Simmons & Edward J. Kameenui. Mahwah, NJ: Erlbaum.

## Who is at risk?

**Students who have little at-home experience with books and reading**

## When to Teach and Assess

Most emergent readers learn key print concepts incidentally, as they explore and enjoy books at home and school. For those students who haven't mastered print concepts, the keys to effective instruction are identifying their particular needs and understanding that students do not master these concepts in any predictable order. The Instructional Timeline on the facing page shows a recommended sequence of instruction that supports acquisition of print concept skills.

Teachers should assess Kindergarteners' print awareness in the beginning and middle of the school year. This is especially true of directionality skills, a more complex concept. To master directionality, students must learn several discrete movements that become automatic over time.

Because students find it far easier to show rather than talk about print concepts and directionality, teachers should use assessment techniques that ask students to "point to" or "show" parts of a book, starting points, left-to-right sweeps, and words. Similarly, teachers should always model correct movements whenever they discuss directionality skills with students who are having difficulty.

# INSTRUCTIONAL TIMELINE FOR PRINT CONCEPTS

**Preschool**

▶ Listening to books read aloud

▶ Playing language activity games

▶ Discussing environmental print

▶ Learning book-handling skills

▶ Dictating stories

▶ Learning and recognizing letters

▶ Retelling simple stories from pictures

**Kindergarten**

▶ Learning about the parts of a book

▶ Exploring print in varying forms

▶ Tracking text as it is being read

▶ Learning about the difference between letters and words

▶ Learning about word boundaries and sentences

▶ Learning about punctuation marks

▶ Finding the starting point

▶ Recognizing single letters and locating the first letter in a word

▶ Directionality

  · Tracking words from left to right

  · Tracking text from the top of a page to the bottom of a page

  · Sweeping to the next line

  · Tracking sentences across pages

**Early Grade 1**

▶ Matching spoken words to printed words

▶ Learning additional conventions of print, including titles and authors

# how? *Print Concepts*

**TEACHING STRATEGY FOR**

## Print Concepts

### Benchmarks

- ability to discriminate between a letter and a word
- ability to recognize word boundaries and sentences
- ability to name and understand the role of common punctuation marks
- ability to recognize print in varying forms

### Grade Level

- Kindergarten

### Grouping

- whole class
- small group or pairs
- individual

### Materials

- transparency of "Jack and Jill" (see Appendix)
- copies of "Little Boy Blue" (see Appendix)
- overhead projector

---

## INTRODUCING PRINT CONCEPTS

There are three methods of instruction that teachers can use to help students master print concepts. First, movement: the teacher can, for example, guide a student's finger from the beginning of a line of text to the end. Second, visual modeling: the teacher can point to words during read-alouds. Third, verbal instruction: the teacher can tell a student: *The next word in this sentence is* Jim. *Can you find* Jim?

Reading nursery rhymes is one way to develop emergent readers' concepts about print. Since most children are already familiar with these rhymes, the one-to-one correspondence between the spoken words and the written text will be readily apparent. In addition, nursery rhymes lend themselves to developing the key print concepts of letter vs. word, word boundaries and sentences, punctuation, and recognition of print in varying forms.

- - - - - - - - - - - - - - - - - - - - - - - -

## Warm Up

Have students recite the nursery rhyme "Jack and Jill." If any students have difficulty, ask them to repeat each line after you until they are able to recite the four lines on their own.

**ELL** English language learners will benefit from extra support. Use pantomime and visual cues to preteach key concept vocabulary: *hill, fetch, pail, fell, crown* (head), *tumbling.* You may also want to model the pronunciation of the rhyming word pairs: *Jill/hill, water/after, down/crown.*

## Teach

Using an overhead projector, display "Jack and Jill." Point to the title and explain that this is the name, or title, of the rhyme. Cover all but the first two lines and read the lines aloud slowly as you track the print with your finger. Ask students to identify the names of the children in the rhyme. *(Jack and Jill)* Point to each name and read it aloud. Explain to students that each name is a word, and then ask them to count the words in the title. Lead students to understand that the empty spaces between words help readers know where one word ends and the next word begins.

Next, explain that each word is made up of letters. Ask students to name the letters in the word *Jack.* Finally, direct students' attention to the comma at the end of the first line and the period at the end of the second line. Tell them that the comma tells readers to pause, or stop for a moment, before reading the next words. It is a "slow down" mark. Then tell them that the period is a signal that tells readers they have come to the end of a sentence. This mark is a "stop mark" and tells readers to stop.

To develop students' recognition of print in varying forms, ask them to compare the title of the rhyme (written in all capital letters and boldface) with the first three words of the rhyme. Guide students to understand that the difference in case and typeface does not change what the text says.

Intervention
Strategy

**Practice with magnetic letters
can help reinforce the concepts of *word* and *letter*. Help
students spell their names
with magnetic letters. You
can exaggerate the spaces
between the letters and have
students return them to the
normal spacing.**

5.10

## Practice

Tell students that they are going to have a chance to practice what they just learned. Uncover the last two lines of the rhyme and read these aloud slowly as you track the print with your finger. Have volunteers come up and point to a word, a letter, and a sentence. Encourage them to explain how they identified each one.

## Apply

Tell students that they are going to have a chance to be "print detectives" working with a new nursery rhyme. Distribute copies of "Little Boy Blue," and do a choral reading of the rhyme with students. As you read, use your voice to emphasize the exclamations (lines 1–2 and 7) and the question (lines 5–6). Point out the exclamation marks and question mark. Then have pairs or small groups work together to underline a letter, circle a word, and draw a box around a sentence.

### OBSERVE AND ASSESS

*As students complete the Apply activity, use these questions to assess their progress.*

| Questions for Observation | Benchmarks |
|---|---|
| Can you point to a letter?<br>Can you point to a word? | Student can distinguish between a letter and a word. |
| How many words are in the last sentence? | Student can recognize word boundaries and sentences. |
| Can you show me a "stop mark"?<br>Can you show me a question mark? | Student understands the role of punctuation marks. |
| *(Point to* Boy *in the title.)*<br>Do you see another word that matches this word? | Student can recognize print in varying forms. |

## Print Concepts

**Benchmarks**

- ability to find the starting point
- ability to track lines from left to right
- ability to make a return sweep to the next line
- ability to track each word from left to right

**Grade Level**

- Kindergarten – Early Grade 1

**Grouping**

- small group or pairs
- individual

**Materials**

- small green stick-on dots
- a variety of text formats

5.11

Different text formats present different challenges for beginning readers. Teachers should select texts that gradually increase in complexity, beginning with those that have one line per page, then two, and then three. Other physical features like line breaks and indentation can make it difficult for students to track from left to right. Before introducing a new book, teachers should identify the characteristics of its layout and format that might be challenging for beginning readers.

### Prep Time

Select three to four stories with different text formats. You should have examples with one, two, and three lines per page, and examples of text that is centered on the page and text that is aligned along the left margin.

### Warm Up

Tell students that you are going to read some stories together. Show the students each story you have selected and preview the story titles and illustrations.

### Teach

Begin with a story that has one sentence per page. For each page, ask students to show you where the starting point is. When students identify the correct starting point, give positive reinforcement. When they make a mistake, gently move their fingers to the correct starting point. Say: *We start here.*

**5.12**

Then place a green stick-on dot at the starting point. Tell students that the green dots mean "go." Next, work with pages that have two and three lines of text and tell students that you are going to show them how to "read" with their fingers. Read the words aloud as you use your finger to model correct left-to-right tracking across each line and the return sweep from the end of one line to the beginning of the next line. (If necessary, as you do the return sweep, rest the pointer finger of your other hand on the first word of the next line.) Repeat the procedure, emphasizing the left-to-right tracking across individual words. Then have students use their fingers to show correct movement as you read the lines aloud.

## Practice

Select another story and ask students to show you where the starting point is on each page. Then have them work in pairs to point to each of the words in the story with their fingers as you read it aloud, slowly saying each word. Pause from time to time and say: *Show me which word I should read next.*

## Apply

Give each student a familiar book that has a variety of page layouts. Have students work independently, placing a green dot at the starting point on each page. Then ask them to "read" the pages with their fingers, starting where they have placed the green dots.

Intervention Strategy

**Place in a row three different-colored objects, such as a red, a green, and a yellow cube. Have students touch and name the objects in left-to-right order.**

**ELL** FOR SPANISH-SPEAKING STUDENTS . . .
English language learners who have experience reading in Spanish can transfer directionality skills to reading in English.

| Questions for Observation | Benchmarks |
|---|---|
| Where will you put the green dot on this page? | Student can locate the starting point for reading texts. |
| Read this sentence with your finger. Show me the first word in the sentence. What word comes next? Which way do we go when we read? | Student can track lines of text from left to right. |
| When we come to the end of this line, where do we read next? | Student can sweep from the end of one line to the beginning of the next. |
| Can you show me the first letter in this word? | Student can track letters in a word from left to right. |

5.13

## The Next Step

Once students are comfortable working with simple formats, teachers can introduce books in which sentences break across pages. Model continuing to read the text from one page to the next. Ask students to watch your finger as you track the print and read. Emphasize the pause at the end of each sentence. After you have read a few sentences that continue from one page to the next, go back and point out these sentences. Explain that sentences may continue from one page of a book to the next. Ask: *If I begin reading here, where is the end of the sentence?* Remind students that a period, exclamation mark, or question mark tells them they have reached the end of a sentence.

CHAPTER

6

# Alphabet Recognition

what?
why?
when?
how?

# Alphabet Recognition

## Letter Pairs That Students Often Confuse

| Lowercase | | |
|---|---|---|
| a-d | a-o | b-d |
| b-h | b-p | b-q |
| c-e | c-o | d-g |
| d-p | d-q | f-t |
| g-p | g-q | h-n |
| h-u | i-j | i-l |
| k-y | m-n | m-w |
| n-u | p-q | u-v |
| v-w | v-y | |

| Uppercase | | |
|---|---|---|
| C-G | D-O | E-F |
| I-J | I-L | K-X |
| L-T | M-N | M-W |
| O-Q | P-R | |
| U-V | V-Y | |

Alphabet recognition is the ability to visually recognize the letters of the alphabet and to name the letters in their different contexts and forms. This requires more than merely being able to say the alphabet. Students must be able to match letter names to four written forms—uppercase manuscript, lowercase manuscript, uppercase cursive, and lowercase cursive—and to distinguish among the many letters that are similar in appearance (e.g., d/b, U/V, and M/W). Alphabet recognition is the foundation for reading any alphabetic language. It is the first step toward understanding the alphabetic principle—the principle that the alphabet is a system of letters that stand for the sounds of spoken language.

There is strong agreement among researchers and teachers alike that the most effective alphabet recognition training combines explicit instruction in recognizing and writing letters with frequent exposure to printed texts. This combined approach helps students learn letter names, letter shapes, letter sounds, and letter production in relation to one another.

By the time they enter school, most children are able to say the alphabet, and many are able to identify by name some of the printed letters. Research has shown that the letters most likely identified are those that are used most frequently or that have some personal relevance for students: letters in environmental print and in students' names (Hiebert and Sawyer

1984). Emergent readers not only need to accurately identify alphabet letters, but must be able to do so in and out of sequence and with automaticity.

Although there is no consensus on the best sequence for teaching the alphabet, most teachers and researchers agree that the more common letters should be taught before the less common letters (e.g., *m* and *t* before *q* and *x*). In addition, visually confusing letters should be taught far apart, with teachers making sure that students have learned one before the other is introduced. As students are taught to recognize letters, they should also learn how to write those letters. Letter formation instruction goes hand-in-hand with alphabet recognition.

See also . . .

**Section IV: Decoding**

**Chapter 8: Phonics**

## ALPHABET RECOGNITION DEVELOPMENT SEQUENCE

| 3 to 4 Years | ▶ Knows that letters have names and belong to a special category of graphics<br>▶ Can identify 10 letters, including those in own name<br>▶ Can recognize own name in print |
|---|---|
| **Kindergarten** | ▶ Can identify and name all lowercase and uppercase letters<br>▶ Grasps the alphabetic principle—that letters stand for sounds |
| **Early Grade 1** | ▶ Knows all letter names and shapes |

# *why?* *Alphabet Recognition*

**6.4**

*"Knowing the alphabet is almost like having an anchor for each sound."*

—HALL & MOATS, 1999

Knowing the alphabet and its related sounds is associated with beginning literacy. It enables beginning readers to figure out how printed words correspond to spoken words. According to Blevins (1998), "without a thorough knowledge of letters and an understanding that words are made up of sounds, children cannot learn to read." Knowing the alphabet can help make learning the sounds of the letters easier for students. It is much easier for a student to associate a sound with a letter if he or she already knows the name of the letter. This is especially true for the letter names that are closely related to their sounds. If students can instantly and effortlessly recognize all the letters, they will be able to give all their attention to other emergent literacy tasks, such as learning the sound associated with each letter and how to write each letter correctly (Hall and Moats 1999).

## Research Findings . . .

*Familiarity with the letters of the alphabet is a powerful predictor of early reading success.*

—EHRI & MCCORMICK, 1998

*A child who can recognize most letters with thorough confidence will have an easier time learning about letter sounds and word spellings than a child who also has to work at distinguishing the individual letters. . . . In general, because the names of most letters are closely associated with their sounds, children who learn to name letters also begin to learn their sounds.*

—ADAMS, 1990

*Whether alphabet knowledge is learned at home or at school, it appears to foster the development of subsequent reading strategies.*

—GUNN ET AL., 1998

*Learning to identify letters helps young children focus more precisely on the features of words, so they have more clues with which to remember those individual words.*

—TEMPLETON, 1995

**Suggested Reading . . .**

*Beginning to Read: Thinking and Learning About Print* (1990) by Marilyn Jager Adams. Cambridge, MA: MIT Press.

*Phonics from A to Z* (1998) by Wiley Blevins. New York: Scholastic.

*Straight Talk About Reading: How Parents Can Make a Difference During the Early Years* (1999) by Susan L. Hall & Louisa C. Moats. Lincolnwood, IL: NTC/Contemporary Publishing Group.

*What Reading Research Tells Us About Children with Diverse Learning Needs: Bases and Basics* (1998) edited by Deborah C. Simmons & Edward J. Kameenui. Mahwah, NJ: Erlbaum.

6.6

## When to Teach, Assess, and Intervene

By the end of Kindergarten, students should be able to name all the uppercase and lowercase letters and match all the letters with their associated single consonant and short vowel sounds. The goal of this instruction is to equip students with the rapid, accurate letter recognition they need to begin reading. According to Hall and Moats (1999), most educators recommend teaching the skills in the following order: (1) letter names, (2) letter shapes, and (3) letter sounds. They also recommend teaching uppercase letters first because they are harder to confuse than lowercase letters.

The Instructional Timeline on the facing page shows a recommended sequence of instruction that supports the acquisition of alphabet recognition skills. It is important to keep in mind that students will master alphabet recognition at varying rates. Some students will need as much as one week to master a single letter, while others will learn several letters during that time.

**ELL** Several languages use many of the same letters found in the English alphabet. Among these are Spanish, French, Portuguese, Italian, Tagalog, and German. Encourage students with alphabet recognition in any of these languages to identify similarities and differences in the letter names and shapes.

# INSTRUCTIONAL TIMELINE FOR ALPHABET RECOGNITION

| | |
|---|---|
| **3 to 4 Years** | ▶ Listening to ABC books read aloud <br> ▶ Singing songs with the letter names <br> ▶ Discussing environmental print <br> ▶ Learning to recognize own name in print <br> ▶ Learning about uppercase letters <br> ▶ Playing with magnetic letters |
| **Kindergarten** | ▶ Singing songs with the letter names <br> ▶ Reading and writing own name <br> ▶ Discussing environmental print and reading classroom labels <br> ▶ Learning about lowercase letters <br> ▶ Printing uppercase and lowercase letters <br> ▶ Experimenting with magnetic letters <br> ▶ Matching letters in words <br> ▶ Playing games with letter cards <br> ▶ Echo reading of ABC books <br> ▶ Making own ABC books <br> ▶ Learning to recognize classmates' names in print |
| **Early Grade 1** | ▶ Reading and writing all letters of the alphabet (uppercase and lowercase) |

See also . . .

CORE Assessing Reading

"CORE Phonics Surveys: Parts 1 and 2"

Intervention
Strategy

**Students can work independently in learning centers with magnetic letters or alphabet tiles.**

**Assessment of Alphabet Recognition**   Students' alphabet recognition skills should be assessed when they enter and exit Kindergarten and again when they enter first grade. A good starting point is to show a lowercase and an uppercase alphabet in random order and to ask students to point to and name each letter. Students can do a matching activity in which they draw lines to match lowercase letters to their uppercase counterparts.

Students who have difficulty learning letter names, who confuse letters, or who have difficulty recognizing uppercase and lowercase counterparts need intervention.

# how?

## *Alphabet Recognition*

**TEACHING STRATEGY FOR**

## Recognizing and Naming Letters

### Benchmarks

• ability to recognize letters in printed form
• ability to identify names of letters

### Grade Level

• Kindergarten – Grade 1

### Grouping

• whole class
• small group or pairs
• individual

### Materials

• two ABC books
• copies of pages from a variety of texts with the target letters (e.g., story book, math book, picture dictionary, magazine, advertisement)

## READ-ALOUD ABC BOOKS

Alphabet books provide an excellent opportunity for students to hear, say, and see the alphabet. Focus on only one or two letters each day and use the book as a springboard for follow-up games and activities.

• • • • • • • • • • • • • • • • • • • • • • • • •

### Warm Up

Help students to learn the letter names by singing an alphabet song. Since the letters *l, m, n, o, p* are slurred in the traditional version, it is more effective to break up the alphabet by pausing in different places: ABCDEFG; HIJKLMN; OPQ; RST; UVW; XYZ. Another way to deal with letter-slurring is to point to the letters on an alphabet chart while students sing the traditional version of the song.

### Teach

Ask students to listen carefully as you read aloud an alphabet book. Encourage them to talk about the illustrations and the parts of the book that they especially liked. Help students enjoy the rhythm and sound of the book's language by reading it in its entirety. Now tell students that they are going to have a chance to see the letters of the alphabet and say the letter names.

## Multisensory Approach

**Teachers should use a multisensory approach to teach alphabet recognition. Visual, auditory, tactile, and kinesthetic activities allow students to see, hear, touch, and move letters of the alphabet.**

Display selected pages of the book, which focus on the targeted letters. Reread the pages and have students repeat each line after you. Point to a letter of the alphabet and ask: *What is this letter? What do you notice about its shape?*

### Practice

Select a different alphabet book and have students work in pairs to find the targeted letters. Ask students to point to the letters and say their names aloud.

**6.9**

### Apply

Have students work independently to find the letters you have selected in a variety of texts. Ask students to circle the letters and to say the letter names aloud. You may also want to have students use some of the words they find to create pages for their own ABC books.

---

**OBSERVE AND ASSESS**

*As students complete the Apply activity, use these questions to assess their progress.*

| Questions for Observation | Benchmark |
|---|---|
| *(Pointing to the circled letter)* What is this letter? *(Pointing to the same letter circled in two places)* Is this letter the same as this letter? | Student can recognize and name letters of the alphabet. |

**TEACHING STRATEGY FOR**

## Recognizing Letter Shapes

6.10

### Benchmarks

• ability to recognize similarities and differences in letter shapes
• ability to correctly write letters of the alphabet

### Grade Level

• Kindergarten – Grade 1

### Grouping

• whole class
• small group or pairs
• individual

### Materials

• magnetic letters
• unlined paper and pencils
• bags of small objects whose names begin with the target letters
• glue

## WRITE IT! BUILD IT!

Writing practice is the best way to help students learn and recall letter shapes. The two most common handwriting styles are Zaner-Bloser and D'Nealian. Whichever style is taught, use it consistently. Students should do their beginning writing practice on unlined paper.

### Warm Up

Provide a set of magnetic letters, with three or four examples of the same letter mixed in different lines. Have students find all the examples of the letter and arrange the letters in one line. Then have students run their fingers over the letter and describe its shape. Encourage them to compare and contrast its shape with that of the other letters that are displayed.

### Teach

Tell students that they are going to practice writing letters of the alphabet. Model writing the target letter as you explain the correct starting point, direction, and line and curve strokes.

**ELL** Directional terms like *under, over, up, down, on, right,* and *left* are challenging for many English language learners. Teachers may need to use visual cues and pantomime to convey the meaning of these key terms.

A B C

## Teach About Similarities and Differences

**For students having difficulty, use three-dimensional letters to point out similarities in the letters they know (for example, both *a* and *b* contain small circles). Then discuss the difference between similar-looking letters—the direction of extenders (*b* vs. *p*), whether the letters face right or left (*b* vs. *d*), their top–bottom orientation (*m* vs. *w*), and the letters' line-curve features (*u* vs. *v*).**

## Practice

Distribute paper and pencils to each student. Then have students print the target letter across the page, from left to right. Encourage them to tell you the movements they used to write the letter.

## Apply

6.11

Distribute drawing paper and the bags of small objects and glue to pairs or small groups of students. Ask them to identify the objects in the bags. Explain that the object names begin with the letter students have been practicing. Then have students print the letter on their paper and then glue the objects in the shape of the letter.

---

**O B S E R V E   A N D   A S S E S S**

*As students complete the Apply activity, use these questions to assess their progress.*

| Questions for Observation | Benchmarks |
| --- | --- |
| *(Pointing to a magnetic letter)* How is this letter different from the one you wrote? How is it the same? | Student can recognize similarities and differences in letter shapes. |
| Show me how you write the letter. Where do you put the pencil when you start to write it? What do you do next? | Student can correctly write letters of the alphabet. |

**TEACHING STRATEGY FOR**

# Recognizing and Matching Letters in Words

### Benchmarks

6.12

- ability to recognize letters in a word
- ability to match letters
- ability to change letters

### Grade Level

- Kindergarten – Grade 1

### Grouping

- whole class
- small group or pairs
- individual

### Materials

- lowercase letter cards

## MATCH IT! CHANGE IT!

The alphabet letters selected for this activity should be ones that students have already learned to recognize and form.

## Warm Up

Review with students the vocabulary and concepts associated with directionality, such as *top, bottom, left,* and *right.*

## Teach

Distribute an alphabet letter card to each student. (For small groups, students will have more than one card.) Have each student identify his or her letter and describe the letter's features. For example, the student with letter *b* might say, "It has a straight line and then a circle on the right side."

Tell students they are going to do a letter-matching activity. Explain that you will ask students to bring their letters, one at a time, to the front of the room to perform a "live" spelling of a word. Print the word *bat* on the board. Say: *This word is* bat. *Who has the first letter in* bat? As the student holds up the letter *b* card, have him or her say the letter name and then come forward to display the card. Continue this procedure, letter by letter, until the word is spelled out by the students holding the correct letter cards. Have students, in order from left to right, name their letters and then, in unison, say the entire word.

**Intervention Strategy**

If a student incorrectly identifies his or her letter, provide the correct response and point out distinctive letter features.

Then, with students still standing, change one letter in the word on the board. For example, change the letter *a* to an *i*, and say: *I changed one letter and made a new word,* bit. *Which letter holder will need to sit down?* (letter *a*) *That's right. The letter* a *will sit down.* Now say: *Who has this letter?* (Point to the *i*.) Have the student with letter *i* say the name of the letter and come forward to stand between the *b* and the *t*, to form the word *bit*. Again, have students say their letters in order from left to right, and then in unison say the new word, *bit*.

## Practice

Follow the procedure described above with several word families, substituting and adding consonants and vowels in initial, medial, and final positions. For example, use the following words: *on, an, in; man, tan, fan; hug, hut, hum; big, bag, beg.*

## Apply

Working in small groups or individually at "letter centers," have students use their letter cards to build and transform the following words:

did    dad    mad    had    hid

**OBSERVE AND ASSESS**

*As students complete the Apply activity, use these questions to assess their progress.*

| Questions for Observation | Benchmarks |
|---|---|
| *(Pointing to a letter)* What is this letter? | Student can recognize specific letters. |
| What letter changed? | Student can distinguish differences and similarities. |

CHAPTER

7

# Phonemic Awareness

what?
why?
when?
how?

what? *Phonemic Awareness*

7.2

**Section II: Word Structure**

**Chapter 3: Structure of the English Language**

**CORE Reading Research Anthology**

for background information

A *phoneme* is a speech sound. It is the smallest unit of sound that makes a difference in meaning. For example, the phonemes /s/ and /f/ are different; the word *sat* has a different meaning than the word *fat*. *Phonemic awareness* is the conscious understanding that spoken language is composed of phonemes, or speech sounds. It involves the ability to blend, segment, and manipulate phonemes in spoken words. The difference between phonemic awareness and phonics is that phonemic awareness involves sounds in *spoken* words and phonics involves the relationship between these sounds and *written* symbols. *Phonological awareness* is an umbrella term that includes phonemic awareness. In addition to breaking words into phonemes, phonological awareness includes skills such as breaking sentences into words, breaking words into syllables, and recognizing and producing rhyming words.

Phonemic awareness is both a precursor to and a result of learning to read. It begins with auditory development and continues to develop as students connect sounds to print. Phonemic awareness is important in phonics instruction and in learning to read because it helps students: (1) to understand the alphabetic principle—the principle that the letters of the alphabet stand for the sounds in oral language; (2) to notice the regular ways that letters in written words stand for sounds; (3) to blend sounds in order to read words; and (4) to segment words in order to spell them.

Phonological awareness generally follows a developmental sequence. Awareness of words, rhymes, and syllables emerges in

> *"Phonemic awareness instruction is most effective when children are taught to manipulate phonemes by using the letters of the alphabet."*
>
> —AMBRUSTER, LEHR & OSBORN, 2001

the preschool and Kindergarten years; awareness of phonemes occurs in Kindergarten and first grade. The ultimate goal of phonological awareness instruction is to achieve awareness of the phoneme, that is, phonemic awareness.

Minimally, one should expect a student in the latter part of Kindergarten to produce the initial and final sound in a CVC word. However, some Kindergarteners who can perform this task still may not be able to rhyme. This is not a cause for concern, since ultimately it is awareness of phonemes that is important for efficient reading and spelling acquisition. As greater attention is paid to phoneme segmentation and blending skills, many students master the ability to fully segment a CVC or a CCVC word by the middle of Kindergarten. This skill should be mastered early in first grade.

It is important to note that across the entire scope and sequence of phonemic awareness skills, the progression of difficulty is fairly predictable. For example, blending is usually easier than segmentation; isolating initial and final sounds is easier than complete segmentation; and performing various manipulations, such as deletion or substitution, is more difficult than segmentation. The best phonemic awareness instruction focuses on one or two types of manipulations–specifically, blending and segmentation (Put Reading First, 2001; National Reading Panel Report, 2000).

Connect to Theory

**How many sounds, or phonemes, do you hear in the following words? What are they?**

1. cat
2. train

3. thought
4. straight
5. flounder

*(See Appendix for answers.)*

**PHONOLOGICAL AWARENESS DEVELOPMENT SEQUENCE**

| | | |
|---|---|---|
| **Word** | Segmentation | EXAMPLE: How many words are there in the sentence *Linda likes pizza*? *(3)* <br> Typically mastered about Age 3 |
| **Rhyme** | Recognition | EXAMPLE: Does *pie* rhyme with *sky*? *(yes)* <br> Typically mastered about Age 4 |
| | Production | EXAMPLE: What rhymes with *sky*? (pie) <br> Typically mastered in Kindergarten |
| **Syllable** | Blending | EXAMPLE: Listen to the two word parts I say: *star…fish*. Now say the whole word. (starfish) <br> Typically mastered about Age 4 |
| | Segmentation | EXAMPLE: Say the two word parts in *starfish*. (star…fish) <br> Typically mastered in Kindergarten |
| | Deletion | EXAMPLE: Say *starfish* without the *fish*. (star) <br> Typically mastered in Kindergarten |
| **Onset and Rime** | Blending | EXAMPLE: What word am I trying to say: /l/…*unch*? (lunch) <br> EXAMPLE: What word am I trying to say: /st/…*op*? (stop) <br> Typically mastered in mid-Kindergarten |
| **Phoneme** | Matching and Isolating: Initial | EXAMPLE: Which two words begin with the same sound: *cat, cup, dog*? (cat, cup) <br> EXAMPLE: What is the first sound you hear in *cup*? *(/k/)* <br> Typically mastered in mid-Kindergarten |
| | Matching and Isolating: Final | EXAMPLE: Which two words end with the same sound: *hat, cup, mop*? (cup, mop) <br> EXAMPLE: What is the last sound you hear in *cup*? *(/p/)* <br> Typically mastered in late Kindergarten and early Grade 1 |
| | Matching and Isolating: Medial | EXAMPLE: Which two words have the same middle sound: *cup, cap, but*? (cup, but) <br> EXAMPLE: What is the middle sound you hear in *cup*? *(/u/)* <br> Typically mastered in late Kindergarten |

## PHONOLOGICAL AWARENESS DEVELOPMENT SEQUENCE

| | | |
|---|---|---|
| **Phoneme** | Blending | EXAMPLE: Can you guess the word I am trying to say: /k/ /u/ /p/? (cup) <br> Typically mastered in late Kindergarten and early Grade 1 |
| **Phoneme** | Segmentation | EXAMPLE: How many sounds do you hear in *cup*? *(3)* <br> EXAMPLE: What sounds do you hear in *cup*? *(/k/ /u/ /p/)* <br> Typically mastered in Grade 1 |
| **Phoneme** | Manipulation: Initial and Final Phoneme Deletion | EXAMPLE: Say *seat* without the /s/. (eat) <br> EXAMPLE: Say *seat* without the /t/. (sea) <br> Typically mastered in Grade 1 |
| | Manipulation: Initial Phoneme in Blend Deletion | EXAMPLE: Say *clap* without the /k/. (lap) <br> Typically mastered in late Grade 1 and early Grade 2 |
| | Manipulation: Phoneme Substitution | EXAMPLE: Say *mat*. Now instead of /t/, say /p/. What's the new word? (map) <br> EXAMPLE: Say *map*. Now instead of /a/, say /o/. What's the new word? (mop) <br> Typically mastered in Grades 1 to 2 |
| | Manipulation: Second Phoneme in Blend Deletion | EXAMPLE: Say *clap* without the /l/. (cap) <br> Typically mastered in Grade 2 |

NOTE: Phonics instruction is most effective when students can recognize initial phonemes in words. The most crucial phonemic awareness skills—blending and segmentation—should be the focus of instruction rather than earlier phonological awareness skills such as rhyme recognition and production. The ability to fully segment and manipulate phonemes typically develops alongside phonics instruction.

# why? *Phonemic Awareness*

7.6

**CORE Reading Research Anthology**

for background information

The concept that spoken language is made up of sequences of abstract sounds, or phonemes, does not come naturally. The problem, in large measure, is that people do not attend to the sounds of phonemes as they produce or listen to speech. Instead, they process the phonemes automatically, directing their active attention to the meaning and to the word as a whole burst of sound (Adams, Foorman, Lundberg, and Beeler 1998). Phonemes are difficult to isolate; they are not easily pronounced without adding another sound. For example, try saying /p/, /b/, or /k/ without adding another sound, such as a schwa.

A child's level of phonemic awareness on entering school is widely held to be the strongest single determinant of the success that he or she will experience in learning to read—or, conversely, the likelihood that he or she will fail (Adams 1990). This is also true for Swedish (Lundberg, Olofsson, and Wall 1980), Norwegian (Hoen, Lundberg, Stanovich, and Bjaalid 1995), Spanish (Manrique and Gramigna 1984), French (Alegria, Pignot, and Morais 1982), Italian (Cossu, Shankweiler, Liberman, Tola, and Katz 1988), Portuguese (Cardoso-Martins 1995), and Russian (Elkonin 1973) students. Research clearly indicates that phonemic awareness can be developed through instruction and, furthermore, that doing so significantly accelerates children's subsequent reading and writing achievement (Ball and Blachman 1991).

**Research Findings . . .**

*Phonemic awareness is more highly related to learning to read than are tests of general intelligence, reading readiness, and listening comprehension.*

—STANOVICH, 1993

*Children who have phonme awareness skills are likely to have an easier time learning to read and spell than children who have few or none of these skills.*

—AMBRUSTER, LEHR & OSBORN, 2001

*Phonological awareness instruction will accelerate the reading growth of all children, and it appears to be vital in order for at least 20 percent of children to acquire useful reading skills.*

—TORGESEN & MATHES, 1998

**Suggested Reading . . .**

*Beginning to Read: Thinking and Learning About Print* (1990) by Marilyn Jager Adams. Cambridge, MA: MIT Press.

*Let's Listen: A Phonological Awareness Program for Young Children* (2000). Waterbury, CT: Abrams and Company.

*Phonemic Awareness in Young Children* (1998) by Marilyn Jager Adams, Barbara Foorman, Ingvar Lundberg & Terri Beeler. Baltimore, MD: Brookes Publishing.

*Put Reading First: The Research Building Blocks for Teaching Children to Read* (2001) by Bonnie Ambruster, Fran Lehr & Jean Osborn. The Partnership for Reading. CIERA, U.S. Dept. of Education.

*Preventing Reading Difficulties in Young Children* (1998) edited by Catherine E. Snow, M. Susan Burns & Peg Griffin. Washington, DC: National Academy Press.

*What Reading Research Tells Us About Children with Diverse Learning Needs: Bases and Basics* (1998) edited by Deborah C. Simmons & Edward J. Kameenui. Mahwah, NJ: Erlbaum.

7.8

## Student Risk Factors for Phonemic Awareness Deficiency

.....................................

**Phonological processing problems**

.....................................

**Speech or hearing impairments**

.....................................

**English language learners**

.....................................

**Literacy-deprived environment**

.....................................

## When to Teach

It is not necessary for students to fully master a particular phonemic awareness task before moving on to another. Rather, a mix of phonemic awareness tasks in an appropriate sequence provides students with ample practice. Generally, instruction in blending phonemes should begin before phoneme segmentation; instruction in matching and isolating phonemes should begin before complete phoneme segmentation; and instruction in phoneme manipulation should begin after phoneme segmentation.

**Kindergarten**   Throughout Kindergarten, students should receive at least 10 to 15 minutes a day of phonological awareness instruction. For students who need further assistance, provide instruction in a small-group setting for an additional 15 minutes per day, 3 to 4 times per week, for about 10 weeks.

**Grade 1**   In first grade, students should receive instruction 10 minutes a day for about three months in conjunction with phonics instruction. For students who need further assistance, provide instruction in a small-group setting for an additional 15 minutes per day, 3 to 4 times per week, for about 10 weeks.

**Grade 2 and Above**   In second grade and above, phonemic awareness instruction may only be necessary for students who do not automatically recognize words and who are not reading at grade level. For students who need further assistance, provide instruction in a small-group setting for an additional 15 minutes per day, 3 to 4 times per week, for about 10 weeks.

The following Instructional Scope and Sequence chart is designed for PreKindergarten and Kindergarten, but can be adjusted for first-grade and older students. For students in second grade and above, introduce the letter/sound correspondences earlier in the sequence. Refer to the Phonological Awareness Development Sequence earlier in this chapter for information about when each of the skills is typically mastered.

## INSTRUCTIONAL SCOPE AND SEQUENCE

| SKILL | Week 1 | Week 2 | Week 3 | Week 4 | Week 5 | Week 6 | Week 7 | Week 8 | Week 9 | Week 10 | Week 11 | Week 12 | Week 13 | Week 14 | Week 15 | Week 16 | Week 17 | Week 18 | Week 19 | Week 20* |
|---|---|---|---|---|---|---|---|---|---|---|---|---|---|---|---|---|---|---|---|---|
| Word Segmentation | ● | ● | ● | | | | | | | | | | | | | | | | | |
| Rhyme Recognition | ● | ● | ● | | | | | | | | | | | | | | | | | |
| Rhyme Production | | | ● | ● | ● | ● | ● | | | | | | | | | | | | | |
| Syllable Blending | ● | ● | ● | ● | | | | | | | | | | | | | | | | |
| Syllable Segmentation | | ● | ● | ● | ● | | | | | | | | | | | | | | | |
| Syllable Deletion | | | ● | ● | ● | ● | | | | | | | | | | | | | | |
| Onset and Rime Blending | | | ● | ● | ● | ● | ● | ● | | | | | | | | | | | | |
| Onset and Rime Segmentation | | | | ● | ● | ● | ● | ● | ● | | | | | | | | | | | |
| Initial Phoneme Matching and Isolating | | | | ● | ● | ● | ● | ● | ● | ● | ● | | | | | | | | | |
| Final Phoneme Matching and Isolating | | | | | ● | ● | ● | ● | ● | ● | ● | | | | | | | | | |
| Medial Phoneme Matching and Isolating | | | | | | | ● | ● | ● | ● | ● | ● | | | | | | | | |
| Phoneme Blending | | | | | | | ● | ● | ● | ● | ● | ● | ● | ● | ● | ● | ● | ● | ● | ● |
| Phoneme Segmentation | | | | | | | | ● | ● | ● | ● | ● | ● | ● | ● | ● | ● | ● | ● | ● |
| Initial and Final Phoneme Deletion | | | | | | | | | | | | | | | | ● | ● | ● | ● | ● |
| Initial Phoneme in Blend Deletion | | | | | | | | | | | | | | | | | | ● | ● | ● |
| Second Phoneme in Blend Deletion | | | | | | | | | | | | | | | | | | | ● | ➜ |
| Initial and Final Phoneme Substitution | | | | | | | | ● | ● | ● | ● | ● | ● | ● | ● | ● | ● | ● | ● | ➜ |
| Letter/Sound Correspondences | | | | | | | | | | | | | | | | | | ● | ● | ➜ |

*Chart shows only 20 of a typical 36-week school year. Arrows indicate that instruction continues through all 36 weeks of instruction.

See also...

**Section II: Word Structure**

**Section IX: Differentiated Instruction**
**Chapter 21: Assessment**

7.10

**For all English language learners, provide practice "feeling" how English sounds are formed, and discuss English articulation similarities and differences from their native languages.**

## When to Assess and Intervene

Begin phonemic awareness assessment in mid-Kindergarten and continue to assess throughout the early elementary grades, as needed. Generally, once a student demonstrates decoding ability, it is not necessary to assess phonemic awareness.

**Upper-Grade Intervention**   Upper-grade students who are either poor readers or nonreaders may lack phonemic awareness. If phonemic awareness is not developed early, learning to read may become an insurmountable task. If a lack of phonemic awareness is diagnosed, swift intervention is crucial. For the older student, this intervention should involve frequent, intensive sessions with auditory practice focused on acoustical differences of the phonemes, along with kinesthetic attention to the way the sounds are produced (lips and tongue position; whether a sound is voiced or unvoiced). As soon as possible, auditory practice should include active manipulations and blending exercises with sound/spellings. Intervention for the older student is best accomplished in a small group or, preferably, one on one.

## Phonological Awareness Tests

| CORE Assessing Reading | Other |
|---|---|
| Phonological Awareness Screening Test | Lindamood Auditory Conceptualization Test |
| CORE Phoneme Deletion Test | Test of Auditory Analysis Skills (TAAS) |
| CORE Phonological Segmentation Test | Test of Awareness of Language Segments |
| CORE Phoneme Segmentation Test | Test of Phonological Awareness (TOPA) |
| CORE Spanish Phonemic Awareness Test | Comprehensive Test of Phonological Processing |

See also...

CORE Assessing Reading
"Resources for Assessing Reading"

 FOR SPANISH-SPEAKING STUDENTS . . .
Use CORE Spanish Phonemic Awareness Test in *CORE Assessing Reading.*

| When | Mid-Kindergarten |
| --- | --- |
| Who | All students |
| Assessment Tool | *CORE Assessing Reading,* Phonological Awareness Screening Test |
| Intervene if ... | Student cannot identify words that begin with the same sound. |
| How | Small-group intervention, 15 minutes, 3 to 4 times per week for about 10 weeks. |

7.11

| When | Late Kindergarten to early Grade 1 |
| --- | --- |
| Who | All students |
| Assessment Tool | Informal or formal phonemic awareness blending and segmentation test |
| Intervene if ... | Student cannot identify words that end with the same sound. <br> Student cannot produce a whole CVC word by blending together the phonemes. |
| How | Small-group intervention, 15 minutes, 3 to 4 times per week for about 10 weeks. |

| When | Mid-Grade 1 |
| --- | --- |
| Who | Students who cannot read CVC words |
| Assessment Tool | *CORE Assessing Reading,* CORE Phonological Awareness Screening Test <br> *CORE Assessing Reading,* CORE Phonological Segmentation Test <br> *CORE Assessing Reading,* CORE Phoneme Deletion Test |
| Intervene if ... | Student cannot segment CVC words into component sounds. |
| How | Small-group intervention, 15 minutes, 3 to 4 times per week for about 10 weeks. |

| When | Late Grade 1 and above |
| --- | --- |
| Who | Students who cannot fluently read grade-level text and exhibit very poor word attack skills |
| Assessment Tool | *CORE Assessing Reading,* Core Phoneme Segmentation Test |
| Intervene if ... | Student cannot successfully complete segmentation tasks. |
| How | Small-group intervention, 15 minutes, 3 to 4 times per week for about 10 weeks. <br> Possible referral to a specialist. |

# how?

## *Phonemic Awareness*

7.12

**TEACHING STRATEGY FOR**

## Word Segmentation

**Benchmark**

- ability to break a sentence into words

**Grade Level**

- PreK – Kindergarten

**Grouping**

- whole class
- small group or pairs
- individual

**Materials**

- self-stick notes
- blocks
- action pictures

## LINDA LIKES PIZZA

### Warm Up

Explain to students that a sentence is a group of words that go together to tell or ask you something, and it names who or what it is talking about. It can have only a few words or many words. Have students listen carefully to the following sentence: *I like bananas.* Explain that the sentence *I like bananas* names a person, me, and tells you about a food that I like. Say the words *likes raisins* and ask students whether this is a sentence. Ask: *Does it name a person? What if I add a word:* Lucy *likes raisins. Now is it a sentence?*

**ELL** FOR SPANISH-SPEAKING STUDENTS . . .
Use the model sentence *Yo como pan* for this activity. Note that in Spanish a sentence does not require a subject pronoun: *Como pan* is a complete sentence.

### Teach

Have students listen carefully to the words in the following sentence: *Linda likes pizza.* Now repeat the sentence, sticking a self-stick note on the board as you say each word. Ask: *How many words do you hear in the sentence?* Tap each self-stick note as you repeat the sentence, having students count along with you. Then point to the first note. Ask: *What is this word?* (Linda) Point to the last note. Ask: *What is this word?* (pizza) Point to the middle note. Ask: *What is this word?* (likes) Reread the sentence pointing to each "word" in the correct left-to-right order.

Intervention
Strategy

**Students can clap as each word in the sentence is identified.**

## Practice

Tell students that they are going to put together words to make sentences about their favorite foods. Give each student some blocks. Have a volunteer name a favorite food and use it in a sentence: for example, *Mark likes apples.* Tell students to place a block in front of them as they hear each word. Model the activity by sticking notes on the board as students place the blocks on their desks. Ask: *How many words do you hear?* (three) Point to the first note. Ask: *What is the first word?* (Mark) Point to the middle note. Ask: *What is the middle word?* (likes) Point to the last note. Ask: *What is this word?* (apples) Repeat the activity, asking other volunteers to suggest sentences.

7.13

## Apply

Distribute action pictures to pairs of students. Ask them to generate a sentence about the picture and then use blocks to show how many words there are in the sentence. Repeat the procedure several times, using different pictures.

**O B S E R V E   A N D   A S S E S S**

*As students complete the Apply activity, use this question to assess their progress.*

| Question for Observation | Benchmark |
| --- | --- |
| Tell me your sentence. Can you use your blocks to show how many words there are? | Student can break a sentence into words. |

## The Next Step

Read a sentence from a Big Book and ask students to segment it. Place self-stick notes on the board to represent each of the words. Now show the Big Book and the sentence you read.

**FOLLOW-UP STRATEGY FOR**

## Word Segmentation

### Benchmarks

- ability to break a sentence into words
- ability to substitute specific words in a given sentence

7.14

### Grade Level

- PreK – Kindergarten

### Prerequisite

- Linda Likes Pizza

### Grouping

- whole class
- small group

### Materials

- family photographs from home

Intervention Strategy

**For students having difficulty, use three-word sentences, replacing only one word at a time. Use blocks to represent the words.**

## SHOW-AND-TELL SENTENCES

### Prep Time

Send a note home asking students to bring in photographs that show them participating in family vacations, gatherings, and other events.

### Warm Up

Post students' photographs on a bulletin board display and have students describe their pictures.

### Teach

Invite a student to make up a short sentence to describe one of the pictures. For example, the student may say: *I went to the beach with my cousins.* Ask students to count the number of words in the sentence as it is repeated. *(eight)* Call eight students to the front of the room and assign each of them one of the words in the sentence. Have students say their words in order. Help students to understand how the meaning of the sentence changes when words are substituted. For example, have the students who were assigned the words *I* and *my,* now say the words *Tom* and *his.* Repeat the procedure with other pictures.

### Try It This Way!

When students are comfortable counting words in Show-and-Tell Sentences, have volunteers add words to a given sentence. For example, *I went to the beach with my cousins and made a sand castle.* The group can identify the number of words that have been added, and that number of students can join the row and repeat the expanded sentence, word by word.

# Rhyme Recognition and Production

## Benchmarks

- ability to recognize words that rhyme
- ability to produce rhyming words

## Grade Level

- PreK – Grade 1

## Grouping

- whole class
- small group or pairs

## Materials

- pairs of pictures of objects whose names rhyme
- two sets of colored cubes
- drawing paper
- crayons or markers

## SWAP A RHYME

Swap a Rhyme is an adaptation of a social game in which participants sit or stand in a circle and swap places based on any given rule, such as: *If you have blue eyes, swap places.* The person who is "it" tries to capture one of the empty spaces or seats.

7.15

### Prep Time

Make a list of words that rhyme with the color or picture names.

### Warm Up

Recite a familiar nursery rhyme, pausing before the word that completes the rhyme: for example, *Jack be nimble, Jack be quick, Jack jumped over the candle . . . stick.* Tell students to listen for the words that have the same ending sound as you recite other familiar nursery rhymes such as "Little Boy Blue," "Mary Had a Little Lamb," and so on. Repeat the nursery rhymes, asking students to fill in the rhyming words at the end of each line.

**ELL** FOR SPANISH-SPEAKING STUDENTS . . .
Use these rhymes as a warm-up: *Pan caliente pide la gente. Piden pan, y no les dan.*

**7.16**

## Teach

Explain that words that have the same ending sounds are called rhyming words. Tell students to listen carefully. Then say: Quick *rhymes with* stick, *and* blue *rhymes with* shoe. *Does* two *rhyme with* moo? Make sure students understand that words rhyme if the ending sounds the same. Hold up three pictures and have students name them: for example, *head, bread,* and *cat.* Ask: *Does* head *rhyme with* bread? *Does* head *rhyme with* cat? *Which picture doesn't belong? What's another word that rhymes with* head *and* bread?

## Practice

Tell students that they are going to play a game called Swap a Rhyme. Have students sit in a circle. Choose someone to be "it." (If you have an even number of students, the teacher should be "it.") The person who is "it" stands in the center of the circle. Distribute a colored cube to each student. Make sure that students with the same color are not sitting next to each other. Have students show their cubes so that the person who is "it" can see them. Say a word that rhymes with one of the colored cube names, such as *bed* for the color *red.* Students who have the red cubes try to swap places while "it" tries to capture one of the empty seats. The student left without a seat becomes "it." Continue reinforcing rhyme recognition by giving students other words that rhyme with color names: *track/black, town/brown, clean/green, kite/white.*

**Have students complete the Apply activity for practice with rhyme recognition and production. Some possible rhyming pairs for their drawings are *gato/pato, taza/plaza, luna/cuna, coche/noche, ropa/sopa, queso/hueso.***

*As students complete the Apply activity, use these questions to assess their progress.*

## Apply

To practice producing rhymes, ask pairs of students to draw pairs of rhyming pictures, such as fish/dish, cat/bat, star/car. Have students show their rhyming pictures to the group and invite classmates to name other words that rhyme. Then have students use their pictures to play Swap a Rhyme. For example, if "it" says the word *wish,* students holding pictures of the fish and dish change places.

7.17

| Questions for Observation | Benchmarks |
|---|---|
| Does *bed* rhyme with *red*? Does *hat* rhyme with *red*? | Student can recognize words that rhyme. |
| Can you think of a word that rhymes with *red*? What is it? | Student can produce rhyming words. |

## Try It This Way!

This game can be adapted to practice recognition of initial or final phonemes. Instead of calling out words that rhyme with a color or an object, the person who is "it" calls out words that begin or end with the same sound as a color name. For example, if "it" says *rabbit,* students holding red cubes switch places.

7.18

**FOLLOW-UP STRATEGY FOR**

## Rhyme Recognition and Production

**Benchmarks**

- ability to recognize words that rhyme
- ability to produce rhyming words

**Grade Level**

- PreK – Grade 1

**Prerequisite**

- Swap a Rhyme

**Grouping**

- whole class
- small group or pairs

**Materials**

- pictures of foods pasted on index cards
- puppet with large mouth
- large envelope for food pictures that says "Feed Me" on one side and "Thank You" on the other

**Sources**

- Adapted from *The Sounds Abound™ Program* (1998) by Orna Lenchner and Blanche Podhajski. East Moline, IL: LinguiSystems, Inc., 800-776-4332.
- *The Hungry Thing* (1988) by Jan Slepian and Ann Seidler.

## THE HUNGRY THING

GRADE LEVEL · PRE K-1 · GRADE LEVEL

This activity developed from a book for children by Jan Slepian and Ann Seidler, *The Hungry Thing.* In the book, a Hungry Thing comes to town. When asked what he wants to eat, he says a word that rhymes with a food. Of all the townspeople, only one little boy can figure out what the Hungry Thing wants.

## Warm Up

Students should be able to identify and name the foods on the cards. Practice asking for some of the foods using a rhyming word (nonsense or real). Ask, for example: *Please may I have some bookies?* (cookies)

## Play the Game

Have students sit in a circle with their food cards facing up in front of them. Tell students that you are going to tell the story of the Hungry Thing. Ask them to listen carefully. Each time the Hungry Thing asks for something, they need to decide if it is their food the Hungry Thing is asking for. For example, if the Hungry Thing asks for a *wanana,* the student with the banana would hold up his or her card and feed the Hungry Thing. Follow this script or use your own variation. Use the puppet to tell the following story.

*Feed me!*

## THE HUNGRY THING

Once upon a time there was a Hungry Thing that came into the town of (school location) and pointed to a sign around his neck that said Feed Me.

And the townspeople asked, "What would you like to eat?"

The Hungry Thing answered [for example], *"Rizza."*

"What is *rizza?*" the townspeople asked.

*(The student with the pizza [or rhyming food] comes up with his or her card to feed the puppet as you continue to narrate.)*

And a little boy [or girl] said, "*Rizza* sounds like . . . *pizza!*"

*(Student feeds the puppet.)*

The Hungry Thing wiped his mouth and pointed again to the Feed Me sign.

And the townspeople asked, "Now, what would you like to eat?"

*(Continue until all the students have fed the puppet.)*

Then the Hungry Thing wiped his mouth, turned his sign around, pointed to it, and said "Thank You!"

### Try It This Way!

Have students take turns thinking of a rhyming food for the Hungry Thing to eat.

**TEACHING STRATEGY FOR**

## Syllable Blending and Segmentation

### Benchmarks

- ability to blend word parts to form multisyllabic words
- ability to recognize parts of multisyllabic words

### Grade Level

- Kindergarten – Grade 2

### Grouping

- whole class
- small group or pairs
- individual

### Materials

- pictures or models of vegetables whose names are multisyllabic: pepper, lettuce, celery, cucumber
- paper salad bowls

---

# CRAZY SALAD TOSS

## Warm Up

Hold up vegetables one at a time and have students name them. Identify vegetables that may be unfamiliar. When possible, invite students to smell and taste the vegetables.

**ELL**   FOR SPANISH-SPEAKING STUDENTS . . .
Instead of vegetable names, use two- and three-syllable names of fruit: *higo, pera, piña, uva, melón, manzana, sandía, banana, naranja.*

## Teach

Show students a picture of a pepper and ask them to name it. Have students say *pepper* and then clap the word parts, or syllables. Ask: *How many times did we clap?* Repeat the word *pepper* a couple of times, clapping as students say the word with you. Next, show students the picture of a cucumber and ask them to name it. Have students say and clap the word. Ask: *How many times did we clap?* Repeat the procedure with the lettuce and celery.

## Practice

On the board, draw two large salad bowls. In one bowl, draw two dots and a carrot. In the other bowl, draw three dots and a tomato.

**Intervention
Strategy**

Students having difficulty can
practice clapping the word
parts of two-syllable compound words.

Point to the salad bowl with the carrot in it. Ask: *What is in
this bowl?* (a carrot) Tell students to clap the word *car•rot.* Ask:
*How many times did you clap?* (two times) Now point to the
other salad bowl. Ask: *What is in this bowl?* (a tomato) Tell
students to clap the word *to•ma•to.* Ask: *How many times did
you clap?* (three times)

Show the picture of a pepper. Ask: *What is the name of this
vegetable?* (pepper) Say: *Clap the word* pepper. (pep•per) Ask:
*How many word parts do you hear in the word* pepper? (two)
Say: *I'm going to put the pepper in the bowl with the carrot
because their names have two word parts.* Tell students to clap
the word *car•rot* and the word *pep•per* several times. Now
repeat the same procedure using the picture of the lettuce.

Show the picture of a cucumber. Ask: *What is the name of
this vegetable?* (cucumber) Say: *Clap the word* cucumber.
(cu•cum•ber) Ask: *How many word parts do you hear in the
word* cucumber? (three) Say: *I'm going to put the cucumber in
the bowl with the tomato because their names have three word
parts.* Tell students to clap the word *to•ma•to* and the word
*cu•cum•ber* several times. Now repeat the same procedure
using the picture of the celery.

Continue by choosing other vegetable pictures at random and
following the procedure described above. Students can tape
the vegetable pictures to the appropriate bowl, prop the vegetable pictures in the chalk tray below the appropriate bowl,
or actually put plastic vegetables into real bowls.

7.22

## Apply

Attach the two paper salad bowls to a bulletin board. On one put two dots and on the other put three dots. Invite students to draw or cut out pictures of things to put in the bowls to make Crazy Salads. For example, items that might go into the two-dot bowl include spider, skateboard, and pencil. Items that might go into the three-dot bowl include computer, elephant, and bicycle. Students can name their ingredients, clapping out the word parts as they add them to the bulletin board. To practice blending syllables, students use the pictures in the bowls to play a guessing game. One student pronounces a picture word by segmenting it into syllables: *ba...na...na.* Other students have to identify the picture by saying the blended word: *banana.*

**OBSERVE AND ASSESS**

*As students complete the Apply activity, use these questions to assess their progress.*

| Questions for Observation | Benchmarks |
| --- | --- |
| Can you say the word *ba...na...na* fast? | Student can blend word parts to form multisyllabic words. |
| Can you tell me the parts you hear in the word *banana*? Let's clap them. | Student can segment parts of multisyllabic words. |

## The Next Step

Challenge students to create a one-dot, four-dot, or five-dot crazy salad.

# Syllable Blending and Segmentation

**Benchmark**

• ability to blend word parts to identify multisyllabic words

**Grade Level**

• Kindergarten – Grade 2

**Prerequisite**

• Crazy Salad Toss

**Grouping**

• whole class
• small group or pairs

**Materials**

• pictures of things whose names have one to four syllables
• large cards with one to four dots

## NAME SORT

### Warm Up

Have each student say his or her name, and tell the class to respond: *Hello [student's name].* Students should clap the word parts they hear as they say each student's name.

7.23

### Play the Game

Select team captains based on the number of syllables in their names: *Bob, Carlos, Harriet,* and so on. Give each of these students a large card marked with dots corresponding to the number of syllables in his or her name. Tell the class that when you count to three, they are to line up behind the team captain whose name has the same number of word parts as their own. They have one minute to find the right captain. After everyone has chosen a captain, give them a short time to clap out the word parts in their names and check with teammates to be sure they are in the right line. They can move to another team if necessary. Invite each team to lead the class in chanting and clapping each team member's name in unison.

### Try It This Way!

Select four students to be captains for the one-, two-, three-, and four-syllable word groups. Have them stand at the front of the room. Select four pictures whose names have one, two, three, or four syllables, such as cat, toothbrush, potato, and helicopter. Distribute to the rest of the class pictures whose names have one to four syllables. Give students time to sort themselves onto the right team, depending on how many word parts they hear in their picture names. Students can check with teammates to be sure they are on the right team and make any last-minute changes before the class checks each team together. To check, have students clap the word parts in the picture names.

## FOLLOW-UP STRATEGY FOR
# Syllable Blending and Segmentation

**Benchmark**

• ability to recognize parts of multisyllabic words

7.24

**Grade Level**

• Kindergarten – Grade 2

**Prerequisite**

• Crazy Salad Toss

**Grouping**

• whole class
• small group or pairs
• individual

**Materials**

• none

**English language learners may need picture prompts.**

## TUMMY TICKLER

### Warm Up
Ask students to name foods they like to eat. Model by clapping out the word parts for each one: *piz•za; milk•shake.* Invite students to join in with you.

### Chant the Rhyme
Have students sit in a circle. Teach them the words to "Yummy, Yummy" and model clapping the word parts. Practice a few times and ask students, one at a time, to say and clap their favorite foods. Students can rub their tummies as they chant the first two lines (the refrain):

---

#### YUMMY, YUMMY

*Class chants:* Yummy, yummy, rub your tummy.
What's a treat you like to eat?

*Student chants:* I like pop•corn.
*(Student supplies a food name,*
*clapping the word parts as they are said.)*

*Class chants:* [Student's name] likes pop•corn.
*(Class repeats food name, clapping the word parts.)*

---

Students should clap the word parts for each food that is named. Encourage them to think of foods that have names with three or more word parts to use in the chant: for example, *cantaloupe, bananas, hamburgers.*

## Syllable Deletion

**Benchmarks**

• ability to identify both syllables in a two-syllable word

• ability to delete one syllable in a two-syllable word

**Grade Level**

• Kindergarten – Grade 1

**Grouping**

• whole class
• small group or pairs
• individual

**Materials**

• objects or pictures of objects whose names have two syllables
• self-stick notes

This activity is based on the work of Jerome Rosner (1993), who developed an entire program around syllable and phoneme deletion.

7.25

### Warm Up

Say the following words and have students identify the word parts in each one: *bookmark* (book•mark); *daytime* (day•time). Ask: *What is the first word part in the word* cowgirl*?* (cow) *What is the second word part in the word* cowgirl*?* (girl) Repeat until students can identify the first and second word parts in two-syllable compound words: for example, *boxtop, haircut.*

**ELL** FOR SPANISH-SPEAKING STUDENTS . . .
Use the song "Debajo de un botón" to introduce students to the concept of syllable deletion: *Debajo de un botón, ton, ton; Que encontró Martín, tin, tin; Había un ratón, ton, ton. Ay qué chiquitín, tin, tin; Era aquel ratón, ton, ton; Que encontró Martín, tin, tin; Debajo de un botón, ton, ton.*

### Teach

Draw a picture of a cupcake on the board. Then draw a two-box grid under the picture, as shown at left.

Ask: *How many word parts do you hear in the word* cupcake*?* (two) *What are the word parts in the word* cupcake*?* (cup•cake) *What is the first word part?* (cup) Put a self-stick note in the first box as students identify the word part. *What is the second word part?* (cake) Put a self-stick note in the second box as students identify the word part. Ask: *If I take away the first word part in the word* cupcake*, what word part is left?* (cake)

Take away the self-stick note in the first box as you ask the question. Then put the self-stick note back. Ask: *If I take away the second word part in the word* cupcake, *what word part is left?* (cup) Take away the self-stick note in the second box as you ask the question. Draw a picture of a rainbow and repeat the questions, taking away the self-stick note for first one word part and then the other.

## Practice

On the board draw a picture of a toothbrush. Then draw a two-box grid under the picture, as shown.

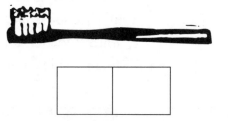

Explain that you want students to find the word parts for some everyday objects, take away one of the word parts, and then say the word part that is left. Point to the picture of the toothbrush. Ask: *What is this?* (toothbrush) Ask: *What are the word parts in the word* toothbrush? (tooth•brush) Put a self-stick note in each box as the word parts are identified. Then take away the self-stick note in the first box. Ask: *If I take away the first word part in the word* toothbrush, *what word part is left?* (brush) Put the self-stick note back in place. Then take away the self-stick note in the second box. Ask: *If I take away the second word part in the word* toothbrush, *what is the word part that is left?* (tooth) Repeat with other pictures or objects, varying the order of the word part that is taken away first. Once students are comfortable with deleting a part of a compound word, use other two-syllable words, such as *pencil, window, curtain, igloo, tulip.*

**7.26**

**If students are having difficulty, have partners work together. Each partner can say one word part of a two-syllable word. For example, ask:** *What word part is left if you take away Joan's part?* **Joan's partner will say his or her word part.**

## Apply

Hold up pictures or objects and have students identify the word parts in each one. Tell students to listen carefully to which part of the word is taken away. Ask: *What is* baseball *without* base? (ball) *What is* baseball *without* ball? (base) *What is* sunshine *without* shine? (sun) *What is* sunshine *without* sun? (shine) Invite students to make up similar word-part takeaway questions of their own. Then challenge students by asking: *What is* napkin *without* nap? (kin) *What is* napkin *without* kin? (nap)

*As students complete the Apply activity, use these questions to assess their progress.*

| Questions for Observation | Benchmarks |
|---|---|
| How many word parts do you hear in *baseball*? Let's clap them. | Student can identify the syllables in a two-syllable word. |
| If I say *sunshine* and take away the *shine*, what is left? | Student can delete one syllable in a two-syllable word. |

## The Next Step

Repeat the activity, using words with more than two syllables. For example, have students identify the word parts in *hamburger* and then delete the second syllable.

**FOLLOW-UP STRATEGY FOR**

## Syllable Deletion

**Benchmark**

• ability to delete one word part in two-syllable words

**7.28**

**Grade Level**

• Kindergarten – Grade 1

**Prerequisite**

• Take It Away

**Grouping**

• whole class
• small group or pairs

**Materials**

• picture cards: football, raincoat, sailboat, pancake, sweatshirt, grapefruit, starfish, umbrella
• self-stick notes

**Source**

• "There's a Starfish Hidden Under My Bed" (1997) by Fran Avni.

## THERE'S A STARFISH HIDDEN UNDER MY BED

### Warm Up

Students should be able to name the items on the picture cards. Invite students to identify and name them with you.

### Chant the Rhyme

Teach students "There's a Starfish Hidden Under My Bed." Then display the picture of the starfish and draw a two-box grid on the board. Place self-stick notes in the boxes.

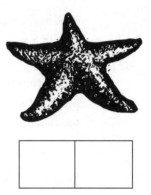

Chant the rhyme slowly, removing the note that represents the deleted syllable *star.*

---

THERE'S A STARFISH HIDDEN UNDER MY BED

There's a starfish hidden under my bed

STARFISH *(clap, clap),* STARFISH *(clap, clap)*

Someone took the star — What's left instead?

Someone took the star — What's left instead?

It's just a . . . fish!  A fish!

Display the picture of a sailboat and chant the rhyme, substituting the word *sailboat* for the word *starfish*. Repeat this procedure with the other pictures (football, pancake), varying the deleted syllable. For example, take the self-stick note out of the second box as you chant the final two lines:

Someone took the foot — What's left instead?

It's just a . . . ball! A ball!

## Try It This Way!
Challenge students to repeat the chant using two-syllable words that are not compounds: for example, *flower* and *rabbit*. Students may then think of three- or four-syllable words and chant the rhyme, deleting one or two syllables.

**Intervention Strategy**

**To make the task more explicit, use two pictures for compound words; one for each syllable. For example, use a picture of a pan and a picture of a cake for *pancake*. Have students name the two word parts and then the whole word. Next remove one of the pictures and ask:** *What is left?*

> There's an umbrella hidden under my bed
>
> UMBRELLA *(clap, clap, clap)*,
>
> UMBRELLA *(clap, clap, clap)*
>
> Someone took the um — What's left instead?
>
> Someone took the um — What's left instead?
>
> It's just a . . . brella! A brella!

**TEACHING STRATEGY FOR**

## Onset and Rime Blending

**Benchmark**

7.30

• ability to blend the onset and the rime to produce a one-syllable word

**Grade Level**

• Kindergarten – Grade 1

**Grouping**

• whole class
• small group or pairs
• individual

**Materials**

• pictures or plastic models of animals whose names have one syllable: for example, bat, bear, bird, deer, fox, skunk, pig, shark, cat, mouse
• kitchen items: spoon, fork, knife, cup, plate, pot, pan

## CRITTER SITTER

A syllable has two primary parts: the onset and the rime. The rime is the vowel and everything after it. The onset is the consonant, consonant blend, or digraph that comes before the rime.

⬤ ⬤ ⬤ ⬤ ⬤ ⬤ ⬤ ⬤ ⬤ ⬤ ⬤ ⬤ ⬤ ⬤ ⬤ ⬤ ⬤ ⬤ ⬤ ⬤ ⬤ ⬤ ⬤ ⬤ ⬤ ⬤ ⬤ ⬤ ⬤

### Warm Up

Students should be able to name the animals and kitchen items. Invite students to identify and name them with you.

### Teach

Introduce students to an imaginary character called the Critter Sitter. Explain that the Critter Sitter works at the zoo. Draw a picture of a large cage on the board. Display pictures or models of the animals. Then tell students that you have gotten a call from the Critter Sitter at the zoo. Some of the animals have escaped. To round them up, you need to help the Critter Sitter say their names. For example, play the part of yourself and the Critter Sitter as you say: *We need to catch the /b/. . . ear. What animal are we trying to catch?* (bear) Set the picture of

the bear in the chalk tray under the cage. *We need to catch the /f/ . . . ox. What animal are we trying to catch?* (fox) Put the picture of the fox in the chalk tray under the cage. Continue until all of the animals are "captured."

## Apply

Tell students that the Critter Sitter has a cousin, a chef, who also likes to play games with words. When the chef asks the kitchen helper for a /k/ . . . *up,* the helper says, "Here's the *cup.*" Distribute kitchen items to pairs of students: for example, spoon, fork, knife, cup, plate, pot, pan. Tell students to take turns being the chef and the kitchen helper. Encourage students to share their "role plays" with the rest of the class.

---

**OBSERVE AND ASSESS**

*As students complete the Apply activity, use this question to assess their progress.*

| Question for Observation | Benchmark |
|---|---|
| Listen to the word parts and then say the word as a whole: /p/ . . . *ot.* What's the word? (pot) | Student can blend onset and rime to produce one-syllable words. |

## TEACHING STRATEGY FOR

# Phoneme Matching and Isolating

### Benchmarks

- ability to identify initial and final phonemes in words
- ability to recognize and match initial and final phonemes in words

### Grade Level

- Kindergarten – Grade 1

### Grouping

- whole class
- small group or pairs
- individual

### Materials

- objects or pictures of objects whose names have the same initial or final sound

Intervention Strategy

**Some students may need more extensive practice "feeling" the voicing and the place and manner of articulation of the consonant phoneme /p/ in *pencil*. For more information, refer to Section II: Word Structure, "What Is a Phoneme?" p. 3.2.**

# SOUND SORT

GRADE LEVEL **K-1** GRADE LEVEL

Initial and final sounds are not to be taught at the same time. Final sounds should be introduced after several initial sound activities.

## Warm Up

Tell students to listen carefully to the words you are going to say. Ask them to tell you whether or not the following pairs of words begin with the same sounds: *cap/cat, dog/pig, hot/cold, sun/sand.*

**ELL** FOR SPANISH-SPEAKING STUDENTS . . .
Use these examples for the Warm Up: *mano/miro, les/dan, sol/pon, fecha/foto.*

## Teach

Display groups of three or four pictures or objects; at least two of them should start with the same sound. For example, display a pencil, a pen, and a ruler. Hold up the pencil. Have students say the word *pencil* aloud. Explain that the word *pencil* begins with /p/. Ask: *What other object do you see whose name begins with /p/?* (pen) Continue in this same manner, using other similar groups of objects. To focus on final sounds, have students choose the pictures or objects with the same final sound: for example, book, flag, desk. For initial vowel phonemes, use groups of pictures such as elbow, envelope, apple.

**ELL** FOR SPANISH-SPEAKING STUDENTS . . .
For the Teach activity, you can display a pencil *(lápiz)*, a book *(libro)*, and a pair of scissors *(tijeras).*

## Practice

Divide the class into groups of two or three students. Give each group a set of objects or pictures that begin or end with two different sounds: for example, pen, pencil, paper, ruler, rubber, and ribbon. Have group members sort the objects, putting objects that begin with the same sound together. Students can re-sort the objects by putting those with the same ending sound together. Ask students to say the first sound in each of the picture groups.

## Apply

Play the game I Spy. Say: *I spy something in the room that begins with /w/.* (window) Repeat for different objects and have students isolate and identify the initial sound. To focus on the final sound, say: *I spy something in the room that ends with /k/.* (desk)

**ELL**

ENGLISH/SPANISH

**This example provides practice using English phonemes that are not found in Spanish words: initial /w/ and final /k/.**

### OBSERVE AND ASSESS

*As students complete the Apply activity, use these questions to assess their progress.*

| Questions for Observation | Benchmarks |
| --- | --- |
| What is the first sound you hear in *pencil*? (/p/) | Student can identify the initial phoneme in a word. |
| What is the last sound you hear in *pen*? (/n/) | Student can identify the final phoneme in a word. |
| What is the sound at the beginning/end of *(item name)*? Can you find other items whose names begin/end with the same sound? | Student can recognize and match the initial or final phoneme in a word. |

## Try It This Way!

Adapt the I Spy game for vowel recognition. Display a bag, a flag, and a rug, and have students identify them. Hold up the bag. Have students say the word *bag* aloud. Tell students to listen to the /a/ sound in the middle of the word *bag*. Have them say the names of the other two objects aloud. Ask: *What other object's name has the /a/ sound?* (flag)

**FOLLOW-UP STRATEGY FOR**

# Phoneme Matching and Isolating

### Benchmarks

- ability to identify initial and final phonemes in words
- ability to isolate initial and final phonemes in words

### Grade Level

- Kindergarten – Grade 1

### Prerequisite

- Sound Sort

### Grouping

- whole class

### Materials

- small toy animals, or pictures of animals: bat, bird, cat, dog, elephant, fish, giraffe, goat, lion, horse, mouse, moose, octopus, ostrich, raccoon, rabbit, seal, shark, sheep, snake, tiger, worm

**Intervention Strategy**

**If a student is unable to isolate a sound, model the correct response and have the student imitate the sound, then let him or her cross the bridge.**

## BRIDGE GAME

Initial and final sounds are best taught separately. Final sounds should be introduced after several initial sound activities.

● ● ● ● ● ● ● ● ● ● ● ● ● ● ● ● ● ● ● ● ● ●

## Prep Time

1. Create a bridge out of chairs or other props.
2. Choose animal names with an initial sound you want to practice. Choose one or two new sounds per lesson.

## Warm Up

Give each student an animal or picture of an animal. Have each student say the name of his or her animal and the first sound in its name.

## Play the Game

Have students gather on one side of the bridge while you stand on the other side. Tell students that you are the lion who guards the bridge. They need to cross the bridge, but you won't let them unless they can answer two questions. Call on the first student. Say, for example: *I am the lion! I am guarding the bridge! What animal are you?* (tiger) *What is the first sound in your name?* (/t/) *You may cross my bridge.* Continue until all the animals have crossed the bridge.

## Try It This Way!

When all the students have crossed the bridge, go to the opposite side and tell students that it is now time for the animals to return to their homes. This time, the lion will ask each animal its name and the last sound in its name. For example, say: *I am the lion! I am guarding the bridge! What animal are you?* (goat) *What is the last sound in your name?* (/t/) Continue until all of the animals have returned home.

## Phoneme Matching and Isolating

**Benchmark**

• ability to isolate initial and final phonemes in words

**Grade Level**

• Grade 2 and above

**Prerequisite**

• Sound Sort

**Grouping**

• whole class
• small group or pairs

**Materials**

• none

## TRAIN GAME

### Warm Up

Make sure students can isolate and identify the first and last sounds in a word. Ask: *What is the first sound you hear in the word* game? (/g/) *What is the last sound you hear in the word* game? (/m/)

7.35

### Play the Game

Tell students that they are going to string words together like train cars on a track. Explain that students will listen for the *last* sound in a word and then think of a word that begins with that sound. Ask: *What is the last sound you hear in the word* cat? (/t/) Say: *Think of a word that begins with /t/.* (Possible answer: *tape*) Next, have the group identify the final phoneme in tape (/p/) and think of a word that begins with /p/. Practice until students understand the concept.

Ask students to stand in a line. Tell them that you are the train engine. Say a word, and have the student next to you identify the final phoneme in that word and use it as the first phoneme in a new word. If the student's response is correct, take the student's hand to link the first train car to the engine. Continue until all of the train cars are hooked together. A student who can't think of a word can go to the caboose and try again.

### Try It This Way!

Choose a category, such as pets, things you find in a particular place (home, school, garage, grocery store), things in nature, and so on. Responses must be words that fit the category. For example: *cat, turtle, lizard, duck, coyote, eagle, leopard, dog,* and so on. Challenge students to string together as many words in a category as possible without any repeats.

**TEACHING STRATEGY FOR**

# Phoneme Blending

### Benchmark

• ability to blend phonemes to correctly say one-syllable words

7.36

### Grade Level

• Kindergarten – Grade 1

### Grouping

• whole class
• small group or pairs
• individual

### Materials

• pictures of objects whose names have three to four phonemes: pin, pot, pen; or block, clock, book

**ELL**

**ENGLISH/SPANISH**

**Here are some one-syllable nouns that can be used in the Warm Up, Teach, and Practice activities: *mar, luz, sol, pan, mes, sal, pez, red, tos, tren, flor, tres, flan.***

---

**OBSERVE AND ASSESS**

*As students complete the Apply activity, use this question to assess their progress.*

---

## SOUND BITES

### Warm Up

Tell students that they are going to play a guessing game. Then say: *I'm thinking of something in this room. You can read it. It is a /b/ /o͝o/ /k/. What am I thinking of?* (book) Continue with classroom items, such as desk, pen, tape, tack.

### Teach

Display three pictures or items: for example, cap, box, coat. Say the individual sounds in one of the words and ask students to guess what word you are thinking of. You say /k/ /a/ /p/, and they say *cap*. Do the same with box and coat. Follow the same procedure using pin, pot, pen, and block, clock, book.

### Practice

Play a riddle game. Say: *I am thinking of something that is red, white, and blue. It is the American /f/ /l/ /a/ /g/.* (flag) *I am thinking of something that swims in a lake. It is a /f/ /i/ /sh/.* (fish) Continue following the same procedure. Some students may be interested in making up their own riddles.

### Apply

Tell a story, such as the following, asking students to blend each segmented word as you say it. *My friend's name is /b/ /i/ /l/.* (Bill) *He likes to eat /f/ /r/ /o/ /g/ /z/.* (frogs) *His favorite color is /g/ /r/ /ē/ /n/.* (green) *He likes to /j/ /u/ /m/ /p/.* (jump)

| Question for Observation | Benchmark |
|---|---|
| Can you put all the sounds together in [word] and say the word fast? | Student can blend phonemes to correctly say one-syllable words. |

# Phoneme Blending

## SIMON SAYS

**Benchmark**

• ability to blend phonemes to say one-syllable words

**Grade Level**

• Kindergarten – Grade 1

**Prerequisite**

• Sound Bites

**Grouping**

• whole class
• small group or pairs

**Materials**

• none

**Have English language learners work with a partner to identify names of body parts.**

### Warm Up

Play a warm-up round of Simon Says to make sure students know body part names and the rules of the game.

LEADER: Simon says, "Touch your wrist."
*(Students touch their wrists.)*
LEADER: Simon says, "Touch your nose."
*(Students touch their noses.)*
LEADER: Touch your leg.
*(Students do nothing.)*
LEADER: Simon says, "Touch your leg."
*(Students touch their legs.)*

7.37

### Play the Game

Tell students that they are going to play a different version of Simon Says.

LEADER: Simon says, "Touch your /l/ /e/ /g/."
*(Students touch their legs, and say the word leg.)*
LEADER: Simon says, "Touch your /l/ /i/ /p/ /s/."
*(Students touch their lips, and say the word lips.)*
LEADER: Put your finger on your /n/ /ō/ /z/.
*(Students do nothing.)*
LEADER: Simon says, "Put your finger on your /n/ /ō/ /z/."
*(Students put their fingers on their noses, and say the word nose.)*

Continue the game. Use one-syllable body-part names, such as toe, heel, foot, knee, thigh, chest, back, arm, wrist, hand, throat, neck, chin, mouth, cheek, ear, eye, head.

### Try It This Way!

Play the game to reinforce onset and rime blending. In this version, instead of saying /l/ /e/ /g/, you would say /l/... *eg.*

## TEACHING STRATEGY FOR
## Phoneme Segmentation

7.38

### Benchmarks

- ability to break words into phonemes
- ability to blend phonemes to say words

### Grade Level

- Kindergarten and above

### Grouping

- whole class
- small group or pairs
- individual

### Materials

- pictures of objects whose names have three phonemes, such as cat, coat, kite, pen
- self-stick notes
- transparency
- overhead projector

## NAME THAT SOUND

This activity is based on the Elkonin (1963) procedure, an effective way to develop phonemic segmentation skills. It is a strategy for older students who need to develop phonemic awareness. This procedure also can be incorporated into phonics lessons: for example, see The Next Step on p. 7.40.

### Warm Up

Remind students that they have learned how to blend sounds into words. On the board, tape a picture of a cat, a coat, a kite, and a pen. Explain that students are going to play a guessing game. You are going to say some sounds; they will listen and then point to what you are thinking of. Say: /k/ /a/ /t/. Invite students to blend the sounds and point to the correct picture. Repeat the procedure for *coat, kite,* and *pen.*

**ELL** FOR SPANISH-SPEAKING STUDENTS . . .
Some examples of words with three phonemes are *sol, pan, pez,* and *mar.*

### Teach

Draw a three-box grid below each displayed picture. Ask students why there are three boxes under each picture. *(Because there are three sounds in each word)* Explain that the boxes under each picture stand for the sounds in each word. (Note: There may be fewer boxes than there are letters in a word. For example, *coat* has four letters but only three phonemes.)

Point to the picture of the cat and have students name the picture. Ask: *What is the first sound you hear in the word* cat? (/k/)

Place a self-stick note or other marker in the first box. Then ask students to identify the next sound they hear in the word *cat.* (/a/) Place a self-stick note in the middle box. Ask students to identify the last sound they hear in the word *cat.* (/t/) Place a self-stick note in the last box. Point to each box in sequence and have students say the sounds. Then guide them in blending the three sounds together to say the whole word. Ask: *How many sounds do you hear?* (three) Repeat this procedure with the words *coat, kite,* and *pen.*

## Practice

Tell students that they are going to have a chance to practice what they just learned. Display pictures of a cap, bat, boat, kite, bed, and the number ten. Ask students to identify the sounds in each of the objects' names. As they identify each sound, stick the self-stick note in the appropriate box. Guide students in blending the phonemes together to sound out whole words. For the remaining pictures, call on a volunteer to identify the first, middle, and last sound in each word and to place a self-stick note in a box as she or he says each sound aloud.

## Apply

Divide the class into pairs. Give each pair of students a new picture, self-stick notes, and a three-box grid. Ask the pairs to count the sounds, identify the sounds that name their picture,

Intervention
Strategy

**You may want to count boxes aloud with students, pointing from left to right. Some students may also benefit from additional attention to the manner and place of articulation of a phoneme, focusing on tongue and lip position, jaw tension, and whether or not the sound is voiced or unvoiced. For more information, refer to Section II: Word Structure, "What Is a Phoneme?" p. 3.2.**

and then say the sounds in order. Pairs can present their sounds to the class to see if classmates can blend the sounds to say the word. They can then show their picture to the group to check their answers.

7.40

*As students complete the Apply activity, use these questions to assess their progress.*

| Questions for Observation | Benchmarks |
| --- | --- |
| How many sounds do you hear in the picture name? | Student can segment spoken words into sounds. |
| What is the first sound? The middle sound? The last sound? | Student can isolate and identify the positions of phonemes. |
| What word do you say if you blend the sounds together? | Student can orally segment words with three phonemes and blend the sounds together. |

## Try It This Way!

Using an overhead projector, draw Elkonin boxes on a transparency to represent the sounds in a selected word. Then using markers, such as pennies, say each sound as you simultaneously move the penny into one of the boxes. For *cat,* for example, move a penny into the first box while saying /k/; move a second penny into the middle box while saying /a/; and move a third penny into the last box while saying /t/. Then have students say each sound as you point to each penny, starting with the first box. Have students say the entire word, blending the sounds together.

## The Next Step

Adapt the activity for more advanced students by printing the actual sound/spellings on the self-stick notes. Work on specific elements, such as digraphs or long vowels. For example, to demonstrate that the *ir* spelling stands for one sound (/ûr/) in the key word *girl,* place the self-stick note with the letter *g* in the first box, the note with the letters *ir* in the middle box, and the note with the letter *l* in the last box.

## Phoneme Segmentation

### Benchmarks

- ability to orally segment words with three phonemes
- ability to blend phonemes to say words

### Grade Level

- Kindergarten – Grade 2

### Prerequisite

- Name That Sound

### Grouping

- whole class

### Materials

- pictures of objects whose names have three to four phonemes

# SOUND-SOUND-WORD

7.41

## Warm Up

Make sure students know how to play the game Duck-Duck-Goose. Students sit in a circle. The student who is "it" walks around the outside of the circle, tapping each classmate on the head in turn and saying, "Duck, duck, duck . . ." When the student taps a classmate and says, "goose," the "goose" chases her around the outside of the circle. If the student who is "it" makes it around the circle and back to the "goose's" place before being tagged, the "goose" is "it." If the "goose" tags the student who is "it," that student is "it" again.

## Play the Game

Tell students that they are going to play Sound-Sound-Word. Explain that you are going to go around the circle tapping them as you say the separate sounds in a word. Whoever gets tapped when you say the whole word is the "goose" and must chase you around the circle. For example, walk around the circle, tapping students as you say the phonemes several times and then say the word: /k/ /a/ /t/, /k/ /a/ /t/, /k/ /a/ /t/, *cat!* Try the game by segmenting the word *fish* into its three phonemes. (/f/ /i/ /sh/) Repeat the game, tapping out the sounds in the word *kite*.

## Try It This Way!

Display pictures of objects whose names each have three phonemes: for example, cap, kite, fish. Have the student who was "it" in the last round choose a picture, and then go around the circle, tapping classmates and saying the separate sounds of the word that names the pictured object. When the student is ready to be chased, she or he says the whole word. Repeat the game, using words that have four phonemes: for example, *spoon, bread, skate, skirt, paint.*

**TEACHING STRATEGY FOR**

## Phoneme Manipulation: Deletion

7.42

### Benchmarks

• ability to delete the initial and final phonemes in words
• ability to segment onset and rime

### Grade Level

• Grades 1 – 3

### Grouping

• whole class
• small group or pairs
• individual

### Materials

• self-stick notes

## DRESS UP

### Warm Up

Explain that you are going to tell students a story with something missing. They have to listen carefully to find out what you have left out. Then tell the following story, leaving off the initial sound of the last word in each sentence: *This morning I got up and put on a shirt and _ants. I wanted to go to the _ark. I put on my _oat. At the park I fed the _irds. I met some friends and played _ag. It started to _ain. I ran _ome.* Ask students what is missing. Students should be able to explain that you have left off the first sound of the last word in each sentence. Tell the story again and have students fill in the missing sounds.

### Teach

Draw a hat on the board and a three-box grid underneath it. Ask the class to name the picture.

Have students name the three sounds in *hat.* (/h/ /a/ /t/) Put a self-stick note in the first box. Say: *If I cover up the first sound in* hat, *what is left?* (at) *What sound is missing?* Switch the self-stick note to the last box. Say: *If I cover up the last sound in* hat, *what is left?* (ha) *What sound is missing?* Continue using pictures of objects such as ball, cake, and dish.

**ELL** FOR SPANISH-SPEAKING STUDENTS . . .
Draw a moon on the board and a four-box grid underneath it. Follow the same procedure, but ask students to name the four sounds in the word *luna.*

## Practice

Ask a volunteer to stand in front of the class. Choose one thing that the student is wearing and say, for example: *Randy is wearing a sock.* Draw three boxes on the board. Have students name the three sounds in *sock.* (/s/ /o/ /k/) Now say: *Randy is wearing a _ock.* Invite students to name the sound you left out. After students have had practice with initial phoneme deletion, they can practice final sound deletion.

## Apply

Have students pair up and describe a few items of clothing the other student is wearing, deleting the first sound in each item's name. Invite the class to identify the sound that was left out.

STUDENT 1: *(Student 2)* is wearing a _irt.

STUDENT 2: No, I am wearing a shirt.

TEACHER: What sound did *(Student 1)* leave out?

CLASS: /sh/

**OBSERVE AND ASSESS**

*As students complete the Apply activity, use these questions to assess their progress.*

| Questions for Observation | Benchmarks |
| --- | --- |
| What sound did you take away from *shirt* to make *_irt*? | Student can delete the initial phoneme of a word. |
| What sound did you take away from *belt* to make *bell*? | Student can delete the final phoneme of a word. |

**FOLLOW-UP STRATEGY FOR**

## Phoneme Manipulation: Deletion

### Benchmarks

• ability to delete the initial phoneme in a word
• ability to delete the initial phoneme in a blend

### Grade Level

• Grades 1 – 3

### Prerequisite

• Dress Up

### Grouping

• whole class
• small group or pairs
• individual

### Materials

• sets of pictures in categories

# CATEGORY GUESSING GAME

## Warm Up

Tell students that you know someone who always leaves off the first sound when she names the days of the week. Instead of *Sunday,* she says *_unday.* What sound did she leave off? (/s/) Then ask students to say *Monday* without the /m/; *Tuesday* without the /t/; *Wednesday* without the /w/; *Thursday* without the /th/; *Friday* without the /f/; and *Saturday* without the /s/.

## Play the Game

Display sets of pictures that show different categories: for example, colors, sports, food. Have a volunteer choose a category, such as colors. Then have the volunteer say a word that fits that category, leaving off the initial sound. For example, for the color word *green,* the student would say *_reen.* Classmates use the category as a clue to help them identify the color and the missing sound (/g/), and then say the whole word, *green.* Continue by having students take turns saying and identifying the words that fit the category: *_lue, _ellow, _ite, _lack, _urple, _ed, _rown.* Repeat the game with a new category such as sports: *_occer, _aseball, _asketball, _ennis, _ockey, _olleyball.*

## Try It This Way!

For older students, adapt this game to practice deleting the second sound in a consonant blend. For example, for the color category you may say: *geen* for *green, bown* for *brown, bue* for *blue, back* for *black.*

## Phoneme Manipulation: Substitution

**Benchmarks**

- ability to substitute the initial phoneme in a word
- ability to substitute the final phoneme in a word

**Grade Level**

- Grades 1 – 3

**Grouping**

- whole class
- small group or pairs
- individual

**Materials**

- none

# TELEPHONE TALK

## Warm Up

Explain that you are going to tell students a story. They have to listen carefully to find out how you have changed the words. Then tell the following story, substituting /p/ for the initial sound in selected words: *I got up and brushed my peeth and washed my pace. Then I got pressed. I had a puffin with pelly, and then I went to plass.* Students should be able to explain the substitution you have made.

## Teach

Tell students that they are going to use words from the story to make substitutions of their own. Say: *Say the word* muffin. *Now instead of /m/, say /p/. What is the new word?* (puffin) *Say* jelly. *Now instead of /j/, say /p/. What's the new word?* (pelly). Repeat with the other words until students can make the substitutions.

## Practice

Have students choose a consonant sound. Then have them say words that fit a particular category, substituting that sound for the initial sound of each word. For example, if the category is body parts and the sound is /p/, possible responses include *peeth, pips, pose, pouth, pegs, peet, poulders, pest.* If the category is transportation and the sound is /d/, possible responses are *dus, drain, det, dar, druck, doat.* If the category is colors and the sound is /k/, possible responses are *ked, klack, krown, kink, kellow, klue.*

**ELL** FOR SPANISH-SPEAKING STUDENTS . . .
Suggest that students substitute either /t/ or /d/ when naming different body parts: *tientes, toca, trazo, tariz, tombros; doca, drazo, dariz, dombros, delo.*

7.45

**7.46**

*As students complete the Apply activity, use this question to assess their progress.*

Intervention Strategy

**Some students may need more practice "feeling" the voicing and the place and manner of articulation of the consonant phonemes /m/ and /b/ in *arm* and *arb*. For more information, refer to Section II: Word Structure, "What Is a Phoneme?" p. 3.2.**

## Apply

Have pairs of students choose a sound and then act out a question-and-answer phone conversation, substituting the sound they have chosen for the initial sound in key words in the conversation. The conversations can be presented to the group so that the class can guess the sound that has been substituted.

| Question for Observation | Benchmark |
|---|---|
| What sound has been substituted for the initial sound? | Student can substitute the initial phoneme in a word. |

## The Next Step

Have students practice substituting a sound for the final sound in a word. For example, if the sound is /b/ and the category is body parts, possible responses include *arm/arb, leg/leb, feet/feeb, neck/neb, back/bab.* Older students may enjoy this more challenging activity.

## Phoneme Manipulation: Substitution

**Benchmarks**

• ability to substitute the initial phoneme in a word
• ability to substitute the vowel sound in a word

**Grade Level**

• Grades 1 – 3

**Prerequisite**

• Telephone Talk

**Grouping**

• whole class
• small group or pairs

**Materials**

• none

**Source**

• "I'm Playing with a Monster" (1997) by Nancy Schimmel and Fran Avni.

# MONSTER CHANT

### Warm Up

Remind students how to substitute initial and final sounds. For example, have students name things in the classroom, substituting /v/ for the initial sound: vencil, vag, ven. *(pencil, bag, pen)* Repeat, having students substitute a different sound for the final sound: pencit, bat, pet. *(pencil, bag, pen)*

7.47

### Chant the Rhyme

Teach students "I'm Playing with a Monster." Begin by specifying the substitution sound /k/.

---

#### I'M PLAYING WITH A MONSTER

I'm playing with a monster,
My monster comes from Konster.
Right where I have legs,
My monster has . . . kegs.

Right where I have fingers,
My monster has . . . kingers.
Right where I have toes,
My monster has . . . koes.

---

Continue the chant with the words *shoulders, lips, hair, hands.* Then encourage students to suggest body parts, including animal parts like *tail, paws, tusks,* and so on.

At the end of the chant, have each student use his or her name for the last substitution:

**7.48**

> Because my name is [Rudy],
>
> My monster's name is . . . Kudy.

When students understand how to make the substitutions in the chant, divide the class into pairs. Specify a new substitution sound. Then have partners take turns saying a line from the chant that includes the substitution. Repeat the activity using a different substitution sound each time. Students may also name articles of clothing that the monster is wearing:

> Right where I have pants,
>
> My monster has . . . kants.

## Try It This Way!

Advanced students can experiment with vowel substitutions. For example, change all the vowel sounds to /i/. *Legs* become *ligs; neck* becomes *nick; head* becomes *hid.*

# Sound/Letter Correspondence

**Benchmark**

• ability to connect a phoneme to a grapheme

**Grade Level**

• Kindergarten and above

**Grouping**

• whole class
• small group or pairs
• individual

**Materials**

• alphabet letter cards
• pictures of animals whose names begin with /m/

This is a generic teaching strategy for connecting a sound to a letter. The letter *m* is used for modeling purposes only—the same strategy can be used to introduce other letter sounds.

7.49

## Warm Up

Display a group of three objects; at least two of them should start with the same sound. For example, display a book, a ball, and a pencil. Hold up the book. Have students say the word *book* aloud. Explain that the word *book* begins with /b/, the sound made by the letter *b*. Ask: *What other object do you see whose name begins with /b/?* (ball)

## Teach

Display pictures of animals whose names begin with /m/, such as a monkey and a mouse. Have students name them. Then ask: *Do these two animal names begin with the same sound? What sound do they begin with?* After students respond, display the letter *m* and say: *This is the letter* m. *The letter* m *stands for the /m/ sound.* Say: *Let's make the sound /m/.* Pause to have students practice the sound. Encourage them to notice their mouth position and how the sound is produced. Say: *Hold your nose and try saying /m/. Can you do it? The /m/ sound uses air through your nose. Now say /m/ without holding your nose.* Explain that the words *monkey* and *mouse* begin with the letter *m*. Then have students think of other words that begin with the /m/ sound.

**ELL** FOR SPANISH-SPEAKING STUDENTS . . .
Display pictures of a hand *(mano)* and a table *(mesa)*. Then follow the same procedure.

**7.50**

## Practice

Tell students that you are thinking of something that begins with the sound of the letter *m*. For example, you may say: *I am thinking of something whose name starts with the /m/ sound. It is an animal. It likes to eat bananas and swing in the trees. What is it?* (a monkey)

## Apply

Students can look through magazines and catalogs for pictures of things whose names begin with the /m/ sound. Have them cut out the pictures, print a large letter *M* on drawing paper, and paste their pictures around the letter. Some students may wish to add original drawings of things whose names begin with the /m/ sound. Provide an opportunity for students to share their work, naming each of the items in their collage.

**OBSERVE AND ASSESS**

*As students complete the Apply activity, use these questions to assess their progress.*

| Questions for Observation | Benchmarks |
|---|---|
| What letter stands for the /m/ sound? | Student can connect a letter to a sound, or phoneme. |
| What sound does the letter *m* stand for? | Student can connect a sound to a letter, or grapheme. |

## The Next Step

Use the same procedure for introducing other initial single-consonant and short-vowel sound/spellings.

## Sound/Letter Correspondence

**Benchmark**

• ability to connect a phoneme
  to a grapheme

**Grade Level**

• Kindergarten and above

**Prerequisite**

• Swap a Rhyme

**Grouping**

• whole class
• small group or pairs

**Materials**

• pairs of consonant and consonant digraph letter cards

# SWAP A LETTER/SOUND

This game focuses on single consonant letters. Only use letters that have been previously introduced. The game can also be played using consonant digraphs.

7.51

## Warm Up

Review the rules of the Swap a Rhyme game on page 7.15, and then play it with students.

## Play the Game

Tell students that they are now going to play Swap a Letter/ Sound. Have students sit in circle. Choose someone to be "it." (If you have an even number of students, the teacher should be "it.") The person who is "it" stands in the center of the circle. Distribute a consonant letter card to each student, making sure that students with the same letter are not sitting next to each other. Have students show their letter cards so that the person who is "it" can see them. Say a word that begins with a consonant sound, such as *sun*. Students who have the letter *s* cards try to swap places while "it" tries to capture one of the empty seats. The student left without a seat becomes "it." Continue reinforcing letter/sound correspondence by provid- ing words that begin with the other consonant letter sounds.

## Try It This Way!

Play Swap a Letter/Sound with final consonant sounds or short vowels in the initial or medial position. Final consonant sounds that are represented by only one letter include /b/, /d/, /g/, /m/, /n/, /p/, /t/.

## Section References

**7.52**

Adams, M. J. 1990. *Beginning to read: Thinking and learning about print.* Cambridge, MA: MIT Press.

Adams, M. J., B. Foorman, I. Lundberg, and T. Beeler. 1998. *Phonemic awareness in young children.* Baltimore, MD: Brookes Publishing.

Alegria J., E. Pignot, and J. Morais. 1982. Phonetic analysis of speech and memory codes in beginning readers. *Memory and Cognition* 10, pp. 451–456.

Ambruster, B., F. Lehr, and J. Osborn. 2001. *Put Reading First: The Research Building Blocks for Teaching Children to Read.* Partnership for Reading. Washington DC: U.S. Department of Education, p. 7.

Ball, E. W., and B. A. Blachman. 1991. Does phoneme awareness training in kindergarten make a difference in early word recognition and developmental spelling? *Reading Research Quarterly* 26(1), pp. 33–44.

Bear, D., M. Invernizzi, S. Templeton, and F. Johnston. 1996. *Words their way: Word study for phonics, vocabulary, and spelling instruction.* Upper Saddle River, NJ: Prentice-Hall.

Blevins, W. 1998. *Phonics from A to Z.* New York: Scholastic.

Cardoso-Martins, C. 1995. Sensitivity to rhymes, syllables, and phonemes in literacy acquisition in Portuguese. *Reading Research Quarterly* 30, pp. 808–828.

Clay, M. 1993. *Reading recovery: A guidebook for teachers in training.* Portsmouth, NH: Heinemann.

Cossu, G., D. Shankweiler, I. Y. Liberman, G. Tola, and L. Katz. 1988. Awareness of phonological segments and reading ability in Italian children. *Applied Psycholinguistics* 9, pp. 1–16.

Ehri, L. C., and S. McCormick. 1998. Phases of word learning: Implications for instruction with delayed and disabled readers. *Reading and Writing Quarterly* 14.

Elkonin, D. B. 1963. The psychology of mastering the elements of reading. In B. Simon and J. Simon (eds.), *Educational psychology in the U.S.S.R.* London: Routledge and Kegan Paul.

Elkonin, D. B. 1973. U.S.S.R. In J. Downing (ed.), *Comparative reading* (pp. 551–579). New York: Macmillan.

Gunn, B. K., D. C. Simmons, and E. J. Kameenui. 1998. Emergent literacy: Research bases. In D. C. Simmons and E. J. Kameenui (eds.), *What reading research tells us about children with diverse learning needs: Bases and basics.* Mahwah, NJ: Erlbaum.

Hall. S. L., and L. C. Moats. 1999. *Straight talk about reading: How parents can make a difference during the early years.* Lincolnwood, IL: NTC/Contemporary Publishing Group.

Hiebert, E. H., and C. C. Sawyer. 1984. *Young children's concurrent abilities in reading and spelling.* Paper presented at the annual meeting of the American Educational Research Association, New Orleans, LA.

Hoen, T., I. Lundberg, K. E. Stanovich, and I. Bjaalid. 1995. Components of phonological awareness. *Reading and Writing* 7, pp. 171–188.

Juel, C., P. Griffith, and P. Gough. 1986. Acquisition of literacy: A longitudinal study of children in first and second grade. *Journal of Educational Psychology* 78, pp. 243–255.

Lenchner, O., and B. Podhajski. 1998. *The sounds abound™ program.* East Moline, IL: LinguiSystems, Inc., 800-776-4332.

Lundberg, I., A. Olofsson, and S. Wall. 1980. Reading and spelling skills in the first school years predicted from phonemic awareness skills in kindergarten. *Scandinavian Journal of Psychology* 21, pp. 159–173.

Manrique, A. M. B., and S. Gramigna. 1984. La segmentación fonológica y silábica en niños de preescolar y primer grado [Phonological segmentation of syllables in preschool and first-grade children]. *Lectura y Vida* 5, pp. 4–13.

National Institute of Child Health and Human Development. 2000. *Report of the National Reading Panel, Teaching Children to Read: Reports of the Subgroups.* Bethesda, MD: National Institutes of Health.

Rosner, J. 1993. *Helping children overcome learning difficulties.* New York: Walker.

Slepian, J., and A. Seidler. 1988. *The hungry thing.* New York: Scholastic.

Stanovich, K. E. 1993. Romance and reality. *The Reading Teacher* 47(4), pp. 280–291.

Templeton, S. 1995. *Children's literacy: Contexts for meaningful learning.* Boston: Houghton Mifflin.

Torgesen, J. K., and P. Mathes. 1998. What every teacher should know about phonological awareness. In *CORE reading research anthology.* Novato, CA: Arena Press.

Tunmer, W. E., M. L. Herriman, and A. R. Nesdale. 1988. Metalinguistic abilities and beginning reading. *Reading Research Quarterly* 23, pp. 134–158.

# SECTION IV

# Decoding

# INTRODUCTION
## Section IV: Decoding

*"Poorly developed word recognition skills are the most pervasive and debilitating source of reading difficulty."*

—ADAMS, 1990

**CORE Reading Research Anthology**
for background information

**Section V: Spelling**

**ORTHOGRAPHY**
the writing system of a language

Because English is an alphabetic language, teaching students to decode words is a crucial element of an effective reading program. Decoding is the process of converting the printed word into its spoken form. Beginning decoding involves reading simple, new, regular words from left to right by generating sounds for individual letters or letter combinations and then blending those sounds into a recognizable word. The reader uses phonics skills—knowledge of letter/sound correspondences—to pronounce a word and attach meaning to it. As students progress in their reading development, they draw on additional word attack skills to decode words: rapid recognition of high-frequency words including those that are irregular; recognition of word parts (syllables, affixes, base words, phonograms); and the use of context to confirm pronunciation and resolve ambiguity.

Decoding is the tool that enables students to become proficient readers who recognize words effortlessly and rapidly. This automatic recognition of individual words leads to the fluent reading of strings of words, which in turn leads to full comprehension—the long-term goal of reading instruction.

## Reading Development

Students progress through discernible stages in their reading development. These stages are influenced in part by the structure of words themselves. The best decoding instruction is in alignment with the structure of English orthography. English orthography contains three layers of information: alphabetic, pattern, and meaning. Proficient readers and writers are able to access all the layers.

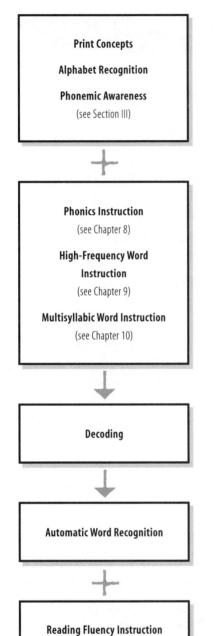

First, words contain an **alphabetic layer** that consists of the relationship between the sounds and letters. This is most easily discerned in basic consonant-vowel-consonant words such as *cat.* This alphabetic layer is the first layer students become aware of as they learn to decode; it is the basic alphabetic principle or insight that students must develop.

Words also contain a **pattern layer** in which groups of letters work as a unit to represent a sound. For example, in the word *mate,* the *a* and the silent *e* work together to produce the long-*a* sound, while in the word *plead,* the *e* and *a* form a pattern that represents the sound of long *e.* Syllables are also part of the English pattern layer of information. Distinct syllable juncture patterns inform the reader as to the correct pronunciation of multisyllabic words. For example, in the word *mitten* two consonants appear between two vowels. Words with this pattern break between the consonants and each syllable is a closed syllable type with a short-vowel sound. As students grow in their decoding development, their awareness of these pattern layers in words also grows.

Finally, all words have a **meaning layer**—that is, groups of letters relate to units of meaning. In the word *construction,* for example, the meaning elements *con, struc,* and *tion* all represent pieces of information about the word as a whole. When students understand this, they find reading much less challenging and use this knowledge as they read increasingly more complex words.

Ultimately, the goal of effective decoding instruction is to equip students with the tools to access all the layers of information contained within a word. To do that efficiently, it is helpful to understand the natural developmental progression students pass through as they develop reading skill.

## READING DEVELOPMENT

| Stages of Reading Development | Layers of English Orthography | Examples |
|---|---|---|
| Pre-alphabetic or Logographic | | Students recognize printed words by visual cues only; for example, the appearance of the two *z*'s in *pizza*. |
| Early Alphabetic | Alphabetic | Students associate sound and letters and begin to read simple words; for example, the CVC words *hat, him, map*. |
| Mature Alphabetic | Pattern | Students know most sound/spellings and the internal structure of words. They recognize recurring "chunks": for example, the phonogram *–ack*. |
| Orthographic | Meaning | Students process larger units of print (syllables and morphemes) and read by analogy to known words: for example, *build → guild*. |

 **Section V: Spelling, "Synchrony of Reading and Spelling Development," p. V.v**

# Align Decoding Instruction with the Stages of Reading Development

*by Louisa C. Moats*

Excerpted from "Teaching Decoding" in the Spring/Summer 1998 issue of *American Educator,* the quarterly journal of the American Federation of Teachers.

That decoding is learned early by good readers is established in studies of reading development (Chall 1983a; Cunningham and Stanovich 1997; Ehri 1994). The ability to sound out new words accounts for about 80 percent of the variance in first-grade reading comprehension, and continues to be a major factor in text comprehension as students progress through the grades (Foorman, Francis, Shaywitz, Shaywitz, and Fletcher 1997). Moreover, a series of studies have traced how beginners learn to read and spell words (e.g., Ehri 1994; Treiman 1993; Wagner and Barker 1994). The learner progresses from global to analytic processing, from approximate to specific linking of

Align Decoding Instruction with the
Stages of Reading Development
*Louisa C. Moats*

sound and symbol, and from context-driven to print-driven reading as proficiency is acquired. The instruction we deliver should be compatible with the emerging competence of the student.

### LOGOGRAPHIC READING

Young children, typically before mid-kindergarten, may learn to recognize a limited vocabulary of whole words through incidental cues such as a picture, color, or shape (Ehri 1994; Gough, Juel, and Griffith 1992) but, in this beginning stage of reading, do not associate sounds with symbols. Children will string letters together when they write and assign changing messages to them, or will look to context to guess at what a word says. A printed word may be remembered for its unique appearance, as in *pizza* or *D'Antoine.* If asked about the sound that begins *pizza,* however, the student might say "hot" or "m m m m." This visual cue reading typically precedes the insight that alphabet letters correspond to speech sounds. Children at this level have not realized that words are composed of phonemes, that letters represent those speech sounds, and that words can be decoded by matching symbol to sound.

Appropriate activities at the pre-alphabetic level include phonological awareness tasks (carried out orally) such as rhyming; counting, adding, and deleting syllables; matching beginning consonants in words; recognizing odd sounds; substituting sounds and identifying that a sound exists in selected words (Adams, Treiman, and Pressley 1998; Brady, Fowler, Stone, and Winbury 1994; Foorman et al. 1997; Torgesen, Wagner, and Rashotte 1997). In addition, the development of print awareness includes alphabet matching and letter naming, following print with the finger during read-alouds, and much interactive engagement with appealing books. All these activities develop awareness of the alphabetic principle: that letters roughly represent segments of one's own speech.

V

IV

Align Decoding Instruction with the
Stages of Reading Development
*Louisa C. Moats*

vi

IV

## NOVICE OR EARLY ALPHABETIC READING

To progress in reading, children must develop the insight that alphabet letters represent abstract speech segments (phonemes) and must be able to compare the likeness and difference of similar-sounding words (Liberman, Shankweiler, and Liberman 1989). Children begin to spell a few salient consonants in words when they write [KR (car); I L T G (I like to go); I LIK LAFFZ (I like elephants)]. Letter sounds and letter names such as /w/ and *y*, and /y/ and *u* may be confused. At this juncture, teaching affects the development of decoding strategies (Tunmer and Chapman 1996); children may not develop the habit of sounding a word out unless they are taught how and are given sufficient practice. Instead, they may learn to rely excessively on pictures or context to decipher the pronunciation of unfamiliar words, a habit of doubtful utility (Adams 1990; Iversen and Tunmer 1993). Once words are pronounced, meaning must be attached. The process of word identification is supported by sound-symbol decoding; the process of learning a word's meaning is supported by contextual analysis.

Once an association between sound and letter(s) is taught, children need cumulative practice building words with letters they know. Systematic programs begin with a limited set of sound-symbol correspondences—a few consonants *(b, f, h, j, k, m, p, t)* and one or two vowels (short *a* and *i*)—so that words can be built right away. Other consonants and vowels are added gradually to those already known. Vowels may be represented in a different color. Coupled with practice dividing words into phonemes and blending them back into wholes, children can build words with letter cards and play "chaining" games in which one sound is changed at a time to make a new word *(hat, bat, bit, hit, him, hip, hap, map)*. The core activity in systematic, explicit decoding instruction is blending single sounds into words. After the children have learned a few sound-letter correspondences through a rhyme or other mnemonic, blending proceeds sequentially:

Align Decoding Instruction with the
Stages of Reading Development
*Louisa C. Moats*

T. (Writing letter *h* on the board.) What's the sound?
S. /h/
T. (Writing letter *a* on the board.) What's the sound?
S. /a/
T. Blend it. (Sweeping hand under the letters.)
S. /ha/
T. (Writing letter *t* on the board.) What's the sound?
S. /t/
T. Blend it. (Sweeping hand under the letters.)
S. /hat/

After ten to fifteen words with known sound-symbol connections are blended, they are used immediately in sentences. Even if the written sentences are short, the teacher can ask the children to expand the sentences verbally, as in "Matt has a hat. Tell me what kind of hat he has!"

### MATURE ALPHABETIC STAGE

At the next stage of early reading, children know associations for the basic sound/spellings and can use them to decipher simple words. Well-taught first graders achieve this by midyear. When associations to letter patterns are secure, children can decode most predictable syllables. Attention to the internal structure of words, in both speech and spelling, supports whole word identification; it is linguistic awareness, not rote visual memory, that underlies memory for "sight" words after children enter this stage (Ehri 1994; Share 1995). As they become more automatic and efficient, children quickly begin to recognize the redundant "chunks" of orthography. Phonograms *(–ell, –ack, –ame, –old)* and word endings *(–ing, –ed, –est)* are read as units.

### ORTHOGRAPHIC STAGE: SYLLABLES AND MORPHEMES

Knowledge of sound-symbol associations and lots of practice reading contribute to fluency in word recognition. As whole words, morphemes, and print patterns become increasingly

Align Decoding Instruction with the
Stages of Reading Development
*Louisa C. Moats*

familiar, knowledge of these larger units of print allows students to read efficiently and spend less and less attention on sounding words out letter by letter (Share 1995). At this stage, students read new words by analogy to known words *(build, guild)* especially if their teachers model and reinforce this strategy (Gaskins, Ehri, Cress, O'Hara, and Donnelly 1996). Beyond phonics, the study of word structures comprises syllables and morphemes, the units from which our Latin- and Greek-derived words are created (Henry 1997). □

## Standards for Decoding and Word Recognition

**KINDERGARTEN**

- Match all consonant and short-vowel sounds to appropriate letters.
- Read simple one-syllable and high-frequency words (i.e., sight words).
- Understand that as letters of words change, so do the sounds (i.e., the alphabetic principle).

**GRADE 1**

- Generate the sounds from all the letters and letter patterns, including consonant blends and long- and short-vowel patterns (i.e., phonograms), and blend those sounds into recognizable words.
- Read common, irregular sight words (e.g., *the, have, said, come, give, of*).
- Use knowledge of vowel digraphs and *r*-controlled letter-sound associations to read words.
- Read compound words and contractions.
- Read inflectional forms (e.g., *–s, –ed, –ing*) and root words (e.g., *look, looked, looking*).
- Read common word families (e.g., *–ite, –ate*).
- Read aloud with fluency in a manner that sounds like natural speech.

### GRADE 2

- Recognize and use knowledge of spelling patterns (e.g., diphthongs, special vowel spellings) when reading.
- Apply knowledge of basic syllabication rules when reading (e.g., vowel-consonant-vowel = *su/per,* vowel-consonant/consonant-vowel = *sup/per*).
- Decode two-syllable nonsense words and regular multi-syllable words.
- Recognize common abbreviations (e.g., *Jan., Sun., Mr., St.*).
- Identify and correctly use regular plurals (e.g., *–s, –es, –ies*) and irregular plurals (e.g., *fly/flies, wife/wives*).
- Read aloud fluently and accurately and with appropriate intonation and expression.

### GRADE 3

- Know and use complex word families when reading (e.g., *–ight*) to decode unfamiliar words.
- Decode regular multisyllabic words.
- Read aloud narrative and expository text fluently and accurately and with appropriate pacing, intonation, and expression.

### GRADES 4, 5, 6

- Read aloud narrative and expository text fluently and accurately and with appropriate pacing, intonation, and expression.

SOURCE
Adapted from *English-Language Arts Content Standards for California Public Schools, Kindergarten Through Grade Twelve* (1999). Sacramento: California Department of Education.

# CONTENTS
## Section IV: Decoding

CONTINUED ▷

CHAPTER

# 8

# Phonics

what?
why?
when?
how?

# what? *Phonics*

8.2

*"The right maxims for phonics are: Do it early. Keep it simple."*

—BECOMING A NATION OF READERS, 1985

**CORE Reading Research Anthology**
for background information

**P**honics is the study and use of sound/spelling correspondences to help students identify written words. *Phonics instruction* teaches students the relationship between letters (graphemes) and speech sounds (phonemes). Phonics instruction can help students learn how to figure out the pronunciation of new words that they encounter in print. It is a technique for getting students off to a fast start in mapping the relationships between letters and sounds (Anderson et al. 1985). The letters and sounds are then connected to the word's meaning. This organized instruction also helps students to understand the *alphabetic principle*—patterns of letters in written words represent the sounds of spoken words.

The two approaches to phonics instruction that have been researched and used most extensively are systematic, explicit phonics and incidental, implicit phonics. These approaches differ in a number of ways.

## APPROACHES TO PHONICS INSTRUCTION

| Systematic, Explicit Phonics | Incidental, Implicit Phonics |
| --- | --- |
| sound/spelling correspondences are directly taught in isolation | sound/spelling correspondences are inferred from reading whole words and analyzing their phonic elements |
| direct instruction and practice in blending together previously introduced sound/spellings to form words | no direct instruction and practice in blending sounds in sequence; primarily uses "teachable moments" |
| | possibly some instruction and practice in blending onset and rime |

| Systematic, Explicit Phonics | Incidental, Implicit Phonics |
|---|---|
| sound/spellings are introduced systematically, following a sequence based on utility and increasing difficulty | sound/spellings are introduced incidentally, as students encounter them in stories or other texts |
| sequential phonics curriculum of increasingly more difficult phonic elements and generalizations | no phonics curriculum of increasingly more difficult phonic elements and generalizations |

8.3

Connect to Theory

The following are examples of instruction for the sound/spelling /a/a. One is an explicit phonics lesson and the other is an implicit phonics lesson. Using the information in the chart above, explain why the first approach is predominantly explicit and the second approach is predominantly implicit.

### EXPLICIT PHONICS

Print the letter *a* on the board. Point to the *a* and tell students that the letter *a* stands for the /a/ sound in the word *at*. Ask students to say the sound with you and then on their own. Have students practice blending together, sound by sound, the short-vowel sound for the letter *a* with previously taught sound/spellings /m/*m*, /p/*p*, /s/*s*, and /t/*t* to form words such as *mat, pat, sat,* and *tap.*

### IMPLICIT PHONICS

Print the word *mat* on the board. Ask students to say the word with you, listening for the middle sound. Point out that the sound in the middle of *mat* is the short sound for the vowel *a*. Invite students to name other words that have the same middle sound as in *mat.* Print suggested words, such as *fat, hat,* and *sat,* on the board and ask volunteers to read them aloud.

*(See Appendix for answer.)*

8.4

*"... programs including systematic instruction on letter-to-sound correspondences lead to higher achievement in both word recognition and spelling, at least in the early grades and especially for slower or economically disadvantaged students."*

—ADAMS, 1990

## Which Approach Works Best?

Major research studies have determined that students who received phonics instruction in early grades—whether explicit or implicit—did better in reading than those who received no phonics instruction. Further, there is compelling evidence that systematic, explicit phonics is the most effective type of instruction, especially for students who are "at risk" for academic failure—those who have fewer literacy experiences at home and those with reading/learning difficulties (Adams 1990; Chall 1996; Chall and Popp 1996; Report of the National Reading Panel 2000; Ambruster, Lehr and Osborn, 2001).

Why do systematic, explicit phonics programs lead to higher achievement? First, learning phonics through explicit teaching requires less inference and discovery on the part of the students and is therefore within the grasp of more of them (Chall and Popp 1996). In addition, implicit phonics requires a high degree of skill in phonemic segmentation. Some students may fail to "discover" the sound/spelling relationships in words because they do not have the level of phonemic awareness needed to isolate the individual sounds. For example, to infer the /m/*m* sound/spelling from the word *map,* students must be able to segment *map* into /m/ . . . *ap.* Explicit phonics requires less sophisticated phonemic awareness because the sounds associated with letters are explicitly taught (Beck and Juel 1992).

Connect to Theory

Examine the Kindergarten and Grade 1 levels of the commercial reading program used in your school or district. What is the program's approach to teaching reading? Does it utilize a predominantly systematic, explicit approach or an incidental, implicit approach to phonics instruction?

## Components of Systematic, Explicit Phonics Instruction

Sound/Spelling Sequence

Blending

Phonograms

Decodable Text

Dictation and Spelling

Word Work

## Phonics instruction should …

• be daily

• be completed by the end of second grade

• be built on a foundation of phonemic awareness

• be systematic and explicit

• be focused

• provide practice with decodable texts

• include regular assessment

• provide for intervention

## Systematic, Explicit Phonics Instruction

Systematic, explicit phonics can be described as an instructional program in which sound/spellings are introduced systematically and sequentially, directly taught in isolation, blended into whole words, and initially practiced in decodable text.

### Phonics Lesson Components

8.5

The "How?" teaching strategies in this chapter follow a simple six-step plan:

① **Phonemic Warm-Up**  Phonemic awareness activities support phonics instruction. These activities include discrimination, oral blending, and segmentation.

② **Teach Sound/Spelling**  Sound/spellings are explicitly taught in isolation. Picture cards and key words are used to exemplify each sound/spelling.

③ **Practice Blending**  This is explicit instruction and practice in the blending together of previously introduced sound/spellings to form recognizable words. Strategies include sound-by-sound, vowel-first, and whole-word blending.

④ **Apply to Decodable Text**  Connected reading practice in decodable texts develops fluency and automaticity. Choose text selections in which most of the words are wholly decodable and the majority of the remaining words are previously taught high-frequency and story words.

⑤ **Dictation and Spelling**  In order to make the reading/writing connection, students must understand that they use sound/spelling knowledge in spelling and writing as well as in reading.

⑥ **Word Work**  These follow-up activities reinforce students' knowledge of sound/spelling patterns by having them build, manipulate, and sort words.

**SOUND/SPELLING**

a phoneme/grapheme pairing

**SLASHES OR VIRGULES**

To distinguish between a letter and a sound in writing, sounds are placed between *virgules,* or slashes. For example, we write /m/ to show the sound for the letter *m.*

8.6

Section II: Word Structure, "What Is a Sound/Spelling?" p. 3.12

"Sound/Spelling Percentages," p. 3.19

## Sound/Spelling Sequence

Explicit phonics instruction involves systematically and sequentially teaching the relationship between sounds (phonemes) and the spellings (graphemes) used to represent them. This systematic instruction allows students to continually build on what they learn. Review and repetition enables students to internalize how the sound/spelling "system" works (Blevins 1998). Students do not need to be taught every single sound/spelling. Although there are hundreds of different sound/spellings for the 42 to 44 English phonemes, it is only necessary to teach those that occur most frequently in words.

Since English has more phonemes than alphabet letters, the same letter or letters may represent different phonemes, or sounds. In addition, different letters may represent the same phoneme, or sound. However, according to a report commissioned by the U.S. Office of Education (Hanna et al. 1966), at least 20 phonemes had spellings that were over 90 percent predictable, and 10 others were predictable more than 80 percent of the time. About 50 percent of English words can be spelled accurately by sound/spelling correspondence rules alone, and an additional 37 percent are off by only one sound.

**ELL** FOR SPANISH-SPEAKING STUDENTS . . .
Explicit Spanish phonics instruction has been shown to improve Spanish-speaking students' reading achievement in both Spanish and English. For further information, see Chapter 4: Structure of Spanish and Other Languages: "What Is the Spanish Letter/Sound System?" p. 4.2; "What Are the Guidelines for Spanish Phonics Instruction?" p. 4.8; "What Are the Differences Between English and Spanish Sound/ Spellings?" p. 4.16; and "What Spanish Phonics Skills Are Transferable to English Phonics?" p. 4.18.

> *"English is an alphabetic language in which there are consistent, though not entirely predictable, relationships between letters and sounds."*
>
> —BECOMING A NATION OF READERS, 1985

**CONTINUOUS CONSONANT**
a sound that can be pronounced for several seconds without distortion: for example, /s/ as in *sun*

**STOP CONSONANT**
a sound that can be pronounced for only an instant: for example, /p/ as in *pop*

Section II: Word Structure, "What Are the Classifications of Consonant Phonemes?" p. 3.4

## Recommendations for Determining a Sound/Spelling Sequence

- Initially introduce only the most common sound for a new letter. The most common sound of a letter is the sound that is usually pronounced for the letter when it appears in a short word, such as the letter/sounds in *man* or *sit*.

- Introduce higher-frequency (and therefore more useful) sound/spellings before less frequent ones. For example, /m/*m* and /a/*a* before /j/*j* and /v/*v*.

- Introduce a few short-vowel sounds early in the sequence, so that students can use letter-sound knowledge to form and read words.

- Introduce a few (about three or four) continuous consonants early in the sequence before introducing stop consonants.

- Introduce early those letter sounds that relate to letter names (/s/, /l/, /m/) to facilitate learning.

- Progress from simple to more complex sound/spellings. Introduce short-vowel sound/spellings before long-vowel sound/spellings, variant vowels, or diphthongs.

- Separate the introduction of easily confused letters as well as sounds that are visually or auditorily similar.

*Visual similarity* (letters that are alike in appearance)
The following pairs are visually confusing: *b* and *d; b* and *p; q* and *p; n* and *m; m, h,* and *n; v* and *w; n* and *r.*

*Auditory similarity* (letters that sound alike)
The following pairs have easily confused sounds: /f/ and /v/, /t/ and /d/, /b/ and /d/, /b/ and /p/, /k/ and /g/, /m/ and /n/, /i/ and /e/, /o/ and /u/, /ch/ and /sh/.

## Phonics Scope and Sequences

Here are examples of a Grades k–2 phonics scope and sequence from two recent basal reading programs.

8.8

| BASAL READING PROGRAM A | |
|---|---|
| **Kindergarten** | Single-consonant and short-vowel letters and sounds |
| **Grades 1–2** | **Grade 1** /m/*m;* /a/*a;* /l/*l;* /t/*t;* /s/*s;* /o/*o;* /h/*h;* /i/*i;* /p/*p;* /f/*f;* /n/*n;* /k/*c;* /b/*b;* /w/*w;* /j/*j;* /z/*z, zz;* /d/*d;* /r/*r;* /e/*e;* /g/*g;* /ks/*x;* /u/*u;* /k/*k, ck;* /th/*th;* /z/*s;* /y/*y;* /kw/*qu;* /v/*v;* /sh/*sh;* /ā/*a_e;* –*ing;* /ē/*e_e;* /ī/*i_e;* /ō/*o_e;* /yo͞o/*u_e;* /ē/*e, ea, ee;* *l*-blends, *r*-blends, *s*-blends; /ch/*ch;* /hw/*wh;* /ô/*all, aw;* /ā/*ai, ay;* /ō/*oa;* /ē/*y, ey;* /ō/*o, ow;* /är/*ar;* –*ed*/*ed*/, /*t*/, /*d*/; /ī/*ild, ind;* /ou/*ou, ow;* /ī/*igh, y;* /ûr/*ir;* /ôr/*or;* /o͞o/*oo;* /o͝o/*oo;* /ûr/*er, ur* <br><br> **Grade 2** 3-letter blends; /s/*c;* /j/*g;* syllabication; /l/*_le;* /ə/*a;* /âr/*air, are, ear;* /oi/*oi, oy;* /n/*kn;* /r/*wr;* /ô/*a, au, aw;* /o͞o/*o, ue, ew, ough;* /e/*ea;* /o͝o/*oo, ou, u;* /ch/*tch;* /f/*gh, ph;* –*tion;* /ôr/*ore, oor, or, our;* /ô/*o;* /ī/*y* |

SOURCE *Scholastic Literacy Place* © 2000. New York: Scholastic.

| BASAL READING PROGRAM B | |
|---|---|
| **Kindergarten** | Single-consonant and short-vowel letters and sounds |
| **Grades 1–2** | **Grade 1** /s/*s;* /m/*m;* /a/*a;* /t/*t;* /h/*h;* /p/*p;* /i/*i;* /n/*n;* /d/*d;* /o/*o;* /b/*b;* /ə/*a;* /k/*c;* /ə/*o;* –*ed*/*ed*/, /*t*/, /*d*/; /k/*_ck;* /r/*r;* syllabication; /u/*u;* /g/*g;* /j/*j, _dge;* /f/*f;* /or/*or;* /e/*e;* /l/*l, _ll, _l;* /l/*_le;* /ks/*x;* /z/*z, zz, s;* /sh/*sh;* /th/*th;* /er/*er, ir, ur;* /ch/*ch, tch;* /ar/*ar;* /w/*w;* /hw/*wh;* /l/*el;* /k/*k;* /ng/*_ng;* /kw/*qu;* /y/*y;* /ā/*a, a_e;* /s/*ce, ci_;* /ī/*i, i_e;* /ō/*o, o_e;* /v/*v;* /ū/*u, u_e;* /j/*ge, gi_;* /ē/*e, e_e;* /ē/*ee, ea;* /ē/*y, _ie_;* long vowels followed by *r;* /ā/*ai_, _ay;* /ī/*igh;* /ī/*_y, _ie;* /ō/*oe;* /ō/*oa_, _ow;* /ū/*_ew, _ue;* /o͞o/*oo, ue, u_e, _ew;* /o͝o/*oo;* /ow/*ow;* /ow/*ou;* /aw/*au, aw;* /n/*kn_;* /oi/*oi, oy;* /r/*wr;* /f/*ph;* /aw/*augh;* /aw/*_ough, wa;* /m/*mb;* /e/*ea;* –*ture, –tion, –ion* <br><br> **Grade 2** Complete review of Grade 1 phonic elements; word parts –*ing, –y, –less, –est, –il, –al, –ous;* /ā/*eigh* |

SOURCE *SRA/Open Court Reading* © 2000. Worthington, OH: SRA/McGraw-Hill.

## Blending

Blending has been described as the "heart and soul" of phonics instruction. The ability to use the sounds of the letters to decode written words is fundamental to learning to read. Teaching students letter/sound correspondences prepares them for sounding out words—just knowing the correspondences alone is insufficient. Beginning in Kindergarten and continuing into first grade, students should be explicitly taught the process of blending individual sounds into words. Students must be able to blend the sounds together from left to right to pronounce a recognizable word. Blending is a difficult process for many students. For instruction to be effective, teachers need to understand how to select words for practice and the strategies, or techniques, used in the actual blending process.

**Section II: Word Structure, "What Are the Classifications of Consonant Phonemes?" p. 3.4**

for a list of continuous and stop sounds

### Progression of Word Difficulty

Successful word reading depends largely on word length and on the configuration of consonants and vowels within a word. Words used in blending instruction and practice should:

- Progress from two- or three-phoneme words in which letters represent their most common sounds to longer, four-, five-, or six-phoneme words in which letters represent their most common sounds.

- Begin with continuous sounds. Words beginning with a stop sound are more difficult for students to sound out than words beginning with a continuous sound. Stop sounds may be used in the final positions of words.

- Present vocabulary and concepts with which students are familiar.

8.9

## PROGRESSION OF WORD DIFFICULTY

| Word Type | Key Words |
|---|---|
| VC and CVC words beginning with a continuous sound and ending with either a stop or a continuous sound | at, am, mop, man |
| VCC and CVCC words beginning with a continuous sound and ending with either a stop or a continuous sound | end, its, sack, fill |
| CVC words beginning with a stop sound and ending with either a stop or a continuous sound | dog, tan |
| CVCC words beginning with a stop sound and ending with a consonant blend | tent, jump |
| CCVC words beginning with a consonant blend in which both consonants are continuous sounds | frog |
| CCVC words beginning with a consonant blend in which one consonant is a stop sound | blob |
| CCVCC, CCCVC, and CCCVCC words beginning with a two- or three-letter consonant blend | slick, split, stress |

**8.10**

(Carnine et al. 1997)

## Practice Word Lists

In addition to selecting the word type for blending instruction, teachers should consider the following criteria when creating the list of practice words:

- Word lists should be limited to the number of words students can master within a five- to seven-minute period.

- The most recently introduced sound/spelling pattern should appear in about one-third to one-half of the words on the list.

- Word lists should be constructed in an unpredictable manner using random mixes of words that contain previously taught patterns.

- Words on the list should be wholly decodable, made up of previously taught sound/spellings.

Connect to Theory

The list of words below is not arranged in order of difficulty. Use the criteria from the Progression of Word Difficulty chart to arrange the words in order of difficulty for blending instruction. Explain your answer.

grab

luck

pink

sip

smog

string

top

Now, assume that the most recently taught sound/spelling is /g/*g*, and that students have been previously introduced to the following sound/spellings: consonants /s/*s*, /m/*m*, /t/*t*, /h/*h*, /p/*p*, /n/*n*, /d/*d*, /b/*b*, /k/*c*, /k/*ck*, /r/*r*, /g/*g*, and vowels /a/*a*, /i/*i*, /o/*o*, /u/*u*. Using the criteria already listed, examine each of the following word lists to determine whether or not it is suitable for blending instruction. Explain your answer.

*(See Appendix for answers.)*

| Word List A | Word List B | Word List C |
|:---:|:---:|:---:|
| mat | rack | at |
| bag | hog | gum |
| sat | run | an |
| gap | tag | rug |
| rack | am | sack |
| sag | got | dog |
| ran | met | hat |

## Blending Strategies

8.12

There are a few basic strategies, or methods, for teaching students to blend sound/spellings to make words: *sound-by-sound blending* and *whole-word*, or *continuous blending*. Commercial reading programs often incorporate one of these strategies. Regardless of the strategy initially used, once students are proficient in oral blending, and after they can blend simple words, they should begin to sound out letter/sound correspondences in their heads, silently producing the whole word.

### Sound-by-Sound Blending

In sound-by-sound blending, each sound is identified and pronounced one at a time through the vowel, then blended with the sounds preceding it. This type of blending begins with the individual sounds; the whole word isn't revealed until all the sounds in the word have been identified and pronounced. The eight steps of sound-by-sound blending are described below, using the word *mat* as an example:

① Print the spelling of the first sound in the word: *m.* Point to the spelling and say the sound: /m/. Have students say the sound with you as you point to the letter and say the sound again: /m/.

② Print the spelling of the next sound: *a.* Point to the spelling and say the sound: /a/. Have students say the sound with you as you point to the letter and say the sound again: /a/.

③ Tell students to listen as you blend the sounds. Demonstrate blending by using your finger or hand to track slowly and smoothly under each letter from left to right as you say the sounds without a break: /ma/. As you make this blending motion, make sure that you point to the letter that corresponds to the sound you are saying at the moment.

④ Now have students join you in saying the sounds as you blend through the vowel again: /ma/.

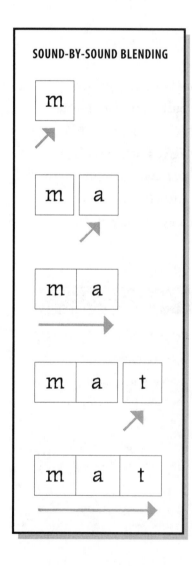

**SOUND-BY-SOUND BLENDING**

m

m a

m a

m a t

m a t

⑤ Print the spelling of the final sound: *t*. Point to the spelling and say the sound: /t/. Have students say the sound with you as you point to the letter and say the sound again: /t/.

⑥ Slowly slide your finger or hand from left to right under the word *mat* as you blend the sounds together and pronounce the word: *mat*.

⑦ Ask students to blend and pronounce the word on their own, modeling as necessary. Have them pronounce the word naturally. It is important for students to realize that blending results in a word. To confirm the response, have a volunteer use the word in a sentence.

*After practice with steps 1–7.*

⑧ To internalize the blending process, direct students to blend the word silently in their heads and then say the word. Model this process by pointing to and quietly saying the sounds in progression, and then loudly saying the whole word. Wait a few seconds and ask for volunteers to say the word aloud.

Intervention Strategy

## Vowel-First Blending

For some students, vowel-first blending is an alternative to sound-by-sound blending. Following are the steps for vowel-first blending for the word *mat:*

① Print the spelling of the vowel in the word: *a*. Point to the spelling and say the sound: /a/. Have students say the sound with you as you point to the letter and say the sound again: /a/.

② Print the spelling of the first sound: *m*, in front of the *a*. Point to the spelling and say the sound: /m/. Have students say the sound with you as you point to the letter and say the sound again: /m/.

*Continue with steps 3 to 8 in sound-by-sound blending.*

**8.14**

**Section II: Word Structure, "What Are the Classifications of Consonant Phonemes?" p. 3.4**

for a list of continuous and stop sounds

## Whole-Word Blending

Whole-word blending is sometimes referred to as continuous, or successive, blending. In this type of blending, students stretch out, or hold, each sound in a word without pausing between the sounds. Unlike sound-by-sound blending, this type of blending begins with the whole word. Here are the steps for whole-word blending of the word *mat:*

① Print the word *mat* on the board. Tell students to listen as you read a word by blending its sounds together. Say: "mmmăăăt." As you blend the word, it is important not to pause between sounds. Use your finger or hand to track under each letter as you say each corresponding sound. Hold each continuous sound for about one full second and each stop sound for only an instant. After blending the sounds in a stretched-out manner, say the whole word quickly, *mat.*

② Have students blend the sounds and then pronounce the word with you. They should say the sound as soon as you point to it and keep holding that sound, without stopping, until you point to the next sound.

③ Have students blend the sounds and then pronounce the word on their own. Ask a volunteer to use the word in a sentence.

④ To internalize the blending process, direct students to blend the word silently in their heads and then say the word. Model this process by pointing to and quietly saying the sounds in progression, and then loudly saying the whole word. Wait a few seconds and ask for volunteers to say the word aloud.

## Blending Words in Sentences

Blending words in sentences helps students move from word fluency to sentence fluency. Irregular words are not sounded out, but must be recognized on sight. The goal is for students to read entire sentences, stopping only to blend words they cannot read otherwise. Following are the steps for blending words in sentences:

① Print a sentence on the board or a transparency. Underline any words that are not wholly decodable because they are irregular or contain sound/spellings that have not been previously introduced. Explain to students that underlined words should not be sounded out.

② Have students join you in reading the sentence, sounding out and blending each word from left to right and reading the underlined words as whole units.

③ Ask students to reread the sentence with natural intonation. Coach students on normal intonation by modeling and having them practice.

④ After reading the sentence, discuss punctuation and capitalization when it seems appropriate.

**Section II: Word Structure, "What Is a Syllable?" p. 3.20**

for more about onset and rime

**"What Is a Phonogram?" p. 3.22**

## Phonograms

A phonogram is a letter (or series of letters) that stands for a sound, syllable, syllable part, or series of sounds. Phonograms are often called word families. A linguistic term sometimes used for phonogram is *rime*. Rime is generally used in combination with the term *onset*. Onset and rime refer to the two parts of a syllable. In a syllable, a rime is the vowel and everything after it. The onset is the consonant, consonant blend, or consonant digraph that comes before the rime in a syllable.

Phonograms should never be the sole focus of early reading instruction. Beginning readers who rely primarily on phonograms to decode by analogy are less skilled at word identification than beginning readers who analyze words fully, sound by sound (Bruck and Treiman 1990). It is less efficient and less generalizable for students to blend only onsets and rimes.

**8.16**

Phonogram instruction should build on the knowledge gained from systematic, explicit phonics instruction in sound/spelling correspondences. Students must know the sounds of the individual letters that make up the rime prior to being introduced to it as a unit. For example, teach students the sound/spellings /a/*a* and /g/*g* before introducing the rime –*ag*. Have students blend the sound/spellings. Next, add the previously taught consonant sound/spelling /b/*b* to the beginning of the rime –*ag*. Have students sound out and then blend the new consonant with the rime to produce the word *bag*.

## Decodable Text

*Decodable text* is an integral part of explicit phonics instruction. Sometimes called "controlled text," decodable text is composed of three types of words: wholly decodable words; sight words; and nondecodable/noninstructed words. For student reading material to be classified as decodable text, most of the words should be wholly decodable and the majority of the remaining words should be previously introduced sight words—including both high-frequency and story words.

Support for the use of decodable text comes from comparative studies showing that code-emphasis programs produce the best results in beginning reading instruction (Adams 1990). A second source of support comes from basic principles of learning: Instruction should always provide students opportunities to apply what they are learning in the context of use.

Decodable text is useful in beginning reading for developing automaticity and fluency. It should be used as an intervening step between explicit skill acquisition and the student's ability to read trade books. Because these controlled texts contain phonic elements that are familiar to students, they give students an opportunity to apply their newly acquired phonics knowledge to what they are reading.

## Decodable Text: Word Types

**Wholly Decodable Words**

Words that can be identified on the basis of letter/sound correspondences, or phonic elements, that have been previously taught.

**Sight Words**

High-frequency and story words that are explicitly taught prior to reading to be recognized as wholes, by sight.

**Nondecodable/ Noninstructed Words**

Words that are neither wholly decodable based on previously taught phonic elements nor preintroduced as sight words.

(Stein, Johnson, and Gutlohn 1999)

How decodable must text be to support learning? Research has not pinned down the extent to which a text should be decodable. Beck (1997) estimated that in order for students to develop reliable word identification strategies, 70 to 80 percent of the text students read early in first grade should be wholly decodable. As students become more proficient readers, the percentage of wholly decodable words may decrease.

## Decodable Text Analysis

The decodability of a particular text can only be determined by examining the relationship between the instructional sequence of phonic elements and the words in the text selections. An example of the text-analysis process follows, using an excerpt from a commercially published decodable text:

Gail and Sue like to hike.

Every year they go to Bass Lake for a week.

They fill their packs with all they will need.

Then they hike in to the lake.

SOURCE From *Bass Lake,* Sound Out Chapter Books (1999) by Matt Sims. Novato, CA: High Noon Books.

For the purpose of this example, assume that the following phonic elements and sight words have been previously taught:

- **Phonic Elements:** All single consonants; /k/*ck;* /th/*th;* /TH/*th;* /a/*a;* /i/*i;* /e/*e;* /ā/*a_e, ai;* /ī/*i_e;* /ō/*o;* /ē/*ea, ee*

- **Sight Words:** *a, all, for, the, their, they, to*

Based on the decodable text word types and the previously introduced phonic elements and sight words, the analysis of the 32 words in this text excerpt reveals that the selection's overall decodability is 94 percent: 56 percent of the words are wholly decodable and 38 percent are previously introduced sight words.

8.18

## DECODABLE TEXT ANALYSIS OF *Bass Lake*

| Word Types | Identified Words in Text | Percentage of Words in Text |
|---|---|---|
| Wholly Decodable Words | and, Bass, fill, Gail, go, hike, hike, in, Lake, lake, like, need, packs, Then, week, will, with, year | 18 words or 56% |
| Sight Words | a, all, for, the, their, they, They, they, they, to, to, to | 12 words or 38% |
| Nondecodable/ Noninstructed Words | Sue, every | 2 words or 6% |

Connect
to Theory

On your own, analyze the same *Bass Lake* decodable text excerpt. Assume that the following phonic elements and sight words have been previously taught. These elements and sight words are different from the previous example. What does this new analysis reveal? What are the percentages of the wholly decodable words and the sight words? Explain your criteria for each of the nondecodable/noninstructed words.

PHONIC ELEMENTS: All single consonants; /k/ck; /a/a; /i/i; /ā/a_e, ai; /ī/i_e; /ō/o; /ē/ee

SIGHT WORDS: *a, all, every, the, their, they, to*

*(See Appendix for answer.)*

Section V: Spelling

Chapter 12: Stages of Spelling

Development

Chapter 13: Spelling Instruction

# Dictation and Spelling

Spelling and word-work activities reinforce decoding and word attack skills. Dictation activities connect the encoding process (writing) to the decoding process (reading) by demonstrating that students not only use sound/spelling knowledge to read, but the same knowledge enables them to communicate with others through writing. Regular dictation of words containing patterns taught in phonics lessons is a useful way to assess student progress. It also develops students' auditory skills. Dictation progresses from individual words to sentences containing previously taught sound/spellings, as well as some previously taught high-frequency irregular words. Students are instructed to write these high-frequency words as a whole.

8.19

## Sound-by-Sound Dictation

"Introducing Single Consonants," p. 8.28

"Introducing Words with a CVCe
   Pattern," p. 8.42

This dictation method is similar to blending instruction in that the teacher dictates words to students one sound at a time. The teacher says each word aloud, uses it in a context sentence, and repeats it again. Students say the word and then write the letter or letter patterns that represent each sound until they make the entire word.

## Whole-Word Dictation

This method gives students the opportunity to practice writing words with previously taught sound/spellings with less help from the teacher. The procedure is the same as that for sound-by-sound dictation, but rather than being guided to spell words sound by sound, students are prompted to "think about" the sounds they hear in the words and write the entire word.

"Introducing Short Vowels," p. 8.33

8.20

## Sentence Dictation

In sentence dictation, the teacher reads the sentence, then dictates the words one by one using either sound-by-sound or whole-word dictation. In addition to spelling individual words, sentence dictation provides students with practice in using correct punctuation and capitalization. After the sentences are written, students proofread their work and make corrections.

## Word Work

Word work is a broad term that describes a range of activities that lead students to practice sound/spelling patterns by building, manipulating, and sorting words.

Chapter 13: Spelling Instruction
"Making Words," p. 13.5

### Word Building

One type of word work is *word building.* Students use letter cards or magnetic letters to make words dictated by the teacher. In the beginning, students are given a limited set of letters representing previously taught sound/spellings. For example, they might be given only a few consonants and one vowel and be asked to make the words *tin, bin,* and *bit* in sequence. After each word is said, the teacher walks around checking for accuracy and then prints the word on the board for the students to self-check. As students get more proficient in word building, they can be given larger sets of letters from which to choose.

Another way to do word building is by having the teacher print a word on the board, saying it aloud, and then asking students to write the word on small, erasable boards. The teacher then says: *If this is* tin, *now make* bin. Students write the new word, and a volunteer is asked to come to the board and make the transformation. Another approach is to ask students who have the *t, i,* and *n* letter cards to come to the front of the class and "become" the word.

**Chapter 13: Spelling Instruction**

**"Word Sorting," p. 13.6**

for a more detailed description

## Word or Picture Sorts

**closed**

teacher defines key word or picture categories and models sorting procedure

**open**

students define key word or picture categories

**blind**

teacher defines key word or picture categories; teacher calls out a word that students do not see, then students point to the key word or picture with same sound

**writing**

teacher defines key word categories; teacher calls out a word, and students write the word below the key word with the same sound/spelling pattern

**speed**

closed, open, blind, and writing sorts completed within a particular time frame

## Word Sorting

In word sorting, students sort words into categories based on sound and/or spelling patterns. After students have been taught specific phonic elements, word sorting reinforces their recognition of words that contain these sound/spelling correspondences. In the early stages of reading development, most word-sorting activities are blind or closed sorts. To help students focus on the sounds in words, sorting should first be done with pictures. For example, students might be shown a series of picture cards that begin with the single-consonant sounds /m/ and /s/ and asked to place the cards under pictures of a monkey or sun. As students progress they might be asked to hold up the key-word card that has the same initial consonant digraph as the words the teacher reads aloud. The teacher records the words under the appropriate key word, and after the sort is complete, students read the words aloud.

In the context of phonics instruction, sorting activities are effective ways to reinforce the contrast between short- and long-vowel sounds and their respective spellings. For example, students can be asked to match the key-word cards *cat* and *cake* with short-*a* and long-*a* words the teacher reads aloud. After the sort is complete and students read the words aloud, they can be asked to do an *open sort* of all the words with the long-*a* sound. They define new categories by sorting the words according to the different spelling patterns for long *a* and thereby review useful spelling generalizations: "The long-*a* sound can be spelled with *a*-consonant–silent *e* or with a vowel team."

**8.21**

# why? *Phonics*

**8.22**

**CORE Reading Research Anthology**

for background information

esearch has shown that good readers do not skim and sample the text when they scan a line in a book. They process the letters of each word in detail, although they do so very rapidly and unconsciously (Share and Stanovich 1995; Adams, Treiman, and Pressley 1998). The ability to sound out words leads to rapid recognition of words. Longitudinal studies of reading and spelling development have shown that students who read well in high school learned early to sound words out and read new words with ease (Moats 1999). When word recognition is fast and accurate, less mental energy is required to decode words and more mental energy can be devoted to making meaning from text (Freedman and Calfee 1984; LaBerge and Samuels 1974).

**Research Findings . . .**

*Sytematic and explicit phonics instruction is more effective than non-systematic or no phonics instruction.*

—AMBRUSTER, LEHR & OSBORN, 2001

*That direct instruction in alphabet coding facilitates early reading acquisition is one of the most well-established conclusions in all of behavioral science.*

—STANOVICH, 1994

*Good readers rely primarily on the letters in a word rather than context or pictures to identify familiar and unfamiliar words.*

—EHRI, 1994

*Focused instruction in phonics is superior to instruction without this focus in teaching students word recognition, oral reading, and spelling.*

—CHALL, 1983b

**Suggested Reading . . .**

*Beginning to Read: Thinking and Learning About Print* (1990) by Marilyn Jager Adams. Cambridge, MA: MIT Press.

*Direct Instruction Reading, 3rd Edition* (1997) by Douglas W. Carnine, Jerry Silbert & Edward J. Kameenui. Upper Saddle River, NJ: Prentice-Hall.

*Phonics from A to Z: A Practical Guide* (1998) by Wiley Blevins. New York: Scholastic.

*Preventing Reading Difficulties in Young Children* (1998) edited by Catherine E. Snow, M. Susan Burns & Peg Griffin. Washington, DC: National Academy Press.

*Put Reading First: The Research Building Blocks for Teaching Children to Read* (2001) by Bonnie Ambruster, Fran Lehr, and Jean Osborn. The Partnership for Reading. CIERA, U.S. Dept. of Education.

*Straight Talk About Reading: How Parents Can Make a Difference During the Early Years* (1999) by Susan L. Hall & Louisa C. Moats. Lincolnwood, IL: NTC/Contemporary Publishing Group.

*Teaching and Assessing Phonics: A Guide for Teachers* (1996) by Jeanne S. Chall & Helen M. Popp. Cambridge, MA: Educators Publishing Service.

*What Reading Research Tells Us About Children with Diverse Learning Needs: Bases and Basics* (1998) edited by Deborah C. Simmons & Edward J. Kameenui. Mahwah, NJ: Erlbaum.

**8.23**

*when?*

*Phonics*

## When to Teach

Formal, basic phonics instruction should begin in Kindergarten and be completed, except in the cases of diagnosed individual need, in second grade (Anderson et al. 1985). Teach two to four sound/spellings per week. As always, ongoing assessment should inform the rate of instruction.

**See also . . .**

**Chapter 10: Multisyllabic Words**

**Kindergarten**    In Kindergarten, students learn to recognize and name all letters of the alphabet and develop their phonemic awareness. They learn to understand the alphabetic principle, that as letters of words change, so do the sounds. Students learn to match all consonant and short-vowel sounds to appropriate letters and to read simple CVC words.

**Grade 1**    In first grade, students learn to generate the sounds for all single consonants; consonant digraphs; short and long vowels; high-utility vowel digraphs; and *r*-controlled vowels. They learn to blend those sounds into single-syllable words. They learn to read and process common long- and short-vowel phonograms (word families).

**Grades 2 and 3**    In second grade, students develop fluency through instruction in advanced phonic elements, such as variant vowels, vowel diphthongs, and more complex spelling patterns. In third grade, students focus on the use of larger orthographic units of text.

## When to Assess and Intervene

Assessment begins in Kindergarten as students are learning consonant sounds. It continues throughout the early elementary grades as students develop their decoding skills. A significant benchmark in early first grade is a student's ability to read simple CVC words. Once students can fluently read authentic text, it is not necessary to continue the assessment of discrete phonics skills. Researchers suggest that the single best measure of student ability to apply knowledge of letter/sound correspondences in decoding words is provided by measures of nonword reading (Share and Stanovich 1995).

**Upper-Grade Intervention**  Intervention is necessary for students in third grade and above who are not yet reading fluently, who struggle to recognize individual words, and who consequently have weak comprehension. Some of these students, non- and very weak readers, will need basic phonics instruction coupled with phonemic awareness development; others will need instruction in word attack skills. For these students, assessment information is crucial in order to efficiently fill in the skill gaps.

8.25

**CORE Assessing Reading**
**"Resources for Assessing Reading"**

## Phonics Tests

| CORE Assessing Reading | Other |
|---|---|
| CORE Phonics Survey | Woodcock Reading Mastery Test-Revised |
| | Durrell Analysis of Reading Ability |
| | Stanford Diagnostic Reading Test |

## ASSESSMENT AND INTERVENTION

8.26

| When | Mid-Kindergarten |
|------|------------------|
| Who | All students |
| Assessment Tool | *CORE Assessing Reading,* CORE Phonics Survey (Items 1, 2) |
| Intervene if . . . | Assessment indicates that student cannot name the letters of the alphabet. |
| How | Teacher-led small-group instruction |
| When | Early Grade 1 |
| Who | All students |
| Assessment Tool | *CORE Assessing Reading,* CORE Phonics Survey (Items 3, 4) |
| Intervene if . . . | Assessment indicates that students cannot match consonant and short-vowel sounds to appropriate letters. |
| How | Teacher-led small-group instruction; phonemic awareness instruction; practice with decodable texts |
| When | Mid-Grade 1 |
| Who | All students |
| Assessment Tool | *CORE Assessing Reading,* CORE Phonics Survey (Item 5: A, B, C, D) |
| Intervene if . . . | Assessment indicates that students cannot read real and pseudo-CVC words; real and pseudo-short-vowel words with digraphs and consonant blends; real and pseudo-long-vowel words. |
| How | Teacher-led small-group instruction; phonemic awareness intervention, if indicated; practice with decodable text |
| When | Early Grade 2 |
| Who | All Students |
| Assessment Tool | *CORE Assessing Reading,* CORE Phonics Survey (Item 5: A, B, C, D, E, F) |
| Intervene if . . . | Assessment indicates that students cannot read all single-syllable phonic elements in real and pseudowords. |
| How | Teacher-led small-group instruction; phonemic awareness intervention, if indicated; practice with decodable text |

| When | Mid-Grade 2 |
|---|---|
| Who | All Students |
| Assessment Tool | *CORE Assessing Reading,* CORE Phonics Survey (Item 5: A, B, C, D, E, F, G) |
| Intervene if ... | Assessment indicates that students cannot read single- and multisyllable real and pseudowords. |
| How | Teacher-led small-group instruction; phonemic awareness intervention, if indicated; practice with decodable text |

| When | Early Grade 3 and above |
|---|---|
| Who | Students who cannot read aloud grade-level text with fluency and accuracy |
| Assessment Tool | *CORE Assessing Reading,* CORE Phonics Survey (Item 5: A, B, C, D, E, F, G) |
| Intervene if ... | Assessment indicates that students cannot read single- and multisyllable real and pseudowords |
| How | Teacher-led small-group instruction; phonemic awareness intervention, if indicated; practice with decodable text |

**ELL** FOR SPANISH-SPEAKING STUDENTS ...
To assess students' phonics knowledge in Spanish, use "CORE Spanish Phonics Survey" in *CORE Assessing Reading.*

# how? *Phonics*

**TEACHING STRATEGY FOR**

## Single Consonant Sound/Spellings

### Benchmarks

- ability to recognize single consonant sound/spellings
- ability to blend previously taught sound/spellings into words

### Grade Level

- Kindergarten – Grade 1 and Intervention

### Prerequisites

- introduced phonic elements: /a/*a*; /l/*l*; /m/*m*; /t/*t*
- introduced high-frequency words: *on, the*

### Grouping

- whole class
- small group or pairs
- individual

### Materials

- picture card: sun
- decodable text

## INTRODUCING SINGLE CONSONANTS

**GRADE LEVEL K-1 GRADE LEVEL**

This generic teaching strategy introduces the consonant /s/*s,* which applies to *s,* pronounced /s/, when it occurs at the end of a word to indicate the plural form or third-person verb tense. The same strategy can be used to introduce other single consonant sounds.

• • • • • • • • • • • • • • • • • • • • • • • • • • • •

## Phonemic Warm-Up

Ask students to listen for the /s/ sound in the following words and to stand up each time they hear it: *sick, kiss, hat, mouse, pot, spot, bird, sorry.* Encourage students to share other words that have the /s/ sound.

## Teach Sound/Spelling

Print the letter *s* on the board. Display a picture of a sun and tell students that the letter *s* stands for the /s/ sound at the beginning of the word *sun.* Ask students to say the /s/ sound, first with you and then on their own. Then have them say the whole word *sun.*

**ELL** FOR SPANISH-SPEAKING STUDENTS . . .
Teachers should point out that the letter *s* also stands for the /s/ sound in the Spanish word for *sun—sol.*

**English language learners can participate in all phonics activities as long as they understand the meanings of the words that they are asked to hear, say, read, and write. Preteach and discuss all new vocabulary words and concepts.**

**"Sound-by-Sound Blending," p. 8.12**

for a more detailed description

## Practice Blending

Have students practice blending words with /s/, sound by sound, using the following example for the word *sat.* Print the letter *s* on the board. Point to the *s* and say /s/. Ask students to say the /s/ sound with you as you point to the letter and say it again. Print the letter *a.* Point to the *a* and say /a/. Now have students say the /a/ sound with you as you point to the letter and say it again. Slowly slide your finger or hand from left to right below the letters *sa* and say /sa/. Then have students join you in blending the two sounds through the vowel. Print the letter *t.* Point to the *t* and say /t/. Have students say the /t/ sound with you as you point to the letter and say it again. Slowly slide your finger or hand from left to right below the word *sat* as you blend the sounds together and pronounce the word. Then have students blend the whole word and pronounce it on their own. Finally, ask a volunteer to use the word in a sentence.

Help students blend the words and sentence shown below. Have them read the sentence, sounding out and blending each word in sequence. The high-frequency words in the sentence are underlined. Students should read these words as a whole; they should not attempt to sound them out.

Sam, mats
Sam sat <u>on</u> <u>the</u> mat.

## Apply

**DECODABLE TEXT** Provide students with connected reading practice. Choose text selections in which most of the words are wholly decodable and the majority of the remaining words are previously taught high-frequency and story words. For strategies to preteach the high-frequency words, see Chapter 9.

**8.30**

Intervention
Strategy

**If students have difficulty spelling the dictated words, see Chapter 7: Phonemic Awareness, "Name That Sound," p. 7.38.**

**DICTATION AND SPELLING**  Dictate the words shown below. Say each word, use it in a sentence, and then say the word again. For example, say: *The word is* sat. *I sat down on the chair . . .* sat. Have students say the word, then guide them in spelling it sound by sound. Ask: *What is the first sound in* sat? (/s/) Say: *Print the letter that stands for the /s/ sound.* Repeat the process for the remaining sounds in each word.

sat, Sam, mats

After the dictation, print the words on the board, and ask students to proofread their work. They should circle any word spelled incorrectly and write the correct spelling next to it.

**OBSERVE AND ASSESS**

*As students complete the Apply activities, use these questions to assess their progress.*

| Questions for Observation | Benchmarks |
| --- | --- |
| *(Point to the letter s.)* What is the sound for this letter? | Student can recognize single-consonant sound/spellings. |
| *(Point to a VC or CVC word with /s/s.)* Can you blend the sounds into a word? | Student can blend previously taught sound/spellings to read words. |

FOLLOW-UP STRATEGY . . .
See the Word Work activities in this chapter.

## Single Consonant Sound/Spellings

### Benchmark

• ability to distinguish the difference between beginning consonant sounds

### Grade Level

• Kindergarten – Grade 1 and Intervention

### Prerequisites

• Introducing Single Consonants
• introduced phonic elements: /a/a; /l/l; /m/m; /s/s; /t/t

### Grouping

• whole class
• small group or pairs
• individual

### Materials

• letter cards  Mm, Ss
• picture cards: mouse, monkey, mitten, money, mask, mirror; sun, sock, scissors, soap, six, soup
• pocket chart

# WORD WORK: CONSONANT PICTURE SORT

Picture sorts help students compare and contrast the sounds in words. This strategy reinforces recognition of the single-consonant sounds /m/*m* and /s/*s*. The same strategy can be used to reinforce other consonant sounds.

8.31

## Phonemic Warm-Up

Read aloud a series of words including some that begin with the consonant *s*, such as *sun, sat, seed, secret*. Tell students to show "thumbs up" when they hear the /s/ sound. Repeat the procedure for words beginning with the consonant *m*, such as *map, many, mitten, mask*.

**ELL** FOR SPANISH-SPEAKING STUDENTS . . .
The Spanish words for *seed* and *secret* also begin with /s/, spelled *s: semilla, secreto*. The Spanish words for *map, many*, and *mask* also begin with /m/, spelled *m: mapa, mucho(s), máscara*.

**Sort the Words**

Display the letter cards for *m* and *s* on a pocket chart, and place a picture card—such as a mouse or a sun—next to the corresponding letter. Shuffle the remaining picture cards. Say: *We're going to listen for the sound at the beginning of each word. We'll decide if it begins like* mouse *or like* sun. Select a picture card and model the whole-word blending process, emphasizing the initial consonant sound. For example, say: *Monkey . . . monkey begins like* mouse, *so I'll put the monkey below the picture of the mouse.* Place the picture of the monkey below the mouse, point to the letter card *m,* and say: Monkey *and* mouse; *they both begin with /m/.* Model the same process with the *s* picture and letter cards. After modeling several picture cards, let students have a turn. After all the pictures have been sorted into letter categories, name each picture. Have students repeat the sort on their own.

**ELL** FOR SPANISH-SPEAKING STUDENTS . . .
Make sure that students can name all of the picture cards in English. Point out that the letter *m* also stands for the /m/ sound in the Spanish words for *monkey* and *mask—mono, máscara.* The letter *s* also stands for the /s/ sound in the Spanish words for *six* and *soup—seis, sopa.*

# Short Vowel Sound/Spellings

### Benchmarks

- ability to recognize short vowel sound/spellings
- ability to blend previously introduced sound/spellings into words

### Grade Level

- Kindergarten – Grade 1 and Intervention

### Prerequisites

- all previously introduced Teaching Strategies in this chapter
- introduced phonic elements: all single consonants; short vowels /a/*a* and /i/*i*
- introduced high-frequency words: *I, when*

### Grouping

- whole class
- small group or pairs
- individual

### Materials

- picture cards: egg, hen, jet
- decodable text

## INTRODUCING SHORT VOWELS

**K-1** GRADE LEVEL

This generic teaching strategy introduces the short vowel /e/*e*. The same strategy can be used to introduce other short vowels. Many students confuse the short-*e* and short-*i* sounds. This is sometimes due to variations in regional pronunciation. In addition, students may be confused by the fact that the short *e* sound can be spelled several ways: *pet, head, said, many.*

8.33

## Phonemic Warm-Up

Display the picture cards egg and hen. Tell students that you are going to say some words with the /e/ sound. Some of the words you say will have the /e/ sound at the beginning of the word, like *egg;* others will have the /e/ sound in the middle, like *hen.* Say the following words and have students raise their hands when they hear the /e/ sound in the middle: *wet, end, bed, fed, edge, neck, elbow, pen.*

## Teach Sound/Spelling

Print the letter *e* on the board. Display a picture of a jet and tell students that the letter *e* stands for the /e/ sound in the middle of the word *jet.* Ask students to say the /e/ sound, first with you and then on their own. Then have them say the whole word *jet.*

**ELL** FOR SPANISH-SPEAKING STUDENTS . . .
In Spanish the letter *e* represents the long-*a* sound in *eight.*

**Chapter 13: Spelling Instruction**
"Single Short Vowels," p. 13.18

8.34

"Sound-by-Sound Blending," p. 8.12

for a more detailed description

**If students have difficulty blending, see "Vowel-First Blending," p. 8.13.**

## Practice Blending

Have students practice blending words with /e/, sound by sound, using the following example for the word *red.* Print the letter *r* on the board. Point to the *r* and say /r/. Ask students to say the /r/ sound with you as you point to the letter and say it again. Print the letter *e.* Point to the *e* and say /e/. Now have students say the /e/ sound with you as you point to the letter and say it again. Slowly slide your finger or hand from left to right below the letters *re* and say /rĕ/. Then have students join you in blending the two sounds through the vowel. Print the letter *d.* Point to the *d* and say /d/. Have students say the /d/ sound with you as you point to the letter and say it again. Slowly slide your finger or hand from left to right below the word *red* as you blend the sounds together and pronounce the word. Then have students blend the whole word and pronounce it on their own. Finally, ask a volunteer to use the word in a sentence.

Help students blend the words and sentence shown below. Have them read the sentence, sounding out and blending each word in sequence. The high-frequency words in the sentence are underlined. Students should read these words as a whole; they should not attempt to sound them out.

wet, pen, fed, men, beg
<u>When</u> can <u>I</u> get in bed?

## Apply

**DECODABLE TEXT**   Provide students with connected reading practice. Choose text selections in which most of the words are wholly decodable and the majority of the remaining words are previously taught high-frequency and story words. For strategies to preteach the high-frequency words, see Chapter 9.

**Intervention Strategy**

If students have difficulty spelling the dictated words, see Chapter 7: Phonemic Awareness, "Name That Sound," p. 7.38.

**DICTATION AND SPELLING**   Dictate the words shown below. Say each word, use it in a sentence, and then say the word again. For example, say: *The word is* pen. *I'll write a letter with this pen . . .* pen. Have students say the word, then guide them in spelling it sound by sound. Ask: *What is the first sound in pen?* (/p/) Say: *Print the letter that stands for the /p/ sound.* Repeat the process for the remaining sounds in each word. After students have written all of the words, read the sentence shown below. Dictate the words one at a time, using the same procedure to guide them in spelling each word sound by sound.

8.35

pen, net, men, red
Ben fed ten pets.

After the dictation, print the words and sentence on the board, and ask students to proofread their work. They should circle any word spelled incorrectly and write the correct spelling next to it.

**OBSERVE AND ASSESS**

*As students complete the Apply activities, use these questions to assess their progress.*

| Questions for Observation | Benchmarks |
|---|---|
| *(Point to the letter* e.*)* What is the sound for this letter? | Student can recognize short vowel sound/spellings. |
| *(Point to a CVC word with /e/e.)* Can you blend the sounds into a word? | Student can blend previously taught sound/spellings to read words. |

**FOLLOW-UP STRATEGY . . .**
See the Word Work activities in this chapter.

**FOLLOW-UP STRATEGY FOR**

## Short Vowel Sound/Spellings

### Benchmarks

- ability to recognize single consonant and short vowel sound/spellings
- ability to build CVC words

### Grade Level

- Kindergarten – Grade 1 and Intervention

### Prerequisites

- Introducing Short Vowels
- introduced phonic elements: all single consonants; short vowels /a/*a*, /i/*i*, /e/*e*

### Grouping

- small group or pairs
- individual

### Materials

- letter cards *b, d, e, f, g, i, l, n, p, s, t* (one set per student)

Intervention Strategy

**If students do not build the word correctly, stop and assist them by having them blend the sounds out loud.**

# WORD WORK: BUILDING CVC WORDS

**GRADE LEVEL · K-1 · GRADE LEVEL**

This strategy reinforces building and reading CVC words with *e* and *i*. The same strategy can be used to reinforce CVC words with other short vowels.

• • • • • • • • • • • • • • • • • • • • • • • • • • •

## Phonemic Warm-Up

Distribute the letter cards *e* and *i* to each student. Read aloud pairs of short-*e* and short-*i* words in random order: *sit/set, beg/big, rid/red, when/win, pit/pet.* Ask students to show the *e* card when they hear the /e/ sound and the *i* card when they hear the /i/ sound.

## Build Words

Distribute sets of letter cards to each student. Say: *Choose three letter cards to make the word* pen *on your desktop.* Watch as students form *pen.* Then say: *Now change one letter in* pen *to make* pin. Watch as students replace the *e* with an *i.* Then say: *Change one letter in* pin *to make* pit. Continue this procedure, having students make the following words in order: *pet, set, sit, bit, big, pig, peg, beg, leg, let, lit, fit, fig, dig.*

## Try It This Way!

Challenge students to use their letter cards to make their own CVC words. Examples include *bet, bed, dip, den, fib, fin, lip, net, sip, tin, tip, ten.* Then help students think of silly sentences with the words they made.

## TEACHING STRATEGY FOR
# Consonant Digraph Sound/Spellings

### Benchmarks

- ability to recognize consonant digraph sound/spellings
- ability to blend previously introduced sound/spellings into words

### Grade Level

- Grade 1 and Intervention

### Prerequisites

- all previously introduced Teaching Strategies in this chapter
- introduced phonic elements: all single consonants and short vowels; /k/ck; /l/ll
- introduced high-frequency words: a, the, I, have, my

### Grouping

- whole class
- small group or pairs
- individual

### Materials

- picture cards: cheese, peach
- decodable text

See also . . .

Chapter 13: Spelling Instruction
"Final-Consonant Patterns," p. 13.26,
and "r-Controlled Vowels," p. 13.23

# INTRODUCING CONSONANT DIGRAPHS

This generic teaching strategy introduces the consonant digraph /ch/*ch* in both initial and final positions. (In the final position, the ending sound /ch/ is usually spelled *tch* when it is preceded by a short-vowel sound, as in *latch, pitch,* and *fetch.* The high-frequency words *which, much,* and *such* are three exceptions.) The same strategy can be used to introduce other consonant digraphs, the phoneme /ng/, the sound/spelling *nk* (/ng/ + /k/), and *r*-controlled vowel patterns.

## Phonemic Warm-Up

Ask students to guess the words you are trying to say by orally blending the sounds in the following segmented words: /ch/ /ē/ /z/ (*cheese*), /ch/ /ûr/ /ch/ (*church*); /p/ /ē/ /ch/ (*peach*); /r/ /i/ /ch/ (*rich*); /ch/ /i/ /p/ (*chip*). Then ask: *What sound did you hear in each word?* (/ch/) Ask students to say other words with the /ch/ sound.

**ELL** FOR SPANISH-SPEAKING STUDENTS . . .
In Spanish the consonant digraph *ch* also represents the /ch/ sound. However, it appears only at the beginning (*chico, chaqueta*) and in the middle of words (*ocho, echan*).

## Teach Sound/Spelling

Print the letters *ch* on the board. Display a picture of a piece of cheese and tell students that the letters *ch* stand for the /ch/ sound at the beginning of the word *cheese.* Ask students to say the /ch/ sound, first with you and then on their own. Then have them say the whole word *cheese.* You may also want to teach that the /ch/ sound can occur at the end of words,

8.38

**Intervention Strategy**

If students confuse the /ch/ and /j/ sounds, help them "feel" the difference between the two sounds by touching their voicebox and noticing that /ch/ is unvoiced, while /j/ is voiced.

*See also . . .*

"Sound-by-Sound Blending," p. 8.12

for a more detailed description

**Intervention Strategy**

If students say a particular sound incorrectly, correct them. For example: If students say /sh/ instead of /ch/, stop them immediately and say /ch/. Next, point to the *ch* and have students identify its sound. Then ask students to blend the word again.

using a picture of a peach and following the same procedure described above.

## Practice Blending

Have students practice blending words with /ch/, sound by sound, using the following example for the word *chin.* Print the letters *ch* on the board. Point to the *ch* pair and say /ch/. Ask students to say the /ch/ sound with you as you point to the letters and say it again. Print the letter *i.* Point to the *i* and say /i/. Now have students say the /i/ sound with you as you point to the letter and say it again. Slowly slide your finger or hand from left to right below the letters *chi* and say /chĭ/. Then have students join you in blending the two sounds through the vowel. Print the letter *n.* Point to the *n* and say /n/. Have students say the /n/ sound with you as you point to the letter and say it again. Slowly slide your finger or hand from left to right below the word *chin* as you blend the sounds together and pronounce the word. Then have students blend the whole word and pronounce it on their own. Finally, ask a volunteer to use the word in a sentence.

Help students blend the words and sentence shown below. Have them read the sentence, sounding out and blending each word in sequence. The high-frequency words in the sentence are underlined. Students should read these words as a whole; they should not attempt to sound them out.

chip, chop, rich, much, such, chill, check
<u>The</u> cup had <u>a</u> chip.

## Apply

**DECODABLE TEXT** Provide students with connected reading practice. Choose text selections in which most of the words are wholly decodable and the majority of the remaining words are previously taught high-frequency and story words. For strategies to preteach the high-frequency words, see Chapter 9.

Intervention Strategy

**If students have difficulty spelling the dictated words, see Chapter 7: Phonemic Awareness, "Name That Sound," p. 7.38**

**DICTATION AND SPELLING**  Dictate the words shown below. Say each word, use it in a sentence, and then say the word again. For example, say: *The word is* chin. *I like to tickle your chin . . .* chin. Have students say the word, then guide them in spelling it sound by sound. Ask: *What is the first sound in* chin? (/ch/) Say: *Print the letters that stand for the /ch/ sound.* Repeat the process for the remaining sounds in each word. After students have written all of the words, read the sentence shown below. Dictate the words one at a time, using the same procedure to guide them in spelling each word sound by sound. The high-frequency words in the sentence are underlined. Students should write these as a whole; they should not try to sound them out.

chin, chop, chest, much
I have chips on my chin.

After the dictation, print the words and sentence on the board, and ask students to proofread their work. They should circle any word spelled incorrectly and write the correct spelling next to it.

**OBSERVE AND ASSESS**

*As students complete the Apply activities, use these questions to assess their progress.*

| Questions for Observation | Benchmarks |
| --- | --- |
| *(Point to the digraph* ch.) What is the sound for these letters? | Student can recognize consonant digraph sound/spellings. |
| *(Point to a one-syllable word with digraph /ch/* ch.) Can you blend the sounds into a word? | Student can blend previously taught sound/spellings to read words. |

FOLLOW-UP STRATEGY . . .
See the Word Work activities in this chapter.

## FOLLOW-UP STRATEGY FOR

# Consonant Digraph Sound/Spellings

**Benchmark**

- ability to recognize and distinguish consonant digraph sound/spellings

**Grade Level**

- Grade 1 and Intervention

**Prerequisites**

- Introducing Consonant Digraphs
- introduced phonic elements: all single consonants and short vowels; /ch/ch; /sh/sh; /k/ck; /l/ll

**Grouping**

- whole class
- small group or pairs
- individual

**Materials**

- index cards (two per student)

# WORD WORK: CONSONANT DIGRAPH WORD SORT

This blind sort reinforces recognition of the initial consonant digraphs /ch/ and /sh/. The same strategy can be used to reinforce recognition of these digraphs at the end of words or as a follow-up to instruction in other consonant digraphs.

## Phonemic Warm-Up

Review the difference between the sounds /ch/ and /sh/ by asking students to substitute the sounds in several words. Say the word *chop* and have students repeat it after you. Then tell them to say the word with the /sh/ sound at the beginning, instead of the /ch/ sound. Ask what the new word is. *(shop)* Repeat this process with the words *chip/ship, cheat/sheet, chew/shoe, chin/shin.*

## Sort the Words

On the board, print the key words *chin* and *ship* and have students copy them on separate index cards. Tell students that you will say a word and—without seeing it—they will tell you whether it starts with /ch/ like *chin* or /sh/ like *ship*.

Model the sort. Say the word *chip.* Then tell students: *The word chip starts with the /ch/ sound like* chin. *It belongs here.* Print the word *chip* under the key word *chin.* Next, say the word *shell* and ask students: *Does this word start with the same sound as* chin *or the same sound as* ship? Place the word in the appropriate column. Say the following words aloud one at a

time, asking students to hold up the key-word card with the matching consonant digraph sound: *shop, chat, chip, she, shelf, chill, shin, chick, chest, shack.* After each student response, print the word under the correct key word. After completing the sort, have volunteers read aloud the words in both columns.

**ELL** FOR SPANISH-SPEAKING STUDENTS . . .
The *sh* digraph does not exist in Spanish and students may have difficulty articulating it. This sorting activity is of special benefit as it provides practice in distinguishing /sh/ from /ch/. Make sure that students know the meanings of all the words used in the sort.

## Try It This Way!

Some students may need to focus on one digraph at a time, sorting words according to initial and final position. For example, to focus on /ch/ use the key words *chin* and *peach* and have students do a blind sort of the following words: *chat, chip, much, chill, rich, chick, chest, such, which.*

## TEACHING STRATEGY FOR
# Long Vowel Sound/Spellings

### Benchmarks

- ability to recognize the long-vowel CVC*e* pattern in words
- ability to blend previously introduced sound/spellings into words

### Grade Level

- Grade 1 and Intervention

### Prerequisites

- all previously introduced Teaching Strategies in this chapter
- introduced phonic elements: all single consonants and short vowels; /sh/*sh*
- introduced high-frequency words: *a, I, two*

### Grouping

- whole class
- small group or pairs
- individual

### Materials

- decodable text

**Chapter 13: Spelling Instruction**
**"Long Vowels," p. 13.21**

---

# INTRODUCING WORDS WITH A CVC*e* PATTERN

This generic teaching strategy introduces CVC*e* words spelled *a_e*. The same strategy can be used to introduce other long-vowel CVC*e* patterns. The CVC*e* pattern with the vowels *e, i, o,* and *u* should be taught directly, one at a time, following this lesson.

## Phonemic Warm-Up

Tell students that they are going to play a word game. You will say three words. You want them to listen closely and tell you what sound they hear in the middle of these words. Use the following words with long and short *a*.

hat, sad, cap
cake, made, late

## Teach Sound/Spelling

Print the word *tap* on the board and have students blend it with you. Point to the *a* in *tap* and ask students to say the sound of the letter. *(/a/)* Next, add an *e* at the end of *tap* to make *tape.* Point to the letter *a* and say: *Adding an* e *at the end of* tap *makes the vowel* a *"say its own name". . . /ā/. The* e *is silent.* Point to the *a* in *tape* and ask students to identify its sound. Then have students say the whole word. Repeat this procedure using the words *cap* and *cape.*

---

✔ **TEACHER TIP** A silent *e* always follows a final *v*, but does not necessarily make the vowel sound long. *(have, give)*

---

## Practice Blending

Have students practice blending words with the CVC*e* pattern using the whole-word blending strategy. Print the word

**See also . . .**

"Whole-Word Blending," p. 8.14

for a more detailed description

Intervention
Strategy

**If students say a particular sound incorrectly, correct them. For example: If students say "tăk" instead of** *take,* **point to the silent** *e* **and say:** *This letter has no sound, but it makes the* a *say its name.* **Next, point to the** *a* **and have students identify its sound. Then ask students to try to blend the word again.**

**If students have difficulty blending the sounds continuously, see "Vowel-First Blending," p. 8.13.**

*make* on the board. Point to the letter *e* and say: *This* e *at the end of the word makes the vowel say its name.* Then say the word, extending its sounds: "mmmāāāk." Do not pause between sounds. For example, do not say /m/ (pause), /ā/ (pause), /k/. Use your finger or hand to track under each letter as you say the corresponding sound. (Since the *e* is silent, do not track under it.) After blending the sounds in a stretched-out manner, say the whole word quickly: *make.* Next, have students blend and pronounce the word with you. Direct them to say each sound as soon as you point to its spelling. Finally, have students blend and pronounce the word on their own. Ask a volunteer to use the word in a sentence.

✔ **BLENDING TIP** When blending words, hold each continuous sound for about one second and each stop sound for only an instant. For a list of continuous and stop sounds see Section II: Word Structure, "What Are the Classifications of Consonant Phonemes?" p. 3.4.

Help students blend the words and sentence shown below. Have them read the sentence, sounding out and blending each word in sequence. The high-frequency word in the sentence is underlined. Students should read the word as a whole; they should not attempt to sound it out.

take, name, same, came, shape, made
Sam made <u>a</u> cake.

## Apply

**DECODABLE TEXT** Provide students with connected reading practice. Choose text selections in which most of the words are wholly decodable and the majority of the remaining words are previously taught high-frequency and story words. For strategies to preteach the high-frequency words, see Chapter 9.

Intervention
Strategy

**If students have difficulty spelling the dictated words, try guiding them in spelling each word sound by sound.**

**DICTATION AND SPELLING**    Dictate the words shown below. Say each word, use it in a sentence, and then say the word again. For example, say: *The word is* hat. *He forgot his hat . . .* hat. Have students say *hat* and ask them to think about the sounds they hear. Say: *Print the letters that stand for the sounds you hear in* hat. Repeat the process for the remaining words. After students have written all of the words, read the sentence shown below. Dictate the words one at a time, using the same procedure to guide them in spelling each word. The high-frequency words in the sentence are underlined. Students should write these as a whole.

hat, hate, cap, cape, mad, made, tap, tape, shake
<u>I</u> can bake <u>two</u> cakes.

After the dictation, print the words and sentence on the board, and ask students to proofread their work. They should circle any word spelled incorrectly and write the correct spelling next to it.

**OBSERVE AND ASSESS**

*As students complete the Apply activities, use these questions to assess their progress.*

| Questions for Observation | Benchmarks |
|---|---|
| *(Point to the vowel* a *in a one-syllable word with the* a_e *pattern.)* What is the sound for this letter? | Student can recognize long-vowel CVCe pattern sound/spellings. |
| *(Point to a one-syllable word with the* a_e *pattern.)* Can you blend the sounds into a word? | Student can blend previously taught sound/spellings to read words. |

## The Next Step

When final silent *e* follows *c* and *g* the consonants have a "soft" sound. Introduce students to words with soft *c* and *g;* for example: *stage, cage, change, face, race, place.*

FOLLOW-UP STRATEGY . . .
See the Word Work activities in this chapter.

## Vowel Digraph Sound/Spellings

### Benchmarks

- ability to recognize vowel digraph sound/spellings
- ability to blend previously introduced sound/spellings into words

### Grade Level

- Grade 1 and Intervention

### Prerequisites

- all previously introduced Teaching Strategies in this chapter
- introduced phonic elements: all single consonants, short vowels, and consonant digraphs; CVC*e* long-vowel pattern
- introduced high-frequency words: *away, from, my, of, out, the*

### Grouping

- whole class
- small group or pairs
- individual

### Materials

- decodable text

Chapter 13: Spelling Instruction
"Long Vowels," p. 13.21

# INTRODUCING VOWEL DIGRAPHS

This generic teaching strategy introduces the vowel digraph /ā/*ai, ay.* The same strategy can be used to introduce other vowel digraphs, diphthongs, and variant vowels.

8.45

## Phonemic Warm-Up

Have students orally blend the following segmented words: /m/ /ā/ /n/ *(main)*, /s//t/ /ā/ *(stay)*, /p//ā/ /n//t/ *(paint)*, /k//l//ā/ *(clay)*, /t//r/ /ā/ *(tray)*.

## Teach Sound/Spelling

Tell students that a vowel can have its long sound when it is part of a vowel team, or a pair of two vowel letters. One of the vowels, usually the first one, "says" its long sound, while the other vowel is silent. Print the word *bait* on the board. Underline the vowel digraph *ai* and tell students that these letters are a team that stand for the sound /ā/. Now print the word *tray* on the board. Underline the vowel digraph *ay* and tell students that these letters are a team that stand for the /ā/ sound at the end of a word.

## Practice Blending

Have students practice blending words with vowel digraphs using the whole-word blending strategy. Print the word *rain* on the board. Then say the word, extending its sounds: "rrrāāānnn." Do not pause between sounds. For example, do not say /r/ (pause), /ā/ ( pause), /n/. Use your finger or hand to track under each letter as you say the corresponding sound. (For the vowel digraph *ai*, be sure to point to both letters as you say the long-vowel sound.) After blending the sounds in a stretched-out manner, say the whole word quickly: *rain.* To

See also...

"Whole-Word Blending," p. 8.14

for a more detailed description

8.46

Intervention
Strategy

**If students say a particular sound incorrectly, correct them. For example, if students say *man* instead of *main*, stop them immediately and say: *These letters are a team. They make one sound: /ā/.* Next, point to the *ai* vowel digraph and have students identify its sound. Then ask students to blend the word again.**

internalize the blending process, direct students to blend the word silently in their heads and then say the word. Model this process by pointing to and quietly saying the sounds in progression, and then loudly saying the whole word. Wait a few seconds and ask for volunteers to say the word aloud and use it in a sentence. Repeat the blending process using the word *say.*

Help students blend the words and sentence shown below. Have them read the sentence, sounding out and blending each word in sequence. The high-frequency words in the sentence are underlined. Students should read these words as a whole; they should not attempt to sound them out.

man, main, ran, rain, dad, day, sat, stay
<u>My</u> cat ran <u>out</u> <u>of</u> <u>the</u> rain.

## Apply

**DECODABLE TEXT** Provide students with connected reading practice. Choose text selections in which most of the words are wholly decodable and the majority of the remaining words are previously taught high-frequency and story words. For strategies to preteach the high-frequency words, see Chapter 9.

**DICTATION AND SPELLING** Dictate the words shown below with the long-*a* sound. Say each word, use it in a sentence, and then say the word again. For example, say *The word is* rain. *I hope it doesn't rain . . .* rain. Have students say the word *rain* and ask them to think about the sounds they hear in the word. Say: *Print the letters that stand for the sounds you hear in* rain. Repeat the process for the remaining words. After students have written all of the words, read the sentence shown

8.47

### Intervention Strategy

If students have difficulty choosing the correct vowel digraph to spell /ā/, remind them to think about where the vowel sound occurs. If it occurs at the end of the word, it is spelled *ay*.

below. Dictate the words one at a time, using the same procedure to guide them in spelling each word. The high-frequency words in the sentence are underlined. Students should write these as a whole.

rain, wait, day, way, sail, play
<u>The</u> dogs ran <u>away</u> <u>from</u> <u>the</u> train.

After the dictation, print the words and sentence on the board, and ask students to proofread their work. They should circle any word spelled incorrectly and write the correct spelling next to it.

### OBSERVE AND ASSESS

*As students complete the Apply activities, use these questions to assess their progress.*

| Questions for Observation | Benchmarks |
|---|---|
| *(Point to the vowel digraph* ai.*)* What is the sound for these letters? | Student can recognize vowel digraph sound/spellings. |
| *(Point to a one-syllable word with /ā/ai.)* Can you sound out the word to yourself and then say it aloud? | Student can blend previously taught sound/spellings to read words. |

FOLLOW-UP STRATEGY . . .
See the Word Work activities in this chapter.

## FOLLOW-UP STRATEGY FOR

# Vowel Digraph Sound/Spellings

### Benchmark

• ability to recognize and distinguish short- and long-vowel sound/spellings

### Grade Level

• Grade 1 and Intervention

### Prerequisites

• Introducing Short Vowels
• Introducing Vowel Digraphs
• introduced phonic elements: all single consonants, short vowels, and consonant digraphs; /kw/*qu*; CVC*e* long-vowel pattern; vowel digraph /ā/*ai, ay*

### Grouping

• small group or pairs

### Materials

• index cards (two per student)
• picture cards: cat, cake
• Word Study Notebooks

# WORD WORK: SHORT- AND LONG-VOWEL WORD SORT

GRADE LEVEL 1 GRADE LEVEL

This blind sort reinforces discrimination of short-*a* and long-*a* vowel patterns. The same strategy can be used to reinforce discrimination of other short- and long-vowel patterns.

## Phonemic Warm-Up

Have students substitute the vowel sound in words with short *a* to create new words with long *a*. For example, ask them to say *pan*. Then say: *Now instead of /a/, say /ā/. What's the new word? (pain)* Repeat the process with the following words: *pal/pail, mad/made, clam/claim, rack/rake.*

## Sort the Words

Display the picture cards of a cat and cake, and ask students to name them. Print the key words *cat* and *cake* on the board, and have students copy the words on separate index cards. Tell students that you will say a word and—without seeing it—they will tell you whether it has the short-*a* sound in *cat* or the long-*a* sound in *cake*. Say the word *pan*. Tell students: *The word* pan *has the /a/ sound like* cat. *It belongs here.* Print the word *pan* under the key word *cat*. Next, say the word *gate* and ask students: *Does this word have the same vowel sound as* cat *or the same vowel sound as* cake? Place the word in the appropriate column.

Say the following words aloud one at a time, asking students to hold up the key-word card with the matching vowel sound: *ran, rain, play, plan, sat, say, date, way, wait, chain, game, shake, flat, quail, patch, take, had.* After each student response, print the word under the correct key word. After completing the sort, have volunteers read aloud the words in both columns.

pan

ran

plan

gate

rain

play

Section V: Spelling

"Word Study Notebooks," p. 13.8

## Try It This Way!

Have students work in pairs or small groups to do an "open sort" of all the words with the long-*a* sound. Ask them to group the words according to their spelling patterns. Students should see that there are three groups: long *a* spelled *a*-consonant-*e*, long *a* spelled *ai*, and long *a* spelled *ay*. When they have finished sorting, ask what they notice about the words. Lead them to make the following generalizations: the long-*a* sound can be spelled with *a*-consonant–silent *e* or with a vowel team. When it appears at the end of a word, it is spelled with the vowel team *ay*. Have students record their sorts and the spelling generalizations in their Word Study Notebooks.

## TEACHING STRATEGY FOR
# Inflectional Ending *–ed*

**Benchmarks**

- ability to read words with inflectional ending *–ed* /t/, /d/, /ed/
- ability to blend previously introduced sound/spellings into words

**Grade Level**

- Grades 1 – 2 and Intervention

**Prerequisites**

- introduced phonic elements: all single consonants, short vowels, and consonant digraphs; CVC*e* long-vowel pattern; vowel digraphs
- introduced high-frequency word: *for*

**Grouping**

- whole class

**Materials**

- none

8.50

# INTRODUCING INFLECTIONAL ENDING *–ed* /t/, /d/, /ed/

GRADE LEVEL 1-2 GRADE LEVEL

This generic teaching strategy introduces the inflectional ending *–ed*. This ending should be introduced in first grade after students have been taught the plural ending *–es*. For English language learners, the *–ed* ending is particularly difficult. These students will need extensive practice hearing, saying, and reading words with the three pronunciations: /t/ in *looked,* /d/ in *played,* and the separate syllable /ed/ in *wanted.*

## Phonemic Warm-Up

Have students clap out the number of syllables they hear in words with the inflectional ending *–ed*. Read aloud the following words in random order: (/t/) *looked, worked, walked, asked;* (/d/) *played, smelled, cleaned, rained;* and (/ed/) *wanted, lifted, painted, batted.* Point out that sometimes the ending *–ed* at the end of a word adds a syllable and sometimes it does not.

## Teach Sound/Spellings

Print the ending *–ed* on the board and tell students that the *–ed* ending can make three sounds: the /t/ sound they hear in *looked,* the /d/ sound they hear in *played,* and the /ed/ sound they hear in *wanted.* Have students repeat the three words. Then ask them to listen as you say the series of words ending in *–ed* shown below, some with /t/, some with /d/, and some with the syllable /ed/. Tell students that you will say a word and then on a signal they will tell you what sound they hear. Remind them that the words are all spelled with the *–ed* ending.

learned, worked, helped, played, wanted, batted

**See also...**

Chapter 13: Spelling Instruction, "Consonant Doubling/Dropping *e*," p. 13.35

"Whole-Word Blending," p. 8.14

for a more detailed description

**Intervention Strategy**

**If students say the sound for –*ed* incorrectly, correct them. For example: If students say *helped* with two syllables, stop them immediately and underline the base word *help* and say it aloud. Next, point to the –*ed* ending and have students identify its sound. Then ask students to blend the word again.**

 **English language learners should be able to distinguish and articulate the different pronunciations of –*ed*. Select words that come from their oral vocabularies.**

Now print the same words on the board. Underline the base word in each of the words. Have students read the list twice. On the first reading, they should say the base word and then the whole word. On the second reading, they should say the whole word.

## Practice Blending

Have students practice blending words with the inflectional ending –*ed* using the whole-word blending strategy. Print the word *asked* on the board. Cover the –*ed* ending and say the base word *ask*, extending its sounds. Use your finger or hand to track under each letter as you say the corresponding sound. After blending the sounds in a stretched-out manner, say the whole base word quickly: *ask*. Then point to the –*ed* ending as you say /t/. Next, blend the base word with the /t/ ending sound and say: *asked*. To internalize the blending process, direct students to blend the word silently in their heads and then say the word. Repeat the blending process using the words *cleaned* and *waited*.

Help students blend the words and sentence shown below. Have them read the sentence, sounding out and blending each word in sequence. The high-frequency words in the sentence are underlined. Students should read these words as a whole; they should not attempt to sound them out.

panted, rained, helped, played
We waited <u>for</u> dad, then walked home.

## Apply

**DECODABLE TEXT**   Provide students with connected reading practice. Choose text selections in which most of the words are wholly decodable and the majority of the remaining words are previously taught high-frequency and story words. For strategies to preteach the high-frequency words, see Chapter 9.

Intervention
Strategy

**If students have difficulty spelling the dictated words, try guiding them in spelling each word sound by sound.**

8.52

PAINT

**DICTATION AND SPELLING** Dictate the words shown below with the *–ed* inflectional ending. Say each word, use it in a sentence, and then say the word again. For example, say: *The word is* rained. *It rained all weekend . . .* rained. Have students say the word *rained* and ask them to think about the sounds they hear in the word. Say: *Print the letters that stand for the sounds you hear in* rained. Repeat the process for the remaining words. After students have written all of the words, read the sentence shown below. Dictate the words one at a time, using the same procedure to guide them in spelling each word. The high-frequency words in the sentence are underlined. Students should write these as a whole.

rained, played, helped, asked, spotted
<u>The</u> paint landed on <u>the</u> rug!

After the dictation, print the words and sentence on the board, and ask students to proofread their work. They should circle any word spelled incorrectly and write the correct spelling next to it.

**OBSERVE AND ASSESS**

*As students complete the Apply activities, use these questions to assess their progress.*

| Questions for Observation | Benchmarks |
|---|---|
| *(Point to a word with the* –ed *ending.)* What is the sound for this ending? | Student can recognize inflectional ending *–ed* sound/spellings. |
| *(Point to a word with the* –ed *ending.)* Can you sound out the word to yourself and then say it aloud? | Student can blend previously taught sound/spellings to read words. |

FOLLOW-UP STRATEGY . . .
See the Word Work activities in this chapter.

## Inflectional Ending *–ed*

**Benchmark**

• ability to read and distinguish the sounds for inflectional ending *–ed*

**Grade Level**

• Grades 1 – 2 and Intervention

**Prerequisites**

• Introducing Inflectional Ending *–ed* /t/, /d/, /ed/
• introduced phonic elements: all single consonants, short vowels, and consonant digraphs; CVC*e* long-vowel pattern; vowel digraphs

**Grouping**

• whole class
• small group or pairs

**Materials**

• index cards (three per student)
• Word Study Notebooks

# WORD WORK: INFLECTIONAL ENDING *–ed* WORD SORT

This blind sort reinforces discrimination of the three sounds represented by the *–ed* ending.

8.53

## Phonemic Warm-Up

Have students select the correct pronunciation when adding the inflectional ending *–ed* to a series of base words. Print _____ + *–ed* on the board. Then prompt students by saying each of the following base words and then pointing to the phrase on the board: *wait, hop, talk, play, turn.*

## Sort the Words

Print the key words *rushed, played,* and *wanted* on the board. Have students repeat the words after you and then copy them on separate index cards. Tell students that you will say a word and—without seeing it—they will tell you whether it ends with the /t/, /d/, or /ed/ sound. Say the word *pushed.* Tell students: *The word* pushed *has the /t/ sound at the end like* rushed. *It belongs here.* Print the word *pushed* under the key word *rushed.* Next, say the word *heated* and ask students: *Does this word have the same ending sounds as* looked, played, *or* wanted? Place the word in the appropriate column.

**8.54**

Say the following words aloud one at a time, asking students to hold up the key-word card with the matching ending sound(s): *pushed, named, heated, smiled, picked, lifted.* After each student response, print the word under the correct key word. After completing the sort, have volunteers read aloud the words in the three columns.

### Try It This Way!

Have students work in pairs or small groups to do a word hunt for words ending in *–ed.* Remind them to look for action words that have the *–ed* ending. Ask them to group the words according to the way they sound. Lead them to make the following generalizations: When *–ed* is added to a base word ending in two consonants, it often has the /t/ sound. When *–ed* is added to a base word with a long-vowel sound, it often has the /d/ sound. When *–ed* is added to a base word ending in *d* or *t,* it often has the /ed/ sound. Have students record their sorts and the spelling generalizations in their Word Study Notebooks.

 See also · · ·

Section V: Spelling
"Word Study Notebooks," p. 13.8

## Variant Vowel Sound/Spellings

### Benchmarks

- ability to recognize variant vowel sound/spellings
- ability to blend previously introduced sound/spellings into words

### Grade Level

- Grades 1 – 2 and Intervention

### Prerequisites

- all previously introduced Teaching Strategies in this chapter
- introduced phonic elements: all single consonants, short vowels, and consonant digraphs; CVCe long-vowel pattern; vowel digraphs
- introduced high-frequency words: *a, to, the, they*

### Grouping

- whole class
- small group or pairs
- individual

### Materials

- picture cards: moon
- decodable text

# INTRODUCING VARIANT VOWELS

This generic teaching strategy introduces spellings of the variant vowel /ōō/*oo, ue, ew.* The same strategy can be used to introduce other spellings of this variant vowel, the variant vowel /ŏŏ/*oo,* and other variant vowels such as /aw/*au, aw.* For older students you may wish to teach both /ōō/*oo* and /ŏŏ/*oo* for contrast.

8.55

## Phonemic Warm-Up

Tell students that they are going to listen for words that have the sound /ōō/ they hear in *moon.* Ask students to put their thumbs up when they hear the sound. Say the following words in random order: *boot, took, blue, cook, stood, chew, wood, smooth.*

## Teach Sound/Spelling

Print the word *moon* on the board. Display a picture of a moon and say the word aloud, emphasizing the vowel sound. Underline the variant vowel *oo* in *moon* and tell students that these letters stand for the sound /ōō/. Point to the *oo* in *moon* and have students repeat the sound and then say the whole word. Now print the words *glue* and *grew* on the board. Underline the *ue* in *glue* and the *ew* in *grew.* Tell students that these spellings can also stand for the /ōō/ sound. Have students repeat the sound and then say the words.

## Practice Blending

Have students practice blending words with /ōō/ using the whole-word blending strategy. Print the word *smooth* on the board and say the word, extending its sounds. Use your finger

**"Whole-Word Blending," p. 8.14**

for a more detailed description

**8.56**

Intervention
Strategy

**Students may need practice hearing and articulating the sound /o͞o/. Remind them that the mouth position should be round and partially open, and the jaw muscles should be tense.**

or hand to track under each letter as you say the corresponding sound. (For the variant vowel *o͞o* be sure to point to both letters as you say the vowel sound.) After blending the sounds in a stretched-out manner, say the whole word quickly: *smooth.* To internalize the blending process, direct students to blend the word silently in their heads and then say the word. Repeat the blending process using the words *true* and *grew.*

Help students blend the words and sentence shown below. Have them read the sentence, sounding out and blending each word in sequence. The high-frequency word in the sentence is underlined. Students should read this word as a whole; they should not attempt to sound it out.

food, true, new, spoon
She drew <u>a</u> blue moon.

## Apply

**DECODABLE TEXT**   Provide students with connected reading practice. Choose text selections in which most of the words are wholly decodable and the majority of the remaining words are previously taught high-frequency and story words. For strategies to preteach the high-frequency words, see Chapter 9.

**DICTATION AND SPELLING**   Dictate the words shown below. Say each word, use it in a sentence, and then say the word again. For example, say *The word is* stew. *I ate the stew . . .* stew. Have students say the word *stew* and ask them to think about the sounds they hear in the word. Say: *Print the letters that stand for the sounds you hear in* stew. Repeat the process for the remaining words. After students have written all of the words, read the sentence shown below. Dictate

**Intervention Strategy**

**If students have difficulty spelling the dictated words, see Chapter 7: Phonemic Awareness, "Name That Sound," p. 7.38.**

the words one at a time, using the same procedure to guide them in spelling each word. The high-frequency words in the sentence are underlined. Students should write these as a whole.

stew, room, spoon, blue, threw, cool
<u>They</u> flew <u>to</u> <u>the</u> moon.

After the dictation, print the words and sentence on the board, and ask students to proofread their work. They should circle any word spelled incorrectly and write the correct spelling next to it.

---

**OBSERVE AND ASSESS**

*As students complete the Apply activities, use this question to assess their progress.*

| Question for Observation | Benchmark |
|---|---|
| (*Point to a word with the variant vowel /o͞o/oo.*) Can you sound out this word to yourself and then say it aloud? | Student can blend previously taught sound/spellings to read words. |

FOLLOW-UP STRATEGY . . .
See the Word Work activities in this chapter.

## Variant Vowel Sound/Spellings

8.58

### Benchmark

- ability to recognize and distinguish different variant vowel sound/spellings

### Grade Level

- Grades 1 – 2 and Intervention

### Prerequisites

- Introducing Variant Vowels
- introduced phonic elements: all single consonants, short vowels, and consonant digraphs; CVCe long-vowel pattern; vowel digraphs; variant vowels

### Grouping

- whole class
- small group or pairs

### Materials

- text selections
- index cards

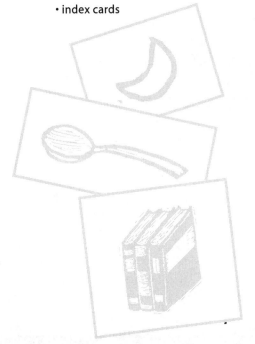

# WORD WORK: VARIANT VOWEL WORD HUNT AND SORT

1-2

This blind sort reinforces discrimination of words with the /ōo/ sound and words with the /ŏo/ sound. The same strategy can be used to reinforce other variant vowel patterns.

## Phonemic Warm-Up

Tell students to listen as you read some words aloud and to stand up if the word they hear has the /ōo/ sound, as in *moon*. Tell them to stay seated if the word has the /ŏo/ sound, as in *book.* Use the following words: *boot, shook, took, pool, wood, spoon, stood.*

## Hunt for Words

On the board, print the key words *hoot* and *book.* Have students look through narrative and expository text selections, poetry, or song lyrics for words that have the same vowel sounds as in *hoot* and *book.* Ask them to write on index cards the words with the /ōo/ sound and those with the /ŏo/ sound.

## Sort the Words

After hunting for the words, have students sort the words into the two categories. Then have students sort words with the long sound of *oo* according to sound/spellings, such as *oo, ew, ue.* After completing the sort, have volunteers share what they found.

## The Next Step

Encourage students to write a poem or story using the words they have found and sorted.

### Benchmarks

- ability to recognize common phonograms in words
- ability to blend onset and rime

### Grade Level

- Kindergarten – Grade 2 and Intervention

### Prerequisites

- all previously introduced Teaching Strategies in this chapter
- introduced phonic elements: all single consonants and short vowels; consonant digraphs
- introduced high-frequency words: *a, by, the*

### Grouping

- whole class
- small group or pairs
- individual

### Materials

- decodable text

See also . . .

Section II: Word Structure, "What Is a Phonogram?" p. 3.22

## PHONOGRAMS WITH SHORT-VOWEL PATTERNS

This generic teaching strategy introduces the *–at* phonogram. The same strategy can be used to introduce other short-vowel and long-vowel phonograms. Introduce a phonogram *after* all the individual sound/spellings that make up that phonogram have been taught.

8.59

## Phonemic Warm-Up

Ask students to brainstorm words that rhyme with *cat*. For example, students might suggest *bat, chat, fat, flat, hat, mat, rat,* or *sat*. Students might enjoy making up silly sentences using their list of brainstormed words.

## Teach the Phonogram

Print the phonogram *–at* on the board. Point to *a* and ask students to say the sound. *(/a/)* Next, point to *t* and ask students to say the sound. *(/t/)* Slowly slide your finger or hand from left to right below the two letters and say *–at*. Have students say *–at* with you, and then on their own. Tell students that *–at* is a word family.

## Practice Onset and Rime Blending

Print the digraph *th* before *–at*. Point to *th* and ask students to say the sound. *(/th/)* Now slowly slide your finger or hand from left to right below the onset *th* and rime *–at* and pronounce the word *that*. Have students blend the word on their own. Repeat the procedure with the digraph *ch*.

**Intervention Strategy**

**If students are having difficulty blending the onset and rime, see Chapter 7: Phonemic Awareness, "Critter Sitter," p. 7.30.**

Help students blend the words and sentence shown below. Have them read the sentence, sounding out and blending each word in sequence. The high-frequency words in the sentence are underlined. Students should read these words as a whole; they should not attempt to sound them out.

cat, sat, scat, bat, brat, hat, fat, flat, rat
<u>The</u> cat sleeps on <u>a</u> flat mat.

## Apply

**DECODABLE TEXT**   Provide students with connected reading practice. Choose text selections in which most of the words are wholly decodable and the majority of the remaining words are previously taught high-frequency and story words. For strategies to preteach the high-frequency words, see Chapter 9.

**WORD HUNT**   Ask students to hunt for words in books and other reading materials that contain the phonogram *–at.* Have them write each word that they find on an index card. After sharing the words and pointing out the phonograms in them, have students post their cards on a classroom bulletin board or word wall.

**OBSERVE AND ASSESS**

*As students complete the Apply activities, use these questions to assess their progress.*

| Questions for Observation | Benchmarks |
| --- | --- |
| *(Point to the phonogram –at.)* What are the sounds for these letters? | Student can read short-vowel phonograms. |
| *(Point to a word with the phonogram –at.)* Can you blend the sounds into a word? | Student can blend onset and rime. |

## The Next Step

To help students to retain what they learn about different phonograms and to read words by analogy, introduce the following study method—a method based on the "self-talk" model developed by Irene Gaskins and her colleagues (1997). Pronounce, for example, the word *chat*. Ask: *How many sounds do you hear in* chat? (three) Ask: *What sounds do you hear?* (/ch/, /a/, /t/) Print the word *chat* on the board. Ask: *How many letters do you see in* chat? (four) Ask: *Does* chat *have the same number of letters as sounds?* (No, there are three sounds and four letters.) Ask: *What letters go with what sounds?* (The letters *ch* make one sound, the letter *a* makes one sound, and the letter *t* makes one sound.) Ask: *In the word* chat, *do you see a word family?* (yes, . . . –at) Ask: *What is the vowel sound in* chat? (/a/ . . . a vowel followed by a consonant is usually short) Ask: *Can you find a word on the bulletin board (or word wall) that has the same vowel sound as in* chat? Now add the word *chat* to the bulletin board (or word wall).

8.61

FOLLOW-UP STRATEGY . . .

See the Word Work activities in this chapter.

**FOLLOW-UP STRATEGY FOR**

## Phonograms

### Benchmark

• ability to recognize and distin-guish phonograms in words

### Grade Level

• Kindergarten – Grade 2 and Intervention

### Prerequisites

• Phonograms with Short-Vowel Patterns
• introduced phonic elements: all single consonants and short vowels; consonant digraphs

### Grouping

• whole class
• small group or pairs
• individual

### Materials

• Word Study Notebooks

# WORD WORK: SHORT-VOWEL PHONOGRAM WRITING SORT

GRADE LEVEL K-2 GRADE LEVEL

This writing sort reinforces the *–ap* and *–op* phonograms. It is used after students have already been explicitly taught the individual sound/spelling correspondences. The same strategy can be used to reinforce other short-vowel phonograms.

## Phonemic Warm-Up

Divide students into two groups: *–ap* and *–op.* Have each group say their word-family aloud. Then tell the groups to listen, as you say aloud the following words in random order: *top, chop, lap, stop, tap, trap, shop, crop, mop, cap, zap.* Ask students to stand up when they hear a word that ends like their word family.

## Sort the Words

Ask students to fold a piece of paper in half lengthwise. Print the key words *cap* and *top* on the board. On their paper, have students write one key word at the top of each column. Say each of the following words aloud and have students write them under the appropriate key word: *clap, tap, hop, lap, stop, chop, map, trap, shop, drop.* When students have finished the sort, have them read aloud what they wrote in each column. Then have them proofread their work and copy the sort in their Word Study Notebooks.

## Try It This Way!

Using the same phonograms, do a word-building activity. Print the phonograms *–ap* and *–op* on index cards. Tell students to add letters to the beginning of the word families to make words. Have them copy the words in their Word Study Notebooks.

### Benchmark

• ability to build words with long-
  vowel phonograms

### Grade Level

• Grades 1 – 2 and Intervention

### Prerequisites

• Phonograms with
  Short-Vowel Patterns
• introduced phonic elements: all
  single consonants, short vowels,
  consonant digraphs, CVCe long-
  vowel pattern; vowel digraphs

### Grouping

• whole class
• small group or pairs

### Materials

• letter cards (one set per
  student)
• phonogram cards –ide, –ice
• Word Study Notebooks

# WORD WORK: LONG-VOWEL PHONOGRAM WORD BUILDING

GRADE LEVEL 1-2 GRADE LEVEL

8.63

This strategy reinforces recognition of words with the long-vowel phonograms *–ice, –ide,* and *–ine.* It is used after students have already been explicitly taught the sound/spellings of the consonants and the *i*-consonant-*e* spelling pattern. The same strategy can be used to reinforce other long-vowel phonograms.

## Phonemic Warm-Up

Have students change the rime *–ide* to *–ice* to create new words. Use the following words: ride *(rice),* slide *(slice),* pride *(price).*

## Build Words

Distribute sets of letter cards to each student. Hold up the phonogram card *–ide* and say: *Choose a letter card that can be added to the beginning of* –ide *to make the word* wide. Have a volunteer come to the front of the classroom and place the *w* card before the phonogram and blend the onset and rime to say the whole word. Repeat the process with the following word families in random order: *ride, slide, pride, glide, side; nice, twice, slice, price, spice.* Have students record the words they make in their Word Study Notebooks.

## Try It This Way!

Repeat this activity using long-vowel phonograms listed on the "'Rhyming' Phonogram Word List" found on page 3.23.

CHAPTER

9

# High-Frequency Words

what?
why?
when?
how?

# what?

*High-Frequency Words*

**9.2**

**HIGH-FREQUENCY WORDS**
a small number of words, both regular and irregular, that appear frequently in print

Only 100 words account for approximately 50 percent of the words in English print (Fry, Fountoukidis, and Polk 1985). These *high-frequency words* are crucial for comprehension, yet are often quite abstract. They include words such as *the, of, to, was, for, at, if,* and *will.* Because it is to a reader's advantage to recognize these high-frequency words on sight, they are sometimes referred to as *sight words.* The Dolch Basic Sight Vocabulary (Dolch 1955) and Instant Words (Fry 1993) are two lists of words that appear most frequently in primary reading texts.

It makes sense that early reading instruction should focus on the words that appear most frequently in print. High-frequency words that follow regular, predictable spelling patterns can be explicitly taught as whole words to beginning readers before they have learned all of the individual letter/sound correspondences. This enables students to begin to practice reading with decodable text containing words that conform to previously introduced letter/sound correspondences, as well as previously introduced high-frequency words and words necessary for story understanding.

**REGULAR WORDS**

words that follow the most common sound/spelling patterns of English and are easily decoded by sounding out

**IRREGULAR WORDS**

words with spelling patterns that do not follow the most common sound/spellings of English and are not readily decoded by sounding out

**SIGHT WORDS**

a term sometimes used to refer to high-frequency words

Section II: Word Structure
"Phonic Elements (Sound/Spelling Categories)," p. 3.13
"Sound/Spelling Percentages," p. 3.19

Many high-frequency words are completely *regular*, spelled with letters and letter patterns that represent their most common sounds. Examples of regular words include *and, that, with, be, not, can,* and *she.* Many of the words that appear most often in English print, however, are *irregular*, containing unique or infrequent letter/sound correspondences. Even the simplest text is filled with words such as *of, you, was, what, said, do,* and *some,* which act as "connecting threads" yet defy predictable phonetic rules. Although students may use these words in their everyday speech, they would expect them to be spelled differently. For example, based on the way the words are pronounced, *of* should be spelled *uv,* and *was* should be spelled *wuz.*

## Instant Words

Instant Words (Fry 1993) are the most common words in English, ranked in frequency order. For fluent reading, students should be able to recognize these words instantly, on sight. It is recommended that students know all of the 300 words by the end of second grade to the beginning of third grade. The sequence of introduction depends on the words that appear most frequently in the literature being used in the classroom. The first 25 Instant Words make up about one-third of all reading material. The first 100 Instant Words make up about one-half, and the first 300 make up 65 percent of all printed text.

9.4

## THE FIRST HUNDRED INSTANT WORDS

| Column 1 Words 1–25 | Column 2 Words 26–50 | Column 3 Words 51–75 | Column 4 Words 76–100 |
| --- | --- | --- | --- |
| the | or | will | number |
| of | one | up | no |
| and | had | other | way |
| a | by | about | could |
| to | words | out | people |
| in | but | many | my |
| is | not | then | than |
| you | what | them | first |
| that | all | these | water |
| it | were | so | been |
| he | we | some | called |
| was | when | her | who |
| for | your | would | oil |
| on | can | make | sit |
| are | said | like | now |
| as | there | him | find |
| with | use | into | long |
| his | an | time | down |
| they | each | has | day |
| I | which | look | did |
| at | she | two | get |
| be | do | more | come |
| this | how | write | made |
| have | their | go | may |
| from | if | see | part |

SOURCE

From Dr. Edward Fry's *1000 Instant Words.* Copyright © Teacher Created Materials, Westminster, CA, 800-557-6241.

# THE SECOND HUNDRED INSTANT WORDS

| Column 5<br>Words 101–125 | Column 6<br>Words 126–150 | Column 7<br>Words 151–175 | Column 8<br>Words 176–200 |
| --- | --- | --- | --- |
| over | say | set | try |
| new | great | put | kind |
| sound | where | end | hand |
| take | help | does | picture |
| only | through | another | again |
| little | much | well | change |
| work | before | large | off |
| know | line | must | play |
| place | right | big | spell |
| years | too | even | air |
| live | means | such | away |
| me | old | because | animals |
| back | any | turned | house |
| give | same | here | point |
| most | tell | why | page |
| very | boy | asked | letters |
| after | following | went | mother |
| things | came | men | answer |
| our | want | read | found |
| just | show | need | study |
| name | also | land | still |
| good | around | different | learn |
| sentence | form | home | should |
| man | three | us | American |
| think | small | move | world |

SOURCE

From Dr. Edward Fry's *1000 Instant Words.* Copyright © Teacher Created Materials, Westminster, CA, 800-557-6241.

9.6

# THE THIRD HUNDRED INSTANT WORDS

| Column 9<br>Words 201–225 | Column 10<br>Words 226–250 | Column 11<br>Words 251–275 | Column 12<br>Words 276–300 |
|---|---|---|---|
| high | saw | important | miss |
| ever | left | until | idea |
| near | don't | children | enough |
| add | few | side | eat |
| food | while | feet | face |
| between | along | car | watch |
| own | might | miles | far |
| below | close | night | Indians |
| country | something | walked | really |
| plants | seemed | white | almost |
| last | next | sea | let |
| school | hard | began | above |
| father | open | grow | girl |
| keep | example | took | sometimes |
| trees | beginning | river | mountains |
| never | life | four | cut |
| started | always | carry | young |
| city | those | state | talk |
| earth | both | once | soon |
| eyes | paper | book | list |
| light | together | hear | song |
| thought | got | stop | being |
| head | group | without | leave |
| under | often | second | family |
| story | run | later | it's |

SOURCE

From Dr. Edward Fry's *1000 Instant Words.* Copyright © Teacher Created Materials, Westminster, CA, 800-557-6241.

Connect to Theory

Regular words follow the most common sound/spelling patterns of English and are easily decoded by sounding out, whereas irregular words contain spelling patterns that do not follow the most common sound/spellings of English and are not readily decoded by sounding out. Use the first 25 Instant Words to answer the following questions: Which words are considered regular? Which words are considered irregular? Explain how you made each decision.

*(See Appendix for answer.)*

## High-Frequency Word Instruction

Beginning with Kindergarten, early reading instruction should include the systematic study, practice, and review of high-frequency words. When introducing words that are irregular, teachers should point out the specific irregularities while focusing student attention on all of the letters that make up the word. This is to keep students in the habit of visually scanning all of the letters, so that they can come up with an approximate pronunciation.

According to Carnine, Silbert, and Kameenui (1997) there are two factors that determine the difficulty of an irregular word. The first factor is the difference between how the word is sounded out and how it is actually pronounced. The greater the number of letters that stray from their most common sounds, the more difficult the irregular word. For that reason, the word *through* will require more practice than the word

**9.8**

*want.* The second factor that determines an irregular word's relative difficulty is familiarity. The more familiar a word is to students, the easier it will be for them to learn to read on sight.

One procedure (Carnine, Silbert, and Kameenui 1997) for introducing high-frequency irregular words involves having the teacher tell students how the irregular word is pronounced, then sounding it out by saying the most common sound for each letter, and saying the whole word again correctly. The teacher then tests the students, asking them to say the word, sound it out, and then say the word again the way it is actually pronounced.

## Guidelines for Teaching High-Frequency Words

- Select the words that are most useful: those that appear frequently in grade-appropriate literature and informational text. If using a basal reader, select the words that will appear in upcoming passages.

- Limit the number of words introduced at one time. In Kindergarten, it may be as few as one or two per week. This number will increase as students begin learning phonics. Generally at the start of first grade, three words per week may be the limit; then five to seven new words per week will be appropriate through second grade.

- Avoid confusion by separating the introduction of similar high-frequency words such as *was* and *saw; were* and *where;* or *them, they,* and *there.* The goal is for students to master a word weeks before they encounter a similar and potentially confusing new word.

- Introduce related irregular words together or one after the other. Examples include *walk, talk, chalk; give, live; would, could, should; other, mother, brother.*

- Teach high-frequency irregular words prior to reading connected text.

- If all the sound/spellings in a high-frequency regular word have not yet been introduced, introduce the high-frequency word prior to reading connected text.

- Provide a cumulative review of important high-frequency words as part of daily reading instruction (2 to 3 minutes).

## Spell-Out Strategy

A spell-out strategy is useful for words that are highly frequent but so irregular that sounding them out will not work well—words such as *was, are,* and *one.* When readers encounter an irregular word such as *was,* they can't just sound it out using the most common sound/spellings—"wwwăăăsss"— and blend the sounds into a recognizable word. Generally, the spell-out method is used to directly teach high-frequency irregular words *prior to students encountering them in texts.* With this method, students (1) see and hear the word, (2) say the word, (3) spell it letter by letter, and (4) repeat the word.

By spelling out a word when it is introduced, students have to attend to all of its letters. They learn the word through a combination of pattern knowledge and memorization. It's important to note that even though these words are not completely regular, readers still store them by attending to the sound/symbol pattern. As is the case in decoding regular words, students scan through a word, connecting all its sounds (expected and unexpected) to its letters or letter combinations, and then consolidate the recognition of the word by reading it successfully several times—preferably in texts (Gough and Walsh 1991; Treiman and Baron 1981; Lovett 1987).

## Sounding Out with Contextual Analysis

Sounding out with contextual analysis is an effective strategy for figuring out high-frequency words *as they are encountered in text*. In this approach, students use phonics and structural cues, combined with context, to arrive at the correct pronunciation of an unfamiliar word. The unfamiliar word may have irregular spelling patterns or may simply contain sound/spellings that have not yet been taught. By itself, contextual analysis has limited utility as a word-recognition strategy; but after decoding a word, students can use context to verify the accuracy and fit of a word in a sentence. For example, when students initially encounter the word *put* they may mispronounce it as *putt*. However, by using the context of the sentence, "I *putt . . . put* the box on the table," they will arrive at the correct word. This strategy is useful because approximately 50 percent of English words are completely regular, and another 37 percent are off by only one letter/sound correspondence (Hanna, Hodges, Hanna, and Rudorf 1966). It works especially well with words such as *have, do,* or *what.* It also works for words that might be ambiguous or have two pronunciations: the present tense of *read* or the past tense of *read.*

## Word Banks and Word Walls

Individual word banks, personal collections of words, are an excellent way for students to store their own high-frequency words. Students can keep their known words in small file boxes or baggies and use them for frequent partner review.

Word walls are a valuable resource that students can use when reading and writing high-frequency words. The word wall is a particularly useful technique for teaching high-frequency irregular words. The words selected should be words students will need often in their reading and writing. Cunningham and Allington (1999) found that most children learn to read and spell almost all of the words on a word wall when some basic guidelines are followed.

See also . . .

**Section VI: Vocabulary Development**
**"External Context Clues," p. 15.24**

9.10

See also . . .

**Section V: Spelling**
**"Word Banks," p. 13.7**

## Basic Guidelines for Using Word Walls

- Teachers should select words that students will need often in their reading and writing, and words that are often confused.

- Words, grouped according to their first letter or other letter patterns, should be added gradually (five per week) and stay in the same spot for the entire year.

- As words are added to the wall, students should discuss their meanings.

- Words should be written in large black letters on colored paper.

- Words that are easily confused should be written on different-colored paper.

- Students should have daily practice finding, writing, and chanting the words.

| A | B | C | D | E | F | G | H | I |
|---|---|---|---|---|---|---|---|---|
| and | be | can | do | each | for | go | he | in |
| are | by | could | down | end | from | give | his | is |
| as | but | called | day | ever | first | good | have | it |

| J | K | L | M | N | O | P | Q | R |
|---|---|---|---|---|---|---|---|---|
| just | know | like | many | not | of | people | | right |
| | kind | look | make | number | on | part | | read |
| | keep | long | more | no | or | place | | run |

| S | T | U | V | W | X | Y | Z |
|---|---|---|---|---|---|---|---|
| said | the | use | very | was | | you | zoo |
| she | to | up | | with | | your | |
| so | that | us | | words | | years | |

# why? *High-Frequency Words*

In order to read and write fluently students must learn to instantly recognize and automatically spell the words that are used most frequently in print. Adding to the challenge is the fact that many of these story-critical words are irregular, with unusual sound/spelling relationships. According to Edward Fry (1997), it makes sense to teach the most common words because they come up all the time.

High-frequency irregular words should be taught systematically and explicitly. Students do not learn irregular words as easily or as quickly as they learn regular words (Cunningham 1995). In addition, many high-frequency words are easily confused. For example, early readers often confuse *of, for, off,* and *from.* They also confuse reversible pairs such as *was/saw* and words starting with *th* and *w* that contain irregular patterns—*there, their, that, then, were, where, what, when.*

**Research Findings...**

*When readers encounter a meaningful word that they have read many times before . . . the word's meaning and phonological image will also be evoked with near instantaneity.*

—ADAMS, 1990

*Only 13 words* (a, and, for, he, is, in, it, of, that, the, to, was, you) *account for more than 25 percent of the words in print.*

—JOHNS, 1980

*Only 100 words account for approximately 50 percent of the words in English print.*

—FRY, FOUNTOUKIDIS & POLK, 1985

*The quick and automatic recognition of the most common words appearing in text is necessary for fluent reading.*

—BLEVINS, 1998

**9.13**

**Suggested Reading . . .**

*Direct Instruction Reading, 3rd Edition* (1997) by Douglas W. Carnine, Jerry Silbert & Edward J. Kameenui. Upper Saddle River, NJ: Prentice-Hall.

*1000 Instant Words* (1994) by Edward Fry. Westminster, CA: Teacher Created Materials.

*Teaching and Assessing Phonics: A Guide for Teachers* (1996) by Jeanne S. Chall & Helen M. Popp. Cambridge, MA: Educators Publishing Service.

*What Reading Research Tells Us About Children with Diverse Learning Needs: Bases and Basics* (1998) edited by Deborah C. Simmons & Edward J. Kameenui. Mahwah, NJ: Erlbaum.

**9.14**

Instructional Scope
and Sequence

## When to Teach

Instruction in high-frequency words should begin as soon as students have grasped the concept of a word and can recognize and name the letters of the alphabet. In some basal programs high-frequency word instruction begins in Kindergarten. Generally, it is recommended that irregular words not be introduced until students can sound out some basic CVC words. The pace of introduction ranges from one new high-frequency word every four to six lessons initially, increasing to one word every three lessons, then to about three to seven words per week in first and second grade.

Researchers and practitioners have given varied recommendations for the total number of high-frequency words to be taught at each grade. The numbers range from about 25 to 50 words in Kindergarten, 50 to 100 by the end of first grade, and 300 words by the end of second to the beginning of third grade. Students should know most of the words in each set of 100 Instant Words before they are taught the next set of 100 words.

| Instructional Scope and Sequence | |
| --- | --- |
| **Kindergarten** | 25–50 high-frequency words (See also "Instant Words," columns 1–2) |
| **Grade 1** | 51–100 high-frequency words (See also "Instant Words," columns 3–4) |
| **Grade 2** | 101–300 high-frequency words (See also "Instant Words," columns 5–12) |

| When | Mid- to late Grade 1 and above |
| --- | --- |
| Who | All students who are not reading grade-level text with relative ease |
| Assessment Tool | Instant Word List |
| Intervene if . . . | Students cannot rapidly read the high-frequency words appropriate to their grade level. |
| How | Small-group practice sessions with more frequent repetition; spell-out strategy and sounding out with contextual analysis, supported by word walls |

**9.15**

*1000 Instant Words* (1994) by Edward Fry. Westminster, CA: Teacher Created Materials.

## When to Assess and Intervene

Students can be assessed on high-frequency word recognition as soon as they have been taught and can read a number of high-frequency words. Generally this assessment will start in first grade. The purpose of assessment is to monitor progress and intervene as soon as possible. The focus of assessment should be on high-frequency words that cannot be easily sounded out.

**Upper-Grade Intervention**   Generally upper-grade students will be taught high-frequency irregular words as they relate to the literature being read in the classroom, but the upper-grade student who is not reading proficiently will need an intensive program of decoding instruction, coupled with high-frequency irregular word instruction. In order to accelerate this instruction, more words per week will need to be taught.

**Assessment of High-Frequency Words**   Have students read aloud from a high-frequency word list such as Instant Words or the Dolch Basic Sight Vocabulary. Keep track of their errors. Fry (1997) suggests that for a quick assessment, students can be asked to read only every tenth word in the columns of "Instant Words."

# High-Frequency Words

**TEACHING STRATEGY FOR**

## High-Frequency Irregular Words

### Benchmark

• ability to read and write high-frequency irregular words

### Grade Level

• Kindergarten – Grade 3 and Intervention

### Prerequisites

• Introducing Single Consonants (Chapter 8: Phonics)
• Introducing Short Vowels (Chapter 8: Phonics)
• Introducing Consonant Digraphs (Chapter 8: Phonics)

### Grouping

• whole class
• small group or pairs

### Materials

• cereal box
• word cards *of, the, you*
• decodable text

---

**INTRODUCING HIGH-FREQUENCY IRREGULAR WORDS** | GRADE LEVEL **K-3**

This generic teaching strategy can be used the first few times high-frequency irregular words are introduced. It involves modeling the correct pronunciation of a word and then contrasting it with the way a word would sound if each letter had its most common sound (Carnine et al. 1997).

## Teach/Model

Display the card with the word *of* and hold up a cereal box as you say: *I have a box of cereal.* Say the sentence again, pointing to the word card when you read the word *of.* Then tell students that you are going to try to sound out the word using the sound the letter *o* usually stands for (/o/ in *mom*) and the sound for *f* (/f/). Pronounce the word as it would be regularly sounded out—"ŏŏŏfff"—as you point to each letter. Then ask students to repeat this pronunciation. Now pronounce *of* correctly, explaining to students that many words sound differently from the way they are spelled. Have students correctly pronounce *of.*

Show students a card with the word *the* and tell them the word as you point to each letter using the voiced *th* digraph and the short-*e* sound in *pet*—"THTHĕĕĕ." Point to the word and say: *This is a funny word. The word is* the. *What is the word?* Ask students to listen as you sound out the word again. Then explain: *That's how we sound out the word. But this is the way we say it:* the. Have students repeat the correct pronunciation of the word. Call on volunteers to sound it out letter by letter, and then pronounce the word. Repeat the procedure with the word *was,* using the sounds /w/, /a/, and /s/.

## Practice

Help students form pairs and distribute cards with the newly introduced high-frequency irregular words. Have partners take turns displaying the words for each other and reading them by sounding out and then correcting pronunciation. Monitor the pairs as they work. Add the words to the word wall and have students clap and chant the spelling of each word.

## Apply

**DECODABLE TEXT**    Provide students with connected reading practice. Choose text selections in which most of the words are wholly decodable and the majority of the remaining words are previously taught high-frequency and story words.

**DICTATION AND SPELLING**    Dictate the following words in random order: *the, of, you.* Then print the words on the board and have students correct their work. Dictate the following sentence: *You sat on the mat.* Print the sentence on the board, and help students correct their work.

**OBSERVE AND ASSESS**

*As students complete the Apply activities, use these questions to assess their progress.*

| Questions for Observation | Benchmarks |
| --- | --- |
| Can you read this word? | Student can read a high-frequency irregular word. |
| Can you spell these words? | Student can spell high-frequency irregular words. |
| Can you write this sentence? | Student can spell high-frequency regular and irregular words. |

**TEACHING STRATEGY FOR**

## High-Frequency Irregular Words

### Benchmark

- ability to read and write high-frequency irregular words

### Grade Level

- Kindergarten – Grade 3 and Intervention

### Prerequisites

- Introducing Single Consonants (Chapter 8: Phonics)
- Introducing Short Vowels (Chapter 8: Phonics)
- Introducing High-Frequency Irregular Words

### Grouping

- whole class
- small group or pairs

### Materials

- word cards *they, was, one, were, said, about, many, some, would, could, should*
- decodable text

# SPELL-OUT STRATEGY

This generic teaching strategy is for high-frequency irregular words, but it can be used with high-frequency regular words before the sound/spellings have been taught. With this method, students see and hear the word, say the word, spell it letter by letter, and repeat the word. The lesson can be adapted by choosing high-frequency irregular words that appear in upcoming text selections and by increasing the number of words being taught to five.

## Prep Time

On large cards print the words to be reviewed: *they, was, one, were, said, about, many, some,* and the new words to be taught: *would, could, should.*

## Warm Up

Using the word cards, review previously introduced high-frequency irregular words: *they, was, one, were, said, about, many, some.* Stand in front of the students and show them the words one by one in random order. Have students read the words rapidly, and call on volunteers to use each word in a sentence.

**Intervention Strategy**

If students have difficulty automatically recognizing any of the words, spell out the word and discuss its sounds. Direct attention to the sound/spellings that are regular as well as those that aren't; for example, in the word *was*, the *w* has a regular sound but the *a* and *s* are not pronounced in the most common way. The letter *a* is pronounced /u/ as in *up*, and the *s* says /z/, not /s/.

## Teach/Model

Tell students that you are going to show them a way to remember and read some new words that can't easily be sounded out. Hold up the word card *would*. Say: *This word is* would. Then use the word in a sentence: *I would like to play ball.* Print the sentence on the board and underline the word *would* as you reread the sentence. Point out the sounds and the spelling patterns: the letter *w* has a /w/ sound, and *ould* is always pronounced "o͝od." Have students spell the word aloud as you point to each letter: *w-o-u-l-d.* Then ask: *What is the word?* (would) Have students write the word in the air. Then have them spell the word again and write it on a piece of paper.

Tell students that there are other words with the *ould* pattern. Then repeat the procedure with the words *could* and *should.* Have students sound out the sound/spellings that are regular in each of these words: /k/*c*, /sh/*sh*. Then add all of the words to the word wall.

## Practice

Have students form pairs. Distribute word cards with the previously taught and the newly introduced high-frequency irregular words. Have partners take turns displaying the words for each other and reading them, using the spell-out strategy. Monitor the pairs as they work.

**Intervention
Strategy**

**If students have difficulty
with the dictation, try segmenting decodable words
sound by sound and refer
students to the word wall for
the irregular words, remind-
ing them of irregular sound/
spelling patterns.**

9.20

## Apply

**DECODABLE TEXT**   Provide students with connected reading practice. Choose text selections in which most of the words
are wholly decodable and the majority of the remaining words
are previously taught high-frequency and story words.

**DICTATION AND SPELLING**   Dictate the following words
in random order: *was, were, some, would, could, should.* Then
print the words on the board and have students correct their
work. Dictate the following sentence: *Some kids could run
fast.* Print the sentence on the board, and help students to
correct their work.

---

**OBSERVE AND ASSESS**

*As students complete the Apply
activities, use these questions to
assess their progress.*

| Questions for Observation | Benchmarks |
|---|---|
| Can you read this word? | Student can read a high-frequency irregular word. |
| Can you spell these words? | Student can spell high-frequency irregular words. |
| Can you write this sentence? | Student can spell high-frequency regular and irregular words. |

# High-Frequency Irregular Words

### Benchmarks

- ability to instantly recognize high-frequency irregular words
- ability to write high-frequency irregular words

### Grade Level

- Grade 1 and above

### Prerequisite

- Spell-Out Strategy

### Grouping

- whole class
- small group

### Materials

- black marker
- colored construction paper

Section II: Word Structure
"What Is a Phonogram?" p. 3.22

## WORD WALLS

9.21

The word wall needs to be in a location that is visible to all students, so students may use it freely. An average of four to five words should be added each week, although some classes will be able to handle more. As a memory aid you can include a sentence or picture as a clue to a word's sound and/or meaning. Words in the same word family can be written on the same-color paper.

**ELL** INTERVENTION STRATEGY . . .
It is important that the meanings of the words are made clear to students before the words are added to the word wall.

For struggling readers, simply looking at words on a word wall will not be enough to remember the words. They will need practice finding words on the wall, chanting the spellings, and writing the words.

## Prep Time

Create a word wall. Use a black marker to print the words on colored construction paper.

## Warm Up

Have students print the numbers 1 through 5 on a sheet of paper. Say aloud five words from the word wall and use each one in a sentence. Ask volunteers to find and point to the words on the wall. Then have the entire group clap and chant the spelling of each word before writing it. When students have finished, point to the words and spell each one aloud as students correct their work.

**Chapter 13: Spelling Instruction**

9.22

Intervention
Strategy

**Add words to the word wall that are commonly misspelled, including homophones. Also add words to the word wall from word hunts and from students' Word Study Notebooks.**

## Practice Words

Use the word wall to practice selected words at least once daily. Guessing games are a good way to engage students' interest. Ask them to say, spell out, and write words that match certain clues: for example, *Number one begins with* s *and rhymes with* bed. (said) You can make the game more challenging by having students try to guess each word before you give them all of the clues.

## Try It This Way!

Make up sentences using only words from the word wall. Dictate the sentences. Tell students to listen as you say the whole sentence. Then repeat the sentence slowly, one word at a time. Students should have ample time to find each of the dictated words on the word wall and to write the whole sentence. Students may enjoy making up their own word wall sentences and dictating them to their classmates.

# High-Frequency Irregular Words

## Benchmark

- ability to use sounding out supported by context to recognize an unfamiliar word

## Grade Level

- Grade 2 and above

## Prerequisites

- all Grades 1 and 2 phonic elements (see p. 8.8)
- Spell-Out Strategy

## Grouping

- whole class
- small group or pairs

## Materials

- "When I Come to a Word I Don't Know" (see Appendix)
- word cards *enough, busy, young, second, every, answer*
- grade-appropriate passages that students have not read previously
- Word Study Notebooks

## SOUNDING OUT WITH CONTEXTUAL ANALYSIS

This generic teaching strategy is for high-frequency irregular words, but it can be used with high-frequency regular words whose sound/spellings have not been taught. It shows students how to make use of decoding knowledge and context clues. This lesson focuses on the high-frequency irregular words *answer, away, enough, young, second, every.*

### Warm Up

Print the sentence *I cut the paper* on the board and ask a volunteer to read it aloud. Then add the phrase *and put it on the desk,* and ask another student to read the expanded sentence aloud. Underline the words *cut* and *put.* Have students sound out *cut* and then sound out *put.* Discuss the similarities and differences between these two words, focusing on the middle vowel sound. Ask how they know to say *put.* Discuss how they used the sounds of the letters and the other words in the sentence to help them figure out the word was /p/ /o͝o/ /t/ and not /p/ /ŭ/ /t/.

### Teach/Model

Print the following sentence on the board: *My teacher asked if I knew the answer.* Cover up the sentence. Then reveal each word one by one, from left to right, asking students to sound out each word. Point to the word *answer.* Say: *Some of you may already know this word, but I don't want you to say it. I am going to show you a way you could figure it out while you were reading if you didn't recognize it.* Use the following Think Aloud procedure to model the strategy.

## Think Aloud Strategy

**An effective strategy is to model the analysis process by "thinking aloud" for students. This is a way to demonstrate the internal thought processes that go on automatically in most good readers.**

9.24

**THINK ALOUD**    *First, let's try to sound it out. This is the first step. Let's use the most common sounds we know: /a/ /n/ /s/ /w/ /ûr/. Now let's blend the sounds together. That doesn't sound right. Let's look for little words inside the big word. I see a word I know:* an. *So, the beginning of the word is* an. *Now let me say the whole sentence and think about the meaning of the other words. "My teacher asked if I knew the* (point to the word answer)." *Do the other words give us a clue to what this word is? That's the last step in figuring out a new word that's hard to sound out.*

Encourage students to say *answer* with the correct pronunciation. Then print the sentence on the board and have them read it silently and ask themselves, "Does the word make sense in this sentence?" Say the sentence again and model sounding out the regular words *(teacher, if, I)* and rapidly reading the high-frequency words students have been previously taught *(my, asked, knew, the).* Ask students which words in the sentence helped them figure out *answer.* Finally, show the word *answer* on a word card, and have students read the word, using the spell-out strategy, and then have them write it again in a new sentence.

**Appendix**

*"When I Come to a Word I Don't Know"*

---

### When I Come to a Word I Don't Know

❶ Try to sound out the word.

❷ Look for letter patterns you know.
Try to sound out the word.

❸ Read the whole sentence. Ask yourself,
"Does the word sound right and make sense?"

Make sure students are famil-
iar with the meanings of all
the words used in the passage
for contextual analysis practice. The lesson should focus
on using context to recognize
a word from students' oral
vocabularies.

**See also...**

Section V: Spelling
"Word Study Notebooks," p. 13.8

## Practice

Display the chart "When I Come to a Word I Don't Know."
Tell students that this chart lists the steps they followed to figure out the word *answer*. Have them work in pairs using these
steps to figure out some other high-frequency irregular words
they may know orally but may not have seen in print. The
following sentences contain high-frequency irregular words.

- Max had *enough* work to keep him *busy* all day.

- The *young* birds could not fly.

- Our team won *second* place!

- She eats an apple *every* day.

Display the word cards and have students read each one using
the spell-out strategy. Ask students to write each word after
they read it and use it in a new sentence.

## Apply

Have students select a short passage from grade-level text that
they have not previously read. Ask them to read the passage
silently and then aloud to a partner. Have them choose two
unfamiliar words and explain to their partner how they figured
out the words. Monitor pairs, making sure that they provide
specific information about the phonic and context clues that
they used. Have students add the new words to their Word
Study Notebooks. Encourage them to write sentences using
the new words.

**OBSERVE AND ASSESS**

*As students complete the Apply activities, use these questions to assess their progress.*

| Questions for Observation | Benchmarks |
|---|---|
| What words did you figure out? | Student can correctly pronounce irregular words by sounding out supported by context. |
| Can you write the words and use them correctly in a sentence? | Student can spell irregular words and use them accurately in a sentence. |

## Try It This Way!

Contextual analysis is also useful when students come across word pairs that have the same spelling but different pronunciations. Using context can confirm correct pronunciation when there is some ambiguity; for example, *live* can be pronounced with either a long- or short-*i* sound, depending on whether it is being used as an adjective or a verb.

Print a few words with varying pronunciations on the board such as *read, tear, close, use, lead, live.* Ask volunteers to pronounce the words. Then ask if students know a different way to say them. Point out that the correct pronunciation and meaning of these words can only be determined through context. Have students write original sentences with the words. Ask them to exchange sentences with a partner, read the partner's sentence aloud, and tell how meaning helped them choose the correct pronunciation.

CHAPTER

10

# Multisyllabic Words

what?
why?
when?
how?

# what? *Multisyllabic Words*

**10.2**

*"Facility with big words is essential for students as they read, write, and learn in all areas of school and life. Many big words occur infrequently, but when they do occur they carry a lot of the meaning and content of what is being read."*

—CUNNINGHAM, 1998

**Section II: Word Structure**
**"What Is a Syllable?" p. 3.20**

A *syllable* is a unit of pronunciation containing a single vowel sound. Multisyllabic words are strings of syllables, which themselves are made up of onsets and rimes. Students who can read one-syllable words often find reading multisyllabic words a daunting task (Just and Carpenter 1987; Samuels, LaBerge, and Bremer 1978). Yet for students in second grade and beyond, knowing how to decode unfamiliar multisyllabic words is essential because most of the new words they will encounter in print are "big" words.

Research shows that when good readers encounter a long, unfamiliar word, they assign the word a pronunciation by chunking letter patterns into manageable units (Adams 1990; Mewhort and Campbell 1981). In the Mature Alphabetic stage, the units can be recurring phonograms *(–ell, –ack, –ame)* or inflectional endings *(–s, –es, –ing, –ed)*. In the Orthographic stage, students begin to recognize larger units, drawing on their knowledge of which letters "pull together" in syllables *(dr)* and which letters "pull apart" into separate syllables *(dn)*. As Hall and Moats (1999) explain, "Once a reader perceives a syllable, he begins searching the memory for a word that matches those letters, simultaneously beginning to sound out the letter combinations." As students' word attack skills mature in the Orthographic stage, they also begin to recognize morphemes—identifying compound words and isolating prefixes and suffixes.

Section IV: Decoding

"Align Decoding Instruction with the

Stages of Reading Development," p. IV.iv

While phonics instruction gives students the basic tools to decode most single-syllable words, explicit instruction in recognizing syllables and morpheme units will give students effective multiple strategies to read longer, unfamiliar words. Syllabication instruction is particularly useful for students who are able to decode single-syllable words but struggle with multisyllabic words. Generally, students' reading development progresses from reading words having one-to-one letter/sound correspondences, to reading patterns of multiple letters representing a sound or blended sounds, and ultimately to a growing awareness that the vowel pattern in particular, and its position in a word, affects pronunciation. Syllabication instruction supports this last important concept. In addition, recognizing affixes (e.g., *un–, re–, –ly, –er, –ful*) as units helps students with word recognition.

## Syllabication

*Syllabication* is the process of analyzing the patterns of vowels and consonants in a word to determine where the word breaks into syllables. This enables readers to identify *syllable types* and their vowel sounds, recognize consonant digraphs and blends, and thus arrive at an approximate pronunciation of the word.

In English, syllables have a great deal of regularity both in *type* of syllable and *pattern* of syllable breaks. These syllabication generalizations provide insight into the way many English words are structured. Although there are exceptions, learning some important generalizations will greatly support students' word attack skills. In an instructional-intervention study, Shefelbine (1990) found that when intermediate students were shown how to use vowels and affixes to pronounce multisyllabic words and then practiced decoding words after identifying these parts,

**SYLLABICATION**

(sĭ•lăb'•ə•kā•shən)

The separation of multisyllabic words into smaller units that can be decoded. The term is synonymous with *syllabification*.

## How to Mark Syllables

① **Label the vowels (all letters that make a vowel sound) with a *v*:**

```
picnic
 v   v
```

**10.4**

② **Label the consonant(s) between the vowels with a *c*:**

```
picnic
 vccv
```

③ **Mark the syllable division(s) with a slash.**

```
pic/nic
vc/cv
```

See also . . .

**Section V: Spelling**

**"Stages IV and V: Syllable Juncture Spelling and Derivational Constancy Spelling," p. 12.14**

the students later demonstrated significantly greater ability to pronounce multisyllabic words that had not been included in their practice.

In order to be able to read most multisyllabic words with ease, students must be able to

- quickly recognize as "chunks" the phonic patterns they have learned in single-syllable words

- understand the concept of a syllable and how to identify vowels and consonants

- recognize the various syllable types and their pronunciations

- know where the syllables divide—syllable patterns

- recognize common prefixes, suffixes, and base words

- possess the necessary "mental flexibility" to break a word and arrive at an approximate pronunciation, then use context to resolve ambiguity and confirm the word.

In second grade, students should be taught a few basic marking procedures to learn how to recognize syllable junctures (for example, VCCV, VCV, VCCCV) and their *division patterns* (VC/CV, V/CV or VC/V). These marking procedures will help make transparent the underlying word structure. When students have internalized how to read multisyllabic words, they will no longer need the marking system.

## TYPES OF SYLLABLES

| | |
|---|---|
| **closed** | A syllable in which a single vowel is followed by a consonant. The vowel sound is usually short. (cat, rabbit, picnic) |
| **open** | A syllable ending with a single vowel. The vowel sound is usually long. (me, veto) |
| ***r*-controlled** | A syllable in which the vowel(s) is followed by the single letter *r*. The vowel sound is neither long nor short. (chart, fern, pour, target, whisper) |
| **vowel team** | A syllable containing two letters that together make one vowel sound. The vowel sound can be long, short, or a diphthong. (plain, show, heavy, boy, cow, cloudy, boiling) |
| **vowel–silent *e*** | A syllable with a long vowel–consonant–silent *e* pattern. (shape, cube, slide, behave) |
| **consonant-*le*** | An unaccented final syllable containing a consonant plus –*le*. (apple, table) |

10.5

**See also . . .**

Section II: Word Structure
"What Are the Syllable Types and Patterns in Spanish?" p. 4.10

## Types of Syllables

English spelling consists of six basic syllable types, described in the chart above. These types represent most of the basic phonic concepts students learn in order to decode single-syllable words. Some students intuitively transfer their understanding of vowel patterns from single-syllable to multisyllable word reading; others, however, need more systematic instruction to generalize this learning to longer, more complex words.

- **closed and open**  These syllable types are the most common. They both contain one vowel letter for one vowel sound. In closed syllables, the single vowel letter is followed by a consonant. The vowel sound is usually short. Open syllables end with a single vowel letter. The vowel sound is usually long. Adding a single consonant letter can change open-syllable words to closed-syllable words: *me → men, hi → him, go → got.*

10.6

- **r-controlled**   An *r*-controlled syllable contains a vowel letter or letters followed by the letter *r*. To identify this syllable type, students train their eyes and ears to recognize that the *r* and the vowel(s) that precedes it remain together as a unit.

- **vowel team**   This syllable contains two letters that together make one vowel sound. The syllable may include a vowel digraph *(painted)*, variant vowel digraph *(looking)*, or diphthong *(cowboy)*. When students recognize this type of syllable, they will tend to keep the vowel team functioning as a unit within a syllable.

- **vowel–silent *e***   In this syllable type, the silent *e* serves as a signal, or marker, indicating that the preceding vowel sound is long.

- **consonant-*le***   When *le* appears at the end of a word and is preceded by a consonant, the consonant + *le* form the final syllable. Whether the preceding syllable is closed or open depends on the number of consonants that come before *le*. If there are two consonants, the first consonant is part of the preceding syllable and the vowel sound is usually short: *ăp•ple*. If there is only one consonant, that consonant plus *le* form the last syllable, and the preceding syllable usually has a long-vowel sound: *tā•ble*.

Connect to Theory

Use the "Types of Syllables" chart to identify the syllable types in the following words.

| | |
|---|---|
| scratch | harvest |
| sharp | seeker |
| tree | candle |
| beside | napkin |

*(See Appendix for answer.)*

## SYLLABLE PATTERNS

| Pattern | Division | Key Word | Definition |
|---------|----------|----------|------------|
| VCCV | VC/CV | rab • bit | If a word has two consonants in the middle, divide between them. When a consonant digraph stands between two vowels, divide the syllables before or after the digraph. |
| VCV | V/CV<br>VC/V | mu • sic<br>clos • et | If a word has one consonant between two vowels, divide the word before or after the consonant. The V/CV division is the most common. |
| VCCCV | VC/CCV | hun • dred | Words with three or more consonants in the medial position almost always contain a blend, and almost always have a closed first syllable. |
| VCCCCV | VC/CCCV | in • struct | Words with four or more consonants in the medial position almost always contain a blend, and almost always have a closed first syllable. |
| VV | V/V | ne • on | If a word has two vowels together that make two different sounds, divide between the two vowels. |

**Section II: Word Structure**
"Spanish Syllable Patterns," p. 4.11

## Syllable Patterns

Recognizing syllable patterns helps students know where to divide a multisyllabic word and how to pronounce it based on the resulting syllable types. The common syllable juncture patterns are VCCV, VCV, VCCCV, VCCCCV, and VV.

- **VCCV**  This syllable pattern is very common in English. It is found in words with two consonants between two vowel sounds. Since words with this pattern are usually divided between the two consonants, the first syllable will generally be closed (*hap•py* and *rab•bit*).

**10.8**

- **VCV** Words with the VCV pattern can break before or after the consonant. The most common division is V/CV as in *mu•sic,* which leaves the first syllable open. When the break comes after the consonant, as in *clos•et,* the first syllable is closed. Students should be instructed to first try to read words with this pattern in the most typical way—V/CV—and to use context clues to confirm the resulting pronunciation. If the word does not make sense in context, they should try dividing it VC/V and again use context to confirm the pronunciation.

- **VCCCV and VCCCCV** Words with three or more consonants together between vowels almost always contain a consonant blend that acts as a unit and generally break after the first consonant (*hun•dred, in•struct*). Sometimes the first syllable in these words ends in a blend or digraph. This causes the syllable break to occur after the second consonant: for example, as in *pump•kin* and *bash•ful.*

- **VV** Multisyllabic words may contain adjacent vowels that look like vowel digraphs—*ie, ea, ee, oa*—but have two distinct vowel sounds. These adjacent vowels that appear to be digraphs are seen in words like *cli•ent, cre•ate, re•en•try,* and *o•a•sis.* Other multisyllabic words may contain adjacent vowels that never appear as digraphs—*eo, ia, ua, ao*—each with its own sound. Examples of words with this second pattern include *ne•on, tri•al, gra•du•ate,* and *a•or•ta.* In both patterns, the syllable division is between the vowels, resulting in an open syllable usually followed by a closed syllable. Students benefit from instruction in these word patterns and should be encouraged to use context to confirm the words' pronunciations.

Connect
to Theory

The following word pairs look similar but have different vowel sounds. First, use the "Syllable Patterns" chart to divide the words into syllables. Then use the "Types of Syllables" chart to identify the syllable types. Think about how the syllable patterns and types affect the vowel sound.

10.9

| | |
|---|---|
| robin | robot |
| study | student |
| hoping | hopping |
| hero | herded |
| teacher | temper |
| ladle | ladder |
| monster | moment |
| volcano | volcanic |

*(See Appendix for answer.)*

**Section II: Word Structure**
"What Is a Morpheme?" p. 3.28

**Section VI: Vocabulary Development**
for more information about using
morphemic analysis

## Morphemes and Syllable Divisions

Syllable divisions often occur between units of meaning, also known as *morphemes.* Just as phonograms are useful chunks, morphemic units help students recognize and pronounce multisyllabic words. To decode big words, students need to recognize common affixes (prefixes and suffixes), use them as logical syllable breaks, and pronounce them as whole units. Beginning instruction in affixes should focus on common inflectional endings *(–es, –ed, –ing, –ly, –er)* and prefixes *(un–, re–, in–, dis–)* attached to known base words (for example, *un– + happy*). The goal of instruction is to show students how to use these affixes to pronounce and recognize multisyllabic words. Since these units affect word meaning, instruction in the use and recognition of morphemes generally improves both word recognition and vocabulary knowledge.

10.10

> FOR SPANISH-SPEAKING STUDENTS . . .
>
> ELL Because English and Spanish share many Latin and Greek word roots, students who are able readers in Spanish can tackle multisyllabic words in English with these roots. For these students "simple" compound words of Anglo-Saxon origin like *daytime* and *doghouse* present a greater challenge than words like *transportation* and *multinational.*

## Multisyllabic Word Instruction

Students must apply multiple strategies when decoding multi-syllabic words. The strategies include recognizing and isolating the affixes, identifying syllable boundaries and syllable types, and applying phonics knowledge to blend the syllables in sequence. After students have learned to read CVC*e* words with long vowels, they can be taught to separate compound words into two known words, to look for simple inflectional endings such as *–es* and *–ing,* and to divide VCCV words between the consonants (Chall and Popp 1996). Students should then be taught basic syllable types and a few more useful division patterns. The goal of such instruction is to help students connect a word in print with its oral counterpart.

Students can be taught a strategy for reading new multisyllabic words. First, they should cover any obvious affixes. They then should use their understanding of syllable division patterns and syllable types to try to pronounce the base word. Next, they should blend all the word parts in sequence. Usually the pronunciation will result in an approximation that is close enough to the real word to enable full recognition. If it is not, context along with the approximate pronunciation will often help students recognize the word.

*"The important consideration is whether or not the reader recognizes the written word—not where it is syllabicated."*

—BURMEISTER, 1975

## What I Know About Reading Big Words

**1** Look for familiar word parts—prefixes and suffixes—and cover them.

**2** In the base word, look for familiar vowel and consonant patterns.

**3** Divide the base word into syllables. Sound out and blend the syllables to say the base word.

**4** Uncover the word parts and blend the whole word.

**5** Use the text to check that the word makes sense in the sentence.

**See also . . .**

Section V: Spelling Instruction
"Word Hunts," "Word Banks," and "Word Study Notebooks," pp. 13.7–13.9

### Word Hunts, Word Banks, and Word Study Notebooks

Word hunts are a useful follow-up to syllabication instruction. Students can search for words fitting a particular pattern. In grades K–2, students can use word banks to house the words found during hunts and other word-study activities. In the upper grades, Word Study Notebooks serve a similar purpose.

**See also . . .**

Chapter 8: Phonics
"Blending Strategies," p. 8.12

### Blending Syllables

The basic blending strategy for multisyllabic words is to isolate each syllable or affix, sound out the syllables one at a time, and then blend them to read the entire word. During instruction, the teacher should cover all but the syllable that is being read, have students sound it out based on their knowledge of sound/spellings and syllable types, and then guide students in blending the syllables in sequence. If students have difficulty reading the syllables, they may need to focus on less complex single-syllable words with practice blending them sound by sound. In this case, syllabication instruction should be targeted to small groups of students.

**Section II: Word Structure**
"What Is a Syllable?" p. 3.20
"What Is a Morpheme?" p. 3.28

**10.12**

## Useful Syllable Generalizations

The following generalizations will help students focus on important patterns when reading multisyllabic words. The emphasis should be on having students apply the generalizations during reading, rather than asking students to memorize them as absolute "rules." Be sure to make students aware of important exceptions.

① If a word is a compound word, divide it between the two smaller words *(in•side, pan•cake)*.

② One syllable in a multisyllabic word usually has more stress or emphasis than the others. In two-syllable words, the accent (stress) usually falls on the first syllable *(mo'ment, fa'mous)*.

③ Word parts like prefixes, suffixes, and inflectional endings usually form separate syllables *(re•write, box•es, sing•ing)*. Note: The letters *re, in, un,* and *dis* at the beginning of a word do not always signal a prefix *(reader, diskette)*.

④ When two or more consonants appear in the middle of a word, divide the word between them *(kit•ten, bas•ket)* and try the short sound for the vowel in the first syllable. Exceptions include *ck* and the consonant digraphs *ch, ph, sh,* and *th*, which cannot be divided. *(rock•et, wash•es)*.

⑤ When one consonant appears between two vowels, divide the word after the first vowel *(pi•lot, be•gan)*, and try the long sound for the first vowel. If you don't recognize the word, divide it after the consonant and try the short sound *(plan•et, sec•ond)*.

⑥ When a two-syllable word ends in a consonant plus *–le,* divide the word so that the consonant and *–le* form the last syllable. If the first syllable ends in a consonant, it will generally have a short-vowel sound *(bat•tle, sim•ple).* If the first syllable ends with a vowel, it will generally have a long-vowel sound *(cra•dle, ti•tle).*

⑦ When two vowels represent a single vowel sound or a diphthong, the vowels stay together *(reach•ing, boy•ish).*

10.13

## Syllables and Stress

A stressed syllable is usually said longer, louder, and higher in pitch than unstressed syllables. In the word *open,* for example, the first syllable *(ō)* is longer and its vowel sound is more pronounced than the vowel sound in the unstressed second syllable *(pən).* Different languages have different stress patterns. English language learners who haven't been exposed to models of natural speech often have difficulty hearing and articulating stress correctly.

Sometimes it is difficult even for proficient readers to hear stress. Teachers may need to slow down or speed up pronunciation of words, or even sing them. Dialogue, poetry, or text excerpts can be read aloud with varying degrees of modulation: from monotone to exaggerated accent on syllables or words.

## ELL

# Useful Generalizations About English Stress

**In two-syllable words, one syllable always has more emphasis, or stress. It is usually the first syllable.** *(**sis**ter, **blan**ket, **ta**ble)*

**Prefixes and suffixes usually form separate syllables. The stress generally falls either on or within the base word.** *(un**lock**, **play**ful, **go**ing)*

**In compound words the primary accent falls on or within the first word.** *(**break**fast, **bas**ketball)*

**When the vowel sound in the last syllable is a vowel team, that syllable is usually accented.** *(be**low**, to**day**)*

**In two-syllable words, the vowel sound in the *unaccented* syllable is often a schwa sound.** *(al**low**, **pro**tect)*

# why?

*Multisyllabic Words*

**10.14**

Section V: Spelling

Section VI: Vocabulary Development

Not all students readily transfer the phonic knowledge acquired in reading single-syllable words to reading multisyllabic words (Just and Carpenter 1987; Samuels et al. 1978; Eldredge 1995). They become overwhelmed by long words because they don't know how to approach them. Yet as students progress through the grades, they will encounter growing numbers of longer and more complex words. Fluent reading, therefore, depends on the ability to quickly analyze and recognize multisyllabic words.

To tackle these longer, more difficult words students need to break them down into smaller parts: syllables, affixes, and base words. Direct instruction in syllable types and division patterns trains students' eyes and ears to recognize these parts and then systematically apply learned phonic generalizations to decode an unrecognized long word. In fact, being able to divide a word into syllables may help students figure out a word without reading all of it (Henry 1990). As Cunningham (1998) explains, "Patterns and morphological relationships are the keys to unlocking pronunciation, spelling, and meaning. All students should be issued these master keys."

**Research Findings . . .**

*The average fifth grader is apt to encounter 10,000 new words each year. Most of these words are big words—words of seven or more letters and two or more syllables.*

—NAGY & ANDERSON, 1984

*Skillful readers' ability to read long words depends on their ability to break the words into syllables. This is true for familiar and unfamiliar words.*

—ADAMS, 1990

*Learning the structure of words at the syllable and morpheme levels supports word recognition, spelling, and vocabulary development.*

—NAGY & ANDERSON, 1984

*For some children, their phonic skills break down when confronted by multisyllabic words because they cannot readily identify syllable boundaries.*

—ELDREDGE, 1995

*When students are decoding unknown multisyllabic words, it is to their advantage to know prefixes and suffixes. Such knowledge will also help in learning the meaning of a word.*

—CHALL & POPP, 1996

**Suggested Reading . . .**

*Direct Instruction Reading, 3rd Edition* (1997) by Douglas W. Carnine, Jerry Silbert & Edward J. Kameenui. Upper Saddle River, NJ: Prentice-Hall.

"The Multisyllabic Word Dilemma: Helping Students Build Meaning, Spell, and Read 'Big' Words" (1998) by Patricia M. Cunningham. *Reading & Writing Quarterly* 14(2).

*Teaching and Assessing Phonics: A Guide for Teachers* (1996) by Jeanne S. Chall & Helen M. Popp. Cambridge, MA: Educators Publishing Service.

*Words: Integrated Decoding and Spelling Instruction Based on Word Origin and Word Structures* (1990) by Marcia Henry. Austin, TX: PRO-ED.

**10.16**

*"Knowing how to decode polysyllabic words is essential because reading materials in the third grade, and surely by the fourth grade and beyond, contain an ever increasing number of unfamiliar polysyllabic words."*

—CHALL & POPP, 1996

## When to Teach

Formal multisyllabic word instruction begins after students have learned most of the basic phonic elements. The concept of a syllable is introduced in Kindergarten as part of phonological awareness development. First graders begin to read multisyllabic words in the form of compound words and words with inflectional endings. As students progress through the grades, they will encounter increasingly complex multisyllabic words.

**Kindergarten**   Early in Kindergarten, students will learn to listen for syllables before they listen for phonemes. Students can be made aware that two-syllable compound words contain two "little" words and each word is called a syllable.

**Grade 1**   In first grade, students learn to read common compound words by dividing them into separate base words (syllables). Students also practice recognizing and writing words with common inflectional endings *–es, –ed,* and *–ing.* Students learn to read these endings as phonic elements, rather than as formal syllable patterns.

**Grade 2**   In second grade, students are introduced to closed and open syllables in the VCCV, VCV, and VCCCV patterns. They also learn common prefixes and suffixes that help with word recognition, and spelling changes that occur when inflectional endings are added to base words.

**Grade 3 and Above**   In third grade and above, syllabication instruction includes review of the concepts introduced in Grade 2 and proceeds to the *r*-controlled, vowel team, vowel–silent *e,* and consonant-*le* syllable types. In addition, students are taught to look for affixes and base words to aid in word recognition. They read longer words—from three to five syllables—with affixes.

## When to Assess and Intervene

In the middle of second grade, it is important to assess students' ability to recognize multisyllabic words. Students should be able to recognize simple multisyllabic words, especially compound words and words containing common affixes. Those who cannot should receive direct instruction in syllabication and in recognizing common morphemic units. Students still struggling with single-syllable words will need intervention.

**Upper-Grade Intervention**   Often, upper-grade students who struggle to decode multisyllabic words need instruction and practice in basic phonics. They may also need explicit instruction in syllabication and recognition of morphemic units. These students need ample practice applying word attack strategies to decodable and authentic texts, which should be chosen to fall beneath students' frustration level.

## Multisyllabic Word Tests

**See also . . .**

**CORE Assessing Reading**
"Resources for Assessing Reading"

**10.18**

| CORE Assessing Reading | Other |
|---|---|
| CORE Phonics Survey | Durrell Analysis of Reading Difficulty |
| San Diego Quick Assessment of Reading Ability, Grades 1–8 | Ekwall and Shanker Reading Inventory |
|  | Stanford Diagnostic Reading Test |
|  | Woodcock Reading Mastery Test–Revised |

## ASSESSMENT AND INTERVENTION

| When | Mid- to late Grade 2 |
|---|---|
| Who | All students |
| Assessment Tool | *CORE Assessing Reading,* CORE Phonics Survey (Item G); San Diego Quick Assessment of Reading Ability (Grade 2 word list) |
| Intervene if . . . | Assessment indicates that students cannot read multisyllabic real and pseudowords in Item G; or cannot read, at the independent level, the grade-level word list. |
| How | Teacher-led small-group instruction focused on syllable types and patterns, and affixes; reinforcement of earlier phonic skills |
| When | Early Grade 3 |
| Who | All students |
| Assessment Tool | *CORE Assessing Reading,* CORE Phonics Survey (Item G); San Diego Quick Assessment of Reading Ability (Grade 3 word list) |
| Intervene if . . . | Assessment indicates that students cannot read multisyllabic real and pseudowords in Item G; or cannot read, at the independent level, the grade-level word list. |
| How | Teacher-led small-group instruction focused on syllable types and patterns, and affixes; reinforcement of earlier phonic skills |

# Assessment and Intervention (CONTINUED)

| | |
|---|---|
| **When** | Grade 4 and above |
| **Who** | All students |
| **Assessment Tool** | *CORE Assessing Reading,* CORE Phonics Survey (Item G); San Diego Quick Assessment of Reading Ability (Grades 4–8 word lists) |
| **Intervene if ...** | Assessment indicates that students cannot read multisyllabic real and pseudowords in Item G; or cannot read, at the independent level, the appropriate grade-level word list. |
| **How** | Teacher-led small-group instruction focused on syllable types and patterns, and affixes; reinforcement of earlier phonic skills |

# how?

## *Multisyllabic Words*

**TEACHING STRATEGY FOR**

## Syllabication

### Benchmarks

- ability to identify the number of syllables in spoken and written words
- ability to read two-syllable words

### Grade Level

- Grades 1 – 2 and Intervention

### Prerequisites

- introduced phonic elements: all single consonants and short vowels, consonant digraphs, CVC*e* long-vowel pattern
- introduced high-frequency words: *played, the, they*

### Grouping

- whole class
- small group or pairs
- individual

### Materials

- authentic text
- copies of Word Study Grid (see Appendix)

---

## INTRODUCING SYLLABLES

This generic teaching strategy introduces the concept of a syllable. It is the first step toward making students aware of syllable boundaries, an essential tool for reading longer words. The lesson focuses on compound words with short-vowel sounds, but it can be adapted to focus on two-syllable words with the inflectional endings *–es* and *–ed.* Students should be reminded that these endings signal "more than one" *(–es)* and an action that happened "in the past" *(–ed).* When reading words with inflectional endings, students should be encouraged to blend the endings with the base words as whole units.

### Warm Up

Say each of the following words and ask students to tell you how many syllables they hear: *jumping* (2), *lunch* (1), *raindrop* (2), *banana* (3), *information* (4), *stick* (1), *rollerblade* (3), *school* (1), *laughing* (2), *patted* (2). After you say each word have students repeat it.

### Teach/Model

Work with students to define what a syllable is, making sure they mention that a syllable includes a vowel sound. Print the word *bathtub* on the board. Say it aloud and ask students how many vowel sounds they hear. Put a dot under each of the vowels. Say the word again and ask students to identify the

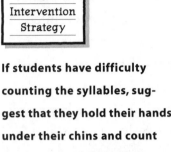

**If students have difficulty counting the syllables, suggest that they hold their hands under their chins and count the number of times their jaws drop for each syllable.**

**If students have difficulty sounding out the base words, see "Whole-Word Blending," p. 8.14.**

number of syllables. Point out that the word *bathtub* has two vowel sounds and two syllables: *bath* and *tub*. Each syllable contains one vowel sound. Next, print the following words on the board: *hotdog, lunchbox, bullfrog.* Have volunteers come to the board and place a dot under each vowel. Ask students how many syllables each word has. Cover the second syllable of *hotdog* and have students sound out the first syllable in unison. Then cover the first syllable and have students sound out the second syllable in unison. Finally, guide them in blending the syllables to say the entire word. Repeat this process with the remaining words.

**10.21**

## Practice Blending

On the board, print the two-syllable words shown below. Have students copy the words on a piece of paper and put a dot under each vowel. Have them identify the number of syllables, sound out each syllable, and then blend the syllables together to pronounce the entire word.

hilltop, sunset, dustpan, backpack, drumstick

Have students read the sentence shown below by sounding out each syllable and then blending the syllables in sequence. The high-frequency words in the sentence are underlined. Students should read these words as a whole; they should not attempt to sound them out.

<u>They</u> <u>played</u> in <u>the</u> sandbox until sunset.

## Apply

**AUTHENTIC TEXT**   Provide students with connected reading practice. Choose text selections at students' independent reading level. For strategies to preteach the high-frequency irregular words found in the text, see Chapter 9.

**10.22**

**SYLLABLE SORT**   For this closed sort, distribute copies of the Word Study Grid with the words shown below printed in the boxes. Have students cut the grid apart and sort the words into two categories: "Words with Two Syllables" and "Words with One Syllable." Model the sort by selecting a few words at random and printing them on the board under the key words *sunset* and *shade.* For the two-syllable words, sound out each syllable and then blend the syllables together to pronounce the entire word. Ask students how the words in the first column are alike. *(Possible answers: All the words have two vowel sounds and two syllables; all the words are made up of two little words.)* Then ask students where the words are divided into syllables. *(between the two base words)* Repeat the process with the words in the second column. Students should note that all of the words have one vowel sound and one syllable. Finally, have students continue the sort on their own. Sorted words can be added to word walls, word banks, or students' Word Study Notebooks.

**sunset,** hilltop, goldfish, snapshot, drumstick, backpack
**shade,** stand, patch, truck, frame, white, shape, phone, brave

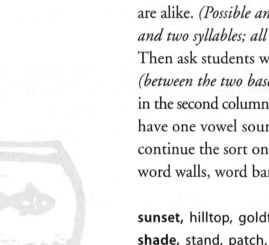

*See also . . .*

"Orthographic Syllable Types," p. 10.40

**OBSERVE AND ASSESS**

*As students complete the Apply activities, use this question to assess their progress.*

| Question for Observation | Benchmark |
|---|---|
| *(Point to a two-syllable compound word.)* Can you blend the syllables to read this word? | Student can use syllable boundaries to read two-syllable words. |

## The Next Step

After students have practice reading two-syllable words with short vowels, they can be introduced to words with other vowel patterns such as silent-*e* long vowels, vowel digraphs, variant vowels, and *r*-controlled words. Examples of compound words with these patterns include *cupcake, raincoat, bedroom,* and *starfish.* Follow the same procedure to help students identify syllable boundaries, but point out that in these syllables more than one letter makes the vowel sound.

## Benchmarks

• ability to recognize the number of syllables in spoken and written words
• ability to read two- to four-syllable words

## Grade Level

• Grade 2 and above

## Prerequisite

• introduced phonic elements: all single consonants and short vowels, consonant digraphs, CVC*e* long-vowel pattern

## Grouping

• whole class
• small group or pairs

## Materials

• list of clue words
• picture cards with words written on the back: *pear, pizza, hamburger, watermelon*

# SYLLABLE SWAP

## GRADE LEVEL 2 AND ABOVE

For this game, students match spoken words to picture cards, based on the number of syllables.

10.23

## Prep Time

Prepare a list of words arranged by number of syllables. For example:

| 1 syllable | 2 syllables | 3 syllables | 4 syllables |
| --- | --- | --- | --- |
| snake | mailbox | telephone | macaroni |
| trees | waited | kangaroo | American |
| swim | sadly | basketball | emergency |

## Warm Up

Show the following picture cards. As you name each picture, have students clap to count the number of syllables they hear: *pear, pizza, hamburger, watermelon.*

## Play the Game

Tell students that they are going to play a Syllable Swap game. Select an odd number of students and have all but one sit in a circle. The remaining student will stand in the center. Distribute a picture card to each seated student, making sure that students with picture cards of words with the same number of syllables are not sitting next to each other. The set you distribute should contain only two pictures representing the same number of syllables (two pictures for two-syllable words, two pictures for three-syllable words, and so on). Ask students to look at their picture cards and name the pictures. Confirm what students say and have them repeat the word without looking at the picture. Have students place their picture cards under their seats face up. When they are ready, call out a number and a *clue word* containing that number of syllables. For example, say: *Three syllables . . .* bicycle. The two students with three-syllable picture words try to swap places while the student in the center tries to capture one of their seats. The player left standing goes in the center of the circle. The newly seated students take over the picture cards under the seats. Play continues with a new number and clue word.

## Try It This Way!

Older students can play a card game with word cards instead of the circle swap activity with picture cards. Deal a set of word cards to three students. This time, make sure that there are *more than two* words with the same number of syllables. Players take turns placing a word face up and pronouncing it. The other players try to be the first to lay down a word with the same number of syllables. The player who is first to throw a correct card takes both cards. Play proceeds to the right. If no player matches the word within one minute, the original player takes back the word. Play proceeds until all the cards are gone, and the winner is the one with the most cards.

# Syllable Types and Patterns

### Benchmarks

- ability to recognize a closed syllable
- ability to read two-syllable words with the VCCV pattern

### Grade Level

- Grades 2 – 3 and Intervention

### Prerequisites

- Introducing Syllables
- all Grades 1 and 2 phonic elements (see p. 8.8)
- introduced high-frequency words: *a, after, the, put*

### Grouping

- whole class
- small group or pairs
- individual

### Materials

- authentic text

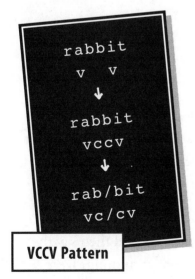

**VCCV Pattern**

## CLOSED SYLLABLES: VCCV PATTERN

This generic teaching strategy introduces students to the *closed syllable,* using VCCV words such as *napkin.* Recognizing this pattern is essential for decoding complex multisyllabic words, including those that contain three or four consonants between the vowels. Such words generally contain two- or three-letter blends and divide after the first consonant: *hun/dred, mon/ster, in/struct.*

10.25

• • • • • • • • • • • • • • • • • • • • • • • • • •

## Warm Up

Review the concept of short- and long-vowel sounds in one-syllable CVC and CV words. Print the following words on the board: *go, got, I, in, she, shed.* Ask students to read the words by blending the sounds in sequence. Then have volunteers come to the board and underline the vowel in each word. Ask them to tell whether the vowel has a long or short sound. Point out that the words that end in a vowel have a long-vowel sound, and those that end in a consonant have a short-vowel sound. Remind students that these words also can be called "syllables" because each has one vowel sound.

## Teach the Pattern

Print the word *rabbit* on the board but don't pronounce it. Ask students how many vowels the word has and mark a *v* under the two vowels. Explain that this tells them that the word has two syllables. Then ask students how many consonants come between the vowels and mark a *c* under the two consonants. Tell students that VCCV is a common syllable pattern and that when they see a word that has this pattern, they should divide the word between the two consonants (VC/CV). Demonstrate the VC/CV division pattern by drawing a slash between the two consonants.

**10.26**

**If students have difficulty sounding out the syllables, they may need instruction in blending sounds in sequence. See "Whole-Word Blending," p. 8.14, for a detailed description.**

**If students have difficulty labeling the vowels and consonants, suggest that they draw a line from each vowel down to the label v.**

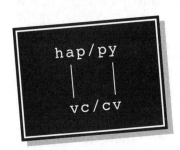

Cover up the second syllable and ask students whether the vowel sound in the first syllable is short or long. *(short)* Point to *rab* and explain that it is called a closed syllable because the single vowel *a* is followed, or "closed in," by the consonant *b*. In a closed syllable the vowel sound is almost always short. Now cover up the first syllable and ask students if the second syllable is also a closed syllable, and why. *(yes, because the single vowel* i *is closed in by the consonant* t*)* Then have students sound out each syllable in sequence and blend them together to read the entire word. Repeat the process with the word *basket* to demonstrate that this pattern also applies when the consonants in the middle are not identical.

## Practice Marking and Blending

On the board, print the words shown below. Have students write the words on a sheet of paper, leaving a blank line under each word. Ask them to label the vowels and consonants and then use what they know about the VCCV pattern to divide the words into syllables. Help students read the words by sounding out and blending the syllables in sequence.

Repeat the process with the sentence shown below. The high-frequency words are underlined. Students should read the words as a whole; they should not attempt to sound them out.

happy, ribbon, tunnel, mitten, pencil
I <u>put</u> <u>a</u> napkin in <u>the</u> picnic basket.

## Apply

**AUTHENTIC TEXT**   Provide students with connected reading practice. Choose text selections at students' independent reading level. For strategies to preteach the high-frequency irregular words found in the text, see Chapter 9.

**DICTATION AND SPELLING**   Dictate the words shown below. Say each word, use it in a sentence, and then say the word again. For example, say: *The word is* running. *We're*

*running to catch the bus . . .* running. Have students say the word, then guide them in spelling it syllable by syllable. After students have written all of the words, read the sentence shown below. Dictate the words one at a time, using the same procedure to guide them in spelling each word syllable by syllable. The high-frequency words in the sentence are underlined. Students should write the words as a whole; they should not attempt to sound them out.

**Section V: Spelling, "Consonant Doubling/Dropping e,"** p. 13.35

running, traffic, happy, basket, bottom, napkin
<u>The</u> kitten ran <u>after</u> <u>the</u> rabbit.

After the dictation, print the words and sentence on the board, and ask students to proofread their work. They should circle any word spelled incorrectly and write the correct spelling next to it.

**OBSERVE AND ASSESS**

*As students complete the Apply activities, use this question to assess their progress.*

| Question for Observation | Benchmark |
| --- | --- |
| *(Point to a word with the VCCV pattern.)* Can you blend the syllables to read this word? | Student can read two-syllable words with the VCCV pattern. |

## The Next Step

Introduce students to words with the VCCCV pattern. Examples include: *hundred, monster,* and *explode.* Explain that words with three consonants between two vowels almost always contain a blend *(dr, st, pl, tr)* that acts as a unit and stays together in the same syllable. Therefore, students should look for these blends and break the word so that the blends remain together. Sometimes the blends are initial blends and the word breaks after the first consonant and before the blend *(hun•dred).* Sometimes the first two consonants are a digraph *(bash•ful)* or an end blend *(pump•kin),* in which case the word breaks after the second consonant.

## TEACHING STRATEGY FOR
# Syllable Types and Patterns

### Benchmarks

10.28

- ability to recognize an open syllable
- ability to read two-syllable words with the V/CV pattern

### Grade Level

- Grades 2 – 3 and Intervention

### Prerequisites

- all previously introduced Teaching Strategies in this chapter
- all Grades 1 and 2 phonic elements (see p. 8.8)
- introduced high-frequency word: *the*

### Grouping

- whole class
- small group or pairs
- individual

### Materials

- authentic text
- copies of Word Study Grid (see Appendix)

# OPEN SYLLABLES: V/CV PATTERN

This generic teaching strategy introduces students to *open syllables* and the syllable-juncture pattern VCV. This pattern can be divided before or after the consonant: V/CV or VC/V. Since the more common pattern is the one with an open first syllable (V/CV), this division pattern should be tried first. Students should then use context to confirm the pronunciation.

⬤ ⬤ ⬤ ⬤ ⬤ ⬤ ⬤ ⬤ ⬤ ⬤ ⬤ ⬤ ⬤ ⬤ ⬤ ⬤ ⬤ ⬤ ⬤ ⬤ ⬤ ⬤ ⬤ ⬤ ⬤ ⬤

## Warm Up

Fold a piece of paper into fourths. (See diagram below.) Print the letter *m* in the first fourth and the letter *e* in the second fourth. Fold over the last fourth (it will cover the third fourth) and print the letter *n* in it. Follow the same procedure for the following words: *men, hit, sob, hen, got.*

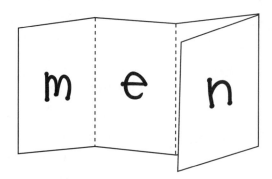

Ask a student to read the CVC word, *men.* Point out that the vowel is "closed in" by the consonant *n* and the vowel sound is short, /e/. Next, unfold the paper, or "open the door," and ask students to say the new word, *me.* Explain that when the single vowel is at the end of the word, "the door is open" and the vowel makes the long sound, /ē/. Tell students an easy way to remember this is to say: *"Door open, vowel at the end, long sound; door closed, vowel not at the end, short sound."* Follow the same procedure for the words *hit, sob, hen,* and *got.*

**V/CV Pattern**

10.29

## Teach the Pattern

Print the word *begin* on the board but don't pronounce it. Ask students how many vowels the word has and mark a *v* under the two vowels. Then ask students how many consonants come between the vowels and mark a *c* under the consonant. Tell students that *begin* has a VCV syllable pattern, and that they should try dividing it after the first vowel and before the consonant. Show the V/CV pattern by drawing a slash before the consonant.

Now, cover up the second syllable and ask students to say the sound of the vowel in the first syllable, /ē/. Point to the first syllable *be* and remind students that "the door is open." The vowel is at the end, so the sound is long, /ē/. Tell students that *be* is called an *open syllable,* because the vowel is not "closed in."

Next, cover up the first syllable and point to the second syllable *gin*. Ask students to say the sound of the vowel, /i/. Remind students that when the vowel is "closed in" by a consonant, the vowel sound is short. Explain that this syllable is called a *closed syllable*. Then have students sound out each syllable in sequence and blend them together to read the entire word. Repeat the process with the word *open*.

## Practice Marking and Blending

On the board, print the words shown below. Have students write the words on a sheet of paper, leaving a blank line under each word. Ask them to label the vowels and consonants and divide the words into syllables. Help students read the words by sounding out and blending the syllables in sequence.

Repeat the process with the sentence shown below. The high-frequency word is underlined. Students should read the word as a whole; they should not attempt to sound it out.

spoken, final, human, music, moment, label
The robot will help the pilot.

---

**Intervention Strategy**

**If students have difficulty reading the syllables as whole units, have them blend each syllable, sound by sound. See "Sound-by-Sound Blending," p. 8.12, for a detailed description.**

**10.30**

## Apply

**AUTHENTIC TEXT**   Provide students with connected reading practice. Choose text selections at students' independent reading level. For strategies to preteach the high-frequency irregular words found in the text, see Chapter 9.

**SYLLABLE SORT**   For this closed sort, distribute copies of the Word Study Grid with the words shown below printed in the boxes. Have students cut the grid apart and sort the words into two categories: "Words with an Open First Syllable" and "Words with a Closed First Syllable." Model the sort by selecting a few words at random and printing them on the board under the key words *music* and *muffin.* Say each syllable, and then blend them together to pronounce the entire word. After you print the words in the appropriate column, ask students how the words in the first column are alike. *(Possible answers: All the words have one consonant between two vowels; all the words have a long-vowel sound.)* Then ask students where the words are divided into syllables. *(before the consonant)* Repeat the process with the VCCV words in the second column. Students should note that all of the words have two consonants between the vowels, have a short-vowel sound, and are divided between the consonants. Finally, have students continue the sort on their own.

**music,** begin, open, student, total, silent, basic, pilot
**muffin,** rabbit, bottom, hidden, basket, traffic, helmet, goblin

**OBSERVE AND ASSESS**

*As students complete the Apply activities, use this question to assess their progress.*

| Question for Observation | Benchmark |
| --- | --- |
| *(Point to a word with the V/CV pattern.)* Can you blend the syllables to read this word? | Student can read two-syllable words with the V/CV pattern. |

# Syllable Types and Patterns

### Benchmarks

- ability to recognize a closed syllable
- ability to read two-syllable words with the VC/V pattern

### Grade Level

- Grades 2 – 3 and Intervention

### Prerequisites

- all Grades 1 and 2 phonic elements (see p. 8.8)
- introduced high-frequency word: *their*
- Open Syllables: V/CV Pattern

### Grouping

- whole class
- small group or pairs
- individual

### Materials

- index cards
- authentic text

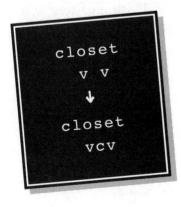

## CLOSED SYLLABLES: VC/V PATTERN

This generic strategy introduces the alternative division of words with the VCV pattern and the idea of flexibility in approaching words with this pattern. Students should become proficient in switching between the two possible syllable pattern divisions when trying to identify an unknown word.

10.31

## Warm Up

Have students print VC/CV on one index card and V/CV on the other. Then on the board, print the words shown below. Ask students to hold up the VC/CV card if the word you point to fits that pattern, or the V/CV card if the word has an open first syllable and fits that pattern.

happen, napkin, shiny, beside, himself, pupil

After students identify the appropriate category for each word, print the division pattern above it. Call on volunteers to come to the board to divide the words into syllables and then blend the syllables together to read the words.

## Teach the Pattern

Print the word *closet* on the board but don't pronounce it. Ask students how many vowels the word has and mark a *v* under the two vowels. Explain that this tells them that the word has two syllables. Then ask students how many consonants come between the vowels and mark a *c* under the consonant. Remind students that if they see a word with the VCV pattern, they should try dividing it after the first vowel (V/CV). Demonstrate the V/CV division pattern by drawing a slash before the consonant. Sound out the first syllable using the long-*o* sound,

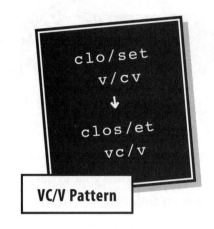

```
clo/set
v/cv
↓
clos/et
vc/v
```

**VC/V Pattern**

10.32

and blend it with the second syllable to say "clō/sĕt." Tell students that this doesn't sound familiar and explain that while the VCV pattern *usually* divides after the first vowel, sometimes the word won't make sense when they try to read it that way. When that happens, they should try the *other* way the VCV pattern can divide, which is after the consonant. Demonstrate the VC/V division pattern by drawing a slash after the consonant.

Now ask whether the first syllable in the word *closet* is open or closed, and whether the vowel sound is short or long. *(closed; short)* Tell students that when they come across a word with the VCV pattern, they should do exactly what you did: try the V/CV division first, and say the word with a long-vowel sound. If they don't recognize the word, they should try the VC/V division, and pronounce the word again with a short-vowel sound.

## Practice Marking and Blending

On the board, print the words shown below. Have students write the words on a sheet of paper, leaving a blank line under each word. Ask them to label the vowels and consonants and then use what they know about the VCV pattern to divide the words into syllables. Help students read the words by sounding out and blending the syllables in sequence. Remind them that they should first try the V/CV division pattern and blend the syllables in sequence. If the words do not sound familiar, they should then try the VC/V division pattern and reblend the syllables.

Repeat the process with the sentence shown below. The high-frequency word is underlined. Students should read the word as a whole; they should not attempt to sound it out.

model, gravy, local, visit, planet
Seven silent whales began <u>their</u> long trip home.

## Apply

**AUTHENTIC TEXT**   Provide students with connected reading practice. Choose text selections at students' independent reading level. For strategies to preteach the high-frequency irregular words found in the text, see Chapter 9.

**SYLLABLE SORT**   For this writing sort, have students sort the words shown below into two categories: "Words with the V/CV Pattern" and "Words with the VC/V Pattern." Print the key words *music* and *closet* on the board. Have students repeat the words after you and then print them at the top of two separate columns on a sheet of paper. Model the sort by reading aloud a few words at random and writing them under the appropriate key word. Say each syllable and then blend the syllables together to pronounce the entire word. Ask students if the vowel sound in the first syllable is long or short and where the words are divided. Read aloud the remaining words, in random order, and have students write each one in the appropriate column. When the sort is complete ask students to use a slash to divide the words into syllables and to read the words aloud. The sorted words can be added to word walls or students' Word Study Notebooks.

label, open, moment, spoken, final, even, total
solid, seven, magic, cabin, metal, planet, finish

**OBSERVE AND ASSESS**

*As students complete the Apply activities, use this question to assess their progress.*

| Question for Observation | Benchmark |
|---|---|
| *(Point to a word with the VCV pattern.)* Can you blend the syllables to read this word? | Student can read two-syllable words with the V/CV and VC/V patterns. |

**TEACHING STRATEGY FOR**

## Affixes as Syllables

**Benchmarks**

- ability to identify syllable boundaries in words with a prefix
- ability to read words with a prefix

**10.34**

**Grade Level**

- Grades 2 – 3 and Intervention

**Prerequisites**

- all Grades 1 and 2 phonic elements (see p. 8.8)
- all previously introduced Teaching Strategies in this chapter
- introduced high-frequency words: *could, the, was, tie*

**Grouping**

- whole class

**Materials**

- authentic text

# INTRODUCING PREFIXES

Identifying common prefixes helps students divide multisyllabic words into recognizable chunks. This generic teaching strategy focuses on the high-utility prefix *un–,* which accounts for nearly one-third of all prefixed words appearing in primary-level materials (Carroll, Davies, and Richman 1971). As is true of many prefixes, *un–* has more than one meaning and students should be made aware of the different meanings. The same strategy can be used to introduce other prefixes.

## Warm Up

Print the letter *u* on the board. Remind students that *u* stands for the /u/ sound at the beginning of the word *up.* Then print the letter *n* on the board. Remind students that *n* stands for the /n/ sound at the beginning of the word *no.* Slowly slide your finger or hand from left to right below the letters as you blend the sounds together and pronounce the prefix. Then have students blend the prefix and pronounce it on their own. Students should repeat this procedure until they become automatic in reading the prefix as a chunk. Tell students that the letters *un–* appear at the beginning of many words.

## Teach/Model

Print the word *happy* on the board and ask a volunteer to read it. Add the word part *un–* to the beginning and say: *I can add these letters to the word* happy *and change its meaning. The letters* un– *form a special word part called a* prefix. *Usually a prefix is the first syllable in a word.* Divide the prefix from the base word with a slash and model blending the prefix with the entire base word to say the word *unhappy.* Ask students what *unhappy* means *(not happy)* and have volunteers use it in a

Intervention
Strategy

**If students are having difficulty automatically recognizing the base words as whole units, encourage them to use sounding out supported by context to say the base word, and then blend it in sequence with the prefix and/or suffix to say the entire word.**

sentence. Tell students that in this case, adding *un–* to the base word changed its meaning to "not," but that *un–* can also mean "do the opposite of" in words like *untie* and *unlock*.

Explain to students that the letters *un* don't always form a prefix. Print the word *uncle* on the board and underline the letters *un*. Tell students that this is the first syllable in the word, but it's not a prefix because if they take it away they aren't left with a recognizable base word. Demonstrate this by erasing the first syllable and circling the letters *cle*. Direct students' attention to the word *unhappy* and erase the letters *un*. Ask them if they are still left with a word and if *un–* is a prefix in *unhappy*. *(yes)*

10.35

## Practice Blending

Help students read the words and sentence shown below. Have them read the words by covering the prefix, identifying the base word, and then blending the two syllables to say the entire word. The high-frequency words in the sentence are underlined. Students should also read these as a whole; they should not attempt to sound them out.

undo, unkind, uncut, unlock, untie
<u>The</u> boy fell but <u>was</u> unhurt.

## Apply

**AUTHENTIC TEXT** Provide students with connected reading practice. Choose text selections at students' independent reading level. For strategies to preteach the high-frequency irregular words found in the text, see Chapter 9.

**DICTATION AND SPELLING** Dictate the words shown below. Say each word, use it in a sentence, and then say the word again. For example, say: *The word is* unlike. *The twins were so unlike each other . . .* unlike. Have students say the

**10.36**

word, then guide them in spelling it syllable by syllable—first the prefix and then the base word. After students have written all of the words, read the sentence shown below. Dictate the words one at a time, using the same procedure to guide them in spelling each word syllable by syllable. The high-frequency words in the sentence are underlined. Students should write the words as a whole; they should not attempt to sound them out.

unlike, unlock, unsafe, uncut, unlucky
The unhappy dog could not un<u>tie</u> <u>the</u> rope.

After the dictation, print the words and sentence on the board, and ask students to proofread their work. They should circle any word spelled incorrectly and write the correct spelling next to it.

**OBSERVE AND ASSESS**

*As students complete the Apply activities, use this question to assess their progress.*

| Question for Observation | Benchmark |
| --- | --- |
| *(Point to a two-syllable word with the prefix un–.)* Can you blend the prefix with the base word to read this word? | Student can read two-syllable words with a prefix. |

## Try It This Way!

Introduce students to the prefix *re–* by having them count the syllables in the words shown below. Print the words on the board and have students listen as you read each one. Ask them to hold up one finger when they hear one syllable and two fingers when they hear two syllables.

real, reach, redo, retell, reef, rewrite

## Affixes as Syllables

### Benchmarks

- ability to identify syllable boundaries in words with a suffix
- ability to read words with a suffix

### Grade Level

- Grades 2 – 3 and Intervention

### Prerequisites

- all Grades 1 and 2 phonic elements (see p. 8.8)
- all previously introduced Teaching Strategies in this chapter
- ability to read words with inflectional endings *–es, –ed,* and *–ing*
- introduced high-frequency word: *the*

### Grouping

- whole class

### Materials

- authentic text
- copies of Word Study Grid (see Appendix)

This generic teaching strategy introduces the suffixes *–ly, –er,* and *–ful.* The same procedure can be used to introduce other suffixes such as *–y, –ness,* and *–tion.* By helping students learn to quickly identify a suffix and visually remove it from a base word, teachers can help students read and recognize many multisyllabic words.

10.37

. . . . . . . . . . . . . . . . . . . . . . . . . . . . . . . . . .

### Warm Up

Review words ending in inflectional suffixes. On the board, print the words shown below. Have students read the words as you point to each one. Then cover the suffix and ask students to identify the base word.

rushing, hopping, missing, batted, handed

### Teach/Model

Print the letters *ly, er,* and *ful* on the board. Have students orally blend the sounds of the letters. Repeat this several times until they become automatic in reading the suffixes as a chunk. Now print the word *slow* on the board and ask a volunteer to read it. Add the suffix *–ly* to the end and say: *I can add these letters to the word* slow *and make a new word. The letters* ly *form a special word part called a* suffix. *Usually a suffix is the last syllable in a word.* Divide the suffix from the base word with a slash and model blending the entire base word with the suffix to say the word *slowly.* Ask students what *slowly* means *("in a slow way")* and have volunteers use it in a sentence. Tell students that in this case, adding *–ly* to the base word changed

**"Consonant Doubling/Dropping e,"**
p. 13.35

for more information about spelling changes
in words with inflectional endings

10.38

an adjective, or describing word, to an adverb—a word that tells how something is done. Ask students to think of other adverbs that end in *–ly*.

Repeat the process with the suffix *–er* in *teacher* and *–ful* in *hopeful*. Explain that in these words the *–er* ending means "a person who does something" and the *–ful* ending means "full of." Remind students that the letters *er* at the end of a word sometimes signal a comparison, as in *smaller* and *softer*.

## Practice Blending

Help students read the words and sentence shown below. Have them read the words by covering the suffix, identifying the base word, and then blending the two syllables to say the entire word. The high-frequency word in the sentence is underlined. Students should read the word as a whole; they should not attempt to sound it out.

safely, player, joyful, sadly, reader
The runner ran quickly past me.

## Apply

**AUTHENTIC TEXT**   Provide students with connected reading practice. Choose text selections at students' independent reading level. For strategies to preteach the high-frequency irregular words found in the text, see Chapter 9.

**WORD SORT**   For this closed sort, distribute copies of the Word Study Grid with the words on the facing page printed in the boxes. Have students cut the grid apart and sort the words into two categories: "Words with Prefixes" and "Words with Suffixes." Print the key words *unlock* and *teacher* on the board. Have students repeat the words after you and then print them at the top of two columns on a sheet of paper. Model the sort by reading aloud a few words at random and writing them under the appropriate key word. Say the prefix or suffix and then blend the affix together with the base word to pronounce the entire word. Ask students how the words in the first column are alike. *(They all have a prefix.)* To confirm their answer, suggest that they cover the prefix and check to see if they are left with a recognizable word. Ask students what they notice about all of the words in the second column. *(They all have a suffix.)* Have students continue the sort. When the sort is complete, ask students to read aloud the words in each column. The sorted words can be added to word walls or students' Word Study Notebooks.

**unlock,** retell, dislike, unwrap, undo, refill, unhappy, rewind
**teacher,** slowly, hopeful, speaker, loudly, painter, seller, neatly

---

## OBSERVE AND ASSESS

*As students complete the Apply activities, use this question to assess their progress.*

| Question for Observation | Benchmark |
|---|---|
| *(Point to a two-syllable word with a suffix.)* Can you blend the base word with the suffix to read this word? | Student can read two-syllable words with a suffix. |

## The Next Step

After students have practice reading two-syllable words with a prefix or suffix, they can be introduced to longer words containing *both* a prefix and a suffix. To read these words, students should isolate the prefix, then the suffix, and identify the base word. They should then blend the syllables in sequence to read the entire word. Examples of words with both a prefix and a suffix include: *unthoughtful, unkindly, rewriting, replanted.*

## TEACHING STRATEGY FOR

# Syllable Types: *r*-Controlled, Vowel Team, Vowel–Silent *e*

**10.40**

### Benchmarks

- ability to recognize syllable types and identify syllable boundaries
- ability to read two-syllable words

### Grade Level

- Grade 3 and above

### Prerequisites

- all previously introduced Teaching Strategies in this chapter
- all Grades 1 and 2 phonic elements (see p. 8.8)
- introduced high-frequency word: *the*

### Grouping

- whole class
- small group or pairs
- individual

### Materials

- index cards (one per student)
- authentic text
- copies of Word Study Grid (see Appendix)

# ORTHOGRAPHIC SYLLABLE TYPES

This generic teaching strategy introduces three orthographic syllable types: *r*-controlled, vowel team, and vowel–silent *e*. The lesson is a demonstration lesson; concepts related to reading these syllable types should be practiced in detail later, or may be fully taught individually.

· · · · · · · · · · · · · · · · · · · · · · · · · · ·

## Warm Up

Review *r*-controlled and long-vowel sounds. Have students print the letter *R* on an index card. On the board, print the compound words shown below. Read the entire word, then say each syllable. Ask students to repeat the syllable and hold up the *R* card if the syllable has an *r*-controlled vowel.

homework, birdseed, grapevine, cornfield, railroad, birthday

## Teach/Model

Tell students that they are going to read words with syllable types other than open and closed, and that they will be surprised at how much they already know.

r-Controlled

### Syllable Type: *r*-Controlled

Print the words *garden* and *whisper* on the board. Underline the vowels, including the *r*. Remind students that the single *r* together with the vowels that come before it make a single vowel sound—/är/ and /ûr/—and for that reason the *r* and the vowel cannot be divided; they stay together in the same syllable. Ask students to count the vowels and tell how many syllables there are in each word. *(two)* Next, use a slash to divide the words into syllables. Have volunteers sound out and blend each syllable in sequence to read the words.

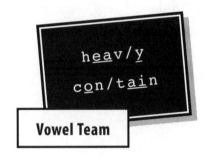

Vowel Team

### Syllable Type: Vowel Team

Print the words *heavy* and *contain* on the board. Underline the single vowel and the vowel teams. Remind students that the vowel pairs *ea* and *ai* work together to make a single vowel sound—/ĕ/ and /ā/—and for that reason the two letters cannot be divided; they stay together in the same syllable. Ask students to count the vowel sounds and tell how many syllables there are in each word. *(two)* Next, use a slash to divide the words into syllables. Have volunteers sound out and blend each syllable in sequence to read the words.

Vowel–Silent *e*

### Syllable Type: Vowel–Silent *e*

Print the words *behave* and *alike* on the board. Remind students that there is a silent *e* in each word and that the letter has no sound but indicates that the preceding vowel is long. Explain that the vowel and silent *e* cannot be divided; they stay together in the same syllable. Then underline the vowels in each word, but do not underline the silent *e*. Ask students to count the vowels and tell how many syllables there are in each word. *(two)* Next, use a slash to divide the words into syllables.

Have volunteers sound out and blend each syllable in sequence to read the words. Point out that the spoken stress in *alike* falls on the second syllable and the vowel sound in the first syllable is /ə/. Explain that other two-syllable words beginning with *a* have this sound, including *about, above,* and *along.*

## Practice Blending

Help students read the words and sentence shown below. Have them read the words by looking for vowel patterns that remain together, identifying the syllable types and boundaries, and then blending the syllables in sequence. The high-frequency word in the sentence is underlined. Students should read the word as a whole; they should not attempt to sound it out.

later, became, corner, locate, turkey, eastern, rainbow
<u>The</u> farmer covered <u>the</u> grapevine before <u>the</u> snowstorm.

## Apply

**AUTHENTIC TEXT**   Provide students with connected reading practice. Choose text selections at students' independent reading level. For strategies to preteach the high-frequency irregular words found in the text, see Chapter 9.

**SYLLABLE SORT**   For this closed sort, distribute copies of the Word Study Grid with the words on the facing page printed in the boxes. Have students cut the grid apart and sort the words into two categories: "Words with Vowel Teams" and "Words with Vowel–Silent *e*." Model the sort by selecting a few words at random and printing them on the board under the key words *complain* and *became.* Say each syllable and then blend the syllables together to pronounce the entire word. After you print the words in the appropriate column, ask students how the words in the first column are alike. *(Possible answer: All the words have two letters that stand for one vowel*

10.42

Intervention
Strategy

**If students say a particular vowel sound incorrectly, correct them. For example: If students say *became* with the short-*a* sound, stop them immediately and say:** *The silent e tells us that the a has a long sound—/ā/.* **Have students correctly say the second syllable and then blend the syllables in sequence to say the entire word.**

*sound.)* Then ask students where the words are divided into syllables. Repeat the process with the words in the second column. Students should note that all of the words have a long-vowel sound spelled with a vowel and silent *e.* Finally, have students continue the sort on their own. The sorted words can be added to word walls or students' Word Study Notebooks.

**complain,** mermaid, greedy, afraid, sneaker, touchdown
**became,** divide, awoke, surprise, skyline, include, trombone

| **OBSERVE AND ASSESS** | Question for Observation | Benchmark |
|---|---|---|
| *As students complete the Apply activities, use this question to assess their progress.* | *(Point to a word with an r-controlled, vowel team, or vowel–silent* e *syllable.)* Can you blend the syllables to read this word? | Student can read words with various syllable types. |

## The Next Step

After students have practiced reading two-syllable words with *r*-controlled, vowel team, and vowel–silent *e,* they can be introduced to longer words containing these syllable types. Examples of three- and four-syllable words with *r*-controlled vowels include the compound words *overflow, storyteller, underwater,* and *supermarket.*

10.44

## TEACHING STRATEGY FOR
# Syllable Types and Patterns

### Benchmarks

- ability to recognize the consonant-*le* syllable type and identify syllable boundaries
- ability to read two-syllable words ending in consonant-*le*

### Grade Level

- Grade 3 and above

### Prerequisites

- all Grades 1 and 2 phonic elements (see p. 8.8)
- introduced high-frequency words: *his, my, the*

### Grouping

- whole class
- small group or pairs
- individual

### Materials

- word cards (one set per pair of students)
- plastic bags (one bag per set of word cards)
- two-minute timer
- authentic text

**Consonant-*le***

---

# SYLLABLE TYPE: CONSONANT-*le*

**GRADE LEVEL 3 AND ABOVE**

This generic teaching strategy introduces students to a common syllable type in English: a final syllable consisting of a consonant and the letters *le*. Students will learn that whether or not the preceding syllable is closed or open depends on the number of consonants that come before *le*.

## Warm Up

Have students do a speed sort of the words shown below. Print the key words *rabbit, music,* and *planet* on the board. Model sorting one word below each key word, based on the syllable division patterns VC/CV, V/CV, and VC/V. Distribute plastic bags with the VCCV and VCV words to pairs of students. Tell them to work as quickly as possible using the key words to sort the words into three categories. Have pairs time themselves and then do the sort again trying to "beat" their initial times.

**rabbit,** muffin, carry, hidden, dinner, bottom; **music,** diver, major, student, paper, hotel; **planet,** river, seven, legend, study, wagon

## Teach the Pattern

Print the following common consonant-*le* patterns on the board: *ple, cle, tle, fle, ble, gle, zle, kle.* Tell students that many words end in this type of syllable: a consonant and the letters *le.* Underline the consonant in each pattern. Then point to the syllable and say: *In this syllable the* e *is silent, and the* le *pair is pronounced /əl/.* Model sounding out the syllables by blending the initial consonant with the sounds of *le.* Say each syllable again and have students repeat it after you.

**English language learners may need practice articulating the final syllable of words ending in consonant-*le*. Students should be shown how to "feel" the sound of /əl/, with their tongues behind their teeth touching the alveolar ridge.**

**Intervention Strategy**

**If students say a particular vowel sound incorrectly in the first syllable, correct them. For example: If students say *apple* with the long-*a* sound, stop them immediately and say: *This syllable is closed, so this sound is short* a, /a/. Have students correctly say the first syllable and then blend it with the second syllable to say the entire word.**

Next, print the words *table* and *little* on the board. Point to the word *table* and say: *When only one consonant comes before* le, *the word breaks after the first vowel because* le *always has to have a consonant with it. This makes the first syllable open, with a long-vowel sound /ā/.* Demonstrate the division pattern by drawing a slash after the vowel *a*. Sound out the first syllable using the long-*a* sound, and blend it with the second syllable to say the entire word. Next, point to the word *little* and say: *When two consonants come before* le, *the word breaks between the consonants. This makes the first syllable a closed syllable, with a short-vowel sound /i/.* Demonstrate the division pattern by drawing a slash after the first *t*. Sound out the first syllable using the short-*i* sound, and blend it with the second syllable to say the entire word.

## Practice Blending

Help students read the words and sentence shown below. Have them read the words by looking for the consonant-*le* syllable type, identifying the syllable boundaries and then blending the syllables in sequence using what they know about open and closed syllables and their pronunciations. The high-frequency words in the sentence are underlined. Students should read the words as a whole; they should not attempt to sound them out.

apple, title, noodle, puzzle, fable, noble
<u>My</u> uncle hurt <u>his</u> ankle when he fell off <u>the</u> table.

## Apply

**AUTHENTIC TEXT**    Provide students with connected reading practice. Choose text selections at students' independent reading level. For strategies to preteach the high-frequency irregular words found in the text, see Chapter 9.

**DICTATION AND SPELLING**    Dictate the words shown below. Say each word, use it in a sentence, and then say the word again. For example, say: *The word is* simple. *That model*

**10.46**

*will be simple to build . . .* simple. Have students say the word, then guide them in spelling it syllable by syllable. After students have written all of the words, read the sentence shown below. Dictate the words one at a time, using the same procedure to guide them in spelling each word syllable by syllable. The high-frequency word in the sentence is underlined. Students should write the word as a whole; they should not attempt to sound it out.

simple, title, needle, purple, cradle, shuttle
<u>The</u> gentle horse rested in its stable.

After the dictation, print the words and sentence on the board, and ask students to proofread their work. They should circle any word spelled incorrectly and write the correct spelling next to it.

### OBSERVE AND ASSESS

*As students complete the Apply activities, use this question to assess their progress.*

| Question for Observation | Benchmark |
|---|---|
| *(Point to a two-syllable word ending in consonant-le.)* Can you blend the syllables to read this word? | Student can read two-syllable words ending in consonant-*le*. |

# Syllable Types and Patterns

### Benchmarks

- ability to identify syllable boundaries
- ability to read multisyllabic words with VV pattern

### Grade Level

- Grades 3 – 4 and Intervention

### Prerequisites

- all previously introduced Teaching Strategies in this chapter
- all Grades 1 and 2 phonic elements (see p. 8.8)
- introduced high-frequency words: *about, of, to, the, a*

### Grouping

- whole class
- small group or pairs
- individual

### Materials

- authentic text

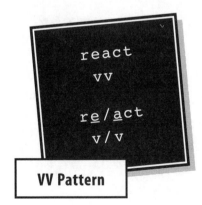

**VV Pattern**

This generic teaching strategy introduces students to words with adjacent vowels that do not function as a vowel digraph. These are words in which each vowel retains its individual sound and appears in a separate syllable.

**10.47**

## Warm Up

Have students do a writing sort to review syllabication. Ask them to fold a piece of paper in half and to print the key words *coat* and *boa* at the top of the columns. Then read aloud in random order the word pairs shown below. Have students write each word in the appropriate column based on the number of syllables they hear.

blue, duet; voice, doing; goes, poem; scream, create

## Teach the Pattern

Tell students that they are used to seeing vowel digraphs like *ea, ai,* and *ie* working together in a syllable to make a single vowel sound. Print the words *wheat, strain,* and *thief* on the board. Underline the vowel digraphs and call on volunteers to identify the vowel sound and read the words aloud. Tell students that in some words these familiar vowel pairs have separate sounds and each sound falls in a different syllable. Print the word *react* on the board and say it aloud. Ask students how many vowel sounds they hear in the word *react. (two)*

Tell students that this is the VV syllable pattern: the word breaks between the two vowels (V/V). Demonstrate the V/V division pattern by drawing a slash between the two vowels. Explain that when they see a multisyllabic word with two adjacent vowels they should first try sounding it out with one vowel sound. If it doesn't make sense in context, they should try two vowel sounds.

Point to the first syllable in *react* and ask if it is open or closed. *(open)* Then point to the second, and ask if it is open or closed. *(closed)* Have students use what they know about these syllable types to blend the syllables in sequence and say the entire word.

## Practice Blending

Help students read the words and sentence shown below. Have them read the words using the V/V division pattern and blending the syllables in sequence. The high-frequency words in the sentence are underlined. Students should read the words as a whole; they should not attempt to sound them out.

quiet, fluid, create, mosaic, museum, oasis, fluent
<u>The</u> theater showed <u>a</u> film <u>about</u> <u>the</u> influence <u>of</u> science.

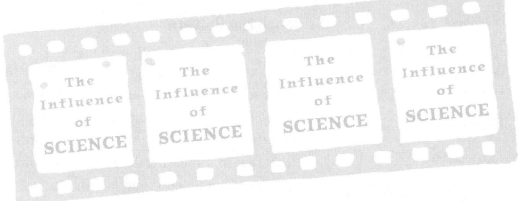

## Apply

**AUTHENTIC TEXT** Provide students with connected reading practice. Choose text selections at students' independent reading level. For strategies to preteach the high-frequency irregular words found in the text, see Chapter 9.

**10.48**

**Intervention Strategy**

**If students have difficulty distinguishing between a vowel-team syllable and adjacent vowels with individual sounds, suggest that they use context to confirm pronunciation.**

**DICTATION AND SPELLING**    Dictate the words shown below. Say each word, use it in a sentence, and then say the word again. For example, say: *The word is* being. *She is used to being the boss* . . . being. Have students say the word, then guide them in spelling it syllable by syllable. After students have written all of the words, read the sentence shown below.

Dictate the words one at a time, using the same procedure to guide them in spelling each word syllable by syllable. The high-frequency words in the sentence are underlined. Students should write the word as a whole; they should not attempt to sound them out.

being, theater, poetry, client, create, museum, quiet, reinforce
<u>The</u> museum is looking for scientists <u>to</u> cooperate on <u>a</u> project.

After the dictation, print the words and sentence on the board, and ask students to proofread their work. They should circle any word spelled incorrectly and write the correct spelling next to it.

**OBSERVE AND ASSESS**

*As students complete the Apply activities, use this question to assess their progress.*

| Question for Observation | Benchmark |
| --- | --- |
| *(Point to a word with the VV pattern.)* Can you blend the syllables to read this word? | Student can read words with the VV pattern. |

## The Next Step
Introduce students to words with adjacent vowels that are never seen together as digraphs yet also follow the V/V division pattern. Examples include *neon, diary, pioneer,* and *medium.*

TEACHING STRATEGY FOR

## Multisyllabic Words in Context

**10.50**

### Benchmarks

- ability to use syllabication and affix knowledge supported by context to read an unfamiliar word
- ability to use context to confirm the pronunciation of multisyllabic words

### Grade Level

- Grade 2 and above

### Prerequisites

- all previously introduced Teaching Strategies in this chapter, through Introducing the Syllable Type Consonant-*le*
- all Grades 1 and 2 phonic elements (see p. 8.8)

### Grouping

- whole class
- small group or pairs

### Materials

- copies of "Naming Living Things" (see Appendix)
- authentic text

# READING MULTISYLLABIC WORDS IN CONTEXT

This generic teaching strategy reinforces the concept of flexibility in approaching multisyllabic words. It shows students how to use their knowledge of affixes, syllabication, and sound/spelling correspondences to pronounce complex words and how to use context clues to confirm pronunciation. The passages are designed for third-grade students. The lesson can be adapted for other grades by using different passages.

## Warm Up

Print the following sentence on the board: *I want to make a* **record** *of all the music I* **record.** Have students read the sentence to themselves, then call on volunteers to read it aloud. Underline the word *record.* Discuss the similarities and differences between these two words, focusing on the first vowel sound and the syllable that is stressed. Discuss how students used what they know about syllable types and context to figure out how to pronounce these words.

Point out that students have learned different strategies to help them divide long words into manageable, recognizable chunks. Help them create a chart that lists these strategies for reading multisyllabic words. Display the chart in the classroom, so that students can refer to it throughout the year.

## What I Know About Reading Big Words

**1** Look for familiar word parts—prefixes and suffixes—and cover them.

**2** In the base word, look for familiar vowel and consonant patterns.

**3** Divide the base word into syllables. Sound out and blend the syllables to say the base word.

**4** Uncover the word parts and blend the whole word.

**5** Use the text to check that the word makes sense in the sentence.

### Teach/Model

Print the following sentences on the board:

We can trace the beginnings of many medicines used today to plants that grow in the jungles of the world. The first travelers to the New World left records telling how quinine was used to cure people suffering from malaria.

Tell students that these are the first two sentences from a paragraph about medicines made from plants. Have students follow along as you read up to the word *beginnings*. Point to the word and say: *Some of you may already know this word, but I don't want you to say it. I am going to show you how you could figure it out while you were reading if you didn't recognize it.* Use the following Think Aloud procedure to model the strategy.

**THINK ALOUD** *Here's a word I haven't seen before. First, I'm going to look for any familiar part—a prefix or suffix. Or it might be a compound word made up of two small words. Okay, I see the –ing and –s endings. Now I'll look at what's left. (Underline the letters* beginn.) *I know there are two vowels, so there must be two syllables. There is a consonant* g *between the two vowels. But I wonder if the first syllable breaks before or after the* g. *I recognize the VCV pattern, so I'll try breaking it before the* g *and sound it out with a long vowel /ē/. I also notice that the second syllable ends with the consonant* n *after the vowel* i. *So the vowel sound must be short.* Bē-gin . . . beginnings. *That sounds right.*

Provide time for students to read the rest of the excerpt to themselves. Then underline several words that students may not have seen in print before but were part of their oral vocabularies, such as *jungles* and *travelers.* Call on volunteers to explain how they used their knowledge of affixes, syllable patterns and types, and context to figure out how to say these words. For example, to read the word *jungles,* students should have noted the consonant-*le* final syllable and closed first syllable.

Students must use context to make sure that the new words they are reading make sense. Point out that especially in the case of *records,* with two possible pronunciations, they have to think about the way the words are being used: meaning and part of speech. Help them compare the differences in vowel sounds and stress depending on how the word *records* is used.

## Practice

Have students work in pairs to read the passage "Naming Living Things." Suggest that they use the chart "What I Know About Reading Big Words" to help them figure out new words. Call on volunteers to read the passage aloud.

## Apply

Have students select a short passage from grade-level text that they have not previously read. Ask them to read the passage silently and then aloud to a partner. Have them choose three new words and explain to their partner how they figured out the words. Monitor pairs, making sure that they provide specific information about the phonic, syllabic, and contextual clues that they used. Have students add the new words to their Word Study Notebooks.

**OBSERVE AND ASSESS**

*As students complete the Apply activity, use these questions to assess their progress.*

| Questions for Observation | Benchmarks |
|---|---|
| What new words did you figure out? How did you divide the words to read them? | Student can use syllabication and affix knowledge supported by context to read unfamiliar words. |
| How did you know these words made sense? | Student can use context to confirm the pronunciation of multisyllabic words. |

CHAPTER

# 11

# Reading Fluency

what?
why?
when?
how?

# what?

## Reading Fluency

11.2

*"Word recognition fluency, while not the goal of reading instruction, is necessary for good comprehension."*

—CARNINE ET AL., 1997

The long-term goal of reading instruction is comprehension. In order to achieve this goal, students need to become *fluent readers* able to (1) recognize words automatically, (2) group individual words into meaningful phrases, and (3) apply rapid phonic, morphemic, and contextual analyses to identify unknown words. Allington (1983) has described fluency as the "neglected goal" of reading instruction. In his review of the research, he concluded that: (1) fluency should be regarded as a necessary feature of good reading, (2) readers can improve fluency through explicit training, and (3) fluency training improves overall reading ability.

*Fluency* is often defined as the *rate* (words per minute) and *accuracy* (number of words correctly identified) with which students perform reading tasks. An additional dimension to fluency is known as *prosody,* or the rhythms and tones of spoken language. Whether text is being read silently or aloud, much of its meaning comes from the way it sounds. Students who read with expression are able to segment text into meaningful units, marking phrase and sentence boundaries with pauses, vowel lengthening, and changes in pitch and emphasis (Dowhower 1991).

At the earliest stage of reading development, students' oral reading is usually slow and labored, or disfluent. This is to be expected in late Kindergarten through early first grade because students are just beginning to "break the code" of written English, learning how to phonologically decode words into their constituent sounds and then *recode* or blend those sounds

## Foundation for Fluency

**a solid base of phonological knowledge**

**automatic word recognition**

**the ability to apply phonic, morphemic, and contextual analysis skills to recognize unfamiliar words**

**the ability to segment text into meaningful syntactic chunks**

**extensive practice with materials that are easy to read**

*See also . . .*

Section VIII: Reading and Responding
Chapter 19: Independent, Wide Reading

back together to pronounce a recognizable word. However, when students have learned to decode and automatically recognize many words by sight, they begin to read simple text aloud in a way that sounds like natural speech. This achievement, usually toward the end of first grade, is an important benchmark of fluent reading. By second grade, fluent reading is generally expected, yet a great deal of foundation building must occur in order to make it happen. Students in the upper grades who read aloud word by word or with little attention to commas or periods require intervention.

## Ways to Build Fluency

Students become fluent readers by reading. Struggling readers spend less time reading, and when they do read they read fewer words and often give up altogether because they make so many errors. Thus, poor fluency can become a self-perpetuating problem, with an ever-widening gap between disfluent readers and their peers. There are, however, several strategies that teachers can use to develop students' reading fluency.

### Independent Practice and Rereading

Fluency develops as a result of multiple opportunities to practice reading skills with a high rate of success. Therefore, the primary strategy for developing reading fluency is to provide extensive reading opportunities with manageable texts: decodable texts in the early part of first grade and beneath-frustration level, authentic readers from mid–first grade on. According to Martinez, Roser, and Strecker (1999), "By definition, text within a reader's instructional range reduces word recognition demands and allows for more rapid reading. As rate increases, the reader is able to devote more attention to meaning and the interpretation of meaning through phrasing and expressiveness." Rereading of texts is an effective way to provide repeated practice and thereby enhance fluency. There are many

## Strategies to Promote Independent Reading and Rereading

ways to incorporate rereading into the classroom and students' homes. All strategies that encourage rereading and independent reading will aid fluency.

- Match books available in the classroom and the school library to students' independent reading level. Text to develop fluency should contain a high proportion of words students are able to readily decode or that are already known to them.

- Encourage rereading activities that require repeated practice with the same text, such as partner rereading of decodable text, older students reading aloud stories to younger students, performing a play, rereading a passage to support answers given during class discussions, and so on. At home, students can work with family members to reread books they read several months ago, or they can alternate reading pages aloud and then reread the story switching pages.

## Auditory Modeling

**choral reading**

reading aloud simultaneously in a group

**echo reading**

reading aloud phrase by phrase, slightly after a live or taped model

**shared reading**

teacher reading aloud with all the students

**partner reading**

reading aloud taking turns with a partner who provides word identification help and feedback

## Auditory Modeling

According to Allington (1983), one of the reasons children fail to read fluently is that they have never been exposed to fluent reading models. Auditory modeling, either live or taped, may be the most powerful technique for developing prosodic reading (Dowhower 1991). By listening to good models of fluent reading, students learn how a reader's voice makes sense out of written text. As Dowhower explains, "Modeling shows the reader explicitly where to pause, where to change pitch, which words to stress, and which segments to elongate. It gives the reader a sense of what reading with expression sounds like." There are many forms of auditory modeling, including having students simply follow along in the text as they listen to a live or audiotaped model and having students do choral, echo, shared, and paired reading. Auditory modeling can be combined with the fluency-building techniques of repeated readings and phrase-cued text.

## Readers Theatre

Readers Theatre is a natural and fun way to encourage rereading of familiar text and to enhance students' phrasing and oral expression of written text. Students read text aloud, using their voices to bring the characters to life. No sets, costumes, props, or memorization of lines is necessary. When preparing to present a story, students "rehearse" by rereading their lines over the course of five days, in 30-minute practice sessions. Rehearsals can provide an opportunity for teacher and peer feedback about pace, phrasing, and expression. By bringing the text to life, performers gain a deeper understanding of the text, the characters' feelings, and the author's choice of words. Stories that have straightforward plots with an adequate amount of dialogue can be easily adapted as scripts to be read aloud.

During their 10-week Readers Theatre project with second graders, Martinez, Roser, and Strecker (1999) found that nearly all of the children made gains in their rate of reading. At the beginning of the project 76 percent of the students fell below the grade-level standard of 78 words per minute. By the end of the ten weeks, 75 percent of students approached or exceeded the standard for oral reading fluency.

## Repeated Readings

Intervention Strategy

Repeated readings is an effective intervention strategy for struggling readers who fall below established fluency norms. This method of repeated readings involves having a student read aloud a short, meaningful passage a number of times until a predetermined level of fluency is reached. Repeated reading can be implemented using available classroom materials, as long as the chosen text is relatively short (50–300 words) and readily decodable (text that students can read with about 95 percent accuracy or miss only about 1 out of every 20 words). When the desired rate of speed and accuracy is reached, the

**CORE Reading Research Anthology**

for background information

**11.6**

student moves on to a new passage. Dowhower (1989) found that the greatest percentage of fluency increase seems to come between the third and fifth rereadings.

By reading the same passage several times, students become familiar and automatic with the words it contains. In addition, there is evidence that repeated reading improves not only reading rate and accuracy, but comprehension as well (Dowhower 1987; O'Shea, Sindelar, and O'Shea 1985). This is because practice enables beginning readers to achieve a level of automaticity that allows them to focus on the meaning of the text. Research also points to the fact that repeated reading builds confidence and motivation in students, especially when they have an opportunity to chart their own progress (Koskinen and Blum 1984; Topping 1987; Trachtenberg and Ferrugia 1989). The real benefit of this practice is that student reading rates have been shown to increase with the first reading of each new passage. Gillet and Temple (1994) have explained that this happens because "all that rereading has helped them acquire more sight words and helped them learn to read aloud fluently and confidently."

## Phrase-Cued Texts

Students with good word-recognition skills may have poor fluency because they have difficulty grouping words that go together. As a result their oral reading is slow, word by word, and expressionless. Using *phrase-cued* text is another effective intervention strategy for improving students' phrasing ability and overall comprehension (Frase and Schwartz 1979; Mason and Kendall 1979; Kirby and Gordon 1988). Phrase-cued, or segmented, text is a written passage that is divided according to the natural pauses that occur within and between sentences. The phrase breaks can help students whose oral reading is disfluent, choppy, or monotone.

**CORE Reading Research Anthology**

for background information

By physically marking phrase boundaries, teachers can help students recognize the syntactic chunks that are formed by prepositional phrases, verbal phrases, and other clauses. There are several different ways to segment text. It can be done by adding vertical lines, diagonal slashes, or blank spaces to a standard paragraph format. Another way to segment text is to write each phrase on a separate line in a column format. Since passages are meant to be practiced orally, they should be brief (100–250 words) and well within students' instructional reading level. Narrative prose, poems, newspaper articles, and speeches are good choices for phrase-cued lessons. As students practice with segmented texts and become more adept in phrasing, they should be given conventional versions of the same passages. Rasinski (1994) cautions that the use of phrase-cued text is "no panacea for reading problems." It is, however, an appropriate intervention strategy that can be used as a 10- to 15-minute warm-up for other reading activities.

Connect to Theory

What do you do that enables students to develop fluency? What are your strategies to encourage independent reading and rereading of familiar texts? How do you incorporate auditory modeling into reading instruction? Make a list of your current classroom "fluency development" practices.

**NORMS**
performance standards

**ORF**
oral reading fluency

11.8

See also...

"Assessing Oral Reading Fluency,"
p. 11.16

## Oral Reading Fluency Norms

The data on the facing page represent the results of a one-minute timed sampling of students' oral reading of at least three carefully constructed passages given under consistent administration conditions. Students came from a variety of school districts, including large urban, racially mixed suburban, small city, and rural districts. The curriculum materials used for reading instruction in these districts also were varied and included both skill-based and literature-based basal programs.

Oral reading fluency (ORF) norms are highly indicative of reading comprehension ability. Given the data-collection procedures, these norms can serve as stable benchmarks for oral reading fluency. Teachers can use the norms to rank student performance and tailor instruction to students' individual needs. The percentiles represent the percentage of students that received scores equal to or lower than the given raw score. Generally, students reading at the 50th percentile in fluency have good reading comprehension of grade-level texts. A fifth-grade student who reads 165 wcpm (words correct per minute) late in the school year is very likely to have excellent comprehension ability; a fifth grader reading 130–140 wcpm will be able to handle most grade-level text. A fifth-grade student who reads 110 wcpm will likely have difficulty comprehending most grade level texts. For this student, it is important to give further diagnostic assessment to determine underlying foundation skill needs, such as decoding and phonemic awareness. Inefficiencies in the underlying component skills will impede fluency and ultimately will impede comprehension.

In addition to providing a way to assess a student's current reading level, the ORF norms can be used to monitor student progress over time. This is especially important for students whose fluency is in the at-risk range of the 25th percentile or below. The norms can identify target fluency rates. For example, to become an average reader, an early Grade 2 student reading 20 wcpm will need to gain roughly 70 wcpm by the end of the school year. With about 24 weeks between the first and third test administration, the student needs to improve by roughly 2.9 wcpm per week to realize the average fluency.

## Edformation Educational Averages Norm Table Report on Oral Reading Fluency – Graded Passages for Grades 1-8

| Grade | Percentile | Fall WCPM* | Winter WCPM | Spring WCPM |
|-------|-----------|------------|-------------|-------------|
| 1 | 90 | 0 | 62 | 104 |
|   | 75 | 0 | 38 | 77 |
|   | 50 | 0 | 22 | 52 |
|   | 25 | 0 | 12 | 33 |
|   | 10 | 0 | 0 | 21 |
| 2 | 90 | 96 | 124 | 141 |
|   | 75 | 71 | 100 | 118 |
|   | 50 | 49 | 77 | 94 |
|   | 25 | 28 | 53 | 71 |
|   | 10 | 15 | 32 | 52 |
| 3 | 90 | 125 | 152 | 168 |
|   | 75 | 97 | 125 | 139 |
|   | 50 | 74 | 97 | 111 |
|   | 25 | 52 | 72 | 85 |
|   | 10 | 31 | 52 | 62 |
| 4 | 90 | 143 | 166 | 180 |
|   | 75 | 118 | 140 | 152 |
|   | 50 | 95 | 115 | 125 |
|   | 25 | 72 | 91 | 101 |
|   | 10 | 49 | 67 | 80 |
| 5 | 90 | 168 | 183 | 189 |
|   | 75 | 142 | 157 | 166 |
|   | 50 | 116 | 131 | 137 |
|   | 25 | 89 | 107 | 111 |
|   | 10 | 65 | 81 | 88 |
| 6 | 90 | 171 | 184 | 200 |
|   | 75 | 143 | 161 | 172 |
|   | 50 | 115 | 133 | 145 |
|   | 25 | 91 | 106 | 116 |
|   | 10 | 71 | 82 | 91 |
| 7 | 90 | 200 | 206 | 212 |
|   | 75 | 174 | 182 | 193 |
|   | 50 | 148 | 158 | 167 |
|   | 25 | 124 | 133 | 145 |
|   | 10 | 104 | 115 | 124 |
| 8 | 90 | 206 | 217 | 223 |
|   | 75 | 183 | 193 | 198 |
|   | 50 | 155 | 165 | 171 |
|   | 25 | 128 | 141 | 146 |
|   | 10 | 101 | 112 | 118 |

**11.9**

*Words Correct Per Minute

SOURCE Copyright © 2001, Edformation, Inc. All rights reserved. Reprinted by permission.

PHONICS　　　HIGH-FREQUENCY WORDS　　　MULTISYLLABIC WORDS　　　READING FLUENCY　　　**DECODING**

# why?

## *Reading Fluency*

**11.10**

**CORE Reading Research Anthology**

for background information

Accurate, effortless, and expressive reading is regarded by most educators as the mark of proficient reading. Yet many teachers fail to develop it through instruction. If students' reading is slow and labored, they cannot remember what they read or relate the material to their own background knowledge to comprehend it. In general, less-fluent readers have poorer comprehension (Carnine, Silbert, and Kameenui 1997). In a study of elementary students referred for reading intervention, researchers found that an overwhelming majority of students had significant difficulties in fluency and that these difficulties were more apparent than those in word recognition or comprehension (Rasinski, Padak, and Dallinga 1991). Fluency affects the amount of material students are able and willing to read in a given amount of time. In one first-grade study, the average skilled reader read about three times as many words in group reading sessions as the average less-skilled reader (Allington 1983).

**Research Findings . . .**

*A fluent reader decodes text automatically, and therefore can devote his/her attention to comprehending what is read.*

—LABERGE & SAMUELS, 1974

*Achieving fluency is recognized as an important aspect of proficient reading, but it remains a neglected goal of reading instruction.*

—ALLINGTON, 1983

*With greater fluency, readers can concentrate on comprehending what they read, develop greater self-confidence, and enjoy reading more.*

—GILLET & TEMPLE, 1994

*If we provide diverse learners with the tools and strategies for achieving automatic and fluent word recognition, we increase their chances for successful reading experiences.*

—CHARD, SIMMONS & KAMEENUI, 1998

*Fluency is important because it provides a bridge between word recognition and comprehension.*

—AMBRUSTER, LEHR & OSBORN, 2001

## Suggested Reading . . .

*Beginning to Read: Thinking and Learning About Print* (1990) by Marilyn Jager Adams. Cambridge, MA: MIT Press.

"Oral Reading Fluency as an Indicator of Reading Competence: A Theoretical, Empirical, and Historical Analyses" (2001) by Lynn S. Fuchs, Douglas Fuchs & Michelle K. Hosp. *Scientific Studies of Reading, 5(3), 239-256.*

*Put Reading First: The Research Building Blocks for Teaching Children to Read* (2001) by Bonnie B. Ambruster, Fran Lehr & Jean Osborn. The Partnership for Reading. CIERA, U.S. Dept. of Education.

Report of the National Reading Panel, Teaching Children to Read (2000) NICHD. Bethesda, MD: National Institute of Health.

"Speaking of Prosody: Fluency's Unattended Bedfellow" (1991) by Sarah L. Dowhower. *Theory Into Practice* 30(3).

Using Timed Oral Readings of Predict Student Performance of Statewide Achievement Tests (2000) by Lindy Crawford, Gerald Tindal & Steve Stieber. University of Oregon.

*What Research Tells Us About Children with Diverse Learning Needs* (1998) edited by Edward Kameenui & Deborah Simmons. Mahwah, NJ: Erlbaum.

## *when?* Reading Fluency

**11.12**

"Edformation Educational Averages Norm Table Report on Oral Reading Fluency – Graded Passages" Grades 1–8, p. 11.9

Good teaching practices in the early grades lay the foundation for fluency. For many students, reading fluency develops naturally as they gain increasing familiarity with words, establish regular independent reading habits, and gain confidence with written text. Most students should be fluent readers by the end of second grade. For those who aren't, explicit fluency training intervention is indicated.

**Kindergarten and Grade 1** Starting at the end of Kindergarten, students may reread familiar, predictable text and decodable text to build fluency. In first grade, as they learn phonics, students should reread decodable text on their own, with partners, and with family members. Students also should have opportunities to listen to books being read aloud with natural intonation and rhythm and then practice imitating the model of fluent reading.

On the average, first graders increase their reading fluency approximately 2.10 correct words per minute per week (Fuchs, Fuchs, Hamlett, Walz, and Germann 1993). In an estimated 30 weeks of instruction, students should exit the first grade reading betweem 50-60 words per minute correctly (California State Board of Education 1999, Edformation, Inc. 2001).

**Grades 2 and 3**  In second grade, students should be able to read grade-level material aloud with accuracy and expression. To develop as fluent readers, students should practice independently with easy-to-read books that present few word-identification and comprehension problems. Teachers should encourage rereading through Readers Theatre and choral and paired reading. Students can also work in listening centers, imitating taped readings of texts. In third grade, students should continue with fluency-building reading practice, using increasingly longer and more complex texts.

Research indicates that, on the average, second graders increase their reading fluency approximately 1.46 correct words per minute per week (Fuchs et al. 1993), and that those reading at the 50th percentile late in the school year read 90–100 words per minute correctly (Hasbrouck and Tindal 1992, G. German 2001). The target rate for early Grade 3 students is roughly 74 words correct per minute and 111 by the end of the school year (G. German 2001). On average, a third grader's weekly reading fluency increases approximately 1.08 correct words per minute (Fuchs et al. 1993).

See also...

**AIMSweb assessment system**

**available through CORE**

www.edformation.com

**11.14**

See also...

**CORE Assessing Reading**

**"Resources for Assessing Reading"**

## Reading Fluency Tests

## When to Assess and Intervene

Starting in the middle of first grade and then again in the spring, teachers can ask students to do a formal timed reading using carefully prepared passages designed for this purpose. In second through eighth grade, students should be formally assessed three times a year for accurate benchmarking. Teachers record the number of words read correctly per minute on each of three one-minute timed readings and then record the median (middle, not average) score. This is repeated each time using the same three benchmark passages. In between the benchmark assessments, students who are not at the target score can be part of ongoing self-assessment, setting oral reading fluency goals, timing their repeated readings of a passage, and charting their progress over time. Students who need help "chunking" words into meaningful phrases should have opportunities to practice with phrase-cued text to improve expression.

**Upper-Grade Intervention**   In the upper grades, students should be reading fluently. If they are not, further assessment will be necessary to pinpoint the particular area(s) of weakness and to target instruction. Generally, intervention will be a combination of decoding instruction and practice with decodable text and high-interest, easy-reading authentic text. Students will also benefit from timed repeated readings, practice with phrase-cued texts, and listening to taped passages of

| CORE Assessing Reading | Other |
| --- | --- |
| Fry Oral Reading Test | AIMS web (CORE) |
| | Read Naturally |

## Assessment and Intervention

| | |
|---|---|
| **When** | Winter and spring Grade 1; fall, winter, and spring Grades 2-8 (every 10-12 weeks) for Benchmark passages. Weekly for below target progress monitoring. |
| **Who** | All students |
| **Assessment Tool** | Prepared passages |
| **Intervene if ...** | Students fall below established fluency norms (see "Edformation Educational Averages Norm Table Oral Reading Fluency-Graded Passages" for Grades 1–8, p. 11.9). |
| **How** | If students can decode but lack fluency, establish partner rereading practice, opportunities to practice reading and rereading phrase-cued text, and listening centers for small-group taping and retaping. |

# *how?* *Reading Fluency*

## Reading Fluency

**Grade Level**

• Grade 1 and above

**Grouping**

• individual

**Materials**

• three prepared benchmark passages
• copies of reading passages for assessor and student
• one-minute timer

**Resource**

• "Edformation Educational Averages Norm Table Report Oral Reading Fluency – Graded Passage" in Grades 1 through 8 (2001) by Gary German

### ASSESSING ORAL READING FLUENCY

In order for students to become fluent readers, they must spend time reading out loud, so their progress can be gauged. Curriculum-based measurement of oral reading fluency involves taking one-minute samples of students' oral reading of three brief passages and then recording the median (middle) score. Timed samples are taken three times a year using the same three benchmark passages for a consistent measurement of growth.

## Select the Passages

Select three specially prepared grade-level passages for each grade to be assessed regardless of students' instructional levels. (A fourth-grade student who reads at the third-grade level or who is receiving intervention instruction at the third-grade level will still read passages from fourth-grade text.) Well designed passages should contain roughly 250 words. The passages should be preserved for testing only and are not to be used for instruction. The same passages are used within the grade for each of the benchmark testing periods, two times in grade 1 and three times in grades 2-8.

## Administer the Test

Before the timed reading begins, instruct students to do their best reading and to try to read each word. Explain that you will tell them any words they do not know. Students are to begin reading aloud when you say *start.* As the student reads, follow along in a copy of the text, marking words that are incorrect. To be correct, words must be pronounced correctly in context; for example, *live* with a long-*i* sound in "There was a live audience during this show." Self-corrections within three seconds and correct phrasal or word repetitions are counted as correct. Additions do not count as errors. Mispronounciations, substitutions of any sort, or omissions are counted as incorrect. The same word read incorrectly is considered an error each time. If a student hesitates for three seconds in reading a word, supply the word and count it as an error. At the end of one minute, make a vertical line after the last word read. Repeat the procedure with the remaining two passages.

## Interpret the Data

For each passage, count the number of words up to the last word read. Then subtract the number of errors from the total words read to arrive at the number of words correct per minute (wcpm). For example, if a student in mid-Grade 2 reads 95 words in one minute, but mispronounces or omits 8 words, the wcpm for the passage is 87. Repeat this process for the remaining two passages and then record the median or middle score. For example, if a student reads passage 1 at 87 wcpm, then passage 2 at 89 wcpm and passage 3 at 84 wcpm, the median score is that for passage 1 – 87 wcpm. Then check this score against the oral reading fluency norms shown on page 11.9. To use the norms, find the grade level of the student who was tested and the season during which the testing took place. Compare the student's wcpm with the numbers given. The

**11.18**

top number shows the average fluency of students who are at or above the 90th percentile in reading fluency, the next number shows the fluency of students who are at the 75th percentile in fluency, the next shows students who are at the average or 50th percentile in reading fluency, the next shows students who are at the 25th percentile in reading fluency, and the bottom number indicates students whose fluency ranges below the last decile. Determine the percentile rank of the student's reading fluency. For example, the second-grade students whose average wcpm is 87 at midyear is between the 50th and 75th percentiles in reading fluency.

## Set Instructional Goals

You can use the results of the assessment to set instructional goals and monitor students' performance over time. Any student who falls significantly below the 50th percentile needs systematic instruction to increase reading fluency. You can use the table to set target fluency rates and calculate the weekly gain in wcpm that is necessary to achieve the target rate. Intervention strategies such as repeated readings and phrase-cued texts can then be incorporated into reading instruction. Periodic reassessment will help give parents concrete information about student progress and achievement in relation to established norms.

## READERS THEATRE

GRADE LEVEL
2
AND ABOVE
GRADE LEVEL

### Benchmarks

· ability to read text quickly and effortlessly
· ability to read with accurate word recognition, natural syntactic phrasing, and expression

### Grade Level

· Grade 2 and above

### Grouping

· whole class
· small group

### Materials

· copies of "TV Dinner" (see Appendix)

### Source

· "TV Dinner" (1979) by the San Francisco Mime Troupe

### Resource

· "'I Never Thought I Could Be a Star': A Readers Theatre Ticket to Fluency" (1999) by Miriam Martinez, Nancy L. Roser, and Susan Strecker.

This is a generic teaching strategy for developing fluency through Readers Theatre. The play "TV Dinner" is at the independent reading level of most students in Grade 4. Other text could be used for lower grade levels.

**11.19**

Selected stories should be within readers' instructional level and have straightforward plots, an adequate number of characters, and sufficient dialogue. In some cases adding brief narration may be needed to describe story action shown in the illustrations.

## Prep Time

1. Make copies of "TV Dinner" for each student to read at home.

2. Prepare rehearsal copies, one for each of the five speaking parts. Highlight one character's lines in each copy. If you want the whole class to perform the play in small groups, you will need to make a set for each group.

3. Practice reading the script aloud for effective modeling.

**11.20**

English language learners may not be familiar with the following idioms used in the play: *be behind on, cutting you off, pulling the plug, get out of sight, like a dream come true, fast food, bust in, aren't into it.* In addition to teaching students these idioms before they read the play, you may want to discuss the meanings of the following technical terms: *monitor, experiment, invention, subject, guinea pig, to beam programs.*

CORE Assessing Reading
"CORE Phonics Surveys"

## Teach/Model

On Monday, read aloud "TV Dinner" as students follow along in the text. Discuss the message of the play with students and how Pauline changes from the beginning to the end. Then focus on some aspect of oral reading fluency: how you used your voice to convey the characters' feelings, where you read slowly and where you read more quickly, how you interpreted punctuation to indicate pauses or emphasis. Tell students that they are going to have a chance to perform this as Readers Theatre on Friday, and that before then they are going to have many opportunities to rehearse the play. Have students take home the unmarked copy of the text and practice reading aloud all of the parts. This at-home practice should continue throughout the week.

## Practice

On Tuesday, divide students into small groups and distribute the copies that have individual parts highlighted. Have students practice reading the play aloud from beginning to end. Circulate among the groups, providing feedback and coaching to enhance students' oral expression. When groups have read through the play once, they should pass their scripts to a different member of the group and repeat the process with a new part. On Wednesday, have group members practice reading aloud two new roles. At the end of the session, either assign or have students choose the parts they will read before an audience in Friday's performance. Encourage students to pay special attention to their performance role when they practice with their at-home copy of the script. On Thursday, students should work together to read and reread their parts. They may want to make character labels and discuss where they will stand during the performance. Using this model of instruction, each performer will have read the play about 15–20 times by Friday.

## Apply

Have students perform their readings in front of a live audience. The reading can be performed for other classrooms or for parents and family members. The anticipation of an audience will increase student motivation.

*As students complete the Apply activity, use these questions to assess their progress.*

| Questions for Observation | Benchmarks |
|---|---|
| Can students read their lines effortlessly? | Students read the text with accuracy and at an appropriate rate. |
| Can students read their lines with expression? | Students use appropriate pauses, lower and raise the pitch of their voices, and emphasize certain words for stress. |

## The Next Step: Respond

According to the 1998 National Assessment of Educational Progress (NAEP), students who reported watching three or fewer hours of television each day had higher average reading scores than those who watched more.

Have students estimate how many hours of television they watch per week. Then ask them how many of those hours are advertisements. To confirm their estimates, have them keep a TV diary for one week. Students can brainstorm a list of things they could do instead of watching TV.

INTERVENTION STRATEGY FOR

## Reading Fluency

### Benchmarks

- ability to read with accuracy, speed, and appropriate intonation
- ability to read at selected target rate

11.22

### Grade Level

- Grade 1 and above

### Grouping

- pairs

### Materials

- copies of short passages for practice reading
- audiotape of selected passages
- one-minute timer
- copies of "Timed Reading Chart" (see Appendix)
- blue and red pencils
- tape recorder

**See also . . .**

**CORE Reading Research Anthology**

for background information

# REPEATED READING

Intervention Strategy

Rereading of familiar text is an excellent way to develop fluency. This generic teaching strategy uses auditory modeling, timed self-assessments, and partner feedback to motivate and engage students. It can be adapted by having students practice reading independently with an audiotape or do unassisted repeated readings, with partners providing word-identification help, feedback, and encouragement. Note that partners need not be reading at the same level or practicing their oral reading with the same passage.

## Prep Time

1. Help each student select an easy, interesting passage for practice reading. The passage should be too long to memorize: 50–100 words for younger children and 200 words or more for older students.

2. Prepare an audiotape of the selected passages.

## Teach/Model

Model reading aloud a different passage from the same story that one of the students selected for practice reading. Discuss your oral reading performance, prompting students to comment on the speed, accuracy, and expression with which you read. Tell them that they are going to have a chance to practice reading, so that they can become fluent readers.

## First Timed Reading

Using a one-minute timer, have each student do an unrehearsed first reading of the passage. Ask the student to read the passage aloud, underline any words she or he does not know, and make a vertical line after the last word read when the timer goes off. Help the student count the number of words read correctly, and color the Timed Reading Chart with a blue pencil up to that number. Discuss the words that the student underlined, focusing on the specific letters, letter patterns, or word structures that were confusing. Then work with the student to set a new target rate for the passage. The initial goal should be sufficiently high to require the student to practice rereading the passage several times. For example, using Hasbrouck and Tindal's ORF norms, 80 words correct per minute would be a reasonable target rate for an early Grade 2 student.

## Reading Practice

Have pairs of students listen to an audiotape of a passage as they follow along in the text. Students should play the tape again, and this time the student who selected the particular passage should read aloud with the tape. The student can practice with the audiotape several times before reading the passage aloud without the tape. Partners should listen carefully to each reading and rate the reader's improvement. As pairs work together, circulate to monitor word identification and comprehension. After the first partner has practiced reading the passage three times, partners should switch roles and work with the passage selected by the second student. Daily practice can continue for one or two days both at school and at home.

## Second and Third Timed Readings

Do a second timed reading of the passage and help students record the results on the Timed Reading Chart with a red pencil. As the rate increases, help students set a new goal for their target rate and continue practicing the passage over the course of several days. If the student is able to reach the end of the passage before the minute is up, instruct the student to start again at the beginning of the passage and mark the last word read.

Help the student record the results of the third timed reading with a red pencil on the Chart. When the reader reaches the set goal, begin a new passage and repeat the practice. Successive portions of a long story work well for repeated readings.

**11.24**   "Timed Reading Chart"

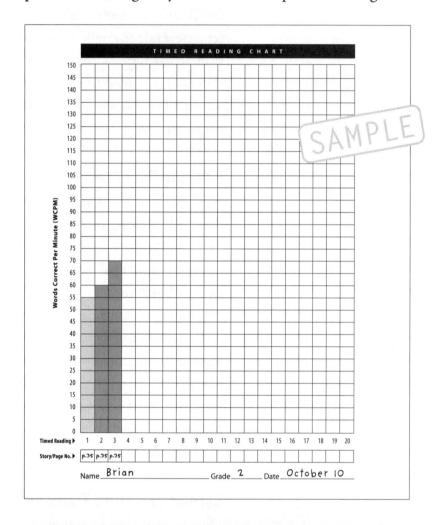

**OBSERVE AND ASSESS**

*As students complete the Timed Readings, use these questions to assess their progress.*

| Questions for Observation | Benchmarks |
|---|---|
| Can you read the passage quickly and accurately? | Student demonstrates increased rates with each timed reading, until the target rate goal is reached. |
| Can you read the passage with good expression? | Student uses appropriate pauses and stress to convey meaning of the passage. |

## Reading Fluency

### DEVELOPING PROSODY WITH PHRASE-CUED TEXT

**11.25**

### Benchmarks

- ability to read with accurate word recognition and natural syntactic phrasing
- ability to mark the phrase boundaries in conventional text

### Grade Level

- Grade 2 and above

### Grouping

- whole class
- small group or pairs

### Materials

- copies of "The Fourth of July Parade"—with phrase cues and without phrase cues (see Appendix)
- copies of another short passage at students' independent reading levels

**CORE Reading Research Anthology**

for background information

---

**Intervention Strategy**

This generic teaching strategy is intended as a 10- to 15-minute warm-up for other reading activities. The sample passage is designed to be read with 90 percent accuracy by students at the end of second grade. Different passages can be used to match particular students' independent reading levels.

### Prep Time

Select a short passage. It should be 100–250 words, with no less than a 90 percent accuracy level for most students in the class. For very young readers, it should be at 95 percent accuracy level and controlled for phonic elements and high-frequency words that have been taught.

### Warm Up

Read aloud a nursery rhyme, such as "Jack and Jill," in a flat, expressionless monotone, inserting unnatural pauses between words. Ask students to comment on your reading, telling what you were and were not doing correctly. Explain that when we read aloud with natural expression, we show which words go together by pausing, raising and lowering the pitch of our voices, and emphasizing certain words and sounds.

### Teach/Model

On the board, print "Jack and Jill went up the hill to fetch a pail of water" as one long sentence on a single line. This time read the line with expression and ask students which words were said louder or with more emphasis (*Jack, Jill, hill, pail, water*) and after which words there is a pause (*Jill/hill/*

*pail/water).* As students respond, put a slash (/) after the words to indicate the pause. Print the next sentence of the nursery rhyme on the board and repeat the procedure. Point out that there is a longer pause—a full stop—between the two sentences. Indicate the full stop with two slashes (//).

**11.26**

Distribute copies of the phrase-cued text passage "The Fourth of July Parade" and explain to students that the story has already been broken into phrases for them. Explain that at first it may be difficult to read the story with the slash marks, but it will get easier with practice. Explain that whether good readers are reading aloud or silently, they automatically read words that go together in "chunks." This helps them read more fluently and better understand what they are reading.

Read the passage aloud, modeling the "chunking" of syntactic phrases in an expressive voice, while students follow along. Discuss why particular words go together and how you use your voice to indicate the breaks between the phrases. Point out that often these chunks tell what the subject does and where the action takes place: for example, *decided to ride; in our town.* Discuss how you also used punctuation as a clue to meaning: for example, stressing the word *fun* to emphasize the exclamation, or raising the pitch to indicate the question in the second paragraph.

## Practice

Have students practice reading the phrase-cued passage "The Fourth of July Parade" aloud with you chorally. Do this two times. Then distribute copies of "The Fourth of July Parade" without phrase cues and have students read it aloud. Ask them to compare their final reading with their first attempts.

## Apply

Distribute copies of the second short passage that you have selected and tell students that they are going to work in small groups (or pairs) to decide where the natural pauses between phrases should go. They should pencil in the slashes to show the pauses and then check their work by reading the passage aloud. Have students work together to assess their oral expression, deciding if their phrasing makes sense when it is read aloud. Suggest that they make adjustments until they are satisfied.

Later in the day or on the following day, bring students back to the whole group. Have them compare phrasing by reading aloud and listening to each other's oral phrasing. Lead discussions about differences in student phrasing, and give explicit information about clauses and other syntactic units as appropriate.

**Intervention Strategy**

**Students who have difficulty with this activity may benefit from listening to and reading along with an audiotape of the story several times.**

**OBSERVE AND ASSESS**

*As students complete the Apply activity, use these questions to assess their progress.*

| Questions for Observation | Benchmarks |
|---|---|
| How do you group words together to make sense of the passage? | Student can mark natural phrase breaks in unsegmented text. |
| Can you read the passage in a way that sounds smooth and natural? | Student reads aloud by grouping words in syntactic phrases. |

## The Next Step

Have students test their skill by trying to read other classroom material, indicating phrasing with prosody.

## Section References

**11.28**

Adams, M. J. 1990. *Beginning to read: Thinking and learning about print.* Cambridge, MA: MIT Press.

Adams, M. J., R. Treiman, and M. Pressley. 1998. Reading, writing, and literacy. In I. E. Sigel and K. A. Renninger (eds.), *Handbook of child psychology.* (5th ed.) Vol. 4: *Child psychology in practice* (pp. 275–355). New York: Wiley.

Allington, R. L. 1983. Fluency: The neglected goal. *The Reading Teacher* 36, pp. 556–561.

Ambruster, B., F. Lehr, and J. Osborn. 2001. *Put Reading First: The Research Building Blocks for Teaching Children to Read.* Partnership for Reading. Washington, DC: U.S. Dept. of Education.

Anderson, R. C., E. H. Hiebert, J. A. Scott, and I. A. G. Wilkinson. 1985. *Becoming a nation of readers: The report of the Commission on Reading.* Champaign, IL: Center for the Study of Reading and National Academy of Education.

Beck, I. L. 1997. Response to "overselling phonics." *Reading Today* 17 (Oct./Nov.).

Beck, I. L., and C. Juel. 1992. The role of decoding in learning to read. In S. J. Samuels and A. E. Farstrup (eds.), *What research has to say about reading instruction.* Newark, DE: International Reading Association.

Blevins, W. 1998. *Phonics from A to Z: A practical guide.* New York: Scholastic.

Brady, S., A. Fowler, B. Stone, and N. Winbury. 1994. Training phonological awareness: A study with inner-city kindergarten children. *Annals of Dyslexia* 44, pp. 26–102.

Bruck, M., and R. Treiman. 1990. Phonological awareness and spelling in normal children and dyslexics: The case of initial consonant clusters. *Journal of Experimental Child Psychology* 50.

Burmeister, L. D. 1975. *Words—From print to meaning.* Reading, MA: Addison-Wesley.

California State Board of Education. 1999. *Reading/language arts framework for California public schools: Kindergarten through grade twelve.* Sacramento: California Department of Education.

Carnine, D. W., J. Silbert, and E. J. Kameenui. 1997. *Direct instruction reading.* (3rd ed.) Upper Saddle River, NJ: Prentice-Hall.

Carroll, J. B., P. Davies, and B. Richman. 1971. *Word frequency book.* Boston: Houghton Mifflin.

Chall, J. S. 1983a. *Stages of reading development.* New York: McGraw-Hill.

Chall, J. S. 1983b. Literacy: Trends and explanations. *Educational Researcher* 12, pp. 3–8.

Chall, J. S. 1996. *Learning to read: The great debate.* (3rd ed.) New York: McGraw-Hill.

Chall, J. S., and H. M. Popp. 1996. *Teaching and assessing phonics: A guide for teachers.* Cambridge, MA: Educator's Publishing Service.

Chard, D. J., D. Simmons, and E. Kameenui. 1998. Word recognition: Research bases. In E. Kameenui and D. Simmons (eds.), *What research tells us about children with diverse learning needs* (pp. 141–167). Mahwah, NJ: Erlbaum.

Cunningham, A. E., and K. E. Stanovich. 1997. Early reading acquisition and its relation to reading experience and ability ten years later. *Developmental Psychology* 33(6), pp. 934–945.

Cunningham, P. M. 1995. *Phonics they use: Words for reading and writing.* (2nd ed.) New York: HarperCollins.

Cunningham, P. M. 1998. The multisyllabic word dilemma: Helping students build meaning, spell, and read "big" words. *Reading and Writing Quarterly* 14(2), pp. 189–218.

Cunningham, P. M., and R. L. Allington. 1999. *Classrooms that work.* New York: HarperCollins.

Dolch, E. W. 1955. *Methods in reading.* Champaign, IL: Garrad.

Dowhower, S. L. 1987. Effects of repeated reading on second-grade transitional readers' fluency and comprehension. *Reading Research Quarterly* 22, pp. 389–406.

Dowhower, S. L. 1989. Repeated reading: Research into practice. *The Reading Teacher* 42, pp. 502–507.

Dowhower, S. L. 1991. Speaking of prosody: Fluency's unattended bedfellow. *Theory Into Practice* 30(3).

Durrell, D. 1963. *Phonograms in primary grade words.* Boston: Boston University Press.

Ehri, L. 1994. Development of the ability to read words: Update. In R. Ruddell, M. Ruddell, and H. Singer (eds.), *Theoretical Models and Processes of Reading.* Newark, DE: International Reading Association.

Eldredge, J. L. 1995. *Teaching decoding in holistic classrooms.* Englewood Cliffs, NJ: Merrill.

Foorman, B. R., D. J. Francis, S. E. Shaywitz, B. A. Shaywitz, and J. M. Fletcher. 1997. The case for early reading intervention. In B. Blachman (ed.), *Foundations of reading acquisition and dyslexia* (pp. 243–264). Mahwah, NJ: Erlbaum.

Frase, L. T., and B. J. Schwartz. 1979. Typographical cues that facilitate comprehension. *Journal of Educational Psychology* 71, pp. 197–206.

Freedman, S. W., and R. C. Calfee. 1984. Understanding and comprehending. *Written Communication* 1.

Fry, E. 1993. *Reading teacher's book of lists.* (3rd ed.) Upper Saddle River, NJ: Prentice-Hall.

Fry, E. 1997. Common reading problems and tools to diagnose them. In Lillian R. Putnam (ed.), *Readings on language and literacy: Essays in honor of Jeanne S. Chall.* Cambridge, MA: Brookline Books.

Fry, E., D. Fountoukidis, and J. Polk. 1985. *The new reading teacher's book of lists.* Upper Saddle River, NJ: Prentice-Hall.

Fuchs, L. S., D. Fuchs, C. L. Hamlett, L. Walz, and G. Germann. 1993. Formative evaluation of academic progress: How much growth can we expect? *School Psychology Review* 22, pp. 27–48.

Gaskins, I., L. Ehri, C. Cress, C. O'Hara, and K. Donnelly. 1996. Procedures for word learning: Making discoveries about words. *The Reading Teacher* 50(4), pp. 312–327.

Gillet, J. W., and C. Temple. 1994. *Understanding reading problems: Assessment and instruction.* (4th ed.)

Germann, G. 2001. Edformation Educational Averages: Reading – General Outcome Measure. *Personal Communications.* www.edformation.com

Gough, P. B., and M. A. Walsh. 1991. Chinese, Phoenicians, and the orthographic cipher of English. In S. A. Brady and D. P. Shankweiler (eds.), *Phonological process in literacy: A tribute to Isabelle Y. Liberman.* Mahwah, NJ: Erlbaum.

Gough, P. B., C. Juel, and P. Griffith. 1992. Reading, spelling and the orthographic cipher. In P. Gough, L. Ehri, and R. Treiman (eds.), *Reading Acquisition* (pp. 35–48). Hillsdale, NJ: Erlbaum.

Hall, S. L., and L. C. Moats. 1999. *Straight talk about reading: How parents can make a difference during the early years.* Lincolnwood, IL: NTC/Contemporary Publishing Group.

Hanna, P. R., R. E. Hodges, J. L. Hanna, and E. H. Rudorf, Jr. 1996. *Phoneme-grapheme correspondences as cues to spelling improvement.* Washington, DC: U.S. Office of Education.

Hasbrouck, J. E., and G. Tindal. 1992. Curriculum-based oral reading fluency norms for students in grades 2 through 5. *Teaching Exceptional Children* (Spring), pp. 41–44.

Henry, M. 1990. *Words: Integrated decoding and spelling instruction based on word origin and word structures.* Austin, TX: PRO-ED.

Henry, M. 1997. The decoding/spelling continuum: Integrated decoding and spelling instruction from pre-school to early secondary school. *Dyslexia* 3, pp. 178–189.

Iversen, S., and W. Tunmer. 1993. Phonological processing skills and the Reading Recovery program. *Journal of Educational Psychology* 85, pp. 112–126.

Johns, J. L. 1980. First graders' concepts about print. *Reading Research Quarterly* 15.

Just, M. A., and P. A. Carpenter. 1987. *The psychology of reading and language comprehension.* Needham Heights, MA: Allyn & Bacon.

Kirby, J. R., and C. J. Gordon. 1988. Text segmenting and comprehension: Effects of reading and information processing abilities. *British Journal of Educational Psychology* 58, pp. 287–300.

Koskinen, P. S., and I. H. Blum. 1984. Repeated oral reading and the acquisition of fluency. In J. Niles and L. Harris (eds.), *Changing perspectives on research in reading/language processing and instruction.* 33rd yearbook of the National Reading Conference. Rochester, NY: National Reading Conference.

LaBerge, D., and S. J. Samuels. 1974. Toward a theory of automatic information processing in reading. *Cognitive Psychology* 6, pp. 292–323.

Liberman, I. Y., D. Shankweiler, and A. M. Liberman. 1989. The alphabetic principle and learning to read. In D. Shankweiler and I. Y. Liberman (eds.), *Phonology and reading disability: Solving the reading puzzle* (IARLD Research Monograph Series). Ann Arbor, MI: University of Michigan Press.

Lovett, M. W. 1987. A developmental approach to reading disability: Accuracy and speed criteria of normal and deficient reading skill. *Child Development* 58.

Martinez, M., N. Roser, and S. Strecker. 1999. "I never thought I could be a star": A Readers Theatre ticket to fluency. *The Reading Teacher* 52(4), pp. 326–334.

Mason, J. M., and J. R. Kendall. 1979. Facilitating reading comprehension through text structure manipulation. *Alberta Journal of Educational Research* 25, pp. 68–76.

Mewhort, D. J. K., and A. J. Campbell. 1981. Toward a model of skilled reading: An analysis of performance in tachistoscoptic tasks. In G. E. Mackinnon and T. G. Walker (eds.), *Reading research: Advances in theory and practice* 3 (pp. 39–118). New York: Academic Press.

Moats, L. C. 1999. Teaching reading is rocket science: What expert teachers of reading should know and be able to do. *American Educator.*

Nagy, W., and R. C. Anderson. 1984. How many words are there in printed school English? *Reading Research Quarterly* 19, pp. 304–330.

National Institute of Child Health and Human Development. 2000. *Report of the National Reading Panel, Teaching Children to Read: Reports of the Subgroups.* Bethesda, MD: National Institutes of Health.

O'Shea, L. J., P. T. Sindelar, and D. J. O'Shea. 1985. The effects of repeated readings and attentional cues on reading fluency and comprehension. *Journal of Reading Behavior* 17, pp. 129–142.

Rasinski, T. V. 1994. Developing syntactic sensitivity in reading through phrase-cued texts. *Intervention in School and Clinic* 29(3).

Rasinski, T. V., N. D. Padak, and G. Dallinga. 1991. *Incidences of difficulty in reading fluency.* Paper presented at the annual meeting of the College Reading Association, Crystal City, VA.

Reitsma, P. 1983. Printed word learning in beginning readers. *Journal of Experimantal Child Psychology* 36.

Samuels, S. J., D. LaBerge, and C. D. Bremer. 1978. Units of word recognition: Evidence for developmental change. *Journal of Verbal Learning and Verbal Behavior* 17, pp. 715–720.

San Francisco Mime Troupe. 1979. *TV dinner.* Performed by the San Francisco Mime Troupe, San Francisco.

*Scholastic literacy place.* 2000. New York: Scholastic.

Share, D. 1995. Phonological recoding and self-teaching: Sine qua non of reading acquisition. *Cognition* 55, pp. 155–218.

Share, D., and K. E. Stanovich. 1995. Cognitive processes in early reading development: Accommodating individual differences into a mode of acquisition. *Issues in Education: Contributions for Educational Psychology* 1, pp. 1–57.

Shefelbine, J. 1990. A syllable-unit approach to teaching decoding of polysyllabic words to fourth- and sixth-grade disabled readers. In J. Zutell and S. McCormick (eds.), *Literacy theory and research: Analysis from multiple paradigms* (pp. 223–230). Chicago: National Reading Conference.

Sims, M. 1999. *Bass Lake,* Sound Out Chapter Book. Novato, CA: High Noon Books.

*SRA/Open Court Reading.* 2000. Worthington, OH: SRA/McGraw-Hill.

Stanovich, K. E. 1994. Romance and reality. *The Reading Teacher* 47(4), pp. 280–291.

Stein, M., B. Johnson, and L. Gutlohn. 1999. Analyzing beginning reading programs: The relationship between decoding instruction and text. *Remedial and Special Education* 20.

Topping, K. 1987. Paired reading: A powerful technique for parent use. *The Reading Teacher* 40, pp. 608–614.

Torgesen, J. K., R. Wagner, and C. Rashotte. 1997. Approaches to the prevention and remediation of phonologically based reading disabilities. In B. Blachman (ed.), *Foundations of reading acquisition and dyslexia* (pp. 287–304). Mahwah, NJ: Erlbaum.

Trachtenberg, P., and A. Ferrugia. 1989. Big books from little voices: Reaching high-risk beginning readers. *The Reading Teacher* 42, pp. 284–289.

Treiman, R. 1993. *Beginning to spell.* New York: Oxford University Press.

Treiman, R., and J. Baron. 1981. Segmental analysis ability: Development and relation to reading ability. In G. E. MacKinnon and T. G. Waller (eds.), *Reading research: Advances in theory and practice.* Vol. 3. New York: Academic Press.

Tunmer, W., and J. Chapman. 1996. Language prediction skill, phonological reading ability, and beginning reading. In C. Hume and R. M. Joshi (eds.), *Reading and spelling: Development and disorder.* Mahwah, NJ: Erlbaum.

Wagner, R., and T. Barker. 1994. The development of orthographic processing ability. In V. Berninger (ed.), *The varieties of orthographic knowledge I: Theoretical and developmental issues* (pp. 243–276). Dordrecht, The Netherlands: Kluwer.

**11.30**

# SECTION V

# Spelling

# INTRODUCTION

## Section V: Spelling

*"Learning to spell isn't only about having a good memory. It's about mastering the patterns, principles, and rules that enable us to spell nearly 90 percent of all words in English."*

—MOATS, 1997

A basic definition of *spelling* is "the ability to write words with the proper letters in correct sequence." To educators spelling is this, but more: *spelling* refers to the *developmental process* of moving from temporary or transitional spelling approximations to formal or traditional spelling used in publication and final copies. Regardless of how one defines spelling, current theories have found order where for four hundred years critics could see only confusion and whimsy. Researchers including Chomsky and Halle (1968), Taylor (1981), and Venezky (1970) have found evidence that while English spelling is complex, it is also orderly and patterned.

There are three layers at work in English orthography: (1) the Alphabetic Layer, (2) the Pattern Layer, and (3) the Meaning Layer (Bear, Invernizzi, Templeton, and Johnston 1996). The English spelling system is alphabetic because letters (either singly or in pairs) can be matched to sounds and written in left-to-right sequence. There is also a pattern layer in English spelling that goes beyond a one-to-one letter/sound correspondence. Letters combine to form patterns within syllables (CVC, CVC*e*, CVVC), and there are also patterns that occur where syllables meet within a word. The third layer comes into play because English spelling is *morphophonemic;* that is, spelling relates letters and letter patterns not only to sounds, but also to units of meaning. Understanding these layers helps us address the problems that children experience as they learn to read and write the English language.

Section II: Word Structure, "Useful
Spelling Generalizations," p. 3.26

Section IV: Decoding, "Align
Decoding Instruction with the Stages
of Reading Development," p. IV.iv

Section II: Word Structure
Chapter 4: Structure of Spanish
and Other Languages

for more on Spanish spelling issues

Children's understanding of spelling patterns and rules has an
enormous impact on their reading ability. Researchers including Bear (1982; 1991), Gentry (1998), Henderson (1981), Gill
(1992), Ehri (1992), and Zutell (1992) have found a correlation
between children's spelling and their (1) reading accuracy and
fluency, (2) comprehension, (3) articulation, and (4) vocabulary and concept development. In fact, the only two factors
known to be *causally related* to reading achievement—knowledge of the alphabet and phonemic awareness—are spelling
skills. Marilyn Jager Adams (1990) has explained how the orthographic (letter identification) processor in the brain is connected to the phonological and meaning processors. *Learning
to spell a word correctly reinforces automatic recognition when
reading* because *all* the graphemes become embedded in our
mind and get attached to sound and meaning. When the eye
sees a word—and its pronunciation and meaning come automatically—all attention can be focused on comprehending
the text. Because spelling knowledge involves structural and
morphemic information about words, spelling also expands
vocabulary and reinforces word-analysis strategies.

As children develop spelling (encoding) and reading (decoding)
skills, they progress through a series of discernible stages. The
chart on page V.v shows the "synchrony" of development that
takes place as children experiment with written language and
gradually master the various layers of English orthography.
Chapter 12 discusses the stages of spelling development.
Spelling requires a higher level of precision than reading. This
is because in written language many different orthographic
patterns can represent the same sound. When teachers take

**CORE Reading Research Anthology**

for background information

**Section II: Word Structure**

**Chapter 4: Structure of Spanish and Other Languages**

for problematic English sound/spellings and sound contrasts

into account the synchrony of reading and spelling development, they are able to implement instructional strategies that foster overall literacy development. Chapter 13 discusses teaching strategies for effective spelling instruction.

Over the past twenty years formal spelling instruction has fallen out of favor, with spelling being viewed as something that is naturally "caught" during the reading and proofreading process. Yet research shows that being immersed in reading does not guarantee that students will learn to spell, and in places where teachers stopped providing formal spelling instruction, test scores dropped and schools began to experience failure with literacy education (Peters 1985; Ehri 1992; Hughes and Searle 1996; Colvin 1995). There is now wide agreement among teachers that for many children spelling is not *caught*—it must be *taught*.

**ELL** English language learners benefit from formal English spelling instruction for all the reasons that native speakers do. However, since they learn to spell more quickly when teachers build on their first language, it is important that teachers know where writing systems overlap and where they differ.

# SYNCHRONY OF READING AND SPELLING DEVELOPMENT

| Stages of Reading Development | Layers of English Orthography | Stages of Spelling Development | Examples |
|---|---|---|---|
| Pre-alphabetic | | Preliterate | Students learn that text is read from left to right. They recognize the letters of their names in environmental print and use pictographic writing: for example, for *bug,* or for *house.* |
| Early Alphabetic | Alphabetic | Early Letter Name | Students begin to read CVC words and represent words with a single predominant sound, usually a consonant. Later they spell first and last consonant sounds: for example, KR for *car.* |
| | | Middle and Late Letter Name | Students include a vowel in each syllable. They spell regular short-vowel patterns, but use the letter name for long-vowel sounds: for example, CAK for *cake.* |
| Mature Alphabetic | Pattern | Within Word Pattern | Students know most sound/spellings and recognize common "chunks" like phonograms and word endings. They begin to experiment with long-vowel markers: for example, SNAIK for *snake.* |
| Orthographic | | Syllable Juncture | Students process words using syllable and morphemic information. They read unknown words by analogy to known words: for example, *should → would.* They join syllables correctly by doubling or changing letters when using inflectional endings. |
| | Meaning | Derivational Constancy | Students focus on meaning and correctly spell derived forms with affixes and roots. |

*Based on Moats 1998 and Bear et al. 1996.*

## Standards for Spelling

**KINDERGARTEN**

- Spell independently by using prephonetic knowledge, sounds of the alphabet, and knowledge of letter names.

**GRADE 1**

- Spell three- and four-letter short-vowel words and grade-level–appropriate sight words correctly.

**GRADE 2**

- Spell frequently used, irregular words correctly (e.g., *was, were, says, said, who, what, why*).
- Spell basic short-vowel, long-vowel, *r*-controlled, and consonant-blend patterns correctly.

**GRADE 3**

- Spell correctly one-syllable words that have blends, contractions, compounds, orthographic patterns (e.g., *qu,* consonant doubling, changing the ending of a word from *–y* to *–ies* when forming the plural), and common homophones (e.g., *hair/hare*).
- Arrange words in alphabetic order.

**GRADE 4**

- Spell correctly roots, inflections, suffixes and prefixes, and syllable constructions.

**GRADE 5**

- Spell roots, suffixes, prefixes, contractions, and syllable constructions correctly.

**GRADE 6**

- Spell frequently misspelled words correctly (e.g., *their, they're, there*).

SOURCE
Adapted from *English-Language Arts Content Standards for California Public Schools: Kindergarten Through Grade Twelve* (1999). Sacramento: California Department of Education.

**GRADE 7**

- Spell derivatives correctly by applying the spellings of bases and affixes.

**GRADE 8**

- Use correct spelling conventions.

# CONTENTS

## Section V: Spelling

CHAPTER

12

# Stages of Spelling Development

what?
why?
when?
how?

# what? *Stages of Spelling Development*

**12.2**

**CORE Reading Research Anthology**

for background information

Years ago most educators believed that spelling was a matter of visual memory, mastered by rote one word at a time. In the past thirty years, research has had a dramatic impact on the way we think about the English spelling system and the way children learn to spell. Although visual memory does play a part in spelling, orthographic knowledge is mostly a matter of concept development. We now know that a child learns to spell in a roughly predictable series of *developmental stages,* or steps, and that these steps build on one another. Researchers found that the types of spelling errors children make are *systematic and common* from child to child (Chomsky 1970; Read 1971; Henderson and Beers 1980). These temporary or "invented" spellings are not random, but rather evolve as children develop their orthographic knowledge.

*Cognitive development* plays an important part in this process. If a child understands that words are made up of sounds and that these sounds can be represented by letters, words become easier to spell (Moats 1995, 1997). At more advanced levels, students draw on their knowledge of sound/spelling pattern variations, syllable types, and word structure—inflectional endings, affixes, and roots. According to Hughes and Searle (1997), proficient spellers use these multiple logics to spell unknown words. As students mature in their spelling development they also begin to rely on the visual features of words (length, letter order, patterns) and their knowledge of parts of speech and word meaning.

Connect
to Theory

To promote concept development, spelling instruction should lead students to discover the recurring patterns of English orthography. Think about the patterns that the following groups of words represent. What spelling generalizations can you deduce from each group of words?

GROUP 1
lid
sit
rip
thin
chip

GROUP 2
read
leaf
seat
meal
team

GROUP 3
hope
rode
smoke
coat
soap

GROUP 4
running
hopping
swimming
patted
hugged

GROUP 5
legal
illegal
legality
legalization
legalize

*(See Appendix for answer.)*

read

leaf

seat

meal

team

## 12.4 Stages of Spelling Development

Many researchers have uncovered stages of spelling development. These stages are relevant for students from preschoolers through adults. While different researchers have given the stages different names, the characteristics of each stage remain remarkably the same across research groups (Henderson and Templeton 1986; Beers, Cramer, and Hammond 1995; Bear et al. 1996; Moats 1995). Bear and his associates (1996) describe students' spelling behaviors in terms of five stages of spelling development.

One way to understand these stages of development is by examining three levels of learning at each stage: (1) What students do correctly, (2) What students use but confuse, and (3) What is absent in students' spelling. It is the second level that informs instruction—when teachers see that students are *using* a concept but confusing it, they know which spelling rules and patterns students are ready to learn (Invernizzi, Abouzeid, and Gill 1994). For example, a child who writes MEEL to spell *meal* is using the idea that vowel sounds can be spelled by a pair, or team, of letters and therefore is ready to learn the most common ways of spelling the long-*e* sound. In contrast, a child who spells *meal* as ML doesn't yet understand that vowels are needed in every syllable and therefore won't be able to assimilate information about vowel teams.

## Sequence of Spelling Development

The following chart shows examples of how orthographic knowledge develops, as seen in five students' spelling inventories. The students' spellings provide teachers with useful information about their stage of spelling development.

### EXAMPLES OF STUDENTS' SPELLING—SEPTEMBER

| WORDS | SARAH | MICHAEL | LUCAS | ANNA | AMANDA |
|---|---|---|---|---|---|
| ▶ bed | BD | bed | bed | bed | bed |
| ▶ ship | SP | SEP | ship | ship | ship |
| ▶ drive | JRV | DRIV | drive | drive | drive |
| ▶ bump | B | BOP | BUNP | bump | bump |
| ▶ when | WN | WHAN | when | when | when |
| ▶ train | | TRAN | TRANE | train | train |
| ▶ closet | | CLAST | CLOZIT | CLOSIT | closet |
| ▶ chase | | CAS | chase | chase | chase |
| ▶ float | | FLOT | FLOTE | FLOTE | float |
| ▶ beaches | | BECIS | BECHES | BEACHS | beaches |
| ▶ preparing | | | PREPRING | PREPEARING | preparing |
| ▶ popping | | | POPING | popping | popping |
| ▶ cattle | | | CATOL | CATTEL | cattle |
| ▶ caught | | | COUT | COT | COUGHT |
| ▶ inspection | | | INSPECSIN | INSPECSHIN | inspection |
| ▶ puncture | | | PUCSHR | PUNKSHER | PUNCHER |
| ▶ cellar | | | SELR | SELLER | CELLER |
| ▶ pleasure | | | PLESER | PLEJER | PRESHER |
| ▶ squirrel | | | SKWEL | SKWREL | SQURRIEL |
| ▶ fortunate | | | FREHNIT | FOOHINIT | FORCHENT |
| Spelling Stage | Early Letter Name | Middle Letter Name | Within Word Pattern | Syllable Juncture | Syllable Juncture |

From *Words Their Way: Word Study for Phonics, Vocabulary, and Spelling Instruction,* by Donald R. Bear, Marcia Invernizzi, Shane Templeton, and Francine Johnston. © 1996.

**12.6**

## Stage I: Preliterate Spelling

In the Preliterate stage students' "spellings" are characterized by scribbles, drawings, and arbitrary numbers and letters of the alphabet. Students in Preschool and early Kindergarten who use these signs understand that written symbols represent words and that print carries a message. As students' writing progresses, their scribbles begin to look like real writing with repeated strokes going up and down, and eventually they use only real letters of the alphabet. According to Marie Clay (1975), this type of writing reveals an understanding of two important concepts: (1) letters occur over and over again; and (2) a finite number of letters can be used to create an infinite number of words.

The key element that is missing at the Preliterate stage is sound/symbol correspondence. In order to move to the next stage, Letter Name spelling, students have to grasp the alphabetic principle—the idea that letters represent sound and that words can be segmented into sounds (Bear et al. 1996).

**See also . . .**

**Section III: Sound/Print Connection**

for Preliterate-stage activities that develop alphabet recognition and phonemic awareness.

---

**An Evolution of a Preliterate Child's Writing**

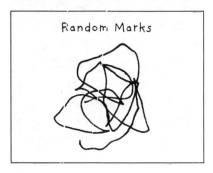

Random Marks

Representational Drawing

"This is my sister"

Drawing Distinct from writing

"A flower for my Mom"

Mock Linear or
Letter-like

*eeeeeelee*

*t/ɔʎɔʎL*

"A note for Daddy"

Symbol Salad
Random Letters and
Numbers

*RS294S*

"Macaroni"

Syllabic / Phonetic

K        "cat"

BB       "baby"

ILU      "I love you"

**12.7**

From *Words Their Way: Word Study for Phonics, Vocabulary, and Spelling Instruction* © 1996.

## Characteristics of the Preliterate Stage of Spelling

|  | What Students Do Correctly | What They Use but Confuse | What Is Absent |
|---|---|---|---|
| ▶ EARLY | • Write on the page<br>• Hold the writing implement | • Drawing and scribbling for writing | • Sound/symbol correspondence<br>• Directionality |
| ▶ MIDDLE | • Horizontal movement across page<br>• Clear distinction between writing and drawing<br>• Use lines and dots for writing<br>• Use letter-like forms | • Use letters, numbers, and letter-like forms<br>• Writing may wrap from right to left at the end of a line | • Sound/symbol correspondence |
| ▶ LATE | • Consistent directionality<br>• Use some letter/sound matches | • Substitute letters that sound, feel, and look alike: *b* and *p*; *b* and *d* | • Complete sound/symbol correspondences<br>• Consistent spacing between words |

From *Words Their Way: Word Study for Phonics, Vocabulary, and Spelling Instruction* © 1996.

## Stage II: Letter Name Spelling

The Letter Name Spelling stage is divided into two parts: Early Letter Name spelling and Middle and Late Letter Name spelling.

### Early Letter Name Spelling

In the Early Letter Name stage students often write the sounds they feel and hear at the beginning and end of words. Students write only the most salient sounds in words, represented by consonants, but they often confuse the "feel" of similar consonant sounds when they make choices about what letters to use. This can be seen in the sample spellings in Sarah's choice of the letter *j* when writing the consonant blend in the word *drive*. Other commonly confused sounds are /f/ and /v/, /b/ and /p/, /d/ and /t/, and /s/ and /z/.

These substitutions, often seen in students' writing in Kindergarten to early Grade 1, underscore how important articulation and phonemic awareness are to spelling proficiency. Students' experience with particular sight words, such as their names, also affects how accurately they represent consonant sounds and the inclusion of vowels. Even at this stage, a child named *Peter* may have no difficulty spelling his name.

**12.8**

*Sarah*

| Early Letter Name Spelling | |
| --- | --- |
| ▸ bed | BD |
| ▸ ship | SP |
| ▸ drive | JRV |
| ▸ bump | B |
| ▸ when | WN |

From *Words Their Way* © 1996.

**See also...**

**Section II: Word Structure, "Consonant Phoneme Articulation," p. 3.5**

for other frequently confused consonant sounds

**Section III: Sound/Print Connection**

**Chapter 7: Phonemic Awareness**

| Early Letter Name Spelling with Word Boundaries |
| --- |

i K hskpen

"I like housekeeping"

From *Words Their Way: Word Study for Phonics, Vocabulary, and Spelling Instruction* © 1996.

## Characteristics of the Early Letter Name Stage of Spelling

| | What Students Do Correctly | What They Use but Confuse | What Is Absent |
|---|---|---|---|
| ▶ **EARLY** | • Write syllabically, spelling most salient feature of the syllable or word<br>• Use several letters of alphabet | • Substitute letters based on point of articulation<br>• Y for *when*, J for *drive* | • Beginning and end of syllables<br>• Vowels in syllables<br>• Some spacing between words |
| ▶ **MIDDLE** | • Directionality<br>• Use most letters of the alphabet<br>• Clear letter/sound correspondences | • Substitute letters based on point of articulation | • Vowels in syllables<br>• Some spacing between words |
| ▶ **LATE** | • Use most beginning and ending consonants<br>• Clear letter/sound correspondences | • Continue to substitute consonants based on point of articulation<br>• BD for *bed*, YN or WN for *when*, SP for *ship*, JRF for *drive*<br>• Use some vowels | • Consistent use of vowels<br>• Consistent use of consonant blends and digraphs |

From *Words Their Way: Word Study for Phonics, Vocabulary, and Spelling Instruction* © 1996.

## Middle and Late Letter Name Spelling

| Middle Letter Name Spelling | |
| --- | --- |
| ▶ bed | bed |
| ▶ ship | SEP |
| ▶ drive | DRIV |
| ▶ bump | BOP |
| ▶ when | WHAN |
| ▶ train | TRAN |
| ▶ closet | CLAST |
| ▶ chase | CAS |
| ▶ float | FLOT |
| ▶ beaches | BECIS |

12.10

From *Words Their Way* © 1996.

See also...

Section II: Word Structure

Chapter 4: Structure of Spanish and Other Languages

By the Middle Letter Name stage students have learned that syllables have vowels and they make the connection between short-vowel sounds and their standard spellings. They often use letter names to spell long-vowel sounds, so that *came* is spelled CAM. In the Late Letter Name stage, students correctly spell most initial consonant blends and digraphs, as seen in the sample spellings where Michael has written DRIV, WHAN, TRAN, CLAST, and FLOT. In the Letter Name stage the nasal sounds /m/ and /n/, which are difficult to feel and hear, are often missing. When students begin to include a vowel marker and the letters *m* and *n* in words like *bump* and *went,* it is a sign that they are progressing from this stage to the Within Word Pattern stage. This usually takes place sometime between late Grade 1 and Grade 3.

**ELL** FOR SPANISH-SPEAKING STUDENTS . . .
For background information about English spelling errors commonly made by Spanish-speaking students, see *CORE Reading Research Anthology.*

---

✎ MIDDLE LETTER NAME — KINDERGARTENER

My FAvT AnML is A DoG
AnD i hoP viT i Love MY
FrST GAD Te Thr  onFA You

"My favorite animal is a dog. And I hope that I love
my first grade teacher — one of you."

> ✏ LATE LETTER NAME — 1ST GRADER
>
> Snow pants and cowt and hat and glavs
> my mom stufsme up on cowld wntr days.
> She stufs me and stafs me I cant even
> bryth. mom y do you do thes to me?
> you stuf me up sow moch you make me
> loock like a frye menstr. I hat to cinpan
> bot mom. ples stop the pan. now mom,
> stop and I wount loock lik e frye monstr
> enymore.

## Characteristics of the Middle and Late Letter Name Stage of Spelling

|  | What Students Do Correctly | What They Use but Confuse | What Is Absent |
|---|---|---|---|
| ▸ **EARLY** | • Most initial and final consonants<br>• A vowel in most syllables | • Use letter name for vowels: CAM for *came*, LIK for *like*<br>• Substitute letter name closest in point of articulation for short vowels: NAT for *net*, SEP for *ship* | • Long-vowel markers<br>• Vowels in unstressed syllables: SISTR for *sister*<br>• Most consonant blends and digraphs |
| ▸ **MIDDLE** | • Initial and final consonants<br>• Frequently occurring short-vowel words | • Include some consonant blends and digraphs | • Preconsonantal nasals: BOB for *bump* |
| ▸ **LATE** | • All of the above plus:<br>• Regular short-vowel patterns<br>• Most consonant blends and digraphs<br>• Preconsonantal nasals | • Regular pattern for a low-frequency short vowel: COT for *caught*<br>• Spell some common long-vowel words: *time, hope* |  |

From *Words Their Way: Word Study for Phonics, Vocabulary, and Spelling Instruction* © 1996.

**12.12**

| Lucas | |
| --- | --- |
| **Within Word Pattern Spelling** | |
| ▶ bed | bed |
| ▶ ship | ship |
| ▶ drive | drive |
| ▶ bump | BUNP |
| ▶ when | when |
| ▶ train | TRANE |
| ▶ closet | CLOZIT |
| ▶ chase | chase |
| ▶ float | FLOTE |
| ▶ beaches | BECHES |
| ▶ preparing | PREPRING |
| ▶ popping | POPING |
| ▶ cattle | CATOL |
| ▶ caught | COUT |
| ▶ inspection | INSPECSIN |
| ▶ puncture | PUCSHR |
| ▶ cellar | SELR |
| ▶ pleasure | PLESER |
| ▶ squirrel | SKWEL |
| ▶ fortunate | FREHNIT |

## Stage III: Within Word Pattern Spelling

In this stage students focus on the vowel within syllables. They correctly spell short-vowel sounds, as well as *r*-controlled vowels, and begin to experiment using long-vowel markers—CVC*e (late)*, CVVC *(nail)*, and CVV *(day)* patterns—but tend to overgeneralize. This can be seen in the sample spellings where Lucas has written TRANE and FLOTE. Generally students in Grades 2–3 have a more abstract understanding of orthography, recognizing that English spelling involves more than a one-to-one correspondence between sounds and letters. Lucas's invented spellings of these two words with long-vowel sounds include five letters even though the words have only four sounds. In the Within Word Pattern stage, students realize that letter sequences relate to sound and meaning (Henderson 1990). When they have clearly understood the differences between long- and short-vowel patterns, they enter the next stage—ready to focus on the spelling conventions of multi-syllabic words.

---

✍ WITHIN WORD — 3RD GRADER

### MY LOG

I have a right to look at the SS fish. I have a right to RAED. I have a right to play. I have a right to lerne. I have a right to help frends. I have a right to lerne slfe Defens! I have a right to go to school. (stamp)

## Characteristics of the Within Word Pattern Stage of Spelling

|  | What Students Do Correctly | What They Use but Confuse | What Is Absent |
|---|---|---|---|
| ▶ **EARLY** | • Initial and final consonants<br>• Consonant blends and digraphs<br>• Regular short-vowel patterns and preconsonantal nasals<br>• Good accuracy on *r*-controlled single-syllable short-vowel words: *fur, bird*<br>• Some infrequently used short-vowel words and frequently used long-vowel words: *like, see* | • Long-vowel markers: SNAIK/*snake* | • Consonant doubling: POPING, STOPED |
| ▶ **MIDDLE** | • All of the above plus:<br>• Slightly more than half of the single-syllable, long-vowel words: *hike, nail* | • Long-vowel markers: NITE/*night*<br>• Consonant patterns: SMOCK/*smoke*<br>• Inventive substitutions in frequent, unstressed syllable patterns: TEACHAUR/*teacher*<br>• *–ed* and other common inflections: BATID/*batted* |  |
| ▶ **LATE** | • All of the above plus:<br>• Single-syllable, long-vowel words<br>• May know some common Latin suffixes | • Low-frequency, long-vowel words: HIEGHT/*height*<br>• *–ed* and other common inflections<br>• Represent some common Latin suffixes phonetically | • Consonant doubling<br>• *e*-drop: AMAZZING/*amazing* |

From *Words Their Way: Word Study for Phonics, Vocabulary, and Spelling Instruction* © 1996.

## Stages IV and V: Syllable Juncture Spelling and Derivational Constancy Spelling

Many of the features of the last two developmental stages overlap. For example, in both stages students focus on the connection between spelling patterns and word meaning (Templeton 1983). They also begin to notice how a change in accent on two syllables can affect the word's syntactic and semantic function (Bear et al. 1996). Students may begin to compare the stress and vowel sounds in the verb *compose* and the related noun *composition*.

### Syllable Juncture Spelling

In the Syllable Juncture stage students begin to drop, double, and change letters as needed at the point where syllables meet. Both Anna and Amanda have doubled the *p* in *popping* to preserve the short-vowel sound in the first syllable. Amanda also has correctly dropped the *e* at the end of *prepare* before adding *–ing*. This concern with base words and inflectional endings and suffixes brings into focus the level of meaning related to syntax or grammar and affixation (Bear et al. 1996). Students may be working in the Syllable Juncture stage from late Grade 2 to Grade 5. In the next stage, they begin to examine word roots and the origins of multisyllabic words.

12.14

**Anna**

| Syllable Juncture Spelling | |
|---|---|
| ▸ train | train |
| ▸ closet | CLOSIT |
| ▸ chase | chase |
| ▸ float | FLOTE |
| ▸ beaches | BEACHS |
| ▸ preparing | PREPEARING |
| ▸ popping | popping |
| ▸ cattle | CATTEL |
| ▸ caught | COT |
| ▸ inspection | INSPECSHIN |
| ▸ puncture | PUNKSHER |
| ▸ cellar | SELLER |
| ▸ pleasure | PLEJER |
| ▸ squirrel | SKWREL |
| ▸ fortunate | FOOHINIT |

From *Words Their Way* © 1996.

**Amanda**

| Syllable Juncture Spelling | |
|---|---|
| ▸ preparing | preparing |
| ▸ popping | popping |
| ▸ cattle | cattle |
| ▸ caught | COUGHT |
| ▸ inspection | inspection |
| ▸ puncture | PUNCHER |
| ▸ cellar | CELLER |
| ▸ pleasure | PRESHER |
| ▸ squirrel | SQURRIEL |
| ▸ fortunate | FORCHENT |

From *Words Their Way* © 1996.

---

✎ BEGINNING SYLLABLE JUNCTURE — 7TH GRADER

### Changes in 7th grade

I half to get up earlyer and spent more time on homwork. At home I will try to keep all my stuff togther and stay ornagized. And I want to make mor firends and do more thing in school.

## Derivational Constancy Spelling

During this stage students continue to integrate the consonant doubling principle and begin to examine how spelling patterns remain constant among related words—*photograph, photographer, photography; sign, signature, resignation.* Despite pronunciation differences in stressed syllable and vowel sound, students recognize that the spelling patterns remain the same because the words are part of the same family, related in etymology and meaning. Generally students in Grades 4–5 begin to think about common roots and "keep" the *music* in *musician* and the *magic* in *magician.* The Derivational Constancy stage is a lifelong stage of spelling development, lasting from about age 10 to 100 (Bear et al. 1996).

**12.15**

---

### ✍ DERIVATIONAL CONSTANCY — 4TH GRADER

My experience intervewing
a first grader

My experience was surprising because Simon did not speek english. He was from a diffirent country. And when I was intervewing him I was startled because he had such an axent! He speeks aribic. He likes basebal, baskitbal, and hocky.

---

**Characteristics of the Syllable Juncture and Derivational Constancy Stages of Spelling**

| | What Students Do Correctly | What They Use but Confuse | What Is Absent |
|---|---|---|---|
| **▶ EARLY** | • Initial and final consonants<br>• Consonant blends and digraphs<br>• Short-vowel patterns<br>• Long-vowel patterns<br>• *–ed* and most common inflections | • Consonant doubling<br>• Long-vowel patterns in accented syllables: PERAIDING/*parading*<br>• Reduced vowel in unaccented syllables: CIRCUL/*circle*<br>• Doubling + *e*-drop: AMAZZING/*amazing*<br>• Common Latin suffixes: ATTENSHUN/*attention* | • Occasional deletion of middle syllables<br>• Assimilated prefixes<br>• Root constancies in derivationally related pairs |
| **▶ MIDDLE** | • All of the above plus:<br>• Consonant doubling: *stopping*<br>• Doubling + *e*-drop: *amazing*<br>• Common Latin suffixes: *attention* | • Assimilated prefixes: ACOMODATE/*accommodate*<br>• Vowel alternations in derivationally related pairs: COMPUSITION/*composition*<br>• Consonant alternations in derivationally related pairs: SPACIAL/*spatial* | |
| **▶ LATE** | • All of the above plus:<br>• Long-vowel patterns in accented syllables<br>• Doubling + *e*-drop (except where overlaps with assimilated prefixes)<br>• Most vowel and consonant alternations | • Same as above | |

From *Words Their Way: Word Study for Phonics, Vocabulary, and Spelling Instruction* © 1996.

**12.16**

Connect to Theory

Look at the following words from Victor's writing sample.

oppizit (opposite)

absents (absence)

carrige (carriage)

coperation (cooperation)

ammusement (amusement)

conclussion (conclusion)

Use the questions on the following chart to analyze Victor's spellings. Based on your observations, what is Victor's stage of spelling development?

| What is Victor doing correctly? | What does Victor use but confuse? | What is absent from Victor's spelling? |
|---|---|---|
|  |  |  |

(See Appendix for answer.)

# why? *Stages of Spelling Development*

**12.18**

**CORE Reading Research Anthology**

for background information

There are two compelling reasons for teaching spelling based on the unique developmental level of each student. First, students grasp English spelling patterns and principles at different rates. When they are presented with spelling words that they are not ready to learn, spelling becomes a matter of memorization rather than concept development. This is what occurs when teachers report that students "know" a word on Friday and forget it on Monday. A child who is just beginning to spell short vowels in a CVC pattern isn't ready to grapple with a list of words that have long *a* spelled *ai* and *a*-consonant-*e* because words like *paid* and *make* require more than the basic understanding that letters map to sounds.

Second, teachers have long been aware that among students in any given classroom, there is a wide range of spelling achievement. When students are forced to deal with word patterns that are too advanced, they become frustrated and begin to make desperate "stabs" at correct spellings. This is seen when students miss more than 50 percent of the words in a given list and their invented spellings deteriorate in quality, making it difficult for teachers to see error patterns (Morris, Nelson, and Perney 1986; Schlagal 1986). In addition, students quickly lose their motivation to learn correct spelling patterns when they are asked to work at levels that are too advanced. Similarly, they may lose interest when given words that are too easy or already well understood. By adapting instruction to each child's individual stage of development, teachers can support the synchrony of learning in all areas of literacy—reading, writing, and spelling.

**Research Findings . . .**

*If a child can spell a word, he or she can usually read the word. Spelling knowledge is an amalgam of an understanding of how one's writing system works and an understanding of the sound structure of one's language.*

—EHRI, 1992

*Many people think that spelling is memorizing all the words in a dictionary. That would truly be a daunting task! However, we have a useful and efficient alphabet. In English, there are patterns, principles, and rules for organizing spelling words.*

—FOORMAN, 1997

*When children have an inadequate base in word knowledge, they rely heavily on rote memory to learn assigned words. But if what is learned by rote does not fit with the child's current intuitions about how words are built, such a strategy fails in the long term.*

—SCHLAGAL & SCHLAGAL, 1992

*Students who are taught at their developmental level learn how to spell better than those students who are plugged into an arbitrary sequence of spelling features.*

—MORRIS ET AL., 1995

**Suggested Reading . . .**

*Development of Orthographic Knowledge and the Foundations of Literacy: A Memorial Festschrift for Edmund Henderson* (1992) edited by Shane Templeton & Donald Bear. Mahwah, NJ: Erlbaum.

*Spelling: Development, Disability, and Instruction* (1995) by Louisa Cook Moats. Timonium, MD: York Press.

*Words Their Way: Word Study for Phonics, Vocabulary, and Spelling Instruction, Second Edition* (2000) by Donald R. Bear, Marcia Invernizzi, Shane Templeton & Francine Johnston. Upper Saddle River, NJ: Prentice-Hall.

# Assessing Stages of Spelling Development

**12.20**

**CORE Assessing Reading**
**"Resources for Assessing Reading"**

Helping students to grow as spellers begins with assessment. An effective way to determine how students are progressing in their early spelling knowledge is to administer a spelling inventory at regular intervals—for example, at the beginning, middle, and end of the school year. The focus of an inventory is to examine the types of errors made by students as well as to take note of correctly spelled words. The same inventory can be used each time as long as the words are not taught directly or assigned for weekly word-study practice and spelling tests.

## Spelling Inventories

| CORE Assessing Reading | Other |
| --- | --- |
| "Words Their Way" Elementary Qualitative Spelling Inventory (Grades K–6) | Qualitative Inventory of Word Knowledge (QIWK) |
| "Words Their Way" Upper Level Qualitative Spelling Inventory (Grades 6–8) | Diagnostic Spelling Potential Test |
| CORE Spanish Spelling Inventory (Grades K–6) | Diagnostic Screening Test–Spelling |

# ASSESSMENT AND INTERVENTION

| When | Late Kindergarten |
|---|---|
| Who | All students |
| Assessment Tool | *CORE Assessing Reading,* "Words Their Way" Elementary Qualitative Spelling Inventory (first five words) |
| Intervene if ... | Assessment indicates that student is at the Preliterate stage of spelling development. |
| How | Small-group intervention, 10–15 minutes, 3–4 times per week for as long as needed |
| When | Mid-Grade 1 |
| Who | All students |
| Assessment Tool | *CORE Assessing Reading,* "Words Their Way" Elementary Qualitative Spelling Inventory (first five to ten words) |
| Intervene if ... | Assessment indicates that student is at or before the Early Letter Name stage of spelling development. |
| How | Small-group intervention, 10–15 minutes, 3–4 times per week for as long as needed. If student shows no progress, phonemic awareness assessment and intervention may be indicated. |
| When | Early Grade 2 |
| Who | All students |
| Assessment Tool | *CORE Assessing Reading,* "Words Their Way" Elementary Qualitative Spelling Inventory |
| Intervene if ... | Assessment indicates that student is at or before the Middle Letter Name stage of spelling development. |
| How | Small-group intervention, 10–15 minutes, 3–4 times per week for as long as needed. If student shows no progress, phonemic awareness assessment and intervention may be indicated. |

CONTINUED ▷

## ASSESSMENT AND INTERVENTION (CONTINUED)

| | |
|---|---|
| **When** | Early Grade 3 |
| **Who** | All students |
| **Assessment Tool** | *CORE Assessing Reading,* "Words Their Way" Elementary Qualitative Spelling Inventory |
| **Intervene if . . .** | Assessment indicates that student is at or before the Late Letter Name stage of spelling development. |
| **How** | Small-group intervention, 10–15 minutes, 3–4 times per week for as long as needed. If student shows no progress, phonemic awareness assessment and intervention may be indicated. |
| **When** | Early Grade 4 |
| **Who** | All students |
| **Assessment Tool** | *CORE Assessing Reading,* "Words Their Way" Elementary Qualitative Spelling Inventory |
| **Intervene if . . .** | Assessment indicates that student is at or before the early point in the Within Word Pattern stage of spelling development. |
| **How** | Small-group intervention, 10–15 minutes, 3–4 times per week for as long as needed. If student shows no progress, phonemic awareness assessment and intervention may be indicated. |
| **When** | Early Grade 5 |
| **Who** | All students |
| **Assessment Tool** | *CORE Assessing Reading,* "Words Their Way" Elementary Qualitative Spelling Inventory |
| **Intervene if . . .** | Assessment indicates that student is at or before the middle point in the Within Word Pattern stage of spelling development. |
| **How** | Small-group intervention, 10–15 minutes, 3–4 times per week for as long as needed. If student shows no progress, phonemic awareness assessment and intervention may be indicated. |

| | |
|---|---|
| **When** | Early Grade 6 |
| **Who** | All students |
| **Assessment Tool** | *CORE Assessing Reading,* "Words Their Way" Upper Level Qualitative Spelling Inventory, and analysis of students' writing samples |
| **Intervene if . . .** | Assessment indicates that student is at or before the early to middle point in the Syllable Juncture stage of spelling development. |
| **How** | Small-group intervention, 10–15 minutes, 3–4 times per week for as long as needed. If student shows no progress, phonemic awareness assessment and intervention may be indicated. |
| **When** | Mid-Grade 7 and above |
| **Who** | All students |
| **Assessment Tool** | *CORE Assessing Reading,* "Words Their Way" Upper Level Qualitative Spelling Inventory |
| **Intervene if . . .** | Assessment indicates that student is at or before the late point in the Syllable Juncture stage of spelling development. |
| **How** | Small-group intervention, 10–15 minutes, 3–4 times per week for as long as needed. If student shows no progress, phonemic awareness assessment and intervention may be indicated. |

12.23

**CORE Reading Research Anthology**

for background information

ELL  FOR SPANISH-SPEAKING STUDENTS . . .
To assess students' orthographic knowledge in Spanish, see "CORE Spanish Spelling Inventory" in *CORE Assessing Reading.*

# how?

## *Assessing Stages of Spelling Development*

**12.24**

While all students pass through the five developmental stages, it is important to keep in mind that the rate of progress through the sequence of stages varies enormously and that there is generally an overlap between stages (Moats 1995). The type, amount, and intensity of instruction a child receives influence how quickly and how well he or she will learn conventional spellings (Tangel and Blachman 1995; Uhry and Shepherd 1993; Hughes and Searle 1997). Teachers can recognize the mastering of patterns when they see that students overgeneralize their use: for example, using the silent-*e* marker to indicate all long-vowel sounds. Gradually students begin to automatize the words that actually follow this pattern and those that don't. When they learn to spell long-vowel sounds in other ways, they show that their spelling strategies and orthographic knowledge have matured. Assessing the spelling stage and characteristics of each student may seem labor-intensive at first, but as teachers become more accustomed to the various stage indicators, the stages become easier to determine and provide valuable information for planning instruction.

## Step 1: Collect Samples of Student Work

Samples from daily writing activities are a good starting point for assessing students' knowledge of spelling rules and patterns. Sometimes, however, samples from students' writing do not contain enough invented spellings because students limit their word choices to words they know they can spell correctly (Bear et al. 1996). The best approach is to gather invented

See also . . .

CORE Assessing Reading

"'Words Their Way' Qualitative Spelling Inventory"

"CORE Spanish Spelling Inventory"

spellings from both formal inventories and writing samples. This provides a sufficient sampling size and enables the teacher to compare students' spelling performance in different contexts. If teachers or students are uncomfortable with formal testing, a broad sample of student writing can be collected and examined using the Qualitative Spelling Checklist, shown later in this chapter.

## Step 2: Administer the Spelling Inventories

The "Words Their Way" Elementary Qualitative Spelling Inventory and the "Words Their Way" Upper Level Inventory have been specially designed to provide teachers of students in grades K–8 with a large enough sample of invented spellings to determine each student's stage of development. Words were selected for the inventories based on their frequency of occurrence and the orthographic patterns that are characteristic of each stage. In each inventory words are presented from the easiest to the hardest to spell.

## Step 3: Correct the Inventories

First, teachers should correct the inventories by circling each error and writing the word correctly beside it. They should then count the number of words spelled correctly to come up with a ratio of correct to total. (Letters written backward should not be counted as errors.) It is important to compare the invented spellings on the inventories to those in daily writing samples to ensure that you get an accurate picture of students' spelling knowledge. Counting the number of words spelled correctly is the first step, but teachers need more qualitative information than in the inventories to determine a student's stage of development and plan appropriate word-study activities.

**Intervention Strategy**

Student self-assessment plays an important part in developing good spelling habits, or "spelling consciousness." Meet with students and ask them to identify a word they think they may have misspelled. Discuss the strategies they used to spell the word and focus on (1) what is correct about the misspelling and (2) how they can remember to spell the word correctly in the future.

See also . . .

Chapter 13: Spelling Instruction "Do-It-Yourself Spelling"

## Step 4: Analyze the Results

Teachers can analyze the results of the spelling inventories and students' writing samples to determine a stage of development by using: (1) Qualitative Spelling Checklist (p. 12.27), (2) Spelling-by-Stage Assessment Scale (p. 12.28), and (3) Inventory Error Guide (Elementary and Upper Levels).

**12.26**

See also...

Core Assessing Reading

"Elementary Level Inventory Error Guide"

"Upper Level Inventory Error Guide"

### Qualitative Spelling Checklist and Spelling-by-Stage Assessment Scale

The checklist asks a series of questions about what the student knows. It presents a progression of spelling skills and asks teachers to indicate whether these skills are present always, often, or never in the spellings found in students' writing. In this way, teachers identify what students do correctly, what they use but confuse, and what is absent in their spelling knowledge. The last place where "Often" is checked is the student's stage of spelling development.

The numbers 1–15 on the checklist correspond to the substages listed in the Spelling-by-Stage Assessment Scale. This scale is a visual aid that tells teachers where students are within a given stage: the early, middle, or late point of the stage. For example, if a student is beginning to use the key elements of a stage but still has some remnants from the previous stage, the student is in an early point of the stage. If a student has worked through most of the features relevant to a stage, then the student is in a late point of the stage. The scale is a useful tool for grouping students for word study. It is most useful in conjunction with the previously mentioned checklist. Assigning an exact number on the scale is not critical. Bear and his colleagues advise that the wisest course is to "take a step backward" when planning instruction. "Teachers take this step backward because students need to learn how to sort words and to play the word-study games, and clearly it is easier to teach students how to sort when they can read the words easily" (Bear et al. 1996).

# QUALITATIVE SPELLING CHECKLIST

Student _____ Observer _____ Date(s) _____

Consider the following progression, and note when certain features are observed in students' spelling and writing. When a feature is always present, check Yes. The last place where you check Often is the stage of spelling development to report. The numbers on the checklist refer to the Spelling-by-Stage Assessment Scale. How many words were spelled correctly? Report as a percentage of total correct to total spelled.

**Preliterate**

| | | | | |
|---|---|---|---|---|
| 1 | Marks on the page. [          ] | Yes ___ | Often ___ | No ___ |
| | Scribbling followed the conventional direction. [ ———>] | Yes ___ | Often ___ | No ___ |
| | Symbols or known letters represented in pretend writing. [bybcl] | Yes ___ | Often ___ | No ___ |

**Early Letter Name**

| | | | | |
|---|---|---|---|---|
| 2 | Syllabic writing. Key sounds are spelled. [P for *stop*] | Yes ___ | Often ___ | No ___ |
| 3 | Beginning. Check Yes if ending sounds are included. | Yes ___ | Often ___ | No ___ |

**Middle and Late Letter Name**

| | | | | |
|---|---|---|---|---|
| 4 | A vowel in each word. | Yes ___ | Often ___ | No ___ |
| 5 | Consonant blends and digraphs in *SHIP, DRIVE, WHEN, TRAIN, CHASE, FLOAT* | Yes ___ | Often ___ | No ___ |
| 6 | Short vowels spelled correctly. [BED, SHIP, WHEN] | | | |
| | Includes preconsonantal nasals. [BUMP] | Yes ___ | Often ___ | No ___ |

**Within Word Pattern**

| | | | | |
|---|---|---|---|---|
| 7 | Uses but confuses long vowels. [DRIEV, TRAN, FLOTE, BEECHS] | Yes ___ | Often ___ | No ___ |
| 8 | Spells many single-syllable long vowels correctly. [DRIVE, TRAIN, FLOAT, BEACHES] | Yes ___ | Often ___ | No ___ |
| | Still experiments with long-vowel patterns. [DRIEV, TRAN, FLOTE, BEECHS] | | | |
| | Spells most consonant blends and digraphs correctly. [*SHIP, DRIVE, WHEN, TRAIN, CHASE, FLOAT*] | Yes ___ | Often ___ | No ___ |
| 9 | Spells long vowels, consonant blends and digraphs, and low-frequency consonant blends and digraphs. [CAUGHT] | Yes ___ | Often ___ | No ___ |

**Syllable Juncture**

| | | | | |
|---|---|---|---|---|
| 10 | Consonant doubling [POPPING, CATTLE, SQUIRREL, CELLAR] | Yes ___ | Often ___ | No ___ |
| 11 | Plurals and other endings [BEACHES, POPPING, PREPARING] | Yes ___ | Often ___ | No ___ |
| 12 | Less frequent affixes: suffixes [PUNCTURE, CELLAR, PLEASURE, FORTUNATE, CONFIDENT, CIVILIZE, FLEXIBLE]; prefixes [PREPARING, CONFIDENT, OPPOSITION] | Yes ___ | Often ___ | No ___ |

**Derivational Constancy**

| | | | | |
|---|---|---|---|---|
| 13 | Knowledge of derived spellings [PLEASURE, FORTUNATE] | Yes ___ | Often ___ | No ___ |
| 14 | Knowledge of derived spellings [CONFIDE, CIVILIZE] | Yes ___ | Often ___ | No ___ |
| 15 | Knowledge of derived spellings [OPPOSITION, EMPHASIZE] | Yes ___ | Often ___ | No ___ |

Adapted from Bear (1988). From *Words Their Way: Word Study for Phonics, Vocabulary, and Spelling Instruction* © 1996.

12.28

| Spelling-by-Stage Assessment Scale | |
|---|---|
| Late Derivational Constancy | 15 |
| Middle Derivational Constancy | 14 |
| Beginning Derivational Constancy | 13 |
| Late Syllable Juncture | 12 |
| Middle Syllable Juncture | 11 |
| Beginning Syllable Juncture | 10 |
| Late Within Word Pattern | 9 |
| Middle Within Word Pattern | 8 |
| Beginning Within Word Pattern | 7 |
| Late Letter Name | 6 |
| Middle Letter Name | 5 |
| Beginning Letter Name | 4 |
| Early Letter Name | 3 |
| Early Letter Name | 2 |
| Preliterate | 1 |

Adapted from Bear (1988). From *Words Their Way: Word Study for Phonics, Vocabulary, and Spelling Instruction* © 1996.

**Michael**

| Middle Letter Name Spelling | |
|---|---|
| ▶ bed | bed |
| ▶ ship | SEP |
| ▶ drive | DRIV |
| ▶ bump | BOP |
| ▶ when | WHAN |
| | |
| ▶ train | TRAN |
| ▶ closet | CLAST |
| ▶ chase | CAS |
| ▶ float | FLOT |
| ▶ beaches | BECIS |

From *Words Their Way* © 1996.

## Michael's Qualitative Spelling Checklist

The following checklist is a qualitative assessment of Michael's sample spellings. (Note that testing was stopped after ten words.) According to this assessment, Michael is in the Middle Letter Name stage, with a point assignment of 5 on the 15-point Spelling-by-Stage Assessment Scale. His spellings indicate that he has mastered the concepts of the Early Letter Name stage, correctly representing initial and final consonant sounds. In addition, he includes a vowel in each syllable, except for the word *closet*. He also spells most of the consonant blends correctly and even uses the consonant digraph *wh*. Where his orthographic knowledge fades is in the spelling of short and long vowels, seen in his use of the letter *e* to represent the short-*i* sound in SEP *(ship)* and his use of the letter *a* to represent the short-*e* sound in WHAN *(when)*. The use of long-vowel markers is completely absent in his spelling attempts, as is the use of the preconsonantal nasal in BOP *(bump)*, and

Student **Michael**          Observer _____ Date(s) _____

Consider the following progression, and note when certain features are observed in students' spelling and writing. When a feature is always present, check Yes. The last place where you check Often is the stage of spelling development to report. The numbers on the checklist refer to the Spelling-by-Stage Assessment Scale. How many words were spelled correctly? Report as a percentage of total correct to total spelled.

12.29

### Preliterate

1   Marks on the page. [          ]                                    Yes _X_ Often ___ No ___
    Scribbling followed the conventional direction. [ ———>]            Yes _X_ Often ___ No ___
    Symbols or known letters represented in pretend writing. [bybcl]   Yes _X_ Often ___ No ___

### Early Letter Name

2   Syllabic writing. Key sounds are spelled. [P for *stop*]           Yes _X_ Often ___ No ___
3   Beginning. Check Yes if ending sounds are included.                Yes _X_ Often ___ No ___

### Middle and Late Letter Name

4   A vowel in each word.                                              Yes _X_ Often ___ No ___
5   Consonant blends and digraphs in
    SHIP, (DR)IVE, (WH)EN, (TR)AIN, CHASE, (FL)OAT                      Yes ___ Often _X_ No ___
6   Short vowels spelled correctly. [B(E)D, SHIP, WHEN]
    Includes preconsonantal nasals. [B**U**MP]                         Yes ___ Often ___ No _X_

### Within Word Pattern

7   Uses but confuses long vowels. [DRIEV, TRAN, FLOTE, BEECHS]        Yes ___ Often ___ No _X_
8   Spells many single-syllable long vowels correctly. [DRIVE, TRAIN, FLOAT, BEACHES]   Yes ___ Often ___ No _X_
    Still experiments with long-vowel patterns. [DRIEV, TRAN, FLOTE, BEECHS]
    Spells most consonant blends and digraphs correctly. [SHIP, DRIVE, WHEN,
    TRAIN, CHASE, FLOAT]                                               Yes ___ Often ___ No _X_
9   Spells long vowels, (consonant blends) and digraphs, and low-frequency
    consonant blends and digraphs. [CAU**GH**T]                        Yes ___ Often ___ No _X_

### Syllable Juncture

10  Consonant doubling [PO**PP**ING, CA**TT**LE, SQUI**RR**EL, CE**LL**AR]   Yes ___ Often ___ No ___
11  Plurals and other endings [BEACH**ES**, POPP**ING**, PREPAR**ING**]      Yes ___ Often ___ No ___
12  Less frequent affixes: suffixes [PUNC**TURE**, CELL**AR**, PLEA**SURE**, FORTUN**ATE**,
    CONFID**ENT**, CIVIL**IZE**, FLEX**IBLE**]; prefixes [**PRE**PARING, **CON**FIDENT, **OP**POSITION]   Yes ___ Often ___ No ___

### Derivational Constancy

13  Knowledge of derived spellings [**PLEA**SURE, **FORTUN**ATE]      Yes ___ Often ___ No ___
14  Knowledge of derived spellings [**CON**FIDE, **CIVIL**IZE]        Yes ___ Often ___ No ___
15  Knowledge of derived spellings [OP**POSITION**, **EMPHA**SIZE]    Yes ___ Often ___ No ___

Adapted from Bear (1988). From *Words Their Way: Word Study for Phonics, Vocabulary, and Spelling Instruction* © 1996.

the consonant digraph *ch* in CAS *(chase)* and BECIS *(beaches)*. Given these results, the starting point for instruction is what Michael uses but confuses—he uses some short vowels but confuses them, and he uses the letter name for long-vowel sounds.

### Elementary and Upper Level Spelling Inventory Error Guides

The Error Guides are an efficient way to determine a student's stage of spelling development. The guides list the most commonly observed misspellings for each of the two inventories. Errors are arranged in order of increasing sophistication and classified under the stage they represent. Teachers should circle the errors on the students' inventories and match them to those listed in the Error Guide. If the exact misspelling does not appear, you should note the invented spelling next to the error listed in the guide that is most similar. The resulting assessment can then be used to confirm the rating on the Qualitative Spelling Checklist. (All of Michael's invented spellings appear in the Elementary Error Guide under the Letter Name category.)

See also...

**Core Assessing Reading**
**"Elementary Level Inventory Error Guide"**
**"Upper Level Inventory Error Guide"**

**ELL** FOR SPANISH-SPEAKING STUDENTS...
The "CORE Spanish Spelling Inventory" measures students' orthographic knowledge in Spanish. The 20 words in the list represent a wide range of orthographic features including consonant digraphs and blends, phoneme/grapheme variations, open vs. closed syllables, silent *h,* preconsonantal nasal, diphthongs, and accentuation. To assess students' knowledge, teachers can use the "Spelling Skills Summary," which lists 17 discrete skills and the words from the inventory that measure the application of those skills. Based on the results, teachers can design Spanish word lists and plan appropriate word-study activities.

See also...

**CORE Assessing Reading**
**"CORE Spanish Spelling Inventory"**

**CORE Reading Research Anthology**
for background information

**12.30**

Connect to Theory

Tina was given the "Words Their Way" Elementary Qualitative Spelling Inventory. Look at her Spelling Inventory below. Then use the Qualitative Spelling Checklist and Spelling-by-Stage Assessment Scale to analyze it.

---

### TINA'S SPELLING INVENTORY

---

1. bed
2. ship
3. drive
4. bump
5. when

6. train
7. closit
8. chase
9. float
10. beaches

11. praparring
12. popping
13. cattel
14. cawt
15. inspecsion

16. punckter
17. celler
18. pleshur
19. squirrle
20. forchunit

Based on your assessment, what is Tina's stage of spelling development? Does the Elementary Level Inventory Error Guide confirm your assessment? What would your word study focus be for Tina?

*(See Appendix for answer.)*

CHAPTER

13

# Spelling Instruction

what?
why?
when?
how?

**13.2**

*"Over the last decade I think we've learned that spelling really does matter and that, as educators, we need to teach it."*

—GENTRY, 1998

**CORE Reading Research Anthology**

for background information

**Section II: Word Structure, "What Are Some Spelling Generalizations?" p. 3.26**

During the late 1980s and early 1990s many school systems moved away from formal spelling instruction, dissatisfied with the traditional drill-and-skill approach and its emphasis on rote memorization. Many educators believed that students would learn to spell "naturally" if they read widely and had experiences proofreading their writing. As part of this approach, spelling was viewed as a subset of writing, and the sole focus of study became the words students happened to misspell in their writing.

Yet research has shown that many students need explicit instruction focused on word concept and pattern understanding. This instruction has several components:

- Spelling words should be linked to students' developmental levels and, therefore, should be somewhat individualized.

- Spelling lists should be made up of high-utility words grouped by pattern and presented in a systematic sequence.

- Word study should be active and engaging, leading students to analyze and categorize words, and thereby to discover spelling rules and generalizations.

- In the classroom, 12 to 15 minutes of spelling activities per day is sufficient for most students to master a week's spelling lesson of 20 words or less. (The number of words students can be expected to learn each week depends on the child and the type and amount of instruction.)

- Students need frequent practice writing words they are able to read. Once they reach the Within Word Pattern stage, there is a several-month lag between reading and spelling mastery.

- Formal instruction with weekly tests and word lists generally begins in second grade. A "pretest-study-posttest" method is desirable, especially if students immediately correct the pretests themselves and use the information to focus their study.

## Word Lists

Learning words in lists is more efficient than learning to spell individual words presented in context. Students learn words faster, remember them longer, and transfer them more readily to a new context when the words are grouped together in a list (Horn 1954; White, Power, and White 1989; Wysocki and Jenkins 1987). Whether teachers use their own spelling lists or those provided by commercial programs, there are several factors to keep in mind:

**See also...**

**Section II: Word Structure**

**"'Rhyming' Phonograms," p. 3.22**

for a list of 37 common rhyming phonograms

① Words on a word list should be grouped by sound, visual, or meaning pattern.

**SOUND PATTERN** Grouping words by sound pattern (for example, words that end in the phonogram *–ack* or words that start with *th–*) introduces students to a large body of words to use when they need to write an unfamiliar word with the same sound. Teaching word families (words with a common phonogram) is extremely efficient because so many words can be generated from just a few phonograms.

**VISUAL PATTERN** Remembering the visual form of a word is one key to being able to spell it. One useful visual pattern is double consonants, which can appear at either the end (*call, fell, pull*) or the middle of words (*supper, hopping, ripped*). Word study that focuses on visual pattern might include words that are grouped together on the basis of a common spelling pattern that has different pronunciations: for example, the —*ough* pattern in *tough, cough, enough; thought, fought;* and *through.*

**MEANING PATTERN** Mature spellers figure out how to spell an unknown word by thinking of its meaning relationship to a known word. Spelling lists that group words with common base words or structural patterns help students focus on this meaning layer. Word study might focus on common verbs with their inflectional endings: *walks, walking, walked; drives, driving, drove;* or base and root words and their derivations: *tooth, toothache, toothpaste; please, pleasant, pleasure.*

② Word lists should include words for review that students consistently misspell. Even when they are able to spell much more difficult words, many students continue to have trouble with such spelling "demons" as *their, about, too, says, lose,* and *would.*

③ Word lists should include words from content-area reading and literature *that fit the patterns being taught.* For example, a list that focuses on the visual pattern of double consonants could include content-area words such as *add, adding, addition; pollute, community, traffic.* Lists should avoid words that are uncommon or unusual since the goal is to help students develop useful spelling strategies and to apply generalizations based on known words.

## Word Lists from Basal Spelling Programs

If teachers choose to use word lists provided by basal spelling programs, they may find that a single grade level's lists do not work for all the students in their classroom. In order to use the basal lists, you have to have several consecutive levels of the same series available. Each student should be given the

---

**13.4**

## Resources for Word Lists

**In Other Words: A Resource of Word Lists for Phonics, Spelling, and Vocabulary Study** (1996) by Kathy Ganske.

...................................................

**The New Reading Teacher's Book of Lists** (1995) by Edward Fry et al.

...................................................

**The Scholastic Rhyming Dictionary** (1994) by Sue Young.

...................................................

**The Spelling Teacher's Book of Lists** (1996) by Jo Phenix.

grade-level pretest or diagnostic placement test that accompanies the series. Students who spell 50 to 75 percent of the words correctly would be appropriately placed at that level. Those who spell fewer words correctly should be given the test for the lower level; and those who score higher than 75 percent should be tested on a higher grade level (Gentry and Gillet 1993).

**CORE Reading Research Anthology**

for background information

**13.5**

## Self-Assessment

At the beginning of each week students should take a pretest of the weekly spelling list and then correct it themselves. Self-assessment is a key ingredient in effective writing and spelling. It enables students to see what they are doing correctly and what they need to work on. They can then set goals for the week, finding and examining words with the pattern(s) they need to learn. At the end of the week, students should take another test, or posttest, to monitor their progress.

## Making Words

Making words with letter cards is an active way for students to study spelling patterns. Students use specific letters and proceed through a series of steps to make bigger words until they make the target word the teacher has selected. For example, students might be given the vowels *a, e, a* and the consonants, *b, f, k, r, s, t.* The teacher could ask them to use three letters to make the word *bat* and then have them add, exchange, and remove letters to create a series of one- and two-syllable words. In the last step students would use all of the letters to make the large word *breakfast.* Students would record all of the words they make and then do a word sort, grouping the words by sound and/or visual pattern (Cunningham 1995).

## Word Sorting

Word-sorting activities are an integral part of spelling instruction. In word sorting, students look at words and sort them into categories based on sound and spelling patterns. Key words identify the orthographic patterns that students will examine while sorting. Research has found that word-sorting activities not only increase students' ability to spell words but to read them as well (Hall, Cunningham, and Cunningham 1995). Sorting words by pattern enables students to see similarities and differences among words and to discover important concepts. Word sorting is *manipulative*—students can move words around and compare them directly to decide which ones fit together. Word sorting is also *flexible*—students can rearrange words as they see patterns and contrasts. Finally, word-sorting activities are, by their very nature, *conceptual*—students classify words based on common features, focusing on the connection between spelling and pronunciation, pattern, or meaning (Zutell 1998).

There are two basic types of word sorts: *closed sorts,* in which teachers ask students to find a specified feature in a group of words, and *open sorts,* in which students classify words according to features that they themselves discover. A *blind sort* is a type of closed sort in which words are called out by either the teacher or a partner, and students point to the key word that has the same pattern. Blind sorts are useful for helping students focus on the sounds in words. *Writing sorts* are a variation of both closed and blind sorts. In writing sorts, words are called out by the teacher, and students write the word in the appropriate category under the model key word. Once they become proficient at open and closed word sorts, many students enjoy the challenge of a *speed sort.* In speed sorts, students work in pairs timing how quickly they are able to sort a group of words. The object is for students to beat their own times, not that of their partners, because partners may be working with a different set of words. Speed sorts develop automaticity, which improves both writing and word attack skills.

---

**13.6**

## Word Sorts

**closed**

teacher defines categories and models sorting procedure

**open**

students define categories

**blind**

teacher defines categories; teacher calls out a word and students point to the key word with same spelling pattern

**writing**

teacher defines categories; teacher calls out a word and students write the word below the key word with the same spelling pattern

**speed**

closed, open, blind, and writing sorts completed within a particular time frame

**Section IV: Decoding**

**Chapter 8: Phonics**

Word sorting is useful across the developmental continuum—from the Letter Name stage to the Derivational Constancy stage. Most word sorting is done in two steps: first by shared sound pattern and then by orthographic pattern. In this way, both sound and sight become part of students' developing orthographic knowledge. Using recognizable words in word sorts makes it easier for students to compare and contrast spelling features.

**13.7**

## Word Hunts

In word hunts students search environmental print (word walls, class lists, signs, and so on) and "hunt" through their reading and writing for words that are examples of the patterns they are studying. In this way, they see the connection between spelling and reading and writing. Word hunts also enhance students' speaking and writing vocabularies.

## Word Banks

Word banks are collections of known words that students use in word sorts and word-study games. The banks are a useful tool for early primary word study. In the Letter Name stage students collect sight words from their Personal Readers (language experience charts, individual dictations, rhymes, poems, and pattern stories) by writing the words on index cards. They keep the word cards in a short-term word bank. This could be an envelope or small plastic bag taped to the inside back cover of the Personal Reader. On the back of each word card students write the number of the story in their readers that the word is from and their own initials, so that the cards can be shared in group activities and later returned to them. Periodically teachers work with students in small groups to read through the words; those they know on sight go into their individualized long-term word bank, which might be a small 3 x 5 file box or an empty food container.

**13.8**

A Personal Reader:
Short-Term and Long-Term Word Banks

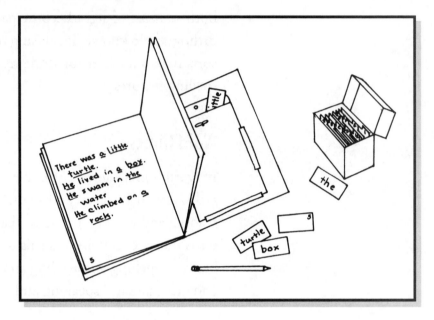

From *Words Their Way: Word Study for Phonics, Vocabulary, and Spelling Instruction* © 1996.

## Word Study Notebooks

Word Study Notebooks are organized collections of words students use in word sorts and games. Students are ready to move on to Word Study Notebooks when they are at the end of the Letter Name stage of spelling, their word banks contain at least 200 words, and they can recognize nearly all of the words in a teacher-made sort. As part of daily practice, students can use the notebooks to (1) record word sorts and write perceptions and generalizations about the sort concepts, (2) draw and label words that match the key words, (3) drop and add letters to make new words, (4) write sentences, paragraphs, and stories using the words they are studying, and (5) do word hunts in trade books and content-area reading. They can also use the notebooks for writing tips for remembering hard-to-spell words: for example, "They went *together to get her.*"

Students also can use their notebooks for a variety of activities and word games to play with partners including crossword puzzles, word searches, Tic-Tac-Toe, and anagrams.

It is helpful if each page of the Word Study Notebook is numbered and referenced in a table of contents. The notebooks can be divided into four sections: (1) regular words, (2) irregular words, (3) homophones, and (4) personal words.

## Word Study Notebook

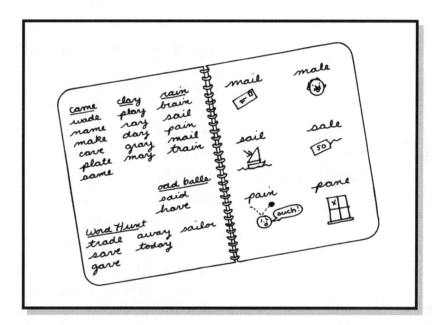

From *Words Their Way: Word Study for Phonics, Vocabulary, and Spelling Instruction* © 1996.

## Spelling Study Strategy

Expert spellers are able to store and retrieve visual images of words. To aid this process teachers use a spelling study strategy based on a technique that was first developed by Ernest Horn in 1919. Although there are variations, one important technique for learning how to spell a word generally involves six simple steps: (1) **Look** at the word, (2) **Say** the word, (3) **Cover** the word and **see** it in your mind, (4) **Write** the word, (5) **Check** your spelling, and (6) **Rewrite** the word correctly.

**"How to Make a Flip Folder," p. 13.18**

for complete directions for making and

using a Flip Folder

**13.10**

The first two steps help students make the connection between visual and sound patterns and also connect meaning to spelling. The third step guides students in seeing a word in their "mind's eye." The fourth step provides practice with retrieving the image and producing letter strings in correct sequence. The final steps allow students to monitor and, if necessary, immediately self-correct their spelling attempts. Many teachers have found Flip Folders to be a convenient way to practice this spelling study strategy.

## Self-Diagnosis of Spelling Errors

Students' spelling will improve if they know how to diagnose and correct their own spelling errors (Moffett and Wagner 1992). Self-diagnosis is possible at any age or stage of spelling development. It begins with teachers helping students to see that spelling errors fall into a limited number of categories: errors made because of the way students pronounce words, errors made because letters are written out of order, errors made because of variations in the way particular sounds can be spelled, and errors made because of a lack of knowledge about English spelling rules and generalizations. Teachers should work with students to examine and classify the misspellings in their written work. Depending on the type of errors, they can give students useful self-monitoring tips. For example, if a student consistently writes letters out of order, the teacher can suggest that when in doubt the student should pronounce the word the way it is written. The student can also work with letter tiles and play word-building games to reinforce correct letter sequence.

**"Do-It-Yourself Spelling," p. 13.47**

## Word Games

Word games are an excellent way to create interest and motivation in students. Popular word games like Scrabble®, crossword puzzles, anagrams, and Hangman develop word knowledge and spelling consciousness. Almost any game can be adapted to help students practice new spelling patterns: just change the rules so that to complete a move, players have to correctly spell one of the words on their weekly lists. Less and more able spellers can play together, with each working on her or his own spelling list. Another benefit from playing games is that opponents check each other's spelling accuracy. In this way, students have a chance to examine a broad range of spelling words. Games to adapt for spelling practice include Jeopardy®, Go Fish, Tic-Tac-Toe, and board games. For students at the Syllable Juncture stage, J. Richard Gentry (1997) suggests using "word scaffolds" to help children visualize spellings by relating letter strings in words with similar spelling patterns. This practice helps children internalize spelling generalizations. An example of a word scaffold is:

13.11

```
        n o

        n o w                       a

    k n o w                       a b l e

a c k n o w l e d g e a b l e

    k n o w l e d g e

            l e d g e

            l e d

            e d
```

# why? *Spelling Instruction*

**13.12**

See also . . .

**CORE Reading Research Anthology**

for background information

While research has confirmed that learning to spell is more complex than memorizing words and rules, researchers and educators now know that in order to become proficient spellers, many students need more than just experience with reading and writing (Peters 1985; Hughes and Searle 1996; Treiman 1996). We now understand that spelling is both a developmental and conceptual process that impacts reading speed and accuracy, writing fluency, pronunciation, and vocabulary. The best spelling practice (1) individualizes instruction by linking it to students' stage of development, (2) actively engages students in discovering spelling patterns, (3) provides opportunities for students to apply what they have learned to reading and writing, and (4) develops spelling consciousness and good spelling habits.

**Research Findings . . .**

*English orthography is often maligned as unpredictable. On the contrary, although there are complexities and irregularities, English orthography is a structured and predictable system in which spelling for phonemes, syllables, and morphemes are rule-governed or explainable according to a word's historical origins, meaning, and sound structure.*

—MOATS, 1995

*The careful examination of words that is part of formal spelling instruction can beneficially affect not only the efficiency and quality of students' writing experiences but of their reading experiences as well.*

—ADAMS, 1990

*Research findings confirm that spelling, for most people, requires something above and beyond experience with reading. . . . The ability to read a word does not always guarantee that a child will be able to spell the word.*

—TREIMAN, 1996

*Word study is* active, *and by making judgments about words and sorting words according to similar features, students devise their own rules for how the features work. The simple act of making judgments about words this way helps teach the relationships among a word's sound, its spelling pattern, and its meaning. Meaningful practice helps students internalize word features and become automatic in using what they have learned.*

—BEAR ET AL., 1996

*Without fluent spelling skills, many students continue to struggle with the mechanics of the writing process and cannot focus their attention and energy on what and why they are writing.*

—HARRIS & GRAHAM, 1996

**Suggested Reading . . .**

*The Spelling Teacher's Book of Lists* (1996) by Jo Phenix. Markham, Ontario: Pembroke Publishers.

*Teaching Kids to Spell* (1993) by J. Richard Gentry & Jean Wallace Gillet. Portsmouth, NH: Heinemann.

*The Violent E and Other Tricky Sounds: Learning to Spell from Kindergarten Through Grade 6* (1997) by Margaret Hughes & Dennis Searle. York, ME: Stenhouse.

*Words Their Way: Word Study for Phonics, Vocabulary, and Spelling Instruction, Second Edition* (2000) by Donald R. Bear, Marcia Invernizzi, Shane Templeton & Francine Johnston. Upper Saddle River, NJ: Prentice-Hall.

# *when?* *Spelling Instruction*

In planning weekly word study, teachers need to consider three scheduling requirements: (1) Students will work in small groups with teacher direction. The grouping is based on students' developmental level. (2) The directed lessons will take an average of 12–15 minutes each day. On one day, students might sort and discuss for 20 minutes and, on the following day, hunt for words in a story for only eight minutes. (3) Students will need time for independent practice in center activities and games. A possible weekly word-study model follows.

**Intervention Strategy ELL**

**English language learners can participate in spelling instruction if they are developmentally ready, learning to read in English, and understand the meanings before being asked to spell words. Students who are learning to read in a language other than English can participate orally to build spelling vocabulary and awareness of English sound patterns in context.**

| Weekly Word-Study Model: Grades K–1 | |
| --- | --- |
| **Monday** | Picture sort |
| **Tuesday** | Drawing and labeling |
| **Wednesday** | Cutting and pasting |
| **Thursday** | Word hunt; Word bank |
| **Friday** | Games |

| Weekly Word-Study Model: Grade 2 and above | |
| --- | --- |
| **Monday** | Pretest, Group sort; Word Study Notebook assignment |
| **Tuesday** | Buddy sort; Word Study Notebook assignment |
| **Wednesday** | Word hunt in trade books; Word Study Notebook assignment |
| **Thursday** | Speed sort; Word Study Notebook assignment |
| **Friday** | Posttest; Word Study Notebook assignment |

**Kindergarten and Grade 1**   Based on this model, on Monday the K–1 teacher does a picture sort and helps students recognize the sound and letters they are studying. On Tuesday, students recall the introduced feature in drawing and labeling activities. On Wednesday, students make judgments about other examples through cutting and pasting tasks. On Thursday, students apply the concepts through word hunts, word bank activities, and other tasks. On Friday students play spelling games in which they recognize patterns, recall examples, and make judgments about spelling features.

**Grade 2 and Above**   From Grade 2 on, pretests provide an opportunity for students to take an active role in planning and monitoring their own spelling progress. Once students' stage of development is assessed, they can be given a pretest that is made up of developmentally appropriate words. By correcting the test themselves and discussing the results with the teacher, students have an opportunity to see what they are doing correctly and what spelling features and patterns need further work. They can then plan their weekly word study, using their Word Study Notebooks to set goals and list the words from their writing, reading, and school experiences that they want and need to learn to spell.

On Fridays, students are tested on the spelling features they have examined over the course of the week. The posttest focuses on only a random sample of words that have been categorized under each key word and those that students missed on the pretest. Depending on the results of the Friday posttest, word study for the next week will include new spelling features as well as a review of those from the previous week.

**See also...**

**CORE Assessing Reading**

**"'Words Their Way' Elementary Qualitative Spelling Inventory"**

**"'Words Their Way' Upper Level Inventory"**

to determine students' stage of spelling development

13.15

The following chart shows a recommended sequence of word study based on teachers' assessment of students' stage of spelling development. It is designed to help teachers match activities to developmental levels.

## SEQUENCE OF WORD STUDY

| | |
|---|---|
| **Stage I:** **Preliterate** | 1 Concept sorts. <br> 2 Learn to recognize alphabet. |
| **Stage II:** **Early Letter Name** | 1 Sort pictures and words by initial consonants. <br> 2 Collect known words for word bank. <br> 3 For most students, final consonants are learned without direct attention unless they are unspoken in dialect. <br> 4 Introduce initial consonant blends *(blend)* and digraphs *(ship)*. Have students see blends and digraphs as a unit *(bl, sh, sp,* etc.). Students spell consonant blends and digraphs correctly during the next stage. |
| **Middle and** **Late Letter Name** | 1 Sort pictures and words by families *(–at, –ed)*. <br> 2 Sort pictures and words by short vowels and CVC pattern. <br> 3 Continue to examine consonant blends and digraphs. <br> 4 Collect known words for word bank. <br> 5 Practice open and closed sorts and games on short vowels. |
| **Stage III:** **Within Word Pattern** | 1 Discontinue word banks and begin a word-study notebook that chronicles sorts; the first entries can come from sorts from the previous stage. <br> 2 Continue with sorts and record sorts and word groups in the word-study notebook. <br> 3 Replace word-bank word sorts with teacher-made word sorts. Students work with known words in sorts and discard unknown words. <br> 4 Examine differences between long and short vowels: for example, CVC versus CVVC or CVC*e*. <br> 5 Examine long-vowel patterns through closed and open sorts and word-study games. Begin with one long vowel and then choose a second long vowel, study it, and compare to the previous one. <br> 6 Examine homographs and homophones *(plain* and *plane)*, low-frequency short-vowel patterns with consonant digraphs *(caught)*, and *r*-controlled vowels *(burst, spark)*. |

| | |
|---|---|
| **Stage IV:** **Syllable Juncture** | 1 Continue with open and closed sorts, word-study notebooks, some word-study games. |
| | 2 Examine consonant doubling and simple suffixes as in plurals. |
| | 3 Focus on words that students bring to word study from their reading and writing. |
| | 4 Join spelling and vocabulary studies; link meaning and spelling. |
| | 5 Engage word study as part of grammar. |
| | 6 Sort and study affixes (prefixes and suffixes). |
| | 7 Study stress and accent in two-syllable words. |
| | 8 Study polysyllabic words and their stressed or unstressed syllables. |
| | 9 Examine increasingly complex affixes and consonant doublings *(occasion)*. |
| **Stage V:** **Derivational Constancy** | 1 Continue with open and closed sorts, word-study notebooks, some word-study games. |
| | 2 Focus on words that students bring to word study from their reading and writing. |
| | 3 Join spelling and vocabulary studies; link meaning and spelling. |
| | 4 Introduce structural consistencies. |
| | 5 Examine vowel alternations. |
| | 6 Use word-study books to examine classical vocabulary, Greek and Latin forms. |
| | 7 Develop an interest in etymology in the content areas. |
| | 8 Examine content-related foreign borrowings. |

**13.17**

From *Words Their Way: Word Study for Phonics, Vocabulary, and Spelling Instruction* © 1996.

**13.18**

**TEACHING STRATEGY FOR**

## Stage II: Letter Name Spelling

### Benchmarks

- ability to spell three-letter short-vowel words
- ability to identify misspellings of three- and four-letter short-vowel words when proofreading

### Grade Level

- Grade 1 and above

### Prerequisites

- Introducing Short Vowels (Chapter 8: Phonics)
- introduced phonic elements: all single consonants and short vowels

### Grouping

- whole class
- small group or pairs
- individual

### Materials

- manila file folders
- copies of Flip Folder Practice Sheet (see Appendix)
- large index cards (3 per student)
- copies of proofreading sample

## SINGLE SHORT VOWELS

This generic teaching strategy focuses on short *a*, short *o*, and short *i*. The same strategy can be used to focus on the spelling of other single vowel sounds in CVC words or to focus on short-vowel sounds in CCVC words.

### How to Make a Flip Folder

1. Cut one side of a manila file folder into thirds lengthwise to obtain three equal "flaps." Each flap should remain connected to the folder at the fold.

2. On the first flap, print LOOK-SAY-COVER-SEE; on the middle flap, print WRITE-CHECK; and on the third flap, print REWRITE.

3. Insert the Flip Folder Practice Sheet horizontally under the flaps, as shown below.

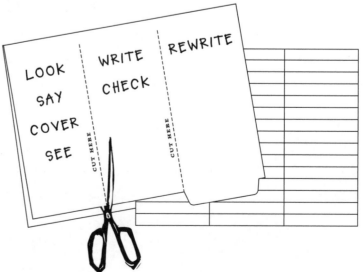

**Intervention Strategy**

Make sure that students pronounce each vowel sound clearly. For students who have difficulty hearing these sounds, ask them to repeat the following sentence after you: *(Name of letter) says (sound).* Have students write the letter each time they say its name. It may also be appropriate to help students feel their jaw and notice their mouth shape as they say the distinctly different vowel sounds.

See also . . .

Section III: Phonemic Awareness "Vowel Phonemes by Mouth Position," p. 3.11

## Introduce the Word List

Introduce the list of spelling words, making sure that students are familiar with the meanings of all the words. Key words are shown in boldface type.

had, **sat**, tap, can, bag; top, not, **box**, fog, mom; big, **did**, sit, him, zip

13.19

## Study the Words

Tell students to print their spelling words in the first column of the Flip Folder Practice Sheet and to proofread the list, making sure each word is spelled correctly. Next, they should insert the practice sheet into the Flip Folder and follow steps 1 through 6: (1) Open flap 1, look at the first word, and then say it aloud. (2) Cover the word by closing flap 1. (3) Close your eyes and visualize the word. (4) Open flap 2 and write the word from memory on the first line. (5) Open flaps 1 and 2 at the same time to check your spelling of the word. (6) Close flaps 1 and 2. (7) Open flap 3 and rewrite the word correctly. (8) Check and correct your spelling again. Follow the same procedure for each of the remaining words in the list.

## Explore the Orthographic Pattern

**WORD SORT** For this blind sort, print the key words *sat, box,* and *did* on the board and have students copy them in large letters on separate cards. Say the rest of the spelling words aloud one at a time, asking students to hold up the word card with the matching vowel sound. After each student response, print the spelling word under the correct key word on the board. After completing the sort, ask students what they notice about the words they have grouped together. Lead them to discover the following spelling generalizations: "The short-*a* sound in *sat* may be spelled *a.* The short-*o* sound in *box* may be spelled *o.* The short-*i* sound in *did* may be spelled *i.*" Finally, invite students to read the words aloud.

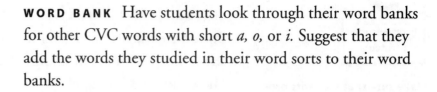

**WORD BANK**  Have students look through their word banks for other CVC words with short *a, o,* or *i.* Suggest that they add the words they studied in their word sorts to their word banks.

Intervention
Strategy

**13.20**

Students who do not attend to all the discrete sounds in a word may have difficulty spelling. Ask them to "stretch" the sounds by counting them on their fingers or by writing out each sound separately using a grid or self-stick notes (see "Name That Sound," p. 7.38).

## Proofread and Write

Distribute copies of the following letter. Have students read the letter, circling all the spelling errors they find. Then ask them to rewrite the words correctly. (There are six misspelled words: *mom, dad, It, swim, Did, not.*)

---

Dear Pat,

I am on a trip with mam and did. We are at the lake. Et is hot. I want to sim. Ded you win the game? I did nat want to miss it!

From, Jed

---

**WRITING IDEA!**  Ask students to write a letter to a friend about a real or imaginary trip. Encourage them to use as many words with the CVC pattern as they can. Help students proofread their letters and then display final corrected drafts.

## Word Game

Print on the board a high-interest multisyllabic word from a content-area lesson or a story being read. Identify the word. Ask pairs of students to select letter cards for all the letters in the word. In a given amount of time, ask pairs to make as many three-letter CVC words as they can. For example, the following words can be made from the word *dinosaur: Dan, din, Don, nod, ran, rid, rod, run, sad, sin, sod, sun.* At the end of the allotted time, have pairs name their words as you write them on the board. The pair with the most words wins.

# Stage III: Within Word Pattern Spelling

### Benchmarks

- ability to spell long-vowel words
- ability to identify misspellings of words with long vowels when proofreading

### Grade Level

- Grade 2 and above

### Prerequisites

- all Teaching Strategies in Chapter 8: Phonics
- all Grade 1 phonic elements (see p. 8.8)

### Grouping

- whole class
- small group or pairs
- individual

### Materials

- Flip Folders (see p. 13.18)
- copies of Flip Folder Practice Sheet (see Appendix)
- copies of Word Study Grid (see Appendix)
- student Word Study Notebooks
- copies of proofreading sample
- letter cards *a, e, b, ch, t*

# LONG VOWELS

This generic teaching strategy contrasts the spelling of short *e* with three spellings of long *e (e, ee, ea)* and can be used after students have learned the various spellings of long *a*. The same strategy can be used to focus on other long-vowel patterns.

13.21

## Introduce the Word List

Introduce the list of spelling words, making sure that students are familiar with the meanings of all the words. Key words are shown in boldface type.

let, men, **get**, pen, yes, then, went, end, when, well;
**we**, the, she; **see**, need, street; **eat**, real, beach, leave

## Study the Words

Have students print their spelling words in the first column of the Flip Folder Practice Sheet and proofread the list, making sure each word is spelled correctly. Then tell them to use their Flip Folders to "look-say-cover-see-write-check-rewrite" each of the words on the list.

## Explore the Orthographic Pattern

**WORD SORT** For this closed sort, distribute copies of the Word Study Grid with the spelling words printed in the boxes. Ask students to read each word aloud and cross out any they do not know. Have them cut the grid apart. Then model the following two-part word sort, first sorting the words by vowel sound (short *e* in one column and long *e* in another column) and then by spelling pattern using the key words *get, we, see, eat.* (There will be four columns: short *e* spelled *e,* and long *e* spelled *e, ee, ea.*)

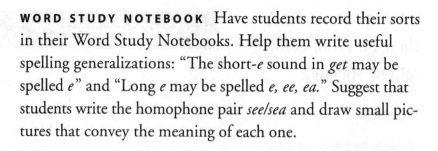

13.22

Intervention Strategy

**Some students may benefit from highlighting the vowel patterns in a different color and emphasizing the long-vowel sound as they say each word aloud.**

**WORD STUDY NOTEBOOK** Have students record their sorts in their Word Study Notebooks. Help them write useful spelling generalizations: "The short-*e* sound in *get* may be spelled *e*" and "Long *e* may be spelled *e, ee, ea*." Suggest that students write the homophone pair *see/sea* and draw small pictures that convey the meaning of each one.

## Proofread and Write

Ask students to imagine that they just found a message in a bottle on the beach. Distribute copies of the message and have students work with partners to proofread and correct the spelling. (There are eight misspelled words: *sea, sail, beach, day, leave, made, need, wait.*)

> Help! I am lost at see. I set sale from the bech on a sunny dae. Then it began to rain. Now I'm on an island and want to leeve. I maid a new boat but I nede help finding my way back. Come quickly. I can't wate!

**WRITING IDEA!** Have partners work together to write a response to the lost sailor, checking their spelling.

## Making Words

Distribute letter cards to each student for vowels *e, a* and consonants *b, ch, t.* Tell students to take two letters and make the word *at.* Then have them add a letter to *at* to make the three-letter word *eat.* Tell them to add another letter to *eat* to make the word *beat.* Now tell them to change the last letter in *beat* to make the five-letter word *beach.*

## Stage III: Within Word Pattern Spelling

### Benchmarks

- ability to spell one-syllable words with *r*-controlled vowels
- ability to identify misspellings of words with *r*-controlled vowels when proofreading

### Grade Level

- Grade 2 and above

### Prerequisites

- all Teaching Strategies in Chapter 8: Phonics
- all Grades 1 and 2 phonic elements (see p. 8.8)

### Grouping

- whole class
- small group or pairs
- individual

### Materials

- Flip Folders (see p. 13.18)
- copies of Flip Folder Practice Sheet (see Appendix)
- copies of Word Study Grid (see Appendix)
- student Word Study Notebooks
- copies of proofreading sample

# *r*-CONTROLLED VOWELS

This generic teaching strategy focuses on three *r*-controlled vowels—*ar*, *or*, and *ir*—by contrasting these with *r*-blends. The same strategy can be used to focus on other *r*-controlled vowels.

13.23

## Introduce the Word List

Introduce the list of spelling words, making sure that students are familiar with the meanings of all the words. Key words are shown in boldface type.

far, hard, park, start; for, horse, short, north; girl, **first**, third, shirt; bread, **from**, drip, grown, bring, tried, print, friend

## Study the Words

Have students print their spelling words in the first column of the Flip Folder Practice Sheet and proofread the list, making sure each word is spelled correctly. Then tell them to use their Flip Folders to "look-say-cover-see-write-check-rewrite" each of the words on the list. Ask students to listen for the /r/ sound as they say each word aloud.

## Explore the Orthographic Pattern

**WORD SORT** For this closed sort, distribute copies of the Word Study Grid with the spelling words printed in the boxes. Ask students to read each word aloud and cross out any they do not know. Have them cut the grid apart. Then model the word sort using the key words *from* and *first*. Tell students to sort the words by the location of the /r/ sound—whether it comes before or after the vowel.

**13.24**

Intervention
Strategy

In certain parts of the United States, the *r* following a vowel is not pronounced. Students, therefore, might not include an /r/ sound when they pronounce such words as *park, for,* or *first.* If pronunciation is affecting correct spelling, encourage students to practice pronouncing these words with the /r/ sound.

**Section IV: Decoding**

**Chapter 10: Multisyllabic Words**

for information about multisyllabic words
with *r*-controlled vowels

**WORD HUNT** Help students focus on the three *r*-controlled spelling patterns by asking them to do a word hunt for words with *ar, or,* and *ir.* Have them add the words they find to those on the word list and sort the words into three columns by spelling pattern. Remind them to keep track of any different sound/spelling patterns they find (such as *hear, near, oar, hair, their*) in a fourth column labeled with a question mark.

**WORD STUDY NOTEBOOK** Have students record their sorts in two columns in their Word Study Notebooks. Suggest that they circle the letter *r* in each word and write the useful spelling tip: "To spell words with *r* listen carefully to hear if the /r/ sound comes before or after the vowel."

## Proofread and Write

Distribute copies of the following Lost Pet sign and have students read through it circling any spelling errors they find. Ask them to rewrite the words correctly. (There are six misspelled words: *bird, third, Park, corn, friend, bring.*)

---

Reward for Lost Pet

Have you seen my lost berd? Lulu was last seen June therd in Forest Prk. She probably flew north but hasn't gone far. She likes apples and curn. She is my best frend. Please birng her back! Call Brad.

---

## Proofreading Checklist

Students can create their own proofreading checklists, with useful self-monitoring hints and reminders. Suggest they follow these good spelling habits:

▶ Sound out the word I want to spell. Then say the word the way I spelled it.

▶ Picture the word. Does it look right the way I spelled it?

▶ Think about the meaning. Do I know another word related to it?

**WRITING IDEA!** Have students write about their favorite animal, using as many of the spelling words as possible. Encourage them to use the Proofreading Checklist in their Word Study Notebooks to proofread their work. Students can draw a picture to go with their final drafts.

## Word Game

Word searches are a good way to reinforce students' knowledge of letter sequences. Have students make a 64-square Word Search Grid in their Word Study Notebooks for a classmate to complete. Students should include a tally of the total number of hidden words. An example is shown below:

| a | x | l | f | a | r | s | g |
|---|---|---|---|---|---|---|---|
| z | r | p | i | o | g | h | a |
| g | u | s | r | p | t | o | v |
| i | o | y | s | t | a | r | t |
| r | p | x | t | u | i | t | h |
| l | a | f | t | h | i | r | d |
| n | r | e | s | r | o | h | m |
| y | k | p | z | e | a | l | r |

*Answer Key: Across*—far, start, third, horse; *Down*—girl, park, first, short

**TEACHING STRATEGY FOR**

## Stage III: Within Word Pattern Spelling

13.26

### Benchmarks

- ability to correctly spell final-consonant patterns *–ch* and *–tch*
- ability to identify misspellings of final-consonant patterns when proofreading

### Grade Level

- Grade 2 and above

### Prerequisites

- all Teaching Strategies in Chapter 8: Phonics
- all Grade 1 phonic elements (see p. 8.8)

### Grouping

- whole class
- small group or pairs
- individual

### Materials

- Flip Folders (see p. 13.18)
- copies of Flip Folder Practice Sheet (see Appendix)
- copies of Word Study Grid (see Appendix)
- student Word Study Notebooks
- copies of proofreading sample

# FINAL-CONSONANT PATTERNS

GRADE LEVEL
2
AND ABOVE
GRADE LEVEL

This generic teaching strategy focuses on two final-consonant patterns (*–ch* and *–tch*) by contrasting short-vowel and long-vowel patterns. The same strategy can be used to introduce other final-consonant patterns (for example, the long-vowel pattern vowel-*g*–silent *e* vs. the short-vowel pattern *–dge*.)

· · · · · · · · · · · · · · · · · · · · · · · · · · · · · · · · ·

## Introduce the Word List

Introduce the list of spelling words, making sure that students are familiar with the meanings of all the words. Key words are shown in boldface type.

each, beach, **teach**, reach, speech, coach, roach, pooch; catch, match, hatch, scratch, fetch, sketch, stretch, **itch**, pitch, witch; much, which

## Study the Words

Have students print their spelling words in the first column of the Flip Folder Practice Sheet and proofread the list, making sure each word is spelled correctly. Then tell them to use their Flip Folders to "look-say-cover-see-write-check-rewrite" each of the words on the list.

**Intervention Strategy**

**Some students may benefit from using colored markers to highlight a single short vowel or a long-vowel team as they say each word aloud.**

## Explore the Orthographic Pattern

**WORD SORT** For this closed sort, distribute copies of the Word Study Grid with the spelling words printed in the boxes. Ask students to read each word aloud and cross out any they do not know. Have them cut the grid apart. Then model the following two-part word sort using the key words *teach* and *itch.* Sort the words into two categories: long-vowel sounds and short-vowel sounds. Ask students what they notice about the spelling of the final-consonant sound. Students should note that the *–ch* ending is used for long-vowel sounds, and the *–tch* ending is used for short-vowel sounds. Point out the two exceptions: the high-frequency words *much* and *which.*

13.27

Then have students do a second sort, dividing the long-vowel words into three categories—long *e,* long *o,* and long *u*—and the short-vowel words into short *a,* short *e,* and short *i.* They should have an "oddball" category that they can add to as they come across additional exceptions in their reading and writing.

**WORD STUDY NOTEBOOK** Have students record their sorts in their Word Study Notebooks. Help them write useful spelling hints or generalizations at the top of each page. To reinforce the idea that spelling is connected to meaning, suggest that students write and draw small pictures for the homophone pair *witch/which.*

## Proofread and Write

Distribute copies of the following ad for a local baseball team. Have students read the ad and circle any spelling errors they find. Then ask them to write each word correctly. (There are eight misspelled words: *coach, stretch, match, catch, Teach, much, each, signed.*)

13.28

Come out and see the Ravens play!

They have a new coatch, a new song, and new team colors. Come early and watch the guys stritch. You can't mach the fun of seeing your team hit, cach, and score. Teech your kids the rules of the game. Remember it doesn't cost mutch to have a good time.

This Sunday only—eech fan gets a sined baseball.

**WRITING IDEA!** Ask students to imagine that they are TV sportscasters writing a script for the evening news about a local baseball game. Challenge them to use as many of the following words as they can: *each, reach, speech, coach, catch, match, stretch, pitch, much, which.* Before writing a final copy, students should proofread their work and make any necessary corrections.

## Word Game

For practice with words ending in *–ch* and *–tch,* students can play a game based on the TV program "Jeopardy®." See *Words Their Way* (Bear et al. 1996, pp. 266–267) for a description of the game.

## Stage III: Within Word Pattern Spelling

# HOMOPHONES

The word *homophone* comes from two Greek words: *homo* meaning "same" and *phone* meaning "sound."

**13.29**

### Benchmarks

- ability to recognize how spelling choices affect meaning
- ability to spell common homophones correctly
- ability to use appropriate resources to verify spelling of homophones

### Grade Level

- Grade 3 and above

### Prerequisites

- all Teaching Strategies in Chapter 8: Phonics
- all Grades 1 and 2 phonic elements (see p. 8.8)

### Grouping

- whole class
- small group or pairs
- individual

### Materials

- Flip Folders (see p. 13.18)
- copies of Flip Folder Practice Sheet (see Appendix)
- copies of Word Study Grid (see Appendix)
- student Word Study Notebooks
- copies of proofreading sample
- index cards

## Introduce the Word List

Tell students that homophones are words that sound the same but have different meanings and are spelled differently. Then introduce the word list and use each word in a sentence, making sure that students are familiar with the meanings of the words: for example, "What can you buy with one dollar? This book is by Dr. Seuss. She said bye-bye before leaving."

buy, by, bye; here, hear; know, no; to, too, two; our, hour; right, write; tail, tale

## Study the Words

Since the correct spelling of homophones depends on meaning, suggest that students draw some pictures or write some clues on their Flip Folder Practice Sheets before they use their Flip Folders to study the spelling words. Here are some examples:

here = this place

hear = There's an ear  in hear.

tail = →

tale = a story

**Memory aids are an excellent way to remember the spelling of some homophones. Help students think of some to add to their Word Study Notebooks: for example, "I hear with my ear." Challenge students to make up some of their own memory aids for common homophones.**

## Explore the Orthographic Pattern

**WORD SORT** For this closed sort, distribute copies of the Word Study Grid with the spelling words printed in the boxes. Have students cut the grid apart and sort the words by vowel sound: long *i*, long *e*, long *o*, long *oo*, diphthong *ou*, and long *a*. Then have them sort the long *i* words into sets of homophones.

**WORD HUNT** Have students search through reading materials for homophones. Tell them to record what they found in their Word Study Notebooks.

**WORD STUDY NOTEBOOK** Ask students to record their sorts and word hunts in their Word Study Notebooks in a special "Homophones" section. Point out that mastering the spelling of homophones takes practice and that this section in their notebooks will be a useful resource. Have students add any homophones from previous spelling lessons.

## Proofread and Write

Distribute copies of the Weather Report. Have students read it, circling any spelling errors they find. Then have them work with a partner to write each word correctly and verify its meaning in a dictionary. (There are five misspelled words: *hear, Two, hour, right, buy.*) Tell students to look for other words in the report that are homophones. *(feet, feat; one, won; new, knew; pair, pear, pare)*

Weather Report

Did you here the latest? To feet of snow fell in one our. And it is still snowing write now! It may be time to bye a new pair of boots.

13.31

**WRITING IDEA!** Challenge students to write sentences using sets of homophones in one sentence: for example, "Our clock chimes every hour."

## Word Game

Have students play a game of "Double Trouble," in which they guess and spell homophone pairs. First, have students write a series of clues on index cards for the homophones they have been studying: for example, "Listen in this place" *(Hear here);* "Spell correctly" *(Write right);* "Tired vegetable" *(Beat beet);* "Visit the butcher" *(Meet meat);* "A sick bucket" *(Pale pail).* Students can then shuffle the cards and work in teams to guess the homophones, tell what they mean, and spell each one correctly.

**TEACHING STRATEGY FOR**

## Stage III: Within Word Pattern Spelling

### Benchmarks

- ability to spell common contractions correctly
- ability to distinguish between contractions and their homophones
- ability to recognize misspellings of contractions when proofreading

### Grade Level

- Grade 3 and above

### Prerequisites

- all Teaching Strategies in Chapter 8: Phonics
- all Grades 1 and 2 phonic elements (see p. 8.8)

### Grouping

- whole class
- small group or pairs
- individual

### Materials

- Flip Folders (see p. 13.18)
- copies of Flip Folder Practice Sheet (see Appendix)
- student Word Study Notebooks
- copies of proofreading sample
- index cards

# CONTRACTIONS

This generic teaching strategy focuses on common contractions with *will, are, is/has, have,* and *not.* It includes the homophones *we'll, they're, you're, who's,* and *it's.* The same strategy can be used to focus on contractions with *had/would* or *am.*

## Introduce the Word List

Tell students that the spelling words are contractions, or words that come from two words that have been joined. Make sure students can identify the apostrophe, and explain that it indicates where letters have been omitted. Then introduce the list of spelling words, making sure that students are familiar with the meanings of all the words.

I'll, we'll, you'll, they're, you're, we're, who's, it's, she's, he's, you've, they've, we've, doesn't, isn't, can't, won't, don't, wouldn't, couldn't

## Study the Words

Have students print their spelling words in the first column of the Flip Folder Practice Sheet and proofread the list, making sure each word is spelled correctly. Then tell them to use their Flip Folders to "look-say-cover-see-write-check-rewrite" each of the words on the list. Help students connect meaning with spelling by asking them to say each contraction, then say the two words from which it is formed, and then repeat the contraction: *You're. You are. You're.* Students may need to be reminded that *won't* is formed from *will + not.*

## Explore the Orthographic Pattern

**WORD SORT** For this writing sort, have students make five columns on a sheet of paper, with the following headings: (1) Contractions with *will,* (2) Contractions with *are,* (3) Contractions with *is* or *has,* (4) Contractions with *have,* and (5) Contractions with *not.* Then say each contraction aloud, while students write it under the appropriate heading: for example, *you're→are; we've→have.* When students have finished the sort, have them share what they wrote down in each of the columns.

**WORD STUDY NOTEBOOK** Have students record their sorts in their Word Study Notebooks. Encourage them to add other words from their reading and writing in the appropriate columns. Students should put the symbol "H" for "homophone" next to the words *we'll, they're, you're, who's,* and *it's* and add these words and their corresponding homophones to the Homophones section in their notebooks.

## Proofread and Write

Distribute copies of the following postcard. Have students read it, circling any spelling errors they find. Then have them correct the misspelled words. (There are eight misspelled words: *won't, It's, your, don't, you've, he's, Who's, I'll.*)

13.33

13.34

*Camp Clover Lake*

Dear Maya,

You wonn't believe who is at Camp Clover Lake. Its that boy who broke you're science fair project! I do'nt know if youve seen him since, but h'es pretty nice. Whose coming with you to see me next week? Ill let you know what time to come.

Love, Rita

**WRITING IDEA!** Have students write a postcard to a friend using as many of the spelling words as they can. Ask them to wait a few days and then proofread their work, using their Proofreading Checklists. Students can copy their corrected messages onto actual postcards and mail them to friends.

## Word Game

Students can play the game "Contraction Concentration." Have them write a series of contractions on index cards and the two words they come from on a separate card. They should then shuffle the cards and lay them face down in rows. Each player turns over two cards per turn, trying to remember each card's position in order to match the contractions with their corresponding word pairs. When a match is made, the player removes the cards until there are no cards left. The player with the most pairs wins.

## Stage IV: Syllable Juncture Spelling

### Benchmarks

- ability to spell one- and two-syllable words ending in *–ed* and *–ing* with correct consonant doubling and e-dropping
- ability to identify misspellings of one- and two-syllable words ending in *–ed* and *–ing* when proofreading

### Grade Level

- Grade 3 and above

### Prerequisites

- all Teaching Strategies in Chapter 8: Phonics Chapter 10: Multisyllabic Words
- all Grades 1 and 2 phonic elements (see p. 8.8)

### Grouping

- whole class
- small group or pairs
- individual

### Materials

- Flip Folders (see p. 13.18)
- copies of Flip Folder Practice Sheet (see Appendix)
- copies of Word Study Grid (see Appendix)
- student Word Study Notebooks
- copies of proofreading sample

# CONSONANT DOUBLING/DROPPING *e*

This generic teaching strategy focuses on the consonant-doubling and *e*-dropping patterns that occur when the inflectional endings *–ing* and *–ed* are added to single-syllable words. The same strategy can be used to introduce the spelling of multisyllabic words with *–ed* and *–ing*.

**13.35**

## Introduce the Word List

Introduce the list of spelling words, making sure that students are familiar with the meanings of all the words. Key words are shown in boldface type.

running, cutting, **hopping**, swimming; hoping, writing, making, losing, changing, coming, giving; patted, hugged, planned, stopped; named, moved, **liked**, stayed, started

## Study the Words

Have students print their spelling words in the first column of the Flip Folder Practice Sheet and proofread the list, making sure each word is spelled correctly. Then tell them to use their Flip Folders to "look-say-cover-see-write-check-rewrite" each of the words on the list.

## Explore the Orthographic Pattern

**WORD SORT** For this closed sort, distribute copies of the Word Study Grid with the spelling words printed in the boxes. Ask students to read each word aloud, cross out any they do not know, and then cut the grid apart. Have them sort the words into two categories: Words with Short-Vowel Sounds and Words with Long-Vowel Sounds. Ask them what they notice about the consonants in most of the words with

See also...

Section II: Word Structure, "Useful
Spelling Generalizations," p. 3.26

**13.36**

Intervention
Strategy

**As they say each word aloud,
ask them to highlight the base
word with a colored marker.
For the words *hoping, writing,
making, losing, changing,
coming,* and *giving,* have them
write the "missing" final *e*
above the highlighted base
word.**

short-vowel sounds. *(Most have a double consonant. The high-frequency words* coming *and* giving *are exceptions.)* Divide the words *hopping* and *hoping* into syllables. *(hop/ping, ho/ping)* Point to the first syllable of *hopping*—the closed syllable *hop.* Explain that doubling the final consonant in *hop* before adding the ending *–ing* acts to preserve the short sound of *o* in the word *hop.* In contrast, point to the first syllable of *hoping*—the syllable *ho.* Explain that the first syllable in *hoping* is an open syllable ending in the long sound of *o.* Tell students that when they're unsure of whether the consonant needs to be doubled, they should think about the vowel sound they hear. If it's long, the syllable is open and a single consonant follows—the V/CV syllable-juncture pattern. If it's short, the syllable needs to be closed by doubling the consonant—the VC/CV syllable juncture pattern.

Next, ask students what they notice about the change made to the base words ending in silent *e* when *–ing* and *–ed* were added. Have them do another sort, grouping the words into three categories according to changes made to the base word: (1) final consonant doubled, (2) final *e* dropped, and (3) no change.

**WORD STUDY NOTEBOOK** Have students record their sorts in their Word Study Notebooks with the spelling generalizations they discovered: "When you add *–ing* or *–ed* to a word that ends with one vowel and one consonant, double the consonant (VC→VCC + *ing*). When you add *–ing* or *–ed* to a word that ends in silent *e*, drop the *e* (VC*e*→VC + *ing*)." Encourage them to add words with *–ed* and *–ing* from their content area reading to their notebooks.

Because the consonant phoneme /ng/ does not exist in some languages, English language learners may have difficulty pronouncing words with *–ing*. Help students practice saying this sound, explaining that it is made by raising the back part of the tongue toward the roof of the mouth.

## Proofread and Write

Distribute copies of the following paragraph from a book report. Have students read the paragraph, and then circle and correct all of the spelling errors. (There are eight misspelled words: *Running, changing, making, cutting, giving, started, planned, hoping.*)

> Do you like scary stories? I really liked "The Runing Robot." The robot is always changeing into a human and makeing trouble. It winds up cuting the phone lines, taping people's windows shut and givving dogs haircuts. When I statred the book, I planed to read it in two days. Then I kept hopping it would never end.

**WRITING IDEA!** Have students write their own book reviews. Ask them to proofread their work, paying special attention to words with *–ing* and *–ed*.

## Word Game

Students can write "math sentences" for classmates to solve. Provide the following examples to help them get started:

1. hop + p + ed =
2. make − e + ing =
3. stay + ed =
4. swim + m + ing =

## Stage IV: Syllable Juncture Spelling

### Benchmarks

• ability to change *y* to *i* when adding a suffix to words ending with a consonant and *y*
• ability to retain *y* when adding a suffix to words ending with a vowel and *y*
• ability to recognize misspelled words ending in *y* to which suffixes have been added

### Grade Level

• Grade 3 and above

### Prerequisites

• all Teaching Strategies in Chapter 8: Phonics Chapter 10: Multisyllabic Words
• all Grades 1 and 2 phonic elements (see p. 8.8)

### Grouping

• whole class
• small group or pairs
• individual

### Materials

• Flip Folders (see p. 13.18)
• copies of Flip Folder Practice Sheet (see Appendix)
• copies of Word Study Grid (see Appendix)
• student Word Study Notebooks
• copies of proofreading sample

13.38

## CHANGING *y* TO *i*

This generic teaching strategy focuses on the change of final *y* to *i* that occurs when the suffixes –*es,* –*ed,* –*er,* and –*est* are added to words ending with a consonant and *y.* The same strategy can be used to focus on the change of *y* to *i* when adding other suffixes, such as –*ness.*

● ● ● ● ● ● ● ● ● ● ● ● ● ● ● ● ● ● ● ● ● ● ● ●

## Introduce the Word List

Introduce the list of spelling words, making sure that students are familiar with the meanings of all the words.

fly, flies, carry, carried, city, cities, happy, happiest, story, stories, study, studied, easy, easiest, crazy, crazier, play, played, monkey, monkeys

## Study the Words

Have students print their spelling words in the first column of the Flip Folder Practice Sheet and proofread the list, making sure each word is spelled correctly. Then tell them to use their Flip Folders to "look-say-cover-see-write-check-rewrite" each of the words on the list. As they say each base word aloud, ask them to notice the sound of the final *y,* and ask them if the vowel sound is the same when the suffixes are added.

## Explore the Orthographic Pattern

**WORD SORT** Distribute copies of the Word Study Grid with the spelling words printed in the boxes and have students do an open sort of the words. Some students may group the words by part of speech; others may divide the words into base words and inflected forms. Discuss with students how they decided to sort the words.

**See also...**

Section II: Word Structure, "Useful Spelling Generalizations," p. 3.26

**Intervention Strategy** ELL

In most Asian languages, the plural form of nouns is signaled by accompanying numbers or quantitative words. Some students may need to review the concept of adding –s or –es to make the plural form. Spanish-speaking students may benefit from a review of words in which the final *y* has a long-*i* sound, as the vowel *y* is pronounced /ē/ in Spanish. Some examples of words to review are *try, dry, cry, fry, fly, sly, reply.*

If students haven't done so, ask them to pair all the base words with their related forms. Have them notice the spelling of the words that end in a consonant + *y* when a suffix is added. (The *y* changes to *i.*) Then tell students to circle the *i* in each word. Direct their attention to the vowel sound in each base word and explain that changing the *y* to *i* preserves this vowel sound; if the letter *y* remained, it would become the first letter in a new syllable and have the consonant sound /y/. Demonstrate this idea by dividing the nonsense word *cit•yes* and asking students to say the word aloud. Then direct students' attention to the words *played* and *monkeys.* Point out that there is no spelling change when *–ed* and *–s* are added to the base words *play* and *monkey.* The vowel sound in these base words is preserved because the *y* and the preceding vowel act together as a vowel team. Then have students sort all the words in which *y* changes to *i* with their corresponding base words into four categories: (1) suffix *–es,* (2) suffix *–ed,* (3) suffix *–est,* and (4) suffix *–er.*

**WORD STUDY NOTEBOOK** Have students record the sorts in their Word Study Notebooks with the spelling generalizations they discovered: "When you add *–es, –ed, –est,* or *–er* to a word that ends with a consonant and *y,* change *y* to *i.*" Encourage them to add words from their own writing projects that follow this pattern.

## Proofread and Write

Distribute copies of the following advertisement for a new game. Have students read it, and then circle and correct all of the spelling errors. (There are six misspelled words: *cities, easiest, crazier, monkeys, flies, happiest.*)

**13.40**

In citys around the world, kids are discovering the easyest way to have a good time. Frantic Frogs is the best game you've ever played. It's crazyer than Leaping Lizards and easy to learn. You start with two monkees, three flys, and a frog. They have to find their way to a fairytale and pick the happyest ending. If you want to have some fun, rush to the store and buy this game!

**WRITING IDEA!** Have students write their own ads for a new game. Challenge them to include as many of the spelling words as they can. Then have students exchange their work with a partner and proofread to correct spelling and the use of punctuation and capitalization.

## Word Game

Have students play "More or Most" Tic-Tac-Toe using words that end in –*er* and –*est* instead of X and O. Players choose to be "more" or "most" and take turns writing words until one player gets three in a row. Before students begin, suggest that they work together to brainstorm a list of words and add these to their Word Study Notebooks. You can provide the following list to help them get started: *tinier, tiniest, scarier, scariest, busier, busiest, dirtier, dirtiest, happier, happiest, stickier, stickiest.*

# Stage V: Derivational Constancy Spelling

### Benchmarks

• ability to use knowledge of base words and word roots to spell words ending in –*able* and –*ible*

• ability to preserve soft *c* and *g* when adding –*able* and –*ible*

• ability to identify misspellings of words ending in –*able* and –*ible* when proofreading

### Grade Level

• Grade 4 and above

### Prerequisites

• all Teaching Strategies in Chapter 8: Phonics Chapter 10: Multisyllabic Words

• all Grades 1 and 2 phonic elements (see p. 8.8)

### Grouping

• whole class
• small group or pairs
• individual

### Materials

• Flip Folders (see p. 13.18)
• copies of Flip Folder Practice Sheet (see Appendix)
• copies of Word Study Grid (see Appendix)
• student Word Study Notebooks
• copies of proofreading sample
• Scrabble® game

## SUFFIXES –*able*, –*ible*

This generic teaching strategy focuses on generalizations about adding –*able* or –*ible* to base words and word roots. Students examine base words ending in silent *e* and base words ending in soft *c* and *g*. The same strategy can be used to introduce less frequent patterns to students in the late Derivational Constancy stage, such as using –*ible* with word roots ending in soft *c* or *g* and –*able* with word roots ending in hard *c* or *g*, or using knowledge of –*ion* forms derived from verb roots to choose between –*able* and –*ible*.

13.41

## Introduce the Word List

Introduce the list of spelling words, making sure that students are familiar with the meanings of all the words. Key words are shown in boldface type.

**enjoyable**, dependable, predictable, laughable, profitable, manageable, noticeable, lovable, comparable; **possible**, visible, terrible, edible; sensible, responsible

## Study the Words

Have students print their spelling words in the first column of the Flip Folder Practice Sheet and proofread the list, making sure each word is spelled correctly. Then tell them to use their Flip Folders to "look-say-cover-see-write-check-rewrite" each of the words on the list. As they say each word aloud, ask them to identify the base word or word root. Discuss how adding the suffix –*able* or –*ible* forms adjectives, and review the meaning of each newly formed word with students.

See also . . .

Section II: Word Structure
"What Is a Morpheme?" p. 3.28

**13.42**

ENGLISH/SPANISH

**Many adjectives in Spanish end in *–able* and *–ible*. Encourage Spanish-speaking students to identify any words in the word list that sound similar and have the same meaning in Spanish:** *predicible, comparable, posible, visible, terrible, responsable.* **(Note that the Spanish word** *sensible* **is a false cognate that means "sensitive.") Students will also benefit from discussing the differences between the suffixes of the cognates** *predic**ible*** **vs.** *predict**able*** **and** *respons**able*** **vs.** *respons**ible.***

## Explore the Orthographic Pattern

**WORD SORT**  For this closed sort, distribute copies of the Word Study Grid with the spelling words printed in the boxes. Point out that although the suffixes *–able* and *–ible* sound alike, their use follows certain patterns. Using *enjoyable* and *possible* as key words, have students sort the words into two groups: those ending in *–able* and those ending in *–ible*. Ask them what they notice about the words with the *–able* suffix. *(The suffix is added to a complete base word.)* Then ask students to compare the spelling of *manageable, noticeable, lovable, comparable.* If necessary, delete the *e* and have students say *manageable* and *noticeable* aloud. Make sure they understand that if a complete base word ends in soft *c* or *g*, the silent *e* is needed before the *–able* suffix.

Next, direct students' attention to the words with the *–ible* suffix and ask them what they notice about most of the words. *(In all but* sensible *and* responsible, *the suffix* –ible *is added to a word root that is not a recognizable word by itself.)* Explain that the two commonly used words *sensible* and *responsible* are exceptions to the general rules: although they are derived from complete base words, they do not retain the silent *e* or take the *–able* ending.

**WORD STUDY NOTEBOOK**  Have students record their sorts and the spelling generalizations they discovered in their Word Study Notebooks: "Use *–able* with a complete base word. Keep the silent *e* if the word ends in *ge* or *ce*," and "Use *–ible* with word roots." Encourage them to add words from their content area reading, and note any exceptions.

## Proofread and Write

Distribute copies of the following letter to the editor. Have students read it, using the proofreading marks to correct any errors they find. Ask them to circle the misspelled words and rewrite them correctly. (There are six misspelled words: *possible, terrible, manageable, profitable, sensible, visible.*)

# Proofreading Marks

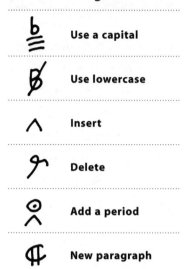

| | |
|---|---|
| b̲ | **Use a capital** |
| ß | **Use lowercase** |
| ∧ | **Insert** |
| ⟍ | **Delete** |
| ⊙̸ | **Add a period** |
| ₵ | **New paragraph** |

To the Editor:

Is it posable to have plastic added to the city recycling program?  It's a terrable waste to just throw all the empty containers in the trash. Our mayor agrees that plastic recycling would be managible and profitible for the city. What we need is citizen support for this sensable plan. Otherwise, garbage will be visable from every corner!

Yours truly,

A Concerned Citizen

13.43

**WRITING IDEA!** Have students write a letter to their school or local newspaper about an important issue. Encourage them to use adjectives ending in *–able* or *–ible* to make their descriptions more vivid. Students can exchange first drafts with a partner and circle any words they think are misspelled. Invite volunteers to read aloud their corrected letters.

## Word Game

Pairs of students can play a game of Scrabble® to practice spelling words with *–able* and *–ible*. A third student's role is to "announce" the words. Player 1 uses letter tiles to spell the base word or word root. Player 2 must then add the appropriate suffix and decide whether or not to preserve the silent *e*. The announcer gives the players one point for each correct spelling.

**TEACHING STRATEGY FOR**

## Stage V: Derivational Constancy Spelling

### Benchmarks

- ability to use meaning to correctly spell derived forms
- ability to retain correct vowel spelling in derived forms with schwa
- ability to recognize misspelled derived forms with schwa when proofreading

### Grade Level

- Grade 6 and above

### Prerequisites

- all Teaching Strategies in Chapter 8: Phonics Chapter 10: Multisyllabic Words
- all Grades 1 and 2 phonic elements (see p. 8.8)

### Grouping

- whole class
- small group or pairs
- individual

### Materials

- Flip Folders (see p. 13.18)
- copies of Flip Folder Practice Sheet (see Appendix)
- copies of Word Study Grid (see Appendix)
- student Word Study Notebooks
- copies of proofreading sample

## DERIVATIVES WITH SCHWA

This generic teaching strategy focuses on the vowel-alteration patterns from long- and short-vowel sounds to schwa (*define → definition, democracy → democratic*). The same strategy can be used at an earlier point in the Derivational Constancy stage to focus on long- to short-vowel changes (*please → pleasant*) or at a later point in the Derivational Constancy stage to focus on the more complex change of long-vowel digraphs to short vowels (*explain → explanation, perceive → perception*).

## Introduce the Word List

Introduce the list of spelling words, making sure that students are familiar with the meanings of all the words.

able, ability, compete, competition, define, definition, inspire, inspiration, compose, composition; democracy, democratic, history, prehistoric, humanity, human, legality, legal, perfection, perfect (adjective)

## Study the Words

After discussing the meaning of each word on the list, have students print their spelling words in the first column of the Flip Folder Practice Sheet and proofread the list, making sure each word is spelled correctly. Then tell them to use their Flip Folders to "look-say-cover-see-write-check-rewrite" each of the words on the list. As they say each word aloud, ask them to underline the stressed syllable.

**All of the words on the list are cognates of Spanish words. Although the vowel sounds and spellings of the derived forms remain the same, the place of stress does change in several Spanish word pairs:** *há*bil*, habi*lidad**; *his*toria**, *prehis*tórico**; *huma*nidad**, *hu*mano**; *lega*lidad**, *le*gal**; *perfec*ción**, *per*fecto**. **Teachers can use these examples with Spanish-speaking students to illustrate shifts in spoken stress.**

# Explore the Orthographic Pattern

**WORD SORT** For this closed sort, distribute copies of the Word Study Grid with the spelling words printed in the boxes. Guide students in sorting the words according to the place of stress. (First syllable: *able, history, human, legal, perfect*; Second syllable: *ability, compete, define, inspire, compose, democracy, humanity, legality, perfection*; Third syllable: *competition, definition, inspiration, composition, democratic, prehistoric*.) Direct their attention to the vowel sound in the unstressed syllables of *history, human, legal,* and *perfect*. Explain that this sound is called "schwa" and can be spelled with any one of the vowel letters. Have students circle the schwa in the words *ability, competition, definition, composition, democratic*.

Invite students to do another sort, matching the ten related word pairs. Point out the pair *compose* and *composition* and ask them what they notice about the words' spelling, meaning, and place of stress. Explain that although the stress and vowel sound changes, the spelling of the shared root *compos* is the same. To correctly spell the unstressed schwa sound in *composition,* students should think of the related word *compose,* and its long-vowel *o* in the second syllable. Have students take another look at the schwa sounds they previously circled and ask them to identify the short and long vowels in the related words that are clues to the spellings of the schwa.

**WORD HUNT** Encourage students to do a word hunt for words that are related in meaning and spelling to those in their word lists (such as ***compose, composition,*** *component, composed, composer, composes, composure, composite, compost, decompose, recomposition*).

**WORD STUDY NOTEBOOK** Have students record their findings in their Word Study Notebooks in a section titled "Words with Schwa." Suggest that they record the spelling strategy: "If you're not sure how to spell a vowel sound, think of a word related in meaning."

13.45

## Proofread and Write

Distribute copies of the following letter from a student to the city council. Have students read it, and then circle and correct all of the spelling errors. (There are six misspelled words: *opposition, decision, perfect, definition, inspiration, competition.*)

13.46

> Dear City Council:
>
> I am writing to express my oppasition to the city council's dicision to eliminate the Arts and Music Program. Lack of money may seem like a perfict excuse, but what is the city's defenition of "education"? Isn't it to provide insperation and prepare children for computition in the workplace? I urge you to reconsider.
>
> Yours truly,
> Art

**WRITING IDEA!** Have students write their own letters to the mayor's office or city council about an important issue. After they have written their first drafts, ask them to check their work for correct spelling, punctuation, and capitalization.

## Word Game

Have students work with a partner to make a crossword puzzle using the spelling words they have been studying. Suggest that they use a dictionary to help them write clues for the puzzle, such as synonyms or related word forms. Have students give the blank puzzles to their classmates to complete.

# Self-Diagnosis of Spelling Errors

### Benchmarks

- recognition of the importance of correct spelling
- ability to judge the logic and accuracy of spelling attempts
- ability to change strategies as needed and use appropriate resources to correct spelling
- ability to diagnose and correct spelling errors

### Grade Level

- Grade 2 and above

### Prerequisite

- all Grades 1 and 2 phonic elements (see p. 8.8)

### Grouping

- whole class
- small group or pairs
- individual

### Materials

- recent samples of students' writing (uncorrected drafts)
- copies of proofreading sample

## DO-IT-YOURSELF SPELLING

*GRADE LEVEL*
*2*
*AND ABOVE*
*GRADE LEVEL*

This generic teaching strategy shows students how to diagnose and correct their own spelling errors. This strategy can be used for students from the Letter Name through Derivational Constancy stages of spelling development.

**13.47**

· · · · · · · · · · · · · · · · · · · · · · · · · · · · · · · · · · · · · · · · · · ·

## Teach/Model

Tell students that it is important to know why they misspell a word and that there are really only three main types of spelling errors:

### wanning or wanting?

1. You may misspell a word because you pronounce it differently than the standard way of saying it. Ask other people to say a word. Then listen to find out if they say it the same way that you do.

### retrop or report?

2. You may misspell a word even though you write down the correct letters if you write them down out of order. You may reverse a couple of the letters. Try to say the word the way you spelled it. Compare your spelling with the right spelling to see if you do this.

### fone or phone?

3. You may misspell a word even though you spell it the way it sounds, because in English many sounds can be spelled more than one way. Most spelling errors are of this kind. For example, the initial /f/ sound can be spelled *f* or *ph*.

## Explore the Orthographic Pattern

**WORD HUNT** Have students select a recent writing sample. Ask students to exchange writing samples with a partner and to look for each other's misspelled words. They should circle any word they think their partner misspelled.

13.48

**WORD SORT** Ask students to look back at each of the words they misspelled and classify each one according to the type of error: (1) Is it because of the way I say the word? Do I leave out or change sounds when I say it? (2) Is it because I wrote the letters out of order? Can I say the word the way I spelled it? (3) Is it because there is more than one way to spell the sounds in the word? Have students group the words according to the kind of spelling error.

Intervention Strategy

**Using a dictionary is part of good spelling habits. Teachers should review dictionary skills with students and have a variety of dictionaries available in the classroom.**

**WORD STUDY NOTEBOOK** Have students check the spelling of the words circled and correctly write the misspelled words in their Word Study Notebooks. Encourage them to use available resources to correct their spelling: a personal spelling dictionary, a classroom dictionary, word walls, class lists, spell checker products, a proofreading partner, or the teacher.

## Proofread and Write

Distribute copies of the following paragraph and ask students to read through it, circling any words they think are misspelled. (There are seven misspelled words: *president, know, always, Just, grandfather, special, get.*)

> Hi. I want to be your class presidint!
> I now I can do a good job. I am alawys
> careful about my work. Jus ask my
> granfather. He gives me a spesial job
> to do every week. And I can git the
> job done right! Vote for me.

Discuss each error, asking students which words were misspelled because of the way the writer pronounces them. *(presidint:* short *i* instead of short *e; jus:* consonant *t* missing from final blend; *granfather:* consonant *d* missing from final blend; *git:* short *i* instead of short *e)* Then ask students which word was misspelled because the writer wrote letters out of order. *(alawys)* Next, ask students which words were misspelled because there is more than one way to spell the sounds in the words. *(now:* initial /n/ can be spelled *n, kn,* or *gn; spesial:* /sh/ can be spelled *s* if it occurs at the beginning of words)

**WRITING IDEA!** Students can write a "spelling error" sentence. The sentence should have examples of each of the three types of spelling errors. Tell students to exchange sentences and identify each type of error.

## Section References

**13.50**

Adams, M. J. 1990. *Beginning to read: Thinking and learning about print.* Cambridge, MA: MIT Press.

Bear, D. 1982. Patterns of oral reading across stages of word knowledge. Unpublished doctoral dissertation. University of Virginia, Charlottesville, VA.

Bear, D. 1988. *"On the hurricane deck of a mule": Teaching adults to read using language experience and oral history techniques* (manual). Reno: Nevada Literacy Coalition and University of Nevada-Reno. (ERIC Document Reproduction Service No. ED 294–155.)

Bear, D. 1991. Determining criteria for the development of a qualitative scale of higher levels of orthographic knowledge. Unpublished study. University of Nevada-Reno, Reno.

Bear, D., M. Invernizzi, S. Templeton, and F. Johnston. 1996. *Words their way: Word study for phonics, vocabulary, and spelling instruction.* Upper Saddle River, NJ: Prentice-Hall.

Beers, J., R. Cramer, and D. Hammond. 1995. *Spelling: An overview of research and current research information and practices.* Glenview, IL: Scott, Foresman.

Chomsky, C. 1970. Reading, writing, and phonology. *Harvard Education Review* 40, pp. 287–309.

Chomsky, N., and M. Halle. 1968. *The sound pattern of English.* New York: Harper & Row.

Clay, M. 1975. *What did I write? Beginning writing behaviour.* Portsmouth, NH: Heinemann.

Colvin, R. L. 1995. State report urges return to basics in teaching reading. *Los Angeles Times* (Sept. 13).

Cunningham, P. M. 1995. *Phonics they use: Words for reading and writing.* New York: HarperCollins.

Ehri, L. C. 1992. Reconceptualizing the development of sight word reading and its relationship to recoding. In P. B. Gough, L. C. Ehri, and R. Treiman (eds.), *Reading acquisition.* Mahwah, NJ: Erlbaum.

Foorman, B. 1997. Why direct spelling instruction is important. *Scholastic Spelling: Research Paper,* Vol. 2. New York: Scholastic.

Fry, E., D. Fountoukidis, and J. Polk. 1995. *The new reading teacher's book of lists.* Upper Saddle River, NJ: Prentice-Hall.

Ganske, K. 1996. *In other words: A resource of word lists for phonics, spelling, and vocabulary study.* Charlottesville: University of Virginia.

Gentry, J. R. 1997. *My kid can't spell!* Portsmouth, NH: Heinemann.

Gentry, J. R. 1998. *Five questions teachers ask about spelling.* Zaner-Bloser Spelling Research Series. Columbus, OH: Zaner-Bloser.

Gentry. J. R., and J. W. Gillet. 1993. *Teaching kids to spell.* Portsmouth, NH: Heinemann.

Gill, J. 1992. Focus on research: Development of word knowledge as it relates to reading, spelling, and instruction. *Language Arts* 69, pp. 444–453.

Hall, D. P., P. M. Cunningham, and J. W. Cunningham. 1995. Multilevel spelling instruction in third grade classrooms. In K. A. Hinchman, D. L. Leu, and C. Kinzer (eds.), *Perspectives on literacy research and practice.* Chicago: National Reading Conference.

Harris, K. R., and S. Graham. 1996. Memo to constructivists: Skills count, too. *Educational Leadership* 53, pp. 26–29.

Henderson, E. H. 1981. *Learning to read and spell: The child's knowledge of words.* DeKalb, IL: Northern Illinois University Press.

Henderson, E. H. 1990. *Teaching spelling* (2nd ed.). Boston: Houghton Mifflin.

Henderson, E. H., and J. W. Beers. 1980. *Developmental and cognitive aspects of learning to spell: A reflection of word knowledge.* Newark, DE: International Reading Association.

Henderson, E. H., and S. Templeton. 1986. The development of spelling ability through alphabet, pattern, and meaning. *Elementary School Journal* 86, pp. 305–316.

Horn, E. 1954. What research says to the teacher. *Teaching Spelling* 3: 32.

Hughes, M., and D. Searle. 1996. Joe and Elly: Sight-based and sound-based approaches to literacy. *Whole Language Umbrella: Talking Points* 7(4), pp. 8–11.

Hughes, M., and D. Searle. 1997. *The violent E and other tricky sounds: Learning to spell from kindergarten through grade 6.* York, ME: Stenhouse.

Invernizzi, M., M. Abouzeid, and T. Gill. 1994. Using students' invented spelling as a guide for spelling instruction that emphasizes word study. *Elementary School Journal* 95(2), pp. 155–167.

Moats, L. C. 1995. *Spelling: Development, disability, and instruction.* Timonium, MD: York Press.

Moats, L. C. 1997. *How children learn to spell* (research paper). New York: Scholastic.

Moats, L. C. 1998. Teaching decoding. *American Educator* (Spring/Summer), pp. 42–49.

Moffett, J., and B. J. Wagner. 1992. *Student-centered language arts: K–12* (4th ed.). Portsmouth, NH: Heinemann.

Morris, D., L. Blanton, W. E. Blanton, J. Nowacek, and J. Perney. 1995. Teaching low-achieving spellers at their "instructional level." *Elementary School Journal* 96, pp. 163–177.

Morris, D., L. Nelson, and J. Perney. 1986. Exploring the concept of "spelling instructional level" through the analysis of error-types. *Elementary School Journal* 87, pp. 181–200.

Peters, M. 1985. *Spelling: Caught or taught?* New York: Routledge.

Phenix, J. 1996. *The spelling teacher's book of lists.* Markham, Ontario: Pembroke Publishers.

Read, D. 1971. Preschool children's knowledge of English phonology. *Harvard Educational Review* 41(1), pp. 1–34.

Schlagal, R. C. 1986. Informal and qualitative assessment of spelling. *The Pointer* 30, pp. 37–41.

Schlagal, R. C., and J. H. Schlagal. 1992. The integral character of spelling: Teaching strategies for multiple purposes. *Language Arts* 69, pp. 418–424.

Tangel, D. M., and B. A. Blachman. 1995. Effect of phoneme awareness instruction on the invented spelling of first-grade children: A one-year follow-up. *Journal of Reading Behavior* 27, pp. 153–185.

Taylor, D. S. 1981. English spelling: A help rather than a hindrance. *English Language Teaching Journal* 35, pp. 316–321.

Templeton, S. 1983. Using the spelling/meaning connection to develop word knowledge in older students. *Journal of Reading* 27(1), pp. 8–14.

Treiman, R. 1996. *Why spelling? The benefits of incorporating spelling into beginning reading instruction.* Paper presented at the Conference on Word Recognition in Beginning Literacy, College Park, MD.

Uhry, J. K., and M. J. Shepherd. 1993. Segmentation/spelling instruction as part of a first-grade reading program: Effects on several measures of reading. *Reading Research Quarterly* 28, pp. 218–233.

Venezky, R. L. 1970. *The structure of English orthography.* The Hague: Mouton.

White, T. G., M. A. Power, and S. White. 1989. Morphological analysis: Implications for teaching and understanding vocabulary growth. *Reading Research Quarterly* 24, pp. 283–304.

Wysocki, K., and J. R. Jenkins. 1987. Deriving word meanings through morphological generalization. *Reading Research Quarterly* 22, pp. 66–81.

Young. S. 1994. *The Scholastic rhyming dictionary.* New York: Scholastic.

Zutell, J. 1992. An integrated view of word knowledge: Correctional studies of the relationships among spelling, reading, and conceptual development. In S. Templeton and D. Bear (eds.), *Development of orthographic knowledge and the foundations of literacy: A memorial festschrift for Edmund Henderson.* Mahwah, NJ: Erlbaum.

Zutell, J. 1998. *A student-active learning approach to spelling instruction.* Zaner-Bloser Spelling Research Series. Columbus, OH: Zaner-Bloser.

# SECTION VI

# Vocabulary Development

# Section VI: Vocabulary Development

*"Our knowledge of words . . . determines how we understand texts, define ourselves for others, and define the way we see the world."*

—STAHL, 1999

Vocabulary development is far more than looking up words in a dictionary and using the words in a sentence. It is a complex process that involves many factors, including students' prior knowledge, their skill in using context, their knowledge of how the English language works, and their general cognitive ability. Adding to the complexity is the issue of what we mean by *vocabulary.* Most often, the term is associated with the body of words students must understand in order to read text with fluency and comprehension. According to Irvin (1998), people have four types of vocabulary: listening, speaking, reading, and writing. The listening and reading vocabularies are receptive, and the speaking and writing vocabularies are expressive.

There is a strong relationship between reading ability and vocabulary acquisition in that the amount of reading students do, both in and out of school, is an indicator of students' vocabulary size (Fielding, Wilson, and Anderson 1986). It follows that students need to develop strong reading skills to be able to engage successfully in the volume of reading necessary for them to learn large numbers of words (Anderson and Nagy 1991).

Vocabulary knowledge is also fundamental to reading comprehension: we cannot understand text without knowing what most of the words mean. In fact, research has shown that the

## Types of Vocabulary

**listening**

all the words a person hears and understands

**speaking**

all the words a person uses in ordinary speech

**reading**

the words in print that a person recognizes or is able to figure out

**writing**

the words a person can use appropriately in his or her own writing

See also...

**CORE Reading Research Anthology**

for background information

proportion of difficult words in text is the single most powerful predictor of text difficulty, and a reader's general vocabulary knowledge is the single best predictor of how well that reader can understand text (Anderson and Freebody 1981).

Most students whose primary language is English enter school with fairly large listening and speaking vocabularies—ranging between 2,500 and 5,000 words (Beck and McKeown 1991). Typical first-grade students can understand and orally use about 6,000 words, but they have very limited reading vocabularies (Chall 1987). By second grade, however, students' reading vocabularies may range between 2,000 and 5,000 words (Graves, Juel, and Graves 1998). Thereafter, reading and writing vocabulary growth increases steadily, with typical students learning an average of 3,000 to 4,000 words a year (Nagy and Anderson 1984; Nagy and Herman 1987).

Learning this number of words a year is an enormous achievement. If teachers were to directly teach students this number of words, it would mean teaching approximately 20 or more words every school day. Yet Stahl and his colleagues have found that, at best, 8 to 10 words a week can be taught directly, for a total of only 300 to 400 words a year. How do students acquire sufficient word knowledge to enable them to read and understand so many new words? In the following excerpt, Stahl (1999) addresses the question of how many words students learn each year and how different estimates inform educators' decisions about vocabulary instruction.

# How Many Words Do People Know?

*by Steven A. Stahl*

Excerpted from *Vocabulary Development* (1999) by Steven A. Stahl. Cambridge, MA: Brookline Books.

At first glance, this question might seem rather esoteric. After all, why should we care how many words people know when our concern is to teach the words they find in the texts they are reading? This question, however, is at the core of many other questions. If an average high school senior knows 45,000 words, according to one estimate (Nagy and Anderson 1984), then it might not be possible to teach someone all the words he or she needs to know through direct instruction. If the estimate is closer to 17,000, as other authors have suggested (D'Anna, Zechmeister, and Hall 1991), or even 5,000 (Hirsh and Nation 1992), then direct teaching might play a more important role. This is especially true for speakers of other languages who are learning English.

There are two ways of looking at the question of how many words people know: looking at texts that people read and testing people. Although estimates vary widely as to how many total words there are in English (unabridged dictionaries can have between 250,000 and 500,000 entries, depending on what they allow as entries), we have good data as to the number of words in books used by elementary and secondary students. Our best estimate, taken from Nagy and Anderson (1984), is that there are roughly 88,500 word families used in books up to 12th grade. A *word family* is defined by Nagy and Anderson as groups of words in which someone knowing one of the words (in the family) could guess or infer the meaning of the others when encountering it in context while reading, such as *add, addition, additive, adding,* and so on.

About half of the texts we read consist of the 107 most common words. Another 5,000 words account for the next 45 percent, so that 95 percent of the texts we read consist of about 5,100 different words (Adams 1990). The rest of the texts we read consist of the remaining 83,000 or so words (Nagy and

How Many Words Do People Know?

*Steven A. Stahl*

Anderson 1984). If this is so, then why do we not just teach the 5,100 most common words and not worry about the relatively rare words? There are two problems with this logic. First, these "rare" words are not so rare. They are words that every literate adult should know and assumes that other literate adults should know. Words in this group might include *beneficial, advocate, accountant, cancer,* and so on. The second problem is that these "rare" words carry most of the content of the texts. How much would one understand in a biology text dealing with the discovery of penicillin without knowing such rare words as *penicillin, antibiotic, bacterium,* and so on? Many, but not all, of the uncommon words have to do with the particular topic of the text. This is especially true in the content areas. Words such as *abiotic, ecosystem,* and *niche* are relatively uncommon, but also very useful to have a suitable understanding of ecology.

It is instructive to look at the number of words in texts that students read, but this does not tell us how many words an average student knows. We do know that this number is considerably less than 88,500, but it is not clear how much less. Early estimates varied wildly, from 17,000 to more than 200,000 words estimated as known by university undergraduates, or from 2,562 to 26,000 words estimated as known by first-graders (Lorge and Chall 1963). Since one cannot ask a person every word he or she knows (can you imagine sitting down to a 90,000-item multiple choice test?), tests need to be based on samples. But the larger the dictionary that is used to sample from, the larger the estimate will be of a person's word knowledge; therefore, dictionaries of different sizes are partly responsible for these differences (see Lorge and Chall 1963 for an explanation).

Even with a low estimate of 17,000 words, a researcher cannot ask students to define every word they supposedly should know. Even a test of 100 words is likely to be so fatiguing that

How Many Words Do People Know?
*Steven A. Stahl*

**vi**

the test would not be accurate. Thus every study that estimates the number of words known uses a sample. Usually this sample comes from a dictionary, possibly the fifth word from every 40th page.

The differing estimates of vocabulary knowledge are crucial to making decisions about vocabulary instruction. Because my experience and those of my colleagues suggest that 300–500 words per year can reasonably be taught through direct instruction (8–10 words per week, 50 weeks a year), the figure accepted is important in determining how to plan for vocabulary growth. If a teacher accepts Nagy and Anderson's (1984) estimate that there are 88,500 word types in English, and that students learn about half of them, this suggests that the average child learns about 3,000 new words each year. (There is other independent evidence that, indeed, children do learn about 3,000 new words per year; White, Graves, and Slater 1990). Even doubling or tripling our estimate for direct vocabulary teaching, we cannot reach 3,000 words per year through direct teaching alone. Most of these words learned must come from context (Sternberg 1987). However, if you accept a lower figure, such as the 17,000 words suggested by D'Anna et al. (1991), or about 1,000 new words per year, then it may be possible to teach all the words that a person needs to learn. This distinction is especially important in teaching English as a second language (Gouldman, Nation, and Read 1990). ESL students rely more heavily on direct instruction than native speakers, because they typically need to make up more ground more quickly to learn English.

If we take this higher estimate for the number of words that children learn each year, will contextual reading be enough to learn 3,000 words per year? This is a monumental task, requiring the learning of about eight words a day, every day, and twice

**How Many Words Do People Know?**
*Steven A. Stahl*

that many if word learning occurs only on school days. Nagy and his colleagues (Nagy, Herman, and Anderson 1985; Nagy, Anderson, and Herman 1987; Herman, Anderson, Pearson, and Nagy 1987) have calculated that much of this annual growth in reading can come from incidental learning of word meanings. Their argument goes as follows:

- We assume that if a fifth-grade child reads for an hour per day (in and out of school) at a rate of 150 words per minute (a conservative estimate; see Harris and Sipay 1990), five days a week, then the child will have encountered 2,250,000 words in the course of all this reading.

- If 2 to 5 percent of those words are unknown (as in instructional-level text; Betts 1946), the child will have encountered from 45,000 to 112,500 unknown words.

- From other research, we know that children will learn between 5 and 10 percent of previously unknown words from a single reading (Nagy and Herman 1987).

- This would account for at least 2,250 new words learned from context each year.

Making all the estimates as conservative as possible, the 2,250 new words is close enough to 3,000 to suggest that context can be a powerful influence on students' vocabulary growth. This suggests that one of the most powerful things we can do to increase children's vocabulary is to encourage them to read as widely as possible. □

See also...

**Section VIII: Reading and Responding**

**Chapter 19: Independent, Wide Reading**

## Support for English Language Learners

Additional instruction time before and after school

Preteaching of essential vocabulary and background knowledge

Emphasis on meaning, rather than pronunciation

Use of pantomime, pictures, and graphic organizers

Flexible grouping and smaller group size

## Effective Vocabulary Instruction

The majority of word meanings are learned through everyday experiences with oral and written language (Baumann and Kameenui 1991). According to Nagy (1988a), "increasing the volume of students' reading is the single most important thing teachers can do to promote large-scale vocabulary growth."

Students face two challenges in vocabulary development: acquiring new word knowledge and increasing the depth of that knowledge over time. For English language learners, these challenges are even greater. Instruction in specific words and concepts is needed to produce word knowledge of any depth (Nagy 1988a). This instruction is most appropriate for words that are conceptually difficult. Students can be taught these word meanings or concepts intentionally, through explicit teaching or modeling. Additionally, explicit instruction in word-learning strategies can help students to determine the meanings of unfamiliar words they encounter while reading. These strategies may focus on morphemic analysis and external context clues.

Older students as well as younger ones can acquire new vocabulary from listening to stories and books read aloud when the teacher stops to quickly define the unfamiliar word and then proceeds with the reading. This, in addition to preteaching words before reading, is especially helpful for English language learners. Stahl, Richek, and Vandevier (1991) found that sixth-grade students were able to learn almost as many word meanings from *listening* to a story once as they learned from *reading* a story once.

### Multiple Exposures to Words

Research has shown that students need to encounter a word about 12 times before they know it well enough to improve their comprehension (McKeown, Beck, Omanson, and Pople 1985).

## Effective Vocabulary Instruction

**Read aloud to students**

**Encourage independent, wide reading**

**Explicitly teach specific words and concepts**

**Explicitly teach strategies to learn new words independently**

**Provide multiple exposure to words**

**Promote word consciousness**

The implication of this finding is that effective vocabulary instruction must not only introduce students to key vocabulary words, but constantly reinforce the meanings of those words. Reinforcement can be in the form of pointing out the words in reading selections, having students use the words in their own writing, and encouraging them to record words in vocabulary notebooks and then refer to the notebooks frequently as they read and write on their own.

## Dictionary Use

Traditionally, instruction in dictionary use has focused on mechanics—how to find an entry, alphabetize words, identify guide words, and use pronunciation keys—and on having students look up words and use information from their definitions to write sentences. Scott and Nagy (1997) contend that such instruction leads only to a superficial understanding and rapid forgetting of a word, and does not provide students with the guidance they need to make dictionary use an efficient independent word-learning strategy.

Nonetheless, dictionaries are powerful aids to word understanding. It appears that students *can* learn quite a bit from simply looking up a word and processing its definition (Jenkins and Dixon 1983). In fact, McKeown and her colleagues have found that the more students are exposed to definitions, the better their word learning (McKeown, Beck, Omanson, and Pople 1985). The most useful dictionaries include sentences that provide clear examples of a word's meaning in context.

Graves and his colleagues (1998) suggest teaching students to use dictionaries to develop the networks of meanings that ensure reading fluency. Teachers need to model how to look up the meaning of an unknown word, choosing the appropriate definition from an entry to make sure it fits a particular context.

**CORE Reading Research Anthology**

for background information

x
VI

## Standards for Vocabulary and Concept Development

## Word Consciousness

Word consciousness is extensive knowledge of and interest in words. Students who are word-conscious know many words, and know and use them well. They are aware of the subtleties of word meaning and of the power words can have. More than that, however, word-conscious students enjoy words and word play, and are eager to hear and learn new words (Graves et al. 1998; Watts and Graves 1995). Stahl (1999) points out that encouraging students to play with words can create an interest in knowing more about them. Focusing on a word's history and searching for instances of a word's usage in everyday life may also foster word consciousness.

### KINDERGARTEN

- Identify and sort common words into basic categories (e.g., colors, shapes, foods).
- Describe common objects and events in both general and specific language.

### GRADE 1

- Classify grade-appropriate categories of words (e.g., concrete collections of animals, foods, toys).

### GRADE 2

- Understand and explain common antonyms and synonyms.
- Use knowledge of individual words in unknown compound words to predict their meaning.
- Know the meaning of simple prefixes and suffixes (e.g., *over–, un–, –ing, –ly*).
- Identify simple multiple-meaning words.

### GRADE 3

- Use knowledge of antonyms, synonyms, homophones, and homographs to determine the meanings of words.
- Demonstrate knowledge of levels of specificity among grade-appropriate words and explain the importance of these relations (e.g., dog/mammal/animal/living things).

> *"The overall goal is for students to learn about 3,000 or more new words per year."*
>
> —HONIG, 1999

- Use sentence and word context to find the meaning of unknown words.
- Use a dictionary to learn the meaning and other features of unknown words.
- Use knowledge of prefixes (e.g., *un–, re–, pre–, bi–, mis–, dis–*) and suffixes (e.g., *–er, –est, –ful*) to determine the meaning of words.

**GRADE 4**
- Apply knowledge of word origins, derivations, synonyms, antonyms, and idioms to determine the meaning of words and phrases.
- Use knowledge of root words to determine the meaning of unknown words within a passage.
- Know common roots and affixes derived from Greek and Latin and use this knowledge to analyze the meaning of complex words (e.g., *international*).
- Use a thesaurus to determine related words and concepts.
- Distinguish and interpret words with multiple meanings.

**GRADE 5**
- Use word origins to determine the meaning of unknown words.
- Understand and explain frequently used synonyms, antonyms, and homographs.
- Know abstract, derived roots and affixes from Greek and Latin and use this knowledge to analyze the meaning of complex words (e.g., *controversial*).
- Understand and explain the figurative and metaphorical use of words in context.

**GRADE 6**
- Identify and interpret figurative language and words with multiple meanings.
- Recognize the origins and meanings of frequently used foreign words in English and use these words accurately in speaking and writing.

- Monitor expository text for unknown words or words with novel meanings by using word, sentence, and paragraph clues to determine meaning.
- Understand and explain "shades of meaning" in related words (e.g., *softly* and *quietly*).

### GRADE 7

- Identify idioms, analogies, metaphors, and similes in prose and poetry.
- Use knowledge of Greek, Latin, and Anglo-Saxon roots and affixes to understand content-area vocabulary.
- Clarify word meanings through the use of definition, example, restatement, or contrast.

### GRADE 8

- Analyze idioms, analogies, metaphors, and similes to infer the literal and figurative meanings of phrases.
- Understand the most important points in the history of the English language and use common word origins to determine the historical influences on English word meanings.
- Use word meanings within the appropriate context and show ability to verify those meanings by definition, restatement, example, comparison, or contrast.

SOURCE

Adapted from *English-Language Arts Content Standards for California Public Schools: Kindergarten Through Grade Twelve* (1999). Sacramento: California Department of Education.

# CONTENTS

## Section VI: Vocabulary Development

CHAPTER

# 14

# Specific Word Instruction

what?

why?

when?

how?

# what?    *Specific Word Instruction*

**14.2**

*"... knowing a word is not an all-or-nothing proposition; it is not the case that one either knows or does not know a word. Rather, knowledge of a word should be viewed in terms of the extent or degree of knowledge that people can possess."*

—BECK & MCKEOWN, 1991

In order to facilitate vocabulary development, intentional vocabulary instruction in specific concepts and word meanings is necessary (Baumann and Kameenui 1991; Nagy 1988a), particularly for those words that are conceptually difficult, or that represent complex concepts that are not part of students' everyday experience. This instruction is most worthwhile when the words or concepts to be covered are important to the understanding of a selection or important because of their general utility in the language.

## Levels of Word Knowledge

Generally, there are three levels of word knowledge: unknown, acquainted, and established (Beck, McKeown, and Omanson 1987). Although it is enough for students to have a superficial acquaintance with some words in a selection, for most words—and *all* important words—students must have an established level of knowledge if they are to attain full reading comprehension (Nagy, Herman, and Anderson 1985).

| Level | Criteria | Example |
|---|---|---|
| **Unknown** | Meaning is completely unfamiliar | gauge |
| **Acquainted** | Basic meaning is recognized, after some thought | yardstick |
| **Established** | Meaning is easily, rapidly, and automatically recognized | ruler |

To illustrate the different levels of word knowledge, Irvin (1998) describes how a youngster might respond if asked about various measuring devices. Asked about a *gauge,* the child is puzzled, because she is completely unfamiliar with the word (unknown). She recognizes *yardstick* because she has heard the word used before in discussions about measuring. However, she is not familiar enough with the term to identify a yardstick (acquainted). She recognizes *ruler* and can identify one, because she has used a ruler to measure her foot (established).

**It is useful to have students analyze and rate their levels of word knowledge. Rate your own level of word knowledge about the following terms related to reading instruction:**

prosody, literacy, comprehension, vowel, syllabication, schema, dyslexia, fricative, morpheme, diphthong, fluency, plosive, automaticity, semantic, orthography, phoneme, schwa, phonics, context, metacognition

## Word-Learning Tasks

Word-learning tasks are not all alike; each one makes different demands on both the teacher and the learner. They differ depending on the actual level of knowledge a student has about a word or concept (unknown, acquainted, established) and the preferred level of word knowledge to be attained. For a given word, the preferred level of word knowledge depends on how important the word is to a selection and how useful the word will be in future reading.

| Word-Learning Task | Explanation |
|---|---|
| Learning a New Meaning for a Known Word | A new meaning for a word that is in students' oral or reading vocabularies: for example, the meaning of *branch* in the context of social studies |
| Learning the Meaning of a New Word Representing a Known Concept | A new word that is not in students' oral or reading vocabularies, but relates to a familiar concept: for example, that the leaf of a palm tree is a *frond* |
| Learning the Meaning of a New Word Representing an Unknown Concept | A new word that is not in students' oral or reading vocabularies and doesn't relate to a familiar concept: for example, *photosynthesis* |
| Clarifying and Enriching the Meaning of a Known Word | Understanding the shades of meaning and usage of known words: for example, the difference between *ancient* and *prehistoric* |

14.4

(Graves, Juel, and Graves 1998; Graves and Slater 1996)

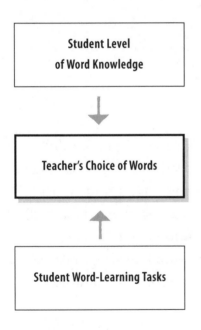

## Selecting Words to Teach

After determining the desired level of word knowledge for students to achieve and the word-learning tasks students face, teachers still need to determine the specific words they will teach. These three steps may be useful.

① Identify the words in the selection that are likely to be unknown to or difficult for students. Make a list of these words.

② Print the list of potential vocabulary words on the board. Point to each word, and have students analyze their level of word knowledge for each one. Research (White, Slater, and Graves 1989) indicates that students can be quite accurate in identifying words they do and do not know.

③ Analyze the word-knowledge data provided by students. Based upon this analysis, make a revised list of potential vocabulary words. From this list, identify the most important words to teach. Use the following questions, along with your own judgment, to inform instruction.

| Question | If the ANSWER Is ... | Then the ACTION Is ... |
| --- | --- | --- |
| ① Is understanding the word necessary for understanding the selection in which it appears? | No | Choose other words. |
| ② Are students likely to be able to identify the word's meaning using context or structural analysis skills? | Yes | Choose other words. |
| ③ Can instruction in this word be helpful in developing a skill that students can later use independently, for example, context, structural analysis, or dictionary skills? | Yes | Teach the word. (The instruction can serve several purposes.) |
| ④ Will knowing the meaning of this particular word be useful in future reading? | Yes | Teach the word. (The more often the word occurs, the greater the chances are that students will retain the word once it is taught.) |

(Graves, Juel, and Graves 1998; Graves and Slater 1996)

## Categories of Language

### Antonyms and Synonyms

*Antonyms* are words that are "opposite or nearly opposite in meaning," although there are different types of opposite relationships. Some antonyms are mutually exclusive word pairs *(girl/boy),* and some are words that reverse or undo the meaning of each other *(stop/go).* Other antonyms allow for gradations of meaning; for example, a more extreme version of *happy/sad* would be *ecstatic/disconsolate* (see, for example, Powell 1986).

Section V: Spelling
"Homophones," p. 13.29

14.6

Screen reading materials for unfamiliar or difficult words and the use of idiomatic language. To reduce students' frustration, these terms and expressions can be directly pretaught. Encourage students to use context to confirm meaning.

*Synonyms* are more challenging for students, as they are words that are "similar but not exact in meaning" *(shy/reticent; slow/languid).* Instruction should help students learn the different shades of meaning and the usage of synonyms (Blachowicz and Fisher 1996).

## Multiple-Meaning Words

Many words in the English language have multiple meanings. Multiple-meaning words include homographs and homonyms. *Homographs* are words that are spelled the same but are usually pronounced differently, such as *bow* ("to bend forward" or "a weapon for shooting arrows"). *Homonyms* include words that are spelled and pronounced the same but differ in meaning, such as *bat* ("a small, furry animal") and *bat* ("a wooden club used to hit baseballs").

Multiple-meaning words pose a challenge for many students, particularly those who are learning English. Often, students do not understand that words with the same spelling and/or pronunciation can have several different meanings, depending upon context. Therefore, they become confused when they look up a word in a dictionary or glossary and find a number of different definitions listed (Stahl 1999).

## Methods of Teaching Specific Words and Concepts

Research has shown that effective instruction uses a variety of techniques to help students make connections between unfamiliar words and their own prior knowledge (Stahl 1999). Providing students with their own vocabulary notebooks for recording new words and word meanings is a valuable supplement to these instructional techniques.

"Concept Picture Sort," p. 14.14

## Categorizing and Classifying

Children have a natural tendency to create simple compare-and-contrast categories, beginning with the very basic "mother-father/*not* mother-father" and "tastes good/tastes bad" categories. Expanding on this natural tendency to sort and classify can be a very effective way to help Kindergarten and first-grade students develop word consciousness and build vocabulary. Picture sorts can reinforce and expand students' understanding of simple concepts. For example, students can sort a stack of pictures into such categories as animals, food, and machines. They might further sort the stack of animal pictures into pets and zoo animals.

**"Semantic Mapping," p. 14.16**

**"Synonym Web," p. 14.26**

**"Word Map: Synonyms and Antonyms," p. 14.30**

for examples of Semantic Maps and Webs

## Semantic Mapping

In Semantic Mapping (or Semantic Webbing), students draw on their prior knowledge of a topic to discuss a targeted word and how it relates to other words. This technique enables teachers to assess students' background knowledge. It also helps students build vocabulary as they categorize new words and enhance their understanding of the selected concept or topic. Semantic Mapping has been found to improve both students' recall of targeted words and their comprehension of selections that contain the targeted words (Johnson, Toms-Bronowski, and Pittelman 1982).

**"Semantic Feature Analysis," p. 14.18**

for an example of a Semantic Feature Analysis grid

## Semantic Feature Analysis

Semantic Feature Analysis uses a grid, rather than a map format, to help students both identify words that belong to a particular category and compare and contrast the features of the words they have identified. Studies have shown this technique to have the same beneficial effects as Semantic Mapping (Johnson et al. 1982), but Semantic Feature Analysis goes beyond Semantic Mapping by focusing on relationships among word meanings. In a study of high school students who were poor readers, Anders, Bos, and Filip (1984) found that Semantic Feature Analysis was especially effective in improving both the learning of word meanings and comprehension of a social studies passage.

**"Possible Sentences," p. 14.20**

14.8

## Possible Sentences

Another approach to teaching word meanings is Possible Sentences. Students are asked to generate sentences containing at least two words that might be in the text they are about to read. The teacher selects ten to twelve words: six to eight of these words are related to key concepts that are likely to be difficult for students; the other four to six are known words. After reading the selection, students reread their sentences to check their accuracy and revise them as needed. Stahl and Kapinus (1991) found that the use of Possible Sentences significantly improved both students' recall of targeted word meanings and their comprehension of selections containing those words.

**"Concept of Definition Map," p. 14.22**
for an example of a Concept Definition Map

## Concept of Definition Maps

A Concept of Definition Map (or Word Map) is a visual representation of a definition. The map includes the three elements of a good definition: (1) the overarching category to which the word belongs: *What is it?*; (2) the important characteristics of the word or concept: *What is it like?*; and (3) some specific examples: *What are some examples?* (Schwartz and Raphael 1985). Students discover what they know and don't know about given words and concepts as they draw on their prior knowledge and dictionaries to complete the map.

**"Antonym Analogies," p. 14.28**

## Analogies

Analogies are an exercise in categorizing word meanings; they serve to establish relationships between sets of things or ideas (Gillet and Temple 1994). Solving word analogies is a suitable activity for upper-grade students. The first step in solving word analogies is identifying the kind of relationship that exists between a given pair of words. Once this relationship is discovered, it can be used to aid identification of the missing word. Here is an example of an antonym-relationship analogy sentence: *In is to out as no is to yes.*

**"PAVE Map," p. 14.24**

## The PAVE Procedure

The PAVE Procedure encourages students to cross-check a word's meaning as defined in a dictionary with the context in which the word appears. The acronym stands for **P**rediction, **A**ssociation, **V**erification, and **E**valuation. Students are asked to (1) write the sentence or context in which the word appears; (2) predict the word's meaning based on the context; (3) write an original sentence using the word to show their grasp of its meaning; (4) verify the word's meaning by consulting a dictionary and selecting and writing the most appropriate definition; (5) evaluate their predicted definition and original sentence, and rewrite the sentence if necessary; and (6) draw an image to create an association with the word's meaning (Blachowicz and Fisher 1996). Blachowicz and Fisher report that students find the procedure to be valuable in helping them remember words and definitions.

**14.9**

Intervention Strategy

## The Keyword Method

The Keyword Method is a mnemonic technique (from *Mnemosyne,* the Greek goddess of memory) that relies on visual imagery. It consists of two stages: in the first stage, students select a keyword that sounds in some way like part of the new, unfamiliar word; in the second stage, students form a visual image to connect the keyword with the meaning of the new word. This technique was originally developed to teach vocabulary to second-language learners, and later adapted for use as part of first-language vocabulary instruction (Levin 1993). In their review of an extensive body of research, Pressley and Lysynchuk (1995) found that the Keyword Method was effective with students across grade levels. It also has been shown to be especially effective with students who have learning difficulties (Mastropieri, Scruggs, and Fulk 1990).

**"Keyword Method," p. 14.34**

# why? *Specific Word Instruction*

**14.10**

*"We use words to think; the more words we know, the finer our understanding is about the world."*

—STAHL, 1999

Specific word instruction provides students with a more complete, in-depth knowledge of word meanings. It is necessary because students who have in-depth word knowledge are more likely to read with fluency, accuracy, and comprehension than are students who have more limited word knowledge. Students who only partially understand certain words in text often cannot fully comprehend what they are reading. Furthermore, it is unlikely that they will be confident enough to use these words in their own speaking or writing (Graves et al. 1998).

Specific word instruction is also necessary to teach new or complex concepts. Nagy, Anderson, and Herman (1987) have found that a reader has about a 5 percent chance of learning a new word fully from encountering it only once in print. Therefore, when specific words are key to understanding a concept, intentional, explicit instruction in word meanings is efficient and productive.

**Research Findings . . .**

*Students who were given direct instruction in word meanings are better able to discern meanings of untaught words.*

—BECK, PERFETTI & MCKEOWN, 1982

*Teaching 350 words each year may augment learning from context by 10 percent to 30 percent, a significant amount.*

—STAHL & FAIRBANKS, 1986

*Comprehension of a text depends crucially on knowledge of specific words that may not be familiar to some students.*

—NAGY, 1988a

*The first reason that vocabulary instruction often fails to produce measurable gains in reading comprehension is that much of the instruction does not produce a sufficient depth of word knowledge.*

**14.11**

—NAGY, 1988a

**Suggested Reading . . .**

*Content Area Reading and Learning* (1996) edited by Diane Lapp, James Flood & Nancy Farnan. Needham Heights, MA: Allyn & Bacon.

*Teaching Vocabulary in All Classrooms* (1996) by Camille Blachowicz & Peter Fisher. Upper Saddle River, NJ: Prentice-Hall.

*Teaching Vocabulary to Improve Reading Comprehension* (1988) by William E. Nagy. Newark, DE: International Reading Association.

*Vocabulary Development* (1999) by Steven A. Stahl. Cambridge, MA: Brookline Books.

*What Reading Research Tells Us About Children with Diverse Learning Needs: Bases and Basics* (1998) edited by Deborah C. Simmons & Edward J. Kameenui. Mahwah, NJ: Erlbaum.

*Words, Words, Words: Teaching Vocabulary in Grades 4–12* (1999) by Janet Allen. York, ME: Stenhouse.

**14.12**

## When to Teach

Specific word instruction should be incorporated into each school day. It should include direct instruction in specific concepts as well as vocabulary essential to understanding content-area and literature-based text. Students should be exposed to new vocabulary by listening to as well as reading text.

**Kindergarten**    In Kindergarten, students learn to categorize common words into basic grade-appropriate concepts: for example, color, shape, and size.

**Grade 1**    In first grade, students continue learning to categorize common words into basic grade-appropriate concepts: for example, animals or transportation.

**Grade 2**    In second grade, students learn about common synonyms and antonyms, and to identify simple multiple-meaning words.

**Grade 3**    In third grade, students extend their understanding and use of antonyms, synonyms, and multiple-meaning words. Students learn to use the dictionary to confirm the meaning and other features of unfamiliar words.

**Grade 4 and Above**    In fourth grade and above, instruction in synonyms, antonyms, and words with multiple meanings continues with an emphasis on content-area vocabulary concepts. Students learn to use other reference materials to confirm the meaning of unfamiliar words.

ELL

**English language learners need extensive vocabulary support through preteaching, modeling, and visual aids. Students in grade 3 and above should receive intensive English-language instruction that focuses on the vocabulary and language structures of grade-level texts.**

## When to Assess and Intervene

To monitor vocabulary growth, starting late in first grade and continuing through succeeding grades, students should be assessed on their knowledge of specific vocabulary and key concepts. Intervene as necessary with teacher-led small group instruction and by encouraging independent reading.

**See also...**

**CORE Assessing Reading**
"Resources for Assessing Reading"

## Vocabulary Inventories

| CORE Assessing Reading | Other |
| --- | --- |
| Critchlow Verbal Language Scales | Brigance Diagnostic Comprehensive Inventory of Basic Skills |
| | Durrell Analysis of Reading Difficulty |
| | Peabody Picture Vocabulary Test–III |

## ASSESSMENT AND INTERVENTION

| | |
| --- | --- |
| **When** | Late Grade 1 and above |
| **Who** | All students |
| **Assessment Tool** | Critchlow Verbal Language Scales |
| **Intervene if ...** | Assessment indicates that the student's vocabulary is not at grade level. |
| **How** | Independent reading and listening to read-alouds. Teacher-led small group instruction in specific words and word-learning strategies (see Chapter 15). |

**ELL** FOR SPANISH-SPEAKING STUDENTS ...
Use the "Critchlow Spanish Verbal Language Scale" in *CORE Assessing Reading.*

# how? *Specific Word Instruction*

**TEACHING STRATEGY FOR**

## Word Meanings as Concepts

### Benchmarks

- ability to classify grade-appro-priate categories of words
- ability to identify and sort common words from within basic categories

### Grade Level

- Kindergarten – Grade 1

### Grouping

- whole class
- small group or pairs

### Materials

- old magazines
- scissors
- key concept pictures

---

## CONCEPT PICTURE SORT

GRADE LEVEL K-1 GRADE LEVEL

This generic teaching strategy focuses on the concept of living and nonliving things. The same strategy can be adapted for further practice with this concept and to introduce other concepts.

### Brainstorm

Have students think of items in a category, such as living things. Help them to understand the category by explaining that plants such as trees, grass, and flowers, and animals such as dogs, squirrels, and snakes, are living things because they grow and change. Say: *Name some things that are alive.* Next, explain that things such as skateboards, computers, and chairs are not living things. Then say: *Now name some things that are not alive.*

### Teach/Model

Distribute copies of old magazines to students and ask them to cut out pictures of living and nonliving things. Say: *Put your pictures into two piles. In one pile, put things that are alive, such as plants and animals. In the other pile, put things that aren't alive, such as chairs and cars.* On a bulletin board, display key concept pictures: for example, a dog and a chair. Point to each picture and have students identify its category. Then call on volunteers to name one of their sorted pictures, identify its category, and then post it under the key concept picture.

## Discuss

Discuss with students how they chose to sort the pictures on the bulletin board. Ask: *Why did you put the picture of the lamp in the group of nonliving things?* Students should be able to explain their reasoning and make comparisons between living and nonliving things. Then ask them to suggest other things that might go in each group.

## Word Consciousness

Have pairs of students play a What's the Category? guessing game. One student chooses a category, such as things with legs, things that make noise, or things with wings. Without naming the category, the student then groups together a set of pictures that belong in the category. The partner studies the set of pictures, names each picture, and tries to guess the category.

**TEACHING STRATEGY FOR**

## Word Meanings as Concepts

### Benchmarks

14.16

- ability to identify words related to a specific concept
- ability to categorize and classify words related to a specific concept

### Grade Level

- Grade 2 and above

### Grouping

- whole class
- small group or pairs

### Materials

- dictionaries
- index cards
- Vocabulary Notebooks

## SEMANTIC MAPPING

This generic teaching strategy focuses on vocabulary related to the study of geography. The same strategy can be adapted for further practice and to introduce vocabulary related to other subject areas.

### Brainstorm

Print the word *geography* on the board and read it aloud. Ask students to brainstorm any word they can think of related to geography, or the study of the features of the earth. They might suggest words such as *continent, ocean, river, bay, island, mountain.* List students' responses on the board.

### Teach/Model

Tell students that the word *geography* comes from the Greek word *geographia,* which means "earth description." Explain that the study of geography includes learning about the features of the earth. Then add other geography-related words to the brainstormed list on the board. Define and discuss the words.

Use the list of words to develop a map that shows the relationships between the words. Tell students to look at the list of words. Say: *You can group these words into categories. For example, what do* ocean, river, *and* bay *have in common?* (They have to do with water.) Print the word *water* on the board and draw a line connecting it to the word *geography.* Next, ask students what other words they could add to this category. (Possible answers include *bay, lake, waterfall.* ) Say: *Can you group the remaining words into a category? For example, what do* continent, island, *and* mountain *have in common?* (They are all landforms.) Print the word *landforms* on the board and draw a line connecting it to the word *geography.* Next, have students add other related words to this category.

**Look It Up!**

Have students use a dictionary to confirm and clarify the meanings of the words on the semantic map. Tell them to look for photographs or illustrations of these terms. Students may record what they learn in their Vocabulary Notebooks.

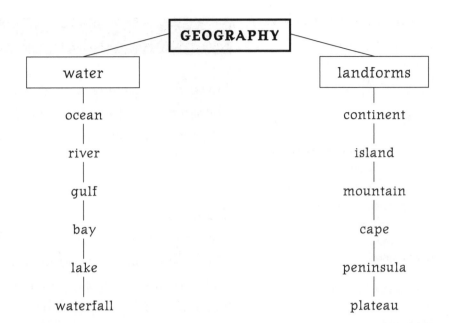

14.17

## Discuss

To deepen students' understanding of geography terms, discuss the differences between the various types of bodies of water and landforms. Ask: *What is the difference between an ocean and a bay? What is the difference between a mountain and a plateau?* Next, encourage students to think of new ways to categorize their responses for a given concept. For example, words listed in the *water* category might be separated according to whether they refer to bodies of fresh water or salt water.

## Word Consciousness

Have the class play a geography quiz game. Divide the class into teams, and provide them with index cards. Have each team use the *Geographical Names* section of a dictionary to look for three geographic categories: for example, rivers, mountains, and islands. Tell students to print each place name on the front of an index card and the geographic category to which it belongs on the back. Have teams read aloud the different place names and challenge opposing teams to identify whether each one is a river, mountain, or island: for example, Monongahela (river), Rainier (mountain), Corfu (island). One point is given for each correct answer.

## TEACHING STRATEGY FOR

# Word Meanings as Concepts

**14.18**

### Benchmarks

• ability to identify words related
  to a specific topic
• ability to categorize and
  compare and contrast features
  of related words

### Grade Level

• Grade 3 and above

### Grouping

• whole class
• small group or pairs
• individual

### Materials

• dictionaries
• Vocabulary Notebooks

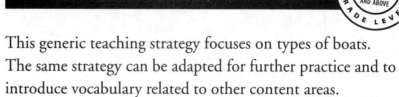

## SEMANTIC FEATURE ANALYSIS

This generic teaching strategy focuses on types of boats. The same strategy can be adapted for further practice and to introduce vocabulary related to other content areas.

### Brainstorm

Encourage students to discuss what they know about boats. This may include their own boating experiences or what they have read in books or seen on television or in the movies. Tell them that "a boat is a small vessel that is used for traveling on water."

### Teach/Model

On the board, copy the following sample Semantic Feature Analysis grid for the category *Boats* (do not include the pluses, minuses, and question marks). Help students to identify and discuss the types of boats that are listed on the left side of the grid. It may be necessary to show photographs or illustrations of the different boats. Then identify and discuss the features that are listed across the top of the grid.

## B O A T S

|  | oars | motor | sails | portable |
|---|---|---|---|---|
| kayak | + | – | – | + |
| canoe | + | – | – | + |
| dinghy | ? | ? | ? | + |
| sailboard | – | – | + | + |
| schooner | ? | – | + | – |
| raft | + | ? | ? | + |
| yacht | – | + | ? | – |

Demonstrate how the grid can be used to show the features of each type of boat. Say: *If the boat has the feature, I'll mark the grid with a plus sign. If it does not, I'll mark it with a minus sign. If the boat might have the feature under some circumstances, I'll mark it with a question mark.* For example, a kayak has oars and is portable, but does not have a motor or sails. Print a plus sign (+) under oars and portable and a minus sign (–) under motor and sails. Demonstrate the use of a question mark (?) by skipping down the chart to *raft.* Say: *Under some circumstances, a raft might have a motor.* Next, discuss the features of each boat with students, marking the grid based on students' responses.

**Look It Up!**

**Have students use a dictionary to confirm and clarify the meanings of the words in the Semantic Feature Analysis grid. Tell them to look for photographs or illustrations of these terms. Students may record what they learn in their Vocabulary Notebooks.**

## Discuss

Let students make their own connections by noting similarities and differences between the types of boats. Ask: *How are a kayak and a canoe alike? How is a dinghy different from a sailboard?* During discussion, encourage students to suggest additional types of boats and features. Boats that might be added include skiff and scull; features that might be added include galley, bunks, and number of masts.

## Word Consciousness

Print the word *portable* on the board and discuss what it means. Underline *port.* Tell students that many words in English contain this word part and are related in meaning. Now print the words *reporter* and *export.* Say each word aloud as you underline *port.* Say: *A reporter carries a story back to tell others. Something that you can carry is portable. When you take or carry something out of a country, you export it.* Then ask students what they think *port* might sometimes mean. *("carry or take")* Have them name other words containing *port:* for example, *import, transportation, airport, important, portrait.* List the words on the board and help students determine which words have a meaning clearly related to "carry or take" and which do not.

14.20

**TEACHING STRATEGY FOR**

## Word Meanings as Concepts

### Benchmark

- ability to use sentence and word context to find the meaning of unknown words

### Grade Level

- Grade 4 and above

### Grouping

- whole class
- small group or pairs

### Materials

- copies of "Studying the Sky" (see Appendix)
- dictionaries
- index cards
- Vocabulary Notebooks

## POSSIBLE SENTENCES

This generic teaching strategy focuses on key concept vocabulary found in a passage about astronomy. In "Studying the Sky," the key concept is that people's ideas about the solar system have changed over the centuries. The same strategy can be adapted for further practice and to introduce vocabulary related to other key concepts in content-area text that students are about to read.

● ● ● ● ● ● ● ● ● ● ● ● ● ● ● ● ● ● ● ● ● ● ●

## Teach/Model

Select six to eight key words from "Studying the Sky" that are related to the key concept and that may cause difficulty for students. Words might include *astronomy, galaxies, ancient, solar system, heliocentric, orbiting, telescope.* List the words on the board, along with four to six other words from the selection that are likely to be known to students, such as *planets, stars, sun, model, center, earth.* Work with students to come up with a short definition of each word.

Next, tell students to think of sentences that contain at least two of the words on the board and that might appear in the selection they are about to read. Print their suggested sentences on the board, making sure to include both accurate and inaccurate sentences. Examples of possible sentences include:

<u>Astronomy</u> is the study of the <u>stars.</u>
The <u>earth</u> is <u>heliocentric.</u>

When students have finished contributing sentences (and all the words have been used), have them read "Studying the Sky."

**Look It Up!**

**Have students use a dictionary to confirm and clarify the meanings of the words they used in the sentences on the board. Point out that dictionary entries sometimes include the abbreviation *Astron.* to indicate that the definition relates to astronomy. Students may record what they learn in their Vocabulary Notebooks.**

## Discuss

Following the reading, have students look again at the sentences on the board. Encourage them to discuss whether, based on their reading, each sentence could or could not be true. If they determine that a sentence is accurate, place a check mark beside it. If a sentence is inaccurate, have students discuss how to rewrite it to make it an accurate statement.

## Word Consciousness

Have students play a Fictionary game. Select five words related to astronomy, such as *gyroscope, implosion, asteroid, nebula,* and *apogee.* Divide the class into groups of five. Print the selected words on index cards (one set per student) and distribute the cards to students. Assign one student in each group to be the leader, who will look up the dictionary definition of one of the words and write it on the back of the card. The other students invent a definition for the word and write it on the back of their cards. The cards for that word are then collected, shuffled, and read aloud by the leader. The other players vote for the definition they think is correct. Leadership rotates until each player has had a chance to lead.

## TEACHING STRATEGY FOR
# Definitional Information

**14.22**

### Benchmarks

• ability to use a dictionary to learn the meaning and other features of an unknown word
• ability to identify elements of a good definition

### Grade Level

• Grade 3 and above

### Grouping

• whole class
• small group or pairs
• individual

### Materials

• dictionaries
• encyclopedia
• Vocabulary Notebooks

# CONCEPT OF DEFINITION MAP

GRADE LEVEL 3 AND ABOVE GRADE LEVEL

This generic teaching strategy is based on the Concept of Definition Map developed by Schwartz and Raphael (1985). The strategy focuses on a definition for the word *drum.* The same strategy can be adapted for further practice and to provide definitional information about other words.

## Brainstorm

Encourage students to discuss what they know about drums, including information about drums they have heard or seen. Record students' responses on the board.

## Teach/Model

Tell students that you are going to work together to come up with a good definition for the word *drum.* Use the information they provide to fill in a Concept of Definition Map like the one on the facing page. Begin by printing the target word *drum* on the board with the heading *What is it?* Read the question aloud and ask students what category a drum belongs to. *(musical instrument)* Point out that to be even more precise they can say that a drum is a *percussion instrument,* or an instrument that makes music by being hit or shaken. Then add the heading *What is it like?* Read the question aloud and tell students to suggest words and phrases that describe the features of a drum; for example, *hollow cylinder* and *has drumhead.* Next, add the heading *What are some examples?* Read the question aloud and ask students to give examples of kinds of drums. *(bass, snare, bongo, tom-tom, conga, timpani)*

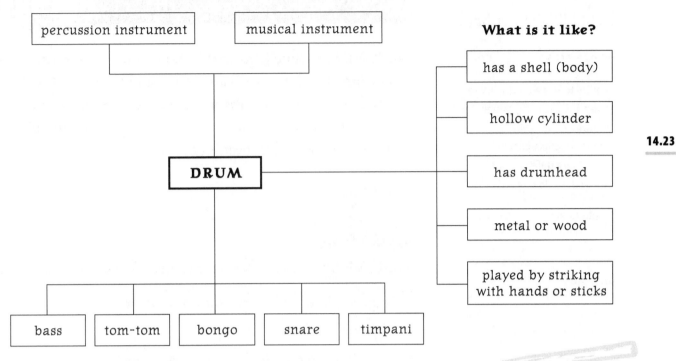

**What is it?**

| percussion instrument | musical instrument |

**What is it like?**

- has a shell (body)
- hollow cylinder
- has drumhead
- metal or wood
- played by striking with hands or sticks

**DRUM**

| bass | tom-tom | bongo | snare | timpani |

**What are some examples?**

**Look It Up!**

**Have students use a dictionary to confirm and clarify their definition of *drum* and to revise or add to their definitions as needed. Students can also be encouraged to use an encyclopedia to find out more about specific types of drums. They can record what they learned in their Vocabulary Notebooks.**

## Discuss

Discuss how students can use the information on the map to write a definition for the word *drum.* For example, "A drum is a percussion instrument. It is cylinder-shaped and hollow. It has a drumhead. Some kinds of drums are bass, snare, and bongo."

## Word Consciousness

Help students identify examples of other percussion instruments, such as a triangle, tambourine, gong, castanets, chimes, cymbals, bells, and maracas. Then ask them to brainstorm a list of descriptive words they could use to convey the sound these instruments make. Examples include *crisp, clattering, thunderous, bellowing,* and *clanging.*

## Definitional Information

**14.24**

**Benchmarks**

• ability to use a dictionary to learn the meaning of unknown words
• ability to cross-check the dictionary definition of a word with its use in context

**Grade Level**

• Grade 3 and above

**Grouping**

• whole class
• small group or pairs
• individual

**Materials**

• dictionaries

# PAVE MAP

The PAVE Procedure (**P**rediction, **A**ssociation, **V**erification, **E**valuation), developed by Bannon, Fisher, Pozzi, and Wessel (1990), helps students to cross-check a word's meaning with the context in which it appeared. This strategy is also useful for words with multiple meanings.

## Teach/Model

The PAVE Map procedure consists of the following steps:

1. Teacher selects a target word from student reading material.

2. Students copy the sentence or context in which the word appears.

3. Students print the target word again.

4. Students predict target word's meaning from the context.

5. Students write a sentence using target word's predicted meaning.

6. Students verify target word's meaning in the dictionary.

7. Students write target word's dictionary definition.

8. If the predicted definition is incorrect, students rewrite sentence using dictionary definition.

9. Students sketch a representational image of the target word to help them remember its meaning.

The following is an example of a completed PAVE Map for the target word *ambush* in an excerpt from *Winnie the Pooh* by A. A. Milne.

**②** They had come to a stream which twisted and tumbled between high rocky banks, and Christopher Robin saw at once how dangerous it was. "It's just the place," he explained, "for an <u>Ambush.</u>" "What sort of bush?" whispered Pooh to Piglet.

Target Word: ambush **③**

Predicted Definition: an accident **④**

Sentence Using Meaning of Predicted Definition:
**⑤** Your bike ambush was not my fault.

"Boo!" **⑨**

Representational Image

**⑥/⑦** Verified Dictionary Definition: a surprise attack made from a hiding place

Another Sentence Using Verified Definition:
**⑧** They hid in the thick grass until it was time for the ambush.

## Discuss

Using information recorded on the PAVE Map, call on volunteers to present the word to the rest of the class. Here is a model:

*The target word was* ambush. *It was in this sentence: "It's just the place," he explained, "for an Ambush." I predicted that* ambush *meant "accident." From the dictionary, I found out that it means "a surprise attack made from a hiding place." So the original sentence meant that this was just the place for a surprise attack. The sentence I wrote was: "They hid in the thick grass until it was time for the ambush." To remember the meaning of the word, I drew a picture of a bush saying, "Boo!"*

## Word Consciousness

Ask students if they think the word *ambush* has anything to do with the meaning of the word *bush*. Suggest that they confirm their predictions by using a dictionary of word origins to find out the history, or origin, of the word *ambush*.

**TEACHING STRATEGY FOR**

## Categories of Language

**14.26**

### Benchmarks

- ability to understand and explain common synonyms
- ability to use knowledge of synonyms to determine word meaning
- ability to distinguish and interpret words with multiple meanings

### Grade Level

- Grade 2 and above

### Grouping

- whole class
- small group or pairs

### Materials

- thesauruses
- dictionaries
- Vocabulary Notebooks

## SYNONYM WEB

This generic teaching strategy focuses on synonyms for the multiple meanings of the word *spot.* The same strategy can be adapted for further practice and to provide definitional information about other words.

### Brainstorm

Ask: *What is a word that means almost the same as* big*?* (large) *What is a word that means almost the same as* good*?* (nice) *What is a word that means almost the same as* fast*?* (quick) Say: *Words that are very close—though not identical—in meaning are called* synonyms. Tiny *and* small *are synonyms.*

### Teach/Model

Print the word *spot* on the board. Have students brainstorm various synonyms for *spot.* List their responses, which may include *stain, mark, place,* and *see,* on the board. Work with students to categorize the synonyms for *spot* according to the different meanings of the word. Explain to students that a word may have different meanings, depending on the sentence or context in which it appears.

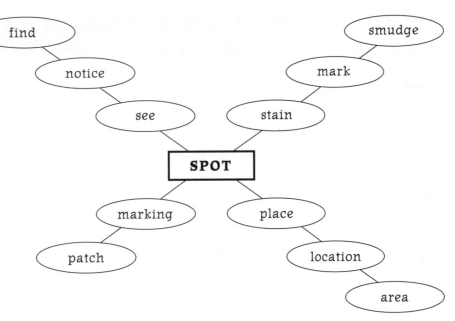

**Have students use a dictionary and/or thesaurus to confirm and clarify synonyms for the multiple meanings of *spot*. Students may record what they learn in their Vocabulary Notebooks.**

## Discuss

Discuss the different meanings for the word *spot.* Have students make up sentences, each using a different meaning of *spot.* Then ask students to replace each use of the word *spot* with a synonym that has almost the same meaning.

I have a <u>spot</u> on my white shirt.
My dog is black with a white <u>spot</u> on his ear.
This is the <u>spot</u> where she found her wallet.
Since he was tall, I was able to <u>spot</u> him in the crowd.

I have a <u>stain</u> on my new white shirt.
My dog is black with a white <u>mark</u> on his ear.
This is the <u>place</u> where she found her wallet.
Since he was tall, I was able to <u>find</u> him in the crowd.

## Word Consciousness

Have students brainstorm a list of computer terms, such as *bug, boot, menu, memory, drive, keys, escape, trash, net, browse, mouse,* and *crash.* Ask them to use each word with its computer-related meaning in a context sentence. Then have them make up sentences using other meanings of the words.

## TEACHING STRATEGY FOR
## Categories of Language

### Benchmarks

- ability to understand and explain common antonyms
- ability to use knowledge of antonyms to determine word meaning

### Grade Level

- Grade 4 and above

### Grouping

- whole class
- small group or pairs
- individual

### Materials

- dictionaries
- Vocabulary Notebooks

# ANTONYM ANALOGIES

This generic teaching strategy focuses on solving analogies with antonym relationships. The same strategy can be adapted for further practice with other antonym pairs or types of analogies.

## Brainstorm

Review the concept of antonyms. Ask: *What is the opposite of* top? (bottom) *What is the opposite of* sweet? (sour) *What is the opposite of* long? (short) *What is the opposite of* asleep? (awake) Explain that words that mean the opposite or nearly the opposite of each other are called *antonyms*.

## Teach/Model

Print the following sentence on the board:

Hot is to cold as on is to off.

Explain to students that the sentence is an analogy. The words *hot* and *cold* are related in the same way as *on* and *off*; they are antonym pairs. Say: *If* cold *is the opposite of* hot, *then* off *is the opposite of* on. Then print the following analogies on the board, asking students to identify the antonym pairs:

Sharp is to dull as full is to empty.
Laugh is to cry as shout is to whisper.

**Look It Up!**

**Have students use a dictionary to confirm and clarify the meanings of the antonym pairs in the analogies they wrote. Students should record what they learned in their Vocabulary Notebooks.**

Print the following incomplete analogies on the board. Help students to select the word that completes the analogy from the three choices given:

<u>In</u> is to <u>out</u> as <u>no</u> is to _____. (up, **yes**, on)

<u>Win</u> is to <u>lose</u> as <u>buy</u> is to _____. (shop, earn, **sell**)

<u>Lost</u> is to <u>found</u> as <u>enter</u> is to _____. (**exit**, come, walk)

<u>Near</u> is to <u>far</u> as <u>wet</u> is to _____. (rain, **dry**, heavy)

<u>Front</u> is to <u>back</u> as <u>strong</u> is to _____. (**weak**, top, side)

<u>Love</u> is to <u>hate</u> as <u>add</u> is to _____. (plus, closed, **subtract**)

Invite pairs of students to work together to create antonym analogies to share with the group.

## Word Consciousness

Print the antonym pair *smallest* and *largest* on the board. Then list the following words in random order: *small, tiny, microscopic, average, large, enormous, gigantic.* Ask groups of students to work together to arrange the words from smallest to largest. Tell them they can consult a dictionary to help them arrange the words.

**FOLLOW-UP STRATEGY FOR**

## Categories of Language

**Benchmarks**

- ability to understand and explain how synonyms and antonyms are related
- ability to use knowledge of antonyms and synonyms

**Grade Level**

- Grade 2 and above

**Prerequisites**

- Antonym Analogies
- Synonym Web

**Grouping**

- whole class
- small group or pairs
- individual

**Materials**

- dictionaries
- Vocabulary Notebooks

# WORD MAP: SYNONYMS AND ANTONYMS

This generic teaching strategy focuses on the relationship between antonyms and synonyms. The same strategy can be adapted for further practice and to provide definitional information about other words.

## Brainstorm

Review the concept of synonyms and antonyms by asking students to name at least one synonym and one antonym for each of the following words: *sad* (miserable/happy); *shout* (yell/whisper); *smile* (grin/frown).

## Teach/Model

On the board, print the target word *laugh* in the center box of a Word Map, as shown below. Ask: *What is a synonym for* laugh? (giggle) *What is an antonym for* laugh? (cry) Have a volunteer share an example of when he or she laughs *(when I hear a funny joke),* then give an example of when he or she does not laugh *(when I see a sad movie).*

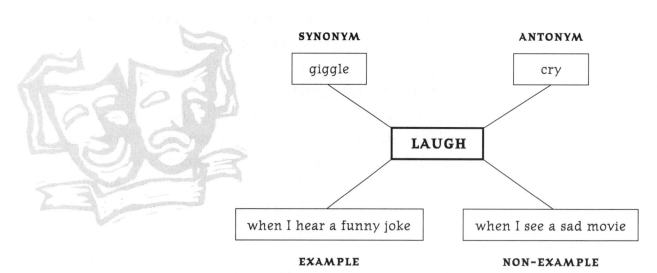

**Look It Up!**

Have students use a dictionary to confirm and clarify the meanings of the antonyms and synonyms. Students may record what they learn in their Vocabulary Notebooks.

## Discuss

Call on students to list additional synonyms and antonyms for the word *laugh* and discuss the different shades of meaning. *(Possible synonyms:* chuckle, chortle, guffaw, snicker. *Possible antonyms:* sob, weep, bawl, whimper.*)*

## Word Consciousness

14.31

Students can use antonyms and synonyms to make up new titles for familiar books and stories. For example, "Giant Red Riding Hood" or "Tiny Crimson Equestrian Cloak" *(Little Red Riding Hood);* "The Feline in the Fedora" *(The Cat in the Hat);* "Where the Tame Things Are" or "Where the Savage Items Exist" *(Where the Wild Things Are);* and so on.

**TEACHING STRATEGY FOR**

## Categories of Language

### Benchmarks

- ability to identify simple multiple-meaning words
- ability to use context to understand and explain common multiple-meaning words

### Grade Level

- Grade 2 and above

### Grouping

- whole class
- small group or pairs

### Materials

- dictionaries
- Vocabulary Notebooks

# MULTIPLE-MEANING WORDS

*GRADE LEVEL* **2** *AND ABOVE* *GRADE LEVEL*

This generic teaching strategy focuses on learning new meanings for known multiple-meaning words. The same strategy can be adapted for further practice with this concept and to introduce other concepts.

● ● ● ● ● ● ● ● ● ● ● ● ● ● ● ● ● ● ● ● ● ● ● ● ●

## Brainstorm

Print the following sentence on the board: *I can open the can.* Ask: *What is the word that has more than one meaning in this sentence?* (can) *What are the meanings of the word* can? (*can* as in "able to" and *can* as in "container") Now print the following sentences on the board: *The boy hit the ball with the bat. The bat flew away.* Ask: *What is the multiple-meaning word in these sentences?* (bat) *What are the meanings of the word* bat? (*bat* as in "baseball bat" and *bat* as in "creature")

## Teach/Model

On the board, print the word *volume* and then say the following sentence: *Please don't play the radio at full volume.* Help students to conclude that in this sentence, *volume* means "the degree of loudness of sound." Now provide a new meaning for the word *volume*. Tell students that in math *volume* can

**Have students use a dictionary to confirm and clarify the multiple meanings of *volume*. Students may record what they learn in their Vocabulary Notebooks.**

mean "the amount of space occupied by a three-dimensional figure." Say the following sentence: *What is the volume of the swimming pool?* Ask students to think of a literature-related meaning for the word *volume*. They might suggest "a book" or "one book in a set."

Challenge students to each write one sentence using at least two meanings of the word *volume*: for example, *There are volumes of math books about volume.* Have students share their sentences and have classmates identify the meanings for each use of the word.

14.33

## Word Consciousness

Students can draw and label cartoons or posters to illustrate phrases that play on words with multiple meanings, such as *baseball fan, official state seal, light rain, pig pen, stamp your feet, post office, home run, square dance,* and so on.

14.34

**INTERVENTION STRATEGY FOR**

## Remembering Word Meanings

**Benchmark**

................................................................

• ability to remember word
  meanings

**Grade Level**

................................................................

• Grade 2 and above

**Grouping**

................................................................

• whole class
• small group or pairs
• individual

**Materials**

................................................................

• Vocabulary Notebooks

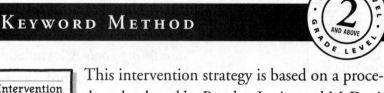

## KEYWORD METHOD

**GRADE LEVEL**
**2**
**AND ABOVE**
**GRADE LEVEL**

> | Intervention | This intervention strategy is based on a proce-
> | Strategy | dure developed by Pressley, Levin, and McDaniel

(1987). The method consists of two stages: an "acoustic link" stage, in which students acquire a key word that sounds in some way like a part of the unfamiliar word; and an "imagery link" stage, in which students form an image that associates the key word with the definition of the unfamiliar word.

• • • • • • • • • • • • • • • • • • • • • • • • • • • • •

## Teach/Model

The Keyword Method consists of the following steps:

1. **Define the Unfamiliar Word**
   Print an unfamiliar word, such as *predator,* on the board. Tell students that *predator* means "an animal that lives by hunting other animals for food."

2. **Select a Keyword for the Unfamiliar Word**
   Have students choose a keyword for *predator.* Tell them that the keyword should be familiar, should sound like an important part of the word *predator,* and should be easy to picture in their minds. For example, the word *tore* is a suitable keyword for *predator.*

3. **Link Keyword with Unfamiliar Word**
   Next, ask students to associate, or relate, the keyword *tore* and the unfamiliar word *predator* by visualizing them interacting. For example, students may form a picture of a large, meat-eating dinosaur tearing apart a small animal.

4. **Recall the Meaning**
   Tell students that the next time they see the word *predator,* they should think of the keyword *tore,* recall the image of a large, meat-eating dinosaur tearing apart a small animal, and link the image to the word's definition.

## Word Consciousness

Incorporate a Word-of-the-Day activity into your daily plan. Display a difficult or unfamiliar word on the bulletin board and have students pronounce and spell it aloud with you. Provide a brief definition, explain why you chose it, and give a few examples of how it relates to everyday life. After you present the word, have students work together to think of a keyword and draw a picture that can be used to associate the definition with an image. Students should record what they learned in their Vocabulary Notebooks.

**14.35**

CHAPTER

15

# Word-Learning Strategies

what?
why?
when?
how?

# what? *Word-Learning Strategies*

**15.2**

*"Skilled reading . . . depends not just on knowing a large number of words, but also on being able to deal effectively with new ones. Skilled readers . . . are readers who cope effectively with words that are new to them."*

—NAGY ET AL., 1994

**CORE Reading Research Anthology**

for background information

Students learn approximately 3,000 to 4,000 words per year during the early grades. Obviously, it is impossible for them to learn a sizable portion of these new words through direct instructional approaches. Instead, students learn word meanings independently through incidental word-learning opportunities—that is, through everyday experiences with oral and written language, including listening to and speaking with others, and wide reading (Baumann and Kameenui 1991; Baker, Simmons, and Kameenui 1998a). Word-learning strategies help students to determine the meanings of unfamiliar words on their own. Word-learning strategies include (1) how to use *dictionaries* and other reference aids to confirm and deepen knowledge of word meanings, (2) how to use information about *word parts* to figure out the meanings of words in text, and (3) how to locate and use *external context clues* to determine word meanings. Directly teaching and modeling these strategies is the key to helping students become independent word learners (Kameenui, Dixon, and Carnine 1987).

## Reading Volume and Vocabulary Growth

Reading volume is the prime contributor to individual differences in children's vocabularies (Hayes and Ahrens 1988; Nagy and Anderson 1984; Stanovich 1986). The typical daily oral language experiences in which children participate—conversations with family members and friends, viewing television programs, and so forth—do not contain enough new or infrequently used words to bring about significant vocabulary growth (Anderson 1996; Cunningham and Stanovich 1998; Hayes and Ahrens 1988).

| Selected Statistics for Major Sources of Spoken and Written Language (Sample Means) | | |
|---|---|---|
| | Rank of Median Word | Rare Words per 1,000 |
| ① **Printed texts** | | |
| Abstracts of scientific articles | 4,389 | 128.0 |
| Newspapers | 1,690 | 68.3 |
| Popular magazines | 1,399 | 65.7 |
| Adult books | 1,058 | 52.7 |
| Comic books | 867 | 53.5 |
| Children's books | 627 | 30.9 |
| Preschool books | 578 | 16.3 |
| ② **Television texts** | | |
| Popular prime-time adult shows | 490 | 22.7 |
| Popular prime-time children's shows | 543 | 20.2 |
| Cartoon shows | 598 | 30.8 |
| *Mr. Rogers* and *Sesame Street* | 413 | 2.0 |
| ③ **Adult speech** | | |
| Expert witness testimony | 1,008 | 28.4 |
| College graduates to friends, spouses | 496 | 17.3 |

**15.3**

SOURCE

Adapted from "Vocabulary Simplification for Children: A Special Case of 'Motherese'?" (1988) by Donald P. Hayes and Margaret G. Ahrens in *Journal of Child Language*, Vol. 15, No. 2.

*"The single most important thing a teacher can do to promote vocabulary growth is to increase students' volume of reading."*

—NAGY, 1988a

Hayes and Ahrens (1988) found that, in terms of exposure to new vocabulary, speech is far more limited than written language. The researchers analyzed three different categories of language: (1) written language from a variety of genres, including children's books and adult scientific journals; (2) language from several different types of television shows for both children and adults; and (3) adult speech in various contexts, including the conversations of college students and court testimony of expert witnesses. They ranked the words from each category according to the frequency with which they appear in written English; a word with a rank of 10,000 or higher is considered to be infrequent, or rare. For example, *the* is number 1, or most frequent word; *amplified* is number 16,000.

In their study, Hayes and Ahrens found that the relative rarity of words in children's books is greater than the words from adult conversation, with the exception of the expert witness testimony. In fact, children's books contained 50 percent more rare words than speech from adult prime-time television or the conversation of college graduates. Therefore, the data indicate that, in terms of vocabulary growth, conversation is not a substitute for reading (Cunningham and Stanovich 1998).

### Reading Aloud

Anderson (1996) notes that one very effective use of oral language is reading aloud to children, especially when it is accompanied by discussion before, during, and after reading. Studies have found that both younger and older students benefit from reading-aloud activities, and that older students are able to learn words as efficiently from having stories read to them as they are from reading stories themselves (Stahl et al. 1991).

With beginning readers, new vocabulary can be taught as a part of the shared reading of Big Books and trade books. Reading aloud to students also gives teachers opportunities to model independent word-learning strategies. Exposing students early on to the use of such strategies helps pave the way for the time when they can apply these strategies on their own.

Connect to Theory

Using Hayes and Ahrens' (1988) data, compare the number of rare words per 1,000 in children's books to prime-time adult television shows. Then compare the number of rare words in comic books to prime-time children's television shows. What do you notice? What other comparisons can you make?

*(See Appendix for answer.)*

15.4

Section II: Word Structure, "What Is a Morpheme?" p. 3.28

**MORPHEMES**
smallest meaningful units of language

**FREE MORPHEMES**
can stand alone as words

**BOUND MORPHEMES**
must be attached or "bound" to other morphemes

**MORPHEMIC ANALYSIS**
identifying morphemes in multisyllabic words

# Word Structure and Meaning

*Morphemes* are units of meaning; they can stand on their own or be part of a word. These word parts include prefixes, suffixes, base words, and word roots. By learning about morphemes, and the ways in which they combine to contribute to the meaning of a word, students build a foundation for independent word learning. Irvin (1998) stresses that, for instruction in morphemic analysis to be most effective, it should be part of a program that also involves instruction in the use of context and prior knowledge. She concludes that students who learn strategies to use word parts, context, and prior knowledge possess powerful tools for expanding their vocabularies.

Cunningham and Stanovich (1998) suggest that teachers help students become "word detectives" by noticing common spelling and pronunciation patterns among related words. One way to do this is to show students how many different words can be made from the same base word like *play* and to discuss how the meaning of the word changes. Examples include *playful, playing, player, playground, ballplayer.*

## Compound Words

A *compound word* is made up of two free morphemes. The meaning of some compound words can be predicted from the meanings of their two smaller word parts: for example, *doghouse* and *bluebird.* Other compound words have a meaning that differs from the meaning of their two smaller word parts: for example, *butterfly* and *airline.*

## Word Parts: Affixes

Prefixes and suffixes are referred to as *affixes.* Affixes are bound morphemes that are "fixed to" other morphemes. Prefixes are "fixed" to the beginning; suffixes are "fixed" to the end. Affixes modify the meaning of the morphemes to which they're

**15.5**

attached. As students read more complex and challenging texts, their understanding of affixes will help them to predict word meanings.

See also . . .

**Section II: Word Structure**
**"Most Frequent Prefixes," p. 3.30**

**Section II: Word Structure**
**"Most Frequent Suffixes," p. 3.31**

**Section IV: Decoding**
**Chapter 10: Multisyllabic Words**

**15.6**

Twenty common prefixes account for 97 percent of the prefixed words in printed school English (White, Sowell, and Yanagihara 1989). The four most common prefixes (*un–, re–, in–,* and *dis–*) account for about 58 percent of all the prefixed words. Prefixes are relatively easy for students to learn because most have a clear meaning, tend to be consistently spelled, and occur at the beginning of words (Graves et al. 1998).

Some researchers (Graves et al. 1998) do not suggest teaching the meanings of derivational suffixes because many of these suffixes have abstract meanings. Stahl (1999) contends that teaching suffixes by providing definitions can often confuse more than help students. Although the definitions of some suffixes, such as *–less* ("without") and *–ful* ("full of"), are predictable and easy for students to understand and apply to words, the definitions of other suffixes are less stable.

## Sequence of Instruction

- Begin with simple compound words made up of words (free morphemes) that are familiar to students, so that they can easily recognize the meaningful parts.

- Next, introduce common prefixes (bound morphemes) with base words.

- Then, introduce Greek and Latin word roots (bound morphemes); introduce Greek roots before Latin roots because their meaning is more apparent and the way they combine with other elements is more understandable.

- Finally, introduce Greek and Latin word roots plus affixes.

- Focus instruction on word parts that occur most frequently, providing ongoing review, practice, and feedback.

## LAYERS OF LANGUAGE

| Greek | Specialized words used mostly in science | photograph, scholar, symphony, microscope |
|---|---|---|
| Latin | Technical, formal words used mostly in literature and textbooks | flexible, structure, immortal, conference, attention |
| Anglo-Saxon | Common, everyday words used in ordinary situations and most often in speech | house, happy, play, boy, girl |

**15.7**

See also...

**Section II: Word Structure, "Common Latin Word Roots," p. 3.32**

**Section II: Word Structure, "Common Greek Word Roots," p. 3.33**

ENGLISH/SPANISH
**Section II: Word Structure, "What Role Do English/Spanish Cognates Play?" p. 4.20**

## Word Parts: Greek and Latin Roots

If you take away a prefix and/or a suffix from a word and what remains is not a word that can stand alone (free morpheme), you probably have found the Greek or Latin word root. Word roots are bound morphemes. The spelling of these word roots varies, and their original Greek or Latin meanings can differ from their meanings in the English words.

Students should understand that word roots are very important meaning elements within words. However, elementary-grade students should not be asked to memorize word roots and their meanings (Templeton 1997). There is no convenient list of Greek and Latin word roots that should be taught. Select word roots from the texts students are reading, choosing those that are most likely to occur again.

Words of Greek and Latin origin are especially prevalent in English. About 60 percent of the words in English text are of Latin and Greek origin (Henry 1997). From the middle grades on, words with Latin and Greek word parts form a large proportion of the new vocabulary that students encounter, primarily in their content-area textbooks. Becoming familiar with Latin and Greek roots and with common affixes lays the groundwork for understanding key concepts in a number of content areas, particularly science and social studies (Bear et al. 1996).

## External Context Clues and Meaning

*Context* refers to the words, phrases, or sentences surrounding an unknown word in a text. *External context clues* are the kinds of "hints" about a word's meaning that are provided by the surrounding text, including devices such as definitions, examples, and restatements. Since most word meanings are learned from context, students should learn to use context effectively. Anderson and Nagy (1991) suggest that teaching students how to use context clues should be the main instructional technique for promoting vocabulary development. Graves and his colleagues indicate that this technique might add as many as 1,000 words per year to students' vocabularies (Graves et al. 1998).

Providing explicit instruction and modeling in how to infer word meaning from context is an extension of the incidental word-learning theory. Because students encounter such an enormous number of words as they read, even a small improvement in their ability to infer the meanings of unknown words can result in a large number of words learned (Fukkink and de Glopper 1998). Therefore, directly teaching students how to use surrounding context to determine word meanings seems to be a logical—and critical—component of any program of vocabulary instruction. Further, given that students often are not able to infer the meanings of unknown words, even when the context contains powerful clues, such direct instruction is especially important (Jenkins, Stein, and Wysocki 1984).

**15.8**

*". . . deliberately deriving word meaning from context is amenable to instruction, and the effect of even relatively short instruction is rewarding."*

—FUKKINK &
DE GLOPPER, 1998

## Guidelines for Selecting Words and Text

**"Selecting Words to Teach," p. 14.4**

- Limit unfamiliar words to a manageable number (about one every two or three sentences).

- Choose target words that are within students' readability level.

- Select text with familiar content.

- Select text in which the meanings of some of the target words can be determined through external context clues and some of the target words need to be looked up in the dictionary or directly taught.

- Select target words of high utility.

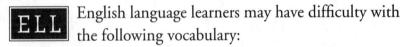 English language learners may have difficulty with the following vocabulary:

- Idioms

- Abstract high-frequency words, such as *an* or *the*

- Words used in inferential questions, such as *would* or *could*

- False cognates (words in a student's first language that are similar in sound or structure but not in meaning to words in English)

15.9

# why? *Word-Learning Strategies*

**15.10**

*"To promote large-scale, long-term vocabulary growth, teachers must aim at increasing students' incidental word learning."*

—NAGY, 1988a

**See also…**

"How Many Words Do People Know?" p. VI.iv

Section I: The Big Picture "Variation in Amount of Independent Reading," p. 1.10

**CORE Reading Research Anthology** for background information

Since reading itself is a major avenue for learning the meanings of unfamiliar words, it is crucial that students learn strategies for learning word meanings independently (Baker et al. 1998a). In addition, there are more words to be learned than can be covered in even the most ambitious program of vocabulary instruction, and there is more to be learned about each word than can be covered in even the most intensive instruction (Nagy 1988a).

To illustrate the importance of teaching word-learning strategies for use during independent, wide reading, it is necessary to look at the amount of reading students do. Anderson, Wilson, and Fielding (1988) have found that the average fifth-grade student reads about 600,000 words annually in books, magazines, and newspapers outside school. This amount of reading is in addition to the 600,000 or so words the student reads in school texts, making the total number of words read each year 1 million or more. Anderson (1996) estimates that in the course of reading 1 million words, a student will encounter some 20,000 new words; and by including idioms and alternate meanings, this number could be as high as 40,000 new words. If a student has a 5 percent chance of learning a word from one encounter, then she or he will learn some 1,000 to 2,000 of the new words. Therefore, if wide reading is the most important vehicle for large-scale vocabulary growth, then helping students to make the most of learning words independently is imperative (Irvin 1998).

**Research Findings . . .**

*Because students derive the meanings of many words incidentally, without instruction, another possible role of instruction is to enhance the strategies readers use when they do in fact learn words incidentally.*

—KAMEENUI ET AL., 1987

*There is no doubt that skilled word learners use context and their knowledge of prefixes, roots, and suffixes to deal effectively with new words.*

—NAGY, 1988a

**15.11**

*About half of the "new" words that students meet in their reading are related to familiar words and can be understood if students see these relationships.*

—ANGLIN, 1993

**Suggested Reading . . .**

*Language and Reading Success* (1999) by Andrew Biemiller. Cambridge, MA: Brookline Books.

*Teaching Reading in the 21st Century* (1998) by Michael F. Graves, Connie Juel & Bonnie B. Graves. Needham Heights, MA: Allyn & Bacon.

*Reading and the Middle School Student* (1998) by Judith L. Irvin. Needham Heights, MA: Allyn & Bacon.

*Vocabulary Development* (1999) by Steven A. Stahl. Cambridge, MA: Brookline Books.

*What Reading Research Tells Us About Children with Diverse Learning Needs: Bases and Basics* (1998) edited by Deborah C. Simmons & Edward J. Kameenui. Mahwah, NJ: Erlbaum.

# *Word-Learning Strategies*

**15.12**

## When to Teach

Throughout the school year, teaching and modeling word-learning strategies should be part of vocabulary instruction. Students should be exposed to broad and diverse vocabulary through listening to and reading narrative and expository text.

**Kindergarten** In Kindergarten, teachers should model word-learning strategies as they read aloud to students, using think-aloud strategies, pictures, and other text clues to help students figure out the meanings of unfamiliar words.

**Grade 1** In first grade, students learn to use pictures and context clues to understand the meaning of unfamiliar words in simple stories and decodable text.

**Grade 2** In second grade, students continue to learn how to use context clues to understand the meaning of unfamiliar words in text. They learn how to use the individual words in compounds and common prefixes and suffixes to assist in word meaning.

**Grade 3** In third grade, instruction focuses on helping students use prefixes and suffixes and external context clues to figure out the meaning of unfamiliar words. They learn to use a dictionary to find and confirm word meanings.

**Grade 4 and Above** In fourth grade and above, instruction focuses on helping students apply knowledge of word origins, Greek and Latin affixes and roots, and common semantic context clues to discover the meaning of unfamiliar words, particularly words found in content-area texts. Students continue to use a dictionary and other reference materials to verify and confirm the meanings of unfamiliar words.

## When to Assess and Intervene

Beginning in the middle of first grade and continuing throughout the grades, students should be assessed for vocabulary knowledge and use of independent word-learning strategies. The best assessment is teacher observation of students as they read and work through texts. In addition, the vocabulary portion of formal achievement tests can be useful in assessing students' vocabulary development.

### ASSESSMENT AND INTERVENTION

| | |
|---|---|
| **When** | Mid-year |
| **Who** | All students |
| **Assessment Tool** | Teacher observation or the vocabulary portion of a standardized reading achievement test |
| **Intervene if . . .** | Students cannot use external context clues and/or morphemic analysis to determine the meaning of unfamiliar words. |
| **How** | Teacher-led small-group instruction in word-learning strategies |

**15.14**

## Word Parts

### Benchmark

- ability to use individual words in a compound word to predict its meaning

### Grade Level

- Grade 2

### Prerequisite

- Introducing Syllables (Chapter 10: Multisyllabic Words)

### Grouping

- whole class
- small group or pairs

### Materials

- overhead projector
- two transparencies: pictures of a shoe and a box
- word cards *shoe, box, bee, hive, class, room, dog, house, fire, wood, home, work, rain, coat, wrist, watch*
- dictionaries
- Vocabulary Notebooks

## COMPOUND WORDS

This generic teaching strategy focuses on compound words whose meaning can be predicted from the two parts: for example, the word *birthday*.

### Brainstorm

Using an overhead projector, display the transparency of the picture of a shoe. Say: *This is a shoe.* Remove the picture and place the word card for *shoe* on the chalktray. Then display the transparency of a picture of a box. Say: *This is a box.* Place the word card for *box* on the chalktray, leaving a large space between the two word cards. Now return the transparency of the shoe to the overhead, overlaying it, so that the shoe is inside the box. Say: *Now, we have a shoebox.* Next, remove the picture of the shoe and say: *What's left?* (a box) Put the picture of the shoe back, and remove the picture of the box. Ask: *What's left?* (a shoe)

### Teach/Model

Tell students that *shoebox* is a compound word—a word made up of two smaller words. Have students read aloud the word cards *shoe* and *box.* Next, slide the cards together to form the word *shoebox.* Have students say the new word and provide a simple definition: for example, "a box for shoes." Say: *The word* shoebox *is made up of two smaller words that can each stand alone. Knowing the meaning of each of the words in a*

*compound word can help you figure out the meaning of the whole word.* Read the following sentences aloud, asking students to suggest the compound word that completes each sentence.

A box for shoes is a _____. (shoebox)

A fish that is gold is a _____. (goldfish)

A boat that sails is a _____. (sailboat)

A bird that is blue is a _____. (bluebird)

A ball made of snow is a _____. (snowball)

Display the following word cards in random order on the chalktray: *bee, hive, class, room, dog, house, fire, wood, home, work, rain, coat, wrist, watch.* Read the words aloud with students. Point out that each word has a meaning of its own, and that each can be used to make part of a compound word. Have students suggest compound words, and as they suggest them slide the two word cards together. Then invite volunteers to take turns making up incomplete sentences (like the ones above) for their classmates to complete. For example, they might suggest: *A house for a dog is a _____.*

## Apply to Text

Print the following sentences on the board and have volunteers read them aloud. Ask students to identify the compound word in each sentence and predict its meaning based on what they know about the two smaller words.

My toolbox is handmade. I keep it on my bookcase.

## Word Consciousness

Challenge students to create their own nonsense compound words. For example, *redtrap, mousecream, treespread, barebird.* Tell them to think of definitions for any made-up compounds. Or, they might say a made-up word and invite classmates to give a definition for it (*redspread:* strawberry jam; *barebird:* a bird that has no feathers).

**Look It Up!**

**Have students use a dictionary to confirm and clarify the meanings of each of the compound words in the sentences. Students may record what they learn in their Vocabulary Notebooks.**

15.16

**TEACHING STRATEGY FOR**

## Word Parts

### Benchmarks

- ability to identify the meaning of simple prefixes
- ability to use knowledge of prefixes to predict the meaning of words

### Grade Level

- Grade 2 and above

### Prerequisite

- Introducing Prefixes (Chapter 10: Multisyllabic Words)

### Grouping

- whole class
- small group or pairs
- individual

### Materials

- dictionaries
- Vocabulary Notebooks

## PREFIXES

This generic teaching strategy focuses on using knowledge of the prefix *re–* to help predict the meaning of words. The same strategy can be used to introduce other common prefixes, such as *un–, dis–, in–,* and *im–.*

- - - - - - - - - - - - - - - - - - - - - - - - - - - - - -

### Brainstorm

Remind students that a *prefix* is a word part that comes at the beginning of a word. Tell them that you are going to name some words that begin with the prefix *re–.* Say the words *replay, redo, rewrite, repay,* and *refill.* Now invite students to generate *re–* words of their own by adding the prefix to action words, including silly words: for example, *recook* and *resleep.*

### Teach/Model

Print the prefix *re–* on the board and say it aloud. Explain to students that the prefix *re–* can mean "again or back." Print the following words on the board: *rewrite, recount, repay.* For each word, underline the prefix *re–* and identify the base word. Point out that *rewrite* means "write again," *recount* means "count again," and *repay* means "pay back."

Print the following sentence on the board, underlining the word *replay.* Ask students to use what they know about the prefix *re–* to predict the meaning of the underlined word.

I wish they would <u>replay</u> my favorite song.

**THINK ALOUD**   *I see the word* replay *begins with* re–, *which can be a prefix, and I know the prefix* re– *can mean "again or back." If I take* re– *away from* replay, *I'm left with the word* play, *which in this sentence means "to put on a tape or CD." Now, I'll try one of the meanings in a sentence: Yes, "play again"* *makes sense in the sentence. "I wish they would play my favorite song again."*

Now, print the following sentence on the board, underlining the word *real:*

That statue looks like a <u>real</u> tiger.

Caution students that the letters *r* and *e* together in a word are not always a prefix, or a separate syllable. For example, if they take the letters *re* away in *real,* they are not left with a word, so the letters are not a prefix and do not have the meaning "again or back."

## Apply to Text

Explain to students that they should always use context clues as well as their knowledge about prefixes to verify a word's meaning. Then ask pairs of students to practice the Think Aloud procedure using the following sentences and underlined target words. After practicing, call on pairs of students to share their Think Alouds with the whole class.

I didn't understand the first part of the story, so I <u>reread</u> it.
I didn't expect the sun to <u>reappear</u> so soon after the storm.

Encourage students to look for examples of words with the prefix *re–* in the texts they are reading. Tell them to bring the examples to class, together with the sentences in which they occur. For each example, students should explain how they arrived at a word's meaning.

## Word Consciousness

Students may enjoy using common prefixes, such as *un–* and *re–,* to invent silly words: for example, *rehamburger, unsuper, resleep, prebig,* and so forth. Encourage them to write definitions for their silly words and share them with the class.

**Look It Up!**

Have students use a dictionary to confirm and clarify the meanings of the affixed words found in their reading materials. Students may record what they learn in their Vocabulary Notebooks.

**TEACHING STRATEGY FOR**

## Word Parts

### Benchmarks

• ability to use knowledge of root words to predict the meaning of unknown words within a passage
• ability to use knowledge of common Greek and Latin roots and affixes to analyze the meaning of complex words

### Grade Level

• Grade 4 and above

### Grouping

• whole class
• small group or pairs

### Materials

• transparency of "Studying the Sky" (see Appendix)
• overhead projector
• dictionaries
• Vocabulary Notebooks

15.18

# WORD ROOTS

This generic teaching strategy focuses on using the Greek word root *tele* to help predict the meaning of words. The same strategy can be used to teach other common Greek word roots, such as *phon, auto,* or *graph,* as well as frequent Latin word roots such as *aud* or *spect.* Generally, Greek roots are introduced before Latin roots because their meaning is more apparent and the way in which they combine with other elements is more understandable.

## Brainstorm

On the board, print the Greek root *tele* in the center of a Word Part Web, as shown below. Identify and pronounce the word part. Then ask students to brainstorm words they know that contain this same word part. Add students' suggestions to the web.

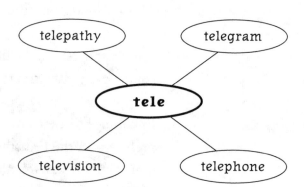

## Teach/Model

Explain to students that they can look at an unfamiliar word and predict its meaning using what they know about other words that contain the same word part. Direct students' attention to the Word Part Web. Ask: *What do these words have in common?* (They all begin with *tele.*) *Think about what the words mean. What do you think the Greek word part they all share might mean?* (Accept any reasonable answer.)

Point to the word *telephone.* Tell students that you assume that they all know what a telephone is and that the word *telephone* is made up of two Greek word parts, or meaning elements. Explain that to the ancient Greeks *tele* meant "distant," and *phon* meant "sound." Say: *From the combination of these two Greek word parts, we get the word* telephone, *or literally "distant sound."* Ask students how this literal definition may apply to the meaning of the word *telephone.* Say: *Now that we know that* tele *means "distant," does this meaning fit all the words on the web?* Ask students to think again about the meanings of the words on the web and to verify that they all have something to do with "distant" or "far away."

Print the following sentence on the board, underlining the word *telephoto.* Remind students that they know what *tele* means. Say: *Now I'm going to show you a way to figure out a new word.*

With my new <u>telephoto</u> lens, I took a great picture of an eagle's nest.

**THINK ALOUD** *I see that the word* telephoto *is made up of two parts. One part is* tele, *which I know can mean "distant"; the other part is* photo. *I know lots of words with* photo—*like* photograph *and* photography. *I think* photo *has something to do with a picture. So maybe a telephoto lens is a camera lens that can take a picture of something at a distance. Now I'll try the meaning in the sentence. It seems to make sense. Now I'll look up my predicted definition in the dictionary. Yes, the dictionary says that a telephoto lens is a photographic lens that can produce a large image of a distant object. I see how knowing something about word parts can help me figure out an unfamiliar word.*

## Apply to Text

Explain to students that it is important to use context clues as well as their knowledge about word parts to verify a word's

**15.20**

![Look It Up!]

**Have students use a dictionary to confirm and clarify the meanings of the words they found in their reading. Students may record what they learn in their Vocabulary Notebooks.**

meaning. On the transparency of "Studying the Sky," highlight the following sentence underlining the word *telescope.*

A <u>telescope</u> can be used to see faraway things more clearly.

Using the overhead projector, display "Studying the Sky." Tell students that you are going to show them how to predict the meaning of the word *telescope.* Remind them that they know the meaning of the word part *tele,* but that they may need to predict the meaning of the word part *scope.* In small groups, have students brainstorm and record in a Word Part Web any words they know that contain *scope.* Based on the meanings of the listed words, ask them to predict a meaning for *scope.* Then have them use their predicted meaning for *scope* along with the known meaning for *tele* to determine a meaning for *telescope.* Ask students to check their predicted meanings in the context of the sentence and share their answers with the whole class. After sharing, guide students to understand that the Greek word part *scope* means "see" and that *telescope,* a device that makes things that are far away look closer and larger, literally means "see from a distance."

Next, ask students to look for examples of words with the word part *tele, phone, photo,* or *scope* in the texts they are reading. Tell them to bring the examples to class, together with sentences in which they occur. For each example, students should explain how they used context and their knowledge of word parts to predict a word's meaning.

## Word Consciousness

Tell students that the English word *phobia* comes from the Greek word part *phobos,* which means "fear." Explain that some common phobias are *claustrophobia,* or "fear of closed places"; *agoraphobia,* or "fear of open places"; and *acrophobia,* or "fear of high places." Invite students to make up names for phobias: *grrophobia* ("fear of growling dogs"), *phewophobia* ("fear of sneakers"), *testtubeophobia* ("fear of science lab").

This generic teaching strategy focuses on common Latin and Greek number morphemes.

**15.21**

### Benchmarks

- ability to use word origins to predict the meaning of unknown words
- ability to recognize Greek and Latin word parts in familiar words

### Grade Level

- Grade 4 and above

### Grouping

- whole class
- small group or pairs
- individual

### Materials

- none

## Brainstorm

On the board, print *bi* in the center of a Word Part Web, as shown below. Identify and pronounce the word part. Tell students that *bi* is a Latin word part that means "two." Then ask students to brainstorm words they know that contain *bi*. Add students' suggestions to the web.

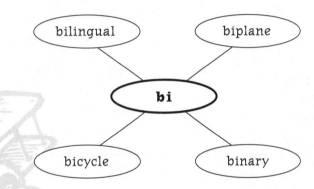

## Teach/Model

Explain to students that many English words are made up of Greek and Latin word parts. Knowing the meaning of some of these word parts can help them to predict the meaning of an English word. Display the following Number Morphemes chart. Read the Latin and Greek word parts and their corresponding meanings. Encourage students to suggest other examples of English words with these number morphemes, and add their suggestions to the chart.

## NUMBER MORPHEMES

| Number | Latin | Greek | Possible Examples |
|---|---|---|---|
| 1 | uni | mono | uniform, monorail |
| 2 | bi, duo | di | bilingual, diploma |
| 3 | tri | tri | triangle |
| 4 | quad | tetra | quadruple, tetrahedron |
| 5 | quint | penta | quintuplet |
| 6 | sex | hex | sextuplet, hexagon |
| 7 | sept | hept | septet |
| 8 | oct | oct | octopus |
| 9 | nove, non | ennea | novena, nonagon |
| 10 | deci | dec, deca, deka | decimeter, decathlon |
| 100 | cent | hect | centennial |
| 1,000 | milli | khilio (kilo) | millipede, kilometer |

15.22

Print the word *bicycle* on the board, underlining the word part *bi.* Ask: *How many wheels does a bicycle have?* (two) Point to the chart and say: *A bicycle has two wheels. The Latin word part* bi *means "two."* Draw two wheels next to the word *bicycle.* Now print the word *unicycle* on the board, underlining the word part *uni.* Ask: *How many wheels does a unicycle have?* (one) Draw one wheel next to the word *unicycle. What do you call a cycle with three wheels?* (a tricycle) Print *tricycle* on the board, underlining *tri.* Draw three wheels next to *tricycle.* Ask: *If you invented a cycle with a thousand wheels, what might you call it?* (a millicycle) Print *millicycle* on the board, underlining the word part *milli.*

**Intervention Strategy** ✔ **ELL**

Invite Spanish-speaking students to share Spanish words they know with these Greek and Latin number morphemes. (Examples: *uniforme, bicicleta, triángulo.*) For other English language learners, use pictures and visual aids to help convey the word meanings to students.

Next, ask students the following number riddles:

- If a *triangle* is a figure with three angles, what is a *quadrangle? (a figure with four angles)*

- If eight people sing in an *octet,* how many people sing in a *quartet? (four)* In a *septet? (seven)*

- How many legs does a *tripod* have? *(three)*

- How many horns does a *unicorn* have? *(one)*

- How many years are there in a *decade? (ten)*

- How many years are there in a *century? (one hundred)*

## Apply to Text

Divide the class into groups. Assign each group a different numeral and ask students to brainstorm words that begin with the corresponding Greek and Latin morphemes. After brainstorming, have students make up their own number riddles. They can write the riddles on chart paper and display them for the rest of the class. Each group can invite the other students to use the Number Morphemes chart to solve the riddles.

## Word Consciousness

Students can use the number morphemes to create nonsense riddles: *What do you call a four-legged octopus?* (a quadropus) They may also use the word parts to write number sentences: *unicycle + bicycle = tricycle; octopus − 5 = tripod.*

**TEACHING STRATEGY FOR**

## Context Clues

**15.24**

### Benchmark

• ability to use context to determine meaning of an unfamiliar word in text

### Grade Level

• Grade 3 and above

### Grouping

• whole class
• small group or pairs
• individual

### Materials

• copies of "Naming Living Things" (see Appendix)
• dictionaries

## EXTERNAL CONTEXT CLUES

GRADE LEVEL **3** AND ABOVE GRADE LEVEL

This generic teaching strategy provides a model for using external context clues to discover the meaning of an unfamiliar word in text. Teach students to first decode the unfamiliar word and then use context to determine its meaning.

● ● ● ● ● ● ● ● ● ● ● ● ● ● ● ● ● ● ● ● ● ● ● ● ● ● ● ●

### Teach/Model

Print the following passage on the board. Then guide students through the process of using context to determine the meaning of unfamiliar words.

(1) We were completely <u>isolated</u> in the cabin. (2) There was no one for miles around. (3) Due to the ice storm, the telephone lines were down. (4) We were wearing our warmest outdoor clothing, but the air was so <u>frigid</u> that our fingers and toes were growing numb. (5) We were hungry, the fire was almost out, and we had only three small pieces of <u>kindling</u>.

Read aloud sentence 1. Then say: Isolated . . . *I don't know the meaning of this word. I'll read the sentence again to see if it helps me.* Reread the first sentence. Say: *Well, that didn't help. Maybe if I read some more.* Read aloud sentences 2 and 3. Say: *Ah, now I see. They're in a cabin, there is no one else around, and the telephone is not working. I get a pretty good idea that* isolated *means something like "cut off." Now I am going to replace the word* isolated *with the words* cut off: "We were completely <u>cut off</u> in the cabin." *That seems to make sense. I think I'll look up* isolated *in the dictionary to be completely sure. The dictionary says that* isolated *can mean "separated from others." OK, that's close to* cut off.

Read aloud sentence 4. Ask students if they know what the word *frigid* means. Even if someone knows that *frigid* means "cold," have students identify the clues in the sentence that could suggest a meaning. Circle the clues. Students might identify the following clues: there's an ice storm; they're wearing warm outdoor clothing; their fingers and toes are numb. Lead students to conclude that *frigid* means something like "cold." Say: *Now I am going to replace the word* frigid *with the word* cold: *". . . but the air was so* <u>cold</u> *that our fingers and toes were growing numb." That works. I think I'll look up* frigid *in the dictionary to be completely sure. The dictionary says that* frigid *means "very cold." OK, that's close to* cold.

Read aloud sentence 5. Say: Kindling *is an unfamiliar word; I'm not sure what it means. I'll read the sentence again.* Reread the sentence. *No luck. Kindling could be some kind of dried food, like beef jerky. Maybe kindling is something like the charcoal we use when we barbecue. I can't make a good prediction. There isn't anything in the rest of the passage to give me more help. I'll have to look* kindling *up in the dictionary. Oh!* kindling *means "dry sticks of wood used to start a fire." That makes sense:* "We were hungry, the fire was almost out, and we had only three small pieces of <u>wood</u>." *See, this time the context didn't help me. In fact, it was misleading.*

## Apply to Text

Provide students with copies of "Naming Living Things." Have them read the passage and use what they know about word parts and context to help them determine the meanings of any unfamiliar words. Students may be unfamiliar with the meanings of the following words: *botany, binomial, genus, species, canine.*

## Word Consciousness

Students might enjoy finding out about the history or origin of the unfamiliar words in "Naming Living Things." If possible, provide a copy of the *Oxford English Dictionary,* or have them access it online.

**Look It Up!**

**Have students use a dictionary to confirm and clarify the meanings of the unfamiliar words in "Naming Living Things." Students may record what they learn in their Vocabulary Notebooks.**

**TEACHING STRATEGY FOR**

## Context Clues

### Benchmark

- ability to clarify word meanings through definitions; examples; restatements; and comparisons and contrasts

### Grade Level

- Grade 4 and above

### Grouping

- whole class
- small group or pairs
- individual

### Materials

- social studies or science textbooks
- copies of "Studying the Sky" (see Appendix)
- Vocabulary Notebooks

15.26

# SEMANTIC CONTEXT CLUES

This generic teaching strategy focuses on some of the common ways that authors of expository text provide contextual support. These semantic context clues include direct definitions or explanations, restatements, and comparisons or contrasts. Each type of semantic clue should be introduced and then applied to text separately, using the following examples and strategies.

## Teach/Model

Point out to students that when textbook authors and authors of informational trade books introduce terms and concepts they often provide contextual support for those terms and concepts. Tell students that there are several types of context clues that may help them figure out an unfamiliar term as they are reading.

**DIRECT DEFINITIONS OR EXPLANATIONS** Explain that direct definitions or explanations are the most obvious type of context clue. Words such as *is* or *means* signal that a definition or explanation of an unfamiliar term will follow. Print the following sentence on the board, underlining the word *kantharos*. Ask a volunteer to read the sentence aloud.

A <u>kantharos</u> is a type of silver cup used by Roman emperors.

Ask: *What is the unfamiliar term in this sentence?* (*kantharos*) *Are there any signal words in the sentence?* (yes, *is*) *Does a definition or explanation follow the word* is? (yes) Circle the definition "a type of silver cup used by Roman emperors." Say: *So now we know that a kantharos is a silver cup used by the Romans.*

Now print the following sentence on the board, underlining the word *environment*. Ask a volunteer to read the sentence aloud.

Environment means the surroundings in which a person, animal, or plant lives.

Ask: *What is the unfamiliar term in this sentence? (environment) Are there any signal words in the sentence? (yes, means) Does a definition or explanation follow the word* means? *(yes) Circle the definition "the surroundings in which a person, animal, or plant lives." Say: So now we know that the word* environment *means the surroundings in which a person, animal, or plant lives.*

To apply their knowledge of this type of semantic context clue, ask students to look through their social studies or science textbooks for examples and share them with the class.

**RESTATEMENTS** Explain that restatements are a type of context clue that uses different words to say the same thing. Tell them that restatements are often signaled by *or, that is,* and *in other words,* and are usually set off by commas. Print the following sentence on the board, underlining the word *gandingan*. Ask a volunteer to read the sentence aloud.

The loud gandingan, or talking gong, was used to send messages from one village to another.

Ask: *What is the unfamiliar term in this sentence? (gandingan) Are there any signal words or commas in the sentence? (yes, or and the two commas) Is there a restatement that explains the unfamiliar word? (yes) Circle the restatement "or talking gong." Say: Now we know that a gandingan is a type of gong.*

Now print the following sentences on the board, underlining the word *compromise*. Ask a volunteer to read the sentence aloud.

The Amish have had to <u>compromise</u> with the modern world. In other words, they have had to give up some of their beliefs.

15.28

Ask: *What is the unfamiliar term in the first sentence?* (*compromise*) *Are there any signal words or phrases in the sentences?* (yes, *in other words*) *Is there a restatement that follows the phrase* in other words? (yes) Circle the restatement "they have had to give up some of their beliefs." Say: *So compromise means "to give up some beliefs."*

To apply their knowledge of this type of semantic context clue, ask students to look through their social studies or science textbooks for examples and share them with the class.

**COMPARISONS OR CONTRASTS**   Explain that comparisons or contrasts are a type of context clue that likens or contrasts an unfamiliar word to a familiar word or concept. Words and phrases, such as *like, just as, similar, different, in contrast,* and *on the other hand* signal that a comparison or contrast of an unfamiliar term will follow. Print the following sentence on the board, underlining the word *tribulations*. Ask a volunteer to read the sentence aloud.

The pioneers' <u>tribulations</u> along the trail were in sharp contrast to their comfortable lives at home.

Ask: *What is the unfamiliar term in this sentence?* (*tribulations*) *Are there any signal words or phrases in the sentence?* (yes, *in sharp contrast*) *Is there a comparison or a contrast that follows the phrase* in sharp contrast? (yes, a contrast) Circle the contrast "their comfortable lives at home." Ask: *What do you think the word* tribulations *means in this sentence?* (Accept any reasonable answer.)

**Look It Up!**

**Have students use a dictionary to confirm and clarify the meanings of the unfamiliar words in "Studying the Sky." Students may record what they learn in their Vocabulary Notebooks.**

To apply their knowledge of this type of semantic context clue, ask students to look through their social studies or science textbooks for examples and share them with the class.

## Apply to Text

After introducing the three types of semantic context clues, provide students with copies of "Studying the Sky." Have them read the passage and use what they know about word parts and context clues to help them determine the meanings of any unfamiliar words. Students may be unfamiliar with the meanings of the following words: *astronomy, ancient, heliocentric, constellations, lunar.*

## Word Consciousness

Students might enjoy finding out about the history or origin of the unfamiliar words in "Studying the Sky." If possible, provide a copy of the *Oxford English Dictionary,* or have them access it online.

## Section References

Adams, M. J. 1990. *Beginning to read: Thinking and learning about print.* Cambridge, MA: MIT Press.

Anders, P. L., C. S. Bos, and D. Filip. 1984. The effect of semantic feature analysis on the reading comprehension of learning disabled students. In J. Niles and L. A. Harris (eds.), *Changing perspectives in research in reading/language processing and instruction* (vol. 33). Rochester, NY: National Reading Conference.

Anderson, R. C. 1996. Research foundations to support wide reading. In V. Greany (ed.), *Promoting reading in developing countries.* Newark, DE: International Reading Association.

Anderson, R. C., and P. Freebody. 1981. Vocabulary knowledge. In J. Guthrie (ed.), *Comprehension and teaching research reviews* (pp. 77–117). Newark, DE: International Reading Association.

Anderson, R. C., and W. E. Nagy. 1991. Word meaning. In R. Barr, M. L. Kamil, P. B. Mosenthal, and P. D. Pearson (eds.), *Handbook of reading research* (vol. 2, pp. 690–724). White Plains, NY: Longman.

Anderson, R. C., P. T. Wilson, and L. G. Fielding. 1988. Growth in reading and how children spend their time outside of school. *Reading Research Quarterly* 23, pp. 285–303.

Anglin, J. M. 1993. Vocabulary development: A morphological analysis. *Monographs of the Society for Research in Child Development* 58 (Serial No. 238).

Baker, S., D. C. Simmons, and E. J. Kameenui. 1998a. Vocabulary acquisition: Instructional and curricular basics and implications. In D. C. Simmons and E. J. Kameenui (eds.), *What reading research tells us about children with diverse learning needs: Bases and basics.* Mahwah, NJ: Erlbaum.

Baker, S., D. C. Simmons, and E. J. Kameenui. 1998b. Vocabulary acquisition: Research bases. In D. C. Simmons and E. J. Kameenui (eds.), *What reading research tells us about children with diverse learning needs: Bases and basics.* Mahwah, NJ: Erlbaum.

Bannon, E., P. J. Fisher, L. Pozzi, and D. Wessel. 1990. Effective definitions for word learning. *Journal of Reading* 34.

Baumann, J. F., and E. J. Kameenui. 1991. Research on vocabulary instruction: Ode to Voltaire. In J. Flood, D. Lapp, and J. R. Squire (eds.), *Handbook of research on teaching the English language arts* (pp. 604–632). New York: Macmillan.

Bear, D. R., M. Invernizzi, S. Templeton, and F. Johnston. 1996. *Words their way: Word study for phonics, vocabulary, and spelling instruction.* Upper Saddle River, NJ: Prentice-Hall.

Beck, I. L., and M. G. McKeown. 1991. Conditions of vocabulary acquisition. In R. Barr, M. L. Kamil, P. B. Mosenthal, and P. D. Pearson (eds.), *Handbook of reading research* (vol. 2, pp. 789–814). White Plains, NY: Longman.

Beck, I. L., M. G. McKeown, and R. Omanson. 1987. The effects and uses of diverse vocabulary instructional techniques. In M. G. McKeown and M. E. Curtis (eds.), *The nature of vocabulary acquisition.* Mahwah, NJ: Erlbaum.

Beck, I., C. Perfetti, and M. G. McKeown. 1982. The effects of long-term vocabulary instruction on lexical access and reading comprehension. *Journal of Educational Psychology* 74.

Betts, E. A. 1946. *Foundations of reading instruction.* New York: American Books.

Blachowicz, C., and P. Fisher. 1996. *Teaching vocabulary in all classrooms.* Upper Saddle River, NJ: Prentice-Hall.

Chall, J. S. 1987. Two vocabularies for reading: Recognition and meaning. In M. G. McKeown and M. E. Curtis (eds.), *The nature of vocabulary acquisition* (pp. 7–18). Mahwah, NJ: Erlbaum.

Cunningham, A. E., and K. E. Stanovich. 1998. What reading does for the mind. *American Educator* 22, pp. 8–15.

D'Anna, C. A., E. B. Zechmeister, and J. W. Hall. 1991. Toward a meaningful definition of vocabulary size. *Journal of Reading Behavior* 23, pp. 109–122.

Fielding, L. G., P. T. Wilson, and R. C. Anderson. 1986. A new focus on free reading: The role of trade books in reading instruction. In T. Raphael and R. E. Reynolds (eds.), *The contexts of school-based literacy.* New York: Random House.

Fukkink, R. G., and K. de Glopper. 1998. Effects of instruction in deriving word meaning from context: A meta-analysis. *Review of Educational Research* 68, pp. 450–469.

Gillet, J. W., and C. Temple. 1994. *Understanding reading problems: Assessment and instruction.* (4th ed.) New York: HarperCollins.

Gouldman, R., P. Nation, and J. Read. 1990. How large can a receptive vocabulary be? *Applied Linguistics* 11, pp. 341–363.

Graves, M. F., and W. H. Slater. 1996. Vocabulary instruction in content areas. In D. Lapp, J. Flood, and N. Farnan (eds.), *Content area reading and learning.* Needham Heights, MA: Allyn & Bacon.

Graves, M. F., C. Juel, and B. B. Graves. 1998. *Teaching reading in the twenty-first century.* Needham Heights, MA: Allyn & Bacon.

Harris, A. J., and E. Sipay. 1990. *How to increase reading ability.* (10th ed.) White Plains, NY: Longman.

Hayes, D. P., and M. Ahrens. 1988. Vocabulary simplification for children: A special case of "motherese"? *Journal of Child Language* 15, pp. 395–410.

Henry, M. 1997. The decoding/spelling continuum: Integrated decoding and spelling instruction from pre-school to early secondary school. *Dyslexia* 3.

Herman, P. A., R. C. Anderson, P. D. Pearson, and W. E. Nagy. 1987. Incidental acquisition of word meanings from expositions with varied text features. *Reading Research Quarterly* 23, pp. 263–284.

Hirsh, D., and P. Nation. 1992. What vocabulary size is needed to read unsimplified tests for pleasure? *Reading in a Foreign Language* 8, pp. 689–696.

Irvin, J. L. 1998. *Reading and the middle school student.* (2nd ed.) Needham Heights, MA: Allyn & Bacon.

Jenkins, J. R., and Dixon, R. 1983. Vocabulary learning. *Contemporary Educational Psychology* 8, pp. 237–280.

Jenkins, J. R., M. L. Stein, and K. Wysocki. 1984. Learning vocabulary through reading. *American Educational Research Journal* 21, pp. 767–787.

Johnson, D. D., S. Toms-Bronowski, and S. D. Pittelman. 1982. *An investigation of the effects of prior knowledge and vocabulary acquisition on passage comprehension* (Program Report 84–5). Madison, WI: Wisconsin Center for Educational Research, University of Wisconsin.

Kameenui, E. J., D. W. Dixon, and D. Carnine. 1987. Issues in the design of vocabulary instruction. In M. G. McKeown and M. E. Curtis (eds.), *The nature of vocabulary acquisition.* Mahwah, NJ: Erlbaum.

Levin, J. R. 1993. Mnemonic strategies in the classroom: A twenty-year report card. *Elementary School Journal* 94, pp. 235–244.

Lorge, I., and J. S. Chall. 1963. Estimating the size of vocabularies of children and adults: An analysis of methodological issues. *Journal of Experimental Education* 32 (2).

Mastropieri, M. A., T. E. Scruggs, and B. J. Fulk. 1990. Teaching abstract vocabulary with the keyword method: Effects on recall and comprehension. *Journal of Learning Disabilities* 23, pp. 92–107.

McKeown, M. G., I. L. Beck, R. C. Omanson, and M. T. Pople. 1985. Some effects of the nature and frequency of vocabulary instruction on the knowledge and use of words. *Reading Research Quarterly* 20, pp. 522–535.

Nagy, W. E. 1988a. *Teaching vocabulary to improve reading comprehension.* Newark, DE: International Reading Association.

Nagy, W. E. 1988b. *Vocabulary instruction and reading comprehension* (Technical Report No. 431). Champaign, IL: Center for the Study of Reading.

Nagy, W. E., and R. C. Anderson. 1984. How many words are there in printed school English? *Reading Research Quarterly* 19, pp. 304–330.

Nagy, W. E., R. C. Anderson, and P. A. Herman. 1987. Learning word meanings from context during normal reading. *American Educational Research Journal* 24, pp. 237–270.

Nagy, W. E., and P. A. Herman. 1987. Breadth and depth of vocabulary knowledge: Implications for acquisition and instruction. In M. G. McKeown and M. E. Curtis (eds.), *The nature of vocabulary acquisition.* Mahwah, NJ: Erlbaum.

**15.32**

Nagy, W. E., P. A. Herman, and R. C. Anderson. 1985. Learning words from context. *Reading Research Quarterly* 20, pp. 233–253.

Nagy, W. E., P. Winsor, J. Osborn, and J. O'Flahaven. 1994. Structural analysis: Some guidelines for instruction. In F. Lehr and J. Osborn (eds.), *Reading, language, and literacy.* Mahwah, NJ: Erlbaum.

Powell, W. P. 1986. Teaching vocabulary through opposition. *Journal of Reading* 29, pp. 626–633.

Pressley, M., J. R. Levin, and M. A. McDaniel. 1987. Remembering versus inferring what a word means: Mnemonic and contextual approaches. In M. G. McKeown and M. E. Curtis (eds.), *The nature of vocabulary acquisition.* Mahwah, NJ: Erlbaum.

Pressley, M., and L. Lysynchuk. 1995. Vocabulary. In M. Pressley, V. Woloshyn, and Associates (eds.), *Cognitive strategy instruction that really improves children's academic performance.* Cambridge, MA: Brookline Books.

Schwartz, R. M., and T. E. Raphael. 1985. Concept of definition: A key to improving students' vocabulary. *The Reading Teacher* 39, pp. 198–203.

Scott, J. A., and W. E. Nagy. 1997. Understanding the definitions of unfamiliar verbs. *Reading Research Quarterly* 32, pp. 184–200.

Stahl, S. A. 1999. *Vocabulary development.* Cambridge, MA: Brookline Books.

Stahl, S., and M. Fairbanks. 1986. The effects of vocabulary instruction: A model-based meta-analysis. *Review of Educational Research* 5.

Stahl, S. A., and B. A. Kapinus. 1991. Possible sentences: Predicting word meanings to teach content area vocabulary. *The Reading Teacher* 45, pp. 36–38.

Stahl, S. A., M. G. Richek, and R. Vandevier. 1991. Learning word meanings through listening: A sixth-grade replication. In J. Zutell and S. McCormick (eds.), *Learning factors/ teacher factors: Issues in literacy research. Fortieth yearbook of the National Reading Conference* (pp. 185–192). Chicago: National Reading Conference.

Stanovich, K. E. 1986. Matthew effects in reading: Some consequences of individual differences in the acquisition of literacy. *Reading Research Quarterly* 21, pp. 360–407.

Sternberg, R. J. 1987. Most words are learned from context. In M. G. McKeown and M. E. Curtis (eds.), *The acquisition of word meanings.* Mahwah, NJ: Erlbaum.

Templeton, S. 1997. *Teaching the integrated language arts.* Boston: Houghton Mifflin.

Watts, S. M., and M. F. Graves. 1995. Fostering word consciousness. *Wisconsin SRA Journal,* 40(2).

White, T. G., M. E. Graves, and W. H. Slater. 1990. Growth of reading vocabulary in diverse elementary schools: Decoding and word meaning. *Journal of Educational Psychology* 82, pp. 281–290.

White, T. G., W. H. Slater, and M. E. Graves. 1989. Yes/No method of vocabulary assessment: Valid for whom and useful for what? *Cognitive and social perspectives for literacy research and instruction.* Chicago: National Reading Conference.

White, T. G., J. Sowell, and A. Yanagihara. 1989. Teaching elementary students to use word-part clues. *The Reading Teacher* 42, pp. 302–308.

# SECTION VII

# Comprehension

# Section VII: Comprehension

## Comprehension Strategies

- **using prior knowledge**
- **predicting**
- **identifying the main idea and summarization**
- **questioning**
- **making inferences**
- **visualizing**

R eading comprehension is the process of constructing meaning from written texts. For proficient readers, comprehension is an expected outcome. In the past few decades, researchers have examined what proficient readers do to reach this expected outcome. Their findings show that the process of comprehension is both interactive (Anderson and Pearson 1984) and strategic (Anderson, Hiebert, Scott, and Wilkinson 1985)—readers make decisions by selecting strategies that fit the kind of text they are reading and their purpose for reading.

Most students require explicit instruction in reading comprehension strategies (Tierney 1982). Certain key comprehension strategies—which students employ before, during, and after reading a selection—need to be taught directly to students in the context of their reading. In explicit comprehension-strategies instruction, students learn *what* the strategy is, *why* it is important, and *how, when,* and *where* to apply it. According to various researchers (Pearson, Roehler, Dole, and Duffy 1992; Pressley, Johnson, Symons, McGoldrick, and Kurita 1989), key comprehension strategies include using prior knowledge, predicting, identifying the main idea and summarization, questioning, making inferences, and visualizing.

Strategic reading comprehension can be developed through reading *and* through listening. For beginning readers with limited word recognition and decoding skills, listening to text read aloud provides opportunities to attend to and comprehend text that they would be unable to read for themselves (Gillet and Temple 1994). Oral reading, combined with teacher-directed discussion, expose students to the widest possible range of literature, familiarize them with various text structures, enrich their vocabularies, and help them become more adept at comprehending *written* texts. As students' reading abilities develop, the gap between their listening comprehension and reading comprehension closes (Gillet and Temple 1994). However, until students can read independently, they continue to benefit from listening to, responding to, and analyzing literature that is read to them.

Students' awareness and understanding of *text organization* plays a key role in reading comprehension (Dickson, Simmons, and Kameenui 1998b). Text organization encompasses both the physical presentation of the text (headings, subheadings, and graphics) and the underlying text structure. There are generally two types of text structures: narrative and expository.

Teachers must understand the demands that various kinds of texts make on the reader. They should use explicit teaching techniques to develop students' understanding of the physical presentation and text structures of both narrative and expository text. In this way, teachers can equip students with the tools that will enable them to make sense of what they read. As students who are learning to read become students who are reading to learn, the goal is to make them increasingly responsible for their own reading comprehension.

## Text Structures

**Narrative Text**

usually a story

**Expository Text**

usually written to communicate information

## Standards for Reading Comprehension

**KINDERGARTEN**

- Students identify the basic facts and ideas in what they have read, heard, or viewed. They use comprehension strategies (e.g., generating and responding to questions, comparing new information to what is already known).

**GRADES 1 THROUGH 4**

- Students read and understand grade-level–appropriate material. They draw upon a variety of comprehension strategies as needed (e.g., generating and responding to essential questions, making predictions, comparing information from several sources).

**GRADES 5 THROUGH 8** *(Focus on Informational Materials)*

- Students read and understand grade-level–appropriate material. They describe and connect the essential ideas, arguments, and perspectives of the text by using their knowledge of text structure, organization, and purpose.

## Standards for Literary Response and Analysis

**KINDERGARTEN**

- Students listen and respond to stories based on well-known characters, themes, plots, and settings.

**GRADES 1 THROUGH 4**

- Students read and respond to a wide variety of significant works of children's literature. They distinguish between the structural features of the text and the literary terms or elements (e.g., theme, plot, setting, characters).

**GRADES 5 THROUGH 8**

- Students read and respond to historically or culturally significant works of literature that reflect and enhance their studies of history and social science. They clarify the ideas and connect them to other literary works.

**SOURCE**

Adapted from *English-Language Arts Content Standards for California Public Schools: Kindergarten Through Grade Twelve* (1999). Sacramento: California Department of Education.

# CONTENTS

## Section VII: Comprehension

CONTINUED ▷

CHAPTER

# 16

# Strategic Reading

what?
why?
when?
how?

# what? *Strategic Reading*

16.2

*"Strategy instruction should be explicit, intensive, and extensive."*

—PRESSLEY & WOLOSHYN, 1995

Recent research has revealed that reading is not an automatic or passive process, but is highly interactive—good readers apply a variety of strategies to process text (Pressley, El-Dinary, Gaskins, Bergman, Almasi, and Brown 1992). Strategic reading, therefore, involves *learner-based* actions, or conscious applications of specific strategies selected from a variety of possibilities. Research also indicates what teachers need to do to produce strategic readers. They need to teach their students a number of cognitive strategies, as well as supply them with the metacognitive knowledge necessary to understand when and how to use these strategies.

*Strategies* are conscious plans that readers apply and adapt to make sense of text and to get the most out of what they read. In other words, a strategy can be thought of as a procedure or set of steps to follow in order to comprehend text. Because these strategies are under the reader's control, they enable the reader to monitor and adjust his or her reading (Dickson, Collins, Simmons, and Kameenui 1998). The goal of strategy instruction is to turn students into interactive readers who are in control of their own reading comprehension. As they interact with different texts, they will choose to apply the different strategies they have been taught.

## Metacognitive Knowledge

Metacognition can be defined as "thinking about thinking." To have metacognitive knowledge is to be aware of one's thought processes and to be able to successfully direct them, adapting one's thinking as needed, toward the accomplishment of a task. Proficient readers, then, are active learners who engage in metacognitive activities as they read. Such activities might include previewing before reading, monitoring understanding during the course of reading, adjusting speed, rereading, reading on, and checking understanding after reading (Brown and Palincsar 1984).

## Key Comprehension Strategies

**Using Prior Knowledge/ Previewing**

**Predicting**

**Identifying the Main Idea and Summarization**

**Questioning**

**Making Inferences**

**Visualizing**

Students typically do not fully develop their metacognitive skills until late adolescence, but much can be done before then to guide them in developing and applying metacognitive knowledge—in particular, in self-monitoring their comprehension of a text (Irvin 1998). During reading, teachers can ask questions that make students "think about their thinking." Such questions might include *How did you know that?* and *What do you do when you don't understand (a word, an event, a passage)?* Teachers also can model self-monitoring techniques for students and encourage students to keep journals about their reading. Until students have internalized the metacognitive process, they need frequent modeling, ample practice, and regular feedback.

Teaching specific strategies equips students with the tools they need to control their reading comprehension (Dickson, Collins, Simmons, and Kameenui 1998). These tools, coupled with an understanding of when, where, and how to use them, help students develop metacognitive knowledge of themselves as learners and readers. Thus, the goal of strategy instruction is twofold:

① To teach students to think metacognitively about the act of reading—to be aware of how well they are understanding what they read and to know what to do to improve their reading comprehension;

② To explicitly teach students a set of effective strategies that they can use when they metacognitively determine the need to do so.

## Comprehension Strategies Instruction

The teaching model that has grown out of recent research emphasizes the planned, purposeful application of strategies to authentic reading tasks. In this model, students are taught to document, monitor, and self-assess their use of strategies "in flight" (Walker 1996a and 1996b).

Comprehension instruction should be aligned with carefully selected texts. New strategies are first taught with familiar narrative and expository texts and then practiced with texts students can easily read.

Research has shown that certain explicit teaching techniques are particularly effective for strategy instruction. These include direct explanation, modeling, guided practice, feedback, and application (Dickson, Collins, Simmons, and Kameenui 1998).

- *Direct explanation:* The teacher explains to students *what* the strategy is and its purpose.

- *Modeling:* The teacher demonstrates *how* to use this strategy by "thinking aloud" while interacting with actual text.

- *Guided practice:* The teacher works with students to help them figure out *how* and *when* to use this strategy, again within the context of reading actual text.

- *Feedback:* As students practice, the teacher may engage them in discussion or ask them to think aloud. During this time, the teacher provides feedback about correct and incorrect responses.

- *Application:* The teacher asks students to apply the strategies to other texts. At this point, students move toward assuming responsibility for determining *what* strategy to use, and *how, when,* and *why* to use it.

**16.4**

*"In learning these strategies, students are internalizing a way of reading and thinking that is active, critical, and reflective."*

—GRAVES, JUEL & GRAVES, 1998

**Students who are able readers in their primary language often have mastered comprehension strategies that they can then transfer to reading in English. For these students, comprehension difficulties may be due to a lack of specific vocabulary or of cultural concepts presented in the text.**

See also...

"DRTA," p. 17.27

"QAR," p. 17.31

"K-W-L Plus," p. 18.21

"Text Organization," p. 18.25

Most researchers agree that students need to master certain key comprehension strategies to become proficient, strategic readers (Pearson et al. 1992). These include using prior knowledge, predicting, identifying the main idea and summarization, questioning, making inferences, and visualizing.

## Using Prior Knowledge/Previewing

16.5

Cognitive research into how the brain acquires and stores knowledge has determined the importance of activating prior knowledge in the comprehension of text. Schema theory proposes that as a person learns about and experiences the world, he or she develops various frameworks (called *schemata*) that expand, are revised, or subdivide to accommodate new information. For example, a young child might develop a broad "doggy" schema that contains the child's accumulated knowledge of furry, four-legged pets. As the child learns more about types of dogs and dog behavior, the schema is refined and becomes more specific. As the child learns that cats are different from dogs, a distinct cat schema is formed.

When students preview text, they begin to determine the prior knowledge needed to help them understand what they are about to read. While previewing a selection, teachers can ask students what they already know about the content of the selection (the topic, concept, genre, or author); the vocabulary used in the text; and what experience they have with the way the text is organized (story grammar, expository text structures). When a reader's prior knowledge is thus "primed," the resulting schema provides a framework for any new information the reader learns (Graves, Juel, and Graves 1998), and increases the likelihood that the reader will recall text afterward (Baldwin, Peleg-Bruckner, and McClintock 1985; Recht and Leslie 1988).

"DRTA," p. 17.27

"K-W-L Plus," p. 18.21

"Reciprocal Teaching," p. 18.29

**16.6**

## Predicting

Making and verifying predictions can be thought of as form-ing a connection between prior knowledge and new informa-tion that comes from the text (Gillet and Temple 1994). Good readers interact with texts by making informed predictions about what they will read, reading to confirm those predictions, and revising or making new predictions as they continue to read. When students make predictions, they set up expectations based on their prior knowledge of similar situations, which set a purpose for reading and motivate them to read on.

Good readers use this strategy routinely. Before they begin a new text, students need to be directed to use all available pieces of information to generate predictions, understanding that even good predictions may turn out to be inaccurate. Teachers can prompt student predictions with the following questions: *Does the title provide a clue to what the text will be about? What do you know about the author? What does the opening artwork suggest? How is the text set up? Is the text likely to be fiction or nonfiction?* If this previewing does not yield much in the way of prediction, students can be asked to read the opening paragraph(s).

The point of the strategy is for students to engage and interact with the text. As they process new information, they may have to partially or completely revise a prediction. Students then read on to test the new hypothesis. An important after-reading aspect of this strategy (and one that improves recall) is review-ing and evaluating the predictions that were generated during reading.

See also...

"Story Grammar Elements," p. 17.20

"Identifying the Main Idea," p. 18.14

"Summarization," p. 18.17

"K-W-L Plus," p. 18.21

"Text Organization," p. 18.25

"Reciprocal Teaching," p. 18.29

## Identifying the Main Idea and Summarization

A *summary* might be defined as a synthesis of the important ideas in a text. Summarizing requires readers to determine what is important, and then condense this information and put it into their own words. The ability to summarize is a crucial reading *and* study strategy, enabling readers to learn in an economical fashion, extract important ideas, and recall text (Bretzing and Kulhavy 1979).

When readers apply the strategy of determining what is important, they are, in essence, trying to determine the author's message and purpose in writing (Garcia and Pearson 1990). Good readers draw on three areas of knowledge to help them: (1) their background knowledge (general knowledge and specific prior knowledge of a topic); (2) their knowledge of author biases, intentions, and goals; and (3) their knowledge of text structure (Baumann 1986; Dole, Duffy, Roehler, and Pearson 1991; Garcia and Pearson 1990).

Traditionally, the strategy of determining what is important has been taught as an isolated skill—identifying the main idea (expository text) or recognizing theme (narrative text). To be strategic, however, students need to be taught the whole process, not just the outcome. Therefore, they need to be shown how to use their own knowledge—their general knowledge about the world and how it works as well as their specific knowledge of a relevant topic or topics—to guide them toward what is important in the text. They need to be trained to figure out an author's purpose or purposes in writing a particular text, and they need to be taught how to use the structure of a text as a signpost for determining what is important.

**16.7**

Teaching students to summarize should begin early on. Young children can begin by identifying the main idea. They can develop a single sentence that tells *who/what* and *what happens.*

> Miguel toasted two slices of bread. He put some mustard on the bread. He then put Swiss cheese on top of one slice. He placed the second slice of bread on top of the cheese.
>
> MAIN-IDEA SENTENCE: Miguel made a cheese sandwich.

> A thread snake is only a few inches long. A giant snake known as the royal python may be over thirty feet long.
>
> MAIN-IDEA SENTENCE: Snakes come in different sizes.

**16.8**

Students begin by identifying the main idea in short passages. They then practice identifying the main idea in a paragraph and an entire selection. Sometimes a main idea will be expressed as a topic sentence; sometimes students will have to infer the main idea. Summarization requires students to be able to eliminate redundant and unnecessary information. In Grade 2 and above, the strategy of summarizing usually involves creating a *written* summary of all or part of a text. An important aspect of instruction in the strategy of summarizing, therefore, is teacher feedback on the quality of a student's written summaries (Hare and Borchardt 1984).

"DRTA," p. 17.27

"QAR," p. 17.31

"K-W-L Plus," p. 18.21

"Reciprocal Teaching," p. 18.29

## Questioning

In this strategy, a reader asks questions about a text before, during, and after reading and then looks for answers. Teaching students to engage in self-questioning has been found to improve their comprehension ability (Andre and Anderson 1978–1979) and ensures that their reading is an interactive process (Graves et al. 1998).

**16.9**

To enable students to learn to generate their own questions, teachers need to pose effective questions and model how to answer them. Answering questions requires an understanding of question-answer relationships—that is, the relationship between a question and where in the text and/or the reader's background knowledge the answer can be found (Raphael and Pearson 1982).

The critical aspect of self-questioning is knowing *which* questions to ask. In Kindergarten, questioning should focus on *who? what?* and *when?* By first grade, however, students can begin to answer the more abstract questions of *why?* and *what if?* As they internalize and apply this self-questioning strategy, students learn to focus on the most important information in a text and to organize it in a meaningful way (Wood, Woloshyn, and Willoughby 1995).

## Making Inferences

"Story Grammar Elements," p. 17.20

"QAR," p. 17.31

"Text Organization," p. 18.25

"Reciprocal Teaching," p. 18.29

Readers must constantly "fill in" information not found in the text by drawing on their prior knowledge and by using textual clues. Good readers do this automatically, so they are usually unaware of the process. To learn this strategy, students must be taught to (1) draw on their prior knowledge and (2) look for clues in the text itself. Asking students inferential-level questions about what they are reading—questions that specifically draw on prior knowledge and/or text clues—is one way to make students conscious of what they need to be doing as they read. For example, students might read the opening of a story that contains the following text:

> It seemed that Tanya and Wynton were always giggling. They giggled every morning when they woke up. They giggled at meals. They giggled at school. And they giggled every night when their parents put them to bed.

After students have read this text, the teacher could ask them if they think Tanya and Wynton are related, and if so, how. When students identify them as sister and brother, the teacher would ask them how they knew: *What clues does the story provide?* (It says that they eat together and their parents put them to bed, and they giggle every night.) *How did your own experience provide clues?* (Children who eat together and have the same parents are usually brothers and sisters.)

## Visualizing

Good readers often form mental pictures as they read; that is, they visualize what is happening. In some cases, they are able to take advantage of visuals provided with the text (illustrations, photographs, graphic organizers), while in other cases they have to rely solely on the text itself. Research has shown that readers who visualize while reading, especially younger readers, have better recall of text than those who do not, and that the strategy of visualizing can easily be taught to young readers (Pressley 1977).

**See also . . .**

"Story Grammar: Beginning, Middle, and Ending," p. 17.16

"Story Grammar Elements," p. 17.20

"DRTA," p. 17.27

**16.10**

When students read stories, they need to be taught to picture what the author is describing. Sometimes this activity will be very straightforward. For example, a student might read this sentence: *The crow cawed twice and flew to the top of the tall tree.* The event described is easily imagined, since most students possess concrete images for *crow* and *tall tree.* Sometimes the text is less detailed, and readers have to create their own images. For example, when reading the sentence *Rita decided to wear her favorite dress to the party,* readers must form their own image of Rita and her party dress.

Visualizing is also effective with complex expository text. If students are reading a content-area passage that describes a process and have no visual aids at their disposal, visualizing the process not only fosters comprehension, but enhances recall of the text. Moreover, Gambrell and Bales (1986) found that by visualizing expository passages, students were able to detect when information was incomplete or inconsistent, and thus were able to determine when they needed further clarification.

# why? *Strategic Reading*

**16.12**

Research has shown that strong readers use comprehension strategies automatically when they read. Thus, teachers can improve the reading of less proficient readers by helping them internalize these effective strategies through explicit comprehension instruction (Kern 1989). In fact, less able readers who have been taught a particular strategy are often indistinguishable from good readers who use the strategy spontaneously (Hansen and Pearson 1983). In addition, researchers have found that students are able to transfer their comprehension-strategies knowledge to their independent reading if they have been carefully instructed (Griffin, Malone, and Kameenui 1995; Pressley, Symons, Snyder, and Cariglia-Bull 1989).

**Research Findings . . .**

*Skilled reading does not involve use of a single potent strategy, but rather coordination of several strategies.*

—PRESSLEY & WOLOSHYN, 1995

*Research supports the benefit of metacognitive strategies instruction for students with reading comprehension difficulties.*

—PARIS ET AL., 1991; SCHUNK & RICE, 1992

*In 89 percent of the reading studies [reviewed], metacognitive knowledge and reading comprehension were related significantly.*

—DICKSON ET AL., 1998a

*A major contribution of research has been to transform reading skills (e.g., summarize, identify main ideas, identify relations between main ideas) into explicit strategies that students can be taught directly.*

—DICKSON, SIMMONS & KAMEENUI, 1998a

**Suggested Reading . . .**

*Children's Literacy: Contexts for Meaningful Learning* (1997) by Shane Templeton. Boston: Houghton Mifflin.

*Cognitive Strategy Instruction That Really Improves Children's Academic Performance, Second Edition* (1995) edited by Michael Pressley & Vera Woloshyn. Cambridge, MA: Brookline Books.

*Cognitive Strategy Instruction for Middle and High Schools* (1995) edited by Eileen Wood, Vera Woloshyn & Teena Willoughby. Cambridge, MA: Brookline Books.

*Teaching Reading in the 21st Century* (1998) by Michael F. Graves, Connie Juel & Bonnie B. Graves. Needham Heights, MA: Allyn & Bacon.

*What Reading Research Tells Us About Children with Diverse Learning Needs: Bases and Basics* (1998) edited by Deborah C. Simmons & Edward J. Kameenui. Mahwah, NJ: Erlbaum.

**16.14**

## When to Teach and Use

Instruction in comprehension skills and strategies should begin as soon as students begin to interact with text. Teachers should start building a foundation in Kindergarten for the strategies that will be developed throughout the school years. They should read aloud a variety of texts and engage students in making predictions, visualizing details, summarizing important events, and using prior knowledge to construct meaning. As students progress through the grades, they will extend and apply these comprehension strategies to increasingly complex texts.

A crucial component of comprehension instruction at each grade is teaching students *when* to use a particular strategy. Although strategic reading must be fluid and flexible, some reading strategies are better suited to certain parts of the comprehension process. Students should be aware that they can use specific strategies in preparation for reading, specific strategies to increase the effectiveness of reading, and specific strategies to increase memory of what they read (Pressley and Woloshyn 1995). Reading instruction is typically divided into Before Reading, During Reading, and After Reading. Teachers can use this framework to implement the key comprehension strategies as shown in the chart on the facing page.

See also...

**Chapter 17: Narrative Text**

**Chapter 18: Expository Text**

for explicit instruction in comprehension strategies

| | Goal | Comprehension Strategy |
|---|---|---|
| **Before Reading** | Preparation | • Using Prior Knowledge<br>• Visualizing<br>• Predicting |
| **During Reading** | Understanding | • Predicting<br>• Identifying the Main Idea and Summarization<br>• Questioning<br>• Visualizing<br>• Making Inferences |
| **After Reading** | Retention | • Questioning<br>• Identifying the Main Idea and Summarization<br>• Visualizing |

16.15

## When to Assess and Intervene

Assessment of comprehension begins early, generally in Kindergarten, through listening and retelling experiences. Teachers read stories aloud to students, who "retell" events, characters, and settings. Teachers may also provide short, verbal instructions for students to follow as a way to assess listening comprehension, which correlates closely with reading comprehension (Duker 1965). Teachers can informally assess students' use of pictures and context to predict story content, and encourage students to ask and answer *who, what, when, where,* and *how* questions; follow written instructions; and restate central ideas.

As students progress through the grades, they can be expected to answer questions that call for facts and details, inferences, and interpretations supported by text evidence. Comprehension may be determined through cloze passage assessments (passages with blanks representing missing vocabulary that must be determined), through multiple-choice assessments, and

**16.16**

through open-ended questions. Student work samples, such as graphic organizers and reading logs, can also provide ways to assess students' comprehension. Finally, listening in on book discussions can be a useful daily check for comprehension.

Intervention should be considered for students who have difficulty repeating information from oral instructions or stories read aloud. Students who have weak comprehension because their decoding skills are not yet sufficiently automatic to enable them to concentrate fully on constructing meaning may simply need more fluency practice. Students who have comprehension difficulty due to limited vocabulary or inefficient use of self-monitoring strategies will benefit from explicit strategies instruction.

**Upper-Grade Intervention**   Comprehension-strategies instruction intervention, especially for struggling upper-grade students, needs to be explicit and scaffolded. The best intervention generally makes use of routines and repeated procedures, organizers, and visual aids. Memory aids, such as mnemonic devices, may help students to recall the steps of a procedure described in text. Recitation has also been shown to improve comprehension. As always, instruction should include ample opportunities for monitored practice.

**See also . . .**

CORE Assessing Reading

"Resources for Assessing Reading"

## Comprehension Assessments

| CORE Assessing Reading | Other |
| --- | --- |
| McLeod Assessment of Reading Comprehension | Informal Reading Inventories (IRIs) |
| | Reading program assessments |
| | Teacher observation |

# Narrative Text

what?
why?
when?
how?

**17.2**

Written text tends to fall into one of two broad categories—expository text, which communicates information, persuades, or explains; and *narrative text,* which tells a story. Narrative text may be the invention of an author, the reporting of factual events, or the retelling of a tale from oral tradition. By the time most children enter school, they have some familiarity with narrative text because they have had stories read to them and watched stories on TV and in the movies. Narrative text reflects the familiar flow of a child's everyday life—each day has a beginning, middle, and ending. For these reasons, comprehension instruction begins with narrative text.

## Story Grammar

Understanding how text is organized helps readers construct meaning (Dickson, Simmons, and Kameenui 1998b). Most narrative texts are organized around a set of elements referred to as *story grammar.* The key story grammar elements of a story are setting, characters, plot, and theme. Instruction in story grammars benefits reading comprehension. Making students aware of story grammar provides them with a schema they can draw on when approaching a new story; it gives them a framework for constructing meaning. Story grammar elements provide students with an "anchor" when they are listening to

See also . . .

**Chapter 16: Strategic Reading**

# Story Grammar Elements

stories, recalling them, and eventually writing their own. In addition, story grammar can be used to teach higher-level comprehension skills (California State Board of Education 1999). Narrative text contains the following story grammar elements:

**Setting**   The setting of a story tells *when* the story takes place and *where* it takes place. Some stories have very specific settings—the date and location are identified by the author. Other stories take place at some indefinite time (e.g., in the future) or in some indefinite place (e.g., an unnamed country). Moreover, the setting can change within a narrative, shifting to another location or shifting in time—moving back (flashback) or jumping ahead (flashforward) before returning to the main time frame of the story.

**Characters**   Characters are the people or animals in a story. The main character can be called the *protagonist* of the story. The main character moves the action forward, sometimes by acting against a villain or rival, the *antagonist.* To understand a character, readers must be able to tap into the author's characterization techniques: what the author states directly about the character; what the character says, does, and thinks; and how other story characters react and respond to the character. In folktales and fables, characters often exhibit exaggerated traits: the clever hero, his foolish but kind friend, and the evil villain. In most narratives, character traits are directly stated *and* implicitly conveyed by what the characters say, think, and do. The main character's motivation drives the plot. The motivations of secondary characters often create complications for the main character. Sometimes the author makes these motives explicit; but often, understanding a character's motivation calls for a reader to make inferences.

**17.4**

**Plot**   The plot of a story tells what happened. It gives the story a beginning, middle, and ending. The plot is the action of the story. As students tackle more complex stories, they will encounter more complicated plots that may contain multiple storylines or that use flashbacks and flashforwards. In general, the plot of a narrative consists of the following:

- a *problem* that the main character has to solve (sometimes referred to as the initiating event);

- the *steps* the character takes to solve this problem (sometimes called the rising action);

- the *resolution* of the character's problem (the *outcome* of the story);

- how the story *ends* (the falling action, or denouement).

**Theme**   The theme is the center of a narrative text. It is the big idea that the author wants the reader to take away from reading the story. Often, the conclusion of a story reveals its underlying theme. In folktales or fables, the theme is usually the moral of the story. In most narratives, however, the reader has to infer the theme.

## When to Teach

In Kindergarten, students begin to identify the setting, the characters, and the beginning, middle, and ending of a simple plot. They use their knowledge of these story grammar elements to retell familiar stories that they have listened to. In first through third grades, students deepen their understanding of setting and characters, and learn about other story grammar elements: for example, problem, outcome, theme. Students incorporate these story grammar elements into written and oral story retellings. In fourth grade and above, students explore character traits and motivations.

## Instructional Techniques and Procedures

To improve and enhance comprehension of narrative text, teachers can use a number of techniques and procedures.

### Story Maps

**See also . . .**

"Story Grammar: Beginning, Middle, and Ending," p. 17.16

"Story Grammar Elements," p. 17.20

A story map is a graphic representation of the story grammar of a narrative. Story maps come in a number of different formats that can be used for particular purposes. For example, some story maps focus on a single story grammar element, while others include multiple elements. According to Shane Templeton (1997), story maps serve two main purposes: (1) For teachers, story maps help to identify the important elements in an upcoming story, thereby helping them focus their instruction; (2) For students, viewing a story map helps them focus on the significant elements of narratives—title, setting, characters, problem, important events, outcome, and theme—and on the relationship among these elements.

## Types of Story Maps

**Appendix**

"Story Map: Beginning, Middle, and Ending"

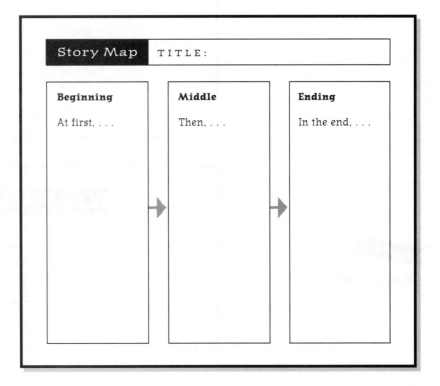

CONTINUED ▷

## Types of Story Maps

**17.6**

**"Story Map: Story Grammar Elements"**

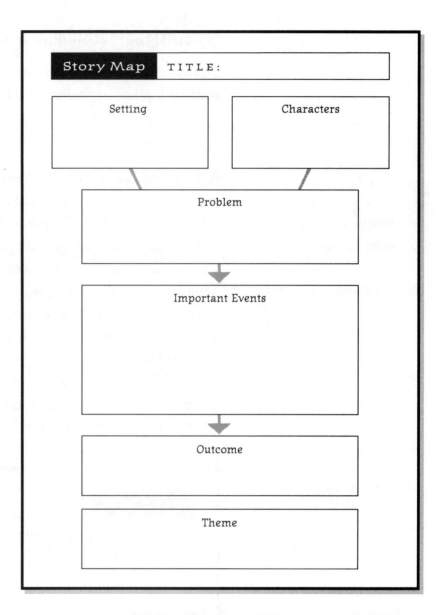

**"Character Weave"**

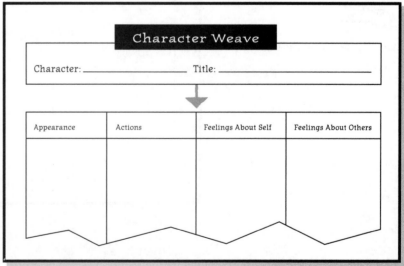

## Retelling

Retelling stories has been shown to help students understand what they read and develop their "sense of story" (Morrow 1986). As they retell what they have just read or heard, students must synthesize and organize information, make inferences, and draw on their prior knowledge. Teachers can use the retelling to gather information about student comprehension and guide the student toward a deeper understanding of a story. For example, a student's retelling may focus strictly on a literal level of understanding. By asking questions that make the student draw conclusions, the teacher can get him or her to explore the story on a more inferential level.

Brown and Cambourne (1987) noticed that as students become more competent readers, their retellings become more sophisticated. This is because students' accumulated experiences with stories and the subjects within them provide the schema to drive their retellings. When evaluating a student's retelling, teachers should look for certain developmental elements.

## Types of Retellings

**Simple descriptive retelling:**
- Has beginning, middle, and ending in order;
- May describe a setting;
- Presents an initiating event and the outcome of a problem.

**More complex retelling:**
- Presents concrete events and facts in sequence;
- Supplies missing information through appropriate inferences;
- Includes some explanations for causes of actions.

**Most complete retelling:**
- Presents a sequence of actions and events;
- Supplies missing information to account for actions;
- Provides explanations for the motivation behind the characters' actions;
- Elaborates points and may comment on or evaluate what was read.

**17.8**

## Retelling Feedback Form

✔ Did my partner tell about the setting?   YES or NO

✔ Did my partner tell about the characters?   YES or NO

✔ Did my partner tell what happened in the story   YES or NO
in the correct order?

✔ The best part of the retelling was . . . _____

_____

Students need explicit instruction on how to construct a retelling, with the teacher explaining why the process is useful, providing a model, and giving practice and feedback. Although students benefit from initially practicing retelling with the teacher—either one-on-one or in a group—they can quickly move on to retell stories to one another, during independent work time. These student retelling sessions are even more effective if they are interactive. For example, after the retelling the listener may provide feedback by using the form above.

"DRTA," p. 17.27

### DRTA (Directed Reading and Thinking Activity)

DRTA (Directed Reading and Thinking Activity) was developed by Russell Stauffer. The purpose of this approach is to teach students how to make and verify predictions throughout their reading. As Stauffer (1975) explains, in a DRTA the students take part in a predict-read-prove cycle to set a purpose for reading, processing ideas, and testing answers. The teacher

# DRTA

**Predict**

What do you think will happen next?

**Read with a Purpose**

Read the next two pages to see if you are right.

**Prove**

Were you right? Can you prove it?

stops at several points throughout the text and asks students to predict what will happen next. To begin, the teacher selects a short, engaging story with a plot that has two or three good stopping points.

**Predict**   The teacher asks questions to help students use the text and their own knowledge to make predictions about what they are going to read. For example, the teacher might ask: *Based on the title, what do you think this story is about?*

**Read with a Purpose**   The teacher directs students to read a prescribed segment of text to find out whether or not their predictions are accurate. Checking the predictions becomes the reader's purpose for reading.

**Prove**   After students have finished reading the prescribed text segment, they are asked to find and read aloud text that supports their findings. For example, the teacher might ask: *Was your prediction right? What makes you think so?* Students either prove why their predictions were accurate or show how the story turned out differently than they had expected.

As the cycle repeats itself, the teacher asks students to review and revise their predictions or formulate new predictions for the upcoming segment. Students then read this segment, stop at the prescribed point, and, with the teacher, examine their most recent predictions, citing proof from the text. Teachers often find it helpful to record students' predictions on the board. Any predictions that are disproved by story events or discarded by students as unlikely are crossed out or erased. At the end of the story, the teacher and students review the predictions and text "evidence."

"QAR," p. 17.31

17.10

## QAR (Question-Answer Relationships)

QAR is a method developed by Taffy Raphael (1982) for enhancing students' ability to answer comprehension questions. It is based on the idea that a three-way relationship exists among the question, the text to which it refers, and the reader's prior knowledge (Pearson and Johnson 1978). The effectiveness of the procedure "lies in the way it clarifies how students can approach the task of reading texts and answering questions" (Raphael 1986). If students understand the distinction between the sources of information for answering questions (In the Text or In My Head), they are on their way to becoming efficient, strategic readers (Templeton 1997). The four types of Question-Answer Relationships are Right There, Think and Search, On My Own, and Author and Me.

## QAR STRATEGY

| Source of Information | Type of QAR (Question-Answer Relationship) |
|---|---|
| **IN THE TEXT** <br> Information comes primarily from the text itself. | **RIGHT THERE** (literal) <br> The answer to the question is "right there" in one sentence; the question and answer have the same wording. |
| | **THINK AND SEARCH** (literal) <br> The answer to the question requires searching across the text; the question and answer have different wordings. |
| **IN MY HEAD** <br> Information comes from students' own prior knowledge. | **ON MY OWN** (inferential and evaluative) <br> The answer to the question comes entirely from students' prior knowledge, without even reading the text. |
| **IN MY HEAD & IN THE TEXT** | **AUTHOR AND ME** (inferential) <br> The answer to the question comes from students' prior knowledge and text clues provided by the author. |

Here is an example of the QAR strategy, using the following short passage:

> Lucy was kayaking down the Snake River.
>
> She was approaching the treacherous rapids.
>
> All of a sudden, she found herself
>
> in the cold swirling water.

| Sample Question | Sample Answer | QAR |
|---|---|---|
| Where was Lucy kayaking? | Lucy was kayaking down the Snake River. | RIGHT THERE |
| Where are the treacherous rapids? | The treacherous rapids are on the Snake River. | THINK AND SEARCH |
| Do you think Lucy will make it safely to shore? Why? | No, she may not be a good swimmer and her clothes might be wet and heavy. | ON MY OWN |
| What caused Lucy to fall into the water? | The kayak tipped over and she fell in. | AUTHOR AND ME |

Connect to Theory

Using the passage about Lucy and the kayak, plus information from the tables on this page and the facing page, explain why you think each question-answer pair represents the identified QAR.

*(See Appendix for possible answers.)*

QAR instructional strategy follows a gradual-release format. Lesson One is totally teacher-directed; the lessons that follow gradually give students more responsibility. Raphael (1982) provides some suggested lesson formats.

**17.12**

## QAR INSTRUCTIONAL STRATEGY

| **Lesson One** | • Explicit instruction and modeling of QAR concepts and terminology<br>• Passage: two to three sentences in length<br>• Number of questions: four per passage (one from each QAR category) |
|---|---|
| | **Stage 1**<br>Teacher provides: passage, questions, answers, and QARs<br>Students will: discuss why question-answer pairs represent their respective QARs |
| | **Stage 2**<br>Teacher provides: passage, questions, answers<br>Students will: identify and explain the QAR for each question-answer pair |
| | **Stage 3**<br>Teacher provides: passage, questions<br>Students will: identify and explain the answer and QAR for each question |
| **Lesson Two** | • Review of QAR concepts and terminology<br>• Passage: 75 to 150 words<br>• Number of questions: up to five per passage (at least one from each QAR category) |
| | Teacher provides: passage, questions, answers<br>Students will: identify and explain the QAR for each question-answer pair |

| **Lesson Three** | • Review of QAR concepts and terminology |
| | • Passage: 150 to 600 words, divided into four sections |
| | • Number of questions: four questions per section |

Teacher provides: passage, questions

Students will: identify, write, and explain the answers and QARs for each question-answer pair

**17.13**

| **Lesson Four** | • Review of QAR concepts and terminology |
| | • Passage: 600 to 800 words |
| | • Number of questions: six questions per QAR category |

Teacher provides: passage

Students will: develop and write the questions and answers, and identify the QAR category

Guidelines for Effective Questioning

- Use clear phrasing.
- Avoid multiple-part questions.
- Allow greater response time before you comment.
- Listen carefully to students' responses.
- Provide tactful modeling of correct grammar.
- Encourage students to elaborate.
- Create a supportive atmosphere.

# why? *Narrative Text*

**17.14**

Teaching students the basic structure of narrative text gives them a frame of reference for processing and storing information (Dickson et al. 1998b). The frame of reference for narrative text is typically story grammar. Studies focusing on the use of story grammars (Pearson and Fielding 1991; Graesser, Golding, and Long 1991) show that they are useful tools for constructing meaning. As readers learn story grammar they become strategic in their reading—predicting upcoming events, confirming their predictions, visualizing characters and setting, and summarizing in order to recall or retell the story at a later time. In short, by applying knowledge of story grammar to uncover the structure of narrative text, students become adept, strategic readers.

**Research Findings . . .**

*Awareness of text structures is an important metacognitive skill that should be made a part of learning to read and write.*

—IRVIN, 1998

*Narrative text instruction has proven to be particularly effective with younger and poorer readers.*

—SHORT & RYAN, 1984

*Narrative text instruction, or story grammar instruction, seems particularly successful for students with learning disabilities.*

—MONTAGUE, MADDUX & DERESHIWSKY, 1990

*The structure of story grammar acts as a model which can be used as a strategy to improve both story comprehension and writing.*

—OLSON & GEE, 1988

**17.15**

**Suggested Reading . . .**

*Cognitive Strategy Instruction for Middle and High Schools* (1995) edited by Eileen Wood, Vera Woloshyn & Teena Willoughby. Cambridge, MA: Brookline Books.

*I Can Fly: Teaching Narratives and Reading Comprehension to African American and Other Ethnic Minority Students* (1999) by Angela Marshall Rickford. Lanham, MD: University Press of America.

*Reading and the Middle School Student: Strategies to Enhance Literacy* (1998) by Judith L. Irvin. Needham Heights, MA: Allyn & Bacon.

*Teaching the Integrated Language Arts* (1997) by Shane Templeton. Boston: Houghton Mifflin.

*What Reading Research Tells Us About Children with Diverse Learning Needs: Bases and Basics* (1998) edited by Deborah C. Simmons & Edward J. Kameenui. Mahwah, NJ: Erlbaum.

**17.16**

### Benchmarks

- ability to identify and describe a story's beginning, middle, and ending
- ability to retell the sequence of events in a story

### Grade Level

- Kindergarten and above

### Grouping

- whole class
- small group or pairs

### Prerequisite

- conceptual understanding of beginning, middle, and ending

### Materials

- drawing paper
- crayons or markers
- masking tape
- copies of "Common Sense: An Anansi Tale" (see Appendix)
- transparency of "Story Map: Beginning, Middle, and Ending" (see Appendix)
- overhead projector

## STORY GRAMMAR: BEGINNING, MIDDLE, AND ENDING

Using the story map format, this generic teaching strategy introduces the three basic parts of a story plot: beginning, middle, and ending.

### Introduce the Strategy

Tell students that they are going to make a story map to help them identify a story's beginning, middle, and ending. Explain that the beginning of a story tells what happened first, the middle of a story tells what happened next, and the ending of a story tells what happened last. Reread or retell a familiar story, such as "The Three Billy Goats Gruff." Divide the class into three groups. Tell one group to draw pictures of three hungry goats (beginning); the second group to draw pictures of the troll on the bridge (middle); and the third group to draw pictures of three goats eating happily (ending).

Print on the board the terms *Beginning*, *Middle*, and *Ending* and read them aloud. Then, one at a time, call on members of each group to tape their drawings on the board below the appropriate term. When all the drawings are displayed, point to each set of drawings, in sequence, and use the following Think Aloud.

For Kindergarten, depending on the ability of your students, you may wish to end this lesson after the Think Aloud.

**THINK ALOUD** *This is what happens at the beginning of the story: Three hungry goats decide to cross the bridge to look for food. When the first two goats try to cross, the troll stops them, but they each convince the troll to let them pass. That's what happens in the middle of the story. Finally, the third and biggest goat knocks the troll off the bridge, and they all happily eat grass on the other side of the bridge. That's what happens in the ending of the story.*

17.17

Using an overhead projector, display the Story Map. Print the title of the story on the map. Point out and discuss the sentence starters *At first, Then,* and *In the end.* Then model for students how to use the terms, sentence starters, and pictures to orally retell the sequence of events in the story. An example of a completed story map is shown below.

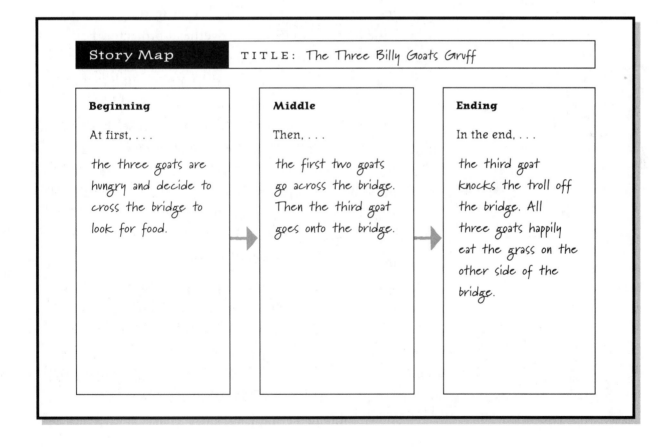

| Story Map | TITLE: The Three Billy Goats Gruff |
| --- | --- |

| **Beginning** | **Middle** | **Ending** |
| --- | --- | --- |
| At first, . . . | Then, . . . | In the end, . . . |
| the three goats are hungry and decide to cross the bridge to look for food. | the first two goats go across the bridge. Then the third goat goes onto the bridge. | the third goat knocks the troll off the bridge. All three goats happily eat the grass on the other side of the bridge. |

17.18

### Common Sense: An Anansi Tale

INDEPENDENT READING LEVEL:

GRADE 3

**BUILD BACKGROUND**   Tell students that Anansi the spider is a West African folk hero known for his cleverness. Anansi loves to plan and scheme, trying to outsmart everyone. Sometimes, Anansi comes up with a clever plan and finds smart solutions to puzzling problems. Other times, he winds up causing lots of mischief.

**INTRODUCE VOCABULARY**   Select and introduce the unfamiliar words and/or concepts in the story. See Section VI: Vocabulary Development for suggestions and strategies.

## Apply the Strategy

Read aloud to students or have students read independently "Common Sense: An Anansi Tale." After reading the story, display the Story Map using the overhead projector. Point out the title of the story and print it on the Story Map. If necessary, explain that common sense is "ordinary good judgment that a person learns from experience, not from school." Remind students that, like most stories, "Common Sense" has a beginning, where the reader meets the main character(s) and learns what problem he faces; a middle, where the character tries to solve the problem; and an ending, where the reader learns if the character is successful or not. Then guide students to identify the beginning, middle, and ending of the story. Start by asking students how the story begins. Use their responses to complete the first section of the map. If students have difficulty recalling or are in disagreement, reread paragraph one of the story aloud. Explain that it is a good idea to look back at a story when filling in a story map. Next, have students determine what happens in the middle and at the ending of the story. Then as a class, complete the remaining sections of the story map. An example of a completed story map is shown on the facing page.

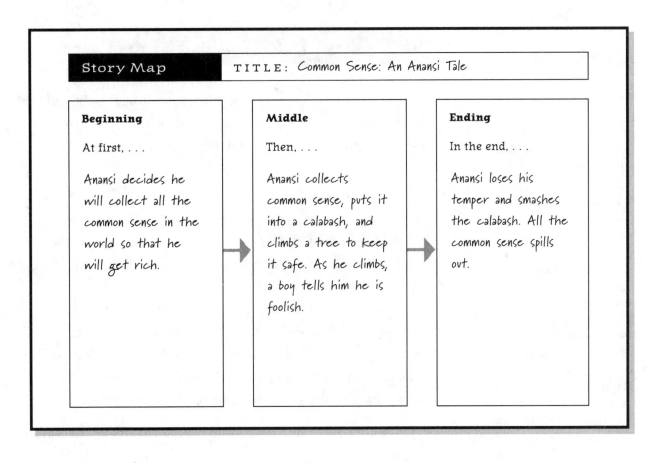

**Story Map**     TITLE: *Common Sense: An Anansi Tale*

**Beginning**

At first, . . .

Anansi decides he will collect all the common sense in the world so that he will get rich.

**Middle**

Then, . . .

Anansi collects common sense, puts it into a calabash, and climbs a tree to keep it safe. As he climbs, a boy tells him he is foolish.

**Ending**

In the end, . . .

Anansi loses his temper and smashes the calabash. All the common sense spills out.

**"Retelling Feedback Form," p. 17.8**

**RETELL THE STORY**    Have pairs of students take turns using the completed Story Map to orally retell the story. Tell pairs to make sure that their partner retells what happened in the story in the correct order, or sequence.

**OBSERVE AND ASSESS**

*As students retell the story, provide feedback and use these questions to assess their retellings.*

| Questions for Observation | Benchmark |
| --- | --- |
| In the story, what happened first? Then what happened? What happened last? | Student can identify the sequence of events by retelling the beginning, middle, and ending of a story. |

## Reflect and Respond

Invite students to tell, dictate, or write a different ending to this story in which Anansi is successful in collecting all the common sense in the world.

# Narrative Text

### Benchmarks

- ability to identify and describe a story's characters, setting, plot, and theme.
- ability to retell the central ideas of a simple narrative passage

**17.20**

### Grade Level

Grade 2 and above

### Grouping

- whole class
- small group or pairs

### Materials

- copies of "Common Sense: An Anansi Tale" (see Appendix)
- copies of "Story Map: Story Grammar Elements" (see Appendix)
- transparency of "Story Map: Story Grammar Elements" (see Appendix)
- copies of "Character Weave" (see Appendix)
- overhead projector

## STORY GRAMMAR ELEMENTS

Using a story map format, this generic teaching strategy introduces the story grammar elements: title, setting, characters, problem, important events, outcome, and theme.

## Introduce the Strategy

Reread or retell a familiar story, such as "The Three Little Pigs." After reading or retelling the story, display the Story Map using the overhead projector. Explain to students that all stories contain the same elements: title, a setting, characters, a plot, and a theme. Tell students that they will use a story map to help them identify key story elements. Then point to and explain each of the story elements on the Story Map.

- Point out that "The Three Little Pigs" is the title of the story.

- Tell students that a setting is where and when a story takes place. Ask: *Where and when does this story take place?* Record students' responses in the Setting box.

- Explain that characters are the people or animals the story is about. The main character is involved in most of the action in a story and often faces a villain. Ask: *Who are the main characters in this story?* Record students' responses in the Characters box.

- Then explain that the plot of a story tells what happened; it gives a story a beginning, middle, and ending. The plot usually involves a problem that the main character or characters face. Ask: *What is the Three Little Pigs' problem?* Record students' responses in the Problem box.

- Now tell students that important events are the things that happen in the story, or what the main characters do. Ask: *What are the main things that happen in the story?* Record students' responses in the Important Events box.

- Next, explain that the outcome of a story tells whether or not the problem was solved, and that it is often the ending of the story. Ask: *Did the Three Little Pigs solve their problem? How?* Record students' responses in the Outcome box.

- Finally, tell students that a theme is the big idea the author wants to make. In a fable, the theme may be a moral or important message. Ask: *What is the theme of the story?* Record students' responses in the Theme box. Use the following Think Aloud to help students understand the theme—the least concrete aspect of the story.

**THINK ALOUD**    *I think this story has a message. The first two pigs were lazy and waited until the last minute to build their houses, wanting to play instead. They used straw and sticks because they are easy to carry. But their houses were weak and the wolf almost got them. The third pig wasn't lazy and didn't mind hard work. Instead of playing, he worked hard to build a solid house. I think the story is trying to say that hard work is important and pays off.*

Model for students how to use the completed Story Map to orally retell the story. An example of a completed story map is shown on the next page.

**17.22**

## Story Map    TITLE: The Three Little Pigs

| Setting | Characters |
|---|---|
| once upon a time<br>the woods | Three Little Pigs<br>Big Bad Wolf |

### Problem

The Big Bad Wolf wants to eat the Three Little Pigs.

### Important Events

1. One Little Pig builds a house of straw, but the wolf huffs and puffs and blows it down.
2. The pig runs to the second Little Pig, who builds a house of sticks. The wolf huffs and puffs and blows his house down, too.
3. The two pigs run to the third Little Pig, who builds a house of bricks. The wolf huffs and puffs but can't blow it down.

### Outcome

The third pig builds a house that is so strong the wolf can't blow it down. The wolf gives up and goes away.

### Theme

Hard work pays off.

**Common Sense:
An Anansi Tale**

INDEPENDENT READING LEVEL:

GRADE 3

**BUILD BACKGROUND** See Build Background, p. 17.18.

**INTRODUCE VOCABULARY** Select and introduce the unfamiliar words and/or concepts in the story. See Section VI: Vocabulary Development for suggestions and strategies.

17.23

## Apply the Strategy

Read aloud to students or have students read independently "Common Sense: An Anansi Tale." After reading the story, distribute copies of the Story Map to students and display it using the overhead projector. Tell students that they are going to use the Story Map to help them understand and remember what they read. Then guide students to identify the title, setting, characters, and problem. Use their responses to complete the first four parts of the map. Then work with students to determine the first important event. Ask students to copy onto their own story maps what you filled in on the transparency.

Then have students work in small groups to complete the rest of the Story Map. Point out that if they have trouble recalling or agreeing on what happened, they can reread portions of the story aloud. Before students begin, direct their attention to the Outcome box. Explain that in some stories the main characters manage to solve their problems, while the characters in other stories fail. When filling in this box, students should ask themselves: "Does Anansi fail or succeed?" An example of a completed story map is shown on the next page.

**17.24**

## Story Map    TITLE: Common Sense: An Anansi Tale

### Setting

jungle

### Characters

Anansi (main)

small boy

### Problem

Anansi wants to collect all the common sense in the world
so that he can sell it and get rich.

### Important Events

1. Anansi travels everywhere, collecting common sense.
2. He puts the common sense in a calabash.
3. He ties the calabash around his neck and begins to climb a tree.
4. A boy tells him to use common sense and tie the calabash
   on his back.
5. Anansi smashes the calabash against the tree.

### Outcome

Anansi's plan fails. The common sense scatters.

### Theme

It is foolish to think that you can "have it all."

"Retelling Feedback Form," p. 17.8

RETELL THE STORY   Using their completed story maps, have students work individually or in pairs to develop an oral or written retelling of the story. Tell students to make sure that their retellings include a description of the story setting.

**17.25**

**OBSERVE AND ASSESS**

*As students complete their story maps, provide feedback and use these questions to assess their progress.*

| Questions for Observation | Benchmarks |
|---|---|
| Where and when does the story take place? | Student can identify the setting of a story. |
| Who is the main character in the story? | Student can identify the main character. |
| What is the main character's problem? | Student can identify the main character's problem. |
| What happens in the story? | Student can identify the plot by retelling important events in sequence. |
| What is the outcome of the story? How was the problem resolved? | Student can identify the outcome of the story. |
| What is the author's message? | Student can identify the theme of a story. |

## Reflect and Respond

A Character Weave map can be useful for stories that focus on a character with distinctive traits. Guide students in filling out the Character Weave for the story. Then have them use the information in the Character Weave to answer questions such as: *How would you describe Anansi? Why does he behave the way he does? What character trait led to Anansi's downfall?* An example of a completed Character Weave is shown on the next page.

17.26

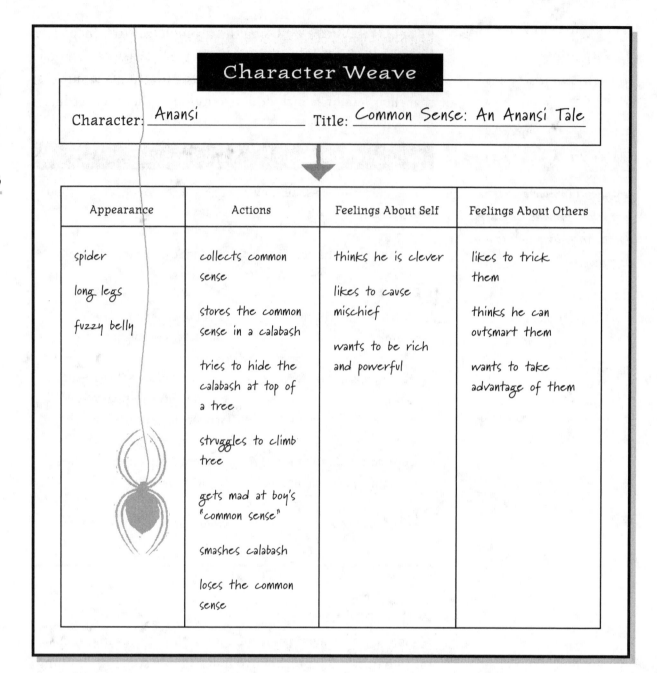

## Character Weave

Character: Anansi          Title: Common Sense: An Anansi Tale

| Appearance | Actions | Feelings About Self | Feelings About Others |
|---|---|---|---|
| spider<br><br>long legs<br><br>fuzzy belly | collects common sense<br><br>stores the common sense in a calabash<br><br>tries to hide the calabash at top of a tree<br><br>struggles to climb tree<br><br>gets mad at boy's "common sense"<br><br>smashes calabash<br><br>loses the common sense | thinks he is clever<br><br>likes to cause mischief<br><br>wants to be rich and powerful | likes to trick them<br><br>thinks he can outsmart them<br><br>wants to take advantage of them |

### Benchmark

• ability to use text information to make, verify, and adjust predictions

### Grade Level

Grade 3 and above

### Grouping

• whole class
• small group or pairs
• individual

### Materials

• copies of "Common Sense: An Anansi Tale" (see Appendix)
• Prediction/Proof Sheets (see p. 17.29)

## DRTA (DIRECTED READING AND THINKING ACTIVITY)

This generic teaching strategy guides students in predicting what a story will be about and what will happen at each stage of the plot. Students make and verify predictions and then explain their reasoning by using the text along with their background knowledge.

17.27

---

**Common Sense: An Anansi Tale**

INDEPENDENT READING LEVEL:

GRADE 3

**BUILD BACKGROUND** See Build Background, p. 17.18.

**INTRODUCE VOCABULARY** Select and introduce the unfamiliar words and/or concepts in the story. See Section VI: Vocabulary Development for suggestions and strategies.

## Introduce and Apply the Strategy

Distribute copies of "Common Sense: An Anansi Tale" to students. Tell them that they are going to learn how to become more active readers, able to understand and retain more of what they read. Explain that they are going to read the story in sections, using the text along with their own knowledge to make predictions about what will happen next. After making their predictions, they will read to find out if their predictions are correct.

Intervention
Strategy

**Depending on student
abilities, students can listen
to the story read aloud, have a
partner read the story, or read
the story independently.**

## READ TITLE AND AUTHOR LINES

*Preview the Story*   Ask students to preview the story by reading the title and author lines aloud, and by giving them an opportunity to skim through the story. Ask students to predict what the story will be about based on their prior knowledge and the text.

## READ PARAGRAPH 1

*Predict*   Ask students to read the first paragraph of the story. Work with them to predict what will happen in the story. List their predictions on the board. If a prediction is totally unfounded, ask students to explain what led to the prediction. Then point out the lack of text evidence. It is helpful to print students' initials beside their predictions.

## READ PARAGRAPHS 2–5

*Read with a Purpose*   Have students read paragraphs 2 through 5 to find out if their predictions are accurate.

*Prove*   When they are ready, ask students whether or not the story is turning out the way they had predicted. Model how to use the text to verify or adjust their predictions. For example, if a student predicted that the story would be about how Anansi collects common sense, direct students' attention to the following lines in the fifth paragraph: "Then he traveled all over the world, collecting common sense from everyone . . . Anansi did not stop until he had all of the common sense he could find." If a student predicted that Anansi would be too lazy to collect the common sense, have the student revise that prediction based on what has just been read. Adjust the predictions listed on the board, crossing out any that students have discarded and revising existing ones as needed.

*Predict*   Have students generate new predictions about what will happen next, based on what they have read so far. They might predict that Anansi will try to find a safe place to keep the common sense. They might be more specific and predict where he will hide it. Again, list students' predictions on the board with their initials.

**READ PARAGRAPHS 6–8**

*Read with a Purpose*   Have students read paragraphs 6 through 8 to find out if their predictions are accurate.

*Prove*   Again, discuss students' predictions, identifying portions of the text that confirm or contradict their predictions. Help students discard or revise their predictions, as needed. Make sure that students always refer to the text to prove their points.

*Predict*   Students can work in small groups for the remaining cycle of predicting, reading with a purpose, and proving. Make and then distribute copies of a Prediction/Proof Sheet such as the one shown below. Ask students to work together to make predictions about what will happen in the ending of the story, based on what they have read so far. Tell them to record their predictions on the sheets. If students have difficulty, suggest that they try to predict the source of the "voice," and whether or not Anansi will succeed in doing what he set out to do. Circulate among the groups as they fill out the sheets, providing assistance and feedback.

## Prediction/Proof Sheet

| Prediction | Proof |
|---|---|
|  |  |
|  |  |
|  |  |
|  |  |
|  |  |

**READ PARAGRAPHS 9–14**

*Read with a Purpose*  To verify their predictions, have students read from paragraph 9 to the end of the story. Suggest that as they read they use the Proof column on their Prediction/Proof Sheets to record the story text that confirms their predictions. Tell them that if they come across text that disproves or contradicts a prediction, they should revise the prediction and record the supporting text.

*Prove*  Discuss students' completed Prediction/Proof Sheets, encouraging them to share predictions that were accurate as well as those that were disproved. Use students' predictions to review the story. Ask: *What did you know about Anansi that helped you predict the ending? Did you expect him to succeed or fail? Why?* Help students see that Anansi's pride and foolishness are evident from the beginning of the story, which is a cue to the reader that Anansi won't be successful in his quest.

**OBSERVE AND ASSESS**

*As students complete their Prediction/Proof Sheets, provide feedback and use these questions to assess their progress.*

| Questions for Observation | Benchmarks |
|---|---|
| What do you predict will happen in the ending of the story? | Student can use the story text to make predictions. |
| Was your prediction accurate? | Student can read and locate evidence to support or disprove the prediction. |
| If your prediction wasn't accurate, how did you revise it? | Student can alter the prediction based on text evidence. |

## Reflect and Respond

Ask students the following question: *If Anansi asked you for three pieces of common sense to add to his calabash, what would you give him?* After discussing various responses, have students make lists naming the three pieces of common sense. Encourage volunteers to share their lists with the class.

## QAR (QUESTION-ANSWER RELATIONSHIPS)

### Benchmarks

- ability to answer factual, inferential, and evaluative questions
- ability to ask factual, inferential, and evaluative questions
- ability to use background knowledge to answer questions

### Grade Level

Grade 3 and above

### Grouping

- whole class
- small group or pairs

### Materials

- copies of "Common Sense: An Anansi Tale" (see Appendix)
- transparency of "Common Sense: An Anansi Tale" (see Appendix)
- overhead projector
- index cards (four per student)

This generic teaching strategy clarifies for students how to approach the task of reading texts and answering questions. It helps them realize the need to consider both information in the text and information from their own background knowledge (Raphael 1984). This procedure can also be used with expository text.

17.31

- - - - - - - - - - - - - - - - - - - - - - - - - - - - -

## Introduce the Strategy

Explain to students that when they are reading, it is important to know how and where to look for answers to questions. Tell them that sometimes an answer to a question might be right there in what they are reading; other times they might have to come up with the answer by putting ideas or information together. At still other times, the answer isn't in their reading at all, but may be what they know already.

Tell students that there are two main places to find answers. Explain that one place to find answers is in what you are reading. The other place to find answers is from what you already know, or in your head.

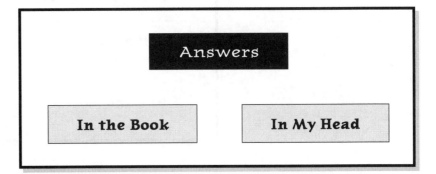

CONTINUED ▷

Explain that there are two types of In the Book answers: Right There, where you can easily find them, or Think and Search, where you may have to look a little harder.

**17.32**

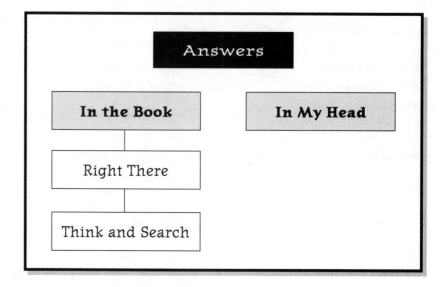

Then explain that there are two types of In My Head answers. On My Own answers come entirely from what you already know. Author and Me answers come from what you already know and what the author of the story tells you.

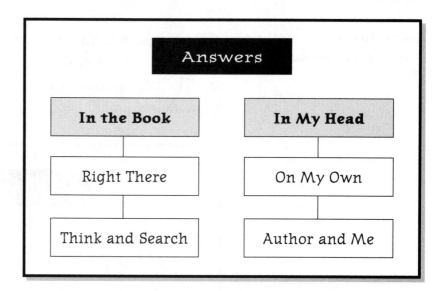

Distribute a set of four index cards to each student. Ask them to print the name of one type of answer on each of the cards: Right There, Think and Search, On My Own, Author and Me.

**Common Sense:
An Anansi Tale**

INDEPENDENT READING LEVEL:

GRADE 3

**BUILD BACKGROUND**   See Build Background, p. 17.18.

**INTRODUCE VOCABULARY**   Select and introduce the unfamiliar words and/or concepts in the story. See Section VI: Vocabulary Development for suggestions and strategies.

17.33

## Apply the Strategy

**READ PARAGRAPHS 1 AND 2**

Distribute copies of "Common Sense: An Anansi Tale." Students should have their index cards available. Using an overhead projector, display the first page of the story. Tell students to read, or read aloud to students, the first two paragraphs of the story (ending with "I can see it all now!").

Ask: *What kind of fellow is Anansi?* Then model finding the answer, circling key words on the transparency. Say: *I looked in the story to see if I could find the same wording as in the question. The second sentence has the words* tricky *and* fellow. *The answer is "Anansi is a tricky fellow." It's right there.* Then have students show the card that names this type of QAR. *(Right There)* Say: *Yes, the answer to this question is right there in the story. The question and the answer have the same wording.*

Ask: *What is Anansi's idea?* Model finding the answer, circling words that together contribute to the answer. Say: *I looked in the story and didn't see those exact words in one sentence, but I saw where it says, "an idea popped into his head," and then it said, "All I need to do is collect all the common sense in the world." So the answer to the question is "Anansi's idea is to collect all the common sense in the world."* Then have students show the card that names this type of QAR. *(Think and Search)* Say: *Yes, to answer this question I had to think and search for and then*

17.34

put together information found in different parts of the paragraph. The question and the answer do not have the same wording.

Ask: *Why is common sense important?* Model this answer. Say: *I can't find the answer to this question in the first paragraph, but I can answer the question using what I already know from my own experience. Common sense is important because good judgment is necessary to get things done.* Then have students show the card that names this type of QAR. *(On My Own)* Say: *Yes, I found the answer to this question in my head.*

Ask: *Why would having all the common sense in the world make Anansi rich?* Model finding the answer, again circling words that contribute to the answer. Say: *I can't find the exact answer to this question in the first paragraph, but the story says "people will need to come to me to find out what to do." And I know common sense is really important. I think Anansi will become rich because people need and use common sense all the time. If Anansi has it all, they will have to pay him for it.* Have students show the card that names this type of QAR. *(Author and Me)* Say: *Yes, I answered the question using what I already know from my own experience and what the author tells me. The answer was partly in the story and partly in my head.*

| Question | Answer | QAR |
|---|---|---|
| What kind of fellow is Anansi? | Anansi is a tricky fellow. | RIGHT THERE |
| What is Anansi's idea? | Anansi's idea is to collect all the common sense in the world. | THINK AND SEARCH |
| Why is common sense important? | Common sense is important because people need it in order to get things done. | ON MY OWN |
| Why would having all the common sense in the world make Anansi rich? | People need and use common sense all the time. If Anansi has it all, they will have to pay him for it. | AUTHOR AND ME |

## READ PARAGRAPHS 3–6

Have students read the next four paragraphs in the story (ending with "... keep it safe and sound."). Use the same procedure as described for paragraphs 1 and 2, but this time provide only the questions and the answers. Ask students to determine and explain the QAR for each question-answer pair. Call on volunteers to mark on the transparency the clues in the text, and to discuss how the clues helped them find the answer to a question.

| Question | Answer | QAR |
|---|---|---|
| What is a calabash? | A calabash is like a great big pumpkin. | RIGHT THERE |
| What does Anansi think will make him a powerful spider? | People will have to pay him for commonsense advice. | THINK AND SEARCH |
| Why does Anansi want to find a hiding place for the common sense? | He wants to keep it safe and sound because he doesn't want anyone to find it and take it from him. | AUTHOR AND ME |
| What are some commonsense answers to the questions that Anansi thinks people will ask him? | Take a nap. Use an umbrella. Eat something. | ON MY OWN |

## READ PARAGRAPHS 7–11

Have students work in small groups to read the next five paragraphs of the story (ending with "... just plain common sense!"). Use the same procedure as described for paragraphs 3 through 6, but this time provide only the questions. Ask students to work together to determine both the answers and the QARs. Circulate from group to group as students work, helping them locate text information to support their answers or articulate information from their experience if the text does not supply the answers.

| Question | Possible Answer | QAR |
|---|---|---|
| What does Anansi think is the perfect hiding place for the common sense? | The top of the tallest tree in the jungle. | RIGHT THERE |
| How does Anansi feel when he hears someone laughing? | He probably feels surprised and maybe afraid. He might be mad. | ON MY OWN |
| What did the thick rope do to Anansi's neck? | It burned his neck. | THINK AND SEARCH |
| Why would tying the calabash around his neck like a necklace be a foolish way for Anansi to climb the tree? | It would get in the way and bang into him. It's hard to climb a tree that way. | AUTHOR AND ME |

**READ PARAGRAPHS 12–14**

Have students continue to work in small groups to read the last three paragraphs of the story. This time, ask students to work together to determine four question-answer pairs and their corresponding QARs. As students work cooperatively, circulate and monitor their discussion.

| Possible Question | Possible Answer | QAR |
|---|---|---|
| Who was sitting on the rock? | A small boy was sitting on the rock. | RIGHT THERE |
| Why did Anansi get mad? | The small boy had a big piece of common sense. | THINK AND SEARCH |
| Why is it common sense to wear a coat on a cold day? | The coat will keep you warm. | ON MY OWN |
| How would you describe Anansi's personality? | He has a bad temper. | AUTHOR AND ME |

## Reflect and Respond

Discuss with students how they would rate their own common sense on a scale from 1 to 10. Ask them to provide examples to support their ratings. Students can write a short essay about the subject.

CHAPTER

# 18

# Expository Text

what?
why?
when?
how?

# what? *Expository Text*

While narrative text tells a story, *expository text* provides an explanation of facts and concepts. Its main purpose is to inform, persuade, or explain. As students progress through school, they devote most of their reading time to expository texts. In each new piece of expository text, readers face the challenge of uncovering its organizational pattern—understanding the presentation, relationship, and hierarchy of ideas. Reading and understanding expository text involves more abstract thinking than does reading and understanding the typical narrative. Students need to compare and contrast ideas, recognize complex causality, synthesize information, and evaluate solutions proposed for problems.

## Text Organization

In textbooks and other expository texts, organizational features and structures help students understand, learn from, and remember what they read. Research has shown that understanding how text is organized helps readers construct meaning (Dickson, Simmons, and Kameenui 1998a). The organization of expository text encompasses both the physical presentation of the text and the underlying text structure.

*Physical presentation* is how the text looks on the page: how it is divided into segments or chapters and visual textual clues such as headings and subheadings, typeface and fonts, signal words, and the location of main-idea sentences.

*Text structure* is the internal organizational pattern the author uses to convey concepts and ideas to the reader. Common text structures include *cause-effect, compare/contrast, description, problem/solution,* and *time order.*

## Physical Presentation

Well-presented text, also known as "considerate" text, includes visual clues that direct readers to the concepts and ideas that are central to comprehension. When students are taught to recognize and use these clues, they are better able to identify the important ideas in textbooks and to understand how those ideas are related (Dickson et al. 1998a).

**Headings and Subheadings**   These elements are common in expository text, especially textbook writing, but are not always present. When used and used well, they function as a map or outline of the main ideas in the text. They alert students who are reading the text for the first time to the important idea(s) in their reading. Headings and subheadings also serve to remind readers what they have just read. In addition, headings and subheadings are valuable tools that students can use when looking for answers to questions. An example of a chapter heading and subheadings from a social studies selection is shown at left.

**Location of Topic/Main-Idea Sentences**   Topic or main-idea sentences at the beginning of a passage or paragraph alert readers to upcoming information. When main ideas are explicitly stated, they provide readers with a framework for understanding and recalling the important ideas in the text. For example, in "Pioneers on the Oregon Trail," the section called "Packing for the Journey" opens with the sentence "Traveling west was not easy." This sets up the expectation that the following sentences in the passage will provide details about how arduous the journey was and the type of supplies pioneers needed. Considerate text contains clearly presented main-idea sentences, usually at the beginning of a paragraph or passage. Less considerate text requires readers to infer the main idea.

**Signal Words**   Certain key words signal the relationship among ideas and point to the underlying structure of the text. For example, students reading the selection "Pioneers on the Oregon Trail" can use the signal words *at first, then, soon after* and *daybreak, morning, noon,* and *evening* as clues to the time-order text structure of the selection. The more considerate the text, the more signal words an author uses.

## Text Structure

Students need to be explicitly and systematically taught that expository text is structured in certain ways. They need to learn what the structures are and what clues they can use to identify the particular organization of a piece of writing. The five text structures that students are most likely to encounter in textbooks are cause-effect, compare/contrast, description, problem/solution, and time order.

The chart on the facing page shows various signal words and their relationship to the five common text structures. Note that some signal words can be used for different structures; for example, the words *first, second,* and *next* can signal description or time order.

**18.4**

## Text Structures

**Compare/Contrast**

presents the similarities and differences between two subjects

**Cause-Effect**

attempts to explain why something occurs

**Description**

uses words to create a picture in the reader's mind

**Problem/Solution**

poses a problem and suggests possible solutions to that problem.

**Time Order**

presents information in chronological, or sequential, order

## SIGNAL WORDS AND TEXT STRUCTURES

| Text Structure | Signal Words | Message to Reader |
|---|---|---|
| Cause-Effect Problem/Solution | because, due to, since, therefore, so, as a result, consequently | These signal words alert the reader to cause(s) leading to effect(s) or problem(s) leading to solution(s). |
| Compare/Contrast | like, just as, similar, both, also, too, unlike, different, but, in contrast, on the other hand | The signal words alert the reader to upcoming comparisons or contrasts. |
| Description | to begin with, first, second, next, then, finally, most important, also, in fact, for instance, for example, in front, beside, near, after | The signal words alert the reader to an upcoming list or set of characteristics. |
| Time Order | before, first, during, while, as, at the same time, after, then, next, at last, finally, now, when | The signal words alert the reader to a sequence of events, actions, or steps. |

18.5

## When to Teach

In Kindergarten, students listen to expository texts. Using big books, teachers explain charts that expand upon ideas presented in the text. In first through third grades, students begin to use headings and other physical features of text. They use titles, tables of contents, charts and graphs, and chapter headings to locate important information and main ideas. In fourth grade and above, students use the main idea and supporting details to learn how to summarize the information they read.

**See also...**

"Identifying the Main Idea and Summarization," p. 16.7

"Identifying the Main Idea," p. 18.14

"Summarization," p. 18.17

18.6

## Instructional Techniques and Procedures

Teachers can use a number of techniques, procedures, and strategies to help students understand expository text and construct meaning from it.

### Identifying the Main Idea and Summarization

Developing a summary helps students clarify, comprehend, and recall what they read. In order to summarize expository text, students must be able to identify the main idea as well as the key details that support that main idea. A summary represents the essence of the information presented, but in an abbreviated form. The sequence of instruction proceeds from developing main-idea sentences for short passages to summaries of entire texts.

### K-W-L Plus

**See also...**

"K-W-L Plus," p. 18.21

K-W-L (Ogle 1986) is the most well known and most frequently used technique for dealing with expository text. The basic K-W-L process involves three steps: What I Know (accessing prior knowledge), What I Want to Know (setting a purpose for reading), and What I Learned (recalling what has been read). A K-W-L chart, like the one shown on the facing page, is used to record student-generated responses before, during, and after reading. After completing the What I Know column, students categorize this information. Teachers may need to model generating Categories of Information I Expect to Use before students can be expected to do so on their own.

Connect to Theory

What do you know about teaching expository text? Using a copy of the K-W-L Chart in the Appendix, fill in the What I Know and What I Want to Know columns now. After you have finished reading this chapter, fill in the What I Learned column.

# K-W-L Chart

**"K-W-L Chart"**

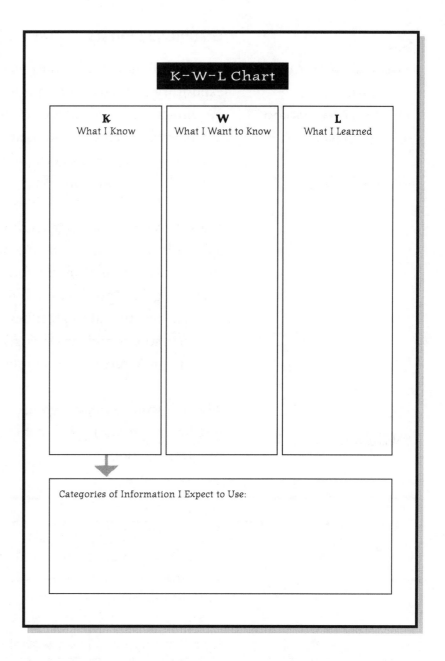

Carr and Ogle (1987) expanded the K-W-L process to create K-W-L Plus for secondary students. Two steps were added at the end of the original process: concept mapping (to group text information) and summarizing. These last steps lead students to reflect on what they have learned, to organize that information, and to express it coherently in their own words.

"Text Organization," p. 18.25

**CORE Reading Research Anthology**
for background information

**18.8**

## Graphic Organizers

One technique for increasing students' understanding of expository text organization is to have them create graphic organizers that represent a text's underlying structure. Graphic organizers highlight how ideas are interrelated, help students understand the most important ideas presented, and facilitate the recall of information (Wood et al. 1995).

Teachers can provide students with graphic organizers that are appropriate to the text structure of a selection they are about to read. Instruction takes the form of modeling and demonstrations, guided practice, and independent application. At first teachers may provide a great deal of direction. As students become more confident using graphic organizers, they can apply them to text independently.

The following graphic organizers represent four common text structures: description, compare/contrast, time order, and problem/solution.

## Description ▽

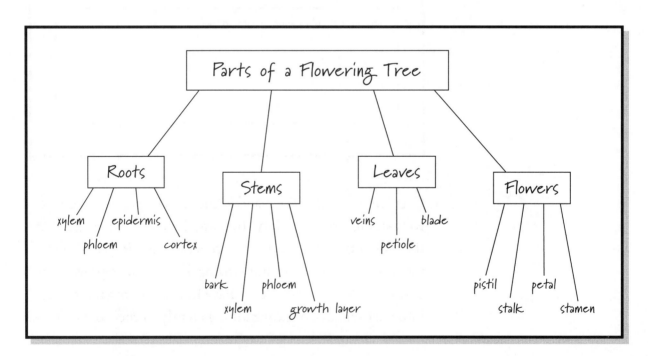

## Compare/Contrast

| TYPE OF FOOD | 1945 | 1950 |
|---|---|---|
| Cornflakes (12 oz.) | 10 cents | 19 cents |
| Bread (1 lb.) | 9 cents | 14 cents |
| Milk (1 qt.) | 16 cents | 21 cents |
| Butter (1 lb.) | 51 cents | 73 cents |
| Sugar (1 lb.) | 7 cents | 10 cents |

**18.9**

## Time Order

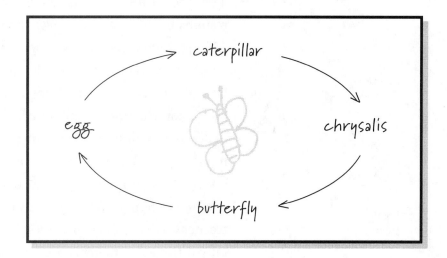

egg → caterpillar → chrysalis → butterfly → egg

## Problem/Solution

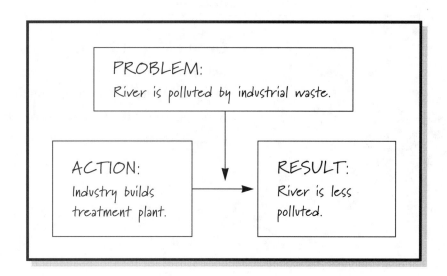

PROBLEM:
River is polluted by industrial waste.

ACTION:
Industry builds treatment plant.

RESULT:
River is less polluted.

"Reciprocal Teaching," p. 18.29

**CORE Reading Research Anthology**
for background information

**18.10**

## Reciprocal Teaching

Brown and Palincsar (1984) originally developed the instructional strategy known as reciprocal teaching "to teach poor comprehenders how to approach text the way successful readers do" (Palincsar, Ransom, and Derber 1989). Reciprocal teaching provides practice in the use of four comprehension strategies: questioning, clarifying, summarizing, and predicting. It involves dividing a text into smaller segments—"chunks" of about two paragraphs.

Another feature of reciprocal teaching is its use of scaffolding. The teacher initially assumes control and gradually releases responsibility to students over the course of several sessions. After students read each segment, a leader (teacher or student) conducts a discussion. Initially, the teacher is the leader, but later, students take turns being leader for a given portion of text. First, the teacher models the leader's tasks, guiding students in applying the four comprehension strategies, monitoring the group's understanding, and providing feedback. After several days of modeling, the teacher turns the leadership role over to students, who take turns leading the discussion. The teacher's role then becomes monitor and facilitator, intervening only if necessary to get students back on track or to jump-start discussion.

**Questioning**   The leader poses questions that direct students' attention to the main ideas of the text. These may include higher-level inferential and evaluative questions. Students' answers to these questions help the teacher check their comprehension.

**Clarifying**   The leader asks students to identify anything that puzzles them, and the group works together to clarify these issues. Items for clarification may include unclear portions of the text or difficult concepts or unfamiliar vocabulary. Clarifying engages students in monitoring their comprehension and helps avoid confusion and misinterpretation.

**Summarizing**   The leader proposes a summary of the passage, which the group can add to or change. Summarizing requires students to synthesize information and determine what is important to remember.

**Predicting**   The leader predicts what the next portion of text will be about, based on what has been read so far and visual clues like subheadings. Again, the group can add to or change the leader's prediction. This process encourages students to review what they have learned and use it as a springboard for predicting what they will learn next. This sets the purpose for reading.

# why? *Expository Text*

While students continue to read a great deal of narrative text, most of the text that they will read for content-area knowledge is expository text. Therefore, expository text increasingly becomes the source of students' new knowledge and information. In addition to expository text found in books and articles, students access information found on the Internet. Research findings indicate a strong link between text comprehension and understanding the way expository text is organized (Seidenberg 1989; Pearson and Fielding 1991; Weaver and Kintsch 1991). Thus, students' success or failure in school is closely tied to their ability to comprehend expository text.

As students learn about the physical presentation and underlying structure of expository text, they become strategic in their reading—using prior knowledge to set a purpose for reading, identifying what is important, questioning and clarifying, making inferences, and summarizing. When students are made aware of structural patterns, they are better able to determine main ideas and to recall text information.

## Research Findings . . .

*Students are simply not garnering much meaning from most of the expository texts they read.*

—BECK, MCKEOWN, HAMILTON & KUCAN, 1997

*Students remember and comprehend narrative text structure more easily than they do expository text structure.*

—ZABRUCKY & RATNER, 1992

*Student awareness of structural patterns in expository text is highly correlated to their recall of text information and of the main ideas contained in that text.*

—PEARSON & FIELDING, 1991

*Explicit instruction in the physical presentation of text and/or text structures facilitates reading comprehension.*

**18.13**

—DICKSON, SIMMONS & KAMEENUI, 1998a

**Suggested Reading . . .**

*Cognitive Strategy Instruction for Middle and High Schools* (1995) edited by Eileen Wood, Vera Woloshyn & Teena Willoughby. Cambridge, MA: Brookline Books.

*Cognitive Strategy Instruction that Really Improves Children's Academic Performance, Second Edition* (1995) edited by Michael Pressley & Vera Woloshyn. Cambridge, MA: Brookline Books.

*Content Area Reading and Learning* (1996) by Diane Lapp, James Flood & Nancy Farnan. Needham Heights, MA: Allyn & Bacon.

*Guiding Readers Through Text: A Review of Study Guides* (1992) by Karen D. Wood, Diane Lapp & James Flood. Newark, DE: International Reading Association.

*Reading and the Middle School Student: Strategies to Enhance Literacy* (1998) by Judith L. Irvin. Needham Heights, MA: Allyn & Bacon.

*Text-Based Learning and Reasoning: Studies in History* (1995) by Charles A. Perfetti, Anne M. Britt & Mara C. Georgi. Mahwah, NJ: Erlbaum.

# how? *Expository Text*

**Benchmark**

• ability to develop a main-idea sentence

**Grade Level**

• Grade 2 and above

**Grouping**

• whole class
• small group or pairs

**Materials**

• none

## IDENTIFYING THE MAIN IDEA

This generic teaching strategy focuses on the main idea of a passage. This lesson utilizes three types of passages: (1) a series of sentences about one person doing a series of actions; (2) a series of sentences about different people doing the same action; and (3) a short paragraph in which some sentences do not relate to the main idea.

● ● ● ● ● ● ● ● ● ● ● ● ● ● ● ● ● ● ● ● ● ● ● ●

### Introduce the Strategy

Tell students that it is impossible to remember everything that they read—especially when they are reading expository text. Explain that learning how to identify the most important, or main, idea of a passage will make it easier for them to remember what they read. Point out that a main idea can be summed up in one sentence. Say: *We are going to figure out the main idea of a group of sentences. The main-idea sentence will name the person and tell the main thing that the person did in all the sentences.* Print the following sentences on the board and read them aloud.

Albert Einstein enjoyed sailing. He liked to play the violin. He had fun putting together jigsaw puzzles. He liked riding his bicycle everywhere.

**THINK ALOUD**   *Let's come up with a sentence that tells the main idea. First, I have to name the person the sentences are about. That's easy. The sentences are about Albert Einstein. Then, I have to figure out how all the things that Albert Einstein did are related to each other. Hmmm, I think he enjoyed all of them. That's it, that's the main idea: Albert Einstein enjoyed doing many different things.*

Now print the following sentences on the board and read them aloud. Providing necessary guidance, ask students to develop a main-idea sentence. Remind them to ask themselves whom all of these sentences are about and the main thing that the person did. *(Benjamin Banneker built clocks.)*

When Benjamin Banneker was twenty-one, he took apart a pocket watch to see how it worked. He built a clock entirely out of wood, carving all the gears by hand. He also built the first American-made striking clock.

Say: *The next group of sentences names different people and tells what they did. To figure out the main idea of these sentences, you have to give the people a group name, and then tell the main thing that the group did.* Print the following sentences on the board and read them aloud.

In 1983, scientist Barbara McClintock won the Nobel Prize for her discovery about cells. In 1992, Rigoberta Menchu won the Nobel Prize for her work to gain peace in Guatemala. In 1993, novelist Toni Morrison won the Nobel Prize for Literature.

**THINK ALOUD**   *Let's figure out a main-idea sentence together. First, we have to name the group of people the sentences are about. I know that these are all women's names, so the sentences are about three women. Now I have to think about the main thing that all three women did. The sentences tell me that they*

**18.16**

*all won Nobel Prizes. So what's the main-idea sentence?* (All three women won a Nobel Prize.)

Tell students that in some passages, there may be one or more sentences that are not related to the main idea. In these passages, the reader has to decide what the person or group did in most—but not all—of the sentences. Most of the sentences in the following passage tell about the main thing a person did. Print the following paragraph on the board:

Garrett Augustus Morgan moved to Cleveland in 1895. He was always busy in his laboratory. In 1912, he developed the first gas mask. After seeing a terrible accident between a car and a horse-drawn carriage, Morgan developed and patented the first traffic light in 1923. Late in his life, he invented an ashtray that automatically put out anything burning. Several schools are named after him.

Ask: *Whom is this passage about?* (Garrett Augustus Morgan) *What is the main thing that he did in most of the sentences?* (He invented things.) *Which sentences don't tell us about Morgan's inventions?* (the first and last sentences) Cross out the two sentences that are unrelated to the main idea. Then say: *What would be a good main-idea sentence for this passage?* (Garrett Augustus Morgan invented safety devices.)

**SUMMARIZATION**

This generic teaching strategy introduces summarization. Students learn to summarize individual paragraphs of a selection first and then to summarize the entire selection by summarizing the summaries. Each of these steps should be introduced separately, providing ample practice.

18.17

### Benchmark

• ability to summarize

### Prerequisite

• Identifying the Main Idea

### Grade Level

• Grades 2–3 and above

### Grouping

• whole class
• small group or pairs

### Materials

• copies of "Albert Einstein Asks a Question" (see Appendix)
• chart paper

---

**Albert Einstein Asks a Question**

INDEPENDENT READING LEVEL:

GRADE 3

**BUILD BACKGROUND** Provide students with background and discuss key concepts related to the selection about Albert Einstein. Explain that many people consider Einstein to be the greatest scientist of the twentieth century. He was born in Germany and fled Nazi persecution to settle in the United States. Einstein's ideas, usually written as mathematical proofs, explored the relationships among motion, light, time, and space. His theories explained how the universe worked. He is most famous for his two theories of relativity and for his mathematical formula $E=mc^2$.

**INTRODUCE VOCABULARY** Select and introduce the unfamiliar words and/or concepts in the selection. See Section VI: Vocabulary Development for suggestions and strategies.

## Introduce and Apply the Strategy

Remind students that learning how to identify the main idea of a selection will help them remember what they read. Tell students that a main-idea sentence is a starting point for a summary. Explain that a summary tells the important information in a selection and includes the important details that support the main idea. It is always shorter than the original selection. Tell students that they are going to work together to develop a summary of "Albert Einstein Asks a Question."

**PREVIEW THE SELECTION**

Distribute copies of "Albert Einstein Asks a Question." Read aloud the title and the first paragraph as students follow along in the text. Ask: *What do the title and the first paragraph tell you about Einstein?* (Possible answer: Albert Einstein liked to ask a lot of questions.) Tell students they are now going to make a Summarizing Map of the selection. Have students print the title of the selection in the center of a piece of paper.

**READ AND SUMMARIZE PARAGRAPH 2**

Read aloud the second paragraph or have students read it independently. Then say: *We are going to learn to summarize this paragraph by identifying its main idea and supporting details. This Summarizing Checklist will help us identify the information to include in our summary.* Print the Summarizing Checklist on chart paper and read it aloud.

Then ask: *Whom is this paragraph about?* (Albert Einstein) *According to this paragraph, what is the main thing that Einstein did?* (He thought about how things worked.) Explain that sometimes you can find a main-idea sentence right in the text. Invite students to identify the sentence that sums up the main idea. *("He wanted to know how everything worked.")* On their papers, tell students to print the main idea, as shown on the Summarizing Map.

---

18.18

## Summarizing Checklist

✔ **Have I identified the main idea of the paragraph?**

✔ **Have I identified the supporting details that tell more about the main idea?**

✔ **Have I included any details that do not tell about the main idea?**

✔ **Have I repeated any information?**

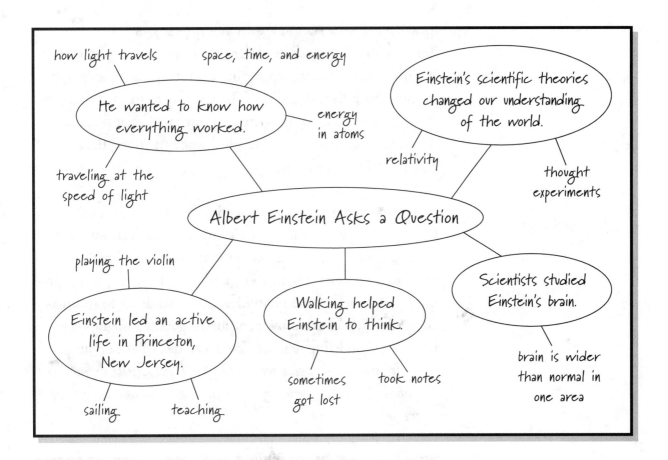

## Summarizing Map △

Then ask: *What are the details that support this main idea?* Tell students to print two or three important supporting details around each main idea. Ask: *Do we now have all the important information? Are there any sentences in the paragraph that don't tell about the main idea?* Lead students to understand that when summarizing the paragraph, they don't need to include the fact that Einstein didn't do well in school or that his teachers thought he was slow.

Have students use the information on their Summarizing Maps to write a summary of the first paragraph. Call on volunteers to read aloud their summaries, having the class use the Summarizing Checklist to evaluate each of the summaries. Here is a possible summary of the second paragraph: *Albert Einstein wanted to know how everything worked. He thought about space, time, and energy. He wondered about traveling at the speed of light.*

18.20

**READ AND SUMMARIZE PARAGRAPHS 3–6**

Tell students to read each of the remaining paragraphs, recording the main idea and supporting details for each paragraph on their Summarizing Maps. Then ask them to use the information on their maps to write a summary of each paragraph. To evaluate each summary, remind students to use the Summarizing Checklist.

After each paragraph in the selection has been summarized, help students write a summary of the entire selection—or to summarize the individual paragraph summaries. First, work together to develop the main idea of the selection. Then, starting with the selection's main idea, direct students to summarize the entire selection by incorporating each paragraph's main idea and supporting details. The main idea might be summed up as follows: *Albert Einstein was a brilliant scientist who spent his whole life asking and trying to answer questions about the universe.*

**OBSERVE AND ASSESS**

*As students summarize, provide feedback and use these questions to assess their progress.*

| Questions for Observation | Benchmarks |
|---|---|
| What is the main idea of this paragraph? | Student can identify the main idea. |
| What are the details that support this main idea? | Student can identify supporting details. |
| How would you summarize the whole selection? | Student can develop a written summary. |

## Reflect and Respond

Invite students to imagine that they had a chance to interview Albert Einstein. Ask them to come up with a list of five questions they would like to ask the famous scientist. Remind them that good interview questions call for more than just simple yes-or-no answers.

### Benchmarks

- ability to use prior knowledge to set a purpose for reading
- ability to identify and recall important information

### Grade Level

- Grade 4 and above

### Grouping

- whole class
- small group or pairs

### Materials

- copies of "Pioneers on the Oregon Trail" (see Appendix)
- copies of the "K-W-L Chart" (see Appendix)
- chart paper

This generic teaching strategy is based on the K-W-L procedure developed by Ogle (1986). It can be used before, during, and after reading most expository texts to help students use prior knowledge, read with a purpose, and clarify what they learned.

---

### Pioneers on the Oregon Trail

**INDEPENDENT READING LEVEL:**

GRADE 4

**BUILD BACKGROUND** Provide students with background and discuss key concepts related to pioneers on the Oregon Trail. Tell students that by the early 1800s, much of the land east of the Mississippi River was settled. The land west of the river, however, was relatively unsettled. After the purchase of the Louisiana Territory and the Lewis and Clark expeditions, fur traders, prospectors, and pioneers began to venture west along trails discovered and mapped out by the various expeditions. The most famous and important of these pioneer trails was the Oregon Trail. After gold was discovered in California in 1848, long lines of covered wagons filled the Oregon Trail.

**INTRODUCE VOCABULARY** Select and introduce the unfamiliar words and/or concepts in the selection. See Section VI: Vocabulary Development for suggestions and strategies.

## Introduce and Apply the Strategy

### BEFORE READING

*What I Know*   Distribute copies of "Pioneers on the Oregon Trail" and copies of the "K-W-L Chart." Tell students that they are going to read the selection and fill in the charts. Direct students to find and read aloud the boldface subheadings for each section: "The Way West," "Packing for the Journey," "Wagons Ho!," "A Day on the Trail," and "The End of the Trail." Ask: *Based on the title and the subheadings, what do you already know about the subject? Do you know anything about pioneers or anything about the Oregon Trail?*

Then draw a K-W-L chart on chart paper. Point to the K column and tell students that you are going to list what they already know in the What I Know column. Then record students' responses. Ask students to copy the What I Know responses onto their own K-W-L charts. In the Categories of Information I Expect to Use section (below the K column), ask students to categorize the information they listed in the What I Know column. Print the category headings in the chart, and then ask students to copy the category names onto their own K-W-L charts.

*What I Want to Know*   Point to the W column of the chart and ask students what they would like to learn by reading the selection. One purpose for reading might be to clarify any conflicting "facts" that different students volunteered when they completed the K column of the chart. For example, students may disagree on the amount of time it took the pioneers to reach the end of the trail. List students' questions in the W column of the chart. Ask students to copy the What I Want to Know questions onto their individual K-W-L charts.

# K-W-L Chart

| **K**<br>What I Know | **W**<br>What I Want to Know | **L**<br>What I Learned |
|---|---|---|
| pioneers went from East to west<br><br>looked for land<br><br>traveled in wagon trains<br><br>wanted to find gold in California<br><br>dangerous and long trip | Where was the Oregon Trail, and how long was it?<br><br>How long did it take to reach the end?<br><br>How many pioneers crossed the Oregon Trail?<br><br>How big were the wagon trains?<br><br>What supplies did the pioneers take?<br><br>What dangers did they face? | Started in Independence, MO, and ended at Ft. Vancouver in the Oregon Territory.<br><br>Trail was thousands of miles long and took 4–6 months to cross.<br><br>In 1843, two hundred families crossed. Soon after gold was discovered, thousands of people crossed.<br><br>10–15 wagons in a group. Up to one mile long and one mile wide.<br><br>They packed food, clothing, candles, soap, eating utensils, tools.<br><br>Dangers included snow, steep mountain passes, dangerous rivers. |

**Categories of Information I Expect to Use:**
- Reasons for heading west
- Dangers on the trail
- How they traveled

**DURING READING**

*What I Learned*   Tell students to read the selection, section by section. When reading each section, they should look for the answers to the questions recorded on the chart. If students have additional questions, they should add them to their charts. Students can take notes as they read—on answers to their questions as well as on new information they learn. Tell students to list the new What I Learned information in the L column of their own K-W-L charts.

**18.24**

**Section VI: Vocabulary Development**
**"Semantic Mapping," p. 14.16**

**AFTER READING**

After students have read each section of the selection, call on volunteers to share what they learned and record their responses on the chart paper. Ask students to look back at each of the questions they listed in the W column. Ask them if their questions were answered and, if so, what the answers are. Then ask students if anything in the text contradicted the "facts" listed in the K column. If disagreements arise, encourage students to refer back to the text. Finally, have students identify any of their questions that weren't answered by the text. Discuss how students might go about finding information that would answer those questions, including research via the Internet and consulting other reference materials.

Finally, guide students to use the "K-W-L Chart" to construct a semantic concept map of the selection. Use Categories of Information as the major heading of the map and the information in the What I Learned column as supporting details. Direct students to use the completed concept map to develop a written summary. Remind them that their summaries should include only the main ideas of the selection and the details that support those ideas.

**OBSERVE AND ASSESS**

*As students complete their K-W-L charts, provide feedback and use these questions to assess their progress.*

| Questions for Observation | Benchmark |
| --- | --- |
| What new information did you learn? Were your questions answered? | Student can identify and recall important information. |

## Reflect and Respond

Ask students to imagine that they are traveling with their families on the Oregon Trail. They have just finished their chores and have some time to write an entry in the diary they are keeping of the trip. Encourage students to draw on information they learned in the selection to write their diary entries.

### Benchmarks

- ability to analyze the structure of expository text
- ability to use physical features of text to understand information

### Grade Level

- Grade 4 and above

### Grouping

- whole class
- small group or pairs

### Materials

- copies of "Pioneers on the Oregon Trail" (see Appendix)
- copies of "'Pioneers on the Oregon Trail' Timeline" (see Appendix)

## TEXT ORGANIZATION

This generic teaching strategy focuses on text organization, which includes physical presentation (headings, signal words, and main-idea sentences) and text structure.

**18.25**

> **Pioneers on the Oregon Trail**
>
> INDEPENDENT READING LEVEL:
>
> GRADE 4

**BUILD BACKGROUND**   See Build Background, p. 18.21.

**INTRODUCE VOCABULARY** Select and introduce the unfamiliar words and/or concepts in the selection. See Section VI: Vocabulary Development for suggestions and strategies.

## Introduce and Apply the Strategy

Tell students that knowing how an author has organized information can help them better understand and remember what they read. Point out that just by looking at how text is laid out on a page can tell them a lot.

**PREVIEW THE SELECTION**

*Physical Presentation*   Distribute copies of "Pioneers on the Oregon Trail." Tell students that the selection is like a chapter of a social studies textbook. Explain to students that expository texts often have subheadings, maps, illustrations, and other graphic aids that help clarify the text. Ask them to skim the selection. Ask: *What special features do you see?* (chapter title, boldface subheadings, a timeline, two boxed lists, a map, italicized text in margins, and illustrations)

Direct students' attention to the timeline. Explain that this timeline shows important historical events that took place before, during, and after pioneers headed west on the Oregon Trail. Ask students to pinpoint on the timeline the year 1848—the year Oregon was made a territory and thousands of pioneers began to cross the Oregon Trail. Next, ask students to look at the supply lists. Ask students why the author has included two different lists. Finally, direct students' attention to the map of the Oregon Trail and ask them to locate the beginning and the end of the trail. Ask students what direction the pioneers traveled to get from Missouri to Oregon. *(northwest)*

*Text Structure*   Have students find the boldface subheadings and read them aloud. Explain that these headings are important clues to how the selection is organized. Use the following Think Aloud procedure to model using headings to identify the organizational pattern of the text.

**THINK ALOUD**   *I know that the chapter is about pioneers on the Oregon Trail. I see that it begins with "The Way West" and "Packing for the Journey." In the middle are sections called "Wagons Ho!" and "A Day on the Trail." The chapter ends with "The End of the Trail." These headings tell me that the author is going to describe what happened before the journey, what happened during the journey, and what happened at the end of the journey. It sounds like the text is written in the order that the events took place. This text structure is called "time order," so I think I'll use a timeline to record the order of events.*

**READ "THE WAY WEST"**

Have students follow along in the text as you read aloud "The Way West." Tell them that as you read you are going to test out your idea about how the text is organized. When you have finished, use the following Think Aloud procedure to model using signal words and a main-idea sentence to identify the author's time order pattern.

**THINK ALOUD**   *In the opening paragraph the author mentions several dates:* early 1800s, 1843, *and* 1848. *I also see words that are clues to when something happened:* as they traveled, before long, *and* at first. *This paragraph describes events in the order they happened, and the last sentence sums up the main idea:* Soon after 1848, thousands of people began heading west, hoping to make their dreams come true at the end of the Oregon Trail.

**READ FROM "PACKING FOR THE JOURNEY" TO "THE END OF THE TRAIL"**

Tell students that they are going to use a timeline to record the order of events in the selection. Distribute copies of the "'Pioneers on the Oregon Trail' Timeline." Ask students to read the rest of the selection in small groups or pairs. Tell them to read section by section, filling in the key events in order on the timeline. Point out that the bottom of the timeline shows which sections of the selection correspond to each part of the timeline. Remind students to look for words in the text, such as dates, names of seasons, and words like *daybreak, noon,* and *evening.* These signal words will help them organize the information on their timelines.

When students have finished reading, ask volunteers to share their completed timelines. An example of a completed timeline is shown on the next page.

18.28

## PIONEERS ON THE OREGON TRAIL

| Before the Journey | Starting Out | On the Trail | End of the Trail |
|---|---|---|---|
| | Independence ★ MISSOURI | | |
| pack food, tools, and supplies for 4- to 6-month journey | join wagon train at Independence, MO or Council Bluffs, IA | do morning chores travel | stake claim in Oregon City |
| use space left for personal belongings | wait for right time to start, to miss the snow | stop to rest, eat, make repairs | build a house before winter |
| say good-bye | set out, watching for landmarks | stop for the day, eat dinner, do chores, relax | use leftover supplies to get through the winter |
| | | go to bed | |
| "Packing for the Journey" | "Wagons Ho!" | "A Day on the Trail" | "The End of the Trail" |

## OBSERVE AND ASSESS

*As students complete their timelines, provide feedback and use these questions to assess their progress.*

| Questions for Observation | Benchmarks |
|---|---|
| How is the selection organized? How do you know? | Student can identify text structure. |
| What did the pioneers experience along the Oregon Trail? | Student can recall important information from the text. |

## Reflect and Respond

Call on a volunteer to tell his or her life story. Then show students how the story can be represented with a simple timeline. Draw a timeline on the board that starts at the student's date of birth. Then work with students to recall key events in the student's life and record these at the appropriate years on the timeline. Finally, use the completed timeline to retell the story, modeling the use of key words that signal time order such as *first, then, later,* and *in 2000.*

# Expository Text

**Benchmarks**

- ability to ask and answer questions about the main ideas in expository text
- ability to ask for clarification of unclear information
- ability to summarize important information
- ability to predict and confirm upcoming information

**Grade Level**

- Grade 4 and above

**Grouping**

- small group

**Materials**

- copies of "Pioneers on the Oregon Trail" (see Appendix)

Intervention Strategy

**Students who are not able to read the text on their own can be paired with a more proficient reader.**

In this generic teaching strategy, discussion leaders (initially the teacher and then the students) guide small groups in questioning, clarifying, summarizing, and predicting as they read segments of "Pioneers on the Oregon Trail." Before students can participate in reciprocal teaching, they must receive explicit instruction in each of these comprehension strategies.

18.29

**Pioneers on the Oregon Trail**

INDEPENDENT READING LEVEL:

GRADE 4

**BUILD BACKGROUND** See Build Background, p. 18.21.

**INTRODUCE VOCABULARY** Select and introduce the unfamiliar words and/or concepts in the selection. See Section VI: Vocabulary Development for suggestions and strategies.

## Introduce and Model the Strategy

**PREVIEW THE SELECTION**

*Predicting* Distribute copies of "Pioneers on the Oregon Trail" and tell students that you are going to read it together in sections. Read aloud the title and ask students to follow along in the text as you read aloud the boldface subheadings. Based on their preview, ask students to predict what the selection will be about. Point to the first heading, "The Way West," and suggest that students read this section to find out why pioneers decided to move west. Allow time for students to read the paragraph to themselves.

18.30

**READ "THE WAY WEST"**

*Questioning*   Provide time for students to write a few questions that will help the group focus on the important information they learned in this section. Ask: *Who would like to start our discussion?* If students have difficulty, ask: *What new discoveries encouraged people to move west of the Mississippi?* (Lewis and Clark made maps and sent back news of how beautiful the land was. Then, in 1848, gold was discovered in California.) Ask: *Why do you think people were willing to pack up and head west?* (They dreamed of owning their own land with good soil for farming; they dreamed of finding gold and getting rich.)

*Clarifying*   Remind students that it is helpful to talk about parts of the text that weren't clear. Ask: *Is there anything in this paragraph that you would like clarified or any words you didn't understand?* If students don't identify something for clarification, you can use the following example. Say: *The article says that pioneers were "hoping to make their dreams come true at the end of the Oregon Trail," but it doesn't say where the end of the trail was.* Explain that expository texts often have maps and illustrations that help clarify things mentioned in the text. Encourage students to look for the map of the Oregon Trail and to locate the end of the trail.

*Summarizing*   Remind students that summarizing paragraphs can help them remember what they read. Explain that their summaries should tell the important ideas of the section they just read. Call on a volunteer to summarize the section. Discuss with students the accuracy and completeness of the summary. Here is a possible summary: *The paragraph is about why pioneers headed west. People learned about the west from Lewis and Clark's maps and journals. First, only a few adventurers traveled the Oregon Trail. Then after gold was discovered in California in 1848, thousands of pioneers crossed the trail in search of a new life.*

*Predicting*   Direct students' attention to the title of the next section and help them make predictions. Ask: *What do you predict the next paragraph will be about?* (The next section will tell what the pioneers packed for their journey.)

Allow time for students to read the second paragraph to themselves. Suggest that they read this section to find out what the pioneers packed.

**READ "PACKING FOR THE JOURNEY"**

*Questioning*   Provide time for students to write a few questions that will help the group focus on the important information they learned in this section. Ask: *Who would like to start our discussion?* If students have difficulty, you can direct their attention to the lists of supplies in the left margin. Then ask: *What did people need to consider as they chose things to pack for their journey west?* (They would need food, clothing, and tools for a long journey, and everything had to fit in a covered wagon.)

*Clarifying*   Ask: *Is there anything in this paragraph that you would like clarified or any words you didn't understand?* If students don't identify something for clarification, you can use the following example. Say: *The article says "the pioneers left behind more than the comforts of home and their special treasures." I'm not sure what the author means by that. What can I do to figure it out?* Lead students to understand that they can reread that part of the text looking for clues to the meaning. The next sentence explains, "They said good-bye to family and friends they never expected to see again." Now ask: *Why are there two lists of supplies?* (The first list shows what each person needed for her- or himself. The second list shows what the members of a family traveling together would share—in addition to the supplies each person needed.)

*Summarizing*   Call on a volunteer to summarize the section. Discuss with students the accuracy and completeness of the summary. Here is a possible summary: *The Oregon Trail was thousands of miles long and took several months to cross. The* pioneers packed all the food, tools, and supplies they would need for the difficult journey. Since the covered wagons were small, the pioneers could only pack necessities.)

18.32

Explain that students could summarize all that they have read to this point by combining the summaries of the two sections: *People learned about the west from Lewis and Clark's maps and journals. First, only a few adventurers traveled the Oregon Trail. Then after gold was discovered in California in 1848, thousands of pioneers crossed the trail in search of a new life. The Oregon Trail was thousands of miles long and took several months to cross. The pioneers packed all the food, tools, and supplies they would need for the difficult journey. Since the covered wagons were small, the pioneers could only pack necessities.*

*Predicting* Direct students' attention to the title of the next section and help them make predictions. Ask: *What do you predict the next section will be about?* (The next section will tell about how wagons set out along the Oregon Trail.)

## Apply the Strategy

Have students read the rest of the selection, pausing after each section to discuss what has been read using the reciprocal teaching strategy. Encourage students to assume as much leadership as they are able to. Typically, students need a great deal of practice before they become adept at using the reciprocal teaching strategy on their own. Here are some possible prompts.

### "WAGONS HO!"

*Questioning* Where did the wagon trains set out from? Where did they end up? What was important about the timing of a trip?

*Clarifying*   Why did most people wind up walking to Oregon, instead of riding in the wagons?

*Summarizing*   Families joined long wagon trains in Independence, Missouri, and at Council Bluffs, Iowa. They left when there would be enough grass on the prairie for grazing and in time to miss snow in the mountains. The trip was long and hard, with pioneers either riding in small bumpy wagons or walking thousands of miles beside the wagons.

18.33

*Predicting*   Read the next section to find out what a day on the trail was like.

**"A DAY ON THE TRAIL"**
*Questioning*   On a typical day, what kinds of things did the pioneers do on the Oregon Trail? How many miles could they travel in a single day?

*Clarifying*   Why was it important to get chores done before nightfall? Why was letting the butter "churn itself" a good idea?

*Summarizing*   A day on the trail was spent doing chores, taking care of the animals, making repairs, preparing and eating meals, and traveling until four or five o'clock. Sometimes pioneers relaxed before bed by singing, dancing, and playing music.

*Predicting*   Read the next section to find out what happened when the pioneers reached the end of the trail.

**18.34**

**"THE END OF THE TRAIL"**

*Questioning*   How long did it take the pioneers to reach the end of the Oregon Trail? Why did the hard work begin at the end of the trail?

*Clarifying*   What does "staked their claims to ranch and farm-land" mean? Why was it important to clear the land and build a house before the start of winter?

*Summarizing*   When pioneers reached the end of the Oregon Trail, they had to claim their land and quickly build a cabin before winter came. The first winter in Oregon could be very hard since their supplies were low and the weather could be wet and cold.

**OBSERVE AND ASSESS**

*As students participate in a reciprocal teaching dialogue, provide feedback and use these questions to assess their progress.*

| Questions for Observation | Benchmarks |
| --- | --- |
| What are some questions about this section? | Student can generate questions about the main ideas. |
| Is there anything in this section that you would like clarified? | Student can ask for clarification. |
| How would you summarize this section? How would you summarize all that you have read to this point? | Student can summarize important information. |
| What do you predict the next section will be about? | Student can predict and confirm upcoming information. |

## Reflect and Respond

Ask students to imagine that they are going to travel across the country today, camping out along the way. Have them make a list of what they would pack for themselves and a second list of what their families would need.

# Section References

Anderson, R. C., and P. D. Pearson. 1984. A schema-theoretic view of basic processes in reading comprehension. In P. D. Pearson, R. Barr, M. Kamil, and P. Mosenthal (eds.), Vol. 1: *Handbook of reading research.* White Plains, NY: Longman.

Anderson, R. C., E. H. Hiebert, J. A. Scott, and A. G. Wilkinson. 1985. *Becoming a nation of readers.* Washington, DC: National Institute of Education.

Andre, M. D. A., and T. H. Anderson. 1978–1979. The development and evaluation of a self-questioning study technique. *Reading Research Quarterly* 14(4), pp. 605–623.

Baldwin, R. S., Z. Peleg-Bruckner, and A. H. McClintock. 1985. The effect of metacognitive instruction in outlining and graphic organization construction on students' comprehension in a tenth-grade world history class. *Journal of Reading Behavior* 18, pp. 153–169.

Baumann, J. F. 1986. Effects of rewritten content textbook passages in middle grade students' comprehension of main ideas: Making the inconsiderate considerate. *Journal of Reading Behavior* 18(1), pp. 1–21.

Beck, I. L., M. G. McKeown, R. L. Hamilton, and L. Kucan. 1997. *Questioning the author: An approach for enhancing student engagement with text.* Newark, DE: International Reading Association.

Bretzing, B. H., and R. W. Kulhavy. 1979. Notetaking and depth of processing. *Contemporary Educational Psychology* 4, pp. 145–153.

Brown, A. L., and A. S. Palincsar. 1984. Reciprocal teaching of comprehension: Fostering and monitoring activities. *Cognition and Instruction* 1, pp. 117–175.

Brown, H., and B. Cambourne. 1987. *Read and retell: A strategy for the whole-language/natural learning classroom.* Portsmouth, NH: Heinemann.

California State Board of Education. 1999. *Reading/language arts framework for California public schools: Kindergarten through grade twelve.* Sacramento, CA: California Department of Education.

Carr, E., and D. Ogle. 1987. K-W-L Plus: A strategy for comprehension and summarization. *Journal of Reading* 30, pp. 626–636.

Dickson, S. V., V. L. Collins, D. C. Simmons, and, E. J. Kameenui. 1998. Metacognitive strategies: Research bases. In D. C. Simmons and E. J. Kameenui (eds.), *What reading research tells us about children with diverse learning needs: Bases and basics.* Mahwah, NJ: Erlbaum.

Dickson, S. V., D. C. Simmons, and E. J. Kameenui. 1998a. Text organization: Instructional and curricular basics and implications. In D. C. Simmons and E. J. Kameenui (eds.), *What reading research tells us about children with diverse learning needs: Bases and basics.* Mahwah, NJ: Erlbaum.

Dickson, S. V., D. C. Simmons, and E. J. Kameenui. 1998b. Text organization: Research bases. In D. C. Simmons and E. J. Kameenui (eds.), *What reading research tells us about children with diverse learning needs: Bases and basics.* Mahwah, NJ: Erlbaum.

Dole, J. A., G. G. Duffy, L. R. Roehler, and P. D. Pearson. 1991. Moving from the old to the new: Research on reading comprehension instruction. *Review of Educational Research Quarterly* 14(4), pp. 239–264.

Duker, S. 1965. Listening and reading. *Elementary School Journal* 65, pp. 321–324.

Gambrell, L. B., and R. J. Bales. 1986. Mental imagery and the comprehension-monitoring performance of fourth- and fifth-grade poor readers. *Reading Research Quarterly* 21.

Garcia, G. E., and P. D. Pearson. 1990. Modifying reading instruction to maximize its effectiveness for all students. *Technical Report #489*. Champaign, IL: Center for the Study of Reading.

Gillet, J. W., and C. Temple. 1994. *Understanding reading problems: Assessment and instruction* (4th ed.). New York: HarperCollins College Publishers.

Graesser, A., J. M. Golding, and D. L. Long. 1991. Narrative representation and comprehension. In R. Barr, M. L. Kamil, P. Mosenthal, and P. D. Pearson (eds.), Vol. 2: *Handbook of reading research*. White Plains, NY: Longman.

Graves, M. F., C. Juel, and B. B. Graves. 1998. *Teaching reading in the 21st century*. Needham Heights, MA: Allyn & Bacon.

Griffin, C. C., L. D. Malone, and E. J. Kameenui. 1995. Effects of graphic organizer instruction on fifth-grade students. *The Journal of Educational Research* 89(2), pp. 98–107.

Hansen, J., and P. D. Pearson. 1983. An instructional study: Improving the inferential comprehension of good and poor fourth-grade readers. *Journal of Education Psychology* 75, pp. 821–829.

Hare, V., and K. M. Borchardt. 1984. Direct instruction in summarization rules. *Reading Research Quarterly* 21, pp. 62–78.

Irvin, J. L. 1998. *Reading and the middle school student: Strategies to enhance literacy* (2nd ed.). Needham Heights, MA: Allyn & Bacon.

Kern, R. G. 1989. Second language reading strategy instruction: Its effects on comprehension and word inference ability. *The Modern Language Journal* 73, pp. 135–149.

Montague, M., C. D. Maddux, and M. I. Dereshiwsky. 1990. Story grammar and comprehension and production of narrative prose by students with learning disabilities. *Journal of Learning Disabilities* 23, pp. 190–197.

Morrow, L. M. 1986. Effects of story retelling on children's dictation of original stories. *Journal of Reading Behavior* 18, pp. 135–152.

Ogle, D. M. 1986. K-W-L: A teaching model that develops active reading of expository text. *The Reading Teacher* 38(6), pp. 564–570.

Olson, M. W., and T. C. Gee. 1988. Understanding narratives: A review of story grammar research. *Childhood Education* 64, pp. 302–306.

Palincsar, A. S., K. Ransom, and S. Derber. 1989. Collaborative research and development of reciprocal teaching. *Educational Leadership* 46(4), pp. 37–41.

Paris, S. C., B. A. Wasik, and J. C. Turner. 1991. The development of strategic readers. In R. Barr, M. L. Kamil, P. Mosenthal, and P. D. Pearson (eds.), Vol. 2: *Handbook of reading research*. White Plains, NY: Longman.

Pearson, P. D., and L. Fielding. 1991. Comprehension instruction. In R. Barr, M. L. Kamil, P. Mosenthal, and P. D. Pearson (eds.), Vol. 2: *Handbook of reading research*. White Plains, NY: Longman.

Pearson, P. D., and D. D. Johnson. 1978. *Teaching reading comprehension*. New York: Holt, Rinehart & Winston.

Pearson, P. D., L. R. Roehler, J. A. Dole, and G. G. Duffy. 1992. Developing expertise in reading comprehension. In S. J. Samuels and A. E. Farstrup (eds.), *What research has to say about reading instruction* (2nd ed.). Newark, DE: International Reading Association.

Pressley, M. 1977. Imagery and children's learning: Putting the picture in developmental perspective. *Review of Educational Research* 47, pp. 586–622.

Pressley, M., P. B. El-Dinary, I. Gaskins, J. L. Bergman, J. Almasi, and R. Brown. 1992. Beyond direct explanation: Transactional instruction of reading comprehension strategies. *The Elementary School Journal* 92, pp. 513–555.

Pressley, M., C. J. Johnson, S. Symons, J. S. McGoldrick, and J. A. Kurita. 1989. Strategies that improve children's memory and comprehension of text. *Elementary School Journal* 90, pp. 3–32.

Pressley, M., S. Symons, B. Snyder, and T. Cariglia-Bull. 1989. Strategy instruction research comes of age. *Learning Disability Quarterly* 12(1), pp. 16–31.

Pressley, M., and V. Woloshyn. 1995. *Cognitive strategy instruction that really improves children's academic performance* (2nd ed.). Cambridge, MA: Brookline Books.

Raphael, T. E. 1982. Question-answering strategies for children. *The Reading Teacher* 36, pp. 186–190.

Raphael, T. E. 1984. Teaching learners about sources of information for answering comprehension questions. *Journal of Reading* 28.

Raphael, T. E. 1986. Teaching question/answer relationships, revisited. *The Reading Teacher* 39, pp. 516–522.

Raphael, T. E., and P. D. Pearson. 1982. The effect of metacognitive awareness training on children's question-answering behavior. *Technical Report #238*. Champaign, IL: Center for the Study of Reading.

**18.36**

Recht, D. R., and L. Leslie. 1988. Effect of prior knowledge on good and poor readers' memory of text. *Journal of Educational Psychology* 80, pp. 16–20.

Schunk, D. H., and J. M. Rice. 1992. Influence of reading-comprehension strategy information on children's achievement outcomes. *Learning Disability Quarterly* 15, pp. 51–64.

Seidenberg, P. L. 1989. Relating text-processing research to reading and writing instruction for learning disabled students. *Learning Disabilities Focus* 5(1), pp. 4–12.

Short, E. J., and E. B. Ryan. 1984. Metacognitive differences between skilled and less skilled readers: Remediating deficits through story grammar and attributional training. *Journal of Educational Psychology* 76, pp. 225–235.

Stauffer, R. G. 1975. *Directing the reading-thinking process.* New York: Harper & Row.

Templeton, S. 1997. *Teaching the integrated language arts.* Boston: Houghton Mifflin.

Tierney, R. J. 1982. Essential considerations for developing basic reading comprehension skills. *School Psychology Review* 11(3), pp. 299-305.

Walker, B. J. 1996a. *Diagnostic teaching of reading.* (3rd ed.) Englewood Cliffs, NJ: Merrill.

Walker, B. J. 1996b. Discussions that focus on strategies and self-assessment. In L. B. Gambrell and J. F. Almasi (eds.), *Lively discussions!* (pp. 256–296). Newark DE: International Reading Association.

Weaver, C. A., and W. Kintsch. 1991. Expository text. In R. Barr, M. L. Kamil, P. Mosenthal, and P. D. Pearson (eds.), Vol. 2: *Handbook of reading research.* White Plains, NY: Longman.

Wood, E., V. E. Woloshyn, and T. Willoughby. 1995. *Cognitive strategy instruction for middle and high schools.* Cambridge, MA: Brookline Books.

Zabrucky, K., and H. H. Ratner. 1992. Effects of passage type on comprehension monitoring and recall in good and poor readers. *Journal of Reading Behavior* 24, pp. 373–391.

# Reading and Responding

# Section VIII: Reading and Responding

*"At all times, developing children's interest and pleasure in reading must be as much a focus as developing their reading skills."*

—LEARNING FIRST ALLIANCE, 1998

Independent, wide reading and classroom discussions about books are an important part of an effective reading program and integral to the literate environment that fosters strong readers. Students should be avid readers, not only because wide reading brings knowledge, but because reading and talking about books brings pleasure. One of the best ways to help children want to read is by providing them with many opportunities to talk about and share books. Interactive discussions about books motivate others to read and lead the readers to consider ideas deeply. Nurturing independent reading and establishing a classroom devoted to reading and talking about books requires careful planning.

## Standards for Reading Comprehension

**GRADES 1 THROUGH 8**

- In addition to their regular school reading, by grade four students read a half million words annually, including a good representation of grade-level–appropriate narrative and expository text (e.g., classic and contemporary literature, magazines, newspapers, online information).

- In addition, by grade eight, students read one million words annually on their own, including a good representation of grade-level–appropriate narrative and expository text (e.g., classic and contemporary literature, magazines, newspapers, online information).

SOURCE
Adapted from *English-Language Arts Content Standards for California Public Schools: Kindergarten Through Grade Twelve* (1999). Sacramento: California Department of Education.

# CONTENTS

# Section VIII: Reading and Responding

CHAPTER

# 19

# Independent, Wide Reading

what?
why?
when?
how?

# what?

## Independent, Wide Reading

**19.2**

*"Reading is a basic life skill. It is a cornerstone for a child's success in school and, indeed, throughout life."*

—BECOMING A NATION
OF READERS, 1985

**CORE Reading Research Anthology**
for background information

**Section I: The Big Picture, "Better
Readers Read More," p. 1.11**

**Section IV: Decoding
Chapter 11: Reading Fluency**

**Section VI: Vocabulary Development**
**Section VII: Comprehension**

Reading achievement is positively related to the amount of time spent reading. "Reading a lot" is one of the most powerful methods of increasing fluency, vocabulary, and comprehension—and becoming educated about the world (Shany and Biemiller 1995; Stanovich 1993). When students read a large amount of material they encounter new ideas, concepts, and knowledge. This, in turn, improves their ability to comprehend. In addition, wide reading builds new background knowledge that students need in order to understand more complex content-area text (Honig 1996).

The excerpt that begins on the facing page provides useful information and suggestions for planning and implementing independent reading programs.

What are you currently doing to encourage your students' independent reading? What else could you do to motivate all students to read?

## Teachers and Independent Reading

From The Center for the Study of Reading, University of Illinois at Urbana-Champaign.

**Section I: The Big Picture**
"Variation in Amount of Independent Reading," p. 1.10

## The Importance of Independent Reading

Independent reading is sustained reading for information or for pleasure. Teachers are familiar with the many kinds of reading that students enjoy on their own, such as a favorite novel; an exciting mystery story; the daily newspaper; the latest sports, entertainment, or electronics magazine; or even comic books. They may not be aware, however, that independent silent reading is one of the most important activities for the reading development of students of all ages. Research shows that students who do a lot of reading "on their own" become better readers because independent reading:

- enhances their reading comprehension;

- provides them with a wide range of background knowledge;

- accounts for one-third or more of their vocabulary growth; and

- promotes reading as a *lifelong activity*.

Alarmingly, while independent reading is so important to reading growth, studies show that many students do not read on their own at all. In fact, some students think that reading is something that is done only with school textbooks. Teachers can help *all* students begin to see independent reading as an *important* activity by allocating classroom time for independent reading; by seeing to it that the classroom contains novels, biographies, children's magazines and newspapers, science and history books, as well as textbooks; and by allowing students opportunities to see their friends, classmates, and teachers immersed in books—in short, by making independent reading an integral part of the scheduled school day.

## Motivating Students to Read

Students' home backgrounds play a major role in the development of their reading habits. Students who come from homes where books are plentiful and where reading is a frequent and valued activity often read earlier, better, and more than do students from homes where literacy is not valued highly.

However, the school is equally important to the development of lifelong reading habits. Classrooms that are filled with books and that offer students ample opportunities to learn about, read, react to, and share books can have much the same effect on reading habits as book-filled homes. Here are some particularly effective ways for teachers to motivate students to read independently:

**Read aloud to students.**   Many teachers read aloud to students as a way of introducing them to books and authors they may enjoy reading on their own. When reading aloud, teachers can keep students' attention and help them to become good listeners by doing the following:

- Prepare students for what they will be reading. Discuss the kind of book you will be reading, talk about its author and illustrator, and introduce the story's main characters, time, and locale.

- Encourage students to react to what they will be reading. Allow students to comment upon the story and illustrations and to discuss their own relevant experiences. Ask occasional questions to check their understanding of the story and of any new vocabulary.

- Let students predict what will happen next. By involving students in this way, teachers are likely to generate so much interest in the book that students will ask to read other copies of it themselves or to read other books by the same author, or on the same theme or topic.

Reading aloud can be *more* than simply a way of motivating students to read. Reading and rereading patterned, predictable books to young children or poor readers, for example, not only makes these books more familiar, but also helps students pay more attention to the words and sentences that will be repeated in other books they read. Older children can derive similar benefits when they are read to; reading to them from novels, for example, introduces them to various writing styles, new vocabulary words, and a variety of sentence and grammatical structures. Most important, it gets them interested in reading those novels.

**Help students select books to read.** Just as they need to learn how to read independently, some students need to learn how to select books. Here are some ways teachers can help students develop this ability.

- Make personalized suggestions based upon what is known about an individual student's interests.

- Treat book selection as part of the regular reading group activity. After students read selections in a basal reader or other textbook, recommend other books by the same author or on the same topic or of the same genre.

- Take students regularly on book-choosing tours of the school library. Teachers can talk to students about what to look for when selecting books for independent reading. Library tours will help students learn to find books that interest them, and acquaint them with the resources of the library. At least once a year take students on a field trip to a local public library.

**19.6**

Teachers and Independent Reading
*The Center for the Study of Reading*

See also...

Section IV: Decoding
"Independent Practice and Rereading,"
p. 11.3

## Independent Reading Plan

**According to Bill Honig, an optimum independent reading plan would include 20–30 minutes of reading in class, plus 20–30 minutes outside class, for a total of 40–60 minutes daily.**

**Encourage book sharing.** Reading "networks" of classmates, friends, and teachers are important because they allow students to become familiar with a wide range of good books. Teachers can encourage the creation of such informal networks in the classroom by doing the following:

- Allow informal discussions for several minutes after group silent reading.

- Make book-sharing sessions a classroom activity once or twice a week ("Let me tell you about a book I just finished reading," or "Has anyone read a good book lately?").

**Read it again!** Reading a book again improves both reading fluency and comprehension, particularly for younger readers and poor readers. Teachers should not hesitate to tell students that it is perfectly all right for them to reread their favorite books; students can derive great pleasure and gain new insights from rereading "oldies but goodies."

## Arranging Classroom Time for Independent Reading

Reading skill will improve significantly if students read for an average of ten minutes a day, or at least one hour per week. Some teachers prefer to set aside a short period of time daily for in-class independent reading, while others prefer to use longer, less frequent periods. There is no evidence that one routine is superior to the other. What is important is that every student read independently in class for *at least one hour per week,* in periods of whatever length and frequency seem most effective.

Finding one hour a week for independent reading may be difficult. It can be done, however, by providing time for independent reading in the following ways:

## CORE's Recommendations for an Independent Reading Program

**Establishing school- or district-wide standards for outside reading (20 to 30 minutes per day or at least 25 books per year)**

**Matching students' reading levels to reading materials**

**Providing a wide variety of reading materials**

**Monitoring the breadth and depth of students' reading (annually and across grade levels)**

**Giving feedback on students' reading growth**

**Motivating and encouraging students to read**

**As an alternative to workbook practice.**  Independent, silent reading can fulfill many of the same functions as workbook activities—it permits students to practice what they are learning, and it keeps the rest of the class occupied while you meet with a small group of students. A surprising amount of time for independent reading can be freed if workbook assignments are trimmed down to an essential core that gives students sound practice on newly taught concepts and a review of important information.

**As an activity during transition times.**  Teachers can identify the longest transition time during the school day and establish it as the one time when everyone (including the teacher) reads a book. Reading should be the only activity permitted during this time.

**As part of a whole-class reading program.**  There is probably no substitute for a whole-class, independent reading period when both students and teachers silently read books of their own choosing. However, teachers should be wary of trying to do too much too soon. They should *gradually* increase the amount of time students spend on independent reading in the classroom. Teachers can start with only five minutes a day and slowly work up to fifteen or twenty minutes a day (or several times a week) over the course of several weeks. Teachers should encourage students to read at home—and have a procedure for allowing students to carry home books that they want to finish.

As teachers plan ways to reallocate time in the classroom schedule, they should remember to pay more than just lip service to independent reading. Telling students that they can read independently when they "finish their work" implies that independent reading is less important than other classroom activities. It also means that the slowest workers—the very ones who may need the most reading practice—will get the shortest amount of time to read.

**19.8**

## Setting Up the Classroom Library

Having books readily available in the classroom is an important way to motivate all students to read, but it is an especially important way to introduce reluctant readers to books and libraries.

Creating a classroom library, however, is not always an easy task, especially in times of tight school budgets. Here are some ways teachers can obtain books for the library.

- Spend discretionary money on books.

- Visit garage sales—they can be veritable gold mines of books for young readers.

- Ask publishers to help stock the classroom library with books at reduced prices—or for free.

- See if the school library will rotate several sets of twenty-five or so titles through the classroom library.

- Work out book exchange agreements with other teachers who have classroom libraries.

- Solicit the support of the Parent-Teacher Association, community book clubs, and other service groups and organizations in the community.

Regardless of how teachers acquire books for the library, they should be sure to let students participate in the selection of titles. Teachers can ask students to recommend particular books or authors or subjects. For additional suggestions, teachers can consult annotated bibliographies that contain summaries and sometimes short reviews of books.

Teachers should choose a specific area of the classroom for the library, then develop a set of clear and simple rules for its operation. Here are some suggestions.

- Set limits on the number of books that can be borrowed and on the length of the borrowing period. Assign two or three students, on a rotating basis, to be library assistants and let them be responsible for such jobs as checking books out and in, issuing overdue book notices, and keeping library shelves in order.

19.9

- Establish times when students are allowed to check out and return books. Such times might be at the beginning and end of the school day, before or after lunch, or during periods when the students are assigned independent work. Students should have frequent access to the library.

*"One of the most powerful ways a school can encourage independent reading is by establishing a policy requiring students to read a set number of minutes outside of class daily."*

—HONIG, 1996

The classroom library will be most effective if it is regarded as a springboard to wider reading. The library is particularly important to students who do not have public library cards and who do not have books at home. By making these students more comfortable with books and library settings, the classroom library may lead them to seek out additional sources of books. Teachers can encourage students further by arranging frequent class trips to the school library or even to a community library.

Finally, teachers should expect that some of the books will get torn or damaged or will disappear into the hands of eager readers; they should be prepared to replenish the library on a regular basis.

## Establishing Schoolwide Reading Programs

Independent reading should not be limited to individual classrooms. In fact, independent reading programs will be most effective if they are implemented on a schoolwide basis.

While individual teachers know best how to encourage their students to read independently, a schoolwide program can

19.10

reinforce what goes on in the classroom by promoting a general attitude that independent reading is an integral part of learning at all grade levels.

There are a few activities the school can do to create and maintain a schoolwide focus on independent reading.

- Maintain hallway bulletin boards that focus on reading.

- Make a "chain of reading" composed of strips of construction paper containing the names of books, authors, and readers and display it in the school library.

- Distribute reading certificates at awards-day ceremonies at the end of the school year.

- Conduct a "battle of the books" in which students compete by answering questions about books they have read.

- Sign up for community and library programs sponsored by federal and state governments, such as Reading Is Fundamental (RIF).

Finally, teachers can extend their in-school independent reading program beyond the school by enlisting the cooperation of parents, Parent-Teacher Associations, and community groups in promoting activities and projects that foster and recognize students' voluntary reading. Many local and national businesses sponsor programs to promote reading. Teachers should investigate these programs and involve students in those that seem appropriate. □

# Book Discussions

what?
why?
when?
how?

# what?

*Book Discussions*

20.2

*"Discussion is an integral part of the comprehension process."*

—ALVERMANN ET AL., 1996

In the recent past, a classroom engaging in "book discussion" would typically read a book together, chapter by chapter, and then respond to a series of questions generated by the teacher. For example, a fourth-grade class that has just read Chapter 11 in *Charlotte's Web* might participate in the following exchange.

TEACHER: All right. Chapter 11 is called "The Miracle." What was the miracle message that appeared in Charlotte's web? Tina?

TINA: "Some Pig."

TEACHER: Right! Ming, what happened as a result of this miraculous web?

MING: People came.

TEACHER: Yes, people came to see the message in the web. What else happened? Chris?

CHRIS: (No answer.)

TEACHER: Well, what about Wilbur, Chris? Did Charlotte manage to save him, as she had promised?

CHRIS: Um, yes.

The teacher in this exchange uses questions to quiz students—to determine whether they have completed their assignment and to test their comprehension. This type of rapid-fire questioning with short answers is best described as *recitation* rather than true discussion.

Alvermann, Dillon, and O'Brien (1987) have identified three criteria that distinguish true discussion from simple recitation: (1) students offering different viewpoints are open to changing their minds based on the evidence presented; (2) students

## Purpose of Book Discussions

**Motivate students to read**

**Provide opportunities to freely explore ideas**

**Deepen students' understanding of what they read**

interact with the teacher and with one another; and (3) most responses, especially those expressing student opinions, are longer than the two- or three-word answers typical of recitations.

Research into discussion (Bridges 1979; Dillon 1984) has built on the extended work of Louise Rosenblatt (1938, 1978). Her reader-response theory defines reading as a transaction between the reader and the writer; both are crucial to the construction of meaning. Discussions, then, become a forum for sharing and validating a reader's personal interpretation of a text and an opportunity for working together to further explore the text and construct additional understandings. Book discussions provide students with opportunities to share and discuss books with others, promote reading achievement, enhance oral language and higher-level cognition, and develop students' desire to read. From these discussions emerge accomplished, enthusiastic, engaged readers.

## Conducting Effective Book Discussions

The size of a given discussion group depends on its purpose, students' abilities, and the teacher's comfort level. Gage and Berliner (1984) found that effective discussion could be conducted in groups of as few as two to as large as twenty students.

When implementing large-group discussions, the teacher should use the discussion purpose to shape the planning. If the teacher wishes to conduct a large-group issue-oriented discussion on a topic such as Global Warming or Proper Role Models, the main consideration would be to assemble heterogeneous, rather than homogeneous, groups. This is because it is important for the participants to have differing opinions on the topic or the discussion will fall flat. Teacher preparation is also critical to these discussions. Since these discussions are likely to be teacher-led, the teacher must spend time prior to discussion deciding what text will best serve the discussion and lead to the important ideas for students to examine.

Teachers must not assume that students "know" how to conduct small-group book discussions on their own or that a simple posting of guidelines will be sufficient. In fact, students require direct instruction in a variety of discussion skills, such as taking turns talking, challenging ideas instead of classmates, and backing up generalizations with specific examples. Direct instruction can take place through modeling, guided practice, and feedback.

In a method developed by Jewell and Pratt (1999), teachers begin the school year by conducting some whole-class discussions, each focusing on a single story that everyone has read. During these sessions, the teacher models how to pose good discussion questions, how to find supporting evidence in text, how to make connections among ideas, and how to elaborate upon one's own ideas. After four to six weeks of whole-class discussions, the class is divided in half, with one group reading or thinking of possible discussion questions while the other group meets under teacher supervision. After two to three weeks of these half-class discussions, students are ready to try meeting in small groups.

## Students' Roles

For effective book discussions students need to know what they are expected to do. Even if a teacher asks probing, open-ended questions, students may be unresponsive, waiting for a cue that will tell them what the "right" answer is. Students tend to view "others" as the ultimate authority—the teacher, or the authors of the books they read. To help them assume responsibility as partners in learning, students can be taught to use and follow a set of Discussion Guidelines:

- Everyone's opinion is important and should be valued. Don't be afraid to say what you think.

- Give everyone a chance to share personal opinions. Don't interrupt!

---

**20.4**

## When setting up discussion groups, consider the…

**Overall purpose of the discussion.**

**Number of participants.**

**Type of grouping (heterogeneous vs. homogeneous).**

**Amount of direct instruction needed.**

**Roles that students will play.**

## Discussion Guidelines

## Student Discussion Group Roles

**discussion director**

**literary luminator or passage master**

**connector**

**illustrator**

## Teacher Discussion Group Roles

**instructor/leader**

**participant**

**consultant/advisor**

**observer**

- When you participate in a discussion, spend as much energy listening to what other students are saying as you do thinking about what you want to say. You might hear something interesting!

- There are many ways to contribute other than offering an opinion or answering a question: share an experience that is connected to something you read; react to what someone else has said; raise a question about something in the text; read a favorite passage aloud.

- Always go back to the text to support what you are saying. Nothing proves your point better than an example right out of the book.

- Good discussions involve sharing ideas. Keep an open mind. Sometimes what someone says may clarify or change what you are thinking. Sometimes what you say affects someone else's thinking. We can all help each other learn!

One way to help students learn how to function within a group is to assign them rotating roles. Cummings (1998) suggests the following roles:

- **discussion director**  This student is responsible for thinking up good, open-ended discussion questions, getting the group together, and making sure that everyone contributes to the discussion.

- **literary luminator or passage master**  This student tends to the text, reminds the group of important or effective moments, and reads selected passages aloud.

- **connector**  This student strives to make connections between the text and the everyday world by using the text itself and the comments that group members make.

- **illustrator**  This student provides graphic, nonverbal responses to the text.

20.5

## Teachers' Roles

Depending on the role they decide to take in a particular discussion, teachers can monitor and guide discussions in a number of ways. There are basically four roles for a teacher to consider, with the teacher moving from role to role as the situation warrants:

- **instructor/leader**   The teacher is in charge—directing, clarifying, telling. When overused, this role can result in a discussion that is more of a recitation and can confuse students by putting the teacher back in the role of ultimate authority.

- **participant**   The teacher becomes a member of the group. As a participant, the teacher is in a position to model good discussion behavior and to help keep discussions focused and interactive. The teacher should take care not to dominate or dictate the discussion, however; students tend to view teachers' comments as more credible than their own and will end up deferring to the teacher or looking to the teacher for discussion cues.

- **consultant/advisor**   The teacher circulates among students, consulting with them on an as-needed basis when problems arise. The goal for the teacher is to direct students toward finding their own answers, rather than simply telling them what to do or how to answer. Students are apt to use the teacher as the "final word" in settling disputes, rather than working out disagreements among themselves.

- **observer**   The teacher stays neutral—not offering opinions, asking questions, or confirming responses. Being an observer, in many ways, is the most desirable role a teacher can play because it indicates that students have taken on full responsibility for managing their learning and conducting their discussion.

20.6

*"For teachers, the neutral role is an ultimate goal because it marks the transfer of their modeled discussion behaviors to students."*

—ALVERMANN ET AL., 1996

> "To have a successful classroom discussion, it is necessary to have the proper setting and climate. Students must feel free to express their opinions and see that what they say will be accepted."
>
> —IRVIN, 1998

Teachers also need to ask themselves whether they are doing everything they can to promote effective discussions:

*Is the environment conducive to discussion?* Certain seating arrangements facilitate student participation and the free flow of ideas. For whole-class or large-group discussions that involve the teacher, a horseshoe arrangement with the teacher at one end is preferable. Row seating prevents students from seeing one another and tends to inhibit students seated toward the back and the sides. For small, student-led discussion groups, an arrangement of chairs around a circular table or a carpeted area in the corner of the room provides the necessary intimacy for students to interact effectively.

*Are there enough opportunities provided for students to discuss what they are reading?* The teacher needs to set aside certain times every week for book discussions. National Merit Scholarship winners stated that teachers who allowed time for classroom discussion contributed the most to their desire to learn (McKeachie 1978). Classroom discussions are just as beneficial for elementary-school students, who need ample opportunity to develop their oral language skills, as they are for middle-school students, who are attempting to master content in various curriculum areas.

*Am I projecting the proper attitude?* Are students encouraged to express themselves? Are they given sufficient time to answer, with strategic prompts to help them along? Are multiple viewpoints on issues accepted? Is the teacher stressing the importance of supporting opinions with textual evidence? Is the teacher modeling being a motivated reader/learner and adhering to the Discussion Guidelines established for students?

## Selection of Reading Material

In large-group discussions, the choice of reading material tends to be under the teacher's control. In small-group discussions, students should be given the freedom to select material so they can feel invested in the book they are about to read. However, *complete* self-selection only works if independent reading is the goal; it does not work as a vehicle for forming discussion groups. A good compromise is for the teacher to select a *set* of books—perhaps organized around a theme or author to lend cohesiveness—and to have students select from among these titles. Providing a mix of reading levels is recommended to accommodate students' varying abilities. Additional options for meeting the individual needs of students include having them listen to audiotapes of the book, reading the book aloud to them, or having them read the book with a partner who is a more accomplished reader.

To help students choose which book to read, the teacher can give a short "book talk" (30 seconds will suffice) to "sell" each title. Below is a sample book talk for *Zeeley,* part of a fifth-grade author study on Virginia Hamilton.

Intervention
Strategy

**20.8**   **Select books that have good picture/text correspondence. Pair students with more able readers or have students listen to an audiotape of the text as they follow along. Allow students to respond to the literature in their first language and have others translate.**

## Book Talk

> Did you ever wish you could be someone else? Does your imagination sometimes get carried away? Do you ever have trouble getting along with your family? With other people? If you do, you have something in common with Elizabeth, the main character in *Zeeley,* who is absolutely fascinated by her mysterious neighbor—a tall, beautiful woman named Zeeley.

After students have listened to the book talks, they are given a chance to examine each book. They then use a sign-up sheet to indicate their first two choices. The teacher then groups students so they can read their first- or second-choice books. On the facing page is a sample sign-up sheet for the Virginia Hamilton author study. Most of the books are written at a fifth-grade level; however, *The House of Dies Drear* is a bit more challenging than *Jaguarundi* and *Drylongso*.

## ✔ Books by Author Virginia Hamilton

| The House of Dies Drear | Zeeley | Jaguarundi | Cousins | Drylongso |
|---|---|---|---|---|
| (1) Heather | (1) Joshua | (1) Eva | (1) Lindsey | (1) Adam |
| (2) Tobias | (1) Kim | (1) Celeste | (1) Selena | (1) Cameron |
| (1) Yuki | (1) Emily | (1) Jamal | (2) Heather | (1) Marco |
| (1) Adolfo | (1) Tyriece | (1) Andrea | (2) Kenesha | (2) Adolfo |
| (2) Aaron | (2) Yuki | (1) Quintin | (2) Vivian | (1) Aaron |
| (1) Kenesha | (2) Ben | (1) Joon Hee | (2) Emily | (2) Kim |
| (2) Matthew | (2) Jamal | (2) Paulina | (2) Eva | (2) Quintin |
| (1) Ben | (2) Lindsey | (2) Tyriece | (2) Celeste | (2) Khan |
| (1) Vivian | (2) Carter | (2) Selena | (1) Tobias | (1) Matthew |
| (1) Carter | (2) Andrea | (2) Jessica | (1) Yuki | (1) Jessica |
| (1) Paulina | | (2) Cameron | | |
| (2) Joshua | | (2) Marco | | |
| (2) Adam | | (1) Khan | | |
| (2) Joon Hee | | | | |

20.10

## Reading Logs

Teachers can also monitor and guide students by using reading logs, sometimes called dialogue or response journals. Students use the logs for recording their personal responses to the literature. Some students find it easy to use this format and need minimal direction or modeling from the teacher. For others, more direction is needed. In such cases, the teacher may suggest prompts for students to use to stimulate their thoughts: *How does this story make you feel? Does anything puzzle you? How do you feel about the characters? Are you enjoying reading this story? Why, or why not? Does anything in this story remind you of something in your life? Has the author used words and images that you particularly like?* Students are invited periodically to share their logs with the teacher, who may respond personally to what the student has recorded. This is an excerpt from a student's reading log for *Zeeley*:

Reading Log ▽

---

Chapter 11:

I was so exsited by this chapter. What would happen to the hogs? What would Geeder do? She was very brave I thougt. And she gets to meet Zeeley too, who is her hero. I would like to be like Geeder—meet my hero and help her and have her proteck me.

Dear Kim,

I totally agree with you. I found this chapter to be extremely exciting! I think the author did a wonderful job of helping the reader see, hear, feel, and smell what was happening. Enjoy the rest of the book.

Sincerely, Mrs. Taber

---

### Literature Circles

Small-group discussions of books selected by the students. Groups meet after students read assigned pages. Discussions are led by the students. Response logs and checklists encourage active participation.

### The Reading Workshop

Begins with a teacher-led, whole-class minilesson. Primary focus is silent self-selected reading and response (journal writing, teacher conference, or small-group discussion). Each workshop ends with student sharing time.

### Questioning the Author (QtA)

Whole-class, teacher-led discussion during the first reading of a portion of text selected by the teacher. The teacher poses queries to launch discussion and help students work collaboratively to construct meaning.

# Instructional Techniques and Procedures

## Literature Circles

Rosenblatt's reader-response theory has generated a number of variations on the theme of small-group discussions including: literature response groups (Reutzel and Cooter 1991), literature discussion groups (Routman 1991), reader response groups (Ruddell and Ruddell 1995), open discussion groups (Sorenson 1993), and literature circles (Short and Klassen 1993). The goal of all these variations is the same: to have a small group of students (usually four or five) read the same piece of literature and then discuss it together.

In the literature circle approach, the teacher gathers multiple copies of several related titles (either on a similar topic, by the same author, or in the same genre). The teacher then presents a short "book talk" for each title, essentially "selling" the book to students, and gives students a chance to look at the individual books. A sign-up sheet is posted, and students are asked to sign up for their first two choices. This is an important feature of literature circles—giving students some degree of choice in the books they read. Research has shown that self-selection is a powerful motivator in getting students interested in their reading (Deci and Ryan 1985; Gambrell 1996).

After students have signed up, the teacher divides the class into small groups (with a maximum of seven members), based on their first and second choices. Group members work with the teacher to plan their reading: *How long will they take to read the book? How many pages will they read each day? When and where will they meet?* As students in each group read and discuss their book, they take turns leading the discussions. The teacher periodically meets with each group, generally as a participant. To ensure student participation, the teacher may have students keep reading logs, where they can comment on what they are reading and note down passages that interest, provoke, or puzzle them. Log entries are then used to launch literature circle discussions. In addition, students can monitor their participation in each group meeting by completing a Literature Circle Checklist.

Although the teacher plays an important role in guiding and monitoring small-group book discussions, it is critical that students assume an increasing role in monitoring their performance. One way to help students self-monitor is by having them complete checklists after each book discussion.

20.12

---

### LITERATURE CIRCLE CHECKLIST

Name: _____

Date: _____

Book (Title and Author): _____

_____

| **Was I Prepared?** | **Yes** | **No** | |
|---|---|---|---|
| Did I read the assigned pages? | _____ | _____ | |
| Did I make note of things I wanted to discuss? | _____ | _____ | |
| Did I bring my book and notes to the literature circle? | _____ | _____ | |

| **How Would I Rate My Performance?** | **Weak** | **Good** | **Excellent** |
|---|---|---|---|
| My participation in the discussion? | _____ | _____ | _____ |
| My comments? | _____ | _____ | _____ |
| My use of text to support ideas? | _____ | _____ | _____ |
| My ability to listen to others? | _____ | _____ | _____ |
| My teamwork overall? | _____ | _____ | _____ |

> *"Only in regular reading workshops can students gain the experience with the printed texts they need to grow to fluency."*
>
> —ATWELL, 1987

## The Reading Workshop

The idea of the reading workshop was first developed by Nancie Atwell (1987) to give students a time when "there isn't anything to do but read; the teacher reads too." Every day at a set time for approximately 45 minutes, she would have her students engage in either a writing workshop (three days a week) or a reading workshop (two days a week).

Each reading workshop began with a teacher-led, whole-class minilesson (five to ten minutes) that usually involved discussing a particular author or piece of writing. The rest of the workshop was devoted to independent reading. For the first ten minutes or so, Atwell would circulate among her students to make sure they were all on task and then settle back to read *her* book for the remainder of the workshop. She had her students keep reading logs (dialogue journals) which were essentially open letters written to her by the students that detailed their personal responses to the literature. From time to time, she would collect the logs, read each student's entries, and write a response in the reading log. In addition, she would set up one-on-one conferences with students to monitor their progress in the workshop. She created and posted a set of "Rules for Reading Workshops" that included such items as "Students must read for the entire period" and "Students may not talk or disturb others."

Various educators have adapted Atwell's original model, giving students opportunities to "break the silence" and engage in book discussions. For example, Graves, Juel, and Graves (1998) have proposed the following structure for a reading workshop:

**Teacher sharing time (5–10 minutes)**  At the beginning of each workshop, the teacher shares his or her personal feelings about reading. The teacher may read aloud from a favorite piece of writing, such as a favorite poem.

**Minilessons (5–15 minutes)**   A tightly focused, whole-class, reading-related minilesson follows the teacher sharing time. The lesson may be procedural (e.g., a review of the rules for conducting the workshop), informational (e.g., background on a reading topic), or skills-based (e.g., a skill or strategy that students need to develop and can apply to their reading).

**20.14**

**Self-selected reading and response (30–40 minutes)**   The core of each workshop is reading—students engaged with texts that they have selected. They may be reading a book on their own, with a partner, or in a small group. At any given point, several activities may be taking place, along with independent silent reading: writing in reading logs, talking about upcoming reading plans, and small-group discussions.

**Student sharing time (5–10 minutes)**   At the end of every reading workshop, the class meets to share and discuss what students have been doing. The typical topic of discussion will be students' experiences with their reading, but other topics may arise. Students may have questions about what they have read that they hope others can answer. They may be looking for partners to read a particular book with. They may have some information they want to pass along (e.g., a favorite author is going to be reading and signing a book at a nearby bookstore).

## Questioning the Author (QtA)

As envisioned by its creators, Isabel Beck and Margaret McKeown, Questioning the Author "is an approach to text-based instruction that was designed to facilitate building understanding of text ideas" (Beck, McKeown, Hamilton, and Kucan 1997). The discussion involved in this approach differs from the book discussions in literature circles and reading workshops in several significant ways:

- The text under discussion is not selected by the students. Typically, it is assigned reading in a content-area textbook.

- The discussion is structured—led and managed by the teacher, who poses queries that engage students in discussing a portion of text. The questioning and discussion is usually done in a whole-class setting.

- The discussion takes place during the initial reading of the text, not before reading begins or after students have completed a chapter in a text. Therefore, the discussion happens "on-line."

> *"In QtA, we teach students that readers must try to 'take on' a text, little by little, idea by idea, and try to understand while they are reading what ideas are there and how they might connect or relate to those ideas."*
>
> —BECK ET AL., 1998

The QtA approach grew out of Beck and McKeown's research into textbook writing. They found that content-area texts often were poorly or confusingly organized, were badly written, and unreasonably assumed knowledge on the part of the reader. The researchers began revising the texts so that students would be better able to extract meaning. As they tested students on the revised material, they realized that the student participants still thought of textbook authors as infallible authorities. As far as the students were concerned, any problem with understanding lay with them, not with the authors. Since Beck and McKeown firmly believe that reading should be a constructive engagement between the reader and the author, they looked for a way to empower their student readers. The procedure they developed can be outlined as follows:

**Philosophy**   The teacher introduces the class to QtA by "deposing the authority of the textbook." Students are led to see that textbook authors are ordinary, fallible people who don't always express themselves as clearly as they should.

**Preparation**   The teacher analyzes the assigned portion of the text to identify the key points and knowledge that students need to grasp. The text is then segmented (segments may be as long as a few paragraphs or as short as a sentence) to reflect those key points/knowledge. For each segment, the teacher generates a set of queries that direct students toward the key points/knowledge and that address potential obstacles to comprehending those ideas.

**Conducting discussions**   The class reads a segment of text. The teacher then poses queries—to initiate discussion, to encourage students to dig deeper, to focus on problems—to help students grapple with the text. Although the teacher encourages students to contribute to the discussion, the focus is kept on the segment of text. The approach includes a set of "discussion moves," which are designed to help the teacher manage and facilitate this focused discussion. Once the teacher feels students have grasped the text segment, they move on to discuss the next segment.

Queries are at the heart of this approach. They are categorized as either *initiating queries* (stimulating discussion) or *follow-up queries* (helping to focus the content and direction of a discussion, helping students integrate ideas). Their intent is very different from the traditional kind of textbook questioning employed by teachers. The table on the facing page sums up these differences and provides examples of the two types of queries.

The queries the teacher prepares prior to a discussion are not a script. Beck and McKeown compare the queries to a rehearsal: The queries are the teacher's attempt to roughly outline how the discussion is likely to go. The teacher responds to the actual discussion and the particular problems that students encounter during that discussion.

Although QtA was developed to help students grapple with "inconsiderate" content-area textbook writing, Beck and McKeown have recently (1997) extended its use to narrative text, providing a modified pattern of queries that the teacher

# QUESTIONING THE AUTHOR (QtA)

| | |
|---|---|
| **Questions** | • Design to evaluate student comprehension of assigned text<br>• Assess individual student responses in a student-to-teacher interaction<br>• Use before or after the full-length reading assignment |
| **Queries** | • Assist students in working together to grapple with the text and actively engage in constructing meaning<br>• Facilitate group discussion of text and prompt student-to-student interactions<br>• Use during the initial reading of a portion of the text |

| | |
|---|---|
| **Initiating Queries**<br>(Stimulate Discussion) | • What is the author trying to say here?<br>• What is the message?<br>• What is the author talking about? |
| **Follow-Up Queries**<br>(Focus Discussion) | • What does the author mean here?<br>• Did the author explain this clearly?<br>• Does this make sense with what the author told us before?<br>• How does this relate to what the author told us here?<br>• Does the author tell us why?<br>• Why do you think the author tells us this now? |

can use. Examples of narrative queries include: *How do things look for this character now? Given what the author has already told us about this character, what do you think he's up to? How has the author let you know that something has changed? How has the author settled this for us?*

Although QtA differs from other book discussion procedures in many ways, it also has something in common with them: The goal of discussion is to have students work together to extract meaning from text, and to have them take responsibility for understanding and appreciating what they are reading.

## *Book Discussions*

**20.18**

Book discussions are pivotal in developing strong readers and learners. During discussions students practice and refine their comprehension strategies and higher-order thinking skills. They also draw upon their understanding of narrative and expository text organization and develop social skills. Research by Gallagher and Pearson (1989) found that discussion not only helped students refine and enrich their understanding of an assigned text, but also promoted recall. When students read a paragraph aloud and then discussed it, they were better able to understand and retain the information than students who had simply read the text on their own.

Another important benefit of book discussions is that they motivate students to read, setting them on the road to becoming lifelong readers. Research by Guthrie, Shafer, Wang, and Afflerbach (1993) has shown that students who engage in frequent discussions about their reading are more motivated to read and have higher reading achievement scores than students who don't participate in discussions. The research team also noted a reciprocal relationship between discussions and independent reading: Book discussions seem to result in more extensive reading, and more extensive reading seems to lead naturally to book discussions.

**Research Findings . . .**

*Our ability to think originates outside ourselves, [so] we must view class discussions as more than just a peripheral part of a thinking-skills [reading] program. Discussion is essential.*

—STERNBERG, 1987

*The use of recitation and lecture . . . cannot compete with discussion in offering opportunities for students to communicate their views to other students with different views.*

**20.19**

—ALVERMANN ET AL., 1987

**Suggested Reading . . .**

*Using Discussion to Promote Reading Comprehension* (1987) by Donna E. Alvermann, Deborah R. Dillon & David G. O'Brien. Newark, DE: International Reading Association.

*In the Middle: Writing, Reading, and Learning with Adolescents* (1987) by Nancie Atwell. Portsmouth, NH: Heinemann.

*Questioning the Author: An Approach for Enhancing Student Engagement with Text* (1997) by Isabel Beck, Margaret G. McKeown, Rebecca L. Hamilton & Linda Kucan. Newark, DE: International Reading Association.

*Teaching Reading in the 21st Century* (1998) by Michael F. Graves, Connie Juel & Bonnie B. Graves. Needham Heights, MA: Allyn & Bacon.

## Section References

Alvermann, D. E., D. R. Dillon, and D. G. O'Brien. 1987. *Using discussion to promote reading comprehension.* Newark, DE: International Reading Association.

Anderson, R. C., E. H. Hiebert, J. A. Scott, and I. A. G. Wilkinson. 1985. *Becoming a nation of readers: The report of the Commission on Reading.* Urbana-Champaign, IL: Center for the Study of Reading and National Academy of Education.

Atwell, N. 1987. *In the middle: Writing, reading, and learning with adolescents.* Portsmouth, NH: Heinemann.

Beck, I. L., M. G. McKeown, R. L. Hamilton, and L. Kucan. 1997. *Questioning the author: An approach for enhancing student engagement with text.* Newark, DE: International Reading Association.

Beck, I. L., M. G. McKeown, R. L. Hamilton, and L. Kucan. 1998. Getting at the meaning. *American Educator* Spring/Summer 1998.

Bridges, D. 1979. *Education, democracy, and discussion.* Windsor, England: NEFR Publishing.

Cummings, N. 1998. Talking about books in collaborative groups. *Scholastic Literacy Research Paper.* New York: Scholastic, Inc.

Deci, E. L., and R. M. Ryan. 1985. *Intrinsic motivation and self-determination in human behavior.* San Diego, CA: Academic Press.

Dillon, J. T. 1984. Research on questioning and discussion. *Educational Leadership* 42, pp. 50–56.

Gage, N. L., and D. D. Berliner. 1984. *Educational psychology.* (3rd ed.) Boston: Houghton Mifflin.

Gallagher, M., and P. D. Pearson. 1989. Discussion, comprehension, and knowledge acquisition in content-area classrooms. *Technical Report #480.* Urbana-Champaign, IL: Center for the Study of Reading.

Gambrell, L. B. 1996. Choice, challenge, control, collaboration: Motivating children to read. *Scholastic Literacy Research Paper.* New York: Scholastic, Inc.

Graves, M. F., C. Juel, and B. B. Graves. 1998. *Teaching reading in the 21st century.* Needham Heights, MA: Allyn & Bacon.

Guthrie, V. T., W. Shafer, Y. Wang, and P. Afflerbach. 1993. Influences of instruction on reading engagement: An empirical exploration of a social-cognitive framework of reading activity. *Research Report #3.* Athens, GA: National Reading Research Center.

Honig, B. 1996. *Teaching our children to read.* Thousand Oaks, CA: Corwin Press.

Irvin, J. L. 1998. *Reading and the middle school student.* Needham Heights, MA: Allyn & Bacon.

Jewell, T. A., and D. Pratt. 1999. Literature discussion in the primary grades: Children's thoughtful discourse about books and what teachers can do to make it happen. *The Reading Teacher* 52(8), pp. 842–850.

Learning First Alliance Board of Directors. 1998. Action paper. Learning First Alliance Summit on Reading and Mathematics, Washington, DC.

McKeachie, W. J. 1978. *Teaching tips.* (7th ed.) Lexington, MA: D.C. Heath.

Reutzel, D. R., and R. B. Cooter. 1991. Organizing for effective instruction: The reading workshop. *The Reading Teacher* 44, pp. 548–554.

Rosenblatt, L. M. 1938/1983. *Literature as exploration.* New York: Modern Language Association.

Rosenblatt, L. M. 1978. *The reader, the text, the poem: The transactional theory of the literary work.* Carbondale, IL: Southern Illinois University Press.

Routman, R. 1991. *Invitations: Changing as teachers and learners K–12.* Portsmouth, NH: Heinemann.

Ruddell, R. B., and M. R. Ruddell. 1995. *Teaching children to read and write.* Needham Heights, MA: Allyn & Bacon.

Shany, M. T., and A. Biemiller. 1995. Assisted reading practice: Effects on performance of poor readers in Grades 3 and 4. *Reading Research Quarterly* 50.

Short, K. G., and C. Klassen. 1993. Literature circles: Hearing children's voices. In B. E. Cullinan (ed.), *Children's voices: Talk in the classroom.* Newark, DE: International Reading Association.

Sorenson, M. 1993. Teach each other: Connecting talking and writing. *English Journal,* pp. 42–47.

Sternberg, R. J. 1987. Most vocabulary is learned from context. In M. G. McKeown and M. E. Curtis (eds.), *The nature of vocabulary acquisition.* Mahwah, NJ: Erlbaum.

**SECTION IX**

# Differentiated Instruction

# INTRODUCTION

## Section IX: Differentiated Instruction

*"When we create effective communities of learners in which the needs of all learners are specifically and systematically addressed, we will go a long way toward addressing both equity and excellence in schools."*

—TOMLINSON, 1999

One basic instructional goal is for every student to meet or exceed grade-level reading expectations. Differentiated instruction accomplishes this goal by tailoring instruction to students' current level of knowledge and skill. A differentiated classroom responds to the needs of all learners. Advanced students, as well as those with learning difficulties, often require systematically planned differentiation to ensure that curriculum and instruction are properly challenging (California Department of Education 1999). Differentiated instruction is determined in large part by assessment, and may be provided in small groups or, for those needing the most help, in individual tutoring sessions. Pacing is perhaps the most commonly used strategy for differentiation: teachers either slow down or speed up instruction. It can be a simple, effective, and inexpensive strategy for many students with special needs (Benbow and Stanley 1996; Geary 1994).

### Diverse Learners

The students who are often most at risk are those described by Edward Kameenui as "diverse learners," children who "by virtue of their instructional, socioeconomic, experiential, physiological, and neurological characteristics bring different and oftentimes additional requirements to instruction and curriculum" (Simmons and Kameenui 1998). Many of these students have identified language and learning disorders, some face linguistic challenges as they learn English, and still others have no particular defined disability but struggle profoundly to read. These are the students who need a well-designed curriculum from the start and strategically initiated and sustained intervention.

## Students with Disabilities or Learning Difficulties

Some students with identified learning problems have difficulty processing information. These students need very clear and explicit instruction with modeling, ample practice, and adequate feedback. For these students, instruction should utilize multimodal approaches and effective memory devices. In addition, for these students carefully planned incremental learning may be more effective than long sessions at a single sitting. Research suggests that the most vulnerable learners need sufficient review and practice to perform a new task automatically. Such review should be distributed over time; should cumulatively integrate simpler and already-learned tasks with newer, more complex activities; and should be applied in varied contexts to ensure internalization and transfer.

## Students Who Are Advanced Learners

Advanced learners are those who demonstrate or are capable of performance at a level significantly ahead of their same-age peers. Advanced learners should be provided with challenges not offered by the regular school curriculum. These students with advanced literacy skills are often overlooked in instructional planning. They need to be challenged by vocabulary extension study and exposure to sophisticated literature, both narrative and informational. Such opportunities can be built into learning centers or small-group instructional time.

Adapted from *Reading/Language Arts Framework for California Public Schools: Kindergarten Through Grade Twelve* (1999). Sacramento: California Department of Education.

## Students Who Are English Language Learners

The goal for English language learners (ELL) is to develop proficiency in English language and literacy skills. Instructional programs for English learners should be planned according to the students' assessed levels of literacy in English and their primary language as well as their proficiency in English. English language proficiency progresses from the students' initial contact with formal instruction in English to the point at which their use of English compares with that of their native English-speaking peers. Because of differing academic backgrounds and ages, some students can be expected to progress more quickly and others to require more support in the English-language arts program.

Three groups of English learners must be considered in program planning: students in Kindergarten through Grade 2; those in Grades 3 through 12 who are literate in their primary language; and those in Grades 3 through 12 who have limited prior academic experience or literacy in their primary language. Typically, primary students who are learning English can participate fully in classroom language arts instruction if provided appropriate reading and writing supports and instruction in oral language. Students in Grades 3 through 12 who have strong literacy skills in their primary language can be expected to transfer many of those skills to English and to progress rapidly in learning English. And students in Grades 3 through 12 with limited prior schooling will require intensive support in beginning literacy instruction as well as learning English.

# CONTENTS

## Section IX: Differentiated Instruction

CHAPTER

21

# Assessment

what?
why?
when?
how?

# what? *Assessment*

**21.2**

See also...

**CORE Assessing Reading**

Assessment is used to inform instruction for both large groups and individuals. Different assessment instruments serve different purposes. For example, statewide achievement tests are useful to inform the public about system-wide instructional efficacy. While such broad-based tests provide useful programmatic information, they are usually less precise in providing information about individual student strengths and weaknesses. Individual diagnostic tests are very useful to the classroom teacher for instructional planning as well as to inform parents of student needs, but are less important for broad public accountability. Regular assessments are needed to guide decisions about such things as grouping, the instructional pace, and individual need for support.

In reading instruction, the content and skills in the early grades are discrete. These specific skills and strategies tend to be "enabling" skills, providing the foundation for long-term outcomes such as comprehension and fluency. Because of the need for mastery of these precursor skills, reading assessment in the early grades needs to be frequent and specific. In the upper grades, assessment is necessary to monitor progress but also to identify causes of reading weakness. Unlike primary-grade measures, which start discrete and then broaden, upper-grade assessment often starts broadly and then becomes more specific in order to pinpoint particular subskills that are causing reading difficulty. As such, assessment in the upper grades becomes increasingly diagnostic.

## Types of Assessment

Within their schools, educators need to organize their assessment toolkits around three broad types of assessment: screening tests; formative, ongoing assessments; and summative assessments. In all cases, teachers need to understand the expected targets of mastery for individual skills in order to identify students at risk of difficulty and to tailor instruction to meet identified needs.

**Screening tests** provide information about the knowledge and skill base of the student. They are useful for determining the most appropriate starting point for instruction and for planning instructional groups. Screening tests usually include formal and informal measures with clear mastery targets. In the primary grades, screening tests should measure phonological awareness, phonics, fluency, vocabulary, spelling, and comprehension. In the upper grades, comprehension is the first screening test, but only as a starting point. Follow-up assessments can be used to target areas for instruction, based on any apparent weaknesses.

**Formative assessment** is ongoing. Examples of formative assessment are teacher observations, informal or formal tests, and curriculum tasks. Formative assessment often looks more like instruction in that it includes tasks typically used during the instructional process; as such, it is often referred to as *curriculum-based assessment.* Ongoing formative assessment may also include diagnostic tests that pinpoint the causes of a particular screening test result or a particular observed reading problem. Formative assessment serves to further define the specific focus of instruction.

**Summative assessment** is often used at the end of major units of instruction and at year's end. It provides data about exiting accomplishments and is useful for planning the next major

21.4

segment of instruction for individual students. It also provides programmatic information for large groups of students. Summative assessment usually leads to summative evaluation, which represents a final annual judgment about a student's strengths and weaknesses.

**Diagnostic assessment** instruments can be used for screening, for formative or summative assessment, to assess students' specific strengths and weaknesses, and/or to plan instruction. These diagnostic tests include the *Woodcock Reading Mastery Test, Durrell Analysis of Reading Difficulty,* and *Stanford Diagnostic Reading Test.*

## TYPES AND FREQUENCY OF EFFECTIVE ASSESSMENT SYSTEMS

| | Screening | Formative Assessment | Summative Assessment |
|---|---|---|---|
| **Kindergarten** | • Midyear and year-end<br>• Can be same tools used for summative | • Frequent, to direct ongoing modification of the curriculum<br>• Informal curriculum-based assessments | • At end of a major instructional sequence<br>• Can be same tools used for screening and formative |
| **Grade 1** | • Two or three times yearly<br>• Can be same tools used for summative | • Frequent, to direct ongoing modification of the curriculum<br>• Informal curriculum-based assessments | • At end of a major instructional sequence<br>• Can be same tools used for screening and formative |
| **Grades 2 and 3** | • Two or three times yearly<br>• Can be same tools used for summative | • Frequent, to direct ongoing modification of the curriculum<br>• Informal curriculum-based assessments | • At end of a major instructional sequence<br>• Can be same tools used for screening and formative |
| **Grades 4 through 8** | • Beginning of year<br>• Can be same tools used for summative | • Frequent, for monitoring formal and informal measures, including assignments as part of regular curriculum | • At end of a major instructional sequence<br>• Can be same tools used for screening and formative |

SOURCE From *CORE Assessing Reading* (1999) by CORE. Novato, CA: Arena Press.

## Assessing Reading

Reading is a complex process. Fluent reading is made up of two major components: (1) the ability to recognize the written word, and (2) the ability to comprehend text as a whole unit. In order to evaluate student progress and to provide help to students with reading difficulties, teachers need to utilize assessments that isolate these two major components.

Many students fail to develop the decoding skills necessary for automatic word recognition because they are not aware that spoken words are composed of units of sound, or phonemes. Because phoneme awareness is a strong correlate of reading skill, it is the basic skill to be assessed in beginning readers (Joshi 1995). Decoding skill can also be directly assessed through tests of real and pseudowords. According to Adams (1990), poorly developed word recognition skills are the most pervasive and debilitating source of reading difficulty. Reading speed is also an important variable that distinguishes good readers from poor readers. For this reason, fluency tests are useful assessment measures.

Spelling knowledge supports fluent reading and writing. For this reason, it is important to monitor students' spelling. A study by Waters, Bruck, and Seidenberg (1985), which examined the question of whether students use similar processes to read and spell words, found that third-grade students, regardless of their ability level, used sound/spelling correspondence in both reading and spelling (Joshi 1995). Tests such as the *"Words Their Way" Qualitative Spelling Inventory* (Bear et al. 1996) provide the means to analyze spelling errors and to identify students' level of mastery of sound/spelling correspondence.

**21.6**

Tests of reading comprehension measure comprehension of passages and whole text—the ultimate goal of reading. Such tests measure reasoning skills through the use of multiple-choice questions, open-ended questions, or cloze passage techniques. To demonstrate comprehension, the student must use word recognition skills, syntactic knowledge, background knowledge, and reasoning skills.

Finally, vocabulary warrants assessment because it is so closely correlated with comprehension. Studies of reading comprehension conducted in 15 different countries show that the correlation between vocabulary and reading comprehension ranges from .66 to .75 (Just and Carpenter 1987; Thorndike 1973; Joshi 1995). The *Critchlow Verbal Language Scales* (Critchlow 1996) assess oral vocabulary, which in turn supports reading vocabulary.

In addition to specific reading assessments, every student should have reading conferences with his or her teacher at designated intervals. The student brings a book she or he is currently reading and shares with the teacher points of interest and information about the characters, events, or ideas. In addition, during a reading conference, the student can select a passage to read aloud to the teacher, thus providing another opportunity for assessing the student's fluency and for monitoring other reading skills. The reading conference can also be used to create a plan between the student and the teacher for follow-up work.

**Appendix**

**"Reading Conference Form"**

## Assessment Plan Sequences

The Assessment Plan Sequence for Primary-Grade Students
(Grades K–3) begins with assessments of the foundation skills.
In contrast, the Assessment Plan Sequence for Upper-Grade
Students (Grades 4–8) begins with the most global skills.
The following charts (pp. 21.8 and 21.9) show the types of
component skills to be assessed. For specific tests of some of
the component skills, see *CORE Assessing Reading*.

Connect to Theory

What reading assessment tools are currently used in your school?
Use copies of the Assessment Plan Sequence for Primary-Grade
Students (Grades K–3) or the Assessment Plan Sequence for
Upper-Grade Students (Grades 4–8) in the Appendix to identify
the tools. Indicate when and how often each assessment is used.
Use your completed forms to identify your plan's strengths and
weaknesses. Now use another copy to show how you would
revise and improve your current assessment plan sequence.

## Assessment Plan Sequence for Primary-Grade Students (Grades K–3)

| READING COMPONENT ASSESSED* | Kindergarten<br>Early  Mid.  Late | Grade 1<br>Early  Mid.  Late | Grade 2<br>Early  Mid.  Late | Grade 3<br>Early  Mid.  Late |
|---|---|---|---|---|
| ▶ Phonological Awareness | First assessment:<br>Middle | Early/Middle | Only if indicated | Only if indicated |
| ▶ Print Concepts | First assessment:<br>Middle | | | |
| ▶ Oral Vocabulary | First assessment:<br>Middle | Every 4–6 weeks<br>until mastery | 3 times a year | 3 times a year |
| ▶ Alphabet Recognition | First assessment:<br>Middle | Only if indicated | | |
| ▶ Phonic Elements | First assessment:<br>Middle (consonant<br>sounds) | Every 4–6 weeks<br>until mastery | Every 4–6 weeks<br>until mastery | Only if indicated |
| ▶ Spelling | | First assessment:<br>Late | 3 times a year | 3 times a year |
| ▶ Word Recognition | | First assessment:<br>Middle | 3 times a year | 3 times a year |
| ▶ Reading Fluency | | 2 times a year | 3 times a year | 3 times a year |
| ▶ Listening Comprehension<br>Oral Retellings | First assessment:<br>Middle | 3 times a year | | |
| ▶ Reading Comprehension | | | 3 times a year | 3 times a year |

*For specific assessment tools, see *CORE Assessing Reading.*

## Assessment Plan Sequence for Upper-Grade Students (Grades 4–8)

| READING COMPONENT ASSESSED* | Grade 4<br>Early    Mid.    Late | Grade 5<br>Early    Mid.    Late | Grade 6<br>Early    Mid.    Late | Grades 7–8<br>Early    Mid.    Late |
|---|---|---|---|---|
| ▶ **Reading Comprehension** | 3 times a year | 3 times a year | 3 times a year | 3 times a year |
| ▶ **Vocabulary** | 3 times a year | 3 times a year | 3 times a year | 3 times a year |
| ▶ **Reading Fluency** | 3 times a year | 3 times a year | 3 times a year | 3 times a year |
| ▶ **Word Recognition** | Early; then only if indicated | Only if indicated | Only if indicated | Only if indicated |
| ▶ **Spelling** | 3 times a year | 3 times a year | 3 times a year | 3 times a year |
| ▶ **Phonic Elements** | Only if indicated | Only if indicated | Only if indicated | Only if indicated |
| ▶ **Phonemic Awareness** | Only if indicated | Only if indicated | Only if indicated | Only if indicated |

*For specific assessment tools, see *CORE Assessing Reading.*

## Conducting Assessment

Teachers should first determine their assessment purpose and then select an appropriate instrument. If assessment is to be ongoing, it will be necessary to have a regular assessment schedule. Teachers who assess students regularly often pull individual students for assessment while others work independently or in small groups. Following is a model for conducting assessment.

**21.10**

## Conducting Assessment

### ① Gather Materials

All necessary materials both for the student and for the teacher should be close at hand. These materials include required word lists, passages, books, a timer, counters or other manipulative objects, record sheets, and so on.

### ② Explain Purpose

Explain the purpose of the assessment and encourage the student to do his or her best work. Direct the student to the materials needed and provide explicit directions. Tell the student in advance if you will be recording information during the process.

### ③ Model the Assessment

Model the assessment carefully and provide practice examples. Give explicit feedback during the practice session. Go over directions a second time.

### ④ Conduct the Assessment

Observe the student carefully, noting tension, anxiety, possible vision or hearing difficulties, and general test-taking behaviors. Do not praise answers that are right, but instead use feedback such as "Keep going . . ." "That's how it works . . ." "I can see you are really trying. . . ." If the student is having a great deal of difficulty, be sure the directions are understood. Discontinue the assessment if the student is having so much difficulty that he or she is becoming frustrated. Try it again at a later time. Thank each student for his or her effort.

### ⑤ Record Student Responses

Note the student's responses during the assessment, following the specific procedures provided. Transfer information to class rosters.

### ⑥ Plan Instruction or Intervention

Use the resulting information to plan or adjust small- or large-group instruction, to make referrals, and to initiate tutoring and at-home follow-up.

## Using Assessment to Inform Instruction

Assessment leads naturally to instruction and, as such, helps monitor and adjust instruction according to student progress. A tight link between assessment and instruction prevents the old "tracking" of students and ensures that each student's needs are met.

**Appendix**

"Class Roster: Kindergarten"

"Class Roster: Grade 1"

"Class Roster: Grades 2–3"

"Class Roster: Grades 4–8"

### Class Rosters

Class rosters enable a teacher to see at a glance which students need certain skills. Class rosters may be useful for parent-teacher conferences, when preparing report cards, and when forming instructional groups. The sample class rosters in the appendix can be used to record data obtained through assessment. By glancing down the skill data columns, the teacher can readily see clusters of students who have the same skill needs. On the rosters, teachers may record either a "+" or a "−" to indicate mastery or nonmastery, or they may record a specific score.

Assessment data informs grouping and intervention. If a critical skill is not mastered, this may indicate a need for intervention.

## MASTERY TARGETS FOR CRITICAL SKILLS (GRADES K–2)

| | | Assessed Skill | Critical Indicator | Intervention |
|---|---|---|---|---|
| **21.12** | **Kindergarten** | Print Concepts and Alphabet Recognition | Can identify parts of a book; knows the basic conventions of directionality; and can recognize most upper- and lowercase letters by midyear | Teacher-led small-group instruction (see Section III) |
| | | Phonemic Awareness | Can identify words that begin with the same sound by midyear | Teacher-led small-group instruction (see Section III) |
| | | Listening Comprehension | Can retell a familiar story by midyear | Teacher-led small-group storytelling (see Section VII) |
| | **Grade 1** | Phonemic Awareness | Can identify words that end with the same sound and blend orally segmented CVC words early in the year | Teacher-led small-group instruction (see Section III) |
| | | Decoding | Can read real and nonsense CVC words and some words with consonant blends by midyear | Teacher-led small-group blending instruction; practice with decodable texts (see Section IV) |
| | | Reading Fluency | Can read correctly about 50–60 words per minute by late in the year | Repeat reading and partner rereading; assessment of decoding skills (see Section IV) |
| | | Listening Comprehension | Can retell main ideas of narratives by midyear | Teacher-led small-group reading-strategy instruction (see Section VII) |
| | **Grade 2** | Reading Comprehension | Can retell main ideas of simple expository or narrative text; can identify story elements early in the year | Teacher-led small-group reading-strategy instruction (see Section VII) |
| | | Reading Fluency | Can read correctly about 77 words per minute by midyear* | Repeat reading and partner rereading; assessment of decoding skills (see Section IV) |
| | | Decoding | Can read real and nonsense single- and multisyllabic words by midyear | Teacher-led small-group blending and syllabication instruction; practice with decodable texts; possible assessment of phonemic awareness (see Sections III and IV) |

*NOTE: For Grades 2–8 reading fluency rates, refer to "Edformation Educational Averages Norm Table Report Oral Reading Fluency -Graded Passages" Grades 1–8, Section IV, Chapter 11.

| | Assessed Skill | Critical Indicator | Intervention |
|---|---|---|---|
| **Grade 3** | Reading Comprehension | Can restate facts and details in the text by midyear | Teacher-led small-group reading-strategy instruction (see Section VII) |
| | Reading Fluency | Can read correctly about 97 words per minute by midyear* | Repeat reading and partner rereading; assessment of decoding skills (see Section IV) |
| | Decoding (only assessed if low fluency and low comprehension) | Can read with ease real and nonsense single- and multi-syllabic words early in the year | Teacher-led small-group blending and syllabication instruction; practice with decodable texts; possible assessment of phonemic awareness (see Sections III and IV) |
| **Grade 4** | Reading Comprehension | Can distinguish main idea and supporting details and identify answers in text to questions early in the year | Teacher-led small-group reading-strategy instruction (see Section VII) |
| | Reading Fluency | Can read correctly about 115 words per minute by midyear* | Repeat reading and partner rereading; assessment of decoding skills (see Section IV) |
| | Decoding (only assessed if low fluency and low comprehension) | Can read with ease real and nonsense single- and multi-syllabic words early in the year | Teacher-led small-group blending and syllabication instruction; practice with decodable texts; possible assessment of phonemic awareness (see Sections III and IV) |
| **Grades 5–8** | Reading Comprehension | Can distinguish fact from opinion, and make and confirm predictions by midyear | Teacher-led small-group reading-strategy instruction (see Section VII) |
| | Reading Fluency | Gr. 5: Can read correctly about 131 words per minute by midyear* Gr. 6: Can read correctly about 133 words per minute Gr. 7: Can read correctly about 158 words per minute Gr. 8: Can read correctly about 165 words per minute | Repeat reading and partner rereading; assessment of decoding skills (see Section IV) |
| | Decoding (only assessed if low fluency and low comprehension) | Can read with ease real and nonsense single- and multi-syllabic words early in the year | Teacher-led small-group blending and syllabication instruction; practice with controlled texts; possible assessment of phonemic awareness (see Sections III and IV) |

**"Intervention Plan"**

## Intervention Plan

The sample Intervention Plan that follows includes the types of diverse learners, some possible instructional interventions, and some delivery methods best suited to the students and the skills being taught.

**21.14**

### SAMPLE INTERVENTION PLAN: GRADES 4–8

| Type of Diverse Learner | Instructional Intervention | Delivery Method |
|---|---|---|
| Students who are English language learners | Vocabulary-development instruction; instruction in similarities and differences between native language structure and English | Teacher-led small group within the class |
| Students reading one to two grade levels below their grade | Decoding-skills instruction and reading-fluency practice | Special reading back-up class or period |
| Students reading at the first-grade level or not reading at all | Intensive decoding instruction | One-to-one tutoring after school |
| Students who can decode adequately but have poor comprehension | Reading-strategy and vocabulary-development instruction | Teacher-led small group within the class |

**Connect to Theory**

What interventions are you using to assist students who need additional support? How are you helping English language learners? Using the Intervention Plan form found in the Appendix of this book, make a chart of your current practices. Use the above example as a guide to help organize your information.

CHAPTER

# 22

# Instructional Organization

what?
why?
when?
how?

# what? *Instructional Grouping*

**22.2**

**CORE Reading Research Anthology**

for background information

Research shows that what students are taught has a far greater effect on their achievement than how they are grouped (Mosteller, Light, and Sachs 1996). The first focus of educators should always be on the quality of instruction; grouping is a secondary concern. . . . [Educators should] use common sense about grouping. Grouping is a tool and an aid to instruction, not an end in itself. As a tool, it should be used flexibly to ensure that all students achieve the standards. Instructional objectives should always be based on the standards, and should dictate grouping strategies. It is perfectly appropriate, even advisable, to group those students who do not understand a concept or skill and to find time to reteach the concept or skill in a different way and provide additional practice. At the same time, those students might be participating with a more heterogeneous mix of students for other classroom activities.

In another setting, teachers may discover that they have a group of students in a grade who have mastered the standards for that grade and are ready to go on to the standards for the next grade. It is appropriate and advisable to group those students for as long as the grouping meets their needs, and to provide the needed accelerated instruction. To promote maximum learning, the teacher should ensure that assessment is frequent, that high-quality instruction is always provided, and that the students are frequently moved into appropriate instructional groups according to their needs.

SOURCE

Adapted from *Reading/Language Arts Framework for California Public Schools: Kindergarten Through Grade Twelve* (1999). Sacramento: California Department of Education.

# Flexible Grouping and Scheduling Options

Flexible grouping is one method of attending to students' differences. The flexible-grouping model uses a variety of instructional practices including whole-class instruction, individual or partner, teacher-directed small groups, and independent small groups or learning centers. Individual student needs can be met through within-class grouping or by cross-class regrouping.

## Grouping Options

**Whole Class**

**Individual or Partner**

**Teacher-Directed Small Groups**

**Independent Small Groups or Learning Centers**

**Cross-Class Regrouping**

**Dedicated Reading Classes**

## Whole Class

Whole-class instruction is most beneficial when the instructional objectives are appropriate for the entire mixed-level group. For example, in early first grade all students may profit from the same initial phonics instruction.

## Individual or Partner

Individual or partner arrangements provide practice and independent application of an acquired skill. Partners may be at different learning levels, as in a peer-tutoring relationship, or at the same level working on a commonly needed skill.

## Teacher-Directed Small Groups

Teacher-directed small groups provide direct instruction to students who share commonly needed skills. During such small-group time, the teacher can closely monitor students and provide structured feedback.

## Independent Small Groups or Learning Centers

Independent small groups or learning centers are appropriate for interest-based and theme-organized instruction, as well as for cooperative learning experiences. Learning centers free the teacher to work directly with students who need special attention. Learning center activities should be aligned with specific instructional outcomes. The group composition may be either heterogeneous, representing mixed skill levels and instructional needs, or homogeneous, in which students share common skill levels and instructional needs. Homogeneous (same-level) groupings, sometimes termed *needs-based groups,* are used to meet individual needs identified by formal and informal assessment. In order to keep the groups flexible, frequent assessment is necessary.

## Cross-Class Regrouping

In some schools, students may be scheduled into another class for skill-based (homogeneous) instruction. This model is often termed *regrouping and replacement* because the regular mixed class is reconstituted into several other classes for targeted instruction. In this regrouping model, teachers in a given grade or even across grades divide up the students based on assessment information and deploy them among groups of teachers. Such grouping maximizes the teacher's ability to focus instruction on a group of students who share common learning needs. Students then return to their heterogeneous home classes for literature-based instruction.

## Dedicated Reading Classes

An effective method for meeting students' needs in middle school is to enhance the regular, mixed-group literature class with a dedicated reading class that focuses on reading instruction at various skill levels. It is important that students in dedicated reading classes are also scheduled into regular, heterogeneous literature classes. In this way, students receive the skills they need to catch up while also getting the literature they need to develop grade-level concepts and vocabulary.

**CORE Assessing Reading**

## Forming and Managing Within-Class Small Groups or Learning Centers

In order to form effective groups and to monitor student progress, teachers must make use of assessment data. This data will provide information about student skill levels and learning needs. After determining the groups, the teacher must manage students during small-group or learning center time, particularly those students working independently.

Before students can begin to work comfortably and effectively in small groups, it is important to teach them how to work independently. The most successful teachers spend the first few weeks modeling for students how to find materials, how to transition to work areas, how to perform the expected task, and how to get help from other students and other sources. Initially, teachers might establish only one or two learning centers or work areas. The content of the centers or small groups needs to relate to familiar strategies and skills. Students should enter the class and see their names posted in a prominent and previously identified location telling them which group to attend. Instructions for those groups or centers should first be modeled with the whole class. Instructions should be clearly visible, with picture directions for the youngest students.

In the first few weeks student work should be carefully monitored, with time built in for whole-class feedback and evaluation about how the independent work has progressed. Students should be instructed in completing forms and records to show their accomplishments each day. Even the youngest student can be taught how to check off boxes or circle pictures representing a completed task.

22.6

In primary grades, a minimum of two to two-and-a-half hours of daily instruction is recommended for language arts. In Grades 4 through 8, two hours of daily instruction is recommended. These two hours may be consecutive or broken up. Additional time beyond the two hours is needed for special one-to-one or small-group intervention. In general, for every grade a student is below his or her level, an additional 15 minutes of daily instruction is warranted. Administrators may need to increase the length of instructional periods devoted to reading or increase the total number of language arts periods, particularly in the upper grades and in middle schools. Teachers may need to reexamine their total daily schedules in order to accommodate increased reading instruction. Other content areas may provide opportunities for additional reading instruction, but dedicated reading time will need to be specifically allocated to assist those students who require intervention.

To maximize instruction in the early grades, schools may need to add personnel in order to maintain small class size for students who need more direct intervention. Specialists and resource teachers may be used for different purposes during different portions of the school day, such as teaming up with teachers in classrooms having large numbers of at-risk students, serving as an additional reading instructor during reading time to reduce group size, or managing teams of tutors.

## Within-Class Scheduling

The sample schedules that follow provide models for managing a comprehensive literacy program during a single day. These schedules accommodate a variety of groupings to maximize small-group and individual skill-based instruction as well as providing for whole-group, literature-based instruction.

### WITHIN-CLASS SCHEDULE: KINDERGARTEN

| | |
|---|---|
| **8:40 to 8:50** | WHOLE CLASS:   Morning Message, Calendar |
| **8:50 to 9:10**<br>WITHIN-CLASS GROUPINGS | **Math Centers**<br>Note: Class is divided into five groups. Student is assigned to a different center each day. Teacher sets up new centers every five days. |
| **9:10 to 9:25** | WHOLE CLASS:   Phonemic Awareness |
| **9:25 to 9:40** | WHOLE CLASS:   Big Book: Print Concepts and Oral Language Development |
| **9:40 to 10:55**<br><br>WITHIN-CLASS GROUPINGS<br><br>(Small group and/or Learning Center Rotation is 25 minutes each.) | **Teacher-Directed Small Group**   Skill Development and/or Assessment<br><br>**Independent Learning Center**   Picture Sorting<br><br>**Independent Learning Center**   Alphabet Writing<br><br>**Independent Learning Center**   Alphabet Recognition |
| **10:55 to 11:10** | WHOLE CLASS:   Recess |
| **11:10 to 11:30** | WHOLE CLASS:   Phonics (Connecting Sound to Symbol); Math Tune-Up |
| **11:30 to 11:50**<br><br>WITHIN-CLASS GROUPINGS | **Teacher-Directed Small Group**   Reading Pre-decodable Text<br><br>**Independent Learning Center**   Art<br><br>**Independent Learning Center**   Science<br><br>**Independent Learning Center**   Listening Center/Computer Lab |
| **11:50 to 12:05** | WHOLE CLASS:   Daily News, Modeled/Interactive Writing, Music |
| **12:05 to 12:10** | WHOLE CLASS:   Dismissal |

Adapted from schedule provided by San Bernardino City Unified School District.

**22.8**

| WITHIN-CLASS LITERACY SCHEDULE: GRADES 1–3 | |
|---|---|
| **8:30 to 8:45** | WHOLE CLASS:  Class Meeting |
| **8:45 to 9:05** | WHOLE CLASS:  Teacher Read-Aloud, Phonemic Awareness |
| **9:05 to 9:25** | WHOLE CLASS:  Sound/Spelling and Blending Instruction |
| **9:25 to 9:45** | WHOLE CLASS:  Reading: Comprehension Strategies, Vocabulary Development, and Book Discussions |
| **9:45 to 10:10** | WHOLE CLASS:  Interactive Writing |
| **10:10 to 10:25** | WHOLE CLASS:  Recess |
| **10:25 to 10:35** | WHOLE CLASS:  Directions for Independent Learning Centers |
| **10:35 to 11:40**  WITHIN-CLASS GROUPINGS | **Teacher-Directed Small Group**   Reading Decodable Text<br>**Independent Learning Center**   Decoding and Word Attack<br>**Independent Learning Center**   Spelling/Writing<br>**Individuals or Partners**   Partner Reading (for fluency) |
| **11:40 to 12:30** | WHOLE CLASS:  Lunch |
| **12:30 to 12:40** | WHOLE CLASS:  Sustained Silent Reading (SSR) |

Adapted from schedule provided by San Bernardino City Unified School District.

## WITHIN-CLASS LITERACY SCHEDULE: GRADES 4–5

|  |  |
|---|---|
| **8:30 to 8:45** | WHOLE CLASS: Class Meeting |
| **8:45 to 9:30** | WHOLE CLASS: Reading Authentic Text: Vocabulary Development and Comprehension Strategies |
| **9:30 to 10:00** | WHOLE CLASS: Writers' Workshop |
| **10:00 to 10:15** | WHOLE CLASS: Recess |
| **10:15 to 10:25** | WHOLE CLASS: Directions for Learning Centers |
| **10:25 to 11:30** WITHIN-CLASS GROUPINGS | **Teacher-Directed Small Group** Word Attack |
| | **Independent Learning Center** Word Sorting/Spelling |
| | **Independent Learning Center** Readers Theatre (for fluency) |
| | **Independent Learning Center** Literature Circle |
| **11:30 to 12:20** | WHOLE CLASS: Lunch |
| **12:20 to 12:40** | WHOLE CLASS: Sustained Silent Reading (SSR) |

Adapted from schedule provided by San Bernardino City Unified School District.

## WITHIN-CLASS LITERACY SCHEDULE: MIDDLE SCHOOL

|  |  |
|---|---|
| **8:30 to 8:40** | WHOLE CLASS: Word Work |
| **8:40 to 8:55** | WHOLE CLASS: Vocabulary Development and Comprehension Strategies |
| **8:55 to 9:20** | WHOLE CLASS: Reading Authentic Text |
| **9:20 to 10:00** WITHIN-CLASS GROUPINGS | **Teacher-Directed Small Group** Reading Intervention |
| | **Independent Small Group** Word Work |
| | **Independent Small Group** Writers' Workshop |
| | **Individuals** Independent Reading |
| **10:00 to 10:15** | WHOLE CLASS: Book Discussions |

Adapted from schedule provided by San Bernardino City Unified School District.

## Cross-Class Scheduling

Some sample cross-class grouping models are provided below. The grouping decisions are based on assessment conducted at the beginning of the year. In the models, students from three classrooms are regrouped, and an added support teacher is provided to work closely with five or more students who need intensive assistance. Assessments will take place every four to six weeks for regrouping in order to keep the groups flexible.

| CROSS-CLASS LITERACY SCHEDULE: GRADE 1 | | |
|---|---|---|
| **Teacher** | **8:30 to 9:30** | **9:30 to 10:30** |
| Teacher A | Whole class; literature-based and writing instruction | Group 1 (20 students from Teachers A, B, and C): Consonant and short-vowel sounds in single-syllable words; spelling (see Sections IV and V) |
| Teacher B | Whole class; literature-based and writing instruction | Group 2 (25 students from Teachers A, B, and C): Consonant blends, long vowels, and variant vowel patterns in single-syllable words; spelling (see Sections IV and V) |
| Teacher C | Whole class; literature-based and writing instruction | Group 3 (25 students from Teachers A, B, and C): Decode multisyllabic words; spelling (see Sections IV and V) |
| Support Teacher | Individual assessment and intervention | Group 4 (5 students from Teachers A, B, and C): Phonemic awareness: consonant and short-vowel sounds (see Sections III and IV) |

## CROSS-CLASS LITERACY SCHEDULE: GRADES 2–3

| Teacher | 8:30 to 9:30 | 9:30 to 10:30 |
|---|---|---|
| Teacher A | Group 1 (20 students from Teachers A, B, and C): Consonant blends, long vowels, and variant vowel patterns in single-syllable words; spelling (see Sections IV and V) | Whole class; literature-based and writing instruction |
| Teacher B | Group 2 (20 students from Teachers A, B, and C): Decode multisyllabic words with and without morphemic elements; fluency practice; spelling (see Sections IV and V) | Whole class; literature-based and writing instruction |
| Teacher C | Group 3 (25 students from Teachers A, B, and C): Fluency practice; reading comprehension strategies; spelling (see Sections IV, V, and VII) | Whole class; literature-based and writing instruction |
| Support Teacher | Group 4 (10 students from Teachers A and B): Phonemic awareness; consonant and short vowel sounds (see Sections III and IV) | Individual assessment and intervention |

## CROSS-CLASS LITERACY SCHEDULE: GRADES 4–5

| Teacher | 8:30 to 9:45 | 9:45 to 10:30 |
|---|---|---|
| Teacher A | Whole class; literature-based and writing instruction | Group 1 (21 students from Teachers A, B, and C): Consonant blends, long vowels, and variant vowel patterns in single-syllable words; spelling (see Sections IV and V) |
| Teacher B | Whole class; literature-based and writing instruction | Group 2 (25 students from Teachers A, B, and C): Decode multisyllabic words with and without morphemic elements; fluency practice; spelling (see Sections IV and V) |
| Teacher C | Whole class; literature-based and writing instruction | Group 3 (26 students from Teachers A, B, and C): Literary analysis (see Section VII) |
| Support Teacher | Individual assessment and intervention | Group 4 (8 students from Teachers A, B, and C): Phonemic awareness; consonant and short-vowel sounds (see Sections III and IV) |

**22.12**

| DEDICATED READING CLASS SCHEDULE: MIDDLE SCHOOL | | |
|---|---|---|
| **Teacher** | **8:30 to 9:30** | **9:40 to 10:40** |
| Teacher A | Whole class; literature-based and writing instruction | Group 1 (25 students from Teachers A, B, and C): Consonant blends, long vowels, and variant vowel patterns in single-syllable words; spelling; literature selection introduction (see Sections IV, V, VII) |
| Teacher B | Whole class; literature-based and writing instruction | Group 2 (30 students from Teachers A, B, and C): Decode multisyllabic words with and without morphemic elements; fluency practice; spelling literature selection introduction (see Sections IV, V, VII) |
| Teacher C | Whole class; literature-based and writing instruction | Group 3 (32 students from Teachers A, B, and C): Literary analysis; extended writing; vocabulary development; spelling (see Sections V, VI, and VII) |
| Support Teacher | Individual assessment and intervention | Group 4 (8 students from Teachers A, B, and C): Phonemic awareness; beginning phonics; decodable text reading; spelling (see Sections III, IV, and V) |

Connect to Theory

What is your Daily Literacy Schedule? How does it work? Does it need improvement? Write down your current daily schedule in the format presented in this chapter. List what you teach chronologically and indicate whether instruction during a given period is for the whole class, a small group, individuals, or partners. Then, revise your schedule to show how you could make it more ideal using the grouping strategies shown in this chapter.

# Section References

Adams, M. J. 1990. *Beginning to read: Thinking and learning about print.* Cambridge, MA: MIT Press.

Bear, D., M. Invernizzi, S. Templeton, and F. Johnston. 1996. *Words their way: Word study for phonics, vocabulary, and spelling instruction.* Upper Saddle River, NJ: Prentice-Hall.

Benbow, C. P., and J. C. Stanley. 1996. Inequity in equity: How 'equity' can lead to inequity for high-potential students. *Psychology, Public Policy and Law* 2, pp. 249–292.

California Department of Education. 1999. *Reading/language arts framework for California public schools K–12.* Sacramento: California Department of Education.

Critchlow, D. E. 1996. *Dos amigos verbal language scales.* Novato, CA: Academic Therapy Publications.

Geary, D. C. 1994. *Children's mathematical development: Research and practical applications.* Washington, DC: American Psychological Association.

Joshi, R. M. 1995. Assessing reading and spelling skills. *School Psychology Review* 24(3), pp. 361–375.

Just, M. A., and P. A. Carpenter. 1987. *The psychology of reading and language comprehension.* Needham Heights, MA: Allyn & Bacon.

Mosteller, F., R. Light, and J. Sachs. 1996. Sustained inquiry in education: Lessons from skill grouping and class size. *Harvard Educational Review* 66 (4), pp. 797–842.

Simmons, D., and E. Kameenui. 1998. *What reading research tells us about children with diverse learning needs.* Mahwah, NJ: Erlbaum.

Thorndike, R. L. 1973. *Reading comprehension education in fifteen countries: An empirical study.* New York: Wiley.

Tomlinson, A. T. 1999. *The differentiated classroom: Responding to the needs of all learners.* Alexandria, VA: Association for Supervision and Curriculum Development.

Waters, G., M. Bruck, and M. Seidenberg. 1985. Do students use similar processes to read and spell words? *Journal of Experimental Student Psychology* 39, pp. 511–530.

# Appendix

# Albert Einstein Asks a Question

BY JOHN ROSS

**A**LBERT EINSTEIN was born in Ulm, Germany, in 1879. When he was five, he was sick in bed for a time. His father gave him a compass. "But why does the needle always point north?" asked the boy. "I don't know why," his dad confessed. Later, the young Einstein studied the subject and found out the answer. And he never stopped asking questions after that. "The most important thing is to keep asking questions," Einstein would always tell young people who wanted to become scientists.

Einstein did not do well in school. His teachers said he was slow to learn. "Albert will never amount to very much," said the principal. But Einstein's mind wasn't slow. It was really working much faster than the school principal could ever have imagined. He wanted to know how everything worked. He thought a lot about space and time. He thought a lot about energy. He thought about atoms and how all the energy inside them could explode outward. He thought about how light travels in waves. He wondered what would happen to a person if he or she traveled at the speed of light, and he guessed that person would never grow old.

Einstein's scientific theories forever changed our understanding of the world. He called his ideas "theories" or "thought experiments." He tested his experiments by making pictures in his mind and using his imagination like a laboratory. These thought experiments were so hard to explain that sometimes only a few people in the whole world could understand what Einstein was thinking. Einstein's most famous theory is the theory of relativity. This is how he explained the theory of relativity: "If you sit with a pretty girl for an hour, it seems like only a minute. But if you sit on a hot stove for a minute, it seems like an hour. That's relativity."

In 1933, Albert Einstein fled Germany and went to the United States. From then until his death in 1955, he taught at Princeton University in New Jersey. There, he enjoyed sailing, playing the violin, putting together jigsaw puzzles, and building houses from playing cards. Einstein rode his bicycle everywhere; he thought driving was way too complicated.

When Einstein wanted to think, he often went for a walk. He usually wore a long overcoat and a black hat on top of his wild white hair (which was always uncombed). He would bring a notepad with him, to take notes on his "thought experiments." Sometimes he would get so lost in his own thoughts that he would get lost for real. Einstein would have to ask neighbors for directions home.

When this famous scientist died at the age of 76, he left his brain to science. Scientists wanted to see if it was different from the average human brain. Nothing unusual turned up—until quite recently. In June 1999, a research team from Canada announced that Einstein's brain is fifteen percent wider than normal in one particular area. This area seems to have something to do with mathematical thinking. Maybe having a wider area *caused* Einstein to be a math genius. Maybe having a wider area is the *result* of Einstein's being a math genius. Or maybe this larger area doesn't mean either of these things. Hmmm. Maybe it has to do with asking all those questions.

Date:

| Assessment Plan Sequence for Primary-Grade Students (Grades K–3) | | | | |
|---|---|---|---|---|
| READING COMPONENT ASSESSED | Kindergarten | Grade 1 | Grade 2 | Grade 3 |
| ▶ **Phonological Awareness**<br>Tool: | | | | |
| ▶ **Print Concepts**<br>Tool: | | | | |
| ▶ **Oral Vocabulary**<br>Tool: | | | | |
| ▶ **Alphabet Recognition**<br>Tool: | | | | |
| ▶ **Phonic Elements**<br>Tool: | | | | |
| ▶ **Spelling**<br>Tool: | | | | |
| ▶ **Word Recognition**<br>Tool: | | | | |
| ▶ **Reading Fluency**<br>Tool: | | | | |
| ▶ **Listening Comprehension**<br>Tool: | | | | |
| ▶ **Reading Comprehension**<br>Tool: | | | | |

Date: _____

| Assessment Plan Sequence for Upper-Grade Students (Grades 4–8) | | | | |
|---|---|---|---|---|
| READING COMPONENT ASSESSED | Grade 4 | Grade 5 | Grade 6 | Grades 7–8 |
| ▶ **Reading Comprehension** <br> Tool: | | | | |
| ▶ **Vocabulary** <br> Tool: | | | | |
| ▶ **Reading Fluency** <br> Tool: | | | | |
| ▶ **Word Recognition** <br> Tool: | | | | |
| ▶ **Spelling** <br> Tool: | | | | |
| ▶ **Phonic Elements** <br> Tool: | | | | |
| ▶ **Phonemic Awareness** <br> Tool: | | | | |

## Character Weave

Character: _____ Title: _____

| Appearance | Actions | Feelings About Self | Feelings About Others |
|---|---|---|---|
|  |  |  |  |

**CLASS ROSTER**
**Kindergarten**

| | Phonological awareness | Print concepts | Letter names— uppercase | Letter names— lowercase | Consonant sounds | Short-vowel sounds | CVC words | Vocabulary/ Oral language | Listening comprehension |
|---|---|---|---|---|---|---|---|---|---|
| 1. | | | | | | | | | |
| 2. | | | | | | | | | |
| 3. | | | | | | | | | |
| 4. | | | | | | | | | |
| 5. | | | | | | | | | |
| 6. | | | | | | | | | |
| 7. | | | | | | | | | |
| 8. | | | | | | | | | |
| 9. | | | | | | | | | |
| 10. | | | | | | | | | |
| 11. | | | | | | | | | |
| 12. | | | | | | | | | |
| 13. | | | | | | | | | |
| 14. | | | | | | | | | |
| 15. | | | | | | | | | |
| 16. | | | | | | | | | |
| 17. | | | | | | | | | |
| 18. | | | | | | | | | |
| 19. | | | | | | | | | |
| 20. | | | | | | | | | |
| 21. | | | | | | | | | |
| 22. | | | | | | | | | |
| 23. | | | | | | | | | |
| 24. | | | | | | | | | |
| 25. | | | | | | | | | |

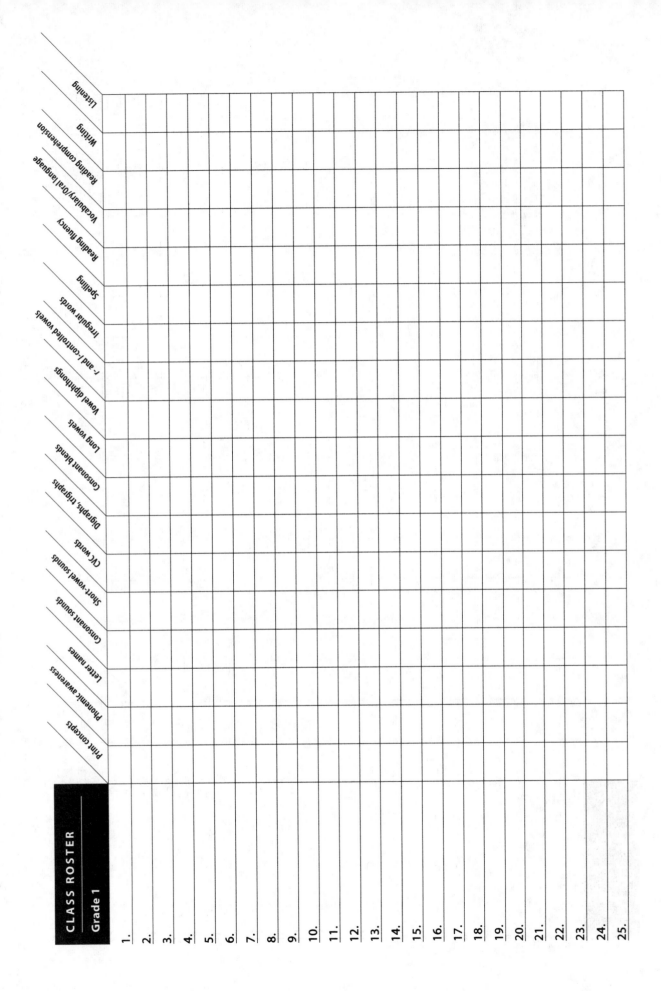

**CLASS ROSTER**
**Grade 1**

Listening
Writing
Reading comprehension
Vocabulary/Oral language
Reading fluency
Spelling
Irregular words
*r-* and *l-*controlled vowels
Vowel diphthongs
Long vowels
Consonant blends
Digraphs, trigraphs
CVC words
Short-vowel sounds
Consonant sounds
Letter names
Phonemic awareness
Print concepts

1.
2.
3.
4.
5.
6.
7.
8.
9.
10.
11.
12.
13.
14.
15.
16.
17.
18.
19.
20.
21.
22.
23.
24.
25.

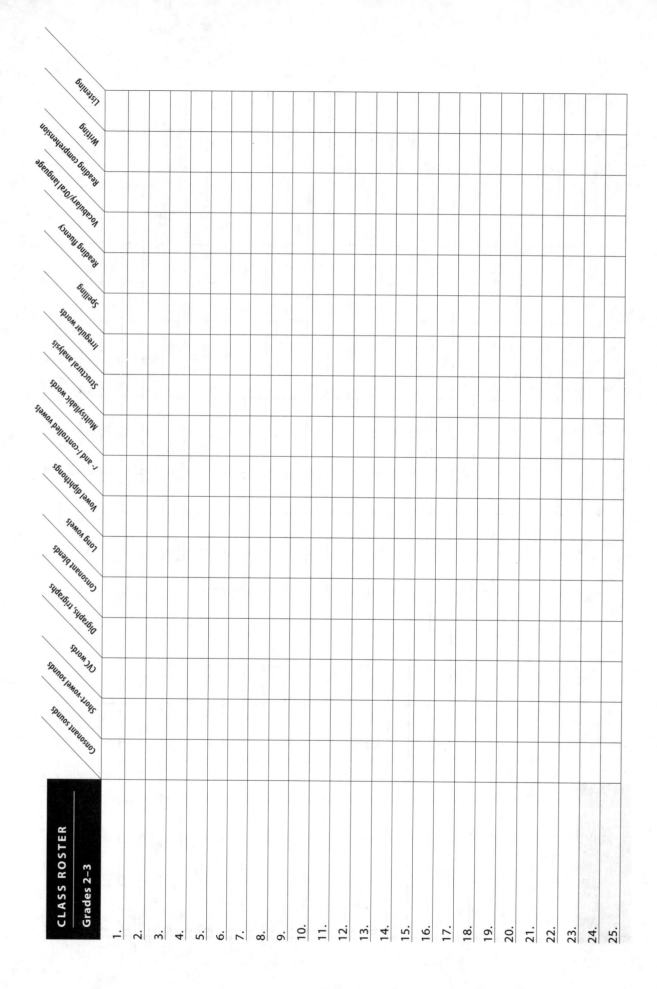

**CLASS ROSTER**
Grades 2–3

Listening
Writing
Reading comprehension
Vocabulary/Oral language
Reading fluency
Spelling
Irregular words
Structural analysis
Multisyllabic words
*r-* and *l-*controlled vowels
Vowel diphthongs
Long vowels
Consonant blends
Digraphs, trigraphs
CVC words
Short-vowel sounds
Consonant sounds

1.
2.
3.
4.
5.
6.
7.
8.
9.
10.
11.
12.
13.
14.
15.
16.
17.
18.
19.
20.
21.
22.
23.
24.
25.

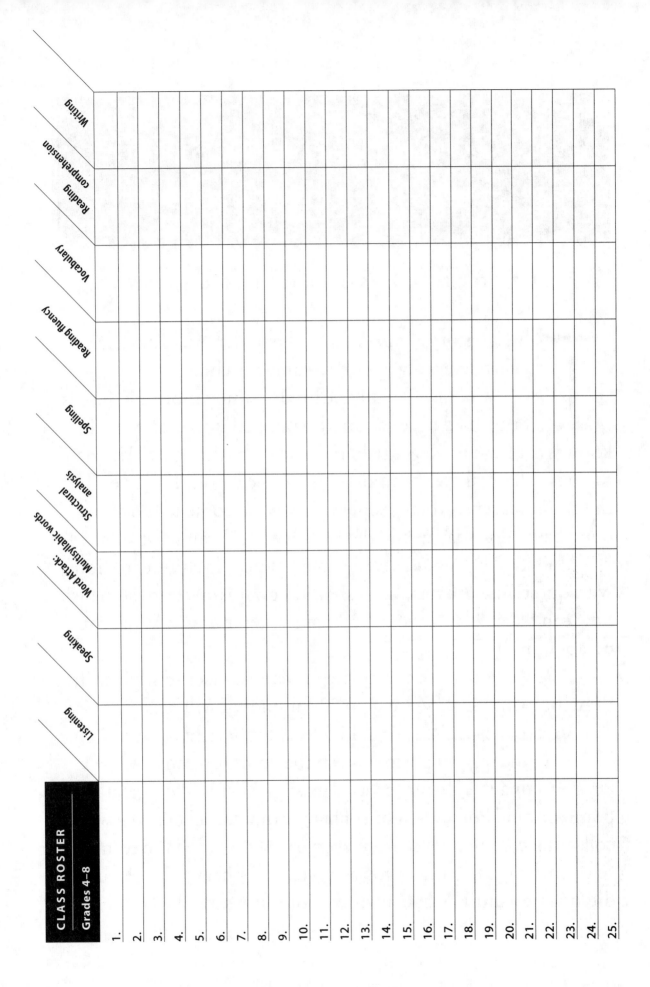

**CLASS ROSTER**
Grades 4–8

Writing
Reading comprehension
Vocabulary
Reading fluency
Spelling
Structural analysis
Word Attack: Multisyllabic words
Speaking
Listening

1.
2.
3.
4.
5.
6.
7.
8.
9.
10.
11.
12.
13.
14.
15.
16.
17.
18.
19.
20.
21.
22.
23.
24.
25.

# Common Sense: An Anansi Tale

RETOLD BY SUSAN BLACKABY

This is a story about Anansi, the spider. Anansi is a tricky fellow. He is always up to some mischief!

Anansi woke up one bright, sunny morning. Just as he opened his eyes, an idea popped into his head. "I know what I can do to get rich, rich, rich!" he thought. "All I need to do is collect all the common sense in the world. If I have all the common sense, then people will need to come to me to find out what to do—day in and day out! Tee hee! I can see it all now!"

In his head, Anansi saw a parade of people coming to him with questions: "Anansi, what should I do if I am sleepy? Anansi, how can I keep dry in the rain? Anansi, I am hungry. What can I do about it?"

"People will have to pay me for commonsense advice," he thought to himself. "What a powerful spider I will be!"

Anansi was excited about his idea. He got right to work. "First I have to find a good place to keep the common sense while I am collecting it." He picked a calabash, which is like a great big pumpkin, and hollowed it out. Then he traveled all over the world, collecting common sense from everyone. He stuffed the common sense into the calabash. It got very, very, *very* heavy. But Anansi did not stop until he had all of the common sense he could find.

When Anansi thought about how rich he would be, he laughed with glee. "I can see it now! Anansi, what shall I do if I am too hot? Help me, Anansi, I am thirsty! They will have the questions, and I will have the answers! All the common sense in the world is mine, mine, mine! Now I just have to find a good place to hide the common sense so that I can keep it safe and sound."

Anansi dragged the calabash all through the jungle as he searched for a hiding place. He went under ferns and over logs. He waded through swamps and streams. He went from shrub to bush to tree.

Finally he came to the tallest tree in the jungle. Its mossy trunk went up, up, up, and disappeared in the leaves that blocked the sky. Anansi decided that the top of the tree would be the perfect hiding place.

Using a thick rope, Anansi tied the calabash around his neck like a necklace. He started to climb the tree. Climbing was so hard! The heavy calabash got in the way. The trunk was slippery. Anansi bruised and scraped his long spider legs. With every step, the calabash banged into his fuzzy spider belly. The rope burned his neck.

Anansi was having a terrible time. But he thought about being rich. And the thought of being rich helped him keep going up, up, up. As he was struggling slowly along, he heard someone laughing down on the ground. Then he heard a voice.

"You are very, very, very foolish," said the voice. "Don't you know that you should carry the calabash on your back? That way, your legs are free, your neck doesn't hurt, and the calabash won't keep hitting you in the belly. Everyone knows that! It is just plain common sense!"

Anansi stopped. He looked down through the branches and spotted a small boy sitting on a rock. Where did that small boy get this piece of common sense? How could Anansi have overlooked this piece? Hadn't Anansi collected *every bit* of common sense that there was? He did not like it that such a saucy little boy had such a big piece of common sense.

It made Anansi so mad that he lost his temper. He forgot about being rich and powerful. He took the calabash and smashed it against the tree. The calabash broke into a million pieces. Out spilled all the common sense that he had collected: Wear a coat on a cold day! Put on your socks before you put on your shoes! When it gets dark, turn on the lights!

As Anansi watched, a breeze came along and carried every bit of common sense away. A little bit went here, and a little bit went there. Before long, common sense was scattered all over the world. Now, everybody, including Anansi, has a little bit of common sense to share. But nobody has all of it.

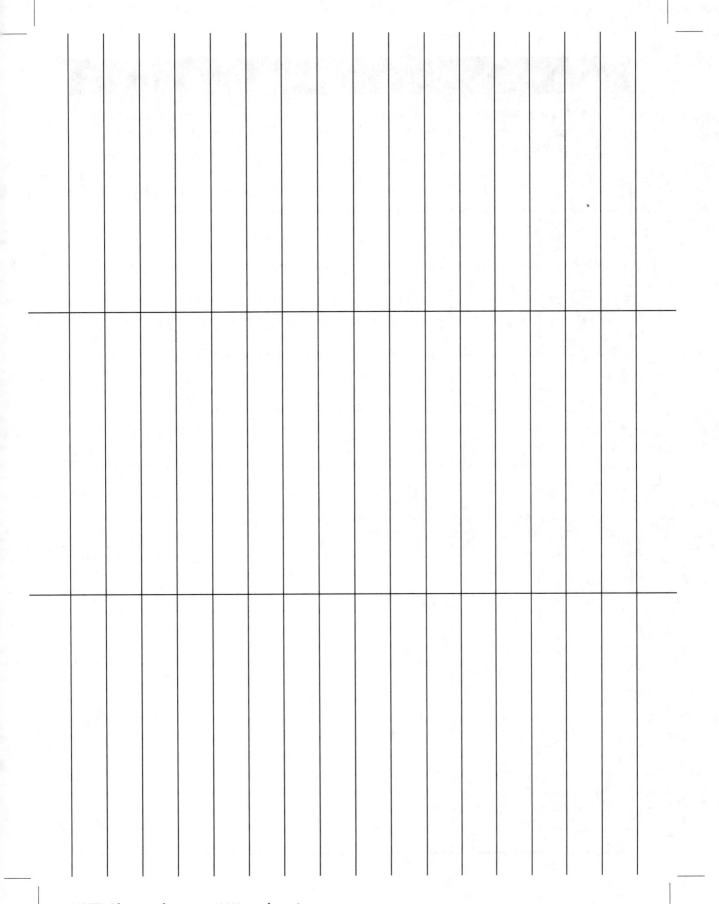

*NOTE: Photocopy this page at 120% onto letter-size paper.*

## INTERVENTION PLAN

| Type of Diverse Learner | Instructional Intervention | Delivery Method |
|---|---|---|
| | | |
| | | |
| | | |
| | | |
| | | |
| | | |
| | | |
| | | |
| | | |

# JACK AND JILL

Jack and Jill went up the hill,

To fetch a pail of water.

Jack fell down, and broke his crown,

and Jill came tumbling after.

# K-W-L Chart

| **K**<br>What I Know | **W**<br>What I Want to Know | **L**<br>What I Learned |
| --- | --- | --- |
| | | |

Categories of Information I Expect to Use:

# LITTLE BOY BLUE

Little Boy Blue, come, blow your

horn!

The sheep's in the meadow, the

cow's in the corn.

Where's the little boy that looks

after the sheep?

Under the haystack, fast asleep!

# Naming Living Things

Carl Linné was born in Sweden in 1707. He was interested in plants, so he studied botany. This study inspired Linné and his fellow scientists to take on a big job. They decided to label every living thing on earth!

To start thinking of names, they invented a binomial, or two-name, system. They borrowed terms from Greek and Latin. In fact, Carl Linné had a Latin binomial of his own, because he was also known as "Carolus Linnaeus."

*Canis Lupus*

The first word in the binomial system gives the genus. The genus tells the general category that the living thing belongs to. The second name gives the species name, which is more specific. If you have a dog, the binomial for your canine companion is *Canis familiaris.* A wolf is *Canis lupus.* Both belong to the same genus, but one is more "familiar" than the other!

Binomial plant names can give you clues about what the plant is like and where it grows. The many different kinds of violets and pansies belong to the genus *Viola. Viola biflora* is a two-flowered variety. *Viola tricolor* has three colors. *Viola labradorika* is from the island of Labrador in North America.

Linnaeus helped people all over the world find a way to talk about living things and share information. His binomial system is still being added to today as new species are discovered and named by scientists.

# Pioneers on the Oregon Trail

*"Ourselves moving on in the general throng, sand reflecting back the heat of the sun in your face and making the sweat trickle down. Oh, this is going to Oregon."*

—HELEN STEWART, 1853

## The Way West

In the early 1800s, Lewis and Clark explored the territory west of the Mississippi. No one knew what they would find. As they traveled, they made maps. They wrote in their journals. They described miles and miles of beautiful land with tall trees, good soil, and rushing rivers. News about the wonders of the west spread. People began to dream about a new life in a new land. And before long, they began traveling west. At first there were only a few adventurers on the trail. In 1843, two hundred families crossed the Oregon Trail. Then in 1848, gold was discovered in California. Soon after, thousands of people began heading west, hoping to make their dreams come true at the end of the Oregon Trail.

## Packing for the Journey

Traveling west was not easy. The Oregon Trail was thousands of miles long and took between four and six months to cross. Pioneers had to pack everything they would need in a covered wagon that was not much bigger than a

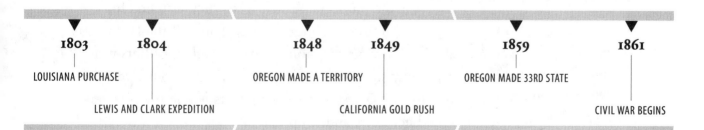

| 1803 | 1804 | 1848 | 1849 | 1859 | 1861 |
|------|------|------|------|------|------|
| LOUISIANA PURCHASE | | OREGON MADE A TERRITORY | | OREGON MADE 33RD STATE | |
| | LEWIS AND CLARK EXPEDITION | | CALIFORNIA GOLD RUSH | | CIVIL WAR BEGINS |

double bed. Once food and tools and supplies for the journey were packed, the wagon was nearly full. As a result, there was no room left for personal belongings. But the pioneers left behind more than the comforts of home and their special treasures. They said good-bye to family and friends they never expected to see again.

## Wagons Ho!

Pioneers gathered at starting points between Independence, Missouri, and Council Bluffs, Iowa, to join up with wagon trains heading west. It was safest to travel with ten to fifteen wagons in a group. Families arrived in the springtime and stayed in camps outside town. Wagon trains did not set out until there was enough grass growing on the prairie to feed the animals along the way. At the same time, they could not wait too long. The wagons had to get over the mountains before it started to snow.

A wagon train on the move could be one mile long and one mile wide. Bumping along in a cramped wagon was a hard and uncomfortable way to travel. Pioneers often trudged beside the wagons instead. Consequently, most people *walked* all the way to Oregon—nearly two thousand miles.

As the pioneers headed west, they watched for famous landmarks along the way. Some of the landmarks showed how far the pioneers had traveled. Others were especially steep mountain passes or dangerous rivers that had to be crossed. Others were forts where the pioneers could get news and supplies.

THE OREGON TRAIL

1. The **Platte River**, which curves through the prairie, had to be crossed several times, with the wagons fording or ferrying across the river.

2. Wagon trains had to reach **Independence Rock** by July 4th in order to stay on schedule; if they were late, they risked being caught in the snow.

3. At the **South Pass**, the pioneers passed into Oregon Territory.

4. Wagon trains came to the **Blue Mountains** late in the trip. This was one place where it was easy to get caught in an early snow.

5. At **The Dalles**, the pioneers could ferry down the Columbia River to Fort Vancouver.

6. Pioneers had to use ropes or chains and inch their wagons down **Laurel Hill**, one of the most terrifying parts of the journey but only a few days away from the end of the trail.

**DID YOU KNOW?**

*Pioneers would milk their cows in the evening. Then in the morning, they would put the cream into the churn and set the churn inside the wagon. The constant rocking motion of the wagon would turn the cream to butter by the time they stopped for supper.*

# A Day on the Trail

If you were traveling in a wagon train on the Oregon Trail, you tried to travel at a steady pace. On a good day, you could go about fifteen miles. On a stormy day or over a bad part of the trail, you might go only one mile. You would wake up at daybreak. Morning chores, including fixing breakfast, milking the cows, taking care of the animals, and packing up the wagon, would take a couple of hours. Then you would hitch up the mules or oxen and set out.

At noon you would find a place to stop and rest. Animals would graze and get water. You would eat a meal and rest and make any repairs that were needed. Then you would set out again and keep going until four or five o'clock. You had to stop in time to get your chores done before nightfall.

Now the evening meal had to be cooked, which might mean gathering firewood, hunting or fishing, picking berries, and so on. Wagon repairs, cleaning and mending clothes, and other chores could be done. If you were lucky, you might find time to rest and relax. Musicians might pull out fiddles and harmonicas for singing and dancing by the campfire. Then it was time to go to bed, so that you could get up and do it again.

# The End of the Trail

After four or five months of traveling, pioneers finally reached the Willamette Valley. Oregon City was the end of the Oregon Trail, where pioneers staked their claims to ranch and farmland. Then the hard work really began.

The first winter in Oregon could be very hard. Supplies were low, and the weather turned rainy and cold. It was important to get busy and clear your land and build a cabin before the start of winter. But the end of the trail was where the dream of living in the west began. The pioneers who survived the trip had risked everything for a new life in the west.

# PIONEERS ON THE OREGON TRAIL

| Before the Journey | Starting Out | On the Trail | End of the Trail |
|---|---|---|---|

MISSOURI

★ Independence

"Packing for the Journey"    "Wagons Ho!"    "A Day on the Trail"    "The End of the Trail"

# READING CONFERENCE FORM

STUDENT NAME: _____

CONFERENCE DATE: _____

BOOK TITLE AND AUTHOR: _____

_____

DECODING: _____

_____

FLUENCY: _____

_____

COMPREHENSION: _____

_____

VOCABULARY: _____

_____

_____

OTHER OBSERVATIONS: _____

_____

_____

_____

FOLLOW-UP RECOMMENDATIONS: _____

_____

_____

_____

# Story Map

TITLE:

**Beginning**

At first, . . . .

**Middle**

Then, . . . .

**Ending**

In the end, . . . .

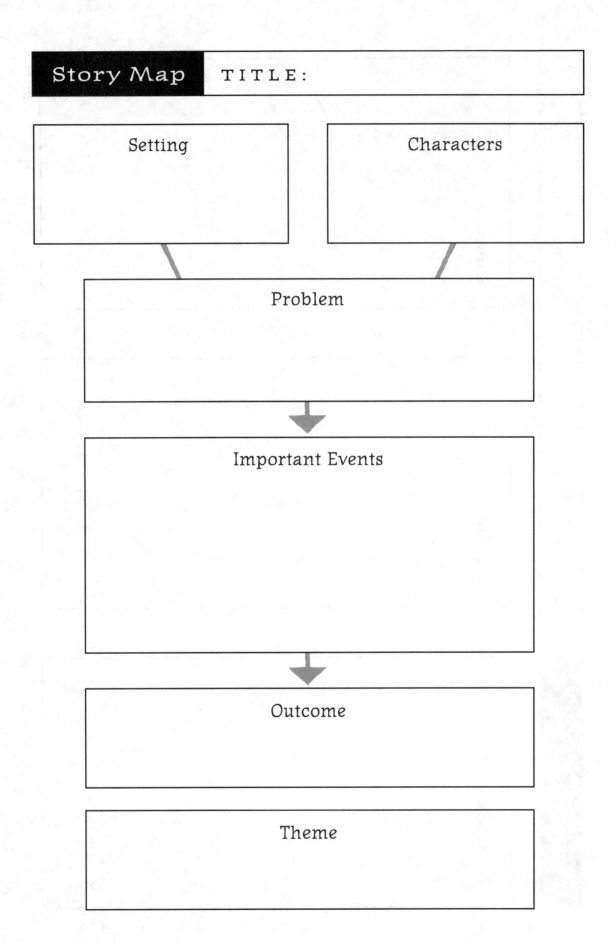

## Story Map    TITLE:

**Setting**

**Characters**

**Problem**

**Important Events**

**Outcome**

**Theme**

# Studying the Sky

STRONOMY is the study of the planets, stars, and galaxies. People have been watching the movement of the sun, moon, planets, and stars since ancient times. So astronomy is a very, very old science.

From early times, people tried to make models of the universe. For many years, no one wanted to believe that the sun was the center of the solar system. It took a long time for people to accept this heliocentric model, with the earth orbiting around the sun with the other planets.

It is interesting to study the night sky like the astronomers from centuries ago. You can see even the most distant stars with your eyes alone. And you may be able to identify constellations, or groups of stars. Constellations make pictures in the sky, such as Canis Major (the Great Dog) or Ursa Minor (the Little Bear).

A telescope can be used to see faraway things more clearly. With a telescope, you can see details like the craters of the moon and other features of the lunar landscape, the moons of Jupiter, and the rings of Saturn.

Astronomy is like taking a trip back in time. This evening you can look at the same planets and stars that ancient astronomers observed so long ago.

# The Fourth of July Parade

Every Fourth of July / there is a parade / in our town. // It is / so much fun! // There are marching bands / and floats. // There are horses, / ponies, / and pets. // There are clowns / and jugglers. // There are wagons / and fire engines. // And most of all, / there are people, / people, / people! //

Can you picture / what it would be like / if everyone in your town / was standing out on Main Street? // Well, / neither could I, / until my friends and I / decided to ride in the parade. // I decorated my bike / with gold and green streamers / on the handlebars. // I put glitter stickers / all over the frame, / and I wove purple ribbons / in and out of the spokes. // My bike looked awesome! // As we rode up the street, / we got to see / all of the babies, / kids, / parents, / and grandparents in the crowd. But / do you know what I didn't see? // I didn't get to see / the parade! //

# The Fourth of July Parade

Every Fourth of July there is a parade in our town. It is so much fun! There are marching bands and floats. There are horses, ponies, and pets. There are clowns and jugglers. There are wagons and fire engines. And most of all, there are people, people, people!

Can you picture what it would be like if everyone in your town was standing out on Main Street? Well, neither could I, until my friends and I decided to ride in the parade. I decorated my bike with gold and green streamers on the handlebars. I put glitter stickers all over the frame, and I wove purple ribbons in and out of the spokes. My bike looked awesome! As we rode up the street, we got to see all of the babies, kids, parents, and grandparents in the crowd. But do you know what I didn't see? I didn't get to see the parade!

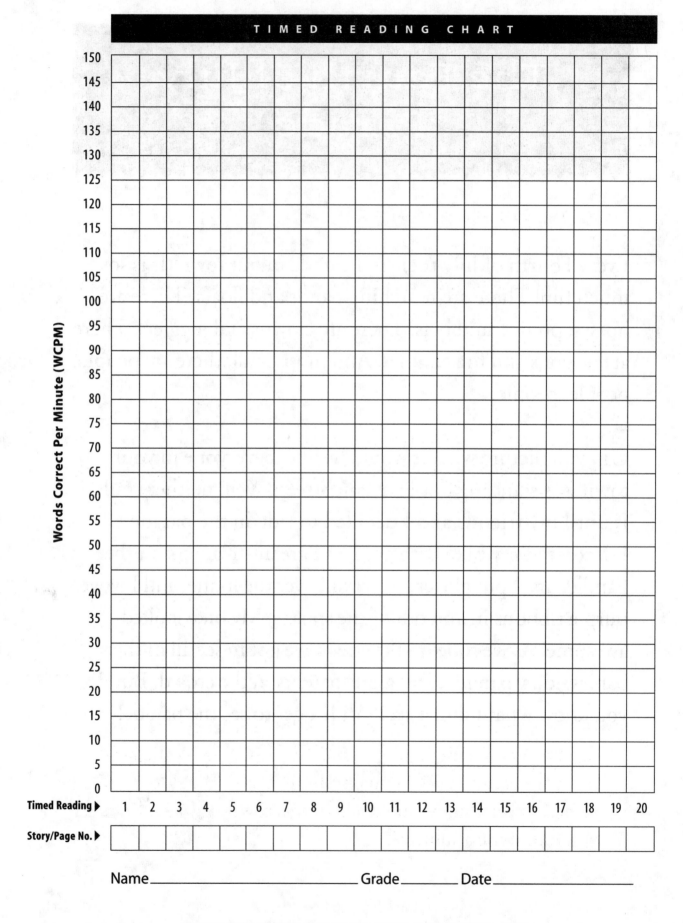

**TIMED READING CHART**

Words Correct Per Minute (WCPM)

150
145
140
135
130
125
120
115
110
105
100
95
90
85
80
75
70
65
60
55
50
45
40
35
30
25
20
15
10
5
0

Timed Reading ▶ 1 2 3 4 5 6 7 8 9 10 11 12 13 14 15 16 17 18 19 20

Story/Page No. ▶

Name_____ Grade_____ Date_____

# TV Dinner

BY THE SAN FRANCISCO MIME TROUPE

Pauline watches too much TV. She's behind on homework, forgets to wash the dishes, and has no time to play with Henrietta, her pet guinea pig. One night Henrietta is "pignapped" by two raccoon servants of Madam Video. Pauline sets out to find her.

**Characters**
Madam Video: Video Central's evil empress
Cosmo and Dodo: two raccoons
Pauline: a twelve-year-old TV fanatic
Henrietta: Pauline's pet guinea pig
Voice: a TV announcer

**Setting:** *Madam Video's control room at Video Central. The walls are lined with TV monitors. Cosmo and Dodo are on stage. Henrietta is strapped to a special chair. Madam Video enters.*

MADAM: *(speaking to audience)* Hi, kids. What a glorious night for my experiment—full moon, low-lying fog—and if my inventions can really bend children's brains, I will rule the mind of every kid within reach of this tower. *(to Cosmo)* Have you found me a subject?

COSMO: A perfect subject, primed and ready, your coldness.

MADAM: *(to Cosmo)* Excellent. Have a Gummy Worm. If all goes well tonight, I'll show you something really special: six segments of "The Simpsons"—uncut, prime stuff.

COSMO: Uncut, ooh, wow! Bart and Homer, Marge and Lisa. Awesome!

MADAM: Place the Video Visor on the subject. *(as Cosmo goes to do so, Madam sees the subject)* What is this?

HENRIETTA: I'm a guinea pig.

COSMO: It is a guinea pig, your monstrosity, just as you ordered.

MADAM: *(chasing raccoons)* You fools! You lazy bums! You, you—animals! I ask for a guinea pig to conduct my experiment and you bring me a . . . a . . .

COSMO: A guinea pig.

MADAM: I can't bear it. The experiment is ruined. It's worthless. You'll pay for this. I'm cutting you off. No TV.

COSMO: No TV? No, please, I can't stand it. *(falls on floor in a fit)*

DODO: Can we have just an hour's worth? Fifteen minutes?

MADAM: I'm pulling the plug.

DODO: No "Wheel of Fortune"?

COSMO: How about educational TV?

MADAM:   Nothing. Not even bowling *(raccoons cry)* . . . until you bring me a real live child. *(an alarm sounds)* The video alarm! *(scans video screen)* A little girl is approaching. Perfect timing. Quick, lock that pig in the pantry. And get out of sight. *(raccoons obey, and Madam also hides)*

PAULINE:   *(peeks in, stage right)* Henrietta? Henrietta? Where are you? *(walks around room)* Wow, look at all those TVs. This place is like a dream come true. *(turns on a TV)*

VOICE:   Hello, America. Welcome to your favorite pastime, "Family Squabble." *(squabbling voices are heard)*

PAULINE:   Oh, this is the game show where people take turns telling family secrets. *(turns off first TV and turns on another)*

VOICE:   Got milk? It's fast food that's good for you.

PAULINE:   *(to audience)* Milk? Yuk. *(turns off second TV)*

MADAM:   *(entering)* Hello, dear.

PAULINE:   Uh, are you real?

MADAM:   As real as anything you'll ever see.

PAULINE:   Hi, uh, my name is Pauline. I, uh, didn't mean to bust in, but . . . I'm looking for my pet. Two raccoons pignapped her and I gotta find her.

MADAM:   Those naughty raccoons—they only wanted to play. But I scolded them, gave them all lettuce sandwiches, and then put them down for a nap. Why don't we let them sleep? *(taking Pauline to chair)* You and I can watch television.

PAULINE: Great—I didn't expect to end up in such a safe place. Can we watch "Tales from the Crypt"? My parents aren't into it.

MADAM: Anything you like, dear. Do you watch a great deal of television?

PAULINE: Not too much—only six hours a day. *(Madam puts Video Visor on her)* What's this?

MADAM: My new Video Visor. It lets you watch more TV in less time.

PAULINE: Wow. *(Madam turns on Visor)* What an awesome monitor! I could watch this forever.

MADAM: *(triumphantly)* You will, you will. *(calls)* Cosmo, Dodo! *(the raccoons enter)*

DODO: Yes, your repulsiveness.

COSMO: Coming, your grease. *(Pauline can tell that something's wrong and begins to struggle)*

MADAM: Program thirty minutes of commercials in ten seconds. *(raccoons bump into each other; Dodo programs the computer and Cosmo goes to read printout)*

COSMO: Maximum and rising.

MADAM: Brain activity?

DODO: Minimum and falling.

MADAM: *(removing Visor)* Little girl, can you hear me?

PAULINE:  Yes.

MADAM:  Hair Club for Men?

PAULINE:  I'm not only president, I'm also a client.

MADAM:  Crunch Cereal is so . . .

PAULINE:  . . . good. Breakfast is back!

MADAM:  What do you want for Christmas, little girl?

PAULINE:  Spice Girls, Tomb Raider V, and Baby Mastercharge. I answered all the questions, what's my prize?

MADAM:  Stupid. *(to audience)* This is thrilling. *(back to Pauline)* What's your favorite food?

PAULINE:  Sugar Smacks, Apple Jacks, Sour Bombs, Pop Tarts, Ding Dongs . . . *(singing)* Ding Dongs, Ding Dongs, Ding Dongs.

MADAM:  It works! It works! My Video Visor works! First the raccoons, then the children. From this tower, I'll beam programs to make everyone in the entire world my obedient slaves.

RACCOONS:  *(dancing and singing)*
  Madam Video will rule the world. Rule the world.
  You will buy things you don't need. You don't need.
  No one will remember how to read. How to read.
  You may think her plan's insane,
  But no one will dare complain.
  You'll all be too busy watching your TVs.

# When I Come to a Word I Don't Know

**1** Try to sound out the word.

**2** Look for letter patterns you know.
Try to sound out the word.

**3** Read the whole sentence. Ask yourself, "Does the word sound right and make sense?"

# "Connect to Theory" Answers

## Section I: The Big Picture

**PAGE 2.16:**
1. three, /k/ /u/ /p/
2. /r/
3. /l/
4. *pot*
5. *funny*

## Section III: Sound/Print Connection

**PAGE 7.3:**
1. three, /k/ /a/ /t/
2. four, /t/ /r/ /ā/ /n/
3. three, /th/ /aw/ /t/
4. five, /s/ /t/ /r/ /ā/ /t/
5. six, /f/ /l/ /ou/ /n/ /d/ /ûr/

## Section IV: Decoding

**PAGE 8.3:**
The first approach is predominantly explicit because the /a/*a* sound/spelling is directly taught in isolation. In addition, students practice blending words that contain previously introduced sound/spellings.

The second approach is predominantly implicit because the /a/*a* sound/spelling must be inferred from reading a whole word; it is not directly taught in isolation. In addition, there is no direct instruction and practice in blending sounds in sequence.

**PAGE 8.11:**
Progression of Word Difficulty: sip, luck, top, pink, smog, grab, string

Word List C is the best list for blending instruction; it meets all criteria. Word List A is too predictable; each of the words contains short *a* in the same position. Word List B contains a word that is not wholly decodable: the word *met*.

| Decodable Text Analysis of *Bass Lake* | | |
| --- | --- | --- |
| **Word Types** | **Identified Words in Text** | **Percentage of Words in Text** |
| Wholly Decodable Words | and, Bass, fill, Gail, go, hike, hike, in, Lake, lake, like, need, packs, week, will | 15 words or 47% |
| Sight Words | a, all, Every, the, their, they, They, they, they, to, to, to | 12 words or 38% |
| Nondecodable/ Noninstructed Words | Sue, for, Then, with, year | 5 words or 15% |

Criteria for Nondecodable/Noninstructed Words
The following sound/spellings have not been introduced: /oō/*ue;* /or/*or;* /th/*th;* /TH/*th;* /ē/*ea.*

**PAGE 9.7:**
Regular Words: and, a, in, is*, that, it, he, for, on, as*, with, his*, I, at, be, this
Irregular Words: the, of, to, you, was, are, they, have, from
*Another common sound for *s* is /z/.

**PAGE 10.6:**

scratch (closed)

sharp (*r*-controlled)

tree (vowel team)

beside (open, vowel–silent *e*)

harvest (*r*-controlled, closed)

seeker (vowel team, *r*-controlled)

candle (closed, consonant-*le*)

napkin (closed, closed)

**PAGE 10.9:**

rob/in (closed, closed)

stud/y (closed, open)

ho/ping (open, closed)

he/ro (open, open)

teach/er (vowel team, *r*-controlled)

la/dle (open, consonant-*le*)

mon/ster (closed, *r*-controlled)

vol/ca/no (closed, open, open)

ro/bot (open, closed)

stu/dent (open, closed)

hop/ping (closed, closed)

herd/ed (*r*-controlled, closed)

tem/per (closed, *r*-controlled)

lad/der (closed, *r*-controlled)

mo/ment (open, closed)

vol/can/ic (closed, closed, closed)

## Section V: Spelling

### PAGE 12.3:

Group 1: The short-*i* sound can be spelled *i*.

Group 2: The long-*e* sound can be spelled *ea*.

Group 3: The long-*o* sound can be spelled *o_e* and *oa*.

Group 4: When the last syllable of a word ends with a short vowel + consonant, double the final consonant when adding *–ing* or *–ed*.

Group 5: Words related in meaning share common spelling patterns, despite differences in stressed syllable and vowel sound.

### PAGE 12.17:

Victor appears to be at the Syllable Juncture stage. He correctly uses consonant and vowel sound/spelling correspondences and the common suffixes *–tion, –sion,* and *–ment.* He uses but confuses consonant doubling, as seen in his overgeneralized spelling of CONCLUSSION and AMMUSEMENT. What is absent in his spelling is an understanding of meaning relationships—he uses an *i* for the unstressed *o* in OPPIZIT. However, his use of the related word *absent* when trying to spell *absence* shows that he's heading in the right direction. Another missing element is the spelling of the less frequent affixes *co–* and *–ite.*

### PAGE 12.31:

Tina's stage of spelling development appears to be Early Syllable Juncture.

## Section VI: Vocabulary Development

### PAGE 15.4:

There were more rare words per 1,000 in children's books than in prime-time adult television shows—30.9 compared to 22.7. There were far more rare words per 1,000 in comic books than in prime-time children's television shows—53.5 compared to 20.2.

## Section VII: Comprehension

### PAGE 17.11:

The first question-answer pair is Right There because the answer to the question is in one sentence and the question and the answer have the same wording. The second question-answer pair is Think and Search because the answer requires information from the first and second sentences in the text. The third question-answer pair is On My Own because the answer depends entirely on students' prior knowledge. The last question-answer pair is Author and Me because the answer comes from students' prior knowledge and clues in the text.

*Acknowledgments, continued from page iv*

Cambridge University Press: "Selected Statistics for Major Sources of Spoken and Written Language," from "Vocabulary Simplification for Children: A Special Case of 'Motherese'?" by Donald P. Hayes and Margaret G. Ahrens in *Journal of Child Language*, Vol. 15, No. 2 (June 1988), pp. 395–410. Reprinted with the permission of Cambridge University Press.

Center for the Study of Reading: "Teachers and Independent Reading" by the Center for the Study of Reading. Adapted with permission of the Center for the Study of Reading, University of Illinois at Urbana-Champaign, 51 Gerty Drive, Champaign, IL. 61820. 217-333-2552.

The Council for Exceptional Children: "Curriculum-Based Norms in Oral Reading Fluency for Grades 2–5 (Medians)," from "Curriculum-Based Oral Reading Fluency Norms for Students in Grades 2 Through 5," by Jan E. Hasbrouck and Gerald Tindal in *Teaching Exceptional Children*, Vol. 24, Spring 1992, p. 42. Copyright © 1992 by The Council for Exceptional Children. Reprinted by permission of The Council for Exceptional Children.

International Reading Association: "Variation in Amount of Independent Reading" figure from Anderson, R. C. (1996). "Research Foundations to Support Wide Reading." In V. Greany (ed.) *Promoting Reading in Developing Countries*. Newark, DE: International Reading Association. Adapted from Anderson, Richard C., Wilson, Paul T., and Fielding, Linda G. (1988, Summer). "Growth in Reading and How Children Spend Their Time Outside School." *Reading Research Quarterly* 23 (3), pp. 285–303. Reprinted by permission of Richard C. Anderson and the International Reading Association.

Lawrence Erlbaum Associates, Inc.: "Correlation Between Decoding and Comprehension in the Connecticut Longitudinal Study," from "The Case for Early Reading Intervention" by Barbara R. Foorman, David J. Francis, Sally E. Shaywitz, Bennett A. Shaywitz, and Jack M. Fletcher, in *Foundations of Reading Acquisition and Dyslexia: Implications for Early Intervention*, edited by Benita A. Blachman. Copyright © 1997 by Lawrence Erlbaum Associates, Inc. Reprinted by permission of Barbara R. Foorman and Lawrence Erlbaum Associates, Inc.

LinguiSystems, Inc.: "The Hungry Thing" activity, adapted from "The Hungry Thing" activity in *The Sounds Abound*™ *Program* developed at the Stern Center for Language and Learning by Orna Lenchner and Blanche Podhajski. Copyright © 1998 by LinguiSystems, Inc. Adapted by permission of LinguiSystems, Inc., East Moline, IL. 800-776-4332.

Prentice-Hall, Inc.: "Examples of Student's Spelling—September," "An Evolution of a Preliterate Child's Writing," "Characteristics of the Preliterate Stage of Spelling," "Early Letter Name Spelling with Word Boundaries," "Characteristics of the Early Letter Name Stage of Spelling," "Characteristics of the Middle and Late Letter Name Stage of Spelling," "Characteristics of the Within Word Pattern Stage of Spelling," "Characteristics of the Syllable Juncture and Derivational Constancy Stages of Spelling," "Qualitative Spelling Checklist," "Spelling-by-Stage Assessment Scale," "A Personal Reader: Short-Term and Long-Term Word Banks," "Word Study Notebook," "Sequence of Word Study," from *Words Their Way: Word Study for Phonics, Vocabulary, and Spelling Instruction* by Donald Bear, Marcia Invernizzi, Shane Templeton, and Francine Johnston. Copyright © 1996 by Prentice-Hall, Inc. Adapted by permission of Prentice-Hall, Inc., Upper Saddle River, NJ. "Problem English Contrasts for Speakers of Other Languages" and "Problem English Sounds for Speakers of Other Languages" excerpted from *The ESL Teacher's Book of Lists*, by Jacqueline E. Kress. Copyright © 1993 by The Center for Applied Research in Education. Reprinted by permission of The Center for Applied Research in Education/Prentice-Hall, Inc.

PRO-ED, Inc.: "Connect to Theory: Teaching Activity" adapted from "Teaching the Mouth Positions Required to Produce Consonant Phonemes" in *Phonological Awareness Training for Reading: Training Manual* (pp. 7, 32, 33–34) by Joseph K. Torgesen and Brian R. Bryant. Austin, TX: PRO-ED. Copyright © 1994 by PRO-ED, Inc. Adapted with permission.

John Ross: "Albert Einstein Asks a Question," by John Ross. Copyright © 1999 by John Ross. Used by permission of the author.

San Francisco Mime Troupe: "TV Dinner," by the San Francisco Mime Troupe. Script by Joaquin Aranda, Daniel Chumley, and Joan Holden. Based on a story by Sophia and Kate Chumley. Songs by Bruce Barthol. Copyright © 1979 by the San Francisco Mime Troupe. Adapted by permission of The San Francisco Mime Troupe. 415-285-1717.

Nancy Schimmel: "I'm Playing With a Monster," by Nancy Schimmel. Copyright © 1997 by Nancy Schimmel and Fran Avni. Reprinted by permission of Nancy Schimmel.

Scholastic, Inc.: "Phonics Scope & Sequence (Grades K–2)," from *Scholastic Literacy Place*. Copyright © 2000 by Scholastic, Inc. Reprinted by permission of Scholastic, Inc.

Ann Seidler: "The Hungry Thing," by Jan Slepian and Ann Seidler. Copyright © 1967 by Ann G. Seidler and Janice B. Slepian. Currently out of print. Reprinted by permission of Ann G. Seidler.

SRA/McGraw-Hill: "Introduction to Sounds (Grades K–2)," from *SRA/Open Court Reading*. Copyright © 2000 by SRA/McGraw-Hill. Reprinted with permission of SRA/McGraw-Hill.

Teacher Created Materials: "First 300 Instant Words," excerpted from *1000 Instant Words*, by Dr. Edward Fry. Copyright © 1994 by Teacher Created Materials, Westminster, CA. Reprinted with permission of the copyright holder. 800-557-6241.

Illustrations: Art Parts™

Every effort has been made to trace the ownership of all copyrighted materials in this book and to obtain permission for their use.

# TEACHING STRATEGY INDEX

*Page numbers in italics indicate charts and other graphics.*

# SUBJECT INDEX

*Words in italics indicate teaching strategies and "connect to theory" features. Page numbers in italics indicate charts and sidebars.*

### CORE Teaching Reading Sourcebook

A comprehensive sourcebook for grades K–8 covering the what, the why, the when, and the how of teaching reading. Includes research-based information as well as practical, hands-on teaching models for all aspects of explicit reading instruction.

**8-1/2 x 11 softcover, 800 pp. [8119-3]**

### CORE Reading Research Anthology, 2nd Edition

A collection of articles that provides background information about reading. Includes the research base for and best practices in the teaching of reading.

**8-1/2 x 11 softcover, 232 pp. [8207-6]**

### CORE Assessing Reading

A collection of formal and informal assessments for the comprehensive monitoring of reading skill development.

**8-1/2 x 11 softcover, 156 pp. [8120-7]**

5855 Christie Avenue, Suite A
Emeryville, CA 94608
TEL: 510-595-3400
FAX: 510-595-3434

**For information about CORE
Call Toll Free** 888-249-6155

**CORE Professional Development**
CORE works collaboratively with schools and districts to implement effective, research-based reading practices by providing workshops, seminars, ongoing coaching, and support for the systemic changes needed for program implementation.

## for ordering and price information:

**Call Toll Free** 800-422-7249
**Call between 8:30 AM and 3:30 PM Pacific Time**

| QUANTITY | PRODUCT NO. | TITLE | UNIT PRICE | TOTAL |
|---|---|---|---|---|
| | 8119-3 | CORE Teaching Reading Sourcebook | | |
| | 8207-6 | CORE Reading Research Anthology | | |
| | 8120-7 | CORE Assessing Reading | | |

**SEND PREPAID ORDERS TO:**

**ARENA PRESS**
20 Commercial Boulevard
Novato, CA 94949-6191
FAX: 415-883-3720

SUBTOTAL _____

Prepaid Orders Only (add $3.00 taxable handling) _____

SUBTOTAL _____

Sales Tax (CA & KY residents only) _____

TOTAL ENCLOSED _____
(U.S. Funds)

❏ Check or Money Order Enclosed
❏ Credit Card:
   ❏ VISA   ❏ MasterCard   ❏ AmEx

Exact Name on Card: _____

CC #: _____

Expiration Date: _____

Signature: _____

➡ **SHIP TO: (PLEASE PRINT)**

NAME _____

ORGANIZATION _____

ADDRESS _____

CITY _____ STATE _____ ZIP _____

PHONE _____